Microsoft Office Excel Complete

2013

A SKILLS APPROACH

Cheri Manning

Catherine Manning Swinson

Triad Interactive, Inc

McGraw Hill Education

MICROSOFT OFFICE EXCEL 2013: A SKILLS APPROACH
Published by McGraw-Hill Education, 2 Penn Plaza, New York, NY 10121. Copyright © 2014 by McGraw-Hill Education. All rights reserved. Printed in the United States of America. No part of this publication may be reproduced or distributed in any form or by any means, or stored in a database or retrieval system, without the prior written consent of McGraw-Hill Education, including, but not limited to, in any network or other electronic storage or transmission, or broadcast for distance learning.

Some ancillaries, including electronic and print components, may not be available to customers outside the United States.

This book is printed on acid-free paper.

1 2 3 4 5 6 7 8 9 0 RMN/RMN 1 0 9 8 7 6 5 4

ISBN 978-0-07-739422-6
MHID 0-07-739422-4

Senior Vice President, Products & Markets: *Kurt L. Strand*
Vice President, Content Production & Technology Services: *Kimberly Meriwether David*
Director: *Scott Davidson*
Senior Brand Manager: *Wyatt Morris*
Executive Director of Development: *Ann Torbert*
Development Editor: *Alan Palmer*
Development Editor: *Allison McCabe*
Digital Development Editor: *Kevin White*
Marketing Manager: *Tiffany Russell*
Content Project Manager: *Rick Hecker*
Content Project Manager: *Brent dela Cruz*
Buyer: *Nichole Birkenholz*
Design: *Lisa King*
Cover Image: *© Burazin/Photographer's Choice/Getty Images*
Content Licensing Specialist: *Joanne Mennemeier*
Typeface: *10.5/13 Garamond Premier Pro Regular*
Compositor: *Laserwords Private Limited*
Printer: *R. R. Donnelley*

All credits appearing on page or at the end of the book are considered to be an extension of the copyright page.

Library of Congress Cataloging-in-Publication Data

Manning, Cheryl.
    Microsoft Office Excel complete 2013 : a skills approach / Cheri Manning, Catherine Manning Swinson,
Triad Interactive, Inc.—1st Edition.
        pages cm
    Includes bibliographical references and index.
    ISBN 978-0-07-739422-6 (alk. paper)
    1. Microsoft Office. 2. Microsoft Excel (Computer file) 3. Business—Computer programs. I. Swinson,
Catherine Manning. II. Title.
    HF5548.4.M525M3496 2014
005.54—dc23   2014019401

The Internet addresses listed in the text were accurate at the time of publication. The inclusion of a website does not indicate an endorsement by the authors or McGraw-Hill Education, and McGraw-Hill Education does not guarantee the accuracy of the information presented at these sites.

www.mhhe.com

brief contents

contents

Contents

preface

How well do you know Microsoft Excel? Many students can follow specific step-by-step directions to re-create a spreadsheet, but do they truly understand the skills it takes to create one on their own? Just as simply following a recipe does not make you a professional chef, re-creating a project step by step does not make you an Excel expert.

The purpose of this book is to teach you the skills to master Microsoft Excel 2013 in a straightforward and easy-to-follow manner. But *Microsoft® Office Excel Complete 2013: A Skills Approach* goes beyond the **how** and equips you with a deeper understanding of the **what** and the **why.** Too many times books have little value beyond the classroom. The *Skills Approach* series has been designed to be not only a complete textbook but also a reference tool for you to use as you move beyond academics and into the workplace.

WHAT'S NEW IN THIS EDITION

This edition of the *Skills Approach* text includes a Let Me Try exercise and student data file for each skill. These exercises are the same as the simulated Let Me Try exercises in SIMnet 2013. We included the student data files to give students the opportunity to explore the skill in the live application in addition to practicing it in a simulated environment (SIMnet).

The Let Me Try exercises are not intended as a running project or case study. Each Let Me Try data file is independent of the others, so the skills may be taught in any order.

ABOUT TRIAD INTERACTIVE

Triad Interactive specializes in online education and training products. Our flagship program is SIMnet—a simulated Microsoft Office learning and assessment application developed for the McGraw-Hill Companies. Triad has been writing, programming, and managing the SIMnet system since 1999.

Triad is also actively involved in online health education and in research projects to assess the usefulness of technology for helping high-risk populations make decisions about managing their cancer risk and treatment.

about the authors

CHERI MANNING

Cheri Manning is the president and co-owner of Triad Interactive. She is the author of the Microsoft Excel and Access content for the *Skills Approach* series and SIMnet. She has been authoring instructional content for these applications for more than 12 years.

Cheri began her career as an Aerospace Education Specialist with the Education Division of the National Aeronautics and Space Administration (NASA), where she produced materials for K–12 instructors and students. Prior to founding Triad, Cheri was a project manager with Compact Publishing, where she managed the development of McGraw-Hill's Multimedia MBA CD-ROM series.

CATHERINE MANNING SWINSON

Catherine Manning Swinson is the vice president and co-owner of Triad Interactive. She is the author of the Microsoft Word and PowerPoint content for the *Skills Approach* series and SIMnet. She also authors SIMnet content for Microsoft Outlook, Windows, and Internet Explorer. She has been authoring instructional content for these applications for more than 12 years.

Catherine began her career at Compact Publishing, one of the pioneers in educational CD-ROM-based software. She was the lead designer at Compact and designed every edition of the *TIME Magazine Compact Almanac* from 1992 through 1996. In addition, she designed a number of other products with Compact, including the *TIME Man of the Year* program and the *TIME 20th Century Almanac*.

acknowledgments

CONTRIBUTORS

Kelly Morber, *Saints Philip and James School, English teacher and Malone University,* M.A.Ed.
Timothy T. Morber, MEd, LPCC-S, *Malone University*

TECHNICAL EDITORS

Menka Brown
Piedmont Technical College

Sylvia Brown
Midland College

Mary Locke
Greenville Technical College

Daniela Marghitu
Auburn University

Judy Settle
Central Georgia Technical College

Pamela Silvers
Asheville-Buncombe Technical College

Candace Spangler
Columbus State Community College

Debbie Zaidi
Seneca College

REVIEWERS

Our thanks go to all who participated in the development of *Microsoft Office 2013: A Skills Approach.*

Sven Aelterman
Troy University

Nick Agrawal
Calhoun Community College

Laura Anderson
Weber State University

Viola Bain
Scott Community College

Greg Ballinger
Miami Dade College

Bill Barzen
Saint Petersburg College

Julia Bell
Walters State Community College

Don Belle
Central Piedmont Community College

Judy Boozer
Lane Community College

Ben Brah
Auburn University

Sheryl Starkey Bulloch
Columbia Southern University

Kate Burkes
Northwest Arkansas Community College

Michael Callahan
Lone Star College

Patricia Casey
Trident Technical College

Wally Cates
Central New Mexico Community College

Jimmy Chen
Salt Lake Community College

Sharon Cotman
Thomas Nelson Community College

Susan Cully
Long Beach City College

Jennifer Day
Sinclair Community College

Ralph De Arazoza
Miami Dade College

Bruce Elliot
Tarrant County College

Bernice Eng
Brookdale Community College

Penny Fanzone
Community College of Baltimore County

Valerie Farmer
Community College of Baltimore County

Jean Finley
Asheville-Buncombe Technical Community College

George Fiori
Tri-County Technical College

Deborah Godwin
Lake-Sumter Community College

Cathy Grant-Churchwell
Lane Community College

Diana Green
Weber State University

Joseph Greer
Midlands Technical College

Debra Gross
Ohio State University

Rachelle Hall
Glendale Community College

Dexter Harlee
York Technical College

Marilyn Hibbert
Salt Lake Community College

Judy Irvine
Seneca College

Sherry E. Jacob
Jefferson Community & Technical College

Linda Johnsonius
Murray State University

Rich Klein
Clemson University

Kevin Lee
Guilford Technical Community College

Mohamed Lotfy
Regis University

Carol Martin
Central Pennsylvania Community College

Sue McCrory
Missouri State University

Ken Moak
Tarrant County College

Cecil Morris
American Intercontinental University

Kathleen Morris
University of Alabama

Patrick J. Nedry
Monroe County Community College

Mitchell Ober
Tulsa Community College

Ashlee Pieris
Raritan Valley Community College

Pamela Silvers
Asheville–Buncombe Technical Community College

W. Randy Somsen
Brigham Young University–Idaho

Bonnie Smith
Fresno City College

Randy Smith
Monterey Peninsula College

Nathan Stout
University of Oklahoma

Carl Struck
Suffolk Community College

Song Su
East Los Angeles College

Kathleen Tamerlano
Cuyahoga Community College

Margaret Taylor
College of Southern Nevada

Debby Telfer
Colorado Technical University

David Trimble
Park University

Georgia Vanderark
Stark State College

Philip Vavalides
Guilford Technical Community College

Dennis Walpole
University of South Florida

Michael Walton
Miami Dade College

Paul Weaver
Bossier Parish Community College

Nima Zahadat
Northern Virginia Community College

Debbie Zaidi
Seneca College

Matthew Zullo
Wake Tech Community College

Instructor Walkthrough

Microsoft Office Excel Complete 2013:
A Skills Approach

SIMnet
Keep IT SIMple!

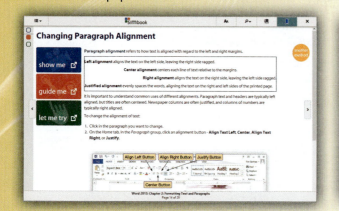

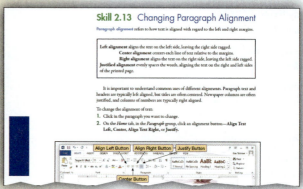

❯ **1-1 Content in SIMnet for Office 2013**

Skill 2.5 Inserting and Deleting Cells

You may find you want to add some extra space or more information into the middle of your worksheet. To do this, you must insert a new cell or group of cells. Any formulas referencing the cell where the insertion takes place will update to reflect the new position of the original cell. Even if the formula uses absolute cell references, it will still update to reflect the updated cell reference.

To insert a cell range, select the range where you want to insert the new cells.

1. If you have a vertical cell range selected, click the **Insert Cells** button and Excel will automatically shift existing cells to the right to make room for the new cells.
2. If you have a horizontal cell range selected, click the **Insert Cells** button and Excel will automatically shift existing cells down to make room for the new cells.

   If you want more control over whether cells are shifted to the right or down, use the *Insert* dialog.

1. Select the cell or cell range where you want to insert the new cells.
2. On the *Home* tab, in the *Cells* group, click the **Insert Cells** button arrow.
3. Click **Insert Cells...** to open the *Insert* dialog.
4. Click the **Shift cells right** or **Shift cells down** radio button.
5. Click **OK.**

Formatting Cells
chapter **2**

In this chapter, you will learn the following skills:

❯ Modify cell data using cut, copy, and paste	Skill 2.1 Cutting, Copying, and Pasting Cells
	Skill 2.2 Using Paste Options
❯ Insert, delete, and merge cells	Skill 2.3 Using Undo and Redo
❯ Work with text and font attributes	Skill 2.4 Wrapping Text in Cells
	Skill 2.5 Inserting and Deleting Cells
❯ Apply borders and shading	Skill 2.6 Aligning Cells
	Skill 2.7 Merging Cells and Splitting Merged Cells
❯ Format cells using cell styles	Skill 2.8 Applying Bold, Italic, and Underline
❯ Copy formatting using Format Painter	Skill 2.9 Changing Fonts, Font Size, and Font Color
❯ Format cells using conditional	Skill 2.10 Adding Borders

❯ **Introduction—Learning Outcomes are clearly listed.**

❯ **At-a-glance Office 2013 skills**

Quick, easy-to-scan pages, for efficient learning

Fix It

fix it 7.6

... salary projections workbook for key departments at a local

... project:
... elements (Skill 7.5)
... pe (Skill 7.9)
... dline (Skill 7.10)
... a Data Series (Skill 7.3)
... pe (Skill 7.11)
... es (Skill 7.12)
... ies (Skill 7.15)
... Chart (Skill 7.1)
... er (Skill 7.17)

...13-FixIt-7-6 and resave the file as:
... **EX-FixIt-7-6**

... Protected View, click the **Enable Editing** button in the
... of the workbook so you can modify the workbook.
... created this workbook made one of the ugliest charts
... to do is a fix th... on the *Salary Projections* worksheet.

On Your Own

on your own 1.5

For Spring Break, you've decided to take a seven-day road trip. Use this Excel workbook to calculate the number of miles you will drive each day and the gas cost for each day. Use the techniques you've learned in this chapter to calculate the total miles and the total gas cost. Don't forget to end the trip at the same location you started! You may want to use the Internet to look up mileage, MPG (miles per gallon), and gas price information.

Skills needed to complete this project:
- Navigating a Workbook (Skill 1.2)
- Working in Protected View (Skill 1.3)
- Entering and Editing Text and Numbers in Cells (Skill 1.4)
- Entering Dates and Applying Date Formats (Skill 1.6)
- Inserting Data Using AutoFill (Skill 1.7)
- Understanding Absolute and Relative References (Skill 1.9)
- Entering Simple Formulas (Skill 1.8)
- Calculating Totals with the Quick Analysis Tool (Skill 1.12)
- Using AutoSum to Insert a SUM Function (Skill 1.11)
- Applying Number Formats (Skill 1.5)
- Checking Spelling (Skill 1.17)

1. Open the start file EX2013-OnYourOwn-1-5 and resave the file as:
   [your initials] EX-OnYourOwn-1-5
2. If the workbook opens in Protected View, click the **Enable Editing** button in the Message Bar at the top of the workbook so you can modify the workbook.

Skill Review

skill review 6.2

In this project, you will create a worksheet to analyze inventory and financial data for a sporting goods store.

Skills needed to complete this project:
- Calculating Totals with SUMPRODUCT (Skill 6.2)
- Finding the Middle Value with MEDIAN (Skill 6.6)
- Finding the Most Common Value(s) with MODE.SNGL and MODE.MULT (Skill 6.7)
- Using SUMIF and SUMIFS (Skill 6.3)
- Using AVERAGEIF and AVERAGEIFS (Skill 6.4)
- Using COUNTIF and COUNTIFS (Skill 6.5)
- Using Database Functions (Skill 6.16)
- Finding Data with MATCH and INDEX (Skill 6.15)
- Managing Errors with the IFERROR Function (Skill 6.17)
- Analyzing Complex Formulas Using Evaluate Formula (Skill 6.18)
- Calculating Future Value with the FV Function (Skill 6.10)
- Calculating the Number of Payments with NPER (Skill 6.13)
- Rounding with Functions (Skill 6.1)
- Using NPV to Calculate Present Value when Payments Are Variable (Skill 6.12)
- Creating an Amortization Schedule (Sk...

❯ **Diverse end-of-chapter projects**

Projects that relate to a broad range of careers and perspectives, from nursing, education, business, and everyday personal uses.

Features

From the Perspective of…

from the perspective of . . .

SPORTING GOODS STORE PURCHASING MANAGER

We chart data from our checkout process using trendlines and Sparklines so we can see which merchandise is in high demand. Our inventory keeps current because we watch the trends over time. We can now better predict which items to order for each upcoming season.

Tips and Tricks

tips & tricks

Be careful when using the *Undo* and *Redo* commands in Excel. In other Office applications, undo and redo actions are confined to the file you are currently working on—even if you have multiple files open. However, in Excel, the undo–redo list of actions includes all the open workbooks. This means that if you are working on multiple Excel files at the same time, using the *Undo* command can actually undo an action in one of the other open workbooks.

another method

〉 To undo an action, you can also press ⌃Ctrl + Z.
〉 To redo an action, you can also press ⌃Ctrl + Y.

Tell Me More

tell me more

To group all the sheets in your workbook together, right-click any sheet tab and then click **Select All Sheets.**

To ungroup sheets, right-click one of the grouped sheet tabs and then click **Ungroup.** If all of the sheets in your workbook are grouped together, you must use this method to ungroup them.

let me try

Open the student data file **EX4-06-PurchaseOrders** and try this skill on your own:
1. Group sheets *PO June* and *PO July.*
2. Change the text in cell **F3** to: **Quantity Ordered**
3. Ungroup the sheets.

Another Method

another method

To add a picture to a header section from the *Page Setup* dialog:
1. On the *Page Layout* tab, in the *Page Setup* group, click the **Page Setup** dialog launcher.
2. In the *Page Setup* dialog, click the **Header/Footer** tab.
3. Click the **Custom Header** button.
4. Click in the section where you want to position the picture.
5. Click the **Insert Picture** button to open the *Insert Picture* dialog.
6. Navigate to the file location. Select the file, and click **Insert.**
7. Click **OK** to close the *Header* dialog, and then click **OK** again to close the *Page Setup* dialog.

let me try

Let Me Try

let me try

Open the student data file **EX3-07-Customers** and try this skill on your own:
1. Enter a formula in cell **C5** to display the text from cell **C2** so the first letter in each word is capitalized.
2. Enter a formula in cell **D5** to display the text from cell **D2** so all the letters display in upper case.
3. Enter a formula in cell **E5** to display the text from cell **E2** so all the letters display in lower case.
4. Save the file as directed by your instructor and close it.

〉 **Instructor materials available on the online learning center, www.mhhe.com/office2013skills**

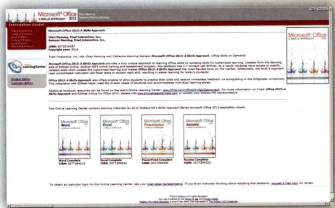

- Instructor Manual
- Instructor PowerPoints
- Test Bank

SIMnet for Office 2013 Online Training & Assessment

❭ Includes:

- Microsoft® Office Suite
- Computer Concepts
- Windows 7
- Windows 8
- Browsers
- File Management

EASY TO USE

SIMnet is McGraw-Hill's leading solution for training and assessment of Microsoft Office skills and beyond. Completely online with no downloads for installation (besides requiring Adobe Flash Player), SIMnet is accessible for today's students through multiple browsers and is easy to use for all. Now, SIMnet offers SIMbook and allows students to go mobile for their student learning. Available with videos and interactive "Guide Me" pages to allow students to study MS Office skills on any device. Its consistent, clean user interface and functionality will help save you time and help students be more successful in their course.

LIFELONG LEARNING

SIMnet offers lifelong learning. SIMnet is designed with features to help students immediately learn isolated Microsoft Office skills on demand. Students can use SIMSearch and the Library to learn skills both in and beyond the course. It's more than a resource; it's a tool they can use throughout their entire time at your institution.

MEASURABLE RESULTS

SIMnet provides powerful, measureable results for you and your students. See results immediately in our various reports and customizable gradebook. Students can also see measurable results by generating a custom training lesson after an exam to help determine exactly which content areas they still need to study. Instructors can use the dashboard to see detailed results of student activity, assignment completion, and more. SIMnet Online is your solution for helping students master today's Microsoft Office Skills.

SIMNET FOR OFFICE 2013

. . . **Keep IT SIMple!** To learn more, visit www.simnetkeepitsimple.com and also contact your McGraw-Hill representative.

office 2013

Essential Skills for Office 2013

In this chapter, you will learn the following skills:

❯ Learn about Microsoft Office 2013 and its applications Word, Excel, PowerPoint, and Access

❯ Demonstrate how to open, save, and close files

❯ Recognize Office 2013 common features and navigation elements

❯ Modify account information and the look of Office

❯ Create new files

❯ Use Microsoft Help

skills

introduction

This chapter introduces you to Microsoft Office 2013. You will learn about the shared features across the Office 2013 applications and how to navigate common interface elements such as the Ribbon and Quick Access Toolbar. You will learn how to open and close files as well as learn how to work with messages that appear when you first open files. You will become familiar with the Office account and learn how to modify the account as well as the look of Office 2013. Introductory features such as creating and closing files and using Office Help are explained.

Skill 1.1 Introduction to Microsoft Office 2013

Microsoft Office 2013 is a collection of business "productivity" applications (computer programs designed to make you more productive at work, school, and home). The most popular Office applications are:

Microsoft Word—A word processing program. Word processing software allows you to create text-based documents, similar to how you would type a document on a typewriter. However, word processing software offers more powerful formatting and design tools, allowing you to create complex documents, including reports, résumés, brochures, and newsletters.

Microsoft Excel—A spreadsheet program. Originally, spreadsheet applications were viewed as electronic versions of an accountant's ledger. Today's spreadsheet applications can do much more than just calculate numbers—they include powerful charting and data analysis features. Spreadsheet programs can be used for everything from personal budgets to calculating loan payments.

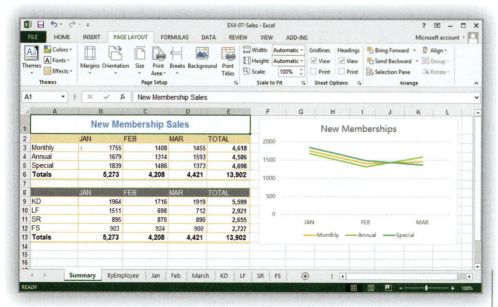

Microsoft PowerPoint—A presentation program. Such applications enable you to create robust, multimedia presentations. A presentation consists of a series of electronic slides. Each slide contains content, including text, images, charts, and other objects. You can add multimedia elements to slides, including animations, audio, and video.

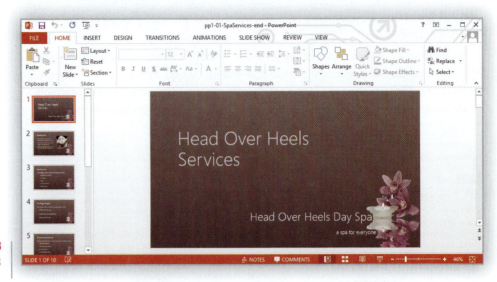

FIGURE OF 1.3
Microsoft PowerPoint 2013

Microsoft Access—A database program. Database applications allow you to organize and manipulate large amounts of data. Databases that allow you to relate tables and databases to one another are referred to as *relational* databases. As a database user, you usually see only one aspect of the database—a *form*. Database forms use a graphical interface to allow a user to enter record data. For example, when you fill out an order form online, you are probably interacting with a database. The information you enter becomes a record in a database *table*. Your order is matched with information in an inventory table (keeping track of which items are in stock) through a *query*. When your order is filled, a database *report* can be generated for use as an invoice or a bill of lading.

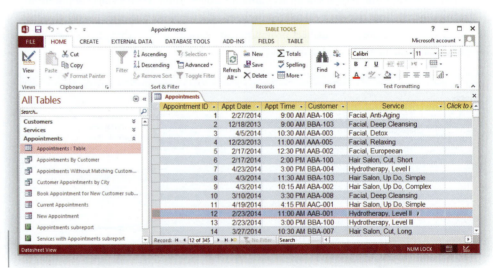

FIGURE OF 1.4
Microsoft Access 2013

To open one of the Office applications using the Windows 8 operating system:

1. Display the **Start screen.**
2. In the *Pinned Apps* section, click the tile of the application you want to open.

To open one of the Office applications using the Windows 7 operating system:

1. Click the Windows **Start** button (located in the lower left corner of your computer screen).
2. Click **All Programs.**
3. Click the **Microsoft Office** folder.
4. Click the application you want to open.

tips & tricks

You can download a free trial version of Microsoft Office from Microsoft's Web site (http://office.microsoft.com). The trial allows you to try the applications before buying them. When your trial period ends, if you haven't purchased the full software license yet, you will no longer be able to use the applications (although you will continue to be able to open and view any files you previously created with the trial version).

tell me more

There are two main versions of Microsoft Office, each offering a different way to pay for the program:

Office 365—This version allows you to download and install Office and pay for it on a yearly or monthly subscription basis. It includes full versions of the different Office applications along with online storage services for your files. When the next version of Office is released, the subscription can be transferred to the new version. If you do not want to install the full version of Office on your computer, you can access limited versions of each application online with an Office 365 subscription.

Office 2013—This version allows you to install Office and pay for it once, giving you a perpetual license for the programs. This means that when the next version of Office is released, you will need to purchase the application suite again. You can associate a Windows Live account with Office 2013, giving you access to online storage for your files.

If you are a home user, business, or a student, there are different purchasing options for both Office 365 and Office 2013. Both versions require that you are running the Windows 7 or Windows 8 operating system.

Skill 1.2 Opening Files

Opening a file retrieves it from storage and displays it on your computer screen. The steps for opening a file are the same for Word documents, Excel spreadsheets, PowerPoint presentations, and Access databases.

To open an existing file from your computer:

1. Click the **File** tab to open Backstage view.
2. Click **Open.**
3. The *Open* page displays listing the recently opened files by default.
4. Click **Computer.**
5. A list of folders you have recently opened files from appears on the right. Click a folder to open the **Open** dialog with that folder displayed.

FIGURE OF 1.5

6. Select the file name you want to open in the large list box.
7. Click the **Open** button in the dialog.

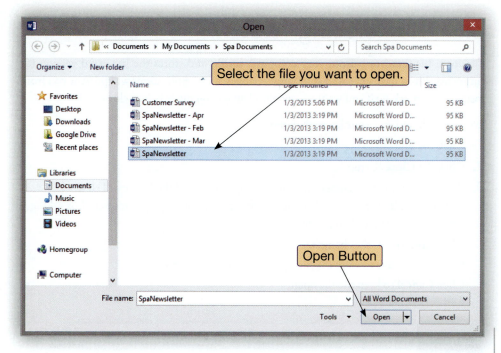

Select the file you want to open.

Open Button

FIGURE OF 1.6

tips & tricks

If you do not see the folder containing the file you want to open, click the **Browse** button. The *Open* dialog will open to your *Documents* folder. Navigate to the location where the file you want to open is located, select the file, and click **Open.**

tell me more

The screen shot shown here is from Word 2013 running on the Microsoft Windows 8 operating system. Depending on the operating system you are using, the *Open* dialog will appear somewhat different. However, the basic steps for opening a file are the same regardless of which operating system you are using.

another method

To display the *Open* page in Backstage view, you can also press ⌃Ctrl + ⓪ on the keyboard.

To open the file from within the *Open* dialog, you can also:

❭ Press the ⏎Enter key once you have typed or selected a file name.

❭ Double-click the file name.

let me try

Try this skill on your own:

1. Open the student data file **of1-SpaNewsletter.**
   NOTE: You may see a yellow security message at the top of the window. See the skill *Working in Protected View* to learn more about security warning messages.
2. Keep the file open to work on the next skill.

Skill 1.3 Closing Files

Closing a file removes it from your computer screen and stores the last-saved version for future use. If you have not saved your latest changes, most applications will prevent you from losing work by asking if you want to save the changes you made before closing.

To close a file and save your latest changes:

1. Click the **File** tab to open Backstage view.

2. Click the **Close** button.

3. If you have made no changes since the last time you saved the file, it will close immediately. If changes have been made, the application displays a message box asking if you want to save the changes you made before closing.

Click **Save** to save the changes.

Click **Don't Save** to close the file without saving your latest changes.

Click **Cancel** to keep the file open.

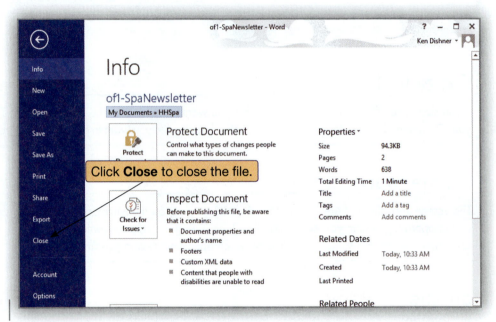

FIGURE OF 1.7

another method

To close a file, you can also press Ctrl + W on the keyboard.

let me try

If necessary, open the student data file **of1-SpaNewsletter** and try this skill on your own:
   Close the file.

Skill 1.4 Getting to Know the Office 2013 User Interface

THE RIBBON

If you have used a word processing or spreadsheet program in the past, you may be surprised when you open one of the Microsoft Office 2013 applications for the first time. Beginning with Office 2007, Microsoft redesigned the user experience—replacing the familiar menu bar/toolbar interface with a new Ribbon interface that makes it easier to find application functions and commands.

The **Ribbon** is located across the top of the application window and organizes common features and commands into tabs. Each **tab** organizes commands further into related **groups**.

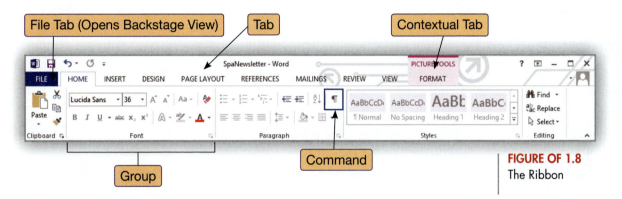

FIGURE OF 1.8
The Ribbon

When a specific type of object is selected (such as a picture, table, or chart), a contextual tab will appear. **Contextual tabs** contain commands specific to the type of object selected and are only visible when the commands might be useful.

Each application includes a **Home tab** that contains the most commonly used commands for that application. For example, in Word, the *Home* tab includes the following groups: *Clipboard, Font, Paragraph, Styles,* and *Editing,* while the Excel *Home* tab includes groups more appropriate for a spreadsheet program: *Clipboard, Font, Alignment, Number, Styles, Cells,* and *Editing.*

tips & tricks

If you need more space for your file, you can minimize the Ribbon by clicking the **Collapse the Ribbon** button in the upper-right corner of the Ribbon (or press (Ctrl) + (F1)). When the Ribbon is minimized, the tab names appear along the top of the window (similar to a menu bar). When you click a tab name, the Ribbon appears. After you select a command or click away from the Ribbon, the Ribbon hides again. To redisplay the Ribbon permanently, click the **Ribbon Display Options** button in the upper-right corner of the window and select **Show Tabs and Commands.** You can also double-click the active tab to hide or display the Ribbon.

BACKSTAGE

Notice that each application also includes a **File tab** at the far left side of the Ribbon. Clicking the *File* tab opens the **Microsoft Office Backstage view,** where you can access the commands for managing and protecting your files, including *Save, Open, Close, New,* and *Print.* Backstage replaces the Office Button menu from Office 2007 and the *File* menu from previous versions of Office.

To return to you file from Backstage view, click the **Back** button located in the upper left corner of the window. ⊖

Many commands available through the Ribbon and Backstage view are also accessible through keyboard shortcuts and shortcut menus.

Keyboard shortcuts are keys or combinations of keys that you press to execute a command. Some keyboard shortcuts refer to F keys or function keys. These are the keys that run across the top of the keyboard. Pressing these keys will execute specific commands. For example, pressing the F1 key will open Help in any of the Microsoft Office applications. Keyboard shortcuts typically use a combination of two keys, although some commands use a combination of three keys and others only one key. When a keyboard shortcut calls for a combination of key presses, such as Ctrl + V to paste an item from the *Clipboard,* you must first press the modifier key Ctrl, holding it down while you press the V key on the keyboard.

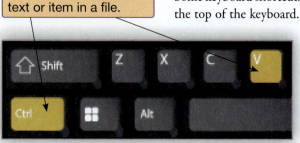

Press and hold **Ctrl** and then press **V** to paste text or item in a file.

FIGURE OF 1.9

tell me **more**

Many of the keyboard shortcuts are universal across all applications—not just Microsoft Office applications. Some examples of universal shortcut keys include:

Ctrl + C = Copy

Ctrl + X = Cut

Ctrl + V = Paste

Ctrl + Z = Undo

Ctrl + O = Open

Ctrl + S = Save

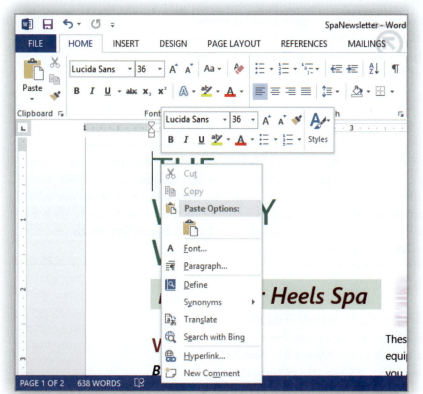

FIGURE OF 1.10
Right-Click Shortcut Menu

SHORTCUT MENUS

Shortcut menus are menus of commands that display when you right-click an area of the application window. The area or object you right-click determines which menu appears. For example, if you right-click in a paragraph, you will see a shortcut menu of commands for working with text; however, if you right-click an image, you will see a shortcut menu of commands for working with images.

THE MINI TOOLBAR

The Mini toolbar gives you access to common tools for working with text. When you select text and then rest your mouse over the text, the Mini toolbar fades in. You can then click a button to change the selected text just as you would on the Ribbon.

another **method**

To display the Mini toolbar, you can also right-click the text. The Mini toolbar appears above the shortcut menu.

The Mini Toolbar

FIGURE OF 1.11

QUICK ACCESS TOOLBAR

The Quick Access Toolbar is located at the top of the application window above the *File* tab. The Quick Access Toolbar, as its name implies, gives you quick one-click access to common commands. You can add commands to and remove commands from the Quick Access Toolbar.

To modify the Quick Access Toolbar:

1. Click the **Customize Quick Access Toolbar** button located on the right side of the Quick Access Toolbar.

2. Options with checkmarks next to them are already displayed on the toolbar. Options with no checkmarks are not currently displayed.

3. Click an option to add it to or remove it from the Quick Access Toolbar.

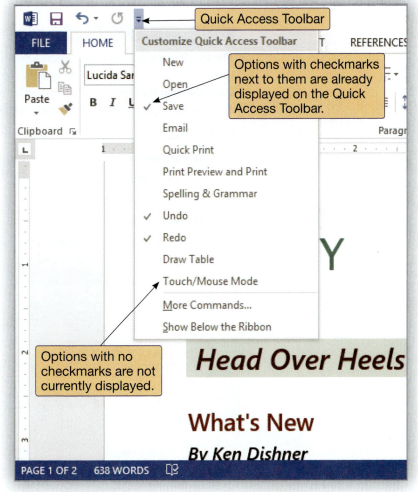

Quick Access Toolbar

Options with checkmarks next to them are already displayed on the Quick Access Toolbar.

Options with no checkmarks are not currently displayed.

FIGURE OF 1.12

tips & tricks

If you want to be able to print with a single mouse click, add the *Quick Print* button to the Quick Access Toolbar. If you do not need to change any print settings, this is by far the easiest method to print a file because it doesn't require opening Backstage view first.

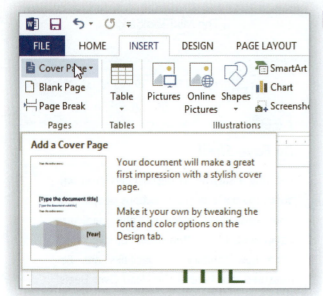

FIGURE OF 1.13
Cover Page
Enhanced ScreenTip

ENHANCED SCREENTIP

A ScreenTip is a small information box that displays the name of the command when you rest your mouse over a button on the Ribbon. An Enhanced ScreenTip displays not only the name of the command, but also the keyboard shortcut (if there is one) and a short description of what the button does and when it is used. Certain Enhanced ScreenTips also include an image along with a description of the command.

USING LIVE PREVIEW

The Live Preview feature in Microsoft Office 2013 allows you to see formatting changes in your file before actually committing to the change. When Live Preview is active, rolling over a command on the Ribbon will temporarily apply the formatting to the currently active text or object. To apply the formatting, click the formatting option.

Use Live Preview to preview the following:

Font Formatting—Including the font, font size, text highlight color, and font color

Paragraph Formatting—Including numbering, bullets, and shading

Quick Styles and Themes

Table Formatting—Including table styles and shading

Picture Formatting—Including correction and color options, picture styles, borders, effects, positioning, brightness, and contrast

SmartArt—Including layouts, styles, and colors

Shape Styles—Including borders, shading, and effects

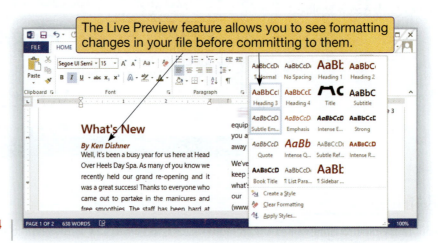

FIGURE OF 1.14

You can enable and disable some of the user interface features through the *Options* dialog.

1. Click the **File** tab to open Backstage view.

2. Click **Options.**

3. Make the changes you want, and then click **OK** to save your changes.

❭ Check or uncheck **Show Mini toolbar on selection** to control whether or not the Mini toolbar appears when you hover over selected text. (This does not affect the appearance of the Mini toolbar when you right-click.)

❭ Check or uncheck **Enable Live Preview** to turn the live preview feature on or off.

❭ Make a selection from the *ScreenTip style* list:

- **Show feature descriptions in ScreenTips** displays Enhanced ScreenTips when they are available.

- **Don't show feature descriptions in ScreenTips** hides Enhanced ScreenTips. The ScreenTip will still include the keyboard shortcut if there is one available.

- **Don't show ScreenTips** hides ScreenTips altogether, so if you hold your mouse over a button on the Ribbon, nothing will appear.

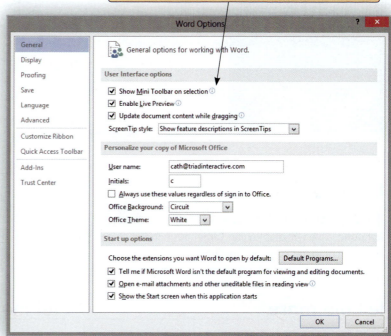

You can enable and disable some of the user interface features through the *Options* dialog.

FIGURE OF 1.15

let me try

Open the student data file **of1-SpaNewsletter** and try this skill on your own:
1. Explore the Ribbon. Click on different tabs and note how commands are arranged together in groups.
2. Click the picture to display the *Picture Tools* contextual tab.
3. Click the **File** tab to display Backstage view. Click the **Back** button to return to the file.
4. Right-click an area of the file to display the shortcut menu.
5. Explore the Mini Toolbar at the top of the shortcut menu. Click away from the menu to hide it.
6. Click the **Customize Quick Access Toolbar** arrow to display the menu of items that can be displayed on the Quick Access Toolbar. Note the ones with checkmarks are the items currently displayed.
7. Click the **Insert** tab. In the *Pages* group, roll your mouse over the **Cover Page** button to display the Enhanced ScreenTip.
8. Click the **File** tab.
9. Click **Options** to open the *Options* dialog.
10. Disable **Live Preview.**
11. Change the ScreenTips so they don't show feature descriptions.
12. Close the file.

Skill 1.5 Using the Start Page

When you launch an Office 2013 application you are first taken to the **Start page**. The *Start* page gives you quick access to recently opened files and templates for creating new files in each of the applications.

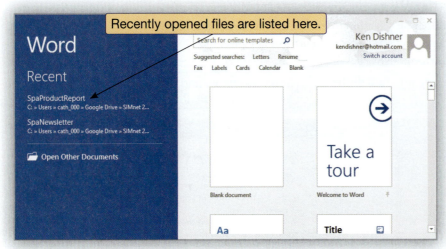

FIGURE OF 1.16

To open a recent file from the *Start* page:

1. Launch the application.
2. The *Start* page displays.
3. Click a file in the left pane to open the file.

tips & tricks

If you do not see the file you want to open in the list of recent files, click **Open Other Documents** at the bottom of the left pane. This will display the *Open* page that includes buttons for finding and opening files from other locations such as your computer or your OneDrive.

tell me more

In previous versions of Office when you launched an application, a blank file opened ready for you to begin working. If you want to start a new blank file, click the blank file template in the list of templates. It is always listed as the first option.

let me try

To try this skill on your own:
1. Launch **Microsoft Word.**
2. If you have files listed under *Recent,* click a file to open it.
3. Close the file.

from the perspective of . . .

A BUSY PARENT

Learning Microsoft Office was one of the best things I did to help manage my family's busy lifestyle. I use Word to write up and print a calendar of everyone's activities for the week. I keep a handle on the family finances with a budget of all expenses in an Excel spreadsheet. I've even learned how to use Excel to calculate loan payments and found the best offer when I had to buy a new family car. I used PowerPoint to create a presentation for my family of our summer vacation pictures. Once I became more familiar with Access, I used it to help organize my family's busy schedule. I created a database with one table for activities, another for parent contact information, another one for carpooling, and another for the schedule. Being able to organize all the information in a database has been invaluable. I always thought Office was only for businesses, but now I can't imagine running my household without it!

Skill 1.6 Changing Account Information

Office 2013 includes an **Account page** that lists information for the user currently logged into Office. This account information comes from the Microsoft account you used when installing Office. From the *Account* page, you can update your user profile, including contact and work information. You can also change the picture associated with the user account.

To change the user information

1. Click the **File** tab.
2. Click **Account.**
3. The current user profile is listed under *User Information*.
4. Click the **Change photo** link.

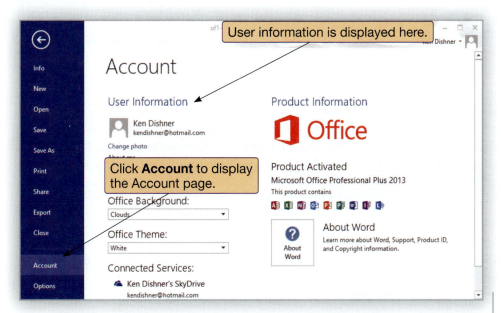

FIGURE OF 1.17

5. The *Profile* page on *live.com* is displayed in the browser window.
6. Click the **Change Picture** link.
7. On the *Picture* page, click the **Browse** button.
8. Navigate to the location of the picture you want to use for you profile and select it.
9. Click the **Open** button.
10. The picture appears on the page. Click the **Save** button to save the profile change.

From the *Profile* page, you can also edit your contact information and work information. Click the **Edit** link under each section to display the edit page. Fill in the form with your information and click the **Save** button.

Click **Change picture** to change the image for the user profile.

Click **Edit** to change other account information.

FIGURE OF 1.18

tell me **more**

Depending on the version of Office 2013 you have, you can have multiple accounts use the same installation of Office. When you switch accounts, any personalization that person has done to Office will be applied. The account will also have access to that person's OneDrive account and all files that have been saved there. To learn more about OneDrive, see the skill *Saving Files to a OneDrive*.

another **method**

To change the user photo, you can also click the arrow next to the user name in the upper right corner of the window and click the **Change photo** link.

let me **try**

Open the student data file **of1-SpaNewsletter** and try this skill on your own:

1. Open the **Account** page in Backstage view.
   NOTE: If you are using this in class or in your school's computer lab, check with your instructor about permissions before completing the following steps.
2. Change the photo for the user account.
3. Change the picture using a photo of your choice.
4. Save the changes to the picture.
5. Close the browser window.
6. Keep this file open for working on the next skill.

Skill 1.7 Changing the Look of Office

In addition to managing the Office account, you can also control the look of Office from the *Account* page. Changing the Office background changes the background image that displays in the upper right corner of the window near the user profile. Changing the Office theme changes the color scheme for Office, affecting the look of the Ribbon and dialogs.

To change the look of Office:

1. Click the **File** tab to open Backstage view.
2. Click **Account.**
3. Click the **Office Background** drop-down list and select an option to display as the background.
4. Click the **Office Theme** drop-down list and select a color option for your applications.

FIGURE OF 1.19

let me try

If necessary, open the student data file **of1-SpaNewsletter** and try this skill on your own:

1. Open the **Account** page in Backstage view.
   NOTE: If you are using this in class or in your school's computer lab, check with your instructor about permissions before completing the following steps.
2. Change the Office background to the **Circuit** background.
3. Change the Office color to **Light Gray.**
4. Close the file.

Skill 1.8 Working in Protected View

When you download a file from a location that Office considers potentially unsafe, it opens automatically in **Protected View**. Protected View provides a read-only format that protects your computer from becoming infected by a virus or other malware. Potentially unsafe locations include the Internet, e-mail messages, or a network location. Files that are opened in Protected View display a warning in the Message Bar at the top of the window, below the Ribbon.

To disable Protected View, click the **Enable Editing** button in the Message Bar.

Click **Enable Editing** to begin working on the file.

FIGURE OF 1.20

tips & tricks

To learn more about the security settings in Office 2013, open the Trust Center and review the options. We do not recommend changing any of the default Trust Center settings.

another method

You can also enable editing from the Info page in Backstage.
1. Click the **File** tab to open Backstage.
2. Click **Info.**
3. The Info page provides more information about the file. If you are sure you want to remove it from Protected View, click the **Enable Editing** button.

let me try

Open the student data file **of1-SpaNewsletter** and try this skill on your own:
1. If you downloaded the file from the Internet, the file will open in Protected View.
2. Click the **Enable Editing** button to begin working with the file.
3. Close the file.

Skill 1.9 Picking Up Where You Left Off

When you are working in a long document or a presentation and reopen it to work on it, you may not remember where you were last working. Office 2013 includes a new feature that automatically bookmarks the last location that was worked on when the file was closed.

To pick up where you left off in a document or presentation:

1. Open the document or presentation.
2. A message displays on the right side of the screen welcoming you back and asking if you want to pick up where you left off. The message then minimizes to a bookmark tag.
3. Click the **bookmark tag** to navigate to the location.

FIGURE OF 1.21

tips & tricks

The bookmark tag only displays until you navigate to another part of the document. If you scroll the document, the bookmark tag disappears.

tell me more

This feature is only available in Word and PowerPoint. Excel and Access do not give you the option of picking up where you left off when you open a file.

let me try

Open the student data file **of1-09-SpaNewsletter** and try this skill on your own:
1. Navigate to the location where the last location the file was at when last closed.
2. Close the file.

Skill 1.10 Creating a New Blank File

When you first open an Office application, the *Start* page displays giving you the opportunity to open an existing file or create a new blank file or one based on a template. But what if you have a file open and want to create another new file? Will you need to close the application and then launch it again? The **New command** allows you to create new files without exiting and reopening the program.

To create a new blank file:

1. Click the **File** tab to open Backstage view.

2. Click **New.**

3. The first option on the *New* page is a blank file. Click the **Blank document** thumbnail to create the new blank file.

FIGURE OF 1.22

tell me **more**

In addition to a blank file, you can create new files from templates from the *New* page.

another **method**

To bypass the Backstage view and create a new blank file, press Ctrl + N on the keyboard.

let me **try**

Open the student data file **of1-SpaNewsletter** and try this skill on your own:
1. Create a new blank file.
2. Close the file but do not save it.

Skill 1.11 Using Help

If you don't know how to perform a task, you can look it up in the **Office Help** system. Each application comes with its own Help system with topics specifically tailored for working with that application.

To look up a topic using the Microsoft Office Help system:

1. Click the **Microsoft Office Help** button. It is located at the far right of the Ribbon.

2. Click in the *Search online help* **box** and type a word or phrase describing the topic you want help with.

3. Click the **Search** button.

4. A list of results appears.

5. Click a result to display the help topic.

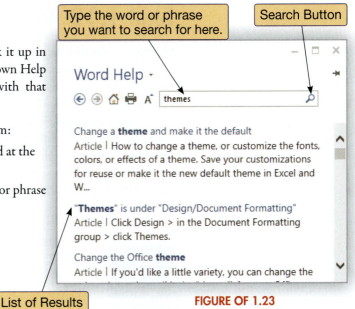

Type the word or phrase you want to search for here.

Search Button

Word Help

themes

Change a **theme** and make it the default
Article | How to change a theme, or customize the fonts, colors, or effects of a theme. Save your customizations for reuse or make it the new default theme in Excel and W...

"**Themes**" is under "Design/Document Formatting"
Article | Click Design > in the Document Formatting group > click Themes.

Change the Office **theme**
Article | If you'd like a little variety, you can change the

List of Results

FIGURE OF 1.23

Help Button

FIGURE OF 1.24

tips & tricks

To search for topics in Microsoft Office Help, you must have an active Internet connection. If you are working offline (not connected to *Office.com*), Help is still available, but it is limited to information about finding buttons of the Ribbon.

tell me more

The Help toolbar is located at the top of the Help window. This toolbar includes buttons for navigating between screens, changing the size of text, and returning to the *Help Home* page. Click the **printer icon** on the toolbar to print the current topic. Click the **pushpin icon** to keep the Help window always on top of the Microsoft Office application.

another method

To open the Help window, you can also press (F1) on the keyboard.

let me try

Open the student data file **of1-SpaNewsletter** and try this skill on your own:

1. Click the **Microsoft Office Help** button.
2. Search for topics about **themes.**
3. Click a link of your choice.
4. Close the **Help** window.
5. Keep this file open for working on the next skill.

Skill 1.12 Working with File Properties

File Properties provide information about a file such as the location of the file, the size of file, when the file was created and when it was last modified, the title, and the author. Properties also include keywords, referred to as **tags,** that are useful for grouping common files together or for searching. All this information about a file is referred to as **metadata**.

To view a file's properties, click the **File** tab to open Backstage view. Properties are listed at the far right of the *Info* tab. To add keywords to a file, click the text box next to *Tags* and type keywords that describe the file, separating each word with a comma. The Author property is added automatically using the account name entered when you installed and registered Office. You can change the author name or add more names by editing the Author property.

FIGURE OF 1.25

tips & tricks

Some file properties are generated automatically by Windows and cannot be edited by the user, such as the date the file was created and the size of the file.

let me try

If necessary, open the student data file **of1-SpaNewsletter** and try this skill on your own:
1. Add a tag to the document that reads **newsletter.**
2. Keep this file open for working on the next skill.

Skill 1.13 Saving Files to a Local Drive

As you work on a new file, it is displayed on-screen and stored in your computer's memory. However, it is not permanently stored until you save it as a file to a specific location. The first time you save a file, the *Save As* page in Backstage view will display. Here you can choose to save the file to your OneDrive, your local computer, or another location.

To save a file to a local drive:

1. Click the **Save** button on the Quick Access Toolbar.
2. The *Save As* page in Backstage view appears.
3. On the left side of the page, click **Computer** to save the file to a local drive.
4. Word displays a list of recent folders; select a folder where you want to save the file.

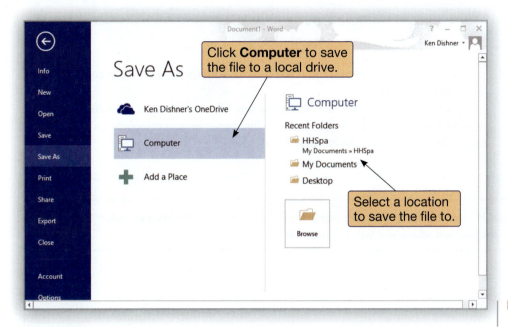

FIGURE OF 1.26

5. The *Save As* dialog opens.
6. If you want to create a new folder, click the **New Folder** button near the top of the file list. The new folder is created with the temporary name *New Folder.* Type the new name for the folder and press **Enter.**
7. Click in the **File name** box and type a file name.
8. Click the **Save** button.

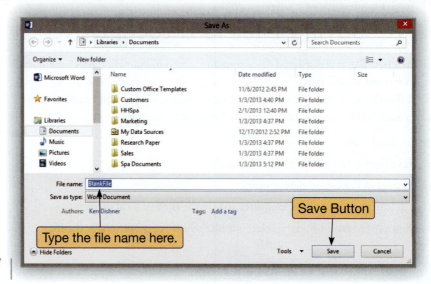

FIGURE OF 1.27

The next time you save this file, it will be saved with the same file name and to the same location automatically.

As you are working with files, be sure to **save often!** Although Office 2013 includes a recovery function, it is not foolproof. If you lose power or your computer crashes, you may lose all the work done on the file since the last save.

tips & tricks

If the location where you want to save the file is not listed under *Recent Folders,* click the **Browse** button to open the *Save As* dialog. Navigate to the location where you want to save the file.

another method

To save a file, you can also:

) Press Ctrl + S on the keyboard.

) Click the **File** tab, and then select **Save.**

) Click the **File** tab, and then select **Save As.**

let me try

Try this skill on your own:

1. Create a new blank file.
2. Save the file to the **My Documents** folder on your computer. Name the file **BlankFile.**
3. Close the file.

Skill 1.14 Saving Files to a OneDrive

NOTE: When Microsoft Office 2013 first published, this feature was named **SkyDrive**. It has since been renamed **OneDrive**.

OneDrive is Microsoft's free cloud storage where you can save documents, workbooks, presentations, videos, pictures, and other files and access those files from any computer or share the files with others. When you save files to your OneDrive, they are stored locally on your computer and then "synched" with your OneDrive account and stored in the "cloud" where you can then access the files from another computer or device that has OneDrive capability.

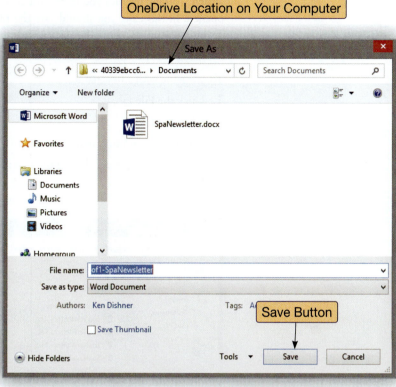

FIGURE OF 1.28

To save a file to your OneDrive:

1. Click the **File** tab.
2. Click **Save As.**
3. Verify the OneDrive account is selected on the left side of the page.
4. Under *Recent Folders,* click the **OneDrive** account you want to save to.
5. The *Save As* dialog opens to your OneDrive folder location on your computer.
6. Click in the **File name** box and type a file name.
7. Click the **Save** button.

tips & tricks

By default, your OneDrive includes folders for documents, pictures, and files you want to make public. You can save your files in any of these folders or create your own. To create a new folder in your OneDrive, click the **New Folder** button near the top of the file list. The new folder is created with the temporary name *New Folder*. Type the new name for the folder and press ⏎ Enter .

tell me more

When you are working on an Excel or Word file that has been saved to your OneDrive, others can work on the file at the same time you are working the file. The application will mark the area being worked on as read only so others cannot modify the same information you are working on. However, if you are sharing a PowerPoint presentation, only one user at a time can work on the presentation.

let me try

If necessary, open the student data file **of1-SpaNewsletter** and try this skill on your own:

1. Save the file to the **Documents** folder on your OneDrive. **NOTE:** If you are using this in class or in your school's computer lab, check with your instructor before completing this step.
2. Keep this file open for working on the next skill.

Skill 1.15   Saving Files with a New Name

When working on files you may want to save a file but not overwrite the original file you opened. In this case, you should save the file with a new name. When you save a file with a new name, the original file still exists in its last saved state and the new file you save will include all the changes you made.

To save a file with a new name:

1. Click the **File** tab.
2. Click **Save As.**
3. Select a location to save the file, either your OneDrive or your local drive.
4. In the *Save As* dialog, click in the **File name** box, type a new name for the file, and click **Save.**

FIGURE OF 1.29

tell me **more**

Beginning with Office 2007, Microsoft changed the file format for Office files. If you want to share your files with people who are using Office 2003 or older, you should save the files in a different file format.

1. In the *Save As* dialog, click the arrow at the end of the *Save as type* box to expand the list of available file types.
2. To ensure compatibility with older versions of Office, select the file type that includes 97-2003 (for example, Word 97-2003 Document or Excel 97-2003 Workbook).

let me **try**

If necessary, open the student data file **of1-SpaNewsletter** and try this skill on your own:
1. Save the file to the **Documents** folder on your computer with the name **SpaNewsletter.**
2. Keep this file open for working on the next skill.

office 2013   chapter 1 Essential Skills for Office 2013

Skill 1.16 Closing the Application

When you close a file, the application stays open so you can open another file to edit or begin a new file. Often, when you are finished working on a file, you want to close the file and exit the application at the same time. In this case, you will want to close the application.

To close an application:

1. Click the **Close** button in the upper-right corner of the application.
2. If you have made no changes since the last time you saved the file, it will close immediately. If changes have been made, the application displays a message box asking if you want to save the changes you made before closing.
   Click **Save** to save the changes.
   Click **Don't Save** to close the file without saving your latest changes.
   Click **Cancel** to keep the file open.

FIGURE OF 1.30

another method

To close the application, you can also:

❯ Right-click the title bar and select **Close.**

❯ Click the application icon in the upper-left corner of the application and select **Close.**

let me try

If necessary, open the student data file **of1-SpaNewsletter** and try this skill on your own:

Close the application.

key terms

Microsoft Word	Quick Access Toolbar
Microsoft Excel	ScreenTip
Microsoft PowerPoint	Enhanced ScreenTip
Microsoft Access	Live Preview
Ribbon	Start page
Tab	Account page
Groups	Protected View
Contextual tabs	New command
Home tab	Office Help
File tab	File Properties
Backstage	Tags
Keyboard shortcuts	Metadata
Shortcut menus	OneDrive
Mini toolbar	

concepts review

1. Microsoft _____ is a spreadsheet program.
   a. Word
   b. Excel
   c. Access
   d. PowerPoint

2. Click the _____ tab to display Backstage view.
   a. File
   b. Home
   c. View
   d. Contextual

3. To display a shortcut menu _____ an area of the file.
   a. left-click
   b. right-click
   c. double-click
   d. None of the above

4. If you have downloaded a file from the Internet and it opens in Protected View, you should never open the file.
   a. True
   b. False

5. The _____ is located across the top of the application window and organizes common features and commands into tabs.
   a. menu bar
   b. toolbar
   c. title bar
   d. Ribbon

6. The _____ provide(s) information about a file such as the location of the file, the size of file, when the file was created and when it was last modified, the title, and the author.

   a. file properties

   b. user profile

   c. account information

   d. Options dialog

7. When you save files to your OneDrive, they are available to access from other computers that have OneDrive capability. If you are working on an Excel or Word file, others can be working on the same file at the same time you are working on the file.

   a. True

   b. False

8. You can change user information from the _____ page in Backstage view.

   a. Account

   b. Options

   c. Share

   d. Info

9. To paste an item from the *Clipboard,* use the keyboard shortcut _____.

   a. (Ctrl) + (C)

   b. (Ctrl) + (X)

   c. (Ctrl) + (V)

   d. (Ctrl) + (P)

10. The _____ gives you quick one-click access to common commands and is located at the top of the application window above the *File* tab.

   a. Ribbon

   b. Quick Access Toolbar

   c. Options dialog

   d. Backstage view

excel 2013

Getting Started with Excel 2013

In this chapter, you will learn the following skills:

- Identify the elements of a Microsoft Excel 2013 workbook
- Navigate a workbook
- Enter and format text, numbers, and dates in cells
- Enter simple formulas
- Understand relative and absolute cell references
- Understand the concept of a function
- Use AutoSum and the Quick Analysis tool to add totals
- Use the status bar to display totals and other values
- Change the zoom level to view more or less of the worksheet
- Create a new workbook from a template
- Arrange multiple workbook windows
- Spell check a worksheet
- Preview and print a worksheet

skills

introduction

This chapter provides you with the basic skills necessary to start working with Excel 2013. The first step is to become familiar with the Excel interface and learn how to navigate a workbook. Next, you'll learn how to enter data and apply simple number and date formats. This chapter introduces the concepts of formulas, functions, and absolute and relative references. Pay close attention to the skill *Understanding Absolute and Relative References*. These concepts are used throughout Excel. You will add totals to worksheet data using the SUM function with a variety of methods including AutoSum and the Quick Analysis tool. To help you start using Excel for your own purposes, you will learn how to create a new workbook from a template and how to manage multiple workbooks at the same time. Finally, the chapter covers how to check a worksheet for spelling errors and how to preview and print.

Skill 1.1 Introduction to Excel 2013

Microsoft Excel 2013 is a spreadsheet program in which you enter, manipulate, calculate, and chart numerical and text data. An Excel file is referred to as a **workbook**, which is a collection of worksheets. Each worksheet (also called a "sheet") is made up of rows and columns of data on which you can perform calculations. It's these calculations that make Excel such a powerful tool.

Some of the basic elements of a Microsoft Excel workbook include:

) **Worksheet**—an electronic ledger in which you enter data. The worksheet appears as a grid where you can enter and then manipulate data using functions, formulas, and formatting. Excel workbooks have one worksheet by default named *Sheet1*. You can rename, add, and delete worksheets as necessary.

) **Row**—a horizontal group of cells. Rows are identified by numbers. For example, the third row is labeled with the number *3*.

) **Column**—a vertical group of cells. Columns are identified by letters. For example, the fourth column is labeled with the letter *D*.

) **Cell**—the intersection of a column and a row. A cell is identified by the **cell address**—its column and row position. For example, the cell at the intersection of column B and row 4 has a cell address of *B4*.

) **Cell Range**—a contiguous group of cells A cell range is identified by the address of the cell in the upper left corner of the range, followed by a colon, and then the address of the cell in the lower right corner of the range. The cell range *B3:D5* includes cells B3, B4, B5, C3, C4, C5, D3, D4, and D5.

) **Formula Bar**—data entry area directly below the Ribbon and above the worksheet grid. Although you can type any data in the formula bar, the *Insert Function* button at the left side of the formula bar was designed to make it easier to create complex formulas.

) **Name Box**—appears at the left side of the formula bar and displays the address of the selected cell. If a group of cells is selected, the *Name* box displays the address of the first cell in the group.

) **Status Bar**—appears at the bottom of the worksheet grid and can display information about the selected data, including the number of cells selected that contain data (count) and the average and sum (total) of the selected values (when appropriate).

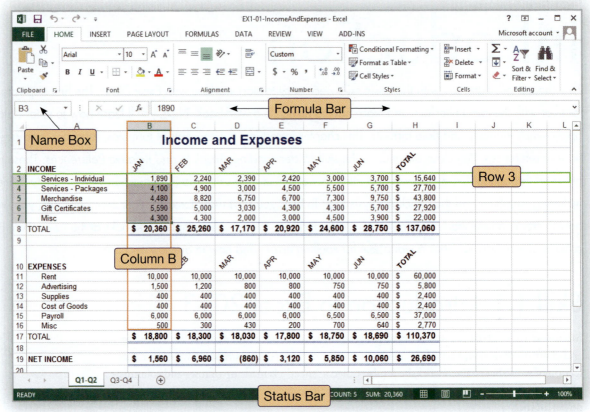

FIGURE EX 1.1

You can use Excel for a wide variety of purposes, from calculating payments for a personal loan, to creating a personal budget, to tracking employee sales and calculating bonuses for your business.

let me try

Open the student data file **EX1-01-IncomeAndExpenses** and explore the Excel workbook on your own:

1. Click the **Q3-Q4** worksheet tab at the bottom of the workbook.
2. Click anywhere in **column B.**
3. Click anywhere in **row 2.**
4. Click cell **B8.**
5. Click the **formula bar.**
6. Click the **Name Box.**
7. Click the **Q1-Q2** worksheet tab.
8. Click the **status bar.**
9. Close the workbook by clicking the **X** in the upper right corner of the window. If Excel asks if you want to save your changes, click **No.**

Skill 1.2 Navigating a Workbook

An Excel 2013 worksheet can include more than one million rows and more than sixteen thousand columns. That's a lot of potential data to navigate! Luckily, most spreadsheets are not quite that large. However, you may encounter workbooks with multiple worksheets and hundreds of rows and columns of data.

The Excel window includes both a **vertical scroll bar** (at the right side of the window) and a **horizontal scroll bar** (at the bottom of the window). Click the arrows at the ends of the scroll bars to move up and down or left and right to see more cells in an individual worksheet. You can also click and drag the scroll box to reposition your view of the spreadsheet. Notice that when you use the scroll bars, the selected cell does not change. Using the scroll bars only changes your view of the worksheet.

The most obvious way to select a cell in a worksheet is to click it with the mouse. Notice that Excel highlights the appropriate column letter and row number to identify the selected cell. When you select a single cell, the cell address appears in the *Name* box in the upper left corner of the spreadsheet, and the cell content appears in the formula bar (immediately below the Ribbon).

FIGURE EX 1.2

To navigate from cell to cell, use the mouse to click the cell you want to go to. You can also use the arrow keys on the keyboard to navigate around the worksheet.

To select a range of cells, click the first cell in the range and drag the mouse until the cells you want are selected. Release the mouse button. You can also click the first cell in the range, press [Shift], and then click the last cell in the range.

To select an entire row, click the **row selector** (the box with the row number at the left side of the worksheet grid).

To select an entire column, click the **column selector** (the box with the column letter at the top of the worksheet grid).

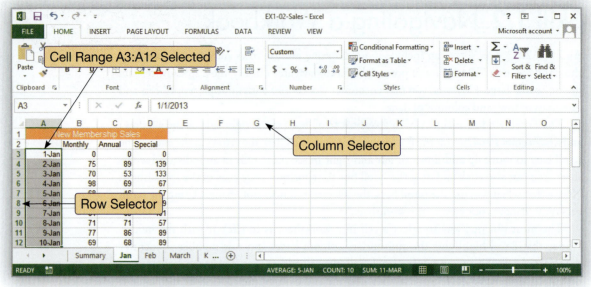

FIGURE EX 1.3

To navigate to another worksheet in the workbook, click the appropriate tab at the bottom of the worksheet grid. If the worksheet tab is not visible, use the navigation arrows located at the left side of the first sheet tab to show one worksheet at a time to the left or the right. These arrows are active only when there are worksheets not visible in your current view.

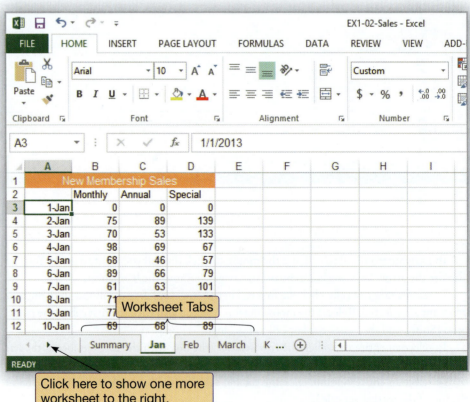

FIGURE EX 1.4

tips & tricks

To make more worksheets visible at one time, adjust the size of the horizontal scroll bar by clicking the dotted line that appears immediately to the left of the scroll bar. Notice that the cursor shape changes to a double-sided arrow. Click and drag to the right to make the horizontal scroll bar shorter and reveal more worksheet tabs.

another method

Another way to navigate to a specific cell location is to type the cell address in the *Name* box, and then press ⏎ Enter.

let me try

Open the student data file **EX1-02-Sales** and try this skill on your own:

1. Select column **A.**
2. Select row **2.**
3. Navigate to the **Summary** worksheet.
4. Select cell **B6.**
5. Move to cell **B7.**
6. Select cells **E3:E5.**
7. Save the file as directed by your instructor and close it.

from the perspective of . . .

SPORTS CLINIC OFFICE MANAGER

I couldn't do my job without Microsoft Excel. All the clinic financial data is kept in Excel spreadsheets, and I use Excel's analysis and formatting tools to visualize our cash flow. Any problem areas are easy to find. We sell rehab equipment directly to our patients, and I also use Excel to track the progress of our orders and sales.

Skill 1.3 Working in Protected View

When you download a workbook from a location that Excel considers potentially unsafe, it opens automatically in Protected View. **Protected View** provides a read-only format that protects your computer from becoming infected by a virus or other malware. Potentially unsafe locations include the Internet, e-mail messages, or a network location. Files that are opened in Protected View display a warning in the **Message Bar** at the top of the window, below the Ribbon.

To disable Protected View, click the **Enable Editing** button in the Message Bar.

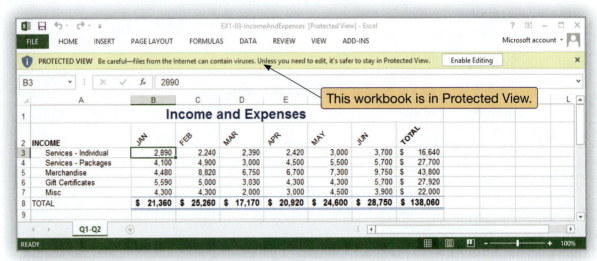

FIGURE EX 1.5

You can also enable editing from the Info page in Backstage.

1. Click the **File** tab to open Backstage.

2. Click **Info.**

3. The Info page provides more information about the file. If you are sure you want to remove it from Protected View, click the **Enable Editing** button.

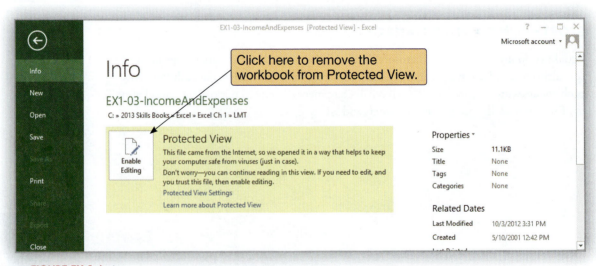

FIGURE EX 1.6

tips & tricks

tell me **more**

You can modify the Protected View settings to add or delete specific locations or types of locations.

To review or modify the Protected View settings for Excel:

1. Click the **File** tab.
2. If you are currently in Protected View, the *Info* tab will include a link to go to the Protected View settings. If you are not currently in Protected View, click the **Options** button to open the *Excel Options* dialog.
3. Click **Trust Center,** and then click the **Trust Center Settings** button.
4. The *Trust Center* dialog opens. Click **Protected View** to enable or disable Protected View for different locations, such as the Internet and Outlook attachments.
5. To exempt specific locations from Protected View, click **Trusted Locations,** and add the location you trust (such as secure network locations).
6. Click **OK** to save your changes and close the *Trusted Locations* dialog.
7. Click **OK** again to close the *Excel Options* dialog.

let me **try**

Open the student data file **EX1-03-IncomeAndExpenses** and try this skill on your own:

This workbook came from a trusted source. If the workbook opens in Protected View, disable Protected View and allow editing. Save the file as directed by your instructor and close it.

Skill 1.4 Entering and Editing Text and Numbers in Cells

The most basic task in Excel is entering data in your workbook. Entering numerical data is as easy as typing a number in a cell. Numbers can be displayed as dates, currency values, percentages, or other formats. (Later skills discuss number formatting and using functions and formulas to automate numerical calculations.)

Excel is not just about numbers, though. Without text headers, descriptions, and instructions, your workbook would consist of numbers and formulas without any structure. Adding text headers to your rows and columns creates the structure for you to enter data into your workbook.

To enter data in a cell:

1. Click the cell where you want the data to appear.

2. Type the number or text.

3. Press ⎆ Enter or Tab ⇥.

   Pressing ⎆ Enter after entering text will move the cursor down one cell.

   Pressing Tab ⇥ will move the cursor to the right one cell.

Excel gives you different ways to edit the data in your worksheet. If you want to change the contents of the entire cell, use **Ready mode**. If you want to change only part of the cell data, use **Edit mode**. The status bar, located at the lower left corner of the Excel window, displays which mode you are in—Ready or Edit.

To use Ready mode to change text:

1. Click the cell you want to change.

2. Type the new contents for the cell.

3. Press ⎆ Enter or Tab ⇥ when you are finished.

4. The old contents are completely removed and replaced with what you've typed.

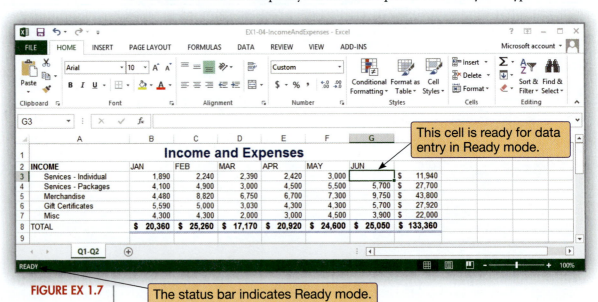

FIGURE EX 1.7

The status bar indicates Ready mode.

To use Edit mode to change text:

1. Double-click the cell you want to change.

2. You should now see a blinking cursor in the cell.

3. Move the cursor to the part of the entry you want to change and make your changes. Use ← Backspace to delete characters to the left of the cursor; use Delete to delete characters to the right of the cursor. You can also click and drag your mouse to select a section of text to delete.

4. Press ← Enter or Tab ⇆ when you are finished making your changes.

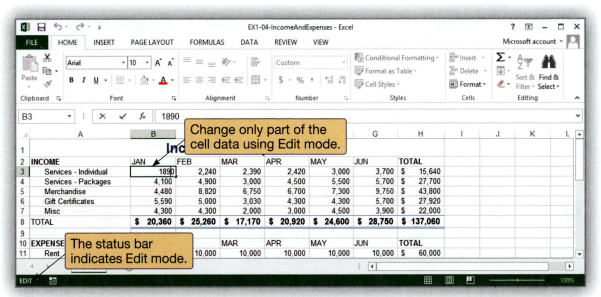

FIGURE EX 1.8

tips & tricks

To add a line break within the cell, press Alt while pressing ← Enter.

another method

As you type in a cell, the entry is displayed in the formula bar as well as in the active cell. Clicking the **Enter** icon ✓ next to the formula bar accepts your entry. Clicking the **Cancel** icon ✗ next to the formula bar removes your entry.

let me try

Open the student data file **EX1-04-IncomeAndExpenses** and try this skill on your own:

1. Add the number **3700** to cell **G3.**

2. Add the word **TOTAL** to cell **H2.**

3. Change the text in cell **B3** to **1870.** You can use ready mode or edit mode.

4. Save the file as directed by your instructor and close it.

Skill 1.5 Applying Number Formats

When you first type numbers in a worksheet, Excel applies the **General number format** automatically. The General format right-aligns numbers in the cells but does not maintain a consistent number of decimal places (43.00 will appear as 43, while 42.25 appears as 42.25) and does not display commas (so 1,123,456 appears as 1123456). For consistency, and to make your worksheet easier to read, you should apply the specific number format that is most appropriate for your data. Excel provides several number formats for you to choose from.

Figure EX 1.9 shows common Excel number formats. All numbers in row 2 contain the number .0567. All numbers in row 3 contain the number 1234. Formatting numbers changes the appearance of the data in your worksheet but doesn't change the numerical values. The formatted number is displayed in the cell, and the actual value is displayed in the formula bar.

Formula bar displays the full number 0.567 while cell B2 formatted using the Number Style format displays 0.57.

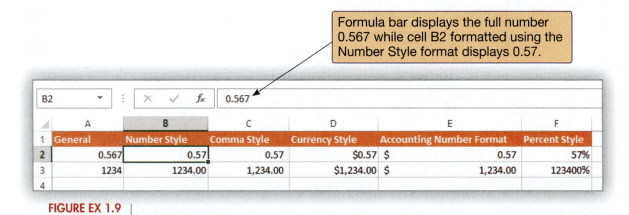

	A	B	C	D	E	F
1	General	Number Style	Comma Style	Currency Style	Accounting Number Format	Percent Style
2	0.567	0.57	0.57	$0.57	$ 0.57	57%
3	1234	1234.00	1,234.00	$1,234.00	$ 1,234.00	123400%
4						

FIGURE EX 1.9

To apply the most common number formats, go to the *Home* tab, *Number* group, and click one of the following buttons:

$ ▾	Click the **Accounting Number Format** button to apply formatting appropriate for monetary values. The **Accounting Number Format** aligns the $ at the left side of the cell, displays two places after the decimal, and aligns all numbers at the decimal point. Zero values are displayed as dashes (–).
%	Click the **Percent Style** button to have your numbers appear as %. For example, the number .02 will appear as 2%. By default, **Percent Style format** displays zero places to the right of the decimal point.
,	Click the **Comma Style** button to apply the same format as the Accounting Number Format but without the currency symbol. **Comma Style format** is a good number format to use if your worksheet includes many rows of numbers, summed in a total row (like a budget or cash flow projection), where too many $ symbols could be distracting. Use Comma Style formatting for all numbers except the total row. Use Accounting Number Format for the total row.

Increase Decimal   Decrease Decimal

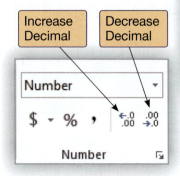

FIGURE EX 1.10

Use *Increase Decimal* and *Decrease Decimal* to increase or decrease the number of digits that appear to the right of the decimal point. For example, if a cell contains the number 1.234 and you click the **Decrease Decimal** button twice, the cell will display 1.2. The formula bar will still display 1.234 because that is the number stored in the worksheet.

For other common number formats, click the **Number Format** arrow above the buttons in the *Number* group to display the *Number Format* menu.

Number—The default Number format shows two decimal places by default (so 43 displays as 43.00) but does not include commas.

Currency—With the Currency format, columns of numbers do not align at the $ and at the decimal as they do with *Accounting Number Format.* Instead, the *Currency* format places the $ immediately to the left of the number.

Percentage—The *Percentage* option on the *Number Format* menu applies the same Percent Style format as clicking the *Percent Style* button.

More Number Formats...—This option opens the *Format Cells* dialog to the *Number* tab, where you can select from even more number formats and customize any format, including adding color, specifying the number of decimal places to display, and setting whether or not negative numbers should be enclosed in parentheses.

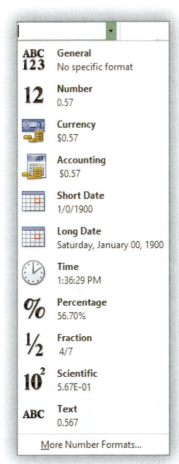

FIGURE EX 1.11
Number Format Menu

tips & tricks

If you type $ before a number, Excel automatically applies the *Currency* number format.

tell me more

On the *Home* tab, in the *Styles* group, click the **Cell Styles** button to expand the *Styles* gallery. At the bottom of the gallery are five number styles. Applying one of these cell styles is the same as applying a number format. However, be aware that applying the Currency cell style actually applies the Accounting Number Format, not the Currency format.

Comma—applies the default Comma Style format with two digits to the right of the decimal.

Comma [0]—applies the Comma Style format but with no digits to the right of the decimal.

Currency—applies the default Accounting Number Format, with two digits to the right of the decimal.

Currency [0]—applies the Accounting Number Format but with no digits to the right of the decimal.

Percent—applies the default Percent Style format.

another method

When you right-click a cell, these formats are available from the Mini toolbar: Accounting Number Format, Percent style, and Comma style.

The *Increase Decimal* and *Decrease Decimal* buttons are also available from the Mini toolbar.

To apply the Percent Style, you can use the keyboard shortcut (Ctrl) + (↑ Shift) + (5).

let me try

Open the student data file **EX1-05-IncomeAndExpenses** and try this skill on your own:

1. Apply the **Accounting Number Format** to cells **B8** through **H8**.
2. Select cells **B3:H7**, and apply the number format to display the numbers in accounting format without the currency symbol.
3. Select cells **B3:H8**. Modify the number format so no decimal places are visible after the decimal point.
4. Select cells **I3:I7** and change the number format to the default percent format.
5. Save the file as directed by your instructor and close it.

Skill 1.6 Entering Dates and Applying Date Formats

When you enter numbers in a date format such as 9/5/1966 or September 5, 1966, Excel detects that you are entering a date and automatically applies one of the date formats. Excel treats dates as a special type of number, so cells formatted as dates can be used in calculations. There are many types of date formats available, but the underlying number for the date will always be the same.

There are two number formats available from the *Number Format* menu. To apply one of these formats, from the *Home* tab, click the **Number Format** arrow above the buttons in the *Number* group, and then click the format you want:

Short Date format—Applies a simple format displaying the one- or two-digit number representing the month, followed by the one- or two-digit number representing the day, followed by the four-digit year (9/5/1966).

Long Date format—Applies a longer format displaying the day of the week, and then the name of the month, the two-digit date, and the four-digit year (Monday, September 05, 1966).

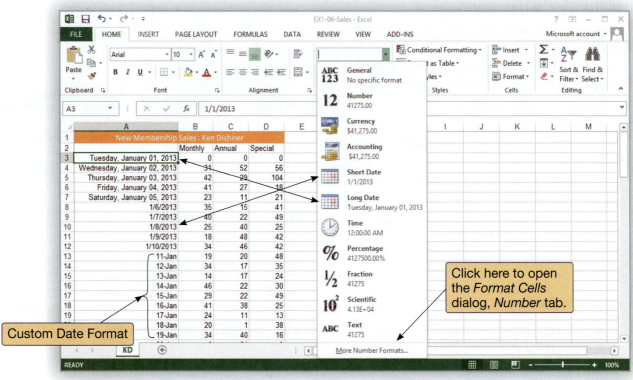

Custom Date Format

Click here to open the *Format Cells* dialog, *Number* tab.

FIGURE EX 1.12

If you would like to use a different date format:

1. Select **More Number Formats...** from the *Number Format* list.

2. In the *Format Cells* dialog, from the *Number* tab, if necessary, click **Date** in the *Category* list. Excel offers a variety of prebuilt date formats to choose from.

3. Notice that as you click each format in the *Type* list, the *Sample* box shows how the active cell will display with the selected format.

4. Click the date format you would like, and click **OK**.

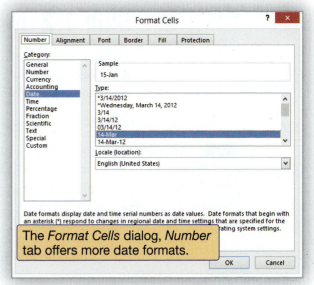

The *Format Cells* dialog, *Number* tab offers more date formats.

FIGURE EX 1.13

tips & tricks

Only dates from January 1, 1900, through December 31, 9999, are stored as numbers. Dates prior to January 1, 1900, are stored as text and cannot be used in calculations. To see the serial number for a date, change the cell format from *Date* to *General* or *Number*. The date will be converted to a "regular" number. For example, December 31, 2009, is the number 40178.

tell me more

Every date format can be expressed as a code. The code for the Short Date format is **m/d/yyy.** The code for the Long Date format is more complicated: **[$ –F800]dddd, mmmm dd, yyyy.** If Excel does not offer the exact date format you want to use, you can modify the date code using the Custom number option.

1. Select **More Number Formats...** from the *Number* list.

2. In the *Format Cells* dialog, from the *Number* tab, click **Custom** in the *Category* list.

3. The *Custom* list includes the code for every number format offered. Click the code for the format closest to the format you want, and then make adjustments to the code in the *Type* box. The *Sample* box shows how the number format will look in your worksheet.

4. Click **OK** to apply your new custom number format.

let me try

Open the student data file **EX1-06-Sales** and try this skill on your own:

1. Select cells **A3:A9** and apply the **Long Date** format.

2. Select cells **A10:A16** and apply the **Short Date** format.

3. Select cells **A17:A23** and apply the date number format to display dates in the format similar to **14-Mar.**

4. Save the file as directed by your instructor and close it.

Skill 1.7 Inserting Data Using AutoFill

Use the AutoFill feature to fill a group of cells with the same data or to extend a data series. With AutoFill, you can copy the same value or formula to a group of cells at once. This is much more efficient than using copy and paste over and over again.

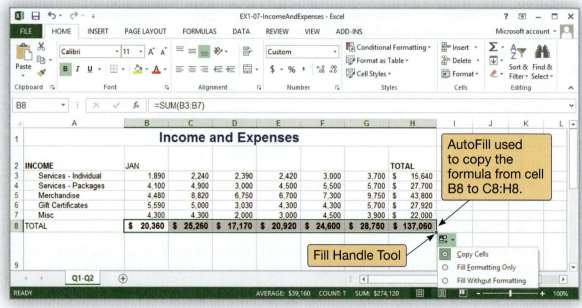

FIGURE EX 1.14

If you have a group of cells with similar data in a series, AutoFill can extend the series automatically. A **data series** is any sequence of cells with a recognizable pattern:

	A	B	C	D	E
1		Numeric Patterns			
2	1	2	3	4	
3	1	3	5	7	
4	Student 1	Student 2	Student 3	Student 4	
5					
6		Date Patterns			
7	January	February	March	April	
8	1/1/2014	2/1/2014	3/1/2014	4/1/2014	
9	7/5/2014	7/12/2014	7/19/2014	7/26/2014	
10					
11					

FIGURE EX 1.15

The easiest way to use AutoFill is to use the **Fill Handle tool** to fill data up or down in a column or to the left or right in a row.

To use the Fill Handle tool:

1. Enter the data you want in the first cell.

2. If you want to fill a series of cells with that same value, skip to step 5.

3. Enter the second value of the series in an adjacent cell.

4. Select the cell(s) you want to base the series on. (Click the first cell. Then holding [Shift] click the last cell you want to select.)

5. Click and drag the **Fill Handle** in the direction you want to fill the series. As you drag the Fill Handle, a tool tip appears displaying the value of the highlighted cell.

6. Release the mouse button when you have highlighted the last cell you want to fill.

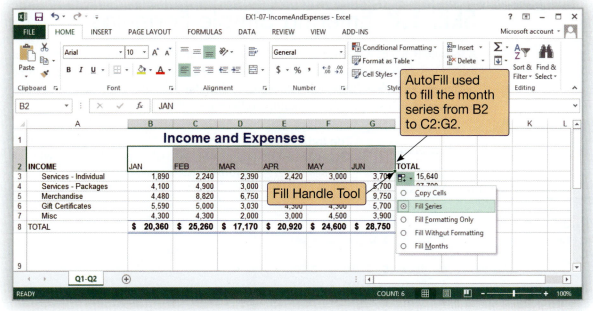

FIGURE EX 1.16

Excel attempts to detect automatically if the data appear to be a series. Sometimes, however, the series doesn't fill with the data you expect or want. To change the type of data Auto-Fill inserts, click the **AutoFill Options** button [icon] and select a different option. From the *AutoFill Options* button, you can choose to copy the cells or fill the series. By default, Excel includes formatting when copying or filling a series; however, you can choose to copy only the cell formatting or to fill or copy the data series without formatting.

tips & tricks

Use AutoFill to enter repetitive data in your worksheet to avoid errors from entering data manually.

tell me more

The Fill Handle tool can be used to fill a series of dates by month as well as year. For example, if you start the series with Jan-2013 and Feb-2013, the Fill Handle will fill in the next cells with Mar-2013, Apr-2013, May-2013, etc. When the series reaches Dec-2013, the next cell will be filled in with Jan-2014. If you are filling a series of dates, the AutoFill Options button will give you the options to fill by day, weekday, month, or year.

another method

❯ You can also use the *Fill* command from the Ribbon. First, select the cells you want to fill. On the *Home* tab, in the *Editing* group, click the **Fill** button and select the type of fill you want: **Down, Right, Up, Left, Across Worksheets…, Series…,** or **Justify.**

❯ Pressing Ctrl + D will fill the selected cell(s) with the value from the cell above it.

❯ Pressing Ctrl + R will fill the selected cell(s) with the value from the cell to the left of it.

let me try

Open the student data file **EX1-07-IncomeAndExpenses** and try this skill on your own:

1. Select cell **B8** (the total income for January) and use AutoFill to copy the formula and formatting to cells **C8:H8.**

2. Select cell **B2** (Jan) and use AutoFill to complete the month series through cell **G2.**

3. Save the file as directed by your instructor and close it.

Skill 1.8 Entering Simple Formulas

A **formula** is an equation used to calculate a value. A formula can perform a mathematical calculation, such as displaying the sum of **35 + 47,** or a formula can calculate a value using cell references, such as displaying a value equal to the value of another cell (= **B3**) or calculating an equation based on values in multiple cells (= **B3 + B4**).

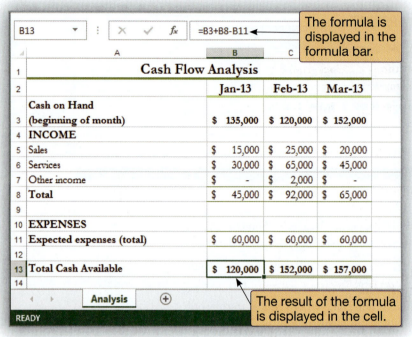

When you select a cell that contains a formula, the cell displays the value and the formula bar displays the formula.

The formula is displayed in the formula bar.

The result of the formula is displayed in the cell.

FIGURE EX 1.17

You can edit the formula in the formula bar, or you can double-click the cell to edit the formula directly in the cell. Notice that when you edit the formula, any referenced cells are highlighted in the same color as the cell reference in the formula.

FIGURE EX 1.18

To enter a formula:

1. Click the cell in which you want to enter the formula.

2. Press [=].

3. Type the formula.

4. To add a cell reference to a formula, you can type the cell address or click the cell. If you are in the middle of typing a formula and you click another cell in the worksheet, Excel knows to add that cell reference to the formula instead of moving to it.

5. Press [←Enter].

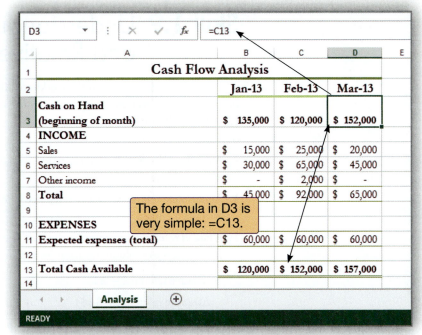

FIGURE EX 1.19

tell me more

When you enter a formula with more than one mathematical operation, the formula is not necessarily calculated from left to right. Excel calculations follow the mathematical rules called the order of operations (also called precedence).

The rules state that mathematical operations in a formula are calculated in this order:

1. Exponents and roots

2. Multiplication and division

3. Addition and subtraction

Adding parentheses around part of a formula will override the order of operations, forcing Excel to perform the calculation within the parentheses first.

$4 + (5 * 2) = 14$—Excel calculates 5 * 2 first (10) and then adds 4.

$(4 + 5) * 2 = 18$—Excel calculates 4 + 5 first (9), and then multiples by 2.

$4 + 5 \char`^ 2 = 29$—Excel calculates 5 to the 2nd power first (25), and then adds 4.

$(4 + 5) \char`^ 2 = 81$—Excel calculates 4 + 5 first (9), and then raises that number to the 2nd power.

another method

To enter a formula, you can click the **Enter** button ✔ to the left of the formula bar.

let me try

Open the student data file **EX1-08-CashFlow** and try this skill on your own:

1. In cell **B13**, enter a formula to calculate total cash available: cash on hand **(B3)** + total income **(B8)** – total expenses **(B11)**.

2. In cell **D3**, enter a formula to make the cash on hand for March **(D3)** equal to the total cash available at the end of February **(C13)**.

3. Save the file as directed by your instructor and close it.

Skill 1.9 Understanding Absolute and Relative References

A cell's address, its position in the workbook, is referred to as a **cell reference** when it is used in a formula. In Excel, the $ character before a letter or number in the cell address means that part of the cell's address is ***absolute*** (nonchanging). Cell references can be relative, absolute, or mixed.

❱ A **relative reference** is a cell reference that adjusts to the new location in the worksheet when the formula is copied.

❱ An **absolute reference** is a cell reference whose location remains constant when the formula is copied.

❱ A **mixed reference** is a combination cell reference with a row position that stays constant with a changing column position (or vice versa).

> Relative reference—A1
>
> Absolute reference—$A$1
>
> Mixed reference with absolute row—A$1
>
> Mixed reference with absolute column—$A1

Here's how relative and absolute references work:

When you type a formula into a cell, it uses ***relative*** references by default. Excel calculates the position of the referenced cell ***relative*** to the active cell. For example, if cell B15 is the active cell and you type the formula **=B13**, Excel displays the value of the cell that is up two rows from the active cell.

If you add another row to your worksheet, shifting the position of cell B15 to cell B16, Excel automatically adjusts the reference in the formula to reflect the new cell address that is up one row from the current position.

If you copy the formula **=B13** from cell B15 and paste it into cell C15, the pasted formula will update automatically to **=C13** to reflect the cell address that is up two rows from the new position.

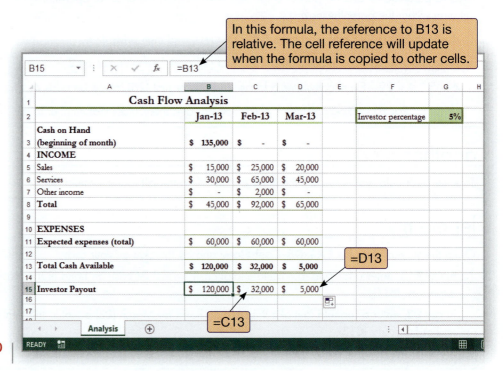

FIGURE EX 1.20

If you cut and paste the formula, Excel assumes that you want the formula to maintain its previous value and treats the formula as if it had included absolute references, pasting the formula exactly as it was.

But what if you don't want the cell reference to adjust? For example, cell G2 contains a value that you want to use in calculations for multiple cells in a row. If you were to copy the formula =B13*G2 from cell B15 to cell C15, the formula would update to =C13*H2 (not what you intended) because both of the cell references are *relative*. Instead, you want the reference to cell G2 to be *absolute*, so it does not update when you copy it. If you use the formula =B13*$G$2 instead and copy it from cell B15 to cell C15, the pasted formula will only update the relative reference B13. The absolute reference $G$2 will remain constant. The formula in cell C15 will be =C13*$G$2.

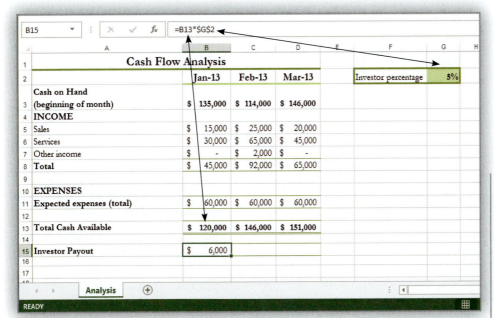

FIGURE EX 1.21
The relative reference to cell B13 will update to the new relative cell position when the formula is copied. The absolute reference to cell G2 will not. When the formula is copied to cell C15, it will be =C13*$G$2.

another method

Another way to change the cell reference type is to select the cell reference in the formula bar, and then press F4 to cycle through the various reference types until you find the one you want (absolute, mixed with absolute row, mixed with absolute column, and then back to relative).

let me try

Open the student data file **EX1-09-CashFlow** and try this skill on your own:

1. Enter a formula in cell **B15** to calculate the investor payout: total cash available **(B13)** * investor percentage **(G2)**. Be sure to use an absolute reference to G2.

2. Use AutoFill to copy the formula to cells **C15:D15**. If you entered the formula in B15 correctly, the reference to G2 will remain constant.

3. Save the file as directed by your instructor and close it.

Skill 1.10 Using Functions in Formulas

Functions are preprogrammed shortcuts for calculating equations. Functions can simplify a straightforward computation such as figuring the total of a list of values. They can also calculate the answer to a complicated equation such as figuring the monthly payment amount for a loan.

Most functions require you to provide input called the **arguments**. For example, when writing a formula using the SUM function to calculate the total of a list of values, each value or range of values to be included in the calculation is an argument. Multiple arguments are separated by commas [,].

This formula will calculate the total of the values in cells B5 through B7:

SUM(B5,B6,B7)

In this example, each cell reference is an argument.

An easier way to write the arguments for this formula is:

SUM(B5:B7)

In the second example, the function requires only one argument—the cell range containing the values. Both formulas will return the same total value.

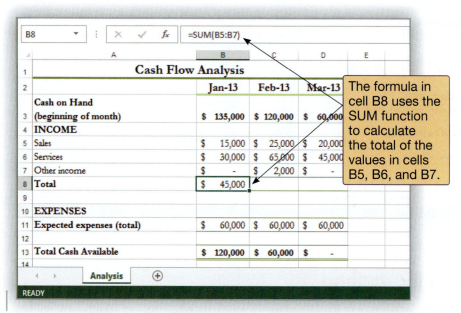

FIGURE EX 1.22

The easiest way to enter a formula using a simple function like SUM is to type the formula directly in the cell or the formula bar. Begin the formula by typing ⬚, and then type the function name. After the function name, type ⬚ followed by the function arguments, separated by commas, and then ⬚. Press ⬚ Enter ⬚ to complete the formula.

tell me **more**

You can also enter functions in formulas using AutoSum, Formula AutoComplete, and the *Function Arguments* dialog. These methods are covered in later skills.

let me **try**

Open the student data file **EX1-10-CashFlow** and try this skill on your own:

In cell **B8,** enter a formula using the SUM function to calculate the total of cells **B5** through **B7.** Save the file as directed by your instructor and close it.

Skill 1.11 Using AutoSum to Insert a SUM Function

If your spreadsheet includes numerical data organized in rows or columns, **AutoSum** can enter totals for you. When you use AutoSum, Excel enters the SUM function arguments using the most likely range of cells based on the structure of your worksheet. For example, if you use AutoSum at the bottom of a column of values, Excel will assume that you want to use the values in the column as the function arguments. If you use AutoSum at the end of a row of values, Excel will use the values in the row.

To insert a SUM function using AutoSum:

1. Select the cell in which you want to enter the function.

2. On the *Home* tab, in the *Editing* group, click the **AutoSum** button.

3. Excel automatically inserts a formula with the SUM function, using the range of cells contiguous to (next to) the selected cell as the arguments for the function. You can increase or decrease the range of cells selected by clicking and dragging the corner of the highlighted cell range

4. Press ⏎ Enter to accept the formula.

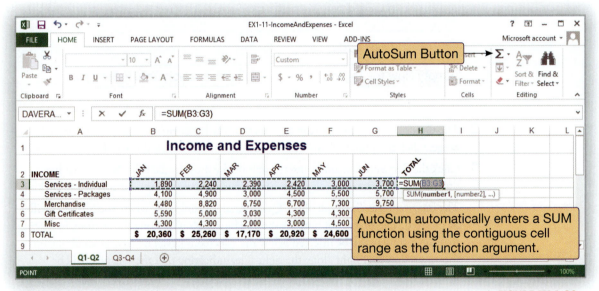

FIGURE EX 1.23

another **method**

❯ AutoSum is also available on the *Formulas* tab, in the *Function Library* group.

❯ You can also click the **AutoSum** button arrow and select **SUM** from the list.

❯ Another way to use the AutoSum function is to select a range of cells, and then click the **AutoSum** button. Excel will insert the SUM function in the next available (empty) cell.

let me **try**

Open the student data file **EX1-11-IncomeAndExpenses** and try this skill on your own:

1. If necessary, select cell **H3**.

2. Use AutoSum to enter a formula using the SUM function to calculate the total of cells **B3:G3.**

3. Save the file as directed by your instructor and close it.

Skill 1.12 Calculating Totals with the Quick Analysis Tool

The **Quick Analysis tool** is a new feature in Excel 2013 to help you easily apply formatting, create charts, and insert formulas based on the selected data. In this skill, we will focus on creating totals with the Quick Analysis tool. You will learn to use the other features of this tool in later skills.

To use the Quick Analysis tool to calculate totals:

1. Select the range of cells. Verify that there are empty cells below or to the right of the selection (where the totals will be inserted).

	A	B	C	D	E	F	G	H	I
1				**Income and Expenses**					
2	INCOME	JULY	AUG	SEPT	OCT	NOV	DEC	TOTAL	
3	Services - Individual	1,890	2,240	2,390	2,420	3,000	5,000	$ 16,940	
4	Services - Packages	4,100	4,900	3,000	4,500	5,500	8,000	$ 30,000	
5	Merchandise	4,480	8,820	6,750	6,700	8,500	15,000	$ 50,250	
6	Gift Certificates	5,590	5,000	3,030	4,300	6,000	9,000	$ 32,920	
7	Misc	4,300	4,300	2,000	3,000	4,500	3,900	$ 22,000	
8	TOTAL								
9									

FIGURE EX 1.24

Empty Row for Totals   Quick Analysis Tool Button

2. The Quick Analysis tool button appears near the lower right corner of the selected range. Click the **Quick Analysis tool** button, and then click the **Totals** tab.

3. Click the first **Sum** button to insert totals below the selected cells. Notice that live preview displays the totals as you hover the cursor over the **Sum** button before clicking.

The images in the *Totals* tab of the Quick Analysis tool show where the formulas will be inserted. The first set of buttons shows a blue highlight along the bottom, indicating that the formulas will be inserted below the selected range. The second set of buttons shows a yellow highlight along the right side, indicating that the formulas will be inserted to the right of the selected range.

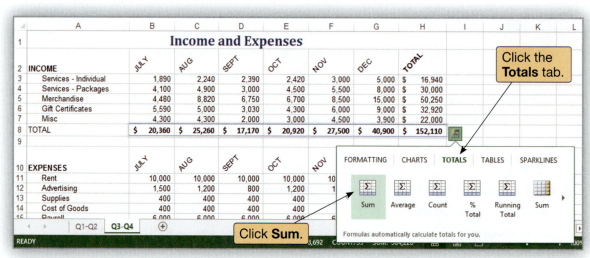

FIGURE EX 1.25

4. Excel inserts formulas using the SUM function into the empty cells below the selected range.

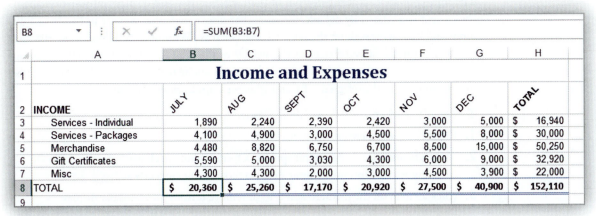

B8	▾	:	✕	✓	*fx*	=SUM(B3:B7)			

⏢	A	B	C	D	E	F	G	H
1				**Income and Expenses**				
2	**INCOME**	JULY	AUG	SEPT	OCT	NOV	DEC	TOTAL
3	Services - Individual	1,890	2,240	2,390	2,420	3,000	5,000	$ 16,940
4	Services - Packages	4,100	4,900	3,000	4,500	5,500	8,000	$ 30,000
5	Merchandise	4,480	8,820	6,750	6,700	8,500	15,000	$ 50,250
6	Gift Certificates	5,590	5,000	3,030	4,300	6,000	9,000	$ 32,920
7	Misc	4,300	4,300	2,000	3,000	4,500	3,900	$ 22,000
8	TOTAL	$ 20,360	$ 25,260	$ 17,170	$ 20,920	$ 27,500	$ 40,900	$ 152,110
9								

> Formulas inserted by the Quick Analysis tool.

FIGURE EX 1.26

tips & tricks

If the Quick Analysis tool button is not visible, move your mouse cursor over the selected cell range, without clicking. This action should make the button appear.

let me try

Open the student data file **EX1-12-IncomeAndExpenses** and try this skill on your own:

1. If necessary, select the cell range **B3:H7.**
2. Click the **Quick Analysis tool** button, and then click the **Totals** tab.
3. Click the first **Sum** button to insert totals in the empty row beneath the selected cell range.
4. Save the file as directed by your instructor and close it.

Skill 1.13 Using the Status Bar

The **status bar** appears at the bottom of the Excel window and displays information about the current worksheet. By default, the status bar displays whether you are in Ready or Edit mode and information about the selected cells (such as the number of cells selected, the sum of the values in the selected cells, or the average of the values in the selected cells). You can customize the status bar to show other information about the worksheet, the minimum or maximum value in the selected cells, and whether Caps Lock is on or off.

To change the information shown on the status bar:

1. Right-click anywhere on the status bar.

2. The *Customize Status Bar* menu appears. Options with checkmarks next to them are currently active. Options without a checkmark are not currently active.

3. Click an item on the menu to add it to or remove it from the status bar display.

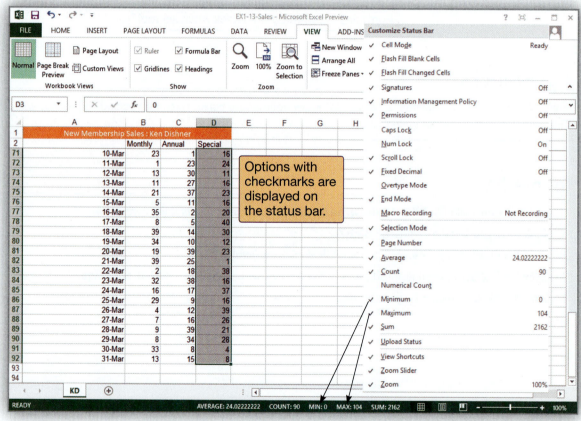

FIGURE EX 1.27

let me try

Open the student data file **EX1-13-Sales** and try this skill on your own:

1. If necessary, select cells **D3:D92.**

2. Right-click anywhere on the status bar.

3. Click **Minimum** to add a checkmark.

4. Click **Maximum** to add a checkmark.

5. Click anywhere to dismiss the menu.

6. Note the minimum and maximum values displayed on the status bar.

7. Save the file as directed by your instructor and close it.

excel 2013   chapter 1 Getting Started with Excel 2013

Skill 1.14 Changing the Zoom Level

If you are working with a large spreadsheet, you may find that you need to see more of the spreadsheet at one time or that you would like a closer look at a cell or group of cells. You can use the **zoom slider** in the lower-right corner of the window to zoom in and out of a worksheet, changing the size of text and images on screen. As you move the slider, the zoom level displays the percentage the worksheet has been zoomed in or zoomed out. Zooming a worksheet only affects how the worksheet appears on screen. It does not affect how the worksheet will print.

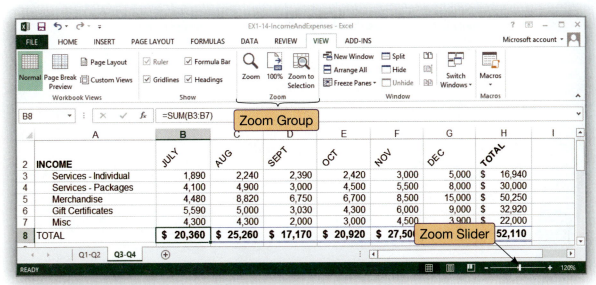

FIGURE EX 1.28

To zoom in on a worksheet, making the text and graphics appear larger:

❯ Click and drag the zoom slider to the right.

❯ Click the **Zoom In** button on the slider.

To zoom out of a worksheet, making the text and graphics appear smaller:

❯ Click and drag the zoom slider to the left.

❯ Click the **Zoom Out** button on the slider.

FIGURE EX 1.29

On the *View* tab, the *Zoom* group includes buttons for two of the most common zoom options:

❯ Click the **Zoom to Selection** button to zoom in as close as possible on the currently selected cell(s).

❯ Click the **100%** button to return the worksheet back to 100% of the normal size.

You can also change the zoom level through the *Zoom* dialog.

1. On the *View* tab, in the *Zoom* group, click the **Zoom** button.

2. In the *Zoom* dialog, click the radio button for the zoom option you want, and then click **OK**.

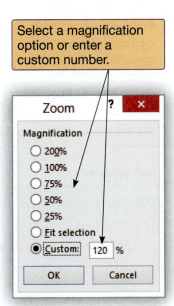

FIGURE EX 1.30

from the perspective of . . .

ACCOUNTING FIRM INTERN

My boss works on two 24″ monitors. She always has her files set at 150% or higher because she has the room to spread the worksheet across two large monitors. I work on a laptop with a 15″ screen. When I open her files, I can only see part of the worksheet until I set the zoom level back to 100%. It is harder to see details when the zoom level is set lower, but for me, it's more important to see the whole worksheet without having to scroll.

tips & tricks

When you save a workbook, Excel saves the zoom setting. However, if you change the zoom level and then close the workbook without making any other changes, Excel will not warn you about saving your change. The next time you open the workbook, it will be back to the zoom level that was set at the time the workbook was last saved.

another method

You can also open the *Zoom* dialog by clicking the zoom level number that appears at the right side of the zoom slider.

let me try

Open the student data file **EX1-14-IncomeAndExpenses** and try this skill on your own:

1. Change the zoom level to 110%.
2. Change the zoom level back to 100%.
3. Change the zoom level to 90%.
4. Save the file as directed by your instructor and close it.

Skill 1.15 Creating a New Workbook Using a Template

A **template** is a file with predefined settings that you can use as a starting point for your workbook. Using an Excel template makes creating a new workbook easy and results in a professional appearance. Many templates use advanced techniques that you may not have learned yet—but you can take advantage of them in a template where someone else has created the workbook framework for you. Templates are available for every imaginable task: from creating budgets to tracking exercise to calculating your grade point average.

To create a new workbook using a template:

1. Click the **File** tab to open Backstage view.

2. Click **New.** Excel 2013 includes a variety of templates that are copied to your computer when you install the application. These templates are always available from the *New* page. Additional templates that you download are also displayed on the *New* page, so your screen may look different than the one in Figure EX 1.31.

3. Click a template picture to open the template preview including a brief description of the template.

4. You can cycle through the template previews by clicking the arrows that appear on either side of the preview.

5. When you find the template you want to use, click the **Create** button.

6. A new workbook opens, prepopulated with all of the template elements.

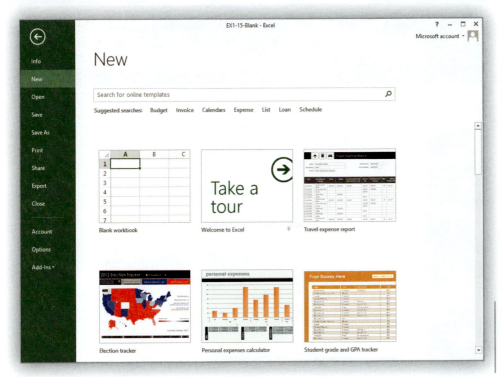

FIGURE EX 1.31
Templates stored on your computer appear on the *New* page.

You can search for more workbook templates online. (You must have an active Internet connection.)

1. Near the top of the *New* page, in the *Search online templates* box, type a keyword or phrase that describes the template you want.

2. Click the **Start searching** button (the magnifying glass image at the end of the *Search online templates* box).

3. The search results display previews of the templates that match the keyword or phrase you entered. To further narrow the results, click one of the categories listed in the *Filter by* pane at the right side of the window. Notice that each category lists the number of templates available.

4. When you find the template you want, click it to display the larger preview with detailed information about the template, and then click **Create.**

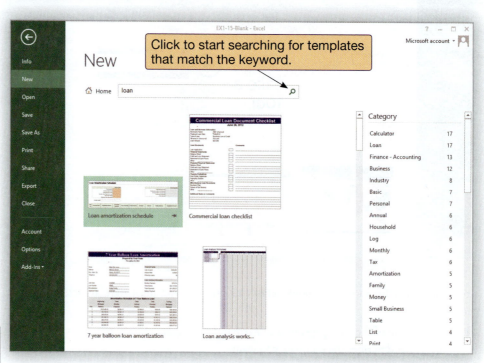

FIGURE EX 1.32

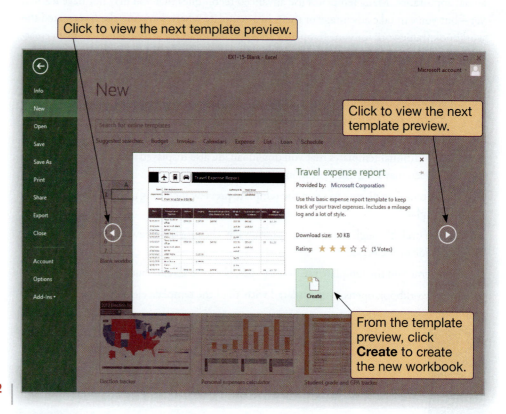

FIGURE EX 1.33
Template Search Results

from the perspective of . . .

COLLEGE STUDENT

I thought Excel was only for business. It's not! I found some really useful templates—one for tracking my day-to-day expenses and another one to help me budget my expenses for the semester. And even though some of the templates look fancy and complicated, I find that I can use them easily by reading the instructions and taking a little bit of time to personalize the data with my own information.

tips & tricks

Many Excel templates have a special worksheet labeled Settings, Instructions, or something similar. Be sure to read all of the instructions before entering data.

let me try

Open the student data file **EX1-15-Blank** and try this skill on your own:

1. Click the **File** tab.
2. Click **New.**
3. Click the **Travel expense report** template. If the *Travel expense report* template does not appear on your *New* page, search for it using the *Search online templates* feature. You may find more than one template named *Travel expense report.* Select one that appeals to you.
4. Click **Create.**
5. Save the file as directed by your instructor and close it.

Skill 1.16 Arranging Workbooks

If you are working with multiple workbooks, you may want to arrange them so you can see them all at the same time. You can arrange workbooks so they are tiled, horizontally, vertically, or in cascading windows.

Tiled Windows

FIGURE EX 1.34

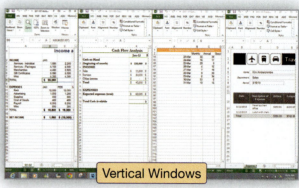

Vertical Windows

FIGURE EX 1.36

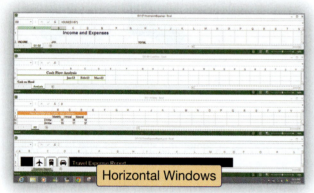

Horizontal Windows

FIGURE EX 1.35

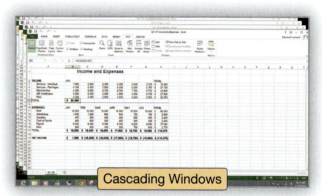

Cascading Windows

FIGURE EX 1.37

To change the arrangement of workbooks:

1. On the *View* tab, in the *Window* group, click the **Arrange All** button.

2. In the *Arrange Windows* dialog, select an arrangement option:
   - **Tiled**—places the windows in a grid pattern
   - **Horizontal**—places the windows in a stack one on top of the other
   - **Vertical**—places the windows in a row next to each other
   - **Cascade**—places the windows in a staggered, overlapping, diagonal arrangement

3. Click **OK**.

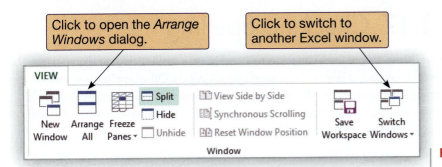

FIGURE EX 1.38

To switch between workbooks, you can:

❱ Click anywhere in the workbook you want to make active.

❱ On the *View* tab, in the *Window* group, click the **Switch Windows** button, then click the name of the workbook you want.

    To undo the arrangement and put the workbooks back in separate windows, maximize any of the workbooks by clicking the **Maximize** button on the title bar.

tell me **more**

If you have two workbooks with similar data, you may want to compare their data row by row. Excel's *Compare Side by Side* feature allows you to compare two workbooks at the same time. When you compare workbooks, the *Synchronous Scrolling* feature is on by default. This feature allows you to scroll both workbooks at once. If you scroll the active workbook, the other workbook will scroll at the same time, allowing you to carefully compare data row by row.

1. Open the workbooks you want to compare.

2. On the *View* tab, in the *Window* group, click the **View Side by Side** button.

3. The two workbooks are displayed one on top of the other.

4. Scroll the active window to scroll both workbooks at once.

5. Click the **View Side by Side** button again to restore the windows to their previous positions.

let me **try**

Open any four Excel workbooks. Practice changing the window arrangement and switching back and forth between the Excel windows. Save the file as directed by your instructor and close it.

Skill 1.17 Checking Spelling

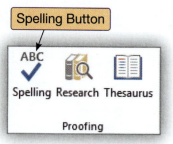

Spelling Button

FIGURE EX 1.39

Regardless of the amount of work you put into a workbook, a spelling error or typo can make the entire workbook appear sloppy and unprofessional. All the Office applications include a built-in spelling checker. In Excel, the *Spelling* command analyzes the current worksheet for spelling errors. It presents any errors it finds in a dialog box, enabling you to make decisions about how to handle each error or type of error in turn.

To check a worksheet for spelling errors:

1. On the *Review* tab, in the *Proofing* group, click the **Spelling** button.

2. The first spelling error appears in the *Spelling* dialog box.

3. Review the spelling suggestions and then select an action:

- Click **Ignore Once** to make no changes to this instance of the word.
- Click **Ignore All** to make no changes to all instances of the word.
- Click **Add to Dictionary** to make no changes to this instance of the word and add it to the spelling checker dictionary, so future uses of this word will not show up as misspellings. When you add a word to the dictionary, it is available for all the Office applications.
- Click the correct spelling in the *Suggestions* list, and click **Change** to correct just this instance of the misspelling in your worksheet.
- Click the correct spelling in the *Suggestions* list, and click **Change All** to correct all instances of the misspelling in your worksheet.

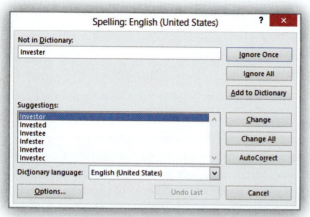

FIGURE EX 1.40

4. After you select an action, the spelling checker automatically advances to the next suspected spelling error.

5. When the spelling checker finds no more errors, it displays a message telling you the check is complete. Click **OK** to close the dialog and return to your worksheet.

tips & tricks

Whether or not you use the Spelling tool, you should always proofread your files. Spelling checkers are not infallible, especially if you misuse a word yet spell it correctly—for instance, writing "bored" instead of "board."

If you misspell a word often, the next time the spelling checker catches the misspelling, use this trick: Click the correct spelling in the *Suggestions* list and then click the *AutoCorrect* button. Now, when you type the misspelled version of the word, it will be corrected automatically as you type.

another method

To open the *Spelling* dialog, you can also press (F7).

let me try

Open the student data file **EX1-17-CashFlow** and try this skill on your own:

Spell check the worksheet and correct any errors you find. Save the file as directed by your instructor and close it.

Skill 1.18 Previewing and Printing a Worksheet

In Excel 2013, all the print settings are combined in a single page along with a preview of how the printed file will look. As you change print settings, the preview updates. To preview and print the current worksheet:

1. Click the **File** tab to open Backstage view.

2. Click **Print.**

3. At the right side of the page is a preview of how the printed file will look. Beneath the preview there is a page count. If there are multiple pages, use the *Next* and *Previous* arrows to preview all the pages in the file. You can also use the scroll bar to the right to scroll through the preview pages.

4. Set the number of copies to print by changing the number in the *Copies* box.

5. Click the **Print** button to send the file to your default printer

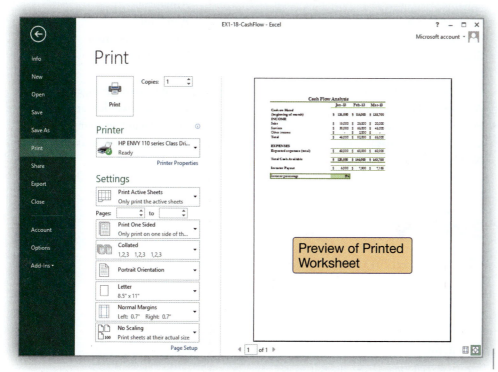

FIGURE EX 1.41

tips & tricks

Add the *Quick Print* command to the Quick Access Toolbar so you can print with a single mouse click. If you do not need to change the default print settings, you can click the *Quick Print* button instead of going through the *Print* tab in Backstage view.

another method

To open the *Print* page in Backstage view, you can use the keyboard shortcut (Ctrl) + (P).

let me try

Open the student data file **EX1-18-CashFlow** and try this skill on your own:

1. Preview how the worksheet will look when printed.

2. If you can, print the worksheet and compare the printed page to the preview.

3. Save the file as directed by your instructor and close it.

key terms

Workbook
Worksheet
Row
Column
Cell
Cell address
Cell range
Formula bar
Name box
Status bar
Vertical scroll bar
Horizontal scroll bar
Row selector
Column selector
Protected View
Message Bar
Ready mode
Edit mode
General number format
Accounting Number Format
Percent Style format
Comma Style format
Number format

Currency format
Short Date format
Long Date format
AutoFill
Data series
Fill Handle tool
Formula
Order of operations (precedence)
Cell reference
Relative reference
Absolute reference
Mixed reference
Function
Argument
AutoSum
Quick Analysis tool
Zoom slider
Template
Tiled window arrangement
Horizontal window arrangement
Vertical window arrangement
Cascade window arrangement

concepts review

1. A new Excel 2013 workbook has _____ worksheet(s).
   a. one
   b. two
   c. three
   d. four

2. The cell D4 refers to the cell at:
   a. The intersection of row D and column 4
   b. The intersection of column D and row 4
   c. The first cell on the D4 worksheet
   d. None of the above

3. Which of these dates uses the Long Date format?
   a. 1/1/2000
   b. January 1, 2000
   c. 01/01/2000
   d. Saturday, January 1, 2000

4. Formulas begin with which character?

    a. $

    b. @

    c. =

    d. *

5. Which of these cell references is an absolute reference?

    a. $G2

    b. G2

    c. $G$2

    d. None of the above

6. Which of these formulas uses a function?

    a. =B4

    b. =B4 + B5

    c. =SUM(B4:B5)

    d. =B4*B5

7. AutoSum is located:

    a. On the *Home* tab, in the *Editing* group

    b. On the *Insert* tab, in the *Formulas* group

    c. On the *Home* tab, in the *Formulas* group

    d. On the *Insert* tab, in the *Tables* group

8. The zoom slider is located:

    a. At the lower right corner of the status bar

    b. On the *View* tab, in the *Zoom* group

    c. In the *Zoom* dialog

    d. On the Ribbon

9. The keyboard shortcut to begin the spelling checker is:

    a. F5

    b. F7

    c. F4

    d. F9

10. Which of these tasks can you **not** perform in Backstage?

    a. Enable Editing when a workbook is in Protected View

    b. Preview how a workbook will look when printed

    c. Create a new workbook from a template

    d. None of the above

projects

Data files for projects can be found on
www.mhhe.com/office2013skills

skill review 1.1

The workbook for this project generates client bills from staff hours in multiple worksheets. In this project, you will complete the worksheet for staff member Marshall to calculate the daily bill, the total billable hours per week, and the total weekly bill. The worksheet for staff member Stevens has been completed. You may use it for reference as necessary.

Skills needed to complete this project:

- Navigating a Workbook (Skill 1.2)
- Working in Protected View (Skill 1.3)
- Entering and Editing Text and Numbers in Cells (Skill 1.4)
- Applying Number Formats (Skill 1.5)
- Entering Dates and Applying Date Formats (Skill 1.6)
- Inserting Data Using AutoFill (Skill 1.7)
- Understanding Absolute and Relative References (Skill 1.9)
- Entering Simple Formulas (Skill 1.8)
- Calculating Totals with the Quick Analysis Tool (Skill 1.12)
- Previewing and Printing a Worksheet (Skill 1.18)

1. Open the start file **EX2013-SkillReview-1-1** and resave the file as:
   `[your initials]EX-SkillReview-1-1`

2. If the workbook opens in Protected View, click the **Enable Editing** button in the Message Bar at the top of the workbook so you can modify the workbook.

3. Explore the workbook. If you accidentally make changes while exploring, press `Ctrl` + `Z` to undo the change.

   a. Click the worksheet tab labeled *Stevens Hours.*

   b. If necessary, use the vertical scroll bar to scroll down so you can see both weeks' of billable hours. (If necessary, use the vertical scroll bar again to return to the top of the worksheet).

   c. Click cell **B3** (the cell displaying the staff member's last name, Stevens). This is the cell at the intersection of column B and row 3.

      i. Note that the column B and row 3 selector boxes highlight.

      ii. Note that the status bar displays *Ready,* indicating that you are in Ready mode.

      iii. On the *Home* tab, in the *Number* group, look at the *Number Format* box at the top of the group. Note that the format for this cell is General.

      iv. Double-click cell **B3** to switch to Edit mode. Note that the status bar now displays *Edit,* and the blinking cursor appears within the cell. If you needed to, you could edit the text directly in the cell.

   d. Press `Esc` to exit Edit mode and return to Ready mode.

e. Press (← Enter) twice to move to cell **B5** (the cell displaying the staff member's billable rate). This cell is formatted with the Accounting Number Format number format.

    i. Look in the *Number Format* box and note that the format for this cell is *Accounting.*

    ii. On the *Home* tab, in the *Styles* group, look in the *Cell Styles* gallery, and note that the cell style *Currency* is highlighted. (If the Cell Styles gallery is collapsed on your Ribbon, click the **Cell Styles** button to display it.)

f. Click cell **B10** (the cell displaying the number of hours for Monday, January 14). This cell is formatted with the Comma Style number format.

    i. Look in the *Number Format* box and note that the format for this cell is also *Accounting.*

    ii. On the *Home* tab, in the *Styles* group, look in the *Cell Styles* gallery, and note that the cell style *Comma* is highlighted for this cell. (If the Cell Styles gallery is collapsed on your Ribbon, click the **Cell Styles** button to display it.)

    iii. Note the style differences between cell **B5** (Accounting Number Format) and cell **B10** (Comma Style format).

g. Click cell **B8** (the cell displaying the date 1/14/2013). This cell is formatted using the Short Date format. Note that the *Number Format* box displays *Date.*

h. Double-click cell **B16.**

    i. Note that the status bar now displays *Edit,* indicating that you are in Edit mode.

    ii. This cell contains a formula to calculate the daily bill for Monday, January 14: =B14*$B$5

    iii. Note that cells B14 and B5 are highlighted with colors matching the cell references in the formula.

    iv. Note that the reference to cell B5 is an absolute reference ($B$5).

i. Press (Esc) to exit Edit mode.

j. Double-click cell **B14.**

    i. Note that once again the status bar displays *Edit,* indicating that you are in Edit mode.

    ii. This cell contains a formula using the SUM function to calculate the total billable hours for Monday, January 14: =SUM(B10:B13)

    iii. In this case, the SUM function uses a single argument B10:13 to indicate the range of cells to total.

    iv. Note that the cell range B10:B13 is highlighted with the color matching the argument in the SUM function formula.

    v. Note that the reference to the cell range B10:B13 uses relative references.

k. Press (Esc) to exit Edit mode.

l. Press (Tab ⇥) to move to cell **C14.** Look in the formula bar and note that this cell contains a similar formula to the one in cell B14: =SUM(C10:C13)

m. Press (→) to move through cells **D14** through **H14.** Note the formula in the formula bar for each cell.

n. Did you notice that the cell references in the formulas in cells C14 through H14 all use relative references?

4. Now you are ready to complete the worksheet for David Marshall. Navigate to the *Marshall Hours* worksheet by clicking the **Marshall Hours** worksheet tab.

5. The staff member's last name is spelled incorrectly. Navigate to cell **B3** and edit the text so the last name is spelled correctly (Marshall—with two Ls). Use Edit mode.

   a. Double-click cell **B3.**

   b. Edit the text to: `Marshall`

   c. Press `← Enter` to accept your changes.

6. The billable rate amount is missing. Navigate to cell **B5** and enter the rate (**150**). Use Ready mode.

   a. Click cell **B5.**

   b. Type: `150`

   c. Press `← Enter`.

7. Modify the billable rate to use the Accounting Number Format.

   a. Press `↑` to return to cell **B5.**

   b. On the *Home* tab, in the *Number* group, click the **Account Number Format** button.

8. The dates are missing from the timesheet. Enter the first date, January 14, 2013.

   a. Click cell **B8.**

   b. Type: `1/14/2013`

   c. Press `← Enter`.

9. Use AutoFill to complete the dates in the timesheet.

   a. Click cell **B8.**

   b. Click the **Fill Handle** tool, and drag to cell **H9.** Release the mouse button.

10. Change the date format to the 1/14/2012 format.

   a. The cell range B8:H9 should still be selected. If not, click cell **B8,** press and hold `↑ Shift`, click cell **H9,** and then release the `↑ Shift` key.

   b. On the *Home* tab, in the *Number* group, expand the *Number Format* list, and click **Short Date.**

11. Use the Quick Analysis tool to enter total hours for each day.

   a. Select cells **B10:H13.** Click cell **B10,** hold down the left mouse button and drag the mouse to cell **H13.** Release the mouse button. The cell range B10 through H13 should now appear selected.

   b. The Quick Analysis tool button should appear near the lower right corner of the selected cell range. (If the Quick Analysis tool button is not visible, move your mouse cursor over the selected cell range again, without clicking. This action should make the button appear.) Click the **Quick Analysis tool** button, and then click **Totals.**

   c. Click **Sum** (the first option).

12. Format the hours billed section to use the Comma Style number format. Be sure to include the total row.

   a. Select cells **B10:H14.** Try another method: Click cell **B10,** press and hold `↑ Shift`, click cell **H14,** and release the `↑ Shift` key.

   b. On the *Home* tab, in the *Number* group, click the **Comma Style** button.

13. Enter a formula in cell **B16** to calculate the daily bill for Monday, January 14. The formula should calculate the total billable hours for the day (cell B14) times the billable rate (B5).

   a. Click cell **B16.**

   b. Type: =

   c. Click cell **B14.**

   d. Type: *

   e. Click cell **B5.**

   f. Press ⌨F4 to change the cell reference **B5** to an absolute reference (**$B$5**).

   g. Press ⌨ ←Enter .

   h. The formula should look like this: **=B14*$B$5**

14. Use AutoFill to copy the formula to the remaining days in the timesheet.

   a. Click cell **B16** again.

   b. Click the **AutoFill handle.** Hold down the left mouse button and drag to cell **H16.** Release the mouse button.

   c. The formulas in cells C16 through H16 should look like this:

	C	D	E	F	G	H
16	=C14*$B$5	=D14*$B$5	=E14*$B$5	=F14*$B$5	=G14*$B$5	=H14*$B$5

FIGURE EX 1.42

   Notice that when AutoFill copied the formula, it updated the relative reference (B14) to reflect the new column position, but it did not change the relative reference ($B$5).

15. Now you can calculate the bill total for the week.by summing the daily bill amounts. Enter a formula using the SUM function with the cell range **B16:H16** as the argument.

   a. Click cell **B17.**

   b. Type: =SUM(B16:H16)

   c. Press ⌨ ←Enter .

16. Preview how the worksheet will look when printed.

   a. Click the **File** tab to open Backstage.

   b. Click **Print** to display the print preview.

17. Save and close the workbook.

skill review **1.2**

In this project you will create a new workbook to track the cost of books for your college classes. For each book, you will enter the purchase price, the potential sell-back price, and the cost difference. You will calculate totals using AutoSum. You will then create a new workbook from a template, and practice changing the zoom level and arranging the workbooks. Skills needed to complete this project:

- Entering and Editing Text and Numbers in Cells (Skill 1.4)
- Navigating a Workbook (Skill 1.2)
- Inserting Data Using AutoFill (Skill 1.7)
- Applying Number Formats (Skill 1.5)
- Using the Status Bar (Skill 1.13)
- Using AutoSum to Insert a SUM Function (Skill 1.11)

- Entering Simple Formulas (Skill 1.8)
- Creating a New Workbook Using a Template (Skill 1.15)
- Checking Spelling (Skill 1.17)
- Arranging Workbooks (Skill 1.16)
- Changing the Zoom Level (Skill 1.14)

1. Start a new blank Excel workbook. Save the file as:
   [your initials]EX-SkillReview-1-2

2. The new workbook opens with one sheet (Sheet1). Cell A1 is selected.

3. In cell A1, type the title for the worksheet: Textbooks

4. Enter data in the worksheet as follows:

	A	B	C	D	E
1	Textbooks				
2					
3	Book	Cost	Value	Difference	
4	Book 1	80.25	40.00		
5	Book 2	74.89	28.00		
6	Book 3	95.26	45.00		
7	Book 4	52.50	25.00		
8					

FIGURE EX 1.43

5. Use AutoFill to add two additional books to the list.
   a. Click cell **A4,** hold down the left mouse button and drag the mouse to cell **A7.** Release the mouse button. The cell range A4 through A7 should now appear selected.
   b. Click the **Fill Handle** tool (located at the lower right corner of the selected cell range).
   c. Drag down to cell **A9,** and release the mouse button.
   d. Excel adds Book 5 and Book 6 to the list.

6. Book 5 cost $65.00 and can be sold for $30.00. Book 6 cost $110.00 and can be sold for $45.00. Add this data to the worksheet.
   a. Click cell **B8** and type: 65
   b. Press → and type: 30
   c. Click cell **B9** and type: 110
   d. Press Tab ⇥ and type: 45
   e. Press ← Enter .

7. Modify the **status bar** to display the minimum value.
   a. Right-click anywhere on the **status bar.**
   b. Click **Minimum** to add a checkmark.
   c. Click anywhere to dismiss the menu.

8. Use the status bar to check the total value of the books and the minimum value.
   a. Click cell **C4.** Press and hold ↑ Shift and click cell **C9.** Release the ↑ Shift key.
   b. Look at the status bar and find the *Sum* value (**213.00**).
   c. Look at the status bar and find the *Min* value (**25.00**).

9. Use **AutoSum** to calculate total cost and total value. The totals should be placed in cells **B10** and **C10.**

   a. Click cell **A10** and type: Total

   b. Press [Tab ⇆].

   c. Cell **B10** should be selected. Press and hold [↑ Shift] and click cell **C10.** Release the [↑ Shift] key.

   d. On the *Home* tab, in the *Editing* group, click the **AutoSum** button.

10. Change the number format for the cost and value numbers to the Accounting Number Format.

   a. Click cell **B4.** Press and hold [↑ Shift]. Click cell **C10.** Release [↑ Shift].

   b. On the *Home* tab, in the *Number* group, click the **Accounting Number Format** button.

11. Enter a formula in cell **D4** to calculate the difference between the cost and the value for Book1. The formula will use only relative references because in the next step, you will use AutoFill to copy the formula down the column.

   a. Click cell **D4.**   **d.** Type: –

   b. Type: =   **e.** Click cell **C3.**

   c. Click cell **B2.**   **f.** Press [← Enter].

12. Use AutoFill to copy the formula to calculate the difference for books 2 through 6 and the total.

   a. Click cell **D4.**

   b. Click the **AutoFill handle.** Hold down the left mouse button and drag to cell **D10.** Release the mouse button.

13. Save the workbook. Do not close it or exit Excel.

14. Create a new file from a template called *Student grade and GPA* tracker.

   a. Click the **File** tab to open Backstage.

   b. Click **New.**

   c. Open a new file based on the *Student grade and GPA tracker* template. (This step may require an active Internet connection.)

   i. The *Student grade and GPA tracker* template may appear in the list of templates automatically. If it does not, you will need to search for it. In the *Search online templates* box, type: student grade tracker

   ii. Click the template preview.

   iii. Click **Create.**

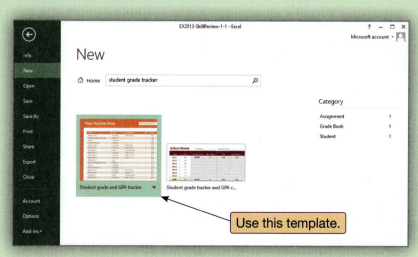

FIGURE EX 1.44

15. The new workbook based on the *Student grade and GPA tracker* template opens. This is a complex workbook using many advanced techniques. The good news is that you don't have to understand how this workbook was created in order to use it.

a. The workbook includes four worksheets. The first worksheet, *Score Tracker,* lists all assignments the student has completed. Navigate to the other worksheets by clicking each of the sheet tabs and review the content of each. When you are finished, return to the first sheet, *Score Tracker,* by clicking that worksheet tab.

b. Click cell **C4** (the cell displaying the text *Modern French*).

c. Click the arrow that appears at the right side of the cell. The list of available classes appears. If you were using this template to actually create your own grade and GPA tracker, this list would display your classes. But where does this list come from?

d. Click the **Settings** tab to go to the *Settings* worksheet.

e. Note the classes listed in cells C9:C15. These are the same classes displayed in the list you saw in the *Score Tracker* sheet.

f. Change the *Modern French* class name to *Conversational Latin.*

    i. Click cell **C9.** Verify that the status bar displays Ready to indicate that you are in Ready mode.

    ii. Type: **Conversational Latin**

    iii. Press ⏎ Enter .

g. Use the spelling checker to verify that you did not misspell *Conversational Latin.*

    i. On the *Review* tab, in the *Proofing* group, click the **Spelling** button.

    ii. Excel should display an informational alert box asking if you want to continue checking spelling from the beginning of the sheet. Click **Yes.**

    iii. If you didn't make any spelling mistakes, Excel will display a message telling you that the spell check is complete. If you did make a mistake, select the correct spelling in the *Suggestions* list and click the **Change** button. Continue correcting mistakes until Excel tells you the spell check is complete. Click **OK.**

h. Now return to the *Score Tracker* sheet and see how your change affected the list. The workbook template author used an advanced technique to create the relationship between the list of classes in the *Settings* sheet and the data entry drop-down list used in the *Score Tracker* sheet. At this stage, you do not need to understand how this was created, but you should understand how the data change on one sheet affects the data in the other sheet.

    i. Click the **Score Tracker** sheet tab. (You could also click the **Score Tracker** button near the top of the *Settings* worksheet.)

    ii. Click cell **C4** again (which still displays *Modern French*).

    iii. Expand the list by clicking the arrow.

    iv. Note the new entry at the top of the list—*Conversational Latin.*

    v. Click **Conversational Latin** to replace the text in the cell.

16. If you think you might like to come back to this workbook later for your personal use, this is a good point to save it. Be sure not to close the file. Use the file name: **[Your Initials]GradesAndGPA**

17. You should still have two workbooks open: the textbooks workbook from the beginning of the project and the grades and GPA workbook based on the template. Arrange the workbooks so you can see both at the same time.

a. On the *View* tab, in the *Window* group, click the **Arrange All** button.

b. In the *Arrange Windows* dialog, click the **Vertical** radio button. Click **OK.**

18. The grades and GPA workbook should be active. If not, click the title bar for that window. Review the *Your Performance* sheet and change the zoom level to 75% so you can see more of the data at once.

    a. Click the **Your Performance** tab.

    b. On the *View* tab, in the *Zoom* group, click the **Zoom** button.

    c. In the *Zoom* dialog, click the **75%** radio button for the zoom option you want. Click **OK.**

    d. Navigate to the *Score Tracker* worksheet again, and note that changing the zoom level of the *Your Performance* sheet did not affect the *Score Tracker* sheet.

19. Close both workbooks. If you made changes to the grades and GPA workbook and you plan to continue using it, be sure to save the changes.

challenge yourself 1.3

In this project, you will complete the timesheet for David Marshall which you worked on in Skill Review 1.1. You will need to enter and format missing dates, correct a data entry mistake, apply number formatting, and enter formulas to calculate the total billable hours per day, the daily total for each day, and the bill total for the week.

Skills needed to complete this project:

- Working in Protected View (Skill 1.3)
- Navigating a Workbook (Skill 1.2)
- Entering and Editing Text and Numbers in Cells (Skill 1.4)
- Applying Number Formats (Skill 1.5)
- Entering Dates and Applying Date Formats (Skill 1.6)
- Inserting Data Using AutoFill (Skill 1.7)
- Understanding Absolute and Relative References (Skill 1.9)
- Entering Simple Formulas (Skill 1.8)
- Calculating Totals with the Quick Analysis Tool (Skill 1.12)
- Previewing and Printing a Worksheet (Skill 1.18)

1. Open the start file **EX2013-ChallengeYourself-1-3** and resave the file as: `[your initials]EX-ChallengeYourself-1-3`

2. If the workbook opens in Protected View, enable editing so you can make changes to the workbook.

3. Verify that the *Marshall Hours* worksheet is active.

4. If necessary, scroll to the bottom of the worksheet so you can see the empty timesheet beginning on **row 20.**

5. The dates are missing from the timesheet. Enter the date `1/21/2013` in cell **B21.**

6. Use **AutoFill** to complete the dates in cells **C21:H21.**

7. Change the date format for **B21:H21** to the Short Date format.

8. The hours reported for the Proctor client on Friday (cell F26) are incorrect. Change the number in cell **F26** to: 6

9. Use the **Quick Analysis** tool to enter total hours for each day. Use the cell range **B23:H26.** The daily totals should be inserted into the range **B27:H27.**

10. Format the hours billed section to use the **Comma Style** number format. Be sure to include the total row.

11. Enter a formula in cell **B29** to calculate the daily bill for Monday, January 21. The formula should calculate the total billable hours for the day (cell **B27**) times the billable rate (**B5**). Be sure to use an absolute cell reference for the billable rate.

12. Use **AutoFill** to copy the formula to the remaining days in the timesheet (cells **C29:H29**).

13. Calculate the bill total for the week.by summing the daily bill amounts. In cell **B30,** enter a formula using the **SUM** function. The function argument should be the range of cells representing the daily bill totals (**B29:H29**).

14. Preview how the worksheet will look when printed.

15. Save and close the workbook.

challenge yourself **1.4**

In this project you will work with a college budget spreadsheet. You will change a few values in the budget, modify number formats, and calculate totals and the difference between expected income and expenses. You will then create a new budget workbook from a template, and practice changing the zoom level and arranging the workbooks.

Skills needed to complete this project:

- Working in Protected View (Skill 1.3)
- Entering and Editing Text and Numbers in Cells (Skill 1.4)
- Navigating a Workbook (Skill 1.2)
- Using AutoSum to Insert a SUM Function (Skill 1.11)
- Calculating Totals Using the Quick Analysis Tool (Skill 1.12)
- Using the Status Bar (Skill 1.13)
- Applying Number Formats (Skill 1.5)
- Understanding Absolute and Relative References (Skill 1.9)
- Entering Simple Formulas (Skill 1.8)
- Checking Spelling (Skill 1.17)
- Creating a New Workbook Using a Template (Skill 1.15)
- Arranging Workbooks (Skill 1.16)
- Changing the Zoom Level (Skill 1.14)

1. Open the start file **EX2013-ChallengeYourself-1-4** and resave the file as: **[your initials]EX-ChallengeYourself-1-4**

2. If the workbook opens in Protected View, enable editing so you can make changes to the workbook.

3. Make the following changes to the *Budget* worksheet:
   a. Change the *Utilities* item to **Electric** (cell **B12**).
   b. Change the Insurance value from *90* to **60** (cell **B19**).

4. The worksheet is missing formulas to calculate totals. Enter formulas using the **SUM** function to calculate the following totals. Use any of the methods you learned in this chapter.
   a. Enter a formula in cell **C7** to calculate the total monthly income.
   b. Enter a formula in cell **C24** to calculate the total monthly expenses.
   c. Enter a formula in cell **F16** to calculate the total semester expenses.
   d. Use the **status bar** to verify that the formula is calculating the correct total for each cell range.

5. Cell **F18** displays the number of months in the semester. Change the number format in this cell to the **Number** format with no numbers showing after the decimal (so the number appears as **4** instead of **$4.00**).

6. The number format in the *Semester Expenses* section does not match the number format in the other sections of the worksheet. Change the number format for cells **F11:F16** to the **Accounting Number Format.**

7. Review the formulas in the *Discretionary Income* section.

   a. Cells **F4:F6** should contain references to the cells where you just entered the formulas to calculate totals. Add the appropriate formula to cell **F6** to reference the value in cell **F16** (the total semester expenses).

   b. The semester is four months long, so the formulas in cells **F4** and **F5** should multiply the total monthly income and total monthly expenses by four. Correct the formulas in cells **F4** and **F6**. Use an absolute reference to the value in cell **F18** (the number of months in the semester).

8. Use spelling checker to find and correct any spelling errors in the *Budget* worksheet.

9. Save the workbook. Do not close it or exit Excel.

10. Create a new file from a template called *Personal Expenses Calculator.* If you do not see this template, search for it using the search phrase *personal expenses.*

FIGURE EX 1.45

11. Explore the worksheets in this workbook.

12. If you think you might like to come back to this workbook later for your personal use, this is a good point to save it. Be sure not to close the file. Use the file name:
    [Your Initials] PersonalExpenses

13. You should still have two workbooks open: the college budget workbook from the beginning of the project and the personal expenses workbook based on the template. Arrange the workbooks so you can see both at the same time.

    a. Try different arrangements until you find the one that works best for you.

    b. Practice moving back and forth between the two workbooks.

14. Make the personal budget workbook active and navigate to the *Dashboard* worksheet. Modify the zoom to **80%.**

15. Close both workbooks. If you made changes to the personal budget workbook and you plan to continue using it, be sure to save the changes.

on your own 1.5

For Spring Break, you've decided to take a seven-day road trip. Use this Excel workbook to calculate the number of miles you will drive each day and the gas cost for each day. Use the techniques you've learned in this chapter to calculate the total miles and the total gas cost. Don't forget to end the trip at the same location you started! You may want to use the Internet to look up mileage, MPG (miles per gallon), and gas price information.

Skills needed to complete this project:

- Navigating a Workbook (Skill 1.2)
- Working in Protected View (Skill 1.3)
- Entering and Editing Text and Numbers in Cells (Skill 1.4)
- Entering Dates and Applying Date Formats (Skill 1.6)
- Inserting Data Using AutoFill (Skill 1.7)
- Understanding Absolute and Relative References (Skill 1.9)
- Entering Simple Formulas (Skill 1.8)
- Calculating Totals with the Quick Analysis Tool (Skill 1.12)
- Using AutoSum to Insert a SUM Function (Skill 1.11)
- Applying Number Formats (Skill 1.5)
- Checking Spelling (Skill 1.17)

1. Open the start file **EX2013-OnYourOwn-1-5** and resave the file as: `[your initials]EX-OnYourOwn-1-5`

2. If the workbook opens in Protected View, click the **Enable Editing** button in the Message Bar at the top of the workbook so you can modify the workbook.

3. Complete the Trip Details section of the *RoadTrip* worksheet:

   a. Enter the dates of your road trip. Use a date format that includes the day of the week.

   b. Enter a start and end location for each day. Remember—the starting location for each day should be the same as the end location for the previous day. If you use a formula with a relative reference rather than retyping the location name for each start location, you can use AutoFill to complete the start location column. Consider using a formula to ensure that the final end location is the same as the first start location.

   c. Look up and enter the miles between each location. Use an appropriate number format for the *Number of Miles* column. (Hint: Use *mapquest.com* or *maps.google.com* to look up the mileage between locations.)

4. Enter your car information including the MPG (miles per gallon). If you don't know your MPG, the government Web site www.fueleconomy.gov has excellent information on average MPG for a variety of car makes, models, and years.

5. Enter the average gas price in your area (or the area of your road trip). Again, the www.fueleconomy.gov Web site has links to this type of information.

6. Enter a formula to calculate the gas cost per mile for your car (gas price per gallon/your car's MPG).

7. Now that you have the gas cost per mile for your car, you can figure the cost of the road trip. Enter a formula to figure the gas cost per day (the number of miles * your gas cost per mile) for the first day of the trip. Be sure to use absolute and relative references as appropriate, so you can use AutoFill to copy the formula to the rest of the cells in the *Gas Cost per Day* column.

8. Apply appropriate number formats to all the cells in the workbook that display costs. Hint: The Accounting Number Format is best for costs that appear in a column. For costs that appear on their own, you may want to use the Currency Style format.

9. Don't forget to spell check the workbook.

10. Save and close the workbook.

fix it 1.6

The workbook for this project tracks how many miles you walked each day for the week of June 2, 2013 through June 8, 2013. Your goal for each day is to walk at least two miles. Use the skills learned in this chapter to fix the workbook.

Skills needed to complete this project:

- Navigating a Workbook (Skill 1.2)
- Working in Protected View (Skill 1.3)
- Entering and Editing Text and Numbers in Cells (Skill 1.4)
- Entering Dates and Applying Date Formats (Skill 1.6)
- Inserting Data Using AutoFill (Skill 1.7)
- Applying Number Formats (Skill 1.5)
- Understanding Absolute and Relative References (Skill 1.9)
- Entering Simple Formulas (Skill 1.8)
- Calculating Totals with the Quick Analysis Tool (Skill 1.12)
- Using AutoSum to Insert a SUM Function (Skill 1.11)
- Checking Spelling (Skill 1.17)

1. Open the start file **EX2013-FixIt-1-6** and resave the file as:
   `[your initials]EX-FixIt-1-6`

2. If the workbook opens in Protected View, click the **Enable Editing** button in the Message Bar at the top of the workbook so you can modify the workbook.

3. The worksheet is missing a title. Type this title in cell **A1: Exercise Log**

4. The weekly goal should be 2, not 20. Correct the value in cell **D1.**

5. The dates are missing from cells **A5:A10.** Use **AutoFill** to complete the dates for the rest of the week.

6. The exercise log would be more useful if the date showed the day of the week in addition to the date. Change the date format for cells **A4:A10** so the date displays in this format: **Sunday, June 02, 2013.**

7. The mileage for each day should use the Comma Style number format. Correct the number format in cells **C4:C10.**

8. Use one of the skills you learned in this chapter to enter formulas using the **SUM** function in cells **B11** and **C11** to calculate the weekly total minutes and miles.

9. The formulas in the *Under/Over Goal* column aren't quite right. Fix the formula in cell **D4,** and then use **AutoFill** to replace the formulas in cells **D5:D10.**

10. There may be spelling errors. Be sure to use spelling checker before you finish the project.

11. Save and close the workbook.

Formatting Cells

In this chapter, you will learn the following skills:

❯ Modify cell data using cut, copy, and paste

❯ Insert, delete, and merge cells

❯ Work with text and font attributes

❯ Apply borders and shading

❯ Format cells using cell styles

❯ Copy formatting using Format Painter

❯ Format cells using conditional formatting

❯ Modify cell data using find and replace

❯ Work with the print area

skills

introduction

This chapter focuses on skills for working with cells and cell ranges. You will learn to use the basic *Cut, Copy,* and *Paste* commands to move data and to insert, delete, and merge cells to create a worksheet structure that fits your data. This chapter also covers the essential skills for formatting cells, including in-depth coverage of conditional formatting. Formatting not only enhances a workbook's appearance, but when used properly, it can make the data easier to understand.

Skill 2.1 Cutting, Copying, and Pasting Cells

The *Cut, Copy,* and *Paste* commands are used to move data within a workbook and from one workbook to another. A cell or range of cells that is **cut** is removed from the workbook and stored for later use. The **Copy** command stores a duplicate of the selected cell or range without changing the workbook. The **Paste** command is used to insert copied or cut cells into a workbook.

If you **copy** and paste a cell containing a formula with relative references, Excel will update the references to reflect the new position in the workbook. However, if you **cut** and paste instead, Excel will treat the formula as if it contained absolute references and will not update the cell reference in the formula.

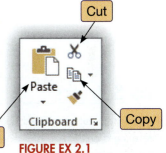

FIGURE EX 2.1

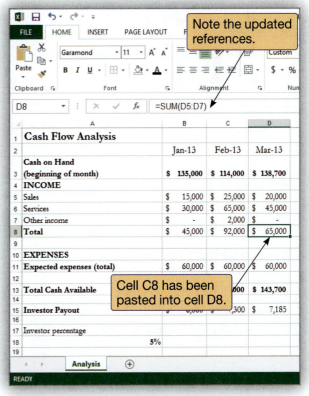

FIGURE EX 2.2

FIGURE EX 2.3

To use *Cut, Copy,* and *Paste:*

1. Select the cell or cells you want to cut or copy.
2. On the *Home* tab, in the *Clipboard* group, click the appropriate button: **Cut** or **Copy.**
3. The selection appears with a flashing dotted line around it, and the cut or copied data are stored temporarily in the computer's memory.
4. Click the cell where you want to paste. If you selected a range of cells to cut or copy, click the cell in the upper-left corner of the area where you want to paste.
5. Click the **Paste** button to paste the cell data and formatting. If the copied or cut cells include formulas, Excel will copy the formulas and update any relative cell references automatically.

These same steps apply whether you are cutting, copying, and pasting text, pictures, charts, or any type of object in an Excel workbook.

If you paste into a cell that contains data, the original cell data will be overwritten. To paste without overwriting existing cells, use the *Insert Copied Cells* or *Insert Cut Cells* command instead.

1. Copy or cut the cells you want to insert.
2. Select the cell where you want to insert.
3. On the *Home* tab, in the *Cells* group, click the **Insert** button arrow and select **Insert Copied Cells** or **Insert Cut Cells.**

tips & tricks

If you insert cut or copied cells into the beginning or end of a data table, be sure to check for formulas that may reference a cell range that does not include the newly inserted cells.

another method

To apply the *Cut, Copy,* or *Paste* command, you can also use the following shortcuts:

> **Cut** = Press (Ctrl) + (X), or right-click and select **Cut.**

> **Copy** = Press (Ctrl) + (C), or right-click and select **Copy.**

> **Paste** = Press (Ctrl) + (V), or right-click and select **Paste.**

let me try

Open the student data file **EX2-01-CashFlow** and try this skill on your own:

1. Copy cell **C7,** and paste to cell **D7.** Note that the formula updated to reflect the new cell range D5:D6.
2. Cut cell **A17,** and paste to cell **B16.** Note that formulas in the workbook that refer to this cell (B14:D14) updated to reflect the new position.
3. Cells **A15:D15** are misplaced. Cut them from their current location and insert them above cell **A6.** Verify that the formulas in cells B8:D8 updated appropriately.
4. Save the file as directed by your instructor and close it.

Skill 2.2 Using Paste Options

When you paste data into Excel, you can use the default *Paste* command to insert the copied data (including formulas and formatting) into the selected cell, or you can select from the paste options to control more precisely what is pasted. The *Paste* button has two parts—the top part of the button pastes the most recent copied or cut data into the current workbook. If you click the bottom part of the button (the *Paste* button arrow), you can control how the item is pasted. Each type of object has different paste options. For example, if you are pasting data that include formulas, you can paste the formulas with or without formatting or just the values without the underlying formulas.

	Paste—The default paste command that pastes all of the source content and formatting.
	Formulas—Pastes the formulas but none of the formatting. The pasted content will use the cell and number formatting of the cell into which it was pasted.
	Formulas & Number Formatting—Pastes the formulas and number formatting but none of the cell formatting such as font size, borders, and shading.
	Keep Source Formatting—Pastes the content, including formulas, and all formatting from the source.
	No Borders—Pastes the content, including formulas, and all formatting except borders.
	Keep Source Column Widths—Pastes the copied cell, including formulas and all number and cell formatting. Also adjusts the column width to match the width of the source column.
	Transpose—Pastes the rows from the source into columns, and the columns from the source into rows.

When your source includes formulas, you have the option to paste the calculated cell values without pasting the underlying formulas.

	Values—Pastes only the values, not the underlying formula or cell formatting.
	Values & Number Formatting—Pastes only the values, not the underlying formulas. Includes number formatting but not other cell formatting such as borders and shading.
	Values & Source Formatting—Pastes only the values, not the underlying formulas. Includes all formatting from the source.

The final group of paste options provides alternatives to pasting the actual contents of one cell into another.

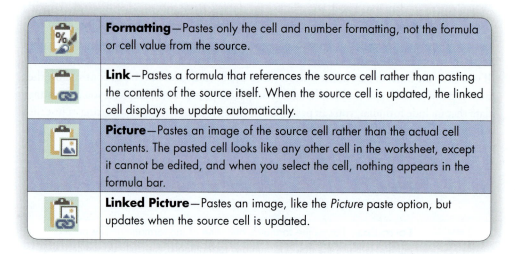

Formatting—Pastes only the cell and number formatting, not the formula or cell value from the source.

Link—Pastes a formula that references the source cell rather than pasting the contents of the source itself. When the source cell is updated, the linked cell displays the update automatically.

Picture—Pastes an image of the source cell rather than the actual cell contents. The pasted cell looks like any other cell in the worksheet, except it cannot be edited, and when you select the cell, nothing appears in the formula bar.

Linked Picture—Pastes an image, like the *Picture* paste option, but updates when the source cell is updated.

To use the *Paste* button on the Ribbon:

1. On the *Home* tab, in the *Clipboard* group, click the bottom part of the **Paste** button (the **Paste** button arrow) to expand the *Paste Options* menu.

2. Move your mouse over the icon for each paste option to see a live preview of how the paste would look, and then click the paste option you want.

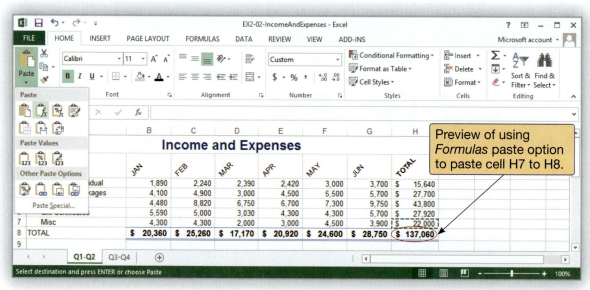

FIGURE EX 2.4

Paste Options Button

FIGURE EX 2.5

To use the keyboard shortcut:

1. Press `Ctrl` + `V`.

2. The source is pasted using the default *Paste* option, and the *Paste Options* button appears.

3. Click the **Paste Options** button or press `Ctrl` to display the *Paste Options* menu. This is the same menu that is available from the *Paste* button on the Ribbon, but moving your mouse over the icons does not show a preview of how the paste would look.

tips & tricks

tell me **more**

If you do not want the *Paste Options* button to appear every time you paste with the keyboard shortcut, you can turn it off:

1. Click the **File** tab to open Backstage.
2. Click **Options** to open the *Excel Options* dialog.
3. Click **Advanced.**
4. In the *Cut, copy, and paste* section near the bottom of the window, click the check box in front of **Show Paste Options button when content is pasted** to remove the checkmark.
5. Click **OK.**

another **method**

You can also access the paste options from the right-click menu. Six of the paste options appear on the right-click menu (*Paste, Values, Formulas, Transpose, Formatting,* and *Paste Link*). To select an option from the full *Paste Options* menu, point to **Paste Special...,** and then click the paste option you want.

let me **try**

Open the student data file **EX2-02-IncomeAndExpenses** and try this skill on your own:

1. Copy cell **H7** and paste only the formula into cell **H8.** Do not paste the original cell formatting.
2. Copy **G17** and paste the formula, formatting, and the source column width into cell **H17.**
3. Save the file as directed by your instructor and close it.

Skill 2.3 Using Undo and Redo

If you make a mistake when working, the **Undo** command allows you to reverse the last action you performed. The **Redo** command allows you to reverse the *Undo* command and restore the file to its previous state. The Quick Access Toolbar gives you immediate access to both these commands.

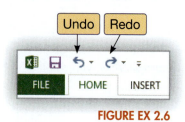

FIGURE EX 2.6

To undo the last action taken, click the **Undo** button on the Quick Access Toolbar.
To redo the last action taken, click the **Redo** button on the Quick Access Toolbar.

To undo multiple actions at the same time:

1. Click the **Undo** button arrow to expand the list of your most recent actions.
2. Click an action in the list.
3. The action you click will be undone, along with all the actions completed after that. In other words, your workbook will revert to the state it was in before that action.

tips & tricks

Be careful when using the *Undo* and *Redo* commands in Excel. In other Office applications, undo and redo actions are confined to the file you are currently working on—even if you have multiple files open. However, in Excel, the undo–redo list of actions includes all the open workbooks. This means that if you are working on multiple Excel files at the same time, using the *Undo* command can actually undo an action in one of the other open workbooks.

another method

⟩ To undo an action, you can also press Ctrl + Z.

⟩ To redo an action, you can also press Ctrl + Y.

let me try

Open the student data file **EX2-03-IncomeAndExpenses** and try this skill on your own:

1. Copy cell **H8** and paste into cell **G8.**
2. Look in the formula bar—that's the wrong formula for this cell. Undo the last action.
3. Copy cell **F8** and paste into cell **G8.**
4. Undo the last action.
5. Redo the last action.
6. Save the file as directed by your instructor and close it.

Skill 2.4 Wrapping Text in Cells

When you type text in a cell, the text will appear to continue to the right as far as it can until there is another cell that contains data. At that point, the text will appear to be cut off. You could increase the width of the cell to show all the text, but do you really want the entire column to be that wide? If your worksheet includes cells with more text than will comfortably fit in the cell, you should use the wrap text feature. When wrap text is enabled for a cell, the text in the cell will automatically wrap to multiple lines, just as a paragraph would.

To wrap text in a cell:

On the *Home* tab, in the *Alignment* group, click the **Wrap Text** button. Notice the button appears selected when text wrapping is active for the cell.

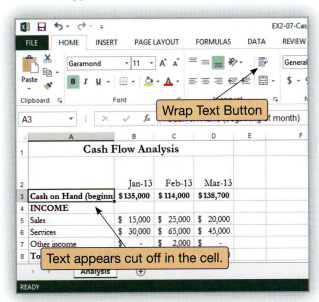

FIGURE EX 2.7

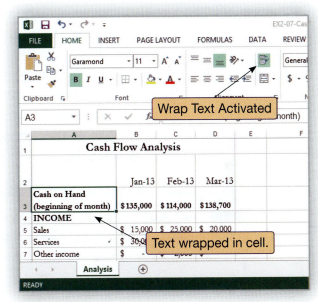

FIGURE EX 2.8

To turn off text wrapping in a cell, click the **Wrap Text** button again to deselect it.

tips & tricks

The text wrapping feature only works for cells that contain text. If a column is too narrow to display its numerical data, Excel will not wrap it. Instead, the cell will show a series of # symbols, indicating that the cell contains numerical data, but the column is too narrow to display it.

another method

You can also turn on the text wrapping feature from the *Format Cells* dialog.

1. On the *Home* tab, in the *Alignment* group, click the **Alignment Settings** Dialog Box Launcher to open the *Format Cells* dialog.
2. In the *Text control* section, click the **Wrap Text** check box.
3. Click **OK**.

let me try

Open the student data file **EX2-04-CashFlow** and try this skill on your own:

Activate text wrapping for cell **A3**. Save the file as directed by your instructor and close it.

Skill 2.5 Inserting and Deleting Cells

You may find you want to add some extra space or more information into the middle of your worksheet. To do this, you must insert a new cell or group of cells. Any formulas referencing the cell where the insertion takes place will update to reflect the new position of the original cell. Even if the formula uses absolute cell references, it will still update to reflect the updated cell reference.

To insert a cell range, select the range where you want to insert the new cells.

1. If you have a vertical cell range selected, click the **Insert Cells** button and Excel will automatically shift existing cells to the right to make room for the new cells.

2. If you have a horizontal cell range selected, click the **Insert Cells** button and Excel will automatically shift existing cells down to make room for the new cells.

If you want more control over whether cells are shifted to the right or down, use the *Insert* dialog.

1. Select the cell or cell range where you want to insert the new cells.

2. On the *Home* tab, in the *Cells* group, click the **Insert Cells** button arrow.

3. Click **Insert Cells...** to open the *Insert* dialog.

4. Click the **Shift cells right** or **Shift cells down** radio button.

5. Click **OK.**

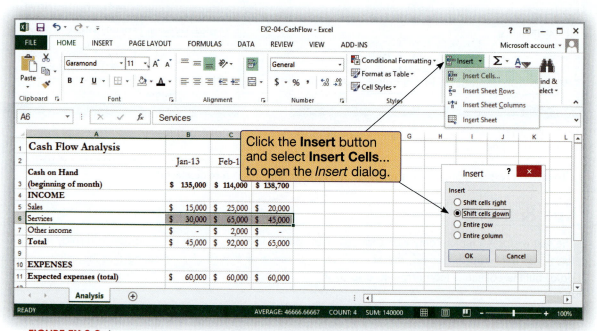

FIGURE EX 2.9

When you insert new cells, the cells will use the same formatting as the cells above (if you shifted cells down) or to the left (if you shifted cells to the right). If you want to use formatting from the cells below or to the left instead, or to insert the cells with no formatting, click the **Insert Options** button that appears at the lower right of the insertion and make a selection from the menu options.

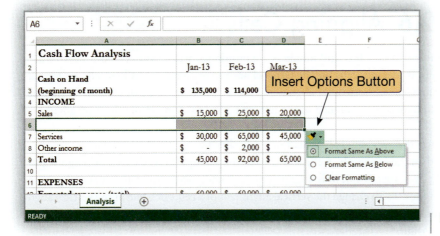

FIGURE EX 2.10

Of course, you can also delete cells. Deleting cells not only deletes the information and formatting in the cell, but also shifts the layout of the worksheet. Even if you delete an empty cell, you shift all the surrounding cells into new positions.

To delete a cell:

1. On the *Home* tab, in the *Cells* group, click the **Delete Cells** button arrow.
2. Click **Delete Cells...** to open the *Delete* dialog.
3. Click the **Shift cells left** or **Shift cells up** radio button.
4. Click **OK**.

tips & tricks

Inserting and deleting cells may have unexpected consequences. Be careful not to delete cells that are referenced in formulas. Even though a new value may shift into the original cell's position, the formula will still be looking for the original cell (now deleted), causing an invalid cell reference error.

another method

Both *Insert...* and *Delete...* commands are available from the right-click menu.

Pressing (Delete) will delete the contents of the cell but not the cell itself.

let me try

Open the student data file **EX2-05-CashFlow** and try this skill on your own:

1. Select cells **A6:D6.**
2. Insert cells so the remaining cells shift down.
3. Delete the inserted cells so the remaining cells shift up.
4. Insert new cells between **A10:D10** and **A11:D11.** Use the formatting from cells A11:D11 for the new cells.
5. Save the file as directed by your instructor and close it.

skill 2.5   Inserting and Deleting Cells

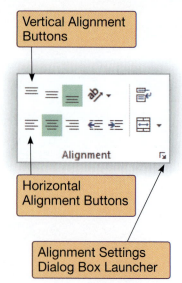

Vertical Alignment Buttons

Horizontal Alignment Buttons

Alignment Settings Dialog Box Launcher

FIGURE EX 2.11

Skill 2.6 Aligning Cells

Alignment refers to how text and numbers are positioned within the cell both horizontally and vertically. By default, cells use the **General horizontal alignment**. When cells are formatted using the General horizontal alignment, Excel detects the type of content in the cell. Cells that contain text are aligned to the left, and cells that contain numbers are aligned to the right.

To change the horizontal alignment of a cell, click one of the horizontal alignment buttons located on the *Home* tab, in the *Alignment* group: **Align Left, Center,** or **Align Right.**

Excel lets you specify not only alignment horizontally across the cell, but also alignment vertically in the cell. To change the vertical alignment of a cell, click one of the vertical alignment buttons located on the *Home* tab, in the *Alignment* group: **Top Align, Middle Align,** or **Bottom Align.**

These options are also available from the *Format Cells* dialog, *Alignment* tab.

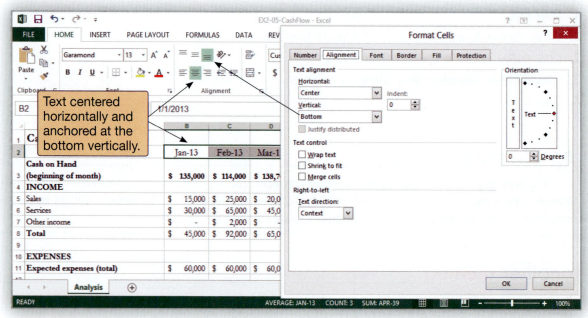

Text centered horizontally and anchored at the bottom vertically.

FIGURE EX 2.12

To change alignment using the *Format Cells* dialog:

1. Click the **Alignment Settings Dialog Box Launcher** at the lower right corner of the *Alignment* group.

2. The *Format Cells* dialog opens to the *Alignment* tab.

3. In the *Text alignment* section, expand the **Horizontal** drop-down list and select the option you want.

4. Click **OK.**

You can also change the angle at which the content displays.

❯ On the *Home* tab, in the *Alignment* group, click the **Orientation** button and select one of the options.

❯ From the *Format Cells* dialog, on the *Alignment* tab, in the *Orientation* section, you can change the angle of rotation by clicking one of the dots on the Orientation dial, by clicking and dragging the Orientation dial to the position you want, or by entering the specific degree of rotation in the *Degrees* box.

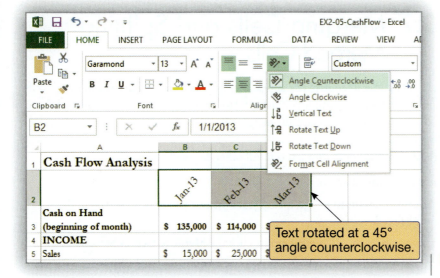

FIGURE EX 2.13

Text rotated at a 45° angle counterclockwise.

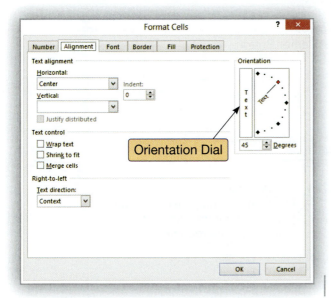

Orientation Dial

FIGURE EX 2.14

tips & tricks

If you have narrow columns of data with descriptive headers, try using one of the orientation options to angle the cells containing the header text.

let me try

Open the student data file **EX2-06-CashFlow** and try this skill on your own:

1. Select cells **B2:D2.**

2. Center the content in each cell horizontally.

3. Center the content in each cell vertically.

4. Change the angle of rotation for these cells to 45°.

5. Save the file as directed by your instructor and close it.

Skill 2.7 Merging Cells and Splitting Merged Cells

Merging cells is one way to control the appearance of your worksheet. You can merge cells to create a header cell across multiple columns of data or center a title across your worksheet. The *Merge & Center* button automatically merges the selected cells and then centers the data from the first cell across the entire merged area. When you merge cells together, Excel will keep only the data in the uppermost left cell. All other data will be lost.

To merge cells and center their content:

1. Select the cells you want to merge, making sure the text you want to keep is in the uppermost left cell.

2. On the *Home* tab, in the *Alignment* group, click the **Merge & Center** button.

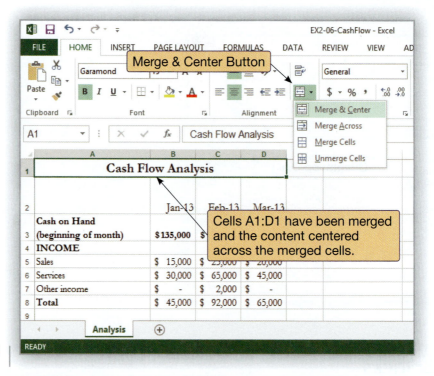

FIGURE EX 2.15

Click the *Merge & Center* button arrow for additional merge commands:

Merge Across—lets you merge cells in multiple rows without merging the rows together. The cells in each row will be merged together, keeping the data in the leftmost cell in each row, but still keeping each row separate.

Merge Cells—lets you merge cells together without centering the data. Like the *Merge & Center* command, *Merge Cells* will combine all the selected cells into one cell, keeping only the data in the uppermost left cell.

Unmerge Cells—splits a merged cell back into its original cells. When the selected cell is a merged cell, clicking the *Merge & Center* button will also undo the merge.

tips & tricks

You cannot really split cells in Excel. You can unmerge a merged cell back into its original cells, but you cannot split a single cell into two new columns or two new rows (like you can with a table in Word or PowerPoint). However, if you have a column of data that you would like to split across multiple cells, you can use the *Text to Columns* command (on the *Data* tab, in the *Data Tools* group).

another method

You can also merge and center cells from the *Format Cells* dialog:

1. On the *Home* tab, in the *Alignment* group, click the **Alignment Settings** Dialog Box Launcher to open the *Format Cells* dialog.

2. On the *Alignment* tab, in the *Text alignment* section, click the **Horizontal** arrow, and select **Center Across Selection** from the drop-down list. (You can also select **Center.** When you merge the cells, it does not matter if the horizontal alignment is *Center Across Selection* or *Center*.)

3. In the *Text control* section, click the **Merge cells** check box.

4. Click **OK.**

To unmerge cells:

1. In the *Format Cells* dialog, on the *Alignment* tab, in the *Text alignment* section, click the **Horizontal** arrow, and select **General** from the drop-down list.

2. In the *Text control* section, click the **Merge cells** check box to uncheck it.

3. Click **OK.**

let me try

Open the student data file **EX2-07-CashFlow** and try this skill on your own:

1. Select cells **A1:D1.**

2. Merge the cells so the text appears centered across the merged cells.

3. Cells **A4:D4** have been merged. Unmerge them.

4. Save the file as directed by your instructor and close it.

Skill 2.8 Applying Bold, Italic, and Underline

You may be familiar with using bold, italic, and underline formatting to emphasize text in a Word document or a PowerPoint presentation. You can use these same techniques in Excel to emphasize cells in your workbook.

To apply bold, italic, and underline formatting:

1. Select a cell or cell range to apply the formatting to all the content in the cell(s). To apply formatting to only part of the content in a cell, double-click the cell to enter Edit mode, and then select the text you want to apply the formatting to.

2. On the *Home* tab, in the *Font* group, click the appropriate button to apply formatting to the selected cell(s).

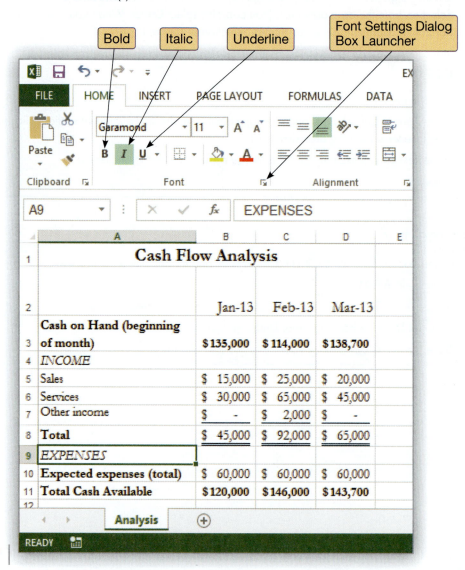

FIGURE EX 2.16

Underline styles used in accounting spreadsheets are slightly different from "regular" underline styles. If you need to apply the accounting style of underline or double underline, do not use the *Underline* button on the Ribbon. Instead, use one of the accounting underline options from the *Format Cells* dialog:

1. On the *Home* tab, in the *Font* group, click the **Font Settings Dialog Box Launcher** to open the *Format Cells* dialog.

2. On the *Font* tab, in the *Underline* section, expand the **Underline** list and select **Single Accounting** or **Double Accounting.**

3. Click **OK.**

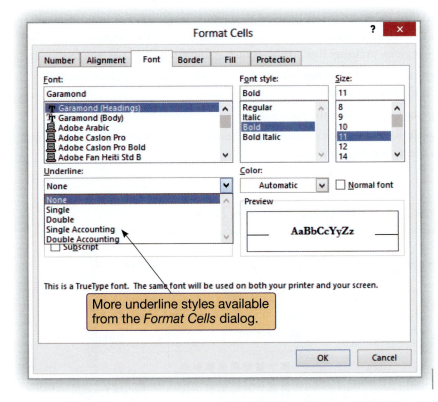

The single and double underline options available when you click the **Underline** button arrow will apply the accounting underline styles only if you recently selected those formats from the *Format Cells* dialog.

tips & tricks

The cell underline formats underline only the content in the cell. The underline does not extend from one edge of the cell to the other. If you want to create an underline that extends across a range of cells without a break in between, use a border instead. (For more information about borders, refer to the skill *Adding Borders.*)

another method

When you right-click a cell, the *Bold* and *Italic* buttons are available on the Mini toolbar.

Bold, italic, and underline font styles are available from the *Format Cells* dialog, *Font* tab.

You can also use the keyboard shortcuts:

❭ Bold: Ctrl + B

❭ Italic: Ctrl + I

❭ Underline: Ctrl + U

let me try

Open the student data file **EX2-08-CashFlow** and try this skill on your own:

1. Apply **Bold** formatting to cells **A3:D3.**

2. Apply the **Single Accounting** underline format to cells **B7:D7.**

3. Apply the **Double Accounting** underline format to cells **B10:D10.**

4. Apply **Italic** formatting to cells **A4** and **A9.**

5. Save the file as directed by your instructor and close it.

Skill 2.9 Changing Fonts, Font Size, and Font Color

A **font**, or typeface, refers to a set of characters of a certain design. The font is the shape of a character or number as it appears on-screen or when printed. Use the commands from the *Home* tab, *Font* group to change font attributes such as font family, font size, and font color.

⟩ To change the font, click the **Font** box arrow to expand the list of available fonts, and then select the font you want.

⟩ To change the font size, click the **Font Size** box arrow and select the size you want.

⟩ To change the font color, click the **Font Color** button arrow to expand the color palette, and then select the color you want.

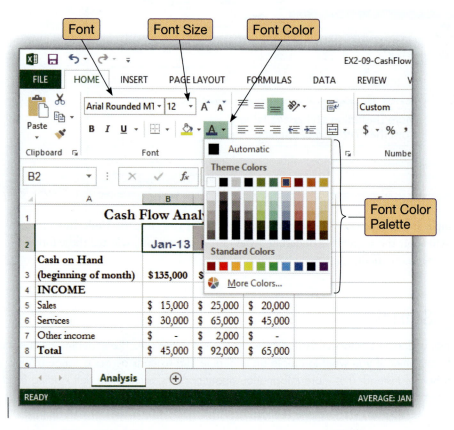

FIGURE EX 2.18

The font color palette is divided into three parts:

1. The top part shows the *Automatic* color choice (black or white, depending on the color of the background).

2. The middle part shows the *Theme Colors* included in the theme that is applied to the workbook. These colors are designed to work together.

3. The bottom part of the palette shows the *Standard Colors* (dark red, red, orange, etc.). These colors are always available, no matter what theme is in use.

tell me **more**

You can pick a custom color by clicking **More Colors**... from the bottom of the font color palette.

another **method**

You can also change the font, font size, or font color by:

❭ Opening the *Format Cells* dialog, clicking the **Font** tab (if necessary), making the font selections you want, and then clicking **OK.**

❭ Right-clicking and making the font, font size, and font color selections you want from the Mini toolbar.

let me **try**

Open the student data file **EX2-09-CashFlow** and try this skill on your own:

1. Select cells **B2:D2.**
2. Change the font to **Arial Rounded MT Bold.** (Bold is part of the font name, not a reference to the font formatting.)
3. Change the font size to **12.**
4. Change the font color to **Blue-Gray, Accent 3** (in the top row of theme colors, the fourth color from the right).
5. Save the file as directed by your instructor and close it.

Skill 2.10 Adding Borders

Add borders to your workbook to emphasize a cell or group of cells. You can use borders to make your workbook look more like a desktop publishing form or to show separation between a column of values and the total row.

To add borders to your workbook:

1. Select the cell(s) you want to add a border to.

2. On the *Home* tab, in the *Font* group, click the **Borders** button arrow and select the border style you want.

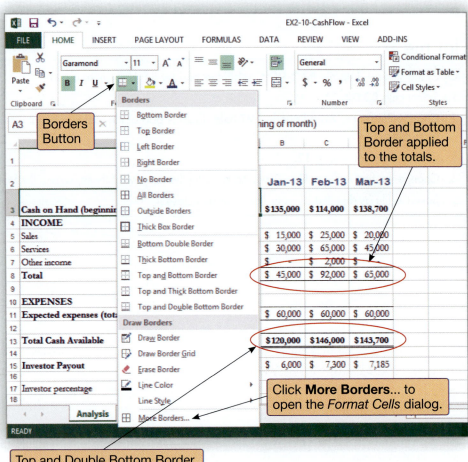

FIGURE EX 2.19

To remove borders:

1. Select the cell(s) you want to remove the borders from.

2. On the *Home* tab, in the *Font* group, click the **Borders** button arrow and select **No Border** from the list of border styles.

For more control over the look of cell borders, select **More Borders...** from the *Borders* menu to open the *Format Cells* dialog. From the *Border* tab, you can specify the line style and color for the border. You can also see a preview of how the border will look.

1. On the *Home* tab, in the *Font* group, click the **Borders** button arrow and select **More Borders...** from the list of border styles.

2. Select a line style from the *Style* section.

3. Expand the **Color** palette and select a color.

4. To add borders around the outside or inside the selected cells, click the appropriate button(s) in the *Presets* section.

5. In the *Border* section, add a border line by clicking the button representing the location of the border or by clicking directly in the area of the preview image where you want the border to appear.

6. Click **OK.**

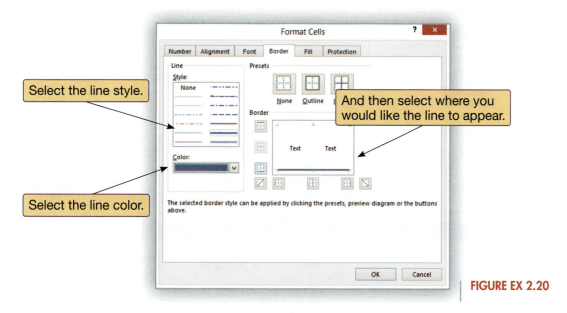

FIGURE EX 2.20

tips & tricks

A properly formatted spreadsheet for accounting purposes should use the cell underline formatting instead of borders on total rows. However, most non-accountant Excel users favor borders above and below total rows instead of using cell underlining.

another method

The *Borders* button displays the most recently used border style. If you want to reuse this style, you can just click the button. You do not need to reselect the border style from the menu again.

The *Borders* button is also available from the Mini toolbar when you right-click a cell.

let me try

Open the student data file **EX2-10-CashFlow** and try this skill on your own:

1. Apply the **Top and Bottom Border** to cells **B8:D8.**

2. Remove the borders from cells **B3:D3.**

3. Add a **Blue-Gray, Accent 3** color, bottom border to cells **B2:D2.** Use the thickest single line style available.

4. Save the file as directed by your instructor and close it.

Skill 2.11 Adding Shading with Fill Color

Another way to emphasize cells in your workbook is to use a **fill color** to change the background color of cells. Fill colors are available in a variety of shades to make it easy to read the cell content. Shading is often used to differentiate alternating rows in a large table or to make the heading row stand out.

To add shading to your workbook:

1. Select the cell(s) you want to add shading to.
2. On the *Home* tab, in the *Font* group, click the **Fill Color** button arrow to display the color palette. The color palette includes colors from the workbook theme as well as a row of standard colors along the bottom. Notice that as you hold the mouse over each color in the palette, a tool tip appears displaying the color name.
3. Click the color you want.

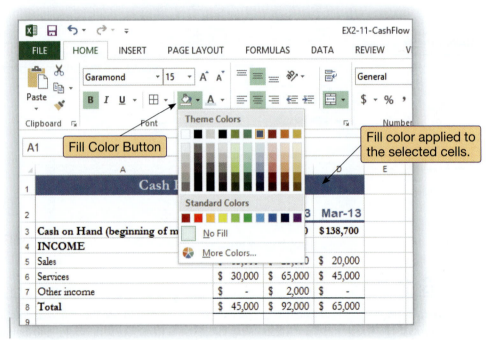

FIGURE EX 2.21

To remove shading:

1. Select the cell(s) you want to remove shading from.
2. On the *Home* tab, in the *Font* group, click the **Fill Color** button arrow to display the color palette.
3. Click **No Fill** to remove the fill color from the selected cells.

tips & tricks

❱ Avoid overusing shading and using too many colors in your workbook. Shading should be used for emphasis and to make the workbook easier to read, not just to make the workbook more colorful.

❱ If you use a dark color for shading, change the font color to white or another light color.

tell me more

In the *Format Cells* dialog, options for fill effects and pattern styles are available under the *Fill* tab.

another **method**

let me **try**

Open the student data file **EX2-11-CashFlow** and try this skill on your own:

1. Add a **Blue-Gray, Accent 3** fill color to cell **A1.** Cells A1:D1 are merged, so you can click anywhere in the merged range to select.

2. Remove the fill color from cell **A17.**

3. Save the file as directed by your instructor and close it.

from the perspective of . . .

HEALTH CLUB OFFICE MANAGER

I use Excel to prepare financial reports for the club owners and their accountant. Proper formatting makes it easier for the owners to read the reports. I would never submit a report without checking for text that appears cut off or titles that aren't centered across columns. And I always use the accounting underline formats instead of borders in my financial reports. Our accountant insists on it!

Skill 2.12 Applying Cell Styles

A **cell style** is a combination of effects that can be applied at one time. Styles can include formatting such as borders, fill color, font size, and number formatting.

Excel includes an extensive gallery of prebuilt cell styles. You can use these styles to help visualize your data by consistently applying them to your worksheet. Use text styles such as *Title* for the title of your worksheet and *Calculation* and *Input* to highlight cells used in formulas. The *Total* style applies borders and font formatting appropriate for a total row in a table.

To apply a cell style:

1. Select the cell or cells you want to apply the style to.
2. On the *Home* tab, in the *Styles* group, click the **Cell Styles** button.
3. Click the style you want to apply to your cells.

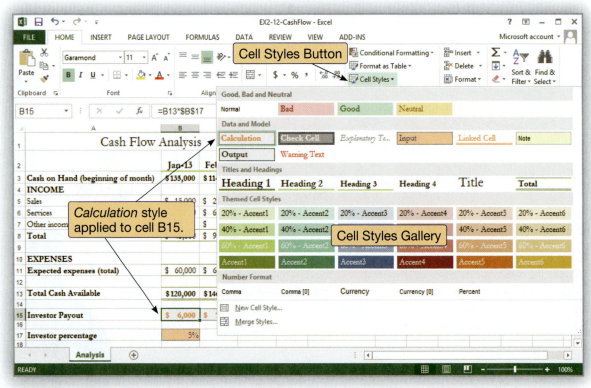

FIGURE EX 2.22

tips & tricks

If you have Live Preview enabled, you can move your mouse over each style in the Cell Styles gallery to see a preview of how that style would look applied to your worksheet.

let me try

Open the student data file **EX2-12-CashFlow** and try this skill on your own:

1. Select cells **A1:D1** (these cells are merged) and apply the **Title** style.
2. Select cells **B13:D13** and apply the **Total** style.
3. Select cells **B15:D15** and apply the **Calculation** style.
4. Select cell **B17** and apply the **Input** style.
5. Save the file as directed by your instructor and close it.

Skill 2.13 Using Format Painter

A professional, well-organized workbook uses consistent formatting. Use the **Format Painter** tool to copy formatting from one part of your worksheet to another, rather than trying to recreate the exact combination of font color and size, number formatting, borders, and shading to reuse.

To use *Format Painter:*

1. Select the cell that has the formatting you want to copy.

2. On the *Home* tab, in the *Clipboard* group, click the **Format Painter** button.

3. Click the cell that you want to apply the formatting to. To apply the formatting to a range of cells, click the first cell in the group, hold down the left mouse button, and drag across the cells. Notice that your mouse cursor changes to the *Format Painter* shape. When you reach the last cell in the group, release the mouse button.

4. The formatting is automatically applied to the selected cell(s).

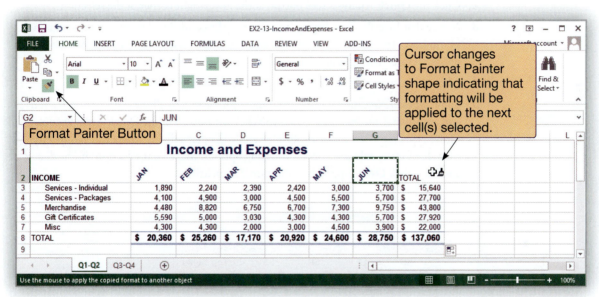

FIGURE EX 2.23

tell me **more**

If you want to apply the formatting to different parts of a worksheet or workbook, double-click the **Format Painter** button when you select it. It will stay on until you click the **Format Painter** button again or press (Esc) to deselect it.

another **method**

To activate *Format Painter,* you can also right-click the cell with formatting you want to copy and click the **Format Painter** button on the Mini toolbar.

let me **try**

Open the student data file **EX2-13-IncomeAndExpenses** and try this skill on your own:

Use **Format Painter** to copy the formatting from cell **G2** and apply it to cell **H2**. Save the file as directed by your instructor and close it.

Skill 2.14 Applying Conditional Formatting Using the Quick Analysis Tool

Conditional formatting provides a visual analysis of data by applying formatting to cells that meet specific criteria (conditions). Excel offers a wide variety of conditional formatting options from the *Conditional Formatting* menu (available on the *Home* tab, in the *Styles* group). However, Excel 2013 offers a new feature from the Quick Analysis tool to quickly apply conditional formatting without opening the menu. The Quick Analysis tool detects whether you've selected numerical or text data and displays only the options appropriate for each type of data. From the Quick Analysis tool, you can also preview conditional formatting before applying it to your data.

To apply conditional formatting with the Quick Analysis tool:

1. Select the cells to which you want to apply conditional formatting.

2. Click the **Quick Analysis** tool button at the lower-right corner of the selection.

3. Notice that Live Preview displays the effect of the conditional formatting on your data as you hover the cursor over each of the formatting options. Review each formatting option before making your selection.

4. Click the button for the type of conditional formatting you want to apply.

5. Some types of conditional formatting apply formatting to all the cells in the selection and are applied automatically when you click the button in the Quick Analysis tool. Other types require a comparison value and will open a dialog where you can specify the value for the rule and select formatting options. Make your selections in the dialog and then click **OK** to apply the conditional formatting.

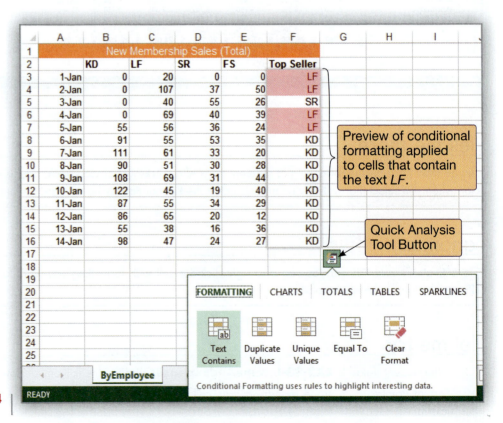

FIGURE EX 2.24

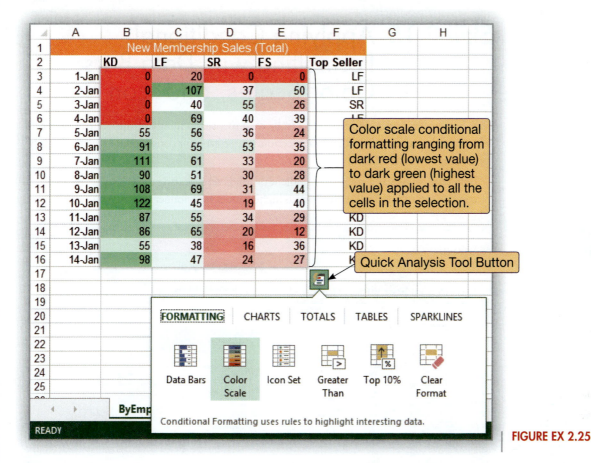

Color scale conditional formatting ranging from dark red (lowest value) to dark green (highest value) applied to all the cells in the selection.

Quick Analysis Tool Button

FIGURE EX 2.25

tips & tricks

You should resist the temptation to overuse conditional formatting. Conditional formatting should be used to highlight important data or data trends, not to colorize the entire worksheet.

another method

You can press Ctrl + Q to open the Quick Analysis tool instead of clicking the *Quick Analysis* tool button.

let me try

Open the student data file **EX2-14-Sales** and try this skill on your own:

1. Use the Quick Analysis tool to apply conditional formatting to cells **F3:F16** to highlight cells containing the text LF. Use the suggested color.
2. Use the Quick Analysis tool to apply conditional formatting to cells **B3:E16** to apply the suggested color scale.
3. Save the file as directed by your instructor and close it.

Skill 2.15 Applying Conditional Formatting with Data Bars, Color Scales, and Icon Sets

Data bars, colors scales, and icon sets can be used to visually represent the value of each cell relative to the other cells in the data selection. These types of conditional formatting apply formatting to all the selected cells.

Data Bars—Display a color bar (gradient or solid) representing the cell value in comparison to other values (cells with higher values have longer data bars).

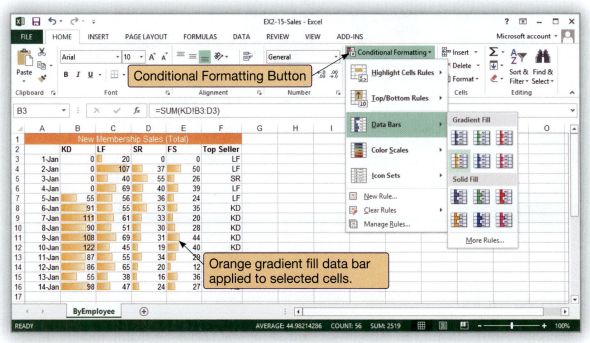

FIGURE EX 2.26

Color Scales—Color the cells according to one of the color scales (e.g., red to green [bad/low to good/high] or blue to red [cold/low to hot/high]).

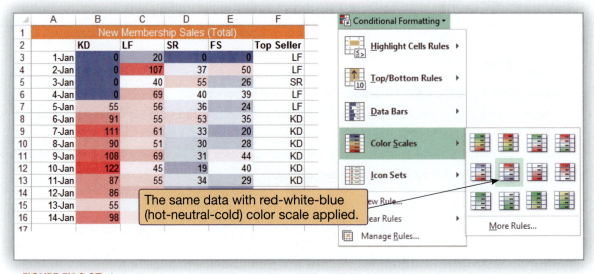

FIGURE EX 2.27

Icon Sets—Display a graphic in the cell representing the cell value in relation to other values.

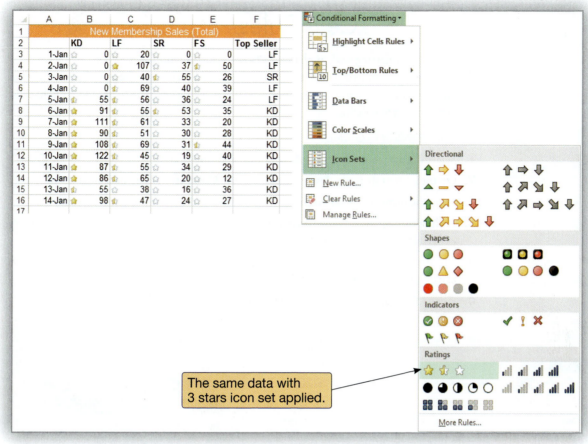

The same data with 3 stars icon set applied.

To apply conditional formatting using data bars, color scales, or icon sets:

1. Select the data you want to apply conditional formatting to.

2. On the *Home* tab, in the *Styles* group, click the **Conditional Formatting** button.

3. From the menu, point to **Data Bars, Colors Scales,** or **Icon Sets,** and then click the specific style of formatting you want. Notice that Live Preview displays the effect of the conditional formatting on your data as you hover the cursor over each of the formatting options.

let me try

Open the student data file **EX2-15-Sales** and try this skill on your own:

Apply conditional formatting to cells **B3:E16** using the orange gradient fill data bar. Save the file as directed by your instructor and close it.

Skill 2.16 Applying Conditional Formatting with Highlight Cells Rules

Conditional formatting with **Highlight Cells Rules** allows you to define formatting for cells that meet specific numerical or text criteria (e.g., greater than a specific value or containing a specific text string). Use this type of conditional formatting when you want to highlight cells based on criteria you define.

To apply *Highlight Cells Rules:*

1. Select the data you want to apply conditional formatting to.
2. On the *Home* tab, in the *Styles* group, click the **Conditional Formatting** button.
3. From the menu, point to **Highlight Cells Rules** and click the option you want.
4. Each option opens a dialog where you can enter a value or date to which the value of each cell will be compared.
5. The default formatting is light red fill with dark red text. To change the formatting, expand the drop-down list in the dialog and select another option.
6. Click **OK** to apply the conditional formatting.

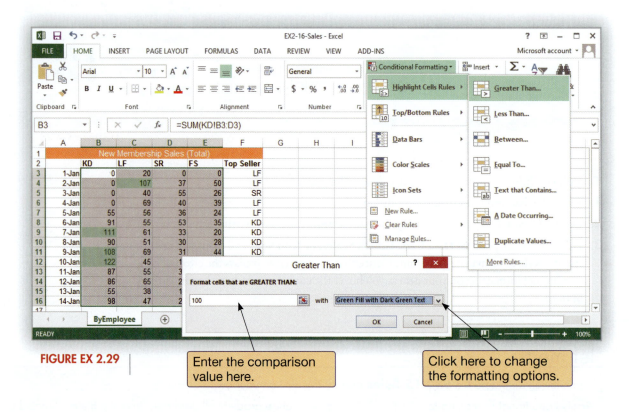

FIGURE EX 2.29

Enter the comparison value here.

Click here to change the formatting options.

tips & tricks

The *Highlight Cells Rules* menu includes an option to highlight duplicate values. This option can be especially helpful when you are trying to find a potential data entry error in a long list of values.

tell me **more**

To highlight unique values (those that are **not** duplicates):

1. Select the data you want to analyze.
2. On the *Home* tab, in the *Styles* group, click the **Conditional Formatting** button.
3. From the menu, point to **Highlight Cells Rules** and click **Duplicate Values...**
4. In the *Duplicate Values* dialog, expand the drop-down box and select **Unique.**
5. Click **OK.**

let me **try**

Open the student data file **EX2-16-Sales** and try this skill on your own:

Apply conditional formatting to cells **B3:E16** so cells with a value greater than 100 are formatted using a green fill with dark green text. Save the file as directed by your instructor and close it.

from the perspective of . . .

HELP DESK COORDINATOR

I love conditional formatting! Every week, each department sends me a spreadsheet of all the help desk calls for each software package we support. I use color scales to identify the software packages with the highest volume of calls. In my spreadsheet that combines the weekly data, I use icon sets to indicate whether the number of calls went up or down for each software package on a week-by-week basis.

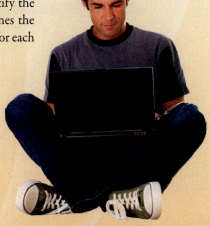

Skill 2.17 Applying Conditional Formatting with Top/Bottom Rules

One way to analyze worksheet data is to compare cell values to other cell values. When analyzing a worksheet, you may want to highlight the highest or lowest values or values that are above or below the average. In these cases, use conditional formatting Top/Bottom Rules. When you use *Top/Bottom Rules,* Excel automatically finds the highest, lowest, and average values to compare values to, rather than asking you to enter criteria (as you do when using *Highlight Cells Rules*).

To highlight cells with conditional formatting *Top/Bottom Rules:*

1. Select the data you want to apply conditional formatting to.
2. On the *Home* tab, in the *Styles* group, click the **Conditional Formatting** button.
3. From the menu, point to **Top/Bottom Rules** and click the option you want.
4. Each option opens a dialog where you can select the formatting to apply when cells meet the condition. The top and bottom options allow you to modify the threshold to a value other than 10 (top/bottom 10 items and top/bottom 10%).
5. Click **OK** to apply the conditional formatting.

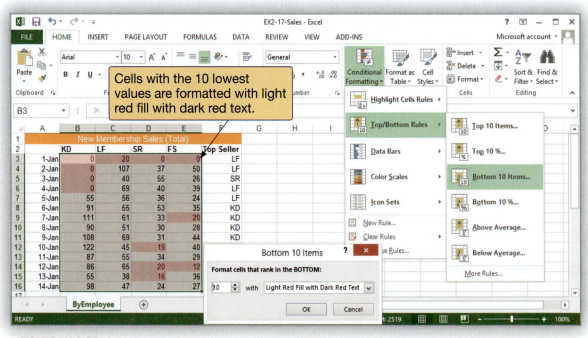

FIGURE EX 2.30

let me try

Open the student data file **EX2-17-Sales** and try this skill on your own:

Apply conditional formatting to cells **B3:E16** so cells with the 10 lowest values are formatted with light red fill and dark red text. Save the file as directed by your instructor and close it.

Skill 2.18 Removing Conditional Formatting

You cannot remove conditional formatting from cells by clearing the data or pressing Delete or ← Backspace . Instead, you must remove the conditional formatting rule from the cells.

To remove conditional formatting:

1. If appropriate, select the cells from which you want to remove conditional formatting.

2. On the *Home* tab, in the *Styles* group, click the **Conditional Formatting** button.

3. Point to **Clear Rules,** and click the option you want from the menu:

   Clear Rules from Selected Cells

   Clear Rules from Entire Sheet

   Clear Rules from This Table (available if the selected cells are part of a table)

   Clear Rules from This PivotTable (available if the selected cells are part of a PivotTable)

FIGURE EX 2.31

tell me **more**

Through the Conditional Formatting Rules Manager, you can view all of your conditional formatting rules at one time and add, modify, or delete rules. Open the Conditional Formatting Rules Manager from the *Manage Rules...* option at the bottom of the *Conditional Formatting* menu.

another **method**

You can also clear conditional formatting from the Quick Analysis tool:

1. Select the cells from which you want to remove conditional formatting.

2. Click the **Quick Analysis** tool button at the lower-right corner of the selection, and click the **Clear Format** button.

let me **try**

Open the student data file **EX2-18-Sales** and try this skill on your own:

Clear the conditional formatting from cells **F3:F16** without clearing conditional formatting from the rest of the worksheet. Save the file as directed by your instructor and close it.

Skill 2.19 Clearing Cell Content

To remove the contents of a cell without removing the cell from the structure of your workbook, use one of the *Clear* commands. In Excel, when you clear a cell, you remove its contents, formats, comments, and hyperlinks, but the blank cell remains in the worksheet. Clearing a cell does not affect the layout of your worksheet.

To clear a cell:

1. Select the cell you want to clear of formats or contents.

2. On the *Home* tab, in the *Editing* group, click the **Clear** button.

3. Click the command for the type of formatting or contents you want to remove from the cell.

    Clear All—clears all cell contents and formatting and deletes any comments or hyperlinks attached to the cell.

    Clear Formats—clears only the cell formatting and leaves the cell contents, comments, and hyperlinks. The *Clear Formats* command does not remove conditional formatting rules from the cell.

    Clear Contents—clears only the contents (including hyperlinks) and leaves the cell formatting and comments.

    Clear Comments—deletes any comments attached to the cell while leaving the cell contents, formatting, and hyperlinks intact.

    Clear Hyperlinks—removes the hyperlink action from the cell without removing the content or the hyperlink style of formatting.

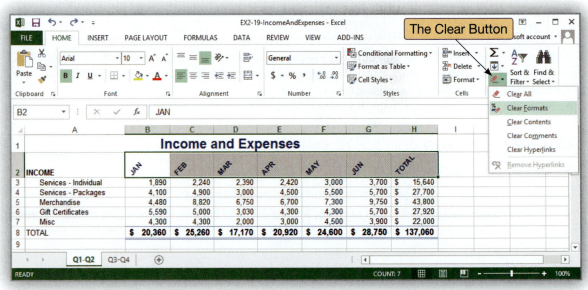

FIGURE EX 2.32

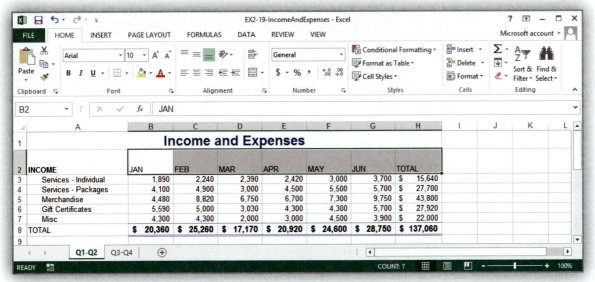

FIGURE EX 2.33
Results after Clearing Formatting Only

another method

To clear the contents of a cell, you can

▸ Right-click the cell and select **Clear Contents** from the menu. Using the right-click method, there are no options to clear formats or comments.

▸ Select the cell and then press (Delete) or (← Backspace) to clear the cell contents but not the cell formatting.

let me try

Open the student data file **EX2-19-IncomeAndExpenses** and try this skill on your own:

1. Clear only the formatting from cells **B2:H2** (leaving the content).
2. Clear only the content from cells **B8:H8** (leaving the formatting).
3. Use a single command to clear everything (content and formatting) from cells **B10:H10**.
4. Save the file as directed by your instructor and close it.

Skill 2.20 Using Find and Replace

All of the Microsoft Office applications include **Find** and **Replace** commands that allow you to search for and replace data in your file. In Excel, these commands can be used to find and replace not only text but also numbers in values and formulas in a single worksheet or across an entire workbook.

Before using the *Replace* command, you should use *Find* to make sure the data you are about to replace are what you expect:

1. On the *Home* tab, in the *Editing* group at the far right side of the Ribbon, click the **Find & Select** button.

2. From the *Find & Select* menu, click **Find...**

3. The *Find and Replace* dialog opens, with the *Find* tab on top.

4. Type the word, phrase, or number you want to find in the *Find what* box.

   a. To go to just the first instance, click the **Find Next** button.

   b. To find all instances, click the **Find All** button. When you click *Find All*, Excel displays a list detailing every instance of the data—workbook file name, worksheet name, cell name, cell address, the value of the cell, and the formula (if there is one).

FIGURE EX 2.34

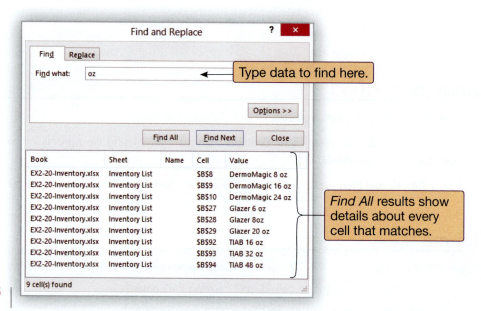

FIGURE EX 2.35

Once you have verified the data you want to replace, switch to the *Replace* tab in the *Find and Replace* dialog:

1. Click the **Replace** tab.

2. Excel keeps the data you typed in the *Find what* box.

3. Now type the replacement text or values in the *Replace with* box.

   a. Click the **Replace** button to replace one instance of the data at a time.

   b. Click the **Replace All** button to replace all instances at once.

4. If you select *Replace All*, Excel displays a message telling you how many replacements were made. Click **OK** to dismiss the message. The results now display details about every cell that was updated with the *Replace* command.

5. Click **Close** to close the *Find and Replace* dialog.

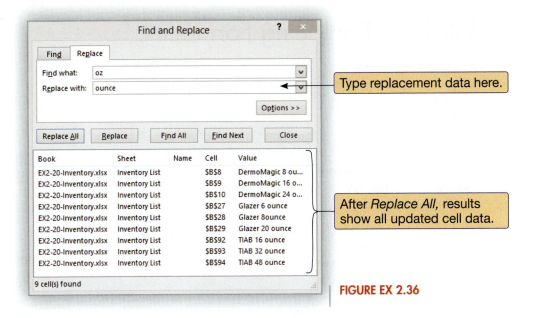

Type replacement data here.

After *Replace All*, results show all updated cell data.

FIGURE EX 2.36

tell me **more**

By default, Excel searches for the data both in cell values and within formulas. If you want to limit the search to only cell values, first click the **Options>>** button in the *Find and Replace* dialog to display the find and replace optional settings. Next, expand the *Look in* list by clicking the arrow, and select **Values.**

another **method**

Use the keyboard shortcut (Ctrl) + (F) to open the *Find and Replace* dialog with the *Find* tab on top.

Use the keyboard shortcut (Ctrl) + (H) to open the *Find and Replace* dialog with the *Replace* tab on top.

let me **try**

Open the student data file **EX2-20-Inventory** and try this skill on your own:

1. Find all instances of the word **oz.**

2. Replace all instances of the word **oz** with **ounce.**

3. Save the file as directed by your instructor and close it.

Skill 2.21 Replacing Formatting

The *Find* and *Replace* commands allow you to find and replace formatting as well as data. This feature is especially helpful when replacing number formats throughout a workbook.

To find and replace formatting:

1. On the *Home* tab, in the *Editing* group, click the **Find & Select** button and select **Replace...** to open the *Find and Replace* dialog.

2. If necessary, click the **Options**>> button to display the find and replace optional settings. Notice that next to the *Find what* and *Replace with* boxes, the preview box displays *No Format Set*.

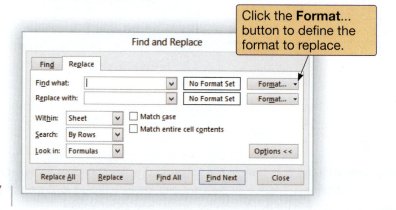

Click the **Format...** button to define the format to replace.

3. If you want to find specific data, enter it in the *Find what* box. If you do not enter anything, Excel will find all cells with the formatting defined in the next step.

4. Click the **Format...** button next to the *Find what* box to open the *Find Format* dialog where you can define the formatting you want to find. The *Find Format* dialog includes all the tabs and formatting options available in the *Format Cells* dialog. Set the formatting to find just as you would set formatting to apply to cells.

   a. To find all cells formatted using the Accounting Number Format, click the **Number** tab and select **Accounting** in the *Category* list.

   b. Click **OK.**

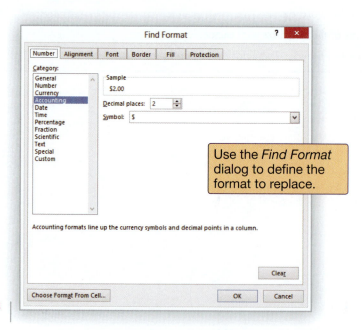

Use the *Find Format* dialog to define the format to replace.

FIGURE EX 2.38

5. The preview box now displays the word *Preview* using the formatting you defined. If you included number formatting, *Preview* will appear with an * after it (because the word *Preview* cannot display number formatting).

6. If you want to replace data as well as formatting, enter the replacement data in the *Replace with* box. If you do not enter anything, Excel will modify the formatting and leave the data in each cell unchanged.

7. Click the **Format...** button next to the *Replace with* box and repeat the same process to define the new format you want to use.

   a. To replace the Accounting Number Format with the Currency number format, click the **Number** tab again (if necessary) and select **Currency** in the *Category* list.

   b. You can also change options for the format such as expanding the **Symbol** list and selecting **None** to remove the $ from the format.

   c. Click **OK.**

8. Click **Replace All.**

9. Click **OK** in the message that appears.

10. Click **Close** to close the *Find and Replace* dialog.

another **method**

You can also define the formatting styles to find and replace by picking cells that are already formatted with those attributes.

1. In the *Find and Replace* dialog, click the **Format button arrow** next to the *Find what* box and select **Choose Format from Cell...**

2. The cursor changes to a picker shape ⊕🖊.

3. Click a cell with the formatting attributes you want to find.

4. Click the **Format button arrow** next to the *Replace with* box and select **Choose Format from Cell...**

5. Click a cell with the formatting attributes you want to apply.

6. Click **Replace All.**

7. Click **OK.**

8. Click **Close** to close the *Find & Replace* dialog.

let me **try**

Open the student data file **EX2-21-Inventory** and try this skill on your own:

Using the *Replace* command, find and replace all cells formatted with the Accounting Number Format with the Currency format with no currency symbol. Save the file as directed by your instructor and close it.

Skill 2.22 Setting and Clearing the Print Area

If you do not want to print your entire worksheet, you can set a print area. The **print area** is a range of cells that you designate as the default print selection. If you have defined a print area for your worksheet, it will be the only part of the worksheet that prints.

To set a print area:

1. Select the area you want to print.
2. On the *Page Layout* tab, in the *Page Setup* group, click the **Print Area** button.
3. Click **Set Print Area.**

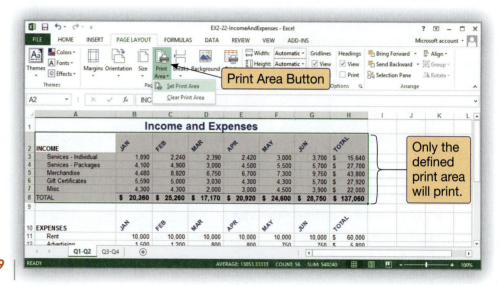

FIGURE EX 2.39

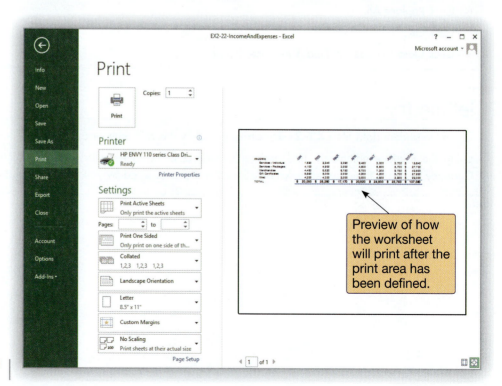

FIGURE EX 2.40

When you save the worksheet, the print area is saved as well. To clear a print area:

1. On the *Page Layout* tab, in the *Page Setup* group, click the **Print Area** button.

2. Click **Clear Print Area.**

tips & tricks

Notice that when the print area is selected, the Name box to the left of the address bar displays *Print_Area*. When you define a print area, Excel automatically creates a named range called *Print_Area*.

tell me more

You can define more than one print area per worksheet. Select the cells you want in the first print area, and then press (Ctrl) and drag the mouse to select the range of cells for the second print area. Each print area will print on a separate page.

let me try

Open the student data file **EX2-22-IncomeAndExpenses** and try this skill on your own:

1. Preview how the worksheet will look when printed. Notice that a print area has been set to print cells **A2:D19** only.

2. Clear the current print area.

3. Modify the workbook so only the *Income* section of the *Q1-Q2* worksheet (**A2:H8**) will print.

4. Preview how the worksheet will look when printed after the new print area has been set.

5. Save the file as directed by your instructor and close it.

key terms

Cut	Format Painter
Copy	Conditional formatting
Paste	Data bars
Undo	Color scales
Redo	Icon sets
Alignment	Highlight Cells Rules
General horizontal alignment	Top/Bottom Rules
Font	Find
Fill color	Replace
Cell style	Print area

concepts review

1. When you cut and paste a cell containing a formula with relative references, Excel
   a. updates the cell references to the new location.
   b. does not update the cell references to the new location.
   c. treats the formulas as if it contained absolute references.
   d. b and c

2. Which paste option pastes formulas and number formatting but none of the cell formatting?
   a. Values
   b. Formulas
   c. Formulas & Number Formatting
   d. Keep Source Formatting

3. To split a cell into two cells:
   a. On the *Home* tab, in the *Alignment* group, click the **Merge & Center** button and select **Unmerge Cells.**
   b. In the *Format Cells* dialog, on the *Alignment* tab, in the *Text Control* section, click the **Merge cells** box to uncheck it.
   c. On the *Data* tab, in the *Data Tools* group, click the **Text to Columns** button.
   d. You cannot split a cell into two cells; you can only unmerge merged cells.

4. To apply the Double Underline accounting underline format:
   a. Press Ctrl + U.
   b. In the *Font* dialog, on the *Font* tab, expand the **Underline** list and select **Double Accounting.**
   c. On the *Home* tab, in the *Font* group, click the **Underline** button.
   d. On the *Home* tab, in the *Font* group, click the **Underline button arrow** and select **Double Underline.**

5. Clicking the *Borders* button on the Ribbon applies which border style?

   a. None

   b. Outline

   c. Bottom border only

   d. The most recently used border style

6. The keyboard shortcut to open the Quick Analysis tool is

   a. Ctrl + A.

   b. Ctrl + Q.

   c. F7.

   d. F10.

7. To highlight cells with values in the top 10% of the select range, use _____ conditional formatting.

   a. Data bars

   b. Highlight Cells Rules

   c. Top/Bottom Rules

   d. Icon sets

8. You can remove conditional formatting using the

   a. *Clear All* command.

   b. Ctrl + X keyboard shortcut.

   c. Delete key.

   d. *Clear Rules from Selected Cells* command.

9. Selecting a cell and pressing Delete clears

   a. cell content only.

   b. cell content and formatting.

   c. cell content, formatting, and formulas.

   d. cell formatting only.

10. Where is the *Set Print Area* command located?

   a. On the *Page Layout* tab, in the *Page Setup* group

   b. In the *Page Layout* dialog

   c. In the *Print* dialog

   d. On the *Home* tab, in the *Print* group

projects

Data files for projects can be found on
www.mhhe.com/office2013skills

skill review 2.1

In this project you will add formatting to a daily vitamin and supplement plan to make the spreadsheet more attractive and easier to read. Throughout the project, use the *Undo* command (Ctrl + Z) if you make a mistake.

Skills needed to complete this project:

- Using Undo and Redo (Skill 2.3)
- Merging Cells and Splitting Merged Cells (Skill 2.7)
- Applying Cell Styles (Skill 2.12)
- Inserting and Deleting Cells (Skill 2.5)
- Aligning Cells (Skill 2.6)
- Changing Fonts, Font Size, and Font Color (Skill 2.9)
- Using Format Painter (Skill 2.13)
- Adding Borders (Skill 2.10)
- Cutting, Copying, and Pasting Cells (Skill 2.1)
- Wrapping Text in Cells (Skill 2.4)
- Applying Conditional Formatting Using the Quick Analysis Tool (Skill 2.14)
- Applying Conditional Formatting with Data Bars, Color Scales, and Icon Sets (Skill 2.15)
- Applying Conditional Formatting with Highlight Cells Rules (Skill 2.16)
- Removing Conditional Formatting (Skill 2.18)
- Applying Conditional Formatting with Top/Bottom Rules (Skill 2.17)
- Replacing Formatting (Skill 2.21)

1. Open the start file **EX2013-SkillReview-2-1** and resave the file as: `[your initials]EX-SkillReview-2-1`

2. If the workbook opens in Protected View, click the **Enable Editing** button in the Message Bar at the top of the workbook so you can modify the workbook.

3. Merge and center the worksheet title across cells **A1:H1.**

   a. Select cells **A1:H1.**

   b. On the *Home* tab, in the *Alignment* group, click the **Merge & Center** button.

4. Apply the **Title** style to the worksheet title.

   a. If necessary, select the merged cells **A1:H1.**

   b. On the *Home* tab, in the *Styles* group, click the **Cell Styles** button.

   c. Click the **Title** style.

5. There are extra cells to the left of the patient name and total cost. Delete them.

   a. Select cells **B2:B3.**

   b. On the *Home* tab, in the *Cells* group, click the **Delete** button.

6. The patient name would look better aligned at the right side of the cell.

    a. Select cell **B2.**

    b. On the *Home* tab, in the *Alignment* group, click the **Align Right** button.

7. Format the **Patient Name** and **Daily Cost** labels with bolding and the **Blue-Gray, Text 2** font color.

    a. Select cells **A2:A3.**

    b. On the *Home* tab, in the *Font* group, click the **Bold** button.

    c. On the *Home* tab, in the *Font* group, click the **Font Color** button arrow, and select the **Blue-Gray, Text 2** color from the first row of the theme colors.

8. Use *Format Painter* to apply the label formatting to the data table header row (cells **A5:H5**).

    a. If necessary, click cell **A2** or **A3.**

    b. On the *Home* tab, in the *Clipboard* group, click the **Format Painter** button.

    c. Click cell **A5** and drag to cell **H5** to apply the formatting.

9. Add a border beneath the data table header row to separate the titles from the data. The border should be the same color as the font.

    a. If necessary, select cells **A5:H5.**

    b. On the *Home* tab, in the *Font* group, click the **Borders** button arrow, and select **More Borders**...

    c. In the *Format Cells* dialog, on the *Border* tab, expand the **Color** palette, and select the **Blue-Gray, Text 2** color from the first row of the theme colors.

    d. Click the bottom border area of the preview diagram to add the border.

    e. Click **OK.**

10. The data in row 13 are misplaced and belong in the data table. Cut it and insert the cut cells above row 8.

    a. Select cells **A13:H13.**

    b. On the *Home* tab, in the *Clipboard* group, click the **Cut** button.

    c. Click cell **A8.**

    d. On the *Home* tab, in the *Cells* group, click the **Insert** button arrow, and select **Insert Cut Cells.**

11. Apply the *Note* cell style to the note in cell **A12.**

    a. Select cell **A12.**

    b. On the *Home* tab, in the *Styles* group, click the **Cell Styles** button.

    c. Click the **Note** style.

12. The note text is much longer than the width of cell A12, and it looks odd with the cell style applied. Apply text wrapping so all the text is visible within the cell formatted with the *Note* style.

    a. If necessary, select cell **A12.**

    b. On the *Home* tab, in the *Alignment* group, click the **Wrap Text** button.

13. Apply conditional formatting using solid blue data bars to cells **H6:H10** to represent the relative daily cost of each supplement.

    a. Select cells **H6:H10.**

    b. Click the **Quick Analysis** tool button.

    c. Click the **Data Bars** button.

14. Apply conditional formatting using **Highlight Cells Rules** to the cost per bottle data (cells **F6:F10**) to format cells with a value greater than 20 with light red fill with dark red text.

    a. Select cells **F6:F10.**

    b. On the *Home* tab, in the *Styles* group, click the **Conditional Formatting** button.

    c. Point to **Highlight Cells Rules,** and select **Greater Than...**

    d. In the *Greater Than* dialog, type 20 in the *Format cells that are GREATER THAN* box.

    e. Click **OK.**

15. There might be too much conditional formatting in this worksheet. Remove the conditional formatting from cells **G6:G10.**

    a. Select cells **G6:G10.**

    b. On the *Home* tab, in the *Styles* group, click the **Conditional Formatting** button.

    c. Point to **Clear Rules,** and select **Clear Rules from Selected Cells.**

16. You would still like to highlight the least expensive cost per pill. Apply conditional formatting to cells **G6:G10** using **Top/Bottom Rules** to format only the lowest value with green fill with dark green text.

    a. If necessary, select cells **G6:G10.**

    b. On the *Home* tab, in the *Styles* group, click the **Conditional Formatting** button.

    c. Point to **Top/Bottom Rules,** and select **Bottom 10 Items...**

    d. In the *Bottom 10 Items* dialog, type 1 in the *Format cells that rank in the BOTTOM* box.

    e. Expand the formatting list and select **Green Fill with Dark Green Text.**

    f. Click **OK.**

17. Click cell **G11** so the cost per pill data is no longer selected.

18. Find all of the values that use the Accounting Number Format with four digits after the decimal and change the formatting to the Accounting Number Format with two digits after the decimal.

    a. On the *Home* tab, in the *Editing* group, click the **Find & Select** button, and select **Replace...**

    b. In the *Find and Replace* dialog, ensure that there are no values in the *Find what* and *Replace with* boxes.

    c. If necessary, click the **Options>>** button to display the find and replace options.

    d. Click the **Format...** button next to the *Find What* box.

    e. In the *Find Format* dialog, on the *Number* tab, click **Accounting** in the *Category* list. If necessary, change the *Decimal places* value to **4.** Verify that the *Symbol* value is $.

    f. Click **OK.**

    g. Click the **Format...** button next to the Replace with box.

    h. In the *Replace Format* dialog, on the *Number* tab, click **Accounting** in the *Category* list. If necessary, change the *Decimal places* value to **2.** Verify that the *Symbol* value is **$.**

    i. Click **OK.**

    j. Click **Replace All.**

    k. Click **OK.**

    l. Click **Close.**

19. Save and close the workbook.

You want to share your recipe for Greek yogurt with friends, but the spreadsheet is a little rough. Use the formatting skills you learned in this chapter to make the recipe look as good as it tastes.

Throughout the project, use the *Undo* command ([Ctrl] + [Z]) if you make a mistake.

Skills needed to complete this project:

- Using Undo and Redo (Skill 2.3)
- Merging Cells and Splitting Merged Cells (Skill 2.7)
- Applying Cell Styles (Skill 2.12)
- Inserting and Deleting Cells (Skill 2.5)
- Using Format Painter (Skill 2.13)
- Changing Fonts, Font Size, and Font Color (Skill 2.9)
- Applying Bold, Italic, and Underline (Skill 2.8)
- Adding Borders (Skill 2.10)
- Using Find and Replace (Skill 2.20)
- Cutting, Copying, and Pasting Cells (Skill 2.1)
- Using Paste Options (Skill 2.2)
- Setting and Clearing the Print Area (Skill 2.22)

1. Open the start file **EX2013-SkillReview-2-2** and resave the file as:
   `[your initials]EX-SkillReview-2-2`

2. Center and merge the recipe title across cells **A1:D1.**

   a. Select cells **A1:D1.**

   b. On the *Home* tab, in the *Alignment* group, click the **Merge & Center** button.

3. Format the title using the **Accent 6** themed cell style.

   a. If necessary, select the merged cells **A1:D1.**

   b. On the *Home* tab, in the *Styles* group, click the **Cell Styles** button.

   c. In the *Themed Cell Styles* section of the gallery, click the **Accent 6** style.

4. Delete cell **B2,** shifting other cells to the left.

   a. Select cell **B2.**

   b. On the *Home* tab, in the *Cells* group, click the **Delete** button arrow and select **Delete Cells...**

   c. Click the **Shift cells left** radio button.

   d. Click **OK.**

5. Use *Format Painter* to copy formatting from the title and apply it to the Ingredients (**A5**) and Directions (**A10**) headers.

   a. Select the merged cells **A1:D1.**

   b. On the *Home* tab, in the *Clipboard* group, double-click the **Format Painter** button.

   c. Click cell **A5.** Notice that *Format Painter* merged cells **A5:D5** and centered the text across the merged cells.

   d. Click cell **A10.** Notice that *Format Painter* merged cells **A5:D5** and centered the text across the merged cells.

   e. On the *Home* tab, in the *Clipboard* group, click the **Format Painter** button again to disable it.

6. The worksheet title should be more prominent than the section headers. Increase the font size to **14** and bold the text.

   a. Select the merged cells **A1:D1.**

   b. On the *Home* tab, in the *Font* group, click the **Font Size** button arrow, and select **14.**

   c. On the *Home* tab, in the *Font* group, click the **Bold** button.

7. Add a bottom border to cells **B6:D6** to separate the headings from the data.

   a. Select cells **B6:D6.**

   b. On the *Home* tab, in the *Font* group, click the **Borders** button arrow and select **Bottom Border.**

8. This recipe is better using organic whole milk. Find and replace all instances of **non fat** with **organic whole.**

   a. On the *Home* tab, in the *Editing* group, click the **Find & Select** button and select **Replace...**

   b. If necessary, display the find and replace options and clear any formats.

      i. Click the **Options>>** button.

      ii. If the button next to the *Find what* box does not display *No Format Set,* click the **Format** button arrow and select **Clear Find Format.**

      iii. If the button next to the *Replace with* box does not display *Not Format Set,* click the **Format** button arrow and select **Clear Replace Format.**

      iv. Click the **Options<<** button to hide the find and replace options.

   c. Type non fat in the *Find what* box.

   d. Type organic whole in the *Replace with* box.

   e. Click the **Replace All** button.

   f. Click **OK.**

   g. Click **Close.**

9. Apply a thick box border around the entire recipe (cells A1:D20).

   a. Select cells **A1:D20.**

   b. On the *Home* tab, in the *Font* group, click the **Borders** button arrow and select **Thick Box Border.**

10. Now that your recipe is formatted, make a copy of it and change the number of servings to **10.** Be sure to retain formulas and column widths.

    a. If necessary, select cells **A1:D20.**

    b. On the *Home* tab, in the *Clipboard* group, click the **Copy** button.

    c. Click cell **F1.**

    d. On the *Home* tab, in the *Clipboard* group, click the **Paste** button arrow.

    e. Select **Keep Source Column Widths.**

11. Change the value in cell **G2** to **10.**

12. Set the print area so only the original version of the recipe will print. Be sure to preview the printed worksheet.

    a. Select cells **A1:D20.**

    b. On the *Page Layout* tab, it the *Page Setup* group, click the **Print Area** button and select **Set Print Area.**

    c. Click the **File** tab.

    d. Click **Print.**

13. Save and close the workbook.

challenge yourself 2.3

In this project, you will format a blood pressure report to make it look less like a spreadsheet and more like a form. You will use conditional formatting to highlight important data. Throughout the project, use the *Undo* command ($\boxed{\text{Ctrl}}$ + $\boxed{\text{Z}}$) if you make a mistake.

Skills needed to complete this project:

- Using Undo and Redo (Skill 2.3)
- Adding Shading with Fill Color (Skill 2.11)
- Merging Cells and Splitting Merged Cells (Skill 2.7)
- Applying Cell Styles (Skill 2.12)
- Changing Fonts, Font Size, and Font Color (Skill 2.9)
- Aligning Cells (Skill 2.6)
- Adding Borders (Skill 2.10)
- Using Format Painter (Skill 2.13)
- Applying Bold, Italic, and Underline (Skill 2.8)
- Applying Conditional Formatting with Data Bars, Color Scales, and Icon Sets (Skill 2.15)
- Applying Conditional Formatting with Top/Bottom Rules (Skill 2.17)
- Setting and Clearing the Print Area (Skill 2.22)

1. Open the start file **EX2013-ChallengeYourself-2-3** and resave the file as: **[your initials]EX-ChallengeYourself-2-3**

2. If the workbook opens in Protected View, enable editing so you can make changes to the workbook.

3. Select cells **A1:F27** and apply the white fill color.

4. Merge and center the title across cells **A1:F1**.

5. Apply the **Title** cell style to the merged cells.

6. Apply the **Indigo, Accent 6, Lighter 40%** fill color to the merged cells.

7. Change the font color to white.

8. Merge cells **C3:D3** and right align the content in the cell.

9. Apply outside borders to the merged cells.

10. Apply the **20%-Accent 2** cell style to cells **C5:D5**.

11. Apply the same formatting to cells **C8:D8**.

12. Apply outside borders to cells **C5:D6** and cells **C8:D9**.

13. Bold cells **B3, B6, B9,** and B11.

14. Merge cells **C11:D11** and right align the content in the cell.

15. Add outside borders to the merged cells.

16. Apply the **Indigo, Accent 6, Lighter 60%** fill color to cells **A13:F13**.

17. Left align the content in cells **A14:A27**.

18. Add all borders to cells **A14:F27**.

19. Add conditional formatting to cells **E14:E27** using the **3 Arrows (Gray)** icon set.

20. Add conditional formatting to cells **C14:C27** to format values greater than 139 with light red fill with dark red text.

21. Add conditional formatting to cells **C14:C27** to format values between 120 and 139 with yellow fill with dark yellow text.

22. Add conditional formatting to cells **D14:D27** to format values greater than 89 with light red fill with dark red text.

23. Add conditional formatting to cells **D14:D27** to format values between 80 and 89 with yellow fill with dark yellow text.

24. Add a thick box border around cells **A1:F27**.

25. Set cells **A1:F27** as the print area.

26. Preview how the worksheet will look when printed.

27. Save and close the workbook.

challenge yourself 2.4

In this project you will add formatting to a college budget spreadsheet and rearrange items that are in the wrong categories.

Skills needed to complete this project:

- Using Undo and Redo (Skill 2.3)
- Merging Cells and Splitting Merged Cells (Skill 2.7)
- Applying Cell Styles (Skill 2.12)
- Adding Shading with Fill Color (Skill 2.11)
- Applying Bold, Italic, and Underline (Skill 2.8)
- Cutting, Copying, and Pasting Cells (Skill 2.1)
- Using Paste Options (Skill 2.2)
- Inserting and Deleting Cells (Skill 2.5)
- Using Format Painter (Skill 2.13)
- Applying Conditional Formatting with Data Bars, Color Scales, and Icon Sets (Skill 2.15)
- Wrapping Text in Cells (Skill 2.7)
- Adding Borders (Skill 2.10)

1. Open the start file **EX2013-ChallengeYourself-2-4** and resave the file as: **[your initials]EX-ChallengeYourself-2-4**

2. If the workbook opens in Protected View, enable editing so you can make changes to the workbook.

3. Center and merge the title across cells **B1:F1**.

4. Apply the **Heading 1** cell style to the merged cells.

5. Merge and center the four section titles across the appropriate cells (**Monthly Income, Discretionary Income, Monthly Expenses,** and **Semester Expenses**).

6. Apply cell styles to the section titles as follows:

   a. Monthly Income—**Accent5**

   b. Discretionary Income—**Accent4**

   c. Monthly Expenses—**Accent1**

   d. Semester Expenses—**Accent6**

7. Add the **Brown, Accent 3, Lighter 80%** fill color to cells **B3:C3**.

8. Bold cells **B3:C3**.

9. Copy only the formatting of cells **B3:C3** to the headers in the other sections. (Hint: Copy the cells and use one of the paste options to paste only the formatting.)

10. The line item for lab fees (cells **B21:C21**) is in the wrong category. Cut the cells and paste them above cell **E12**, shifting the other cells down. Do not overwrite the existing data.

11. Delete the empty cells **B21:C21**, shifting the other cells up.

12. Cell F6 has the wrong number format applied. Copy the formatting from cell **F5** and apply it to cell **F6**.

13. Apply conditional formatting to cells **C11:C23** to display an orange gradient data bar in each cell.

14. The text in cell **B21** appears cut-off. Apply text wrapping to the cell.

15. Apply all borders to the following cell ranges: **B3:C7, E3:F7, B10:C24,** and **E10:F16.**

16. Save and close the workbook.

on your own 2.5

In this project, you will add your own data to a worksheet that tracks the original cost and current resell value for textbooks. As you format the worksheet, keep in mind that you want the worksheet to be visually appealing, but you don't want it to look like a circus! Try a variety of formatting options and keep using the *Undo* command until you find the formats you like best.

Skills needed to complete this project:

- Using Undo and Redo (Skill 2.3)
- Adding Shading with Fill Color (Skill 2.11)
- Merging Cells and Splitting Merged Cells (Skill 2.7)
- Applying Cell Styles (Skill 2.12)
- Inserting and Deleting Cells (Skill 2.5)
- Aligning Cells (Skill 2.6)
- Changing Fonts, Font Size, and Font Color (Skill 2.9)
- Using Format Painter (Skill 2.13)
- Adding Borders (Skill 2.10)
- Cutting, Copying, and Pasting Cells (Skill 2.1)
- Applying Conditional Formatting Using the Quick Analysis Tool (Skill 2.14)
- Applying Conditional Formatting with Data Bars, Color Scales, and Icon Sets (Skill 2.15)
- Replacing Formatting (Skill 2.21)
- Wrapping Text in Cells (Skill 2.4)
- Applying Bold, Italic, and Underline (Skill 2.8)
- Applying Conditional Formatting with Highlight Cells Rules (Skill 2.16)
- Applying Conditional Formatting with Top/Bottom Rules (Skill 2.17)

1. Open the start file **EX2013-OnYourOwn-2-5** and resave the file as: **[your initials]EX-OnYourOwn-2-5**

2. If the workbook opens in Protected View, click the **Enable Editing** button in the Message Bar at the top of the workbook so you can modify the workbook.

3. Update the data in the workbook with an inventory of textbooks you own. Include the purchase price and estimated resell value for each title.

4. Add and delete cells as necessary.

5. Wrap text if any of your book titles are too long to fit in the cell.

6. Format the worksheet title and data table using cell styles, borders, and fill color. Change fonts, font color, and font size as appropriate.

7. Remember to use *Format Painter* to copy formatting from one part of the worksheet to another.

8. You can also use the *Replace* command if you want to change formatting from one style to another in multiple cells at the same time.

9. Apply conditional formatting to identify the most expensive books and the ones with the highest resell values. Use any type of conditional formatting you'd like.

10. When you are satisfied with the appearance of the worksheet, save and close the workbook.

fix it 2.6

In this project you will fix a rather unattractive worksheet that was intended for recording walking/running miles and times.

Skills needed to complete this project:

- Using Undo and Redo (Skill 2.3)
- Adding Shading with Fill Color (Skill 2.11)
- Merging Cells and Splitting Merged Cells (Skill 2.7)
- Applying Cell Styles (Skill 2.12)
- Inserting and Deleting Cells (Skill 2.5)
- Changing Fonts, Font Size, and Font Color (Skill 2.9)
- Using Format Painter (Skill 2.13)
- Adding Borders (Skill 2.10)
- Wrapping Text in Cells (Skill 2.4)
- Applying Conditional Formatting Using the Quick Analysis Tool (Skill 2.14)
- Applying Conditional Formatting with Data Bars, Color Scales, and Icon Sets (Skill 2.15)
- Using Find and Replace (Skill 2.20)
- Applying Bold, Italic, and Underline (Skill 2.8)

1. Open the start file **EX2013-FixIt-2-6** and resave the file as:
   `[your initials]EX-FixIt-2-6`

2. If the workbook opens in Protected View, click the **Enable Editing** button in the Message Bar at the top of the workbook so you can modify the workbook.

3. Begin by removing all the fill color, font colors, and borders from the worksheet. This worksheet has so many different formats, it is probably easier to start from a clean slate.

4. All fonts in the worksheet should be set to **Calibri, 12** point size.

5. Apply appropriate formatting for the title. Consider using a cell style.

6. Add borders and fill color to make the data table easy to follow. Use bold where appropriate to make row and column headers stand out from the data.

7. An entry for June 9 is missing. You walked for 40 minutes that day, and went 3 miles. Insert the data in the appropriate place. (You can copy the formula to calculate miles per hour from one of the other cells.)

8. Apply text wrapping where needed.

9. Apply conditional formatting using data bars to visually compare the distance jogged each day.

10. Ensure that all entries for miles and miles per hour display two digits after the decimal.

11. Ensure that all average calculations display only two digits after the decimal.

12. Find all instances of *walk* and replace with *jog*.

13. Save and close the workbook.

chapter **3**

Using Formulas and Functions

skills

introduction

It is time to go beyond simple formulas. In this chapter you will learn to use the functions built into Excel to compute statistics, modify text, insert dates, work with logical expressions, compute loan payments, and perform table lookups. Also, you will create formulas that reference named ranges and other worksheets for fast replication. Finally, you will learn skills necessary for troubleshooting formulas.

Skill 3.1 Using the Function Arguments Dialog to Enter Functions

In Chapter 1, you learned to enter functions three ways:

1. **Typing the formula directly in the cell or the formula bar.** This method is easiest for simple functions.

2. **Using the *AutoSum* button.** This method works well when your spreadsheet includes numerical data organized in rows or columns. Functions available via AutoSum are limited to simple math and statistical functions (SUM, AVERAGE, COUNT, MIN, and MAX).

3. **Using the Quick Analysis tool.** This method is the easiest way to enter totals for multiple rows or columns of data at once. Like AutoSum, the Quick Analysis tool offers a limited number of functions (SUM, AVERAGE, and COUNT). It has the advantage of including options not available from AutoSum (calculating running totals and calculating the percentage of the overall total for each row or column) and showing a live preview of the totals before you make a selection.

Every function can be entered using its *Function Arguments* dialog. This dialog is different for each function. There are two primary methods for opening the *Function Arguments* dialog.

1. **Select the function from the *Formulas* tab, *Function Library* group.** Each button in this Ribbon group represents a category of functions. Clicking a button displays a menu of functions in that category. Selecting a function opens its *Insert Function* dialog.

2. **Select the function from the Insert Function dialog.** To open the *Insert Function* dialog, on the *Formulas* tab, in the *Function Library* group, click the **Insert Function** button. You can also click the **Insert Function** button to the left of the formula bar.

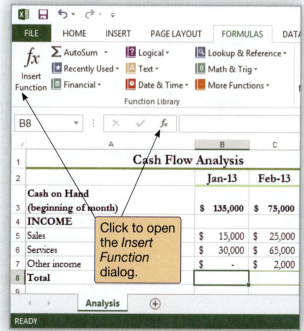

FIGURE EX 3.1

To use the *Insert Function* dialog:

1. Functions in the *Insert Function* dialog are organized in the same categories as the *Function Library* group. By default, the category list will default to the category you last used or it will show the *Most Recently Used* list. To select another category, expand the **Or select a category** list and select the function category you want.

2. Click a function in the *Select a function* box to see a brief description of what it does and the arguments it takes.

3. Click **OK** to open the *Function Arguments* dialog for the selected function.

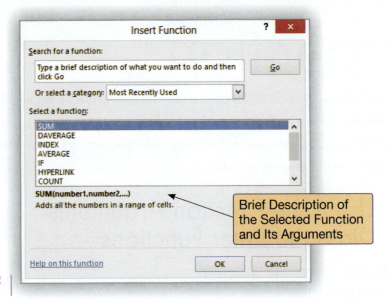

FIGURE EX 3.2

To use the *Function Arguments* dialog:

1. Enter values or cell references in each of the argument boxes as needed by typing or by clicking the cell or cell range in the worksheet. As you click each argument box, a brief description of the argument appears near the bottom of the dialog. The *Function Arguments* dialog also displays a preview of the result of the calculation. This value updates as you add arguments.

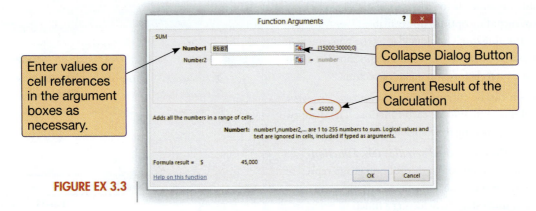

FIGURE EX 3.3

2. If the position of the *Function Arguments* dialog box makes it difficult to click the cell you want, click the **Collapse Dialog** button next to the argument box. The *Function Arguments* dialog collapses to show only the function argument box you are working with. Click the cell to add the reference to the dialog.

3. Click the **Expand Dialog** button to return the *Function Arguments* dialog to its full size.

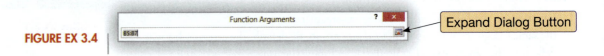

FIGURE EX 3.4

4. When you are finished entering arguments, click **OK.**

tips & tricks

The SUM *Function Arguments* dialog shown in Figure EX 3.3 includes an extra argument box. For functions that calculate a value based on a series of cells, Excel adds a blank argument box each time you enter an argument (up to 256 arguments). Enter values or cell references only in the argument boxes you need.

tell me **more**

If you're not sure of the name of the function you want, open the *Insert Function* dialog and type keywords describing the function in the *Search for a function* box, and then click the **Go** button. The *Or select a category* box changes to *Recommended,* and the *Select a function* box now displays a list of functions that match the keywords you typed.

let me try

Open the student data file **EX3-01-CashFlow** and try this skill on your own:

1. Enter a SUM function in cell **B8** to calculate the total of cells **B5:B7.** Open the *Function Arguments* dialog from the *Formulas* tab, *Function Library* group, **Math & Trig** button. You will have to scroll down the list to find SUM. Because cell B8 is below a list of values, Excel enters that cell range as the function argument for you.

2. Enter a SUM function in cell **C8** to calculate the total of cells **C5:C7.** Use the *Insert Function* dialog. If the SUM function is not listed in the *Select a Function* box, expand the **Or select a category list,** and select either **Math & Trig** or **Most Recently Used.** Again, Excel enters the adjacent cell range as the function arguments for you.

3. Enter a SUM function in cell **E5** to calculate the total of cells **B5:D5.** Use any method you want.

4. Save the file as directed by your instructor and close it.

Skill 3.2 Using Formula AutoComplete to Enter Functions

Formula AutoComplete is a shortcut for entering functions. When you type = and then a letter, Formula AutoComplete displays a list of potential matches (functions and other valid reference names). This is a good method to use if you prefer typing the function arguments, but you need a reminder of what the arguments are or the order in which they should be entered.

Double-click the function you want.

FIGURE EX 3.5

1. Type = in the cell or the formula bar to begin the formula. Formula AutoComplete displays the list of potential matches.
2. Type more letters to shorten the Formula AutoComplete list.
3. Double-click a function name to enter it in your formula.
4. Enter the expected arguments by typing values or selecting a cell or cell range.
5. Press ⏎Enter to complete the formula. Excel enters the closing) for you.

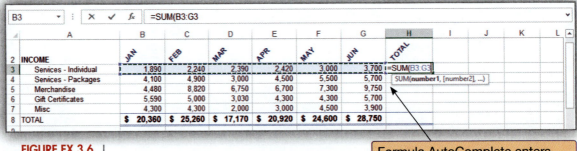

FIGURE EX 3.6

Formula AutoComplete enters arguments as you click and drag.

tips & tricks

When you use Formula AutoComplete, you can click the function name in the ScreenTip to open the Excel help topic for that function.

let me try

Open the student data file **EX3-02-IncomeAndExpenses** and try this skill on your own:

Use Formula Auto Complete to enter a SUM function in cell **H3** to calculate the total of cells **B3:G3**. Save the file as directed by your instructor and close it.

Skill 3.3 Calculating Averages

The **AVERAGE** statistical function is used to calculate the average value of a group of values. Average is calculated by adding the values, and then dividing the sum by the number of values.

A formula using the AVERAGE function looks like this:

=AVERAGE(B3:D3)

The value of this formula is the average of the values of cells B3 through D3: (B3 + C3 + D3)/3.

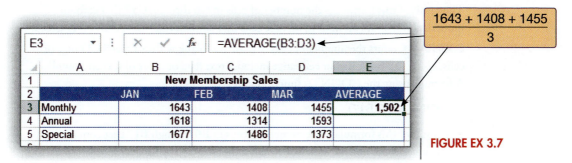

FIGURE EX 3.7

To create a formula with the AVERAGE function, use any of these methods:

❭ If you prefer typing in the cell or the formula bar, try using Formula AutoComplete.

❭ If the data are organized in rows or columns, you can use AutoSum. On the *Home* tab, *Editing* group or on the *Formula* tab, *Function Library* group, click the **AutoSum** button arrow and select **Average.**

❭ If you want to calculate the average for multiple rows or columns at once, use one of the average options in the Quick Analysis tool, *Totals* tab.

❭ If you prefer using the *Function Arguments* dialog, on the *Formulas* tab, in the *Function Library* group, click the **More Functions** button, point to **Statistical,** and click **AVERAGE.**

tips & tricks

When calculating an average, Excel will ignore empty cells. If you want to include those cells in your average calculations, make sure they have a value of zero.

tell me more

What you might think of as the "average" is actually the statistical mean. Average is a general term in statistics that includes **mean** (the sum of a group of values divided by the number of values in the group), **median** (the middle value of a set of values) and **mode** (the value that appears most often in a group of values). In Excel, the AVERAGE function calculates the mean value. Most people say *average* when they really want to calculate the mean value.

let me try

Open the student data file **EX3-03-Sales** and try this skill on your own:

Enter a formula in cell **E3** to calculate the average value of cells **B3:D3.** Use any method you like. Save the file as directed by your instructor and close it.

Skill 3.4 Creating Formulas Using Counting Functions

There are three basic counting functions in Excel. These functions are useful when you need to know how many numbers or items are in a list, or how many rows are missing data for a particular column.

COUNT—Counts the number of cells that contain numbers within a specified range of cells. A formula using the COUNT function looks like this:

=COUNT(G6:G17)

The result of this formula is the number of cells in **G6** through **G17** that contain numerical values. If you want to include cells that contain text, use COUNTA instead.

COUNTA—Counts the number of cells that are not blank within a specified range of cells. Use COUNTA if your cell range includes text data or a mix of text and numbers. A formula using the COUNTA function looks like this:

=COUNTA(B6:B17)

The result of this formula is the number of cells in **B6** through **B17** that contain any data (numerical or text).

COUNTBLANK—Counts the number of blank cells within a specified range of cells. Cells that contain a zero (0) are not considered blank. Use COUNTBLANK to find the number of rows missing values in a column. A formula using the COUNTBLANK function looks like this:

=COUNTBLANK(E6:E17)

The result of this formula is the number of cells in **E6** through **E17** that are blank.

	A	B	C	D	E	F	G	H
1	How many different items in our current inventory?			12	=COUNTA(B6:B17)			
2	How many items are on reorder?			2	=COUNT(G6:G17)			
3	How many items are not in stock?			2	=COUNTBLANK(E6:E17)			
4								
5	Inventory ID	Item	Unit Price	Reorder Time in Days	Quantity in Stock	Reorder Level	Quantity in Reorder	
6	1094	TIAB sampler	$ 22.00	14	18	5		
7	1095	SPF 15 gel	$ 12.00	5	18	8		
8	1096	SPF 30 gel	$ 19.00	5	16	8		
9	1097	SPF 45 gel	$ 18.00	5	22	8		
10	1098	SPF 60 gel	$ 20.00	5	12	8		
11	1099	Yan Can Shampoo	$ 19.00	21	2	5	20	
12	1100	Yan Can Conditioner	$ 7.00	21	28	5		
13	1101	Yan Can Hair Mask	$ 18.00	21	4	5	20	
14	1102	Yan Can Mousse	$ 18.00	21		5		
15	1103	Yan Can Gel	$ 15.00	21	1	5		
16	1104	Yan Can Moulding Gel	$ 25.00	21	12	5		
17	1105	Yan Can Masque	$ 20.00	21		5		
18								
19								

FIGURE EX 3.8

To create a formula with COUNT, COUNTA, or COUNTBLANK, use either of these methods:

❭ If you prefer typing in the cell or the formula bar, try using Formula AutoComplete.

❭ If you prefer using the *Function Arguments* dialog, on the *Formulas* tab, in the *Function Library* group, click the **More Functions** button, point to **Statistical,** and click **COUNT, COUNTA,** or **COUNTBLANK.**

To count numbers, you have two additional options:

❭ If the data are organized in rows or columns, you can use AutoSum to enter the COUNT function. On the *Home* tab, *Editing* group or on the *Formula* tab, *Function Library* group, click the **AutoSum** button arrow and select **Count Numbers.**

❭ If you want to count the numbers in for multiple rows or columns at once, use one of the *Count* options in the Quick Analysis tool, *Totals* tab.

tips & tricks

The COUNT and COUNTA functions can take multiple arguments.

COUNTBLANK accepts only a single argument, so if you want to count across a non-contiguous range of cells, you will need to create a formula adding together the results of multiple functions.

=COUNTBLANK(A1:C1)+COUNTBLANK(B10:C15)

let me try

Open the student data file **EX3-04-Inventory** and try this skill on your own:

1. In cell **D1,** enter a formula using a counting function to count the number of items in the inventory (cells **B6:B17**).

2. In cell **D2,** enter a formula using a counting function to count the number of values in the *Quantity in Reorder* column (cells **G6:G17**).

3. In cell **D3,** enter a formula using a counting function to count the number of blank cells in the *Quantity in Stock* column (cells **E6:E17**).

4. Save the file as directed by your instructor and close it.

Skill 3.5 Finding Minimum and Maximum Values

In addition to AVERAGE and the counting functions, there are a few other statistical functions you may find useful in working with day-to-day spreadsheets.

The **MIN** (minimum) statistical function will give you the lowest value in a range of values. The **MAX** (maximum) statistical function will give you the highest value in a range of values. A formula using the MIN or MAX function looks like this:

=**MIN(A3:A6)**

=**MAX(A3:A6)**

	A	B	C	D	E	F	G
1	What is the minimum reorder time?			5	=MIN(D5:D16)		
2	What is the maximum reorder time?			21	=MAX(D5:D16)		
3							
4	Inventory ID	Item	Unit Price	Reorder Time in Days	Quantity in Stock	Reorder Level	Quantity in Reorder
5	1094	TIAB sampler	$ 22.00	14	18	5	
6	1095	SPF 15 gel	$ 12.00	5	18	8	
7	1096	SPF 30 gel	$ 19.00	5	16	8	
8	1097	SPF 45 gel	$ 18.00	5	22	8	
9	1098	SPF 60 gel	$ 20.00	5	12	8	
10	1099	Yan Can Shampoo	$ 19.00	21	2	5	20
11	1100	Yan Can Conditioner	$ 7.00	21	28	5	
12	1101	Yan Can Hair Mask	$ 18.00	21	4	5	20
13	1102	Yan Can Mousse	$ 18.00	21		5	
14	1103	Yan Can Gel	$ 15.00	21	1	5	
15	1104	Yan Can Moulding Gel	$ 25.00	21	12	5	
16	1105	Yan Can Masque	$ 20.00	21		5	
17							

FIGURE EX 3.9

To create a formula with the MIN or MAX function, use any of these methods:

❯ If you prefer typing in the cell or the formula bar, try using Formula AutoComplete.

❯ If the data are organized in rows or columns, you can use AutoSum. On the *Home* tab, *Editing* group or on the *Formula* tab, *Function Library* group, click the **AutoSum** button arrow and select **Max** or **Min.**

❯ If you prefer using the *Function Arguments* dialog, on the *Formulas* tab, in the *Function Library* group, click the **More Functions** button, point to **Statistical,** and click **MAX** or **MIN.**

let me try

Open the student data file **EX3-05-Inventory** and try this skill on your own:

1. In cell **D1,** enter a formula to find the minimum reorder time (cells **D5:D16**).

2. In cell **D2,** enter a formula to find the maximum reorder time (cells **D5:D16**).

3. Save the file as directed by your instructor and close it.

Skill 3.6 Using Date and Time Functions

Excel includes two functions that insert the current date or date and time. The **NOW** function inserts the current date and time. The **TODAY** function inserts only the current date. Both of these functions are *volatile*—that is, they are not constant. They update with the current date or date and time each time the workbook is opened. This is useful if you want to keep track of the last time the workbook was edited or opened.

A formula using the NOW function looks like this:

   =NOW()

A formula using the TODAY function looks like this:

   =TODAY()

Notice that both of these functions include parentheses, but there are no arguments inside them. These functions do not require arguments.

To create a formula with NOW or TODAY, use either of these methods:

❯ If you prefer typing in the cell or the formula bar, try using Formula AutoComplete.

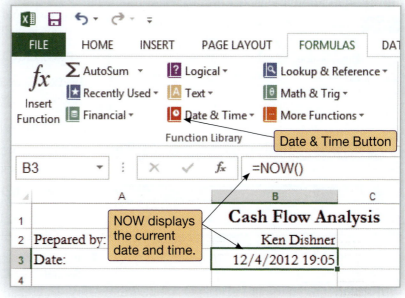

FIGURE EX 3.10

❯ If you prefer using the *Function Arguments* dialog, on the *Formulas* tab, in the *Function Library* group, click the **Date & Time** button and click **NOW** or **TODAY.**

tips & tricks

Both NOW and TODAY use the date and time from your computer's clock. If your computer's clock is wrong, the date and time displayed in your workbook will be wrong as well.

tell me more

If the cell is formatted to use a date format that does not display the time, the result of the NOW and TODAY functions will appear the same. However, the underlying value will still be different. If you change the formatting of the cell to display the time, a cell using the TODAY function will always display a time of 12:00 AM, whereas a cell using the NOW function will display the correct time.

let me try

Open the student data file **EX3-06-CashFlow** and try this skill on your own:

1. Enter a formula in cell **B3** to display only the current date.
2. Modify the formula in cell **B3** to display the current date and time.
3. Save the file as directed by your instructor and close it.

Skill 3.7 Formatting Text Using Functions

Functions can do more than perform calculations. Excel includes a special group of functions to modify text. These text functions are useful for ensuring that text data have a consistent appearance. In functions, text is referred to as a **string** or **text string**.

The most commonly used text functions are:

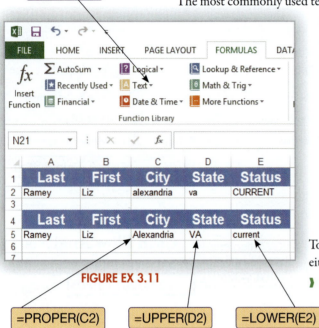

Text Button

FIGURE EX 3.11

=PROPER(C2)   **=UPPER(D2)**   **=LOWER(E2)**

PROPER—Converts the text string to proper case (the first letter in each word is capitalized). A formula using the PROPER function looks like this:

=PROPER(C2)

UPPER—Converts the text string to all uppercase letters. A formula using the UPPER function looks like this:

=UPPER(D2)

LOWER—Converts the text string to all lowercase letters. A formula using the LOWER function looks like this:

=LOWER(E2)

To create a formula with PROPER, UPPER, or LOWER, use either of these methods:

❯ If you prefer typing in the cell or the formula bar, try using Formula AutoComplete.

❯ If you prefer using the *Function Arguments* dialog, on the *Formulas* tab, in the *Function Library* group, click the **Text** button and click **PROPER, UPPER,** or **LOWER.**

tips & tricks

Typically, when you use one of the text functions, you are left with two groups of cells containing the same data: One group has the original incorrectly formatted text; the second group contains the formulas and displays correctly formatted text. There are two options for managing this:

❯ Hide the columns or rows that contain the original text. For information on hiding rows and columns, refer to the skill *Hiding and Unhiding Rows and Columns.*

❯ Copy the cells containing the text formulas; use one of the *Paste Values* options to paste just the values of the text formulas over the original cells, then delete the cells containing the text formulas. For information on using the *Paste Values* commands, refer to the skill *Using Paste Options.*

let me try

Open the student data file **EX3-07-Customers** and try this skill on your own:

1. Enter a formula in cell **C5** to display the text from cell **C2** so the first letter in each word is capitalized.
2. Enter a formula in cell **D5** to display the text from cell **D2** so all the letters display in upper case.
3. Enter a formula in cell **E5** to display the text from cell **E2** so all the letters display in lower case.
4. Save the file as directed by your instructor and close it.

Skill 3.8 Using CONCATENATE to Combine Text

To **concatenate** means to link items together. You can use the **CONCATENATE** function to combine the text values of cells. For example, if you have two columns for first name and last name, but you need a third column displaying the full name, you can use CONCATENATE to combine the values of the first two columns.

In Figure EX 3.12, the customer name in cell C2 is created by concatenating the values in column B (first name) and column A (last name). The formula looks like this:

=CONCATENATE(B2," ",A2)

The argument in the middle (" ") places a one-space text string between the values of cells B2 and A2.

FIGURE EX 3.12

If you are building a long string from multiple cells, you may want to use the Function Arguments dialog until you become familiar with this function. Of course, you can always type directly in the cell or formula bar and use Formula AutoComplete.

1. On the *Formulas* tab, in the *Function Library* group, click the **Text** button.
2. Click **CONCATENATE.**
3. In the *Function Arguments* dialog, enter each cell reference or text string you want to combine in its own argument. If one of the arguments is a blank space, enter " " in the argument box.
4. Click **OK.**

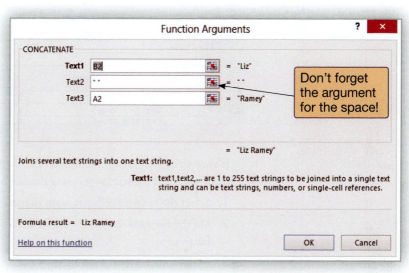

FIGURE EX 3.13

tips & tricks

For sorting purposes, you may want to keep the columns that you concatenate. If you do not want them to display in your worksheet, hide them. Hide the columns or rows that contain the original text. For information on hiding rows and columns, refer to the skill *Hiding and Unhiding Rows and Columns.*

let me try

Open the student data file **EX3-08-Customers** and try this skill on your own:

Enter a formula in cell **C2** to combine the text from cells **B2** and **A2** to display the customer name in the format *Bob Smith.* Don't forget the argument for the space. Save the file as directed by your instructor and close it.

Skill 3.9 Naming Ranges of Cells

Cell references like A4 and J34 do not provide much information about what data the cell contains—they just tell you where the cell is located in the worksheet. However, you can assign names to cells or ranges of cells to give your cell references names that are more user-friendly. These **names** (also called **range names** or **named ranges**) act as a list of short-cuts to the cell locations.

To create a named range:

1. Select the cell or range of cells to which you want to assign a name.
2. Type the name in the *Name* box to the left of the formula bar.
3. Press ← Enter to apply the name to the cell(s).

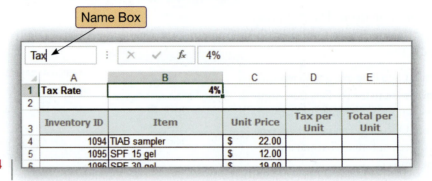

FIGURE EX 3.14

If your worksheet is organized in a table format, with column or row labels, you can automatically create named ranges using the labels as names:

1. Select the range of cells you want to name including the labels.
2. On the *Formulas* tab, in the *Defined Names* group, click the **Create from Selection** button.
3. In the *Create Names from Selection* dialog, click the checkbox to indicate where the names are (*Top row, Left column, Bottom row,* or *Right column*).
4. Click **OK.**

Excel automatically creates named ranges for the groups of cells associated with each label. Because names may not include spaces, Excel will replace the spaces with underscore _ characters. The named ranges will not include the labels. The *Create Names from Selection* command in Figure EX 3.15 will create the following named ranges:

INVENTORY_ID	ITEM	UNIT_PRICE	TAX_PER_UNIT	TOTAL_PER_UNIT
A4:A15	B4:B15	C4:C15	D4:D15	E4:E15

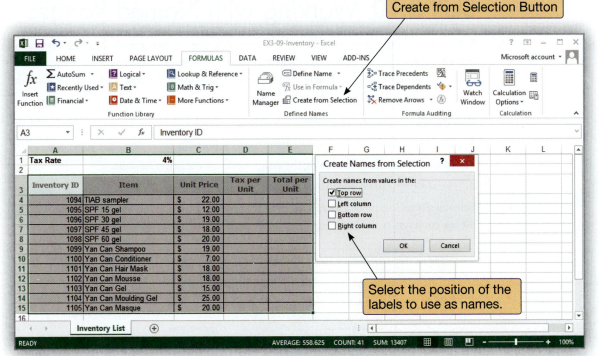

Create from Selection Button

Select the position of the labels to use as names.

FIGURE EX 3.15

another **method**

You can also create new names through the *New Name* dialog.

1. On the *Formulas* tab, in the *Defined Names* group, click the **Define Name** button.

2. The selected cell(s) is entered in the *Refers to* box.

3. Type the name you want in the *Name* box. If the cell to the immediate left or immediately above the selected cell appears to include a label, Excel will pre-populate the *Name* box with that text.

4. Click **OK.**

let me **try**

Open the student data file **EX3-09-Inventory** and try this skill on your own:

1. Name cell **B1** as follows: **Tax**

2. Use the *Create from Selection* command to create named ranges for the data table **A4:E15** using the labels in row **3** as the basis for the names.

3. Save the file as directed by your instructor and close it.

Skill 3.10 Working with Named Ranges

Rather than using a range of cells in your formulas, you can use a named range. The name will always refer to the cells, even if their position in the worksheet changes. Using named ranges in your formulas also makes it easier for others to use your workbook. Which formula is easier to understand: **=C4*B1** or **=C4*Tax**?

To use a named range in a formula:

1. Click the cell where you want to enter the new formula.
2. Type the formula, substituting the range name for the cell references.
3. Press ⏎ Enter to accept the formula.

Formula AutoComplete lists named ranges as well as functions. Using the AutoComplete list is a good way to avoid typographical errors and ensure that you enter the name correctly.

> The name *Tax* refers to cell B1.

To use Formula AutoComplete with names:

1. Type = (an equal sign) to begin the formula. As you type alphabetical characters, Excel will offer name suggestions.
2. When you find the name you want, double-click it.
3. Excel inserts the name into the formula.

FIGURE EX 3.16

tips & tricks

When you copy and paste a formula containing a named range, the name does not change with the new position in the workbook (similar to using an absolute reference).
   If you move a named cell, the name updates with the new cell location automatically.

another method

❯ On the *Formulas* tab, in the *Defined Names* group, click the **Use in Formula** button to display a list of names in your workbook, and then click one of the names to insert it into your formula.

❯ You can also click **Paste Names...** from the bottom of the *Use in Formula* list. The *Paste Names* dialog opens and lists all of the names in your workbook. Click a name and then click **OK** to add it to your formula.

let me try

Open the student data file **EX3-10-Inventory** and try this skill on your own:

1. Enter a formula in cell **D4** to calculate the tax. Multiply the item unit price (cell **C4**) * the value in the cell named **Tax.**
2. Copy the formula to cells **D5:D15.** Notice that while the reference to the item unit price updates for each row, the reference to the name *Tax* remains absolute.
3. Save the file as directed by your instructor and close it.

Skill 3.11 Updating Named Ranges with the Name Manager

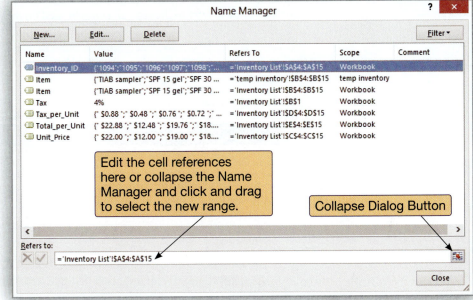

FIGURE EX 3.17

The **Name Manager** lists all the named ranges used in your workbook, the current value for each, the cells to which the name refers (including the sheet name), the scope of the name (whether it is limited to a specific worksheet or applies to the entire workbook), and comments (if there are any).

To open the Name Manager, on the *Formulas* tab, in the *Defined Names* group, click the **Name Manager** button.

To change the cell or range of cells to which a name refers:

1. Open the Name Manager.

2. Select the name you want to modify.

3. Edit the cell references in the *Refers to* box. You can also click the **Collapse Dialog** button to hide the Name Manager, and then click and drag to select the new cell range. When you are finished, click the **Expand Dialog** button to display the Name Manager again.

4. Click the checkmark icon to the left of the *Refers to* box to accept the change.

5. Click **Close** to close the Name Manager. If you forgot to save your change, Excel will ask if you want to save the change you made to the cell reference. Click **Yes.**

FIGURE EX 3.18

tell me **more**

When auditing a workbook for errors, you may find it useful to review a list of the defined names in your workbook.

1. Start with a blank worksheet.

2. Select the cell where you want the list to begin.

3. On the *Formulas* tab, in the *Defined Names* group, click the **Use in Formula** button, and select **Paste Names** from the end of the list.

4. The *Paste Name* dialog opens. Click the **Paste List** button.

A two-column list is pasted into Excel. The first column displays the name, and the second column displays the cell or ranges of cells to which the name refers.

let me **try**

Open the student data file **EX3-11-Inventory** and try this skill on your own:

1. Open the Name Manager.

2. Edit the **Inventory_ID** name so it refers to cells **A4:A18** on the *Inventory List* worksheet.

3. Close the Name Manager.

4. Save the file as directed by your instructor and close it.

Skill 3.12 Editing and Deleting Names with the Name Manager

When you copy data, you may find that some of the names in your workbook are repeated. Remember that names must be unique—but only within their scopes. You can have more than one named range with the same name, but only one can belong to the entire workbook. The others are specific to the worksheet in which they are defined.

In Figure EX 3.19, there are two *Item* names. The first is limited in scope to the *temp inventory* worksheet. If you refer to the name *Item* in a formula in any other sheet in the workbook, it will refer to the second name (located on the *Inventory List* worksheet).

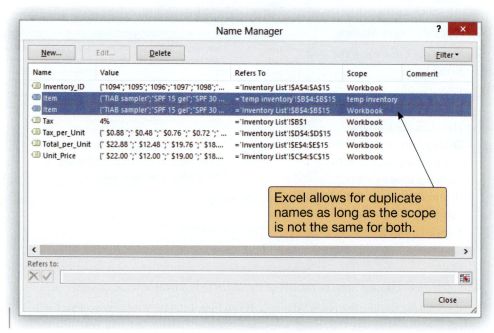

FIGURE EX 3.19

Duplicate names can be confusing. A good practice is to rename duplicates to make them easier to identify and use.

To change a name:

1. Open the Name Manager.
2. Click the name you want to modify, and then click the **Edit** button.
3. The *Edit Name* dialog opens.
4. Type the new name in the *Name* box.
5. Click **OK** to save your changes.
6. Click the **Close** button to close the Name Manager.

When you change a name, Excel automatically updates the name in any formulas that reference that name.

If your workbook includes names you no longer need, you should delete them.

To delete a name:

1. On the *Formulas* tab, in the *Defined Names* group, click the **Name Manager** button.

2. Click the name, and then click the **Delete** button.

3. Excel displays a message asking if you are sure you want to delete the name. Click **OK.**

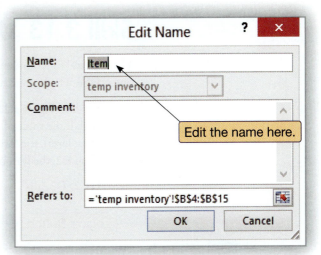

FIGURE EX 3.20

tips & tricks

There are two types of names identified in the Name Manager. **Defined names** are the names you created and names that Excel creates automatically when you define a print area or print titles. Table names are names created automatically when you define a data range as a table. By default, tables are named Table1, Table2, Table3, and so on. To make table names easier to use, consider renaming them through the Name Manager.

let me try

Open the student data file **EX3-12-Inventory** and try this skill on your own:

1. Open the Name Manager.

2. There are two Item names. Rename the one that is limited in scope to the temp inventory list to: **Item_temp**

3. In the Name Manager, review the information about the *Total_Price* name. The name refers to a series of empty cells. You do not need it in this workbook. Delete the **Total_Price** name.

4. Close the Name Manager.

5. Save the file as directed by your instructor and close it.

Skill 3.13 Using the Logical Function IF

The **IF** logical function returns one value if a condition is true and another value if the condition is false. The IF function can return a numerical value or display a text string.

The formula in Figure 3.21 uses the IF function to determine whether or not an item should be ordered. If the value of cell C2 (the quantity in stock) is greater than the value of cell D2 (the reorder level), the formula will return "yes." If the value of cell C2 is not greater than the value of cell D2, the formula will return "no." The formula looks like this:

$$=IF(C2>D2,"no","yes")$$

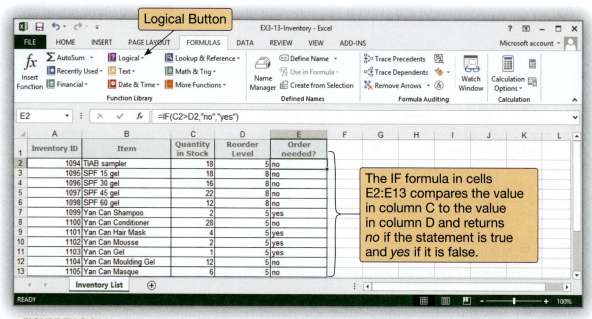

FIGURE EX 3.21

To create a formula using the IF function:

1. Select the cell where you want to enter the formula.

2. On the *Formulas* tab, in the *Function Library* group, click the **Logical** button.

3. Select **IF** to open the *Function Arguments* dialog. IF functions take three arguments as shown in the *Function Arguments* dialog in Figure EX 3.22.

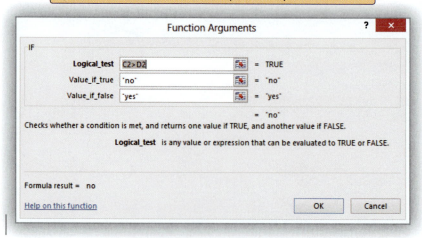

FIGURE EX 3.22

4. Enter the **Logical_test** argument. This argument states the condition you want to test for. The *Logical_test* always includes a comparison operator (=, >, <, etc.).

5. Enter the **Value_if_true** argument. This argument is the text string or value that will be displayed or the formula that will be calculated if the *Logical_test* argument is true.

6. Enter the **Value_if_false** argument. This argument is the text string or value that will be displayed or the formula that will be calculated if the *Logical_test* argument is false.

7. Click **OK.**

tips & tricks

If you use the *Function Arguments* dialog to enter text as the *Value_if_true* or the *Value_if_false* argument, you do not need to include the quotation marks. Excel will add them for you. However, if you type the formula directly in the cell or the formula bar, you must include quotation marks around the text.

let me try

Open the student data file **EX3-13-Inventory** and try this skill on your own:

Enter a formula in cell **E2** using the logical function IF to display **no** if the quantity in stock (cell **C2**) is greater than the reorder level (cell **D2**) and **yes** if it is not. Save the file as directed by your instructor and close it.

from the perspective of . . .

INSTRUCTOR

I use a spreadsheet to keep a grid of class attendance by student and by day. Using formulas and functions for grading gives me the flexibility to add scores, calculate averages, and provide feedback to my students.

Skill 3.14 Calculating Loan Payments Using the PMT Function

One of the most useful financial functions in Excel is **PMT** (payment), which you can use to calculate loan payments. The PMT function is based upon constant payments and a constant interest rate. To calculate a payment using PMT, you need three pieces of information: the interest rate, the number of payments, and the amount of the loan.

PMT(interest rate, number of loan payments, loan principal amount)

Using the values in Figure EX 3.23, the PMT function would look like this:

=PMT(4%/12,36,2500)

The *annual* interest rate is 4%. To calculate monthly payments, the interest rate must be divided by the number of payments per year.

When working with complex functions like PMT, use cell references as arguments rather than entering values directly. This way you can change values in your spreadsheet and see the results instantly without opening the *Function Arguments* dialog again. Using cell references, the PMT function in Figure EX 3.23 looks like this:

=PMT(B4/12,B5,B3)

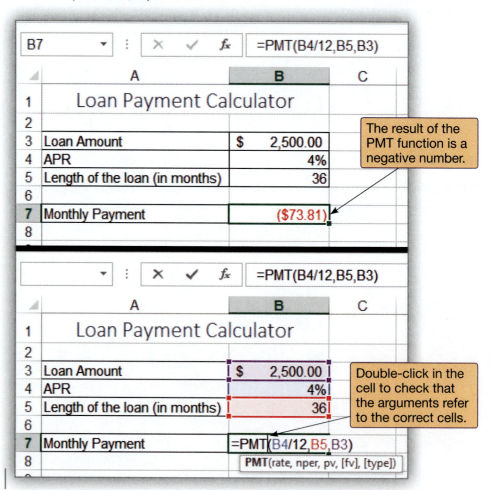

FIGURE EX 3.23

To use the PMT function:

1. Select the cell where you want to enter the formula.

2. On the *Formulas* tab, in the *Function Library* group, click the **Financial** button.

3. Select **PMT** from the list to open the *Function Arguments* dialog. PMT takes three required arguments and two optional arguments as shown in Figure EX 3.24.

4. Enter the **Rate** argument. This argument is the interest rate. Usually, interest rate is expressed as an annual rate. If the loan requires a monthly payment, the annual percentage rate (APR) should be divided by 12.

5. Enter the **Nper** argument. This argument is the total number of payments over the life of the loan.

6. Enter the **Pv** argument. This argument is the present value of the loan—how much you owe now (the loan principal).

7. (Optional) The *Fv* argument is future value of the loan. Excel assumes a value of 0 unless you include the argument and specify a different value. If you will make payments on the loan until it is completely paid off, you can leave this argument blank or enter 0.

8. (Optional) The *Type* argument represents when payments will be made during each loan period. Enter 1 if the payment is at the beginning of the period. If you omit this argument, Excel assumes a value of 0 (meaning each payment is at the end of the period).

9. Click **OK.**

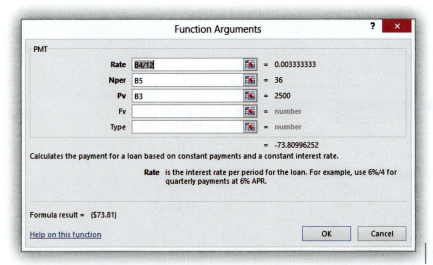

FIGURE EX 3.24

Because the result of the formula is a payment, it is expressed as a negative number. If you want the result expressed as a positive number instead, add a negative symbol before the PMT function: = −PMT(B4/12,B5,B3).

tips & tricks

It can be helpful to name the cells containing data for the function arguments with the same name as the argument. For example, name the cell with the interest rate **Rate.** Then when you build the PMT function, the cell names match the argument names. It makes creating the function easy.

let me try

Open the student data file **EX3-14-Loan** and try this skill on your own:

Enter a formula in cell **B7** using the PMT function to calculate the monthly loan payment. The annual interest rate is in cell **B4,** the number of monthly payments is in cell **B5,** and the amount of the loan is in cell **B3.** Remember, payments will be monthly, so divide the annual interest rate by 12. Save the file as directed by your instructor and close it.

Skill 3.15 Creating Formulas Referencing Data from Other Worksheets

Cell references are not limited to cells within the same worksheet. You can reference cells in other worksheets in your workbook. This feature is useful when you want to create summary sheets or perform analysis on data from multiple sheets at once.

For example, this formula will display the value of cell B34 from the *Jan* worksheet:

=Jan!B34

To include a reference to a cell from another sheet in your workbook:

1. Click the cell where you want the formula.

2. Type (=).

3. Navigate to the cell you want to reference by clicking the sheet tab and then clicking the cell.

4. Press (← Enter) to complete the formula.

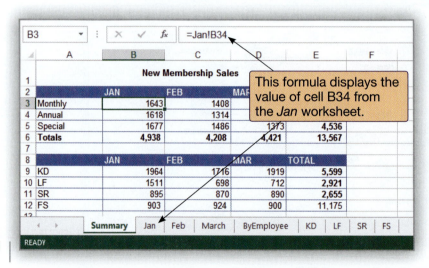

You can also refer to cells in other worksheets within formulas. For example, this formula will calculate the sum of cells B3:D33 from the *KD* worksheet:

=SUM(KD!B3:D33)

To include a reference to another worksheet in a formula:

1. Begin entering the formula as normal.

2. When you want to add a reference to a cell in another sheet, click the sheet tab, then click the cell(s) you want to add to the formula or click and drag to select a cell range.

3. When you are finished with the formula, press (← Enter).

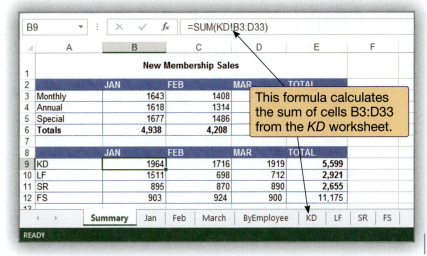

FIGURE EX 3.26

If your workbook includes multiple sheets with the same data structure, you can create a formula that references the same cell(s) on multiple sheets. This is called a **3-D reference**. For example, this formula will calculate the sum of the value of cell D3 on all sheets from KD through FS (sheets KD, LF, SR, and FS).

=SUM(KD:FS!D3)

To add a 3-D reference to a formula:

1. Begin entering the formula as you would normally.

2. Then, when you want to add the 3-D reference, select the sheet tabs for all the sheets you want included and click the specific cell(s) you want.

3. When you are finished with the formula, press ⏎ Enter.

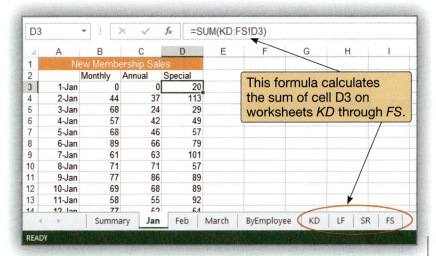

FIGURE EX 3.27

let me try

Open the student data file **EX3-15-Sales** and try this skill on your own:

1. On the *Summary* sheet, in cell **B3,** enter a formula to display the value of cell **B34** from the *Jan* sheet.

2. On the *Summary* sheet, in cell **B9,** enter a formula to calculate the sum of cells **B3:D33** from the *KD* sheet.

3. Go to the *Jan* sheet. Enter a formula using a 3-D reference in cell D3 to calculate the sum of cell **D3** from sheets *KD* through *FS*.

4. Copy that formula to the remaining cells in the column (through cell **D33**). Look at the formulas and note that Excel updated the relative cell reference in each row but did not change the worksheet references.

5. Save the file as directed by your instructor and close it.

Skill 3.16 Finding Data Using the VLOOKUP Function

Excel includes a group of functions that can be used to look up matching values in a cell range. The **VLOOKUP** function finds a value or cell reference in a cell range and returns another value from the same row. VLOOKUP requires you to specify the value you want to find, the cell range that contains the data, and the column that contains the value you want the function to return.

The formula in Figure 3.28 finds the value from cell **B2** in the cell range named **Inventory** and then returns the value from the second column of the range. In other words, VLOOKUP finds the item ID and returns the item name.

=VLOOKUP(B2,Inventory,2,FALSE)

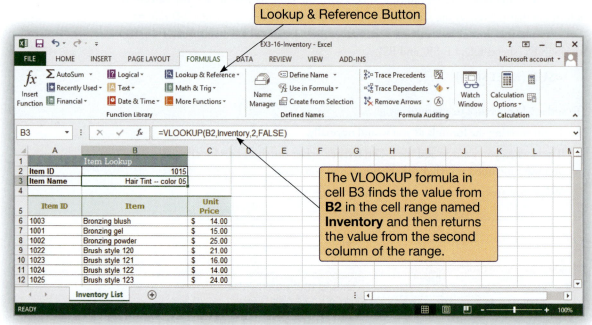

FIGURE EX 3.28

To use the VLOOKUP function:

1. Select the cell where you want to enter the formula.

2. On the *Formulas* tab, in the *Function Library* group, click the **Lookup & Reference** button.

3. Select **VLOOKUP** from the list to open the *Function Arguments* dialog. VLOOKUP takes three required arguments and one optional argument as shown in Figure EX 3.29.

4. Enter the **Lookup_value** argument. Enter the cell reference for which you want to find a corresponding value. In other words, the value you want to look up.

5. Enter the **Table_array** argument. Enter the range of cells (or the range name) that contains the lookup data. If your data include a header row, do not include it in the range used for the *Table_array* argument.

6. Enter the **Col_index_num** argument. This argument is the position of the column in the *Table_array* from which the function should return a matching value. Enter the column number, not the letter or the column heading.

7. (optional) Enter the **Range_lookup** argument. Type **FALSE** if you want to find only an exact match for the value entered in the *Lookup_value* box. If you omit this argument, Excel assumes a value of **TRUE** and will return the value for the closest match in the first column.

8. Click **OK.**

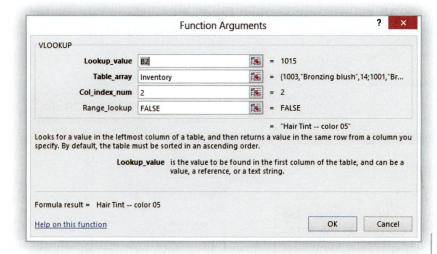

FIGURE EX 3.29

tips & tricks

If you do not specify *False* for the *Range_lookup* argument, make sure the data in the *Table_array* are sorted A–Z by the first column (the lookup column). If your data are not sorted, you may see unexpected results.

tell me more

The examples here all use the VLOOKUP function to find corresponding values in different *columns* within the same row (a *vertical* lookup). The **HLOOKUP** function works similarly, except you use it to find corresponding values in different rows within the same column (a *horizontal* lookup).

Use HLOOKUP when your worksheet uses a horizontal layout—few rows with many columns.

Use VLOOKUP when your worksheet uses a vertical layout—few columns with many rows.

let me try

Open the student data file **EX3-16-Inventory** and try this skill on your own:

Enter a formula in cell **B3** using the VLOOUP function to find the item name for the item number listed in cell **A3.** You can use the name **Inventory** for the lookup table. The item names are located in column **2** of the lookup table. Save the file as directed by your instructor and close it.

Skill 3.17 Checking Formulas for Errors

Some worksheet errors are easily identifiable—such as divide by zero errors, which look like this in your worksheet: **#DIV/0!** (because Excel cannot calculate a value to display). Other potential errors, like formulas that leave out part of a cell range, are harder to find yourself. You can use Excel's error checking features to review your worksheet for errors.

Cells that include potential errors are marked with a green triangle in the upper-left corner of the cell. When you click the cell, Excel displays a **Smart Tag** to help you resolve the error.

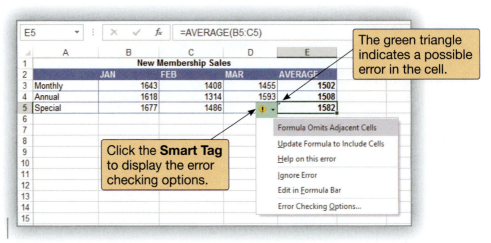

FIGURE EX 3.30

To use Smart Tags to resolve errors in formulas:

1. When a Smart Tag appears, move your mouse over the icon to display a tool tip describing the possible error.

2. Click the **Smart Tag** to display the possible error resolutions.

3. If you want to keep the formula as it is, select **Ignore Error.**

4. If you want to resolve the error, select one of the options:

   • The first option is usually a suggestion of how to resolve the error. Click it to accept Excel's suggestion.

   • Select **Help on this error** to open Microsoft Office Help.

   • Select **Edit in Formula Bar** to manually edit the formula.

   • Select **Error Checking Options...** to open the *Options* dialog and modify the way that Excel checks for errors.

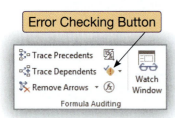

FIGURE EX 3.31

5. Once you have made a selection from the Smart Tag options, the Smart Tag is dismissed.

Error checking is also available from the *Formulas* tab.

The *Error Checking* dialog displays each error it finds, allowing you to resolve or ignore each error in turn.

To use error checking to find errors in your worksheet:

1. On the *Formulas* tab in the *Formula Auditing* group, click the **Error Checking** button.

2. The *Error Checking* dialog displays information about the first error. The buttons available in the dialog box will differ, depending on the type of error found.

   • If Excel is able to offer a solution to the error, the dialog will include a button to accept the suggested fix.

   • Click the **Help on this error** button to open Microsoft Office Help.

- Click **Ignore Error** to dismiss the error. Excel will ignore this error until you manually reset ignored errors through Excel *Options*.
- Click **Edit in Formula Bar** to fix the error manually.

4. Click the **Next** button to see the next error in your worksheet.

5. When you have reviewed all errors, Excel displays a message that the error check is complete. Click **OK** to dismiss the message box.

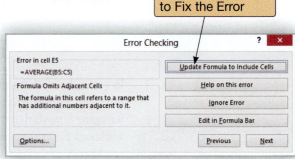

FIGURE EX 3.32

tips & tricks

You can make changes to your worksheet without closing the *Error Checking* dialog. When you click away from the dialog, one of the buttons changes to a *Resume* button and none of the other buttons in the dialog is available. When you are ready to return to error checking, click the **Resume** button.

tell me more

If the error is part of a complex formula, Excel may include a *Show Calculation Steps...* button in the *Error Checking* dialog. This button launches the *Evaluate Formula* dialog where you can walk through the formula step by step to try to find the cause of the error.

If the error is related to a reference to another cell, Excel will offer a *Trace Error* button to display precedent and dependent arrows showing dependencies between formulas in your worksheet.

another method

You can also start the Error Checking feature by clicking the **Error Checking** button arrow and selecting **Error Checking...**

let me try

Open the student data file **EX3-17-Sales** and try this skill on your own:

1. Cell **E5** has an error. Display the **Smart Tag** and accept Excel's suggestion for fixing the error.
2. On the *Formulas* tab, in the *Formula Auditing* group, open the *Error Checking* dialog and check the rest of the worksheet for errors.
3. Review the information about the error and select the option to edit the error in the formula bar.
4. Correct the error and resume error checking until Excel reports that the error check is complete.
5. Save the file as directed by your instructor and close it.

Skill 3.18 Finding Errors Using Trace Precedents and Trace Dependents

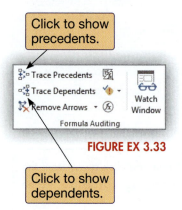

Click to show precedents.

Click to show dependents.

FIGURE EX 3.33

In a complex worksheet where formulas often reference each other, an error in one formula can cause a ripple effect of errors throughout the entire workbook. However, finding and fixing the formula that is the root cause of the errors can be difficult. One way to review your workbook for errors is to display the dependencies between formulas.

There are two types of dependencies: precedents and dependents. A **precedent** is the cell containing the formula or value the selected cell refers to. A **dependent** is the cell containing a formula that references the value or formula in the selected cell. On the *Formulas* tab, the *Formula Auditing* group includes commands for displaying and hiding arrows tracing dependencies.

To trace precedents:

1. Select the cell containing the formula for which you want to trace precedents.
2. On the *Formulas* tab, in the *Formula Auditing* group, click the **Trace Precedents** button.
3. Tracer arrows appear pointing from the selected cell to precedent cells.

To trace dependents:

1. Select the cell containing the formula for which you want to trace dependents.
2. On the *Formulas* tab, in the *Formula Auditing* group, click the **Trace Dependents** button.
3. Tracer arrows appear pointing from the selected cell to dependent cells.

Tracer arrows normally appear blue. If the tracer arrow points to a cell that contains an error, the tracer arrow will appear red. If the tracer arrow points to a cell that references a cell in another worksheet or workbook, the arrow will appear black and include a small worksheet icon. Double-click the tracer arrow to open the *Go To* dialog to navigate to the worksheet or workbook that contains the referenced cell.

Figure EX 3.34 shows both precedent and dependent tracer arrows for cell B8. You can see that the precedent arrow changes from blue to red at cell B6. The formula in that cell is the first error. (However, the error itself is not necessarily in that cell. It could be in another cell that B6 refers to.)

⬜	A	B	C	D	E
1	Loan Payment Calculator			My Budget	
2					
3	Loan Amount	$ 27,000.00		Monthly Income	$ 2,800
4	APR	4%		Expenses	$ 2,200
5	Length of the loan (in years)	5 years		Loan	#VALUE!
6	Length of the loan (in months)	#VALUE!		Savings Target (10%)	$ 280
7					
8	Monthly Payment	#VALUE!		Enough left over for savings?	#VALUE!
9					
10					

FIGURE EX 3.34

Red tracer arrows indicate an error.

To remove the tracer arrows from your worksheet, on the *Formulas* tab, in the *Formula Auditing* group, click the **Remove Arrows** button arrow and select the option you want:

❭ To remove the precedent tracer arrows, select **Remove Precedent Arrows.**

❭ To remove the dependent tracer arrows, select **Remove Dependent Arrows.**

❭ To remove all tracer arrows at once, select **Remove Arrows.** Clicking the *Remove Arrows* button instead of the button arrow will also remove all the tracer arrows.

tips & tricks

Tracer arrows cannot identify cells with incorrect values or values of the wrong type (for example, a text value where a number is expected). However, using the tracer arrows may help you find those errors yourself.

tell me more

There may be multiple layers of dependencies in your workbook. Clicking the **Trace Precedents** button or the **Trace Dependents** button once only displays the immediate dependencies. To display tracer arrows from the precedent and dependent cells to their precedents and dependents, click the appropriate button again. Continue clicking the **Trace Precedents** button or the **Trace Dependents** button until you reach the end of the trail.

Selecting **Remove Precedent Arrows** and **Remove Dependent Arrows** removes the tracer arrows one level at a time.

another method

If the selected cell contains an error, you can display tracer arrows by clicking the **Error Checking** button arrow and selecting **Trace Error.**

let me try

Open the student data file **EX3-18-Loan** and try this skill on your own:

1. Show the precedent arrows for cell **B8.**
2. Show the dependent arrows for cell **B8.**
3. Change the value in cell **B5** to: 5 Note that the arrows change color from red to blue.
4. Hide all of the arrows at once.
5. Save the file as directed by your instructor and close it.

Skill 3.19 Displaying and Printing Formulas

How do you troubleshoot a worksheet that is displaying unexpected values? When you look at a worksheet, you see only the results of formulas—cells display the values, not the formulas themselves. When you click a cell, the formula is displayed in the formula bar. But what if you want to view all of the formulas in your worksheet at once?

To display the formulas in the current worksheet instead of values:

On the *Formulas* tab in the *Formula Auditing* group, click the **Show Formulas** button.

To hide the formulas and display calculated values:

Click the **Show Formulas** button again.

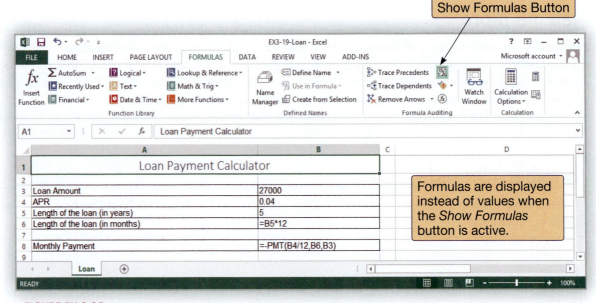

FIGURE EX 3.35

To print a copy of the worksheet with formulas instead of values:

1. First display the formulas in the worksheet by clicking the **Show Formulas** button.
2. Next, print the worksheet:
3. Click the **File** tab.
4. Click **Print.**
5. Click the **Print** button to send the file to your default printer.

tips & tricks

When you show formulas in your worksheet, Excel automatically adjusts the column sizes so the formulas are visible.

another method

The keyboard shortcut to display (or hide) formulas is Ctrl + ` (the ` key is directly to the left of 1 at the top of the keyboard).

let me try

Open the student data file **EX3-19-Loan** and try this skill on your own:

1. Display the formulas in this worksheet.
2. Preview how the worksheet will look when printed.
3. Save the file as directed by your instructor and close it.

Formula AutoComplete
AVERAGE
Mean
Median
Mode
COUNT
COUNTA
COUNTBLANK
MIN
MAX
NOW
TODAY
String
Text string
PROPER
UPPER

LOWER
Concatenate
CONCATENATE
Name
Range name
Named range
Name Manager
Defined name
IF
PMT
3-D reference
VLOOKUP
HLOOKUP
Smart Tag
Precedent
Dependent

concepts review

1. Which of these methods can you use to enter a formula using the AVERAGE function?

   a. Formula Auto Complete

   b. AutoSum

   c. *Function Arguments* dialog

   d. All of the above

2. To count the number of cells that contain text or numerical values, but not blanks, use which function?

   a. COUNT

   b. COUNTALL

   c. COUNTA

   d. COUNTBLANK

3. Which of these functions returns the current date and time?

   a. TIME

   b. DATE

   c. NOW

   d. TODAY

4. What is the definition of *concatenate?*

   a. To link items together

   b. To look up a value

   c. A logical comparison

   d. To convert text to proper case

5. Which of these is **not** an acceptable name for a named range?

    a. BonusRate

    b. Bonus_Rate

    c. Bonus Rate

    d. BONUSRATE

6. Identify the *Value_if_true* argument in this formula: =IF(A1>50,"bonus","no bonus")

    a. A1

    b. 50

    c. bonus

    d. no bonus

7. Identify the *Pv* argument in this formula: =−PMT(B2/12,B3,B4)

    a. B2

    b. B2/12

    c. B3

    d. B4

8. In a PMT function, what is the *Pv* argument?

    a. The interest rate

    b. The present value of the loan

    c. The number of payments

    d. The value of the loan at the end of the loan period

9. A formula to display the value of cell **B2** on the *Sales* worksheet looks like this:

    a. =Sales!B2

    b. =B2,Sales!

    c. =Sales,B2

    d. =Sales(B2)

10. A(n) _____ is the cell containing a formula that references the value or formula in the selected cell.

    a. 3-D reference

    b. argument

    c. precedent

    d. dependent

skill review 3.1

In this project you will complete a staff billing workbook similar to the one you worked on in Chapter 1. This worksheet is more complicated and uses a variety of formulas to calculate information about each staff member's weekly billing and to generate client bills from the staff hours. As you work on the *Marshall Hours* worksheet, you can use the *Luz Hours* or *Stevens Hours* worksheet as a guide. This is a long project. Be sure to save your work often!

Skills needed to complete this project:

- Naming Ranges of Cells (Skill 3.9)
- Using CONCATENATE to Combine Text (Skill 3.8)
- Creating Formulas Referencing Data from Other Worksheets (Skill 3.15)
- Finding Data Using the VLOOKUP Function (Skill 3.16)
- Working with Named Ranges (Skill 3.10)
- Using the Function Arguments Dialog to Enter Functions (Skill 3.1)
- Creating Formulas Using Counting Functions (Skill 3.4)
- Using Formula AutoComplete to Enter Functions (Skill 3.2)
- Calculating Averages (Skill 3.3)
- Finding Minimum and Maximum Values (Skill 3.5)
- Using the Logical Function IF (Skill 3.13)
- Displaying and Printing Formulas (Skill 3.19)
- Using Date and Time Functions (Skill 3.6)
- Checking Formulas for Errors (Skill 3.17)
- Finding Errors Using Trace Precedents and Trace Dependents (Skill 3.18)
- Updating Named Ranges with the Name Manager (Skill 3.11)
- Editing and Deleting Names with the Name Manager (Skill 3.12)
- Calculating Loan Payments Using the PMT Function (Skill 3.14)

1. Open the start file **EX2013-SkillReview-3-1** and resave the file as:
   `[your initials]EX-SkillReview-3-1`

2. If the workbook opens in Protected View, click the **Enable Editing** button in the Message Bar at the top of the workbook.

3. The *Luz Hours* and *Stevens Hours* worksheets are completed, but they contain errors. You'll need to fix the errors before working on the *Marshall Hours* worksheet.

   a. Click the **Luz Hours** sheet tab.

   b. Click cell **C4.**

   c. Notice the #NAME? error. Move your mouse over the **Smart Tag** icon to display a tool tip describing the possible error—*The formula contains unrecognized text.*

   d. The formula =VLOOKUP(C3,BillableRates,4,FALSE) references the named range BillableRates. That name has not yet been defined. That's what is causing the error.

4. Billable rates are kept in the *Rates* worksheet. Create the name **BillableRates** to use in formulas throughout the workbook.

    a. Click the **Rates** sheet tab.

    b. Select cells **A3:D5**.

    c. Type **BillableRates** in the *Name* box.

    d. Press ⟵ Enter .

5. Return to the *Luz Hours* worksheet. Notice all the errors have been fixed. Now you can move on to completing the *Marshall Hours* sheet.

6. Enter a formula in cell **C2** to display Marshall's full name in the format *Bob Smith*. Staff names are kept in the *Rates* worksheet.

    a. Click the **Marshall Hours** sheet tab, and click cell **C2**.

    b. On the *Formulas* tab, in the *Function Library* group, click the **Text** button, and select **CONCATENATE.**

    c. Click the **Rates** sheet tab. If necessary, position the *Function Arguments* dialog so you can click the sheet tabs.

    d. Click cell **C3** to enter the cell reference in the *Text1* argument box.

    e. Press Tab ⇥ to move to the *Text2* argument box.

    f. Type " " to place a space between the first and last names.

    g. Press Tab ⇥ to move to the *Text3* argument box.

    h. Click the **Rates** tab again.

    i. Click cell **B3** to enter the text reference in the *Text3* argument box.

    j. Click **OK.** The completed formula should look like this:

        =CONCATENATE(Rates!C3," ",Rates!B3)

7. Enter a formula in cell **C4** to look up Marshall's current billable rate. Use the employee number as the lookup value.

    a. Click cell **C4**.

    b. On the *Formulas* tab, in the *Function Library* group, click the **Lookup & Reference** button, and select **VLOOKUP.**

    c. Click cell **C3** to enter it in the *Lookup_value* argument box.

    d. Type **BillableRates** in the *Table_array* argument box.

    e. The rates are located in the fourth column of the lookup table. Type **4** in the *Col_index_num* argument box.

    f. Ensure that the function will return only an exact match. Type **false** in the *Range_lookup* argument box.

    g. Click **OK.** The completed formula should look like this:

        =VLOOKUP(C3,BillableRates,4,FALSE)

8. Enter formulas in cells **B17:H17** to calculate the number of clients served each day.

    a. Click cell **B17**.

    b. Type **=COU**

    c. Double-click **COUNT** in the Formula AutoComplete list.

    d. Click cell **B9** and drag to cell **B12**.

    e. Press ⟵ Enter . The completed formula should look like this:

        =COUNT(B9:B12)

    f. Copy the formula in cell **B17** to cells **C17:H17.** Use any method you want.

9. Enter a formula in cell **H19** to calculate the average daily billable hours (B13:H13).

   a. Click cell **H19.**

   b. Type **=AV** and then double-click **AVERAGE** in the Formula AutoComplete list.

   c. Click cell **B13** and drag to cell **H13.**

   d. Press ⏎ Enter. The completed formula should look like this:

   =AVERAGE(B13:H13)

10. Enter a formula in cell **H20** to calculate the total billable hours for the week (B13:H13).

    a. Click cell **H20.**

    b. Type **=SU** and then double-click **SUM** in the Formula AutoComplete list.

    c. Click cell **B13** and drag to cell **H13.**

    d. Press ⏎ Enter. The completed formula should look like this:

    =SUM(B13:H13)

11. Enter a formula in cell **H22** to calculate the lowest daily bill for the week (B15:H15).

    a. Click cell **H22.**

    b. Type **=MIN (** and then click cell **B15** and drag to cell **H15.**

    c. Press ⏎ Enter. The completed formula should look like this:

    =MIN(B15:H15)

12. Enter a formula in cell **H23** to calculate the highest daily bill for the week.

    a. Click cell **H23.**

    b. Type **=MAX(** and then click cell **B15** and drag to cell **H15.**

    c. Press ⏎ Enter. The completed formula should look like this:

    =MAX(B15:H15)

13. Each staff member is required to log a minimum number of billable hours per week. Enter a formula in cell **H3** using an IF statement to display "yes" if the total billable hours for the week (cell H20) is greater than or equal to the required hours (cell H2) and "no" if they are not.

    a. Click cell **H3.**

    b. On the *Formulas* tab, in the *Function Library* group, click **Logical.**

    c. Click **IF.**

    d. If necessary, move the *Function Arguments* dialog to the side so you can see the worksheet data.

    e. In the *Logical_test* argument box, type: **H20>=H2**

    f. In the *Value_if_true* argument box, type: **yes**

    g. In the *Value_if_false* argument box, type: **no**

    h. Click **OK.** The completed formula should look like this:

    =IF(H20>=H2,"yes","no")

14. Display your formulas temporarily to check for accuracy.

    a. On the *Formulas* tab, in the *Formula Auditing* group, click the **Show Formulas** button.

    b. When you are ready to continue, hide the formulas and display formula values by clicking the **Show Formulas** button again.

15. Now that the worksheet for Marshall is complete, you can generate a bill for the Smith client for the week. Click the **Smith Bill** sheet tab.

16. All bills are due thirty days from the date the bill was created. Enter a formula in cell C2 to calculate the due date using the TODAY function.

   a. Double-click cell **C2.**

   b. Type the formula: **=TODAY()+30**

   c. Press ⏎ Enter.

17. Enter formulas to reference the number of hours each staff member billed for Smith.

   a. Click cell **B6** and type **=** to begin the formula.

   b. Click the **Marshall Hours** sheet, and click cell **J12.**

   c. Press ⏎ Enter. The completed formula should look like this:

   =**'Marshall Hours'!J12**

   d. Type **=** to begin the next formula in cell B7.

   e. Click the **Stevens Hours** sheet, and click cell **J12.**

   f. Press ⏎ Enter. The completed formula should look like this:

   =**'Stevens Hours'!J12**

   g. Type **=** to begin the next formula in cell B8.

   h. Click the **Luz Hours** sheet, and click cell **J12.**

   i. Press ⏎ Enter. The completed formula should look like this:

   =**'Luz Hours'!J12**

18. There are errors in the Rate and Bill Amount columns. Use your error checking skills to track down the cause of the error.

   a. On the *Formulas* tab, in the *Formula Auditing* group, click the **Error Checking** button to open the *Error Checking* dialog.

   b. After you've reviewed the first error, click the **Next** button to go to the next error. Continue reviewing each error and clicking **Next** until you receive the message that the error check is complete for the entire sheet. Click **OK.**

19. Did you notice that every error in the worksheet is a "value not available" error? You probably need to dig deeper to find the root cause of the problem.

   a. Click cell **D6** and look at the formula in the formula bar: =B6*C6

   b. Display the Trace Precedent and Trace Dependent arrows for this cell. On the *Formulas* tab, in the *Formula Auditing* group, click both the **Trace Precedents** button and the **Trace Dependents** button.

   c. You can see that the problem appears to start in the precedent cell C6. Hide the arrows for cell **D6** by clicking the **Remove Arrows** button, and then click cell **C6** and click the **Trace Precedents** button.

   d. Notice that one of the precedent arrows for cell C6 refers to another worksheet. Double-click the dashed precedent arrow line.

   e. In the *Go To* dialog, click the worksheet reference and then click the **OK** button.

20. The link takes you to the *Rates* sheet where cells A2:D5 are selected. Notice that the *Name* box displays the name *ClientRates*. (Depending on your screen resolution, the name may be slightly cut-off.) The formula in cell C6 is a lookup formula that uses the named range *ClientRates* as the *Table_array* argument. There are two problems with the definition of the named range: It includes the label row (A2:D2), and it includes the employee number data (A2:A5).

   a. On the *Formulas* tab, in the *Defined Names* group, click the **Name Manager** button.

   b. Click the **ClientRates** name and review the cell range in the *Refers to* box. The range is incorrect. The ClientRates name should refer to cells **B2:D5** on the *Rates* sheet.

c. Edit the range listed in the *Refers to* box to:

    =Rates!$B$2:$D$5

d. Click the **Close** button to close the Name Manager.

e. When Excel asks if you want to save the changes to the name reference, click **Yes.**

21. Now that the total bill amount is computing correctly, you can enter a formula in cell D14 to give the client the option of a monthly payment plan. You are authorized to offer a 6-month payment plan at a 2% annual percentage rate. Use cell references in the formula.

a. If necessary, click the **Smith Bill** sheet.

b. Click cell **D14.**

c. On the *Formulas* tab, in the *Function Library* group, click the **Financial** button.

d. Scroll down the list, and click **PMT.**

e. In the *Function Arguments* dialog, enter the *Rate* argument:

    D13/12

f. Click in the **Nper** argument box, and then click cell **D12** (the number of payments).

g. Click in the **Pv** argument box, and then click cell **D9** (the present value of the loan).

h. In the *Function Arguments* dialog, click **OK.** The completed formula should look like this:

    =PMT(D13/12,D12,D9)

i. The monthly payment amount appears as a negative number. That might be confusing to the client. Modify the formula so the result appears as a positive number.

j. Double-click cell **D14** and type – between = and **PMT.**

k. Press ⏎ Enter . The final formula should look like this:

    =–PMT(D13/12,D12,D9)

22. Save and close the workbook.

skill review **3.2**

In this project you will edit a worksheet to compute student grades and grade statistics. Be sure to save your work often!

Skills needed to complete this project:

- Using Date and Time Functions (Skill 3.6)
- Using CONCATENATE to Combine Text (Skill 3.8)
- Formatting Text Using Functions (Skill 3.7)
- Creating Formulas Using Counting Functions (Skill 3.4)
- Using Formula AutoComplete to Enter Functions (Skill 3.2)
- Displaying and Printing Formulas (Skill 3.19)
- Using the Logical Function IF (Skill 3.13)
- Using the Function Arguments Dialog to Enter Functions (Skill 3.1)
- Finding Minimum and Maximum Values (Skill 3.5)
- Calculating Averages (Skill 3.3)
- Naming Ranges of Cells (Skill 3.9)
- Finding Data Using the VLOOKUP Function (Skill 3.16)
- Working with Named Ranges (Skill 3.10)
- Checking Formulas for Errors (Skill 3.17)

1. Open the start file **EX2013-SkillReview-3-2** and resave the file as: `[your initials]EX-SkillReview-3-2`

2. If the workbook opens in Protected View, click the **Enable Editing** button in the Message Bar at the top of the workbook.

3. Take a look at the two sheets. The first sheet contains the students' names and their scores. The second sheet will be used to look up the letter grade for each student.

4. Enter a function in cell **B3** to display the current date each time the worksheet is opened.

   a. Click cell **B3**.

   b. On the *Formulas* tab, in the *Function Library* group, click the **Date & Time** button.

   c. Click **NOW**.

   d. Click **OK**.

5. The first column should display the full student name. Use CONCATENATE to combine the values from the First Name and Last Name columns.

   a. Click cell **A10**.

   b. On the *Formulas* tab, in the *Function Library* group, click the **Text** button, and select **CONCATENATE**.

   c. Click cell **C10** to enter the cell reference in the *Text1* argument box.

   d. Press (Tab ⇥) to move to the *Text2* argument box.

   e. Type **" "** to place a space between the first and last names.

   f. Press (Tab ⇥) to move to the *Text3* argument box.

   g. Click cell **B10** to enter the text reference in the *Text3* argument box.

   h. Click **OK**. The completed formula should look like this:
   =CONCATENATE(C10," ",B10)

6. Add the PROPER function to the formula so student names do not appear in all upper case.

   a. Double-click cell **A10** to edit the formula.

   b. Create a nested formula by typing **PROPER (** between the = symbol and CONCATENATE.

   c. Type another **)** at the end of the formula.

   d. Press (← Enter). The completed formula should look like this:
   =PROPER(CONCATENATE(C10," ",B10))

7. Copy the formula from cell **A10** to **A11:A28** to fill the list of student names. Use any method you want.

8. Count the number of students to calculate the class size.

   a. Click cell **B2**.

   b. Type **=COU**

   c. Double-click **COUNTA** in the Formula AutoComplete list.

   d. Click cell **A10** and drag to cell **A28**.

   e. Press (← Enter). The completed formula should look like this:
   =COUNTA(A10:A28)

9. Display your formulas to check for accuracy.

   a. On the *Formulas* tab, in the *Formula Auditing* group, click the **Show Formulas** button.

   b. When you are ready to continue, hide the formulas and display formula values by clicking the **Show Formulas** button again.

10. Find out which students have a below C grade at the cut-off point for dropping the class. Enter an IF function in cell **T10** to check if the student's total points divided by the total possible points through the midterm is less than 70% (the lowest percentage for a C grade). Use SUM functions within the IF function. Be sure to use absolute references for the range representing the total possible points. If the student is below a C grade, display **Warning!** in the cell; otherwise leave the cell blank.

    a. Click cell **T10.**

    b. On the *Formulas* tab, in the *Function Library* group, click **Logical.**

    c. Click **IF.**

    d. If necessary, move the *Function Arguments* dialog so you can see the worksheet data.

    e. In the *Logical_test* argument box, type:
       SUM(D10:S10)/SUM($D$7:$S$7)<70%

    f. In the *Value_if_true* argument box, type:
       Warning!

    g. In the *Value_if_false* argument box, type: **" "**

    h. Click **OK.** The completed formula should look like this:
       =IF(SUM(D10:S10)/SUM($D$7:$S$7)<70%,"Warning!"," ")

11. Fill the IF function in cell **T10** down for all students. Use any method you want.

12. Find the highest score for each assignment.

    a. Click cell **D4.**

    b. Type **=MAX (** and then click cell **D10** and drag to cell **D28.**

    c. Press ⏎ Enter . The completed formula should look like this:
       =MAX(D10:D28)

    d. Copy the formula across the row to cell **AE4.** Use any method you want. Be sure to leave cell T4 blank.

13. Find the lowest score for each assignment.

    a. Click cell **D5.**

    b. Type **=MIN (** and then click cell **D10** and drag to cell **D28.**

    c. Press ⏎ Enter . The completed formula should look like this:
       =MIN(D10:D28)

    d. Copy the formula across the row to cell **AE5.** Use any method you want. Be sure to leave cell T5 blank.

14. Calculate the average score for each assignment.

    a. Click cell **D6.**

    b. Type **=AV** and then double-click **AVERAGE** in the Formula AutoComplete list.

    c. Click cell **D10** and drag to cell **D28.**

    d. Press ⏎ Enter . The completed formula should look like this:
       =AVERAGE(D10:D28)

    e. Copy the formula across the row to cell **AE6.** Use any method you want. Be sure to leave cell T6 blank.

15. Compute the students' total points. Enter a SUM function in cell **AF10** to add all the points across for the first student.

   a. Click cell **AF10**.

   b. Type **=SU** and then double-click **SUM** in the Formula AutoComplete list.

   c. Click cell **D10** and drag to cell **AE10**.

   d. Press ⏎ Enter. The completed formula should look like this:

   =SUM(D10:AE10)

   e. Copy the formula from **AF10** through cell **AF28**. Use any method you want.

16. In cell **AG10**, enter a formula to compute the percentage for the first student. Divide the student's total points by the total possible points. You will be copying this formula, so make sure the reference to the total possible points uses an absolute reference. The formula should look like this:

   =AF10/$AF$7

17. Copy the formula from **AG10** through **AG28**. Use any method you want.

18. The grade scale is stored in the *Grades* worksheet. Before calculating students' final grades, create a named range to use in the formula.

   a. Click the **Grades** sheet tab.

   b. Select cells **B5:C9**.

   c. Type **GradeScale** in the *Name* box.

   d. Press ⏎ Enter.

19. Now you are ready to create a lookup formula to display each student's final letter grade.

   a. Return to the *Scores* sheet, and click cell **AH10**.

   b. On the *Formulas* tab, in the *Function Library* group, click the **Lookup & Reference** button, and select **VLOOKUP**.

   c. Click cell **AG10** to enter it in the *Lookup_value* argument box.

   d. Type **GradeScale** in the *Table_array* argument box.

   e. The rates are located in the second column of the lookup table. Type **2** in the *Col_index_num* argument box.

   f. In this case, you do not want to specify an exact match, as the percentage grades do not match the grade scale percentages exactly An approximate match will return the correct letter grade.

   g. Click **OK**. The completed formula should look like this:

   =VLOOKUP(AG10,GradeScale,2)

20. Fill down for all students. Use any method you want.

21. Before closing the project, check your workbook for errors.

   a. On the *Formulas* tab, in the *Formula Auditing* group, click the **Error Checking** button.

   b. If errors are found, use the error checking skills learned in this chapter to find and fix the errors.

   c. When Excel displays a message that the error check is complete, click **OK**.

22. Save and close the workbook.

challenge yourself **3.3**

In this project you will complete a vehicle shopping workbook to compare the purchase of several vehicles. After completing the project, you can make a copy of the file and use it to compare vehicle purchases you are considering for yourself. Be sure to save your work often!

Skills needed to complete this project:

- Naming Ranges of Cells (Skill 3.9)
- Calculating Averages (Skill 3.3)
- Finding Data Using the VLOOKUP Function (Skill 3.16)
- Working with Named Ranges (Skill 3.10)
- Using the Function Arguments Dialog to Enter Functions (Skill 3.1)
- Using the Logical Function IF (Skill 3.13)
- Calculating Loan Payments Using the PMT Function (Skill 3.14)
- Creating Formulas Referencing Data from Other Worksheets (Skill 3.15)
- Displaying and Printing Formulas (Skill 3.19)
- Finding Errors Using Trace Precedents and Trace Dependents (Skill 3.18)
- Finding Minimum and Maximum Values (Skill 3.5)
- Using Formula AutoComplete to Enter Functions (Skill 3.2)
- Updating Named Ranges with the Name Manager (Skill 3.11)
- Editing and Deleting Names with the Name Manager (Skill 3.12)
- Checking Formulas for Errors (Skill 3.17)

1. Open the start file **EX2013-ChallengeYourself-3-3** and resave the file as: `[your initials]EX-ChallengeYourself-3-3`

2. If the workbook opens in Protected View, enable editing so you can make changes to the workbook.

3. The registration fee information in cells **B11:C18** on the *Assumptions* sheet will be used in lookup formulas later in this project. Name the range `RegistrationFees` to make it easier to use later.

4. Return to the *Purchase* worksheet.

5. Calculate the average MPG for each vehicle.

   a. Enter a formula in cell **C11** using the AVERAGE function to calculate the average value of **C9:C10.** Use only one argument.

   b. Copy the formula to the appropriate cells for the other vehicles.

   c. Excel will detect a possible error with these formulas. Use the **SmartTag** to ignore the error. *Hint:* Use the **SmartTag** while cells **C11:F11** are selected and the error will be ignored for all the selected cells.

6. Calculate the registration fee for each vehicle.

   a. Enter a formula in cell **C14** to lookup the registration fee for the first vehicle. Use the vehicle type in cell **C5** as the *Lookup_value* argument. Use the **RegistrationFees** named range as the *Table_array* argument. The registration fees are located in column **2** of the data table. Require an exact match.

   b. Copy the formula to the appropriate cells for the other vehicles.

7. Determine whether or not you will need a loan for each potential purchase.

  a. In cell **C16,** enter a formula using an IF function to determine if you need a loan. Your available cash is located on the *Assumptions* sheet in cell **A3.** If the price of the car is less than or equal to your available cash, display **"no".** If the price of the car is more than your available, cash, display **"yes".** Use absolute references where appropriate—you will be copying this formula across the row.

  b. Copy the formula to the appropriate cells for the other vehicles.

8. Calculate how much you would need to borrow for each purchase.

  a. In cell **C17,** enter a formula to subtract your available cash from the purchase price: Use absolute references where appropriate—you will be copying this formula across the row.

  b. Copy the formula to the appropriate cells for the other vehicles.

9. Calculate the monthly payment amount for each loan.

  a. In cell **C22,** enter a formula using the PMT function to calculate the monthly loan payment for the first vehicle. Use absolute references where appropriate—you will be copying this formula across the row. *Hint:* Don't forget to multiple the number of years by 12 in the *Nper* argument to reflect the number of monthly payments during the life of the loan.

  b. Edit the formula so the monthly payment appears as a positive number.

  c. Copy the formula to the appropriate cells for the other vehicles.

10. Compute the monthly cost of gas.

  a. In cell **C21,** enter a formula to calculate the number of miles you expect to drive each month (*Assumptions* sheet, cell **A5**) / the average MPG for the vehicle (*Purchase* sheet, cell **C11**) * gas price per gallon (*Assumptions* sheet, cell **A6**).

  b. Copy the formula to the appropriate cells for the other vehicles.

  c. If cells **D21:F21** display an error or a value of 0, display formulas and check for errors.

  d. If you still can't find the error, try displaying the precedent arrows.

  e. *Hint:* The references to the cells on the *Assumptions* sheet should use absolute references. If they do not, the formula will update incorrectly when you copy it across the row.

11. Compute the monthly cost of maintenance.

  a. In cell **C23,** enter a formula to calculate the annual maintenance cost (cell **C13**) / 12.

  b. Copy the formula to the appropriate cells for the other vehicles.

12. Compute the monthly cost of insurance.

  a. In cell **C24,** enter a formula to calculate the annual insurance cost (cell **C15**) / 12.

  b. Copy the formula to the appropriate cells for the other vehicles.

13. In cells **C25:F25,** compute the total the monthly cost for each vehicle.

14. Determine which vehicles are affordable.

  a. In cell **C27,** enter a formula using the IF function to display **"yes"** if the total monthly cost (cell **C25**) is less than or equal to the total monthly amount available for vehicle expenses (*Assumptions* sheet, cell **A4**).

  b. Copy the formula to the appropriate cells for the other vehicles.

  c. Display formulas and use the error checking skills learned in this lesson to track down and fix any errors.

15. Complete the Analysis section using formulas with statistical functions. Use named ranges instead of cell references in the formulas.

    a. *Hint:* Select cells **B8:F25** and use Excel's **Create from Selection** command to create named ranges for each row using the labels at the left side of the range as the names.

    b. *Hint:* Open the **Name Manager** and review the names Excel created. Notice that any spaces or special characters in the label names are converted to _ characters in the names.

    c. *Hint:* To avoid typos as you create each formula, try using Formula AutoComplete to select the correct range name.

16. Before finishing the project, check the worksheet for errors.

17. Save and close the workbook.

challenge yourself 3.4

In this project, you will record data about your completed and planned college courses. You will compute your GPA, college course costs, and various statistics. You will compute your expected college loan payment and count down the days to graduation and paying off the loan. Be sure to save your work often!

Skills needed to complete this project:

- Finding Errors Using Trace Precedents and Trace Dependents (Skill 3.18)
- Finding Data Using the VLOOKUP Function (Skill 3.16)
- Using the Function Arguments Dialog to Enter Functions (Skill 3.1)
- Checking Formulas for Errors (Skill 3.17)
- Creating Formulas Referencing Data from Other Worksheets (Skill 3.15)
- Calculating Loan Payments Using the PMT Function (Skill 3.14)
- Using Date and Time Functions (Skill 3.6)
- Finding Minimum and Maximum Values (Skill 3.5)
- Using Formula AutoComplete to Enter Functions (Skill 3.2)
- Calculating Averages (Skill 3.3)
- Using the Logical Function IF (Skill 3.13)

1. Open the start file **EX2013-ChallengeYourself-3-4** and resave the file as: `[your initials]EX-ChallengeYourself-3-4`

2. If the workbook opens in Protected View, enable editing so you can make changes to the workbook.

3. There are three sheets. Start with the *GPA* sheet.

4. There is at least one error on this sheet. Click the cell that displays an error and use the precedent arrows to find the cause of the error. If the error is caused by missing values in other cells in the worksheet, you will probably fix the error by the end of this project. Hide the arrows before continuing.

5. Enter the formulas for the GPA worksheet as follows.

    a. In cell **B14** compute the cost for the first course by multiplying the unit cost (cell **C11**) by the number of units for the course (cell **G14**). Use absolute references where appropriate.

    b. Fill and copy to compute the cost for each course, both semesters (cells **B15:B16** and **B19:B22**).

6. Lookup the grade points for each letter grade as follows:

   a. In cell **I14**, enter a formula using the VLOOKUP function. Use the cell range **J3:K7** as the *Table_array* argument. The grade points are located in column **2** of this table. Use absolute references where appropriate.

   b. Fill and copy to look up the grade points for each courses, both semesters (cells **I15:I16** and **I19:I22**).

7. Multiply the grade points by the units to calculate the quality points for each course, for both semesters.

   a. In cell **J14**, enter a formula to multiply **I14** (the grade points) * cell **G14** (the units).

   b. Copy the formula to cells **J15:J16** and **J19:J22**.

8. Use AutoSum to calculate totals for cost (cells **B17** and **B23**), units (cells **G17** and **G23**), and quality points (cells **J17** and **J23**) for each semester.

9. In cell **K17**, compute the GPA for the first semester by dividing the total quality points by the total units (**J17/G17**).

10. In cell **K23**, compute the GPA for the second semester using the same formula.

11. Check the worksheet for errors. Is the error you found in step 4 fixed now? (It should be!)

12. Next go to the *Loan* worksheet.

13. In cell **B3**, enter a formula to display the total cost shown in cell **B9** on the *GPA* sheet.

14. Enter a formula in cell **B7** to look up the number of years to pay based on the loan amount show in cell **B3**. Use the data table in cells **G6:H11** as the *Table_array* argument. Do not require an exact match.

15. Now that you have the loan amount and the number of payments, enter a formula using the PMT function in cell **B8** to calculate the payment amount. Allow the payment to display as a negative number.

16. In cell **B10**, enter a formula to display the current date (just the date, not the date and time).

17. Enter a formula in cell **B16** to estimate the date of the last loan payment. Take the number of years to pay (cell **B7**) times **365.3** and add that to the date of the first loan payment (cell **B15**).

18. Enter a formula in cell **B17** to estimate the number of days until the loan is paid off.

19. Complete the *Summary* sheet information.

20. On the *Summary* sheet, in cell **B5**, enter a simple formula to reference the *Cumulative GPA* number from the *GPA* worksheet (*GPA* **worksheet, cell B5**).

21. Do the same for Total Units (cell **B6**), Total Cost (cell **B8**), and Total Debt (cell **B9**). For Total Debt, reference the Amount Owed number from the *Loan* sheet.

22. Compute the Average Cost Per Unit by dividing the Total Cost (cell **B8**) by the Total Units (cell **B6**).

23. Compute Average Debt Per Unit in the same way.

24. In cell **B14**, enter a formula using a statistical function to calculate the most paid for any semester. Reference cells **B17** and **B23** in the *GPA* sheet. **Hint:** You will need two arguments.

25. In cell **B16**, enter a formula to calculate the average semester cost. Reference cells **B17** and **B23** in the *GPA* sheet. **Hint:** You will need two arguments.

26. In cell **F1**, enter a formula using the IF function to determine if the student met her GPA goal. Display **"yes"** if the goal was met and **"no"** if it was not.

27. In cell **F2**, enter a formula using the IF function to determine if the student met her unit goal. Display **"yes"** if the goal was met and **"no"** if it was not.

28. Before finishing the project, check each worksheet for errors.

29. Save and close the workbook.

on your own 3.5

In this project you will complete a dental plan workbook. Be sure to save your work often!

Skills needed to complete this project:

- Updating Named Ranges with the Name Manager (Skill 3.11)
- Editing and Deleting Names with the Name Manager (Skill 3.12)
- Naming Ranges of Cells (Skill 3.9)
- Working with Named Ranges (Skill 3.10)
- Finding Data Using the VLOOKUP Function (Skill 3.16)
- Using the Function Arguments Dialog to Enter Functions (Skill 3.1)
- Calculating Averages (Skill 3.3)
- Finding Minimum and Maximum Values (Skill 3.5)
- Using Formula AutoComplete to Enter Functions (Skill 3.2)
- Creating Formulas Using Counting Functions (Skill 3.4)
- Using CONCATENATE to Combine Text (Skill 3.8)
- Creating Formulas Referencing Data from Other Worksheets (Skill 3.15)
- Formatting Text Using Functions (Skill 3.7)
- Using Date and Time Functions (Skill 3.6)
- Using the Logical Function IF (Skill 3.13)
- Calculating Loan Payments Using the PMT Function (Skill 3.14)
- Checking Formulas for Errors (Skill 3.17)
- Finding Errors Using Trace Precedents and Trace Dependents (Skill 3.18)
- Displaying and Printing Formulas (Skill 3.19)

1. Open the start file **EX2013-OnYourOwn-3-5** and resave the file as:
   `[your initials]EX-OnYourOwn-3-5`

2. If the workbook opens in Protected View, click the **Enable Editing** button in the Message Bar at the top of the workbook so you can modify the workbook.

3. Start with the *Pocket Chart* worksheet. This dental chart is designed to be used to record measurements of the depth of gum pockets around the teeth. Each tooth is identified by number and name. The teeth of the upper and lower jaws are arranged across the worksheet from the patient's right side to the left. Pocket depth measurements have been entered.

4. Enter your name as the patient's name and enter the date of the examination. Do not use a function for the date. (You don't want the value to update every time you open the workbook.)

5. Review the information in the *Look Up* worksheet and assign names as necessary to each of the lookup tables to use in formulas in other worksheets. One of the lookup tables already has a name assigned.

6. Return to the *Pocket Chart* worksheet and complete the patient data.

   a. Use VLOOKUP functions to determine the severity level for each tooth.

   b. Use statistical functions to calculate the smallest pocket depth, the largest pocket depth, and the average pocket depth for the upper and lower teeth sections. Use similar formulas in **O2:O4** to calculate the overall statistical information for the patient (the average, minimum, and maximum pocket depths for both upper and lower teeth).

   c. Count the number of cells missing pocket depth information (blank cells). **Hint:** Remember, the COUNTBLANK function accepts only one argument, so you will need to count the blank cells for the upper teeth and the lower teeth and then add those values together.

7. Now switch to the *Treatment Plan* worksheet and fix any errors. **Hint:** Display formulas and then use the **Name Manager** to review names and create missing names as needed. Delete any duplicate names you may have accidentally created.

8. Create a formula to display the patient name in the format Bob Smith. Reference the patient name cells from the *Pocket Chart* sheet. Be sure to include a space between the first and last names.

9. Modify the formula that displays the patient name so the name appears in all upper case.

10. Enter a formula to display today's date in cell **I1.**

11. Cells B7:C9 summarize the number of teeth with each severity level. Use this data table to complete the treatment plan. For each treatment, display **"yes"** if the patient meets the requirement below and **"no"** if he does not.

    a. Sonic Toothbrush: Recommend only if the patient has more than five mild pockets.

    b. Scaling & Planing: Recommend only if the patient has more than seven moderate pockets.

    c. Surgery: Recommend only if the patient has more than three severe pockets.

12. Complete the billing information.

    a. Look up the cost of each treatment.

    b. Compute the amount the insurance company will cover for each treatment. Multiply the treatment cost by the insurance company rate. **Hint:** Use the HLOOKUP function to find the insurance company rate.

    c. Compute the billable amount for each treatment. If the treatment is recommended, compute the billable amount by subtracting the amount insurance will cover from the cost of the treatment. If the treatment is not recommended, display **"N/A"** instead.

    d. Enter a formula to calculate the total bill for the patient.

13. Enter a formula to compute the monthly payment for the payment plan option. Be sure to display the number as a positive value.

14. Display your formulas and check for errors. Use the error checking skills you learned in this chapter as needed.

15. Save and close the workbook.

fix it 3.6

In this project, you will correct function mistakes and other formula errors in a workbook designed for planning a large party or event. Be sure to save your work often!

Skills needed to complete this project:

- Checking Formulas for Errors (Skill 3.17)
- Finding Errors Using Trace Precedents and Trace Dependents (Skill 3.18)

- Displaying and Printing Formulas (Skill 3.19)
- Creating Formulas Using Counting Functions (Skill 3.4)
- Finding Minimum and Maximum Values (Skill 3.5)
- Formatting Text Using Functions (Skill 3.7)
- Using CONCATENATE to Combine Text (Skill 3.8)
- Finding Data Using the VLOOKUP Function (Skill 3.16)
- Using the Function Arguments Dialog to Enter Functions (Skill 3.1)
- Using Formula AutoComplete to Enter Functions (Skill 3.2)
- Calculating Averages (Skill 3.3)
- Naming Ranges of Cells (Skill 3.9)
- Working with Named Ranges (Skill 3.10)
- Updating Named Ranges with the Name Manager (Skill 3.11)
- Editing and Deleting Names with the Name Manager (Skill 3.12)
- Using Date and Time Functions (Skill 3.6)
- Using the Logical Function IF (Skill 3.13)
- Creating Formulas Referencing Data from Other Worksheets (Skill 3.15)
- Calculating Loan Payments Using the PMT Function (Skill 3.14)

1. Open the start file **EX2013-FixIt-3-6** and resave the file as:
   `[your initials]EX-FixIt-3-6`

2. If the workbook opens in Protected View, click the **Enable Editing** button in the Message Bar at the top of the workbook so you can modify the workbook.

3. On the *GuestList* sheet, check all the formulas. Cells to check are filled with the light orange color. Most of them need to be corrected.

   a. In the *Name Tag* column, enter a formula to display the guest name in this format: **BILL SMITH**

   b. Correct the function used in cell **A3** to calculate the sum of the values in the *NumAttending* column.

   c. Correct the function used in cell **A4** to count the number of values in the *Street* column.

   d. Correct the function used in cell **A5** to count the number of blank cells in the *NumAttending* column.

   e. Correct the function used in cell **A6** to display the largest value in the *NumAttending* column.

   f. Correct the function used in cell **A7** to display the smallest value in the *NumAttending* column.

4. Use error checking as needed and/or display the formulas on-screen for easy viewing. When you have them right, it should look like Figure EX 3.36.

5. On the *Shopping List* sheet, check all the formulas. Cells to check are filled with the light orange color. Most of them need to be corrected. Many of the problems on this worksheet can be solved by creating named ranges or using a name that already exists.

   a. The formula in cell **B2** uses the wrong function.

   b. The formulas in cells **A9:A23** reference a named range that doesn't exist. There is more than one correct way to fix this problem using the cell range **A5:H18** on the *Places to Shop* worksheet. You can create the named range referenced in the formulas, or you can change the function arguments to reference the cell range instead.

Guest List

	Title	First Name	Last Name	Name Tag	Street	City	State	Zip	Phone	NumAttending
		90	Total number of guests attending		cost per invitation		$0.89			
		65	Count of invitations sent		postage cost		$0.56			
		6	Count of missing responses		Total cost for purchasing					
		6	Largest group attending		and mailing invitations		$130.50			
		1.53	Average number of guests in each group							

	Title	First Name	Last Name	Name Tag	Street	City	State	Zip	Phone	NumAttending
10	Mr.	Cindy	Jacobs	CINDY JACOBS	417 9th St.	Rocklin	CA	95602	916-598-6952	1
11	Mrs	Larrina	Grande	LARRINA GRANDE	87441 Palace Square	Newcastle	CA	95602	916-741-8526	4
12	Miss	Katherine	Hairless	KATHERINE HAIRLESS	2068 Harry Hill	Auburn	CA	95602	530-888-0805	1
13	Mr	James	Muchley	JAMES MUCHLEY	87543 Baldys Road	Auburn	CA	95602	530-885-6523	1
14	Mr./Mrs	William	Holland	WILLIAM HOLLAND	9225 Marchmont Dr	Saramento	CA	95602	(916)348-9982	2
15	Mr/Mrs	Bethany	Sanchaz	BETHANY SANCHAZ	8852 Jones Lane	Santa Rosa	CA	95602	(707)521-3478	3
16	Mrs	Gerald	Watkins	GERALD WATKINS	446 Chest Ave	San Jose	CA	95602	(415)441-8639	2
17	Mr	Emily	Thatcher	EMILY THATCHER	2275 Oak Park Lane	Rocklin	CA	95602	(916)315-8690	1
18	Mr/Mrs	Louisa	Cater	LOUISA CATER	852 Paly Place	Roseville	CA	95602	(916)789-4470	2
19	Mr.	Harold	Roger	HAROLD ROGER	14 Header Dr	Rocklin	CA	95602	555-1324	

FIGURE EX 3.36

   c. The formula in cell **H9** results in the correct value. However, the workbook author copied this formula to the remaining cells in the column and those values are definitely not correct! Fix the formula in cell H9 so you can copy it to cells **H10:H23.** *Hint:* It might be useful to use the name for H8 the tax rate cell (**Tax**) so you don't have to remember to use an absolute reference when referencing it in a formula.

6. If you've fixed the formulas in cells H9:H23 correctly, the formulas in cells **I9:I23** and **G5** should be calculate properly now. However, the formulas in cells **G2:G4** still have errors that need to be fixed.

   a. Correct the function used in cell **G2** to average value of the *Cost* column.

   b. Correct the function used in cell **G3** to display the largest value in the *Cost* column.

   c. Correct the function used in cell **G4** to display the smallest value in the *Cost* column.

7. Use error checking as needed and/or display the formulas on-screen for easy viewing. When you have it right, it should look like Figure EX 3.37.

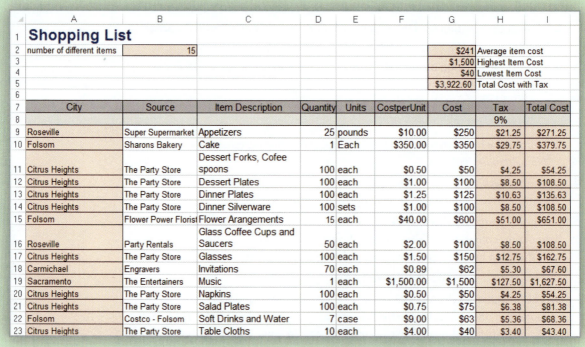

Shopping List

	City	Source	Item Description	Quantity	Units	CostperUnit	Cost	Tax	Total Cost
2	number of different items	15					$241	Average item cost	
3							$1,500	Highest Item Cost	
4							$40	Lowest Item Cost	
5							$3,922.60	Total Cost with Tax	
7	City	Source	Item Description	Quantity	Units	CostperUnit	Cost	Tax	Total Cost
8								9%	
9	Roseville	Super Supermarket	Appetizers	25	pounds	$10.00	$250	$21.25	$271.25
10	Folsom	Sharons Bakery	Cake	1	Each	$350.00	$350	$29.75	$379.75
11	Citrus Heights	The Party Store	Dessert Forks, Cofee spoons	100	each	$0.50	$50	$4.25	$54.25
12	Citrus Heights	The Party Store	Dessert Plates	100	each	$1.00	$100	$8.50	$108.50
13	Citrus Heights	The Party Store	Dinner Plates	100	each	$1.25	$125	$10.63	$135.63
14	Citrus Heights	The Party Store	Dinner Silverware	100	sets	$1.00	$100	$8.50	$108.50
15	Folsom	Flower Power Florist	Flower Arangements	15	each	$40.00	$600	$51.00	$651.00
16	Roseville	Party Rentals	Glass Coffee Cups and Saucers	50	each	$2.00	$100	$8.50	$108.50
17	Citrus Heights	The Party Store	Glasses	100	each	$1.50	$150	$12.75	$162.75
18	Carmichael	Engravers	Invitations	70	each	$0.89	$62	$5.30	$67.60
19	Sacramento	The Entertainers	Music	1	each	$1,500.00	$1,500	$127.50	$1,627.50
20	Citrus Heights	The Party Store	Napkins	100	each	$0.50	$50	$4.25	$54.25
21	Citrus Heights	The Party Store	Salad Plates	100	each	$0.75	$75	$6.38	$81.38
22	Folsom	Costco - Folsom	Soft Drinks and Water	7	case	$9.00	$63	$5.36	$68.36
23	Citrus Heights	The Party Store	Table Cloths	10	each	$4.00	$40	$3.40	$43.40

FIGURE EX 3.37

8. On the *Summary* sheet, you will be entering all the formulas. Cells to complete are filled with the light orange color.

    a. Cell **B2** should use a function that will update the date to the current date every time the workbook is opened.

    b. Cell **B4** references a named range that doesn't exist. It should reference cell **A4** on the *Guest List* sheet. You can create the named range or edit the formula to reference the cell instead.

    c. Cell **B5** references a named range that doesn't exist. It should reference cell **A3** on the *Guest List* sheet. You can create the named range or edit the formula to reference the cell instead.

    d. Cell **B8** is missing the formula to calculate whether or not the total cost with tax on the *Shopping List* sheet + the total cost for purchasing and mailing invitations on the *Guest List* sheet is greater than the available cash. The cell should display **yes** or **no**.

    e. If the result in cell B8 is *yes,* you should add a formula to cell **B9** to calculate the amount to borrow.

    f. If the result in cell B8 is *yes,* you should add a formula to cell **B10** to calculate the monthly loan payment based on the information in cells B9:B11. Remember to display the monthly payment amount as a positive number.

9. Use error checking as needed and/or display the formulas on-screen for easy viewing. When you have the formulas right, the *Summary* sheet should look like Figure EX 3.38.

	A	B
1	**Party Financing**	
2	As of	12/4/2012
3		
4	# of Invitations	65
5	# of Guests	90
6		
7	Cash Available for Event	$1,800.00
8	Do We Need to Borrow?	yes
9	Amount to Borrow	$2,253.10
10	APR	4.5%
11	# Months to Pay	12
12	Monthly Payment Amount	$192.37
13		

FIGURE EX 3.38

10. Save and close the workbook.

chapter 4

Formatting Worksheets and Managing the Workbook

❯ Insert, delete, and format worksheets

❯ Apply themes

❯ Insert, delete, and modify rows and columns

❯ Modify the worksheet view

❯ Manage how the worksheet prints

In this chapter, you will learn the following skills:

skills

introduction

As Excel projects get bigger and more complicated, more formatting skills are required. In this chapter, you will learn how to manage the organization and appearance of worksheets for the optimal display of data both on-screen and when printed.

Skill 4.1 Inserting Worksheets

When you create a new workbook, it contains a single worksheet named *Sheet1*. If you need more than one worksheet, you can add more. It is a good practice to keep all related information in the same workbook by adding more worksheets, rather than starting a new workbook.

❭ To add a new worksheet to the end of your workbook, click the **New Sheet** button to the right of the last worksheet tab.

❭ To add a worksheet to the left of the active worksheet, on the *Home* tab, in the *Cells* group, click the **Insert** button arrow, and select **Insert Sheet.**

FIGURE EX 4.1

The new sheet is given the name Sheet# (where # is the next number available—for example, if your workbook contains *Sheet1* and *Sheet 2*, the next sheet inserted will be named *Sheet3*).

another **method**

To add a worksheet you can also:
1. Right-click on a sheet tab.
2. Select **Insert...** on the shortcut menu.
   ❭ To insert a blank worksheet, click the **Worksheet** icon in the dialog box.
   ❭ To insert a formatted worksheet, click the **Spreadsheet Solutions** tab, and click any of the template icons.
3. Click **OK.**

let me **try**

Open the student data file **EX4-01-IncomeAndExpenses** and try this skill on your own:
1. Add a new worksheet to the right of the *Sheet1* sheet.
2. Add another new worksheet to the left of the new *Sheet2* worksheet.
3. Save the file as directed by your instructor and close it.

Skill 4.2 Naming Worksheets

When you create a new workbook, Excel automatically includes a worksheet named *Sheet1*. Additional worksheets that you insert are automatically named *Sheet2, Sheet3*, and so forth. It is a good idea to rename your worksheets to something more descriptive. Giving your worksheets descriptive names can help organize multiple worksheets, making it easier for you to find and use information.

To rename a worksheet:

1. Right-click the worksheet tab, and select **Rename.**

2. Excel highlights the sheet name, allowing you to replace it as you type.

3. Type the new sheet name, and press ⏎ Enter.

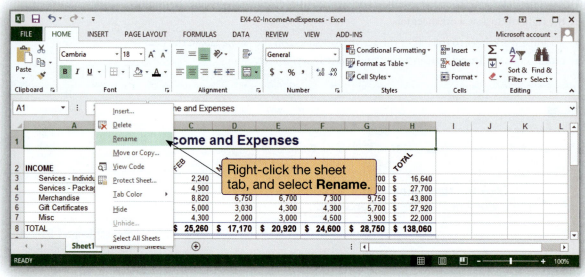

FIGURE EX 4.2

another **method**

You can also use the Ribbon to rename a worksheet.
1. Click the sheet tab you want to rename.
2. On the *Home* tab, in the *Cells* group, click the **Format** button.
3. Click **Rename Sheet.**
4. Type the new sheet name, and press ⏎ Enter.

let me **try**

Open the student data file **EX4-02-IncomeAndExpenses** and try this skill on your own:
1. Rename *Sheet1* using the following name: Q1-Q2
2. Save the file as directed by your instructor and close it.

Skill 4.3 Changing the Color of Sheet Tabs

By default, all the worksheet tabs in Excel are white. If you have many sheets in your workbook, changing the tab colors can help you organize your data.

To change a worksheet tab color:

1. Right-click the sheet tab and point to **Tab Color** to display the color palette.

2. Hover the mouse pointer over each color to preview how the color will look when the worksheet is active.

3. Click the color you want.

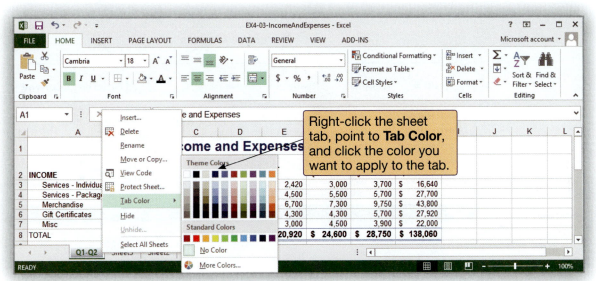

FIGURE EX 4.3

tips & tricks

> The color palette used for worksheet tab color is the same color palette used for font color, fill color, and border color. The colors available change depending on the theme applied to the workbook.
> If you have sheets that contain related data, color them using different shades of the same color.

another method

You can also use the Ribbon to change tab color.
1. Click the sheet tab you want to color.
2. On the *Home* tab, in the *Cells* group, click the **Format** button.
3. Point to **Tab Color** to display the color palette.
4. Click the color you want.

let me try

Open the student data file **EX4-03-IncomeAndExpenses** and try this skill on your own:
1. Change the color of the sheet tab for the *Q1-Q2* worksheet to **Dark Blue, Text 2**.
2. Save the file as directed by your instructor and close it.

Skill 4.4 Moving and Copying Worksheets

You can move worksheets around in a workbook, rearranging them into the most logical order.

To move a worksheet within a workbook:

1. Click the worksheet tab and hold down the mouse button.

2. Notice that the mouse pointer changes to the ⬚ shape.

3. Drag the mouse cursor to the position where you want to move the sheet, and release the mouse button.

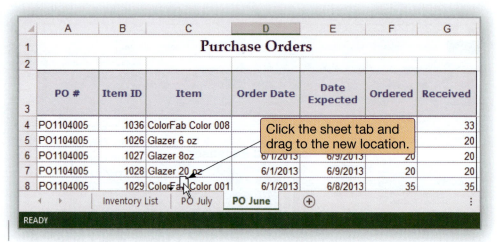

FIGURE EX 4.4

If you want to experiment with worksheet layouts or formulas, you can create a copy of the worksheet in case you want to go back to the original version.

To create a copy of a worksheet:

1. Click the worksheet tab, hold down the mouse button, and press and hold Ctrl.

2. Notice that the mouse pointer changes to the ⬚ shape.

3. Drag the mouse cursor to the position where you want to insert a copy of the selected sheet, and release the mouse button.

To move or copy a worksheet to another workbook or to a new workbook:

1. Right-click the sheet tab, and select **Move or Copy...** to open the *Move or Copy* dialog.

2. In the *Move or Copy* dialog, expand the **To book** list at the top of the dialog. The *To book* list shows all the Excel workbooks you have open. Click the workbook you want. To move or copy the sheet to a new blank workbook, select **(new book).**

3. The list of sheets in the *Before sheet* box will update to show the sheets available in the workbook you selected. Click the name of the sheet you want to move the selected sheet before. If you want to move the sheet to the end of the workbook, select **(move to end)** in the *Before sheet* box.

4. If you want to create a copy of the selected sheet, instead of moving the original, click the **Create a copy** check box.

5. Click **OK.**

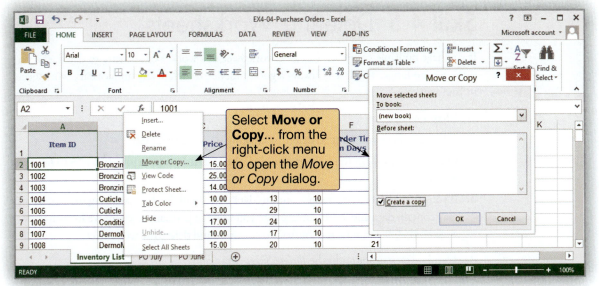

FIGURE EX 4.5

You can use this same method to move or copy worksheets within a workbook by not changing the workbook listed in the *To book* list in the *Move or Copy* dialog.

tips & tricks

Moving a worksheet from one workbook to another deletes the worksheet from the original workbook. Consider copying the worksheet to the second workbook first, and then, once you are confident that formulas work as you intend, delete the worksheet from the original workbook.

tell me more

To move or copy more than one worksheet, press (↑Shift) and click the worksheets you want to move or copy. If the worksheets are not consecutive, then press (Ctrl) instead.

another method

You can also open the *Move or Copy* dialog from the Ribbon:
    On the *Home* tab, in the *Cells* group, click the **Format** button, and select **Move or Copy Sheet...**

let me try

Open the student data file **EX4-04-PurchaseOrders** and try this skill on your own:
1. Move the *PO June* worksheet so it is positioned before the *PO July* worksheet.
2. Make a copy of the *PO June* worksheet and position it before the *PO July* worksheet.
3. Copy the *Inventory List* worksheet to a new workbook.
4. Save the files as directed by your instructor and close them.

Skill 4.5 Deleting Worksheets

If you have multiple copies of the same worksheet in a workbook, be sure to delete the versions you no longer need. It is always a good practice to delete any unnecessary worksheets in your workbook.

To delete a worksheet:

1. Select the sheet you want to delete by clicking the worksheet tab.

2. On the *Home* tab, in the *Cells* group, click the **Delete** button arrow, and select **Delete Sheet.**

3. If you try to delete a sheet that contains data, Excel will display a warning that the sheet may contain data and ask if you are sure you want to permanently remove it from your workbook. Click the **Delete** button to continue and delete the worksheet.

Be careful—you cannot undo the *Delete Sheet* command.

FIGURE EX 4.6

tell me **more**

You can delete multiple worksheets at the same time. First, select all the sheet tabs you want to remove, and then invoke the *Delete Sheet* command.

another **method**

To delete a worksheet you can also right-click on a sheet tab and then select **Delete** from the shortcut menu.

let me **try**

Open the student data file **EX4-05-PurchaseOrders** and try this skill on your own:

1. Delete the *PO June (2)* worksheet.
2. Save the file as directed by your instructor and close it.

Skill 4.6 Grouping Worksheets

If you have multiple worksheets with the same structure, you can make changes to all of the worksheets at the same time by **grouping** them. This is convenient when you are setting up a series of worksheets with the same row or column headings. When sheets are grouped together, you can also change column widths and formatting, add formulas such as totals, or add headers and footers. Using grouping saves time and ensures that the sheets share a consistent format.

To group worksheets:

1. Click the first worksheet tab.

2. Hold down ⇧ Shift and click the tab for the last worksheet you want included in the group. If you want to select noncontiguous worksheets (sheets that are not next to each other), press Ctrl instead, and then click each sheet tab.

3. Notice that the title bar now includes [Group] after the file name.

4. Make the change you want to the sheet. This same change will be made to all sheets in the group.

5. To ungroup, click any sheet tab that is not part of the group.

FIGURE EX 4.7

tell me **more**

To group all the sheets in your workbook together, right-click any sheet tab and then click **Select All Sheets.**

To ungroup sheets, right-click one of the grouped sheet tabs and then click **Ungroup.** If all of the sheets in your workbook are grouped together, you must use this method to ungroup them.

let me **try**

Open the student data file **EX4-06-PurchaseOrders** and try this skill on your own:

1. Group sheets *PO June* and *PO July.*
2. Change the text in cell **F3** to: **Quantity Ordered**
3. Ungroup the sheets.
4. Review cell **F3** in sheets *PO June* and *PO July* to ensure that the change was made to both sheets.
5. Save the file as directed by your instructor and close it.

Skill 4.7 Applying Themes

A **theme** is a unified color, font, and effects scheme. When you apply a theme to the workbook, you ensure that all visual elements work well together, giving the workbook a polished, professional look. When you create a new blank workbook in Excel 2013, the Office theme is applied by default.

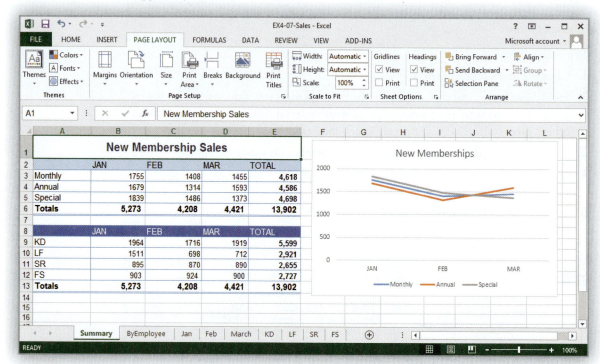

FIGURE EX 4.8
A workbook with the Office theme applied

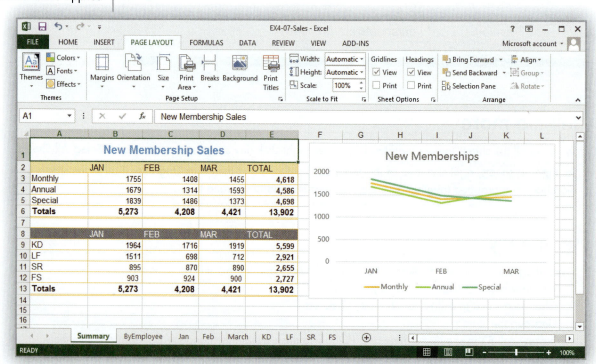

FIGURE EX 4.9
The same workbook with the Banded theme applied

To apply a theme to a workbook:

1. On the *Page Layout* tab, in the *Themes* group, click the **Themes** button to expand the gallery.

2. Roll your mouse over each theme in the gallery to preview the formatting changes.

3. Click one of the themes to apply it to your workbook.

From the *Themes* group, you can apply specific aspects of a theme by making a selection from the *Theme Colors, Theme Fonts,* or *Theme Effects* gallery. Applying one aspect of a theme (for example, colors) will not change the other aspects (fonts and effects).

Theme Colors—Limits the colors available from the color palette for fonts, borders, and cell shading. Notice that when you change themes, the colors in the color palette change.

Theme Fonts—Affects the fonts used for cell styles (including titles and headings). Changing the theme fonts does not limit the fonts available to you from the *Font* group on the Ribbon.

Theme Effects—Controls the way graphic elements in your worksheet appear. Chart styles change according to the theme color and effects.

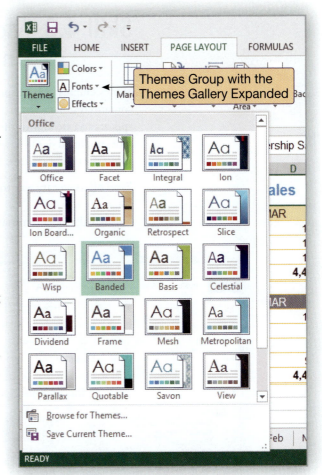

FIGURE EX 4.10

tips & tricks

When you change the workbook theme, the look of the built-in cell styles changes. Be careful, as the change in style may increase the font size, causing some of your data to be too wide for the columns. If you change themes, you may need to adjust some of your column widths or row heights.

let me try

Open the student data file **EX4-07-Sales** and try this skill on your own:

1. If necessary, click the *Summary* sheet tab.
2. Expand the *Themes* gallery and preview how each theme would affect the workbook.
3. Apply the **Banded** theme.
4. Save the file as directed by your instructor and close it.

Skill 4.8 Modifying Column Widths and Row Heights

Some columns in your spreadsheet may be too narrow to display the data properly. If a cell contains text data, the text appears cut off. (If the cell to the right is empty, however, the text appears to extend into the empty cell.) If the cell contains numerical data, Excel displays a series of pound signs (#) when the cell is too narrow to display the entire number. You should adjust the column widths so the spreadsheet is easy to read.

Excel offers an easy way to automatically set columns to the width to best fit the data in the column:

To make the column automatically fit the contents, double-click the right column border.

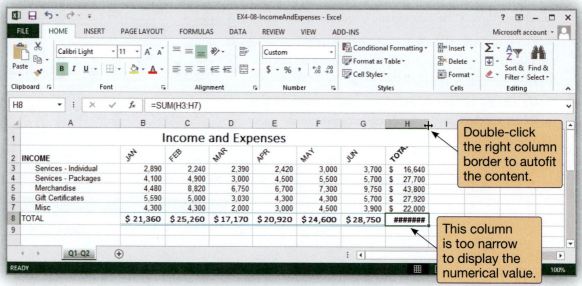

FIGURE EX 4.11

You can also modify column widths manually:

1. Move your mouse over the right column boundary.
2. The cursor will change to a ↔ shape.
3. Click and drag until the column is the size you want, and then release the mouse button.

Rows in Excel are automatically sized to fit the font size. However, if you change the font size or apply a new theme, you may need to modify row heights. Use the same techniques you use for resizing columns:

To make the row automatically fit the contents, double-click the bottom row boundary.

To modify row heights manually:

1. Move your mouse over the bottom row boundary.
2. The cursor will change to a ↕ shape.
3. Click and drag until the row is the size you want, and then release the mouse button.

If your worksheet data are organized in a table format, you should ensure that all columns have the same width. The column width number refers to the number of standard characters that can display in the column.

To specify an exact column width:

1. Select the columns you want to modify. Click the column selector for the first column, press and hold (↑ Shift), and click the column selector for the last column.
2. On the *Home* tab, in the *Cells* group, click the **Format** button.
3. Select **Column Width...**
4. Enter the value you want in the *Column Width* dialog.
5. Click **OK.**

You can use this same technique to specify a row height. From the *Format* button menu, select **Row Height...** and enter the row height value in the *Row Height* dialog.

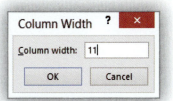

FIGURE EX 4.12

another method

You can also apply the *AutoFit* command from the Ribbon:

To autofit a column:
1. Click the column selector for the column you want to resize.
2. On the *Home* tab, in the *Cells* group, click the **Format** button.
3. Click **AutoFit Column Width.**

To autofit a row:
1. Click the row selector for the row you want to resize.
2. On the *Home* tab, in the *Cells* group, click the **Format** button.
3. Click **AutoFit Row Height.**

let me try

Open the student data file **EX4-08-IncomeAndExpenses** and try this skill on your own:
1. Autofit column **H** to best fit the data.
2. Autofit row **2** to best fit the data.
3. Select columns **B:G** and change the column width to **11.**
4. Save the file as directed by your instructor and close it.

Skill 4.9 Inserting and Deleting Rows and Columns

You may find you need to add rows or columns of new information into the middle of your workbook. Adding a new row will shift other rows down; adding a new column will shift other columns to the right.

To insert a row:

1. Place your cursor in a cell in the row below where you want the new row.

2. On the *Home* tab, in the *Cells* group, click the **Insert** button arrow and select **Insert Sheet Rows.**

3. The new row will appear above the selected cell.

To insert a column:

1. Place your cursor in a cell in the column to the right of where you want the new column.

2. On the *Home* tab, in the *Cells* group, click the **Insert** button arrow and select **Insert Sheet Columns.**

3. The new column will appear to the left of the selected cell.

When you insert a row or column, a Smart Tag will appear. Click the **Smart Tag** to choose formatting options for the new row or column—**Format Same as Above, Format Same as Below,** or **Clear Formatting** for rows and **Format Same as Left, Format Same as Right,** or **Clear Formatting** for columns.

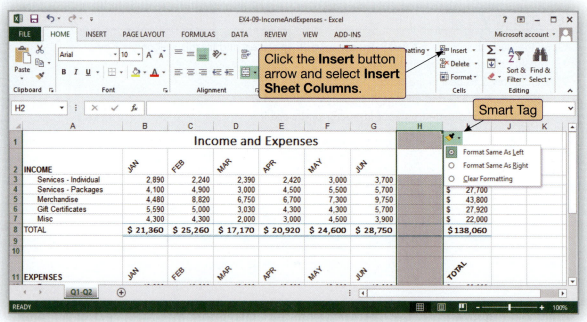

FIGURE EX 4.13

Of course, you can also delete rows and columns. Deleting a row will shift other rows up; deleting a column will shift the remaining columns to the left.

To delete a row:

1. Place your cursor in a cell in the row you want to delete.

2. On the *Home* tab, in the *Cells* group, click the **Delete** button arrow and select **Delete Sheet Rows.**

3. The row will be deleted and the rows below it will shift up.

To delete a column:

1. Place your cursor in a cell in the column you want to delete.
2. On the *Home* tab, in the *Cells* group, click the **Delete** button arrow and select **Delete Sheet Columns.**
3. The column will be deleted, and columns to the right of the deleted column will shift left.

tips & tricks

Depending on whether you have a cell, a range of cells, a row, or a column selected, the behavior of the *Insert* and *Delete* commands will change. If you have a single cell selected and click the **Insert** button instead of the button arrow, Excel will insert a single cell, automatically moving cells down. However, if you select the entire column first, and then click the **Insert** button, Excel will automatically insert a column.

another method

To insert or delete rows and columns, you can also:
1. Right-click in a cell, then select **Insert...** or **Delete...**
2. In the dialog box, select **Entire row** or **Entire column.**
3. Click **OK.**

You can also select an entire row or column by clicking the row or column selector, then right-click and select **Insert** or **Delete** from the menu. Because you have already selected an entire row or column, Excel will not ask you to specify what you want to insert or delete.

let me try

Open the student data file **EX4-09-IncomeAndExpenses** and try this skill on your own:
1. Insert a new column to the left of column **H.** Format the new column the same as the column to its left.
2. Delete row **10.**
3. Save the file as directed by your instructor and close it.

Skill 4.10 Freezing and Unfreezing Rows and Columns

If you have a large spreadsheet (very wide or very tall), you may want to **freeze** part of the worksheet. By doing this, you can keep column headings and row labels visible as you scroll through your data.

To freeze part of the worksheet, so it is always visible:

1. Arrange the worksheet so the row you want to be visible is the top row or the column you want is the first column visible at the left.

2. On the *View* tab, in the *Window* group, click the **Freeze Panes** button.

   ❭ If you want the first row to always be visible, click **Freeze Top Row.**

   ❭ If you want the first column to always be visible, click **Freeze First Column.**

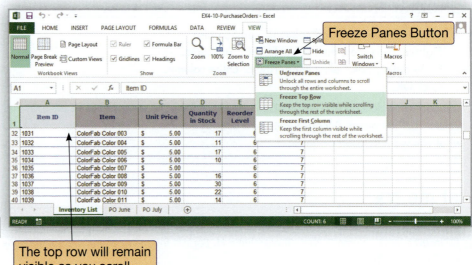

FIGURE EX 4.14

The top row will remain visible as you scroll down the worksheet.

If your worksheet has both a header row and a column of labels in the first column, use the *Freeze Panes* option to freeze the worksheet at the selected cell, so the rows above the cell and the columns to the left of the cell are always visible.

1. Select the cell immediately below the header row and immediately to the right of the label column (usually cell B2).

2. On the *View* tab, in the *Window* group, click the **Freeze Panes** button, and select **Freeze Panes.**

To return your worksheet to normal, click the **Freeze Panes** button and select **Unfreeze Panes.**

let me try

Open the student data file **EX4-10-PurchaseOrders** and try this skill on your own:

1. Verify that the *Inventory List* sheet is selected and the header row (row 1) is visible at the top of the worksheet.
2. Apply the *Freeze Panes* command so the top row will remain visible as you scroll down the worksheet.
3. Save the file as directed by your instructor and close it.

Skill 4.11 Hiding and Unhiding Rows and Columns

When you hide a row or column, the data still remain in your workbook, but they are no longer displayed on-screen and are not part of the printed workbook. Hiding rows can be helpful when you want to print a copy of your workbook for others but do not want to share all the information contained in your workbook.

To hide a row or column:

1. Select any cell in the row or column you want to hide.
2. On the *Home* tab, in the *Cells* group, click the **Format** button.
3. Point to **Hide & Unhide,** and click **Hide Rows** or **Hide Columns.**

To unhide a row or column:

1. Select the rows or columns on either side of the row or column you want to unhide.
2. On the *Home* tab, in the *Cells* group, click the **Format** button.
3. Point to **Hide & Unhide,** and click **Unhide Rows** or **Unhide Columns.**

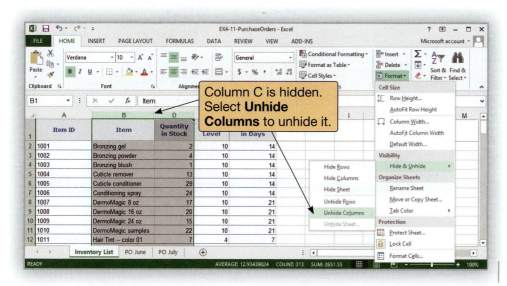

FIGURE EX 4.15

another method

The *Hide* and *Unhide* commands are also available from the right-click menu when columns or rows are selected.

let me try

Open the student data file **EX4-11-PurchaseOrders** and try this skill on your own:

1. Verify that the *Inventory List* sheet is selected.
2. Hide column **C.**
3. Unhide column **C** without using the *Undo* command.
4. Save the file as directed by your instructor and close it.

Skill 4.12 Splitting Workbooks

In Excel, you can split the worksheet view into two or four panes. Each pane scrolls independently of the other(s), so you can see two (or four) different areas of the worksheet at the same time. This can be especially helpful if you want to compare data in multiple parts of the worksheet at the same time.

To split the worksheet view:

1. Click the cell in the worksheet where you would like to split the view. You can select an entire row or column as the split point.

   ❯ If you want to split the worksheet into two horizontal panes, click a cell in column **A.**

   ❯ If you want to split the worksheet into two vertical panes, click a cell in row **1.**

   ❯ If you want to split the worksheet into four panes, click any cell in the worksheet. The cell you selected will be the top left cell in the pane in the lower-right quadrant.

2. On the *View* tab, in the *Window* group, click the **Split** button.

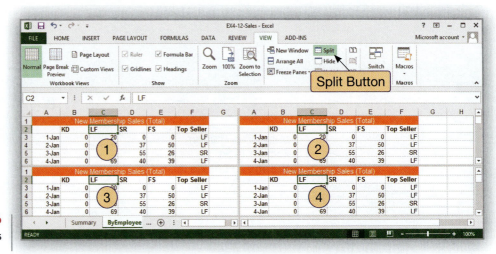

FIGURE EX 4.16
Worksheet split into four panes

To undo the split and return the worksheet to a single view, click the **Split** button again.

tips & tricks

Splitting your worksheet will undo the *Freeze Panes* command.

tell me more

To adjust the size of the panes, click and drag the pane border.

let me try

Open the student data file **EX4-12-Sales** and try this skill on your own:
1. Verify that the *ByEmployee* sheet is selected.
2. Select any cell in the middle of the worksheet, and then split the worksheet into four panes.
3. Save the file as directed by your instructor and close it.

Skill 4.13 Changing the Worksheet View

Excel offers three ways to view a worksheet.

Just as the name implies, **Normal view** is the typical working view. In *Normal* view, Excel shows the aspects of the worksheet that are visible only on-screen. Elements that are visible only when printed (like headers and footers) are hidden.

Page Layout view shows all the worksheet elements as they will print. *Page Layout* view includes headers and footers. You will work with *Page Layout* view when you learn about headers and footers

Page Break Preview view allows you to manipulate where page breaks occur when the worksheet is printed. You will work with *Page Break Preview* view when you learn about inserting page breaks.

To switch between worksheet views, click the appropriate button in the status bar at the bottom of the Excel window, or on the *View* tab, in the *Workbook Views* group, click the button for the view you want.

FIGURE EX 4.17
Page Layout view

let me try

Open the student data file **EX4-13-Sales** and try this skill on your own:
1. Verify that the *Summary* sheet is selected.
2. Switch to **Page Break Preview** view.
3. Switch to **Page Layout** view.
4. Save the file as directed by your instructor and close it.

Skill 4.14 Adding Headers and Footers

A **header** is text that appears at the top of every page, just below the top margin; a **footer** is text that appears at the bottom of every page, just above the bottom margin. Typically, headers and footers display information such as dates, page numbers, sheet names, file names, and authors' names.

To add a header or footer to a worksheet from *Page Layout* view:

1. Switch to *Page Layout* view by clicking the **Page Layout** button on the status bar.
2. The header area has three sections with the text *Click to add header* in the center section. Click the header section where you want to add information (left, center, or right).
3. The *Header & Footer Tools Design* contextual tab appears.
4. In the *Header & Footer* group, click the **Header** button and select one of the predefined headers, or click a button in the *Header & Footer Elements* group to add a specific header element such as the sheet name or the current date. Excel inserts the code for the header element. Once you click away from the header, you will see the actual header text.

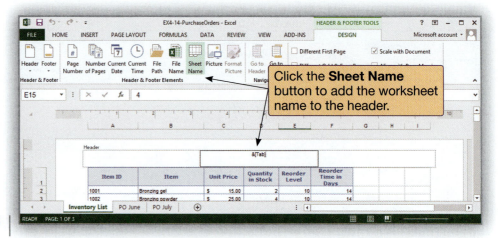

Click the **Sheet Name** button to add the worksheet name to the header.

FIGURE EX 4.18

5. In the *Navigation* group, click the **Go to Footer** button to switch to the footer. Add footer elements the same way you add header elements.
6. When you are finished adding your header and footer elements, click anywhere in the worksheet and then switch back to *Normal* view.

Another method for adding headers and footers uses the *Page Setup* dialog. This method will be familiar to users who have worked with older versions of Excel.

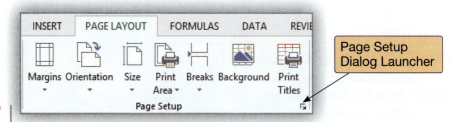

Page Setup Dialog Launcher

FIGURE EX 4.19

To add a header or footer to a worksheet using the *Page Setup* dialog:

1. On the *Page Layout* tab, in the *Page Setup* group, click the **Page Setup Dialog Launcher** to open the *Page Setup* dialog.
2. Click the **Header/Footer** tab.
3. Click the arrow beneath the Header or Footer area to expand the list of predefined header/footer options. Click the option you want to use.

4. You can also customize the header or footer by clicking the **Custom Header...** or **Custom Footer...** button and adding elements through the *Header* or *Footer* dialog.

5. In the *Header* or *Footer* dialog, click the section you want, and then click one of the header/footer element buttons.

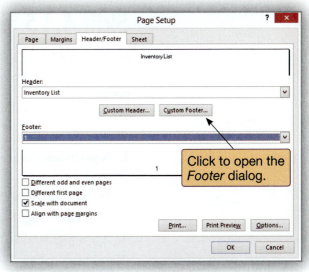

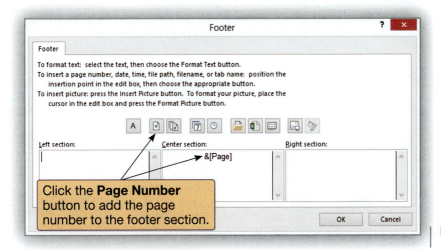

tips & tricks

Page Layout view is not compatible with Freeze Panes. If you have Freeze Panes applied to your worksheet, Excel will warn you before switching to *Page Layout* view. Click **OK** in the message box to continue to *Page Layout* view and undo Freeze Panes.

another method

Another way to add a header or footer to your worksheet is to click the *Insert* tab. In the *Text* group, click the **Header & Footer** button. (The worksheet will automatically switch to *Page Layout* view when you click the *Header & Footer* button.)

let me try

Open the student data file **EX4-14-PurchaseOrders** and try this skill on your own:
1. Verify that the *Inventory List* sheet is active.
2. Add a header that displays the sheet name in the center section.
3. Add a footer that displays the page number in the center section.
4. Click anywhere in the worksheet grid, and then switch back to *Normal* view.
5. Preview how the worksheet will look when printed and note the header and footer.
6. Save the file as directed by your instructor and close it.

Skill 4.15 Inserting Page Breaks

Excel automatically inserts page breaks so columns and rows are not split across pages when you print. However, you may want to control where page breaks happen so your worksheet prints in a more logical order. When the worksheet is in *Normal* view, page breaks appear as faint dotted lines. To view the page breaks more clearly, switch to *Page Break Preview* view.

To manually insert a new page break:

1. Begin by selecting the cell below and to the right of where you want the new page break.

2. On the *Page Layout* tab, in the *Page Setup* group, click the **Breaks** button.

3. Click **Insert Page Break.**

4. A new page break is inserted to the left of the selected column or above the selected row.

When the worksheet is in *Page Break Preview* view, automatic page breaks appear as blue dotted lines and manually inserted page breaks appear as solid blue lines. You can manually move a page break by clicking the page break line, and then dragging to the right or left or up or down. Release the mouse button when the line appears where you want the break. Notice that if you move an automatic page break, the line changes from dotted to solid.

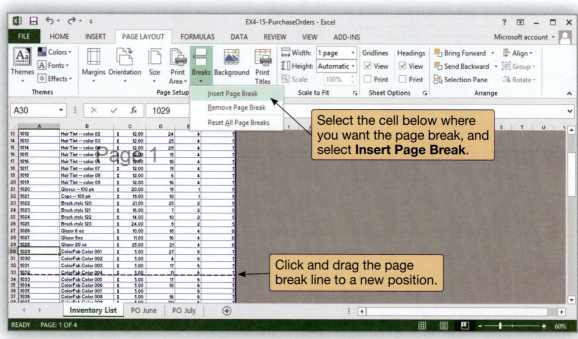

FIGURE EX 4.22
This worksheet is in Page Break Preview view

To remove a manual page break, select any cell adjacent to (to the right of or below) the break, then on the *Page Layout* tab, in the *Page Setup* group, click the **Breaks** button, and click **Remove Page Break.**

tips & tricks

If you insert a page break but nothing seems to happen, check to see if you have the scaling option set for printing. For example, if you have the worksheet set to print all columns on a single page, inserting a new page break between columns will not appear to have any effect on the worksheet. However, if you remove the scaling option, the new manual page break will appear.

tell me **more**

To remove all the manual page breaks at once, on the *Page Layout* tab, in the *Page Setup* group, click the **Breaks** button, and click **Reset All Page Breaks.**

let me **try**

Open the student data file **EX4-15-PurchaseOrders** and try this skill on your own:
1. Verify that the *Inventory List* sheet is active.
2. Switch to *Page Break Preview* view and observe the page breaks.
3. Move the page break between pages 1 and 2 to just below **row 29.**
4. Switch back to *Normal* view.
5. Save the file as directed by your instructor and close it.

from the perspective of . . .

WAREHOUSE LOGISTICS SUPERVISOR

Part of our company's "green" initiative is to minimize paper usage for printing. Using Excel's page break controls and layout controls like scaling, page orientation, and margins, we make sure that the reports we *have* to print use as little paper as possible.

Skill 4.16 Showing and Hiding Worksheet Elements

Gridlines are the lines that appear on the worksheet defining the rows and columns. Gridlines make it easy to see the individual cells in your worksheet. By default, gridlines are visible on-screen when you are working in Excel, but they do not print.

Headings are the numbers at the left of rows and the letters at the top of columns. By default, Excel displays the row and column headings on-screen to make it easy to identify cell references but they do not print.

To hide gridlines or headings on-screen:

On the *Page Layout* tab, in the *Sheet Options* group, click the **View** check box under **Gridlines** or **Headings** to remove the checkmark.

To print the gridlines and headings when you print the worksheet:

On the *Page Layout* tab, in the *Sheet Options* group, click the **Print** check box under **Gridlines** or **Headings.**

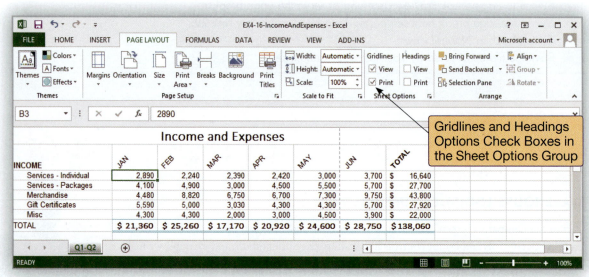

Gridlines and Headings Options Check Boxes in the Sheet Options Group

FIGURE EX 4.23

tips & tricks

Hiding gridlines and headings can make your workbook look less like a spreadsheet and more like a form.

another method

To show or hide gridlines and headings on-screen, you can also check or uncheck the appropriate boxes on the *View* tab, in the *Show* group.

let me try

Open the student data file **EX4-16-IncomeAndExpenses** and try this skill on your own:
1. Modify the *Q1-Q2* worksheet so gridlines will print.
2. Modify the *Q1-Q2* worksheet so headings are hidden on-screen.
3. Save the file as directed by your instructor and close it.

Skill 4.17 Changing Worksheet Orientation

Orientation refers to the direction the worksheet prints. It doesn't affect the way the worksheet looks on your computer screen. The default print setting is for **portrait orientation**—when the height of the page is greater than the width (like a portrait hanging on a wall). If your workbook is wide, you may want to use **landscape orientation** instead, where the width of the page is greater than the height.

You can set the worksheet orientation from the *Page Layout* tab on the Ribbon:

1. On the *Page Layout* tab, in the *Page Setup* group, click the **Orientation** button.
2. Click the **Portrait** or **Landscape** option.

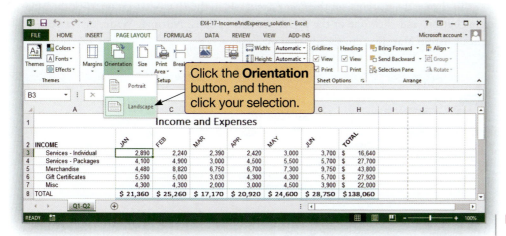

FIGURE EX 4.24

You can also change the worksheet orientation when you print:

1. Click the **File** tab to open Backstage.
2. Click **Print.**
3. In the *Settings* section, click the button displaying the current orientation setting, and then click the orientation setting you want.

tips & tricks

Changing the *Orientation* setting affects only the active worksheet.

another method

You can also use the *Page Setup* dialog box to change the orientation of your worksheet. On the *Page* tab, click the **Portrait** or **Landscape** radio button, and then click **OK.**

let me try

Open the student data file **EX4-17-IncomeAndExpenses** and try this skill on your own:
1. Note the page break line between columns F and G.
2. Change the worksheet orientation to **Landscape.**
3. Note that the page is wider now and the page break line is between columns I and J.
4. Save the file as directed by your instructor and close it.

Skill 4.18 Setting Up Margins for Printing

Margins are the blank spaces at the top, bottom, left, and right of a printed page. You may need to adjust the margins individually for each worksheet in your workbook to ensure they print exactly as you intend. Excel provides three margin settings:

❭ **Normal**—Uses Excel's default margins: 0.75 inch for the top and bottom and 0.7 inch for the left and right.

❭ **Wide**—Adds more space at the top, bottom, left, and right sides.

❭ **Narrow**—Reduces the amount of space at the top, bottom, left, and right sides, so more of your worksheet fits on each printed page.

If none of the automatic margins options is exactly what you want, the *Custom Margins...* option opens the *Page Setup* dialog where you can specify exact margins.

To change the margins, on the *Page Layout* tab, in the *Page Setup* group, click the **Margins** button, and click one of the preset margins options: **Normal, Wide,** or **Narrow,** or click **Custom Margins...** to specify your own values.

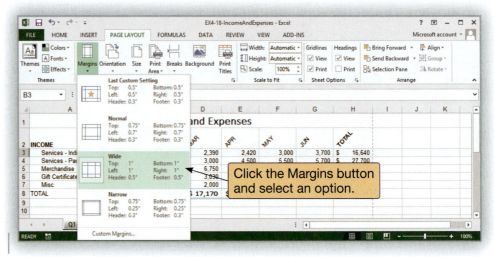

FIGURE EX 4.25

Because you will often want to adjust margins once you are ready to print, Excel allows you to adjust the margins directly from Backstage.

1. Click the **File** tab to open Backstage.

2. Click **Print**.

3. In the *Settings* section, click the button displaying the current margins setting, and then select the option you want.

let me try

Open the student data file **EX4-18-IncomeAndExpenses** and try this skill on your own:
1. Note the page break line between columns I and J.
2. Change the worksheet margins to the **Wide** option.
3. Note the printable area has become smaller and the page break line is between columns H and I.
4. Save the file as directed by your instructor and close it.

Skill 4.19 Scaling Worksheets for Printing

When printing your worksheet, you can set the **scale** and specify that the worksheet prints at a percentage of the original size or at a maximum number of pages wide and/or tall. Each worksheet in the workbook has its own scale settings.

On the *Page Layout* tab, in the *Scale to Fit* group, select the option(s) you want.

❭ Click the **Width** arrow and select the maximum number of pages you want the worksheet to print across.

❭ Click the **Height** arrow and select the maximum number of pages you want the worksheet to print vertically.

❭ Click the **Scale** box and enter a percentage to grow or shrink the worksheet when printed.

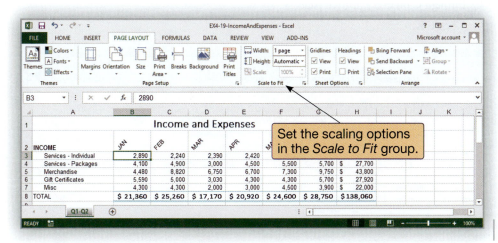

FIGURE EX 4.26

Because you often need to adjust scaling once you are ready to print, Excel has included scaling options on the Print page in Backstage view:

1. Click the **File** tab to open Backstage.

2. Click **Print**.

3. In the *Settings* section, click the button displaying the current scaling setting and select the setting you want to use.

tips & tricks

When scaling your worksheet, be careful not to make the worksheet too small to read.

let me try

Open the student data file **EX4-19-IncomeAndExpenses** and try this skill on your own:

1. If necessary, switch the orientation back to portrait.

2. Set the scaling options so all the columns will print on one page across.

3. Save the file as directed by your instructor and close it.

Skill 4.20 Printing Titles

If your worksheet includes a large table of data that prints on more than one page, you should ensure that the column or row labels print on every page.

To repeat rows and columns on every printed page:

1. On the *Page Layout* tab, in the *Page Setup* group, click the **Print Titles** button.

2. In the *Page Setup* dialog, on the *Sheet* tab, click in the **Rows to repeat at top** box, and then click and drag to select the rows to repeat. You can also type the row reference(s) using the format $1:$1. This example would repeat the first row only. $1:$3 would repeat rows 1 through 3 on every printed page.

3. Click in the **Columns to repeat at left** box, and then click and drag to select the columns to repeat. You can also type the column reference(s) using the format $A:$A. This example would repeat the first column only. $A:$C would repeat columns A through C on every printed page.

4. Click **OK.**

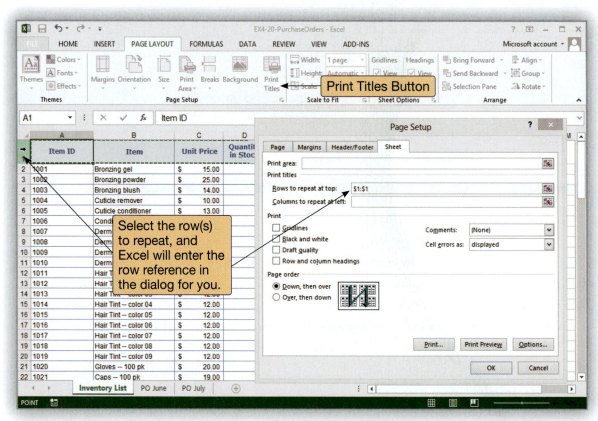

FIGURE EX 4.27

let me try

Open the student data file **EX4-20-PurchaseOrders** and try this skill on your own:

1. Verify that the *Inventory List* worksheet is active.
2. Set row **1** to print on every page.
3. Go to Backstage and preview how the worksheet will look when printed. Verify that the titles from row 1 are included at the top of every page.
4. Save the file as directed by your instructor and close it.

Skill 4.21 Printing Selections, Worksheets, and Workbooks

By default, Excel will print the current, active worksheet. You can change the printing options, however, to print only part of a worksheet or the entire workbook at once.

1. Click the **File** tab to open Backstage.

2. Click **Print.**

3. In the *Settings* section, the first button displays which part of the workbook will print. By default, **Print Active Sheets** is selected. To change the print selection, click the button, and then click one of the other options:

   - **Print Entire Workbook**—Prints all the sheets in the workbook.

   - **Print Selection**—Prints only the selected cells in the active worksheet, overriding any print area definitions in the active worksheet.

   - **Print Selected Table**—Prints the table only (only available if the current selection is within a defined table).

4. If you want to ignore the defined print area, click **Ignore Print Area** at the bottom of the list.

5. Click the **Print** button to print.

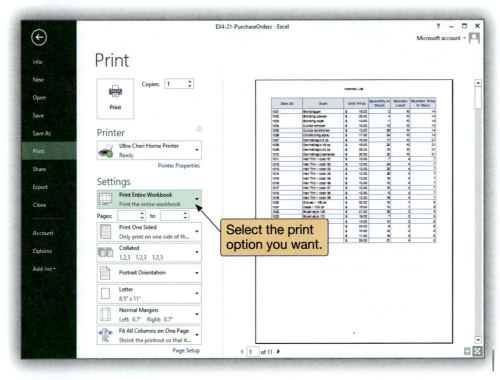

FIGURE EX 4.28

let me try

Open the student data file **EX4-21-PurchaseOrders** and try this skill on your own:

1. Change the print option to print the entire workbook.
2. Verify that all the worksheets in the workbook are included in the print preview.
3. Save the file as directed by your instructor and close it.

key terms

Group	Header
Theme	Footer
Theme Colors	Gridlines
Theme Fonts	Headings
Theme Effects	Orientation
Freeze	Portrait orientation
Normal view	Landscape orientation
Page Layout view	Margins
Page Break Preview view	Scale

concepts review

1. If you delete a worksheet, you can undo the action.

   a. True

   b. False

2. To group worksheets that are not next to each other, select the first worksheet and press the _____ key, and then click the other sheet tabs you want included in the group.

   a. Shift

   b. Alt

   c. Ctrl

   d. None of the above

3. A _____ is a unified color, font, and effects scheme you apply to a workbook.

   a. style

   b. theme

   c. cell format

   d. conditional format

4. To keep column headings as you scroll through a large spreadsheet you should use the _____ command.

   a. Freeze Top Row

   b. Freeze First Column

   c. Split

   d. View Headings

5. When you hide a row or column, the data remain in your workbook. They are no longer displayed on-screen but will be part of the printed workbook.

   a. True

   b. False

6. To display a worksheet in two or four panes, you should _____ the worksheet.

   a. merge

   b. freeze

   c. split

   d. group

7. A _____ is text that appears at the bottom of every page just above the margin.

    a. header

    b. footer

    c. headings

    d. sheet tab

8. _____ are the numbers at the left of rows and the letters at the top of columns.

    a. Headings

    b. Headers

    c. Footers

    d. Gridlines

9. If your worksheet is wide, you may want to use portrait orientation where the height of the page is greater than the width.

    a. True

    b. False

10. If you want more or less white space around your worksheet area when printing, you should adjust the _____.

    a. margins

    b. scaling

    c. orientation

    d. page size

projects

Data files for projects can be found on
www.mhhe.com/office2013skills

skill review 4.1

In this project, you will work on an attendance log for a 16-week college course. For one section of the course, you will set up the sheet to print as an attendance sign-in sheet. For another section, you will set up the sheet to print as an attendance report for the administration office. This is a long project. Be sure to save often!

Skills needed to complete this project:

- Naming Worksheets (Skill 4.2)
- Changing the Color of Sheet Tabs (Skill 4.3)
- Moving and Copying Worksheets (Skill 4.4)
- Grouping Worksheets (Skill 4.6)
- Modifying Column Widths and Row Heights (Skill 4.8)
- Changing the Worksheet View (Skill 4.13)
- Adding Headers and Footers (Skill 4.14)
- Applying Themes (Skill 4.7)
- Splitting Workbooks (Skill 4.12)

- Inserting and Deleting Rows and Columns (Skill 4.9)
- Deleting Worksheets (Skill 4.5)
- Freezing and Unfreezing Rows and Columns (Skill 4.10)
- Hiding and Unhiding Rows and Columns (Skill 4.11)
- Changing Worksheet Orientation (Skill 4.17)
- Setting Up Margins for Printing (Skill 4.18)
- Scaling Worksheets for Printing (Skill 4.19)
- Showing and Hiding Worksheet Elements (Skill 4.16)
- Printing Selections, Worksheets, and Workbooks (Skill 4.21)
- Printing Titles (Skill 4.20)
- Inserting Page Breaks (Skill 4.15)

1. Open the start file **EX2013-SkillReview-4-1** and resave the file as: **[your initials]EX-SkillReview-4-1**

2. If the workbook opens in Protected View, click the **Enable Editing** button in the Message Bar at the top of the workbook.

3. Rename *Sheet1* and change the color of the sheet tab.

   a. Right-click on the *Sheet1* tab, choose **Rename,** and type: **TTH1230**

   b. Press ⏎ Enter.

   c. Right-click the sheet tab again, point to **Tab Color,** and select **Red, Accent 2, Darker 25%.**

4. Make a copy of the *TTH1230* sheet.

   a. Right-click the sheet tab and select **Move or Copy...** to open the *Move or Copy* dialog.

   b. In the *Before sheet* box, select **Sheet2.**

   c. Check the **Create a copy** check box.

   d. Click **OK.**

5. Name the new sheet **TTH340** and change the tab color.

   a. Right-click the new *TTH1230 (2)* sheet tab, choose **Rename,** and type: **TTH340**

   b. Press ⏎ Enter.

   c. Right-click the sheet tab again, point to **Tab Color,** and select **Yellow.**

6. Group sheets *TTH1230* and *TTH340* so you can apply formatting changes to both sheets at once.

   a. Click the **TTH1230** sheet tab, press and hold Ctrl, and click the **TTH340** sheet tab. Now any changes made to one of the sheets will be made to both sheets.

   b. Verify that [Group] appears in the title bar, indicating that the selected sheets are grouped.

7. Resize **column A** in both worksheets at once to best fit the data by double-clicking the right border of the column heading.

8. Add a header and footer to both worksheets at once.

   a. Switch to *Page Layout* view by clicking the **Page Layout** button on the status bar.

   b. Click in the center section of the header.

c. On the *Header & Footer Tools Design* tab, in the *Header & Footer Elements* group, click the **File Name** button. The code **&[File]** will be entered in the center section of the header. Once you click somewhere else, this will display the name of your file.

d. Click in the right section of the header and type your own name.

e. On the *Header & Footer Tools Design* tab, in the *Navigation* group, click the **Go to Footer** button.

f. Click in the center section of the footer.

g. On the *Header & Footer Tools Design* tab, in the *Header & Footer Elements* group, click the **Sheet Name** button. The code **&[Tab]** will be entered. Once you click somewhere else, this will display the name of the sheet.

h. Click in the right section of the footer.

i. On the *Header & Footer Tools Design* tab, in the *Header & Footer Elements* group, click the **Current Date** button. Once you click somewhere else, this will display the current date.

j. Click in any cell of the worksheet and click the **Normal** button on the status bar.

9. Ungroup the sheets by clicking on any other sheet, such as *Sheet3*. Verify that the same formatting was applied to both sheets and that they are now ungrouped.

10. Apply the **Dividend** theme to the workbook.

a. On the *Page Layout* tab, in the *Themes* group, click the **Themes** button to display the *Themes* gallery.

b. Notice that as you hover the mouse pointer over each option in the *Themes* gallery, Excel updates the worksheet to display a live preview of how the theme would affect the worksheet.

c. Click the **Dividend** option.

11. Select the **TTH1230** sheet. It can be difficult to work with such a wide worksheet. Scroll to the right to see the end of the semester, and you can no longer see the student names. Split the screen into two views of different parts of this worksheet.

a. Click cell **D1.** On the *View* tab, in the *Window* group, click the **Split** button. Now you can scroll each pane separately, but it is all still the same worksheet. You can drag the split bar to the right or left as needed.

b. Scroll to show the student names and the last few weeks of the semester on your screen.

c. Click the **Split** button again to return to normal.

12. Insert a new row to add a new student to the list.

a. Right-click on the row heading for row number **9** and select **Insert.**

b. Click the **Insert Options** button that appears immediately below where you right-clicked, and select **Format Same As Below.**

c. Enter the new student name: **Alloy, Craig**

d. Enter his student ID #: **1350699**

13. Justin Parry has decided to drop the class. Delete the entire row for Justin by right-clicking on the row heading for row number **23** and selecting **Delete.**

14. Select the **TTH340** sheet. Because this sheet was copied from the 12:30 pm class worksheet, the student names and ID numbers are not those of the students in the 3:40 pm class. Copy the student data from *Sheet3,* and then delete *Sheet3* when it is no longer needed.

a. Copy the student names and ID numbers from *Sheet3*.

b. Paste the copied names and ID numbers to the *TTH340* sheet, overwriting the existing student names and ID numbers.

c. Delete *Sheet3* by right-clicking on the sheet name and selecting **Delete.**

d. When Excel displays the message telling you that you can't undo deleting sheets, click the **Delete** button to complete the action.

15. Use the *Freeze Panes* option to keep rows 1:8 and columns A:B visible at all times.

a. Verify that the *TTH340* sheet is selected, and click cell **C9.**

b. On the *View* tab, in the *Window* group, click the **Freeze Panes** button, then click the **Freeze Panes** option.

c. Verify that you selected the correct point at which to freeze panes. Scroll down and to the right. Are rows 1:8 and columns A:B visible regardless of where you scroll?

16. Modify sheet *TTH340* to print as an attendance sign-in sheet.

17. First, hide the student ID numbers by right-clicking on the **column B** heading and selecting **Hide.**

18. Set the page layout options.

a. On the *Page Layout* tab, in the *Page Setup* group, click the **Orientation** button, and select **Landscape.**

b. On the *Page Layout* tab, in the *Page Setup* group, click the **Margins** button, and select **Narrow.**

c. On the *Page Layout* tab, in the *Scale to Fit* group, expand the **Width** list and select **1 page,** and expand the **Height** list and select **1 page.**

d. On the *Page Layout* tab, in the *Sheet Options* group, click the **Print** check box under **Gridlines.**

19. Print only the part of the worksheet to use as the attendance sign-in sheet.

a. Select the appropriate cells to print as an attendance sign-in by selecting cells **A1:C29.**

b. Click the **File** tab, and then click **Print** to display the Print page.

c. Under *Settings,* click the **Print Active Sheets** button to expand the options, and select **Print Selection.**

d. If your instructor has directed you to print the attendance sign-in list, click the **Print** button.

e. Click the **Back** button to exit Backstage.

20. At the end of the semester you will need to print all the attendance records to turn in to the administration office. Let's do this for the *TTH1230* class worksheet.

21. First, complete the worksheet data by entering **P** for present or **A** for absent for each day and student.

22. Hide the attendance sign-in column by right-clicking the **column C** heading and selecting **Hide.**

23. Modify the worksheet so column A and rows 1 through 8 will print on every page.

a. On the *Page Layout* tab, in the *Page Setup* group, click the **Print Titles** button.

b. Click in the **Rows to repeat at top** box, and then click and drag with the mouse to select rows **1:8.** When you release the mouse button, you should see $1:$8 in the box.

c. Click in the **Columns to repeat at left** box, and then click with the mouse to select column **A.** When you release the mouse button, you should see $A:$A in the box.

d. Click **OK.**

24. Preview how the worksheet will look when printed and make adjustments from the Print page to keep the report to four or fewer pages.

    a. Click the **File** tab to open Backstage, and then click **Print.**

    b. Under *Settings,* click the **Print Selection** button to expand the options, and select **Print Active Sheets.**

    c. Under *Settings,* click the **Fit All Columns on One Page** button to expand the options, and select **No Scaling.**

    d. Note that the current settings will cause the worksheet to print on six pages.

    e. Under *Settings,* click the **Portrait Orientation** button and switch to **Landscape Orientation** instead.

    f. Under *Settings,* click the **Normal Margins** button, and select **Custom Margins...** to set your own margins.

    g. In the *Page Setup* dialog, on the *Margins* tab, change the **Top, Bottom, Left,** and **Right** values to **.5.** Click **OK.**

    h. Under *Settings,* click the **No Scaling** button, and select **Fit All Rows on One Page.**

25. Modify the worksheet page breaks so weeks 1–8 print on the first page and weeks 9–16 print on the second page.

    a. Click the **Back** button to exit Backstage.

    b. If necessary, scroll to the right so columns T:V are visible. Note that the current page break occurs between columns U and V (after week 9).

    c. Click cell **T1.**

    d. On the *Page Layout* tab, in the *Page Setup* group, click the **Breaks** button, and select **Insert Page Break.** This inserts a page break to the left of the selected cell (after week 8).

    e. Click the **File** tab, and then click **Print** to preview how the change will affect the printed pages.

    f. If your instructor has directed you to print the worksheet, click the **Print** button.

    g. Click the **Back** button to exit Backstage.

26. Save and close the workbook.

skill review **4.2**

In this project, you will be working with a workbook designed to plan employees' or volunteers' work schedules.

Skills needed to complete this project:

- Naming Worksheets (Skill 4.2)
- Changing the Color of Sheet Tabs (Skill 4.3)
- Applying Themes (Skill 4.7)
- Grouping Worksheets (Skill 4.6)
- Modifying Column Widths and Row Heights (Skill 4.8)
- Splitting Workbooks (Skill 4.12)
- Freezing and Unfreezing Rows and Columns (Skill 4.10)
- Moving and Copying Worksheets (Skill 4.4)
- Hiding and Unhiding Rows and Columns (Skill 4.11)

- Showing and Hiding Worksheet Elements (Skill 4.16)
- Deleting Worksheets (Skill 4.5)
- Changing the Worksheet View (Skill 4.13)
- Adding Headers and Footers (Skill 4.14)
- Changing Worksheet Orientation (Skill 4.17)
- Setting Up Margins for Printing (Skill 4.18)
- Scaling Worksheets for Printing (Skill 4.19)
- Inserting Page Breaks (Skill 4.15)
- Printing Titles (Skill 4.20)
- Printing Selections, Worksheets, and Workbooks (Skill 4.21)

1. Open the start file **EX2013-SkillReview-4-2** and resave the file as:
   `[your initials]EX-SkillReview-4-2`

2. If the workbook opens in Protected View, click the **Enable Editing** button in the Message Bar at the top of the workbook.

3. Look at the various worksheets. The monthly schedule worksheets need to be named and color coded.

   a. Double-click the tab for **Sheet1**, type **January** and press ⏎ Enter.

   b. Right-click the tab, point to **Tab Color,** and select **Dark Blue, Text 2, Lighter 40%.**

   c. Double-click the tab for **Sheet2**, type **February** and press ⏎ Enter.

   d. Right-click the tab, point to **Tab Color,** and select **Red, Accent 2, Lighter 40%.**

   e. Double-click the tab for **Sheet3**, type **March** and press ⏎ Enter.

   f. Right-click the tab, point to **Tab Color,** and select **White, Background 1, Darker 50%.**

4. Apply a theme to the workbook.

   a. On the *Page Layout* tab, in the *Themes* group, click the **Themes** button. Slide the mouse over different themes and notice the preview of the theme appearance on the worksheet.

   b. Choose the **Facet** theme.

5. The monthly schedule sheets all need formatting. Group them and then format them all at once.

   a. Click the **January** sheet tab, hold down ⇧ Shift, click the **March** sheet tab, and then release ⇧ Shift. Notice the three sheet tabs' appearance has changed to indicate that the three are selected. The *Regular Schedule* tab is not selected.

   b. Verify that the title bar displays [Group]. Any changes you make to the current sheet will be made to all three of the selected sheets, so be very careful.

6. Adjust column widths and row heights to fit the contents and to make the worksheet more readable.

   a. Look in column **A.** If you see ########## it means that the cell content is too wide for the column. Double-click the right column border to autofit the column to the data.

   b. Select all the time columns (**B:U**). Locate the column that is too narrow to display both the *From* time and the *To* time. Double-click the right column border to best fit the column width to the content. All the selected columns will size to match.

   c. Select all the rows (**5:35**).

d. On the *Home* tab, in the *Cells* group click the **Format** button, and select **Row Height.** In the *Row Height* dialog, change the height value to **18** to make each row a little roomier.

e. Click **OK.**

7. Ungroup the sheets by clicking on any other sheet, such as the *Regular Schedule* sheet.

    a. Look at the *January, February,* and *March* sheets; they should all have been formatted.

    b. Verify that the sheets are now ungrouped.

8. Select just the **Regular Schedule** sheet. It is hard to work with such a wide worksheet. Scroll to the right to see the night shift and you can no longer see the dates. Split the screen into two views of different parts of this worksheet.

    a. Click cell **G1.** On the *View* tab, in the *Window* group, click the **Split** button. Now you can scroll each pane separately, but it is all still the same worksheet. You can drag the split bar to the right or left as needed.

    b. Scroll to show the morning and night shifts on your screen.

    c. Click the **Split** button again to return to normal.

9. Another way to deal with large worksheets is to freeze panes.

    a. Select any one of the month worksheets.

    b. Select cell **B5.** On the *View* tab, in the *Window* group, click **Freeze Panes,** and select **Freeze Panes.**

    c. Now you can scroll up or down and everything above and to the left of B5 remains visibly frozen on the screen.

    d. Freeze panes must be set on each of the month sheets separately. Grouping does not work for freeze panes. Repeat the freeze panes process for each of the month worksheets.

10. Drag the sheet tab for **Regular Schedule** before the sheet tab for **January** so that *Regular Schedule* is the first worksheet in the workbook.

11. Look closely at the *Regular Schedule* sheet. There are two row numbers missing.

    a. Select the rows before and after the missing rows. Select the entire rows by dragging over the row heading numbers at the far left.

    b. With both rows selected, right-click on the selection, and select **Unhide** to reveal the rows for Tuesdays and Wednesdays.

12. Ensure that the worksheet gridlines will print with the worksheet.

    a. On the *Page Layout* tab, in the *Sheet Options* group, click the **Print** check box under *Gridlines.*

    b. Repeat this process for the *January, February,* and *March* worksheets. (If you group the sheets first, be sure to ungroup them when you are finished.)

13. The *Sheet 4* worksheet is unnecessary. Delete it.

    a. Click the **Sheet 4** tab.

    b. On the *Home* tab, in the *Cells* group, click the **Delete** button arrow and select **Delete Sheet.**

14. Prepare to print your worksheets by adding headers and footers.

    a. Group all the worksheets to save time. This way the headers and footers may be added to all the sheets at once. Verify that all the sheets are selected.

    b. Click the **Page Layout** view button in the lower right of your screen. If you see a message about Freeze Panes being incompatible with *Page Layout* view, click **OK** to continue.

c. Click the **Click to add header** text at the top of any of the pages to add information to the center header section.

d. On the *Header & Footer Tools Design* tab, in the *Header & Footer Elements* group, click the **File Name** button. The code **&[File]** will be entered in the center section of the header. Once you click somewhere else, this will display the name of your file.

e. Click in the right section of the header and enter your own name.

f. On the *Header & Footer Tools Design* tab, in the *Navigation* group, click the **Go to Footer** button.

g. Click in the center section of the footer.

h. On the *Header & Footer Tools Design* tab, in the *Header & Footer Elements* group, click the **Sheet Name** button. The code **&[Tab]** will be entered. Once you click somewhere else, this will display the name of the sheet tab.

i. Click in the right section of the footer and click the **Current Date** button.

j. Click in any cell of the worksheet and click the **Normal** view button in the lower right of your screen.

k. Ungroup the sheets. Right-click on any sheet tab and choose **Ungroup Sheets.**

15. Set up printing options for the *Regular Schedule* sheet.

a. Select the **Regular Schedule** sheet. Click the **File** tab, and then click **Print.**

b. Scroll down to see all the pages for your worksheet. Scroll back up to the first page.

c. Click the **Portrait Orientation** button and select **Landscape.**

d. Click the **Normal Margins** button and select **Narrow.**

e. Click the **No Scaling** button, and select **Fit Sheet on One Page.**

16. The monthly schedules would be easier to read if the morning, afternoon, and night shifts each printed on a separate page in a reasonably large font size.

a. Click the **Back** arrow to return to the worksheet.

b. Group sheets **January : March.**

c. On the *Page Layout* tab, in the *Page Setup* group, click the **Orientation** button, and select **Landscape.**

d. On the *Page Layout* tab, in the *Page Setup* group, click the **Margins** button, and select **Narrow.**

e. Review the current page break. Switch to *Page Break Preview* view if you want by clicking the **Page Break Preview** button at the lower right corner of the status bar.

f. Notice that the schedule just barely requires two pages vertically. On the *Page Layout* tab, in the *Scale to Fit* group, click the **Height** box arrow and select **1 Page.**

g. Click cell **I1.** On the *Page Layout* tab, in the *Page Setup* group, click the **Breaks** button. Select **Insert Page Break.** (Note that you cannot drag the page break lines when the worksheets are grouped. You must use the Ribbon method to insert manual page breaks.)

h. Click in cell **N1.** On the *Page Layout* tab, in the *Page Setup* group, click the **Breaks** button. Select **Insert Page Break.**

i. Click the **Normal** button to return to *Normal* view.

17. The days will only show on the first sheet, so the second and third sheets will make no sense. Set the worksheets so column A will print on every page. You must ungroup the sheets first.

a. Click the **Regular Schedule** sheet to ungroup the sheets, and then click the **January** sheet tab again.

b. On the *Page Layout* tab, in the *Page Setup* group, click **Print Titles** button.

c. In the *Columns to repeat at left* box enter **$A:$A** or click in the box and then click anywhere in column **A.**

d. Click **OK** in the *Page Setup* dialog box.

e. Repeat this process with the **February** and **March** worksheets.

18. Preview how the entire workbook will print. Be sure to verify that column A will print at the left side of the *January, February,* and *March* worksheets.

    a. Click the **File** tab to open Backstage.

    b. Click **Print.**

    c. Click the **Print Active Sheets** button and select **Print Entire Workbook.**

    d. Use the **Next Page** button below the print preview to review how every printed page will look. There should be 10 pages. Note the worksheet name in the footer area at the bottom of each page.

19. Save and close the workbook.

challenge yourself 4.3

In this project, you will be working with a workbook designed to keep track of loan repayment.

Skills needed to complete this project:

- Naming Worksheets (Skill 4.2)
- Changing the Color of Sheet Tabs (Skill 4.3)
- Moving and Copying Worksheets (Skill 4.4)
- Freezing and Unfreezing Rows and Columns (Skill 4.10)
- Inserting and Deleting Rows and Columns (Skill 4.9)
- Applying Themes (Skill 4.7)
- Grouping Worksheets (Skill 4.6)
- Modifying Column Widths and Row Heights (Skill 4.8)
- Hiding and Unhiding Rows and Columns (Skill 4.11)
- Changing the Worksheet View (Skill 4.13)
- Adding Headers and Footers (Skill 4.14)
- Showing and Hiding Worksheet Elements (Skill 4.16)
- Deleting Worksheets (Skill 4.5)
- Changing Worksheet Orientation (Skill 4.17)
- Printing Titles (Skill 4.20)
- Scaling Worksheets for Printing (Skill 4.19)
- Printing Selections, Worksheets, and Workbooks (Skill 4.21)

1. Open the start file **EX2013-ChallengeYourself-4-3** and resave the file as:
   [your initials]EX-ChallengeYourself-4-3

2. If the workbook opens in Protected View, enable editing so you can make changes to the workbook.

3. Change the name of *Sheet1* to **Truck 1.**

4. Change the *Truck 1* sheet tab color to **Blue, Accent 1.**

5. Make a copy of the *Truck 1* sheet, placing it before *Sheet2*.

6. Change the name of the new sheet to **Truck 2.**

7. Change the *Truck 2* sheet tab color to **Green, Accent 6.**

8. Change the values in the *Truck 2* worksheet.

   a. Change the amount borrowed (cell **B3**) to **10,000.**

   b. Change the APR (cell **B5**) to **2%.**

9. Freeze panes so rows **1:8** and columns **A:B** remain in place when you scroll through the worksheet.

10. Delete any extra rows at the bottom of the worksheet where the payment due is 0 (row **45**).

11. Apply the **Retrospect** theme.

12. Switch to the *Truck 1* sheet and delete any extra rows at the bottom of the worksheet where the payment due is 0 (rows **43:45**).

13. Apply the **Metropolitan** theme.

14. Group the *Truck 1* and *Truck 2* worksheets. Make the following changes to both sheets at once.

15. Change the width of the Payment Date column (column **C**) to exactly **17.**

16. Delete the extra column (column **H**).

17. Unhide column **G.**

18. Add header and footer information to the worksheet. (You may allow Excel to remove Freeze Panes.)

   a. Enter your name in the right header section.

   b. Set the left header section to display the sheet name.

   c. Add the page number to the center footer section.

   d. Set the right footer section to display the current date.

19. Hide the gridlines so they do not appear on-screen.

20. Ungroup the sheets.

21. Delete the unused worksheets.

22. Change the page orientation for the *Truck 1* sheet to **Landscape.**

23. Modify the *Truck 1* sheet so row **8** will repeat at the top of every printed page.

24. Scale the *Truck 2* sheet so all columns will fit on one page and all rows will fit on one page.

25. Print preview the entire workbook.

26. Save and close the workbook.

challenge yourself 4.4

In this project, you will be working with data about automobile emissions and fuel economy. These green car data were downloaded from the Web site https://explore.data.gov/d/9un4-5bz7 and are explained at this Web site: http://www.epa.gov/greenvehicles/Aboutratings.do. The scores range from 0 to 10, where 10 is best. The vehicles with the best scores on both air pollution and greenhouse gas receive the SmartWay designation. These raw data need formatting in order to be usable.

Skills needed to complete this project:

- Changing the Color of Sheet Tabs (Skill 4.3)

- Naming Worksheets (Skill 4.2)

- Inserting Page Breaks (Skill 4.15)
- Moving and Copying Worksheets (Skill 4.4)
- Inserting Worksheets (Skill 4.1)
- Applying Themes (Skill 4.7)
- Grouping Worksheets (Skill 4.6)
- Modifying Column Widths and Row Heights (Skill 4.8)
- Hiding and Unhiding Rows and Columns (Skill 4.11)
- Showing and Hiding Worksheet Elements (Skill 4.16)
- Changing the Worksheet View (Skill 4.13)
- Adding Headers and Footers (Skill 4.14)
- Setting Up Margins for Printing (Skill 4.18)
- Changing Worksheet Orientation (Skill 4.17)
- Scaling Worksheets for Printing (Skill 4.19)
- Inserting and Deleting Rows and Columns (Skill 4.9)
- Printing Titles (Skill 4.20)
- Printing Selections, Worksheets, and Workbooks (Skill 4.21)

1. Open the start file **EX2013-ChallengeYourself-4-4** and resave the file as:
   `[your initials]EX-ChallengeYourself-4-4`

2. If the workbook opens in Protected View, enable editing so you can make changes to the workbook.

3. Color the *all_alpha_10* worksheet tab **Green, Accent 6, Darker 50%** and rename the worksheet **Raw Data.**

4. In the *Raw Data* worksheet, enter page breaks after the first three manufacturers (Acura, Aston Martin, and Audi). There are really too many cars to continue doing this with reasonable effort.

5. Copy the *Raw Data* worksheet. Place the new worksheet at the end of the workbook.

6. Color the worksheet tab **Green, Accent 6, Darker 25%** and name the worksheet **Formatted All.**

7. Remove all the manual page breaks on this worksheet.

8. Add a new worksheet to the end of the workbook.

9. Copy row **1** from the *Formatted All* worksheet and paste it into row **1** in the new worksheet. Use the **Keep Source Column Widths** paste option.

10. Copy all the rows for Cadillac models (rows **298:334**) from the *Formatted All* worksheet to the new sheet.

11. Name the new sheet: **Cadillac** and color the sheet tab the standard color **Red.**

12. Repeat steps 10–13, copying the rows for Honda (rows **842:903**). Name the sheet **Honda** and color the sheet tab the standard color **Blue.**

13. Apply the **Banded** workbook theme.

14. Group the *Formatted All, Cadillac,* and *Honda* worksheets.

15. AutoFit column **L** to best fit the data.

16. Set the column width for columns **M:O** to **5.**

17. Set the row height for row **1** to **70.**

18. Hide the **Underhood ID** and **Stnd Description** columns.

19. Set the worksheet gridlines to print.

20. Cause Excel to insert the sheet name into the center of the footer and your name in the upper-right section of the header.

21. Set **Narrow** margins.

22. Set the worksheet orientation to **Landscape.**

23. Scale the worksheet so all columns will print on one page.

24. Insert a row at the top for entering sheet titles. Merge and center cells **A1:Q1** and apply the **Title** cell style.

25. Ungroup the sheets.

26. Set the worksheet options so rows **1:2** will print on every page. You will need to do this individually for the *Formatted All, Cadillac,* and *Honda* worksheets.

27. Enter the following titles in cell **A1** of each of the worksheets.

    a. Enter the title for the *Formatted All* sheet: **All Models**

    b. Enter the title for the *Cadillac* sheet: **Cadillac Models**

    c. Enter the title for the *Honda* sheet: **Honda Models**

28. Preview how the *Cadillac* worksheets will print and change the scaling so the entire worksheet will print on one page.

29. Using the *Formatted All* worksheet, select all the data for Acura (rows **A3:Q20**). Change the print settings to print just this data.

30. Save and close the workbook.

on your own 4.5

In this project, you will be working with a workbook designed keep track of hobbies.

Skills needed to complete this project:

- Naming Worksheets (Skill 4.2)
- Changing the Color of Sheet Tabs (Skill 4.3)
- Applying Themes (Skill 4.7)
- Inserting and Deleting Rows and Columns (Skill 4.9)
- Modifying Column Widths and Row Heights (Skill 4.8)
- Grouping Worksheets (Skill 4.6)
- Changing the Worksheet View (Skill 4.13)
- Adding Headers and Footers (Skill 4.14)
- Freezing and Unfreezing Rows and Columns (Skill 4.10)
- Inserting Worksheets (Skill 4.1)
- Deleting Worksheets (Skill 4.5)
- Moving and Copying Worksheets (Skill 4.4)
- Changing Worksheet Orientation (Skill 4.17)
- Setting Up Margins for Printing (Skill 4.18)
- Scaling Worksheets for Printing (Skill 4.19)
- Showing and Hiding Worksheet Elements (Skill 4.16)
- Inserting Page Breaks (Skill 4.15)
- Printing Selections, Worksheets, and Workbooks (Skill 4.21)

1. Open the start file **EX2013-OnYourOwn-4-5** and resave the file as:
   `[your initials]EX-OnYourOwn-4-5`

2. If the workbook opens in Protected View, click the **Enable Editing** button in the Message Bar at the top of the workbook so you can modify the workbook.

3. Change the names of the sheets as follows and apply a different tab color to each.

   a. Rename *Sheet1* to **Running**

   b. Rename *Sheet2* to **Football**

   c. Rename *Sheet3* to **Movies**

4. Apply a theme of your choice to the workbook.

5. Add a row at the top of each sheet and enter an appropriate title.

6. Adjust column widths to best fit the data (all worksheets individually).

7. Group the worksheets.

8. Add header and footer elements of your choice to all the worksheets at once.

9. Ungroup the worksheets.

10. Freeze panes to make it easier to work with each worksheet. Add more Oscar and/or Super Bowl data. (Research to find this information on the Web.)

11. Insert a new worksheet after *Running* and enter data about your own hobby or interest.

    a. Name the worksheet and apply a color to the worksheet tab.

    b. Add an appropriate header and/or footer.

    c. If necessary, freeze panes.

12. Delete unused sheets.

13. Rearrange the worksheets in alphabetical order.

14. Make an attractive readable printout of each worksheet. Each should fit neatly on one page or have logical page breaks and print titles when more than one page is required. Only print the worksheets if directed to do so by your instructor.

    a. Set the worksheets' orientation appropriately.

    b. Set appropriate margins.

    c. Scale the worksheets appropriately.

    d. Add manual page breaks if necessary.

    e. Set at least one of the sheets to print with gridlines and at least one to print without gridlines.

    f. For worksheets that print on more than one page, ensure that the label row will be included on every page.

    g. For one worksheet, adjust the print settings to print a useful selection of just some cells that will fit all on one page.

15. Save and close the workbook.

fix it 4.6

In this project, you will fix a number of formatting errors that prevent this gradebook spreadsheet from displaying and printing properly.

Skills needed to complete this project:

- Moving and Copying Worksheets (Skill 4.4)
- Deleting Worksheets (Skill 4.5)
- Inserting and Deleting Rows and Columns (Skill 4.9)
- Modifying Column Widths and Row Heights (Skill 4.8)
- Hiding and Unhiding Rows and Columns (Skill 4.11)
- Changing Worksheet Orientation (Skill 4.17)
- Scaling Worksheets for Printing (Skill 4.19)
- Inserting Page Breaks (Skill 4.15)
- Printing Titles (Skill 4.20)
- Showing and Hiding Worksheet Elements (Skill 4.16)
- Changing the Worksheet View (Skill 4.13)
- Adding Headers and Footers (Skill 4.14)
- Printing Selections, Worksheets, and Workbooks (Skill 4.21)
- Naming Worksheets (Skill 4.2)

1. Open the start file **EX2013-FixIt-4-6** and resave the file as: `[your initials]EX-FixIt-4-6`
2. If the workbook opens in Protected View, click the **Enable Editing** button in the Message Bar at the top of the workbook so you can modify the workbook.
3. The *Scores* worksheet should be first in the workbook.
4. This workbook has an unnecessary worksheet. Delete it.
5. There are two unnecessary columns in the middle of the worksheet. Delete them.
6. The *Scores* worksheet has at least one column and one row that do not display the data properly. Resize them to best fit the data.
7. Column **S** should not be visible.
8. Review how the *Scores* worksheet will look when printed. Fix the following issues:
   a. The worksheet should print on no more than two pages, with the page break coming after the midterm grades (before column **T**). (Hint: Try changing the worksheet orientation and adjusting the scaling.)
   b. Columns **A:B** should be included on every printed page.
   c. The worksheet gridlines should print.
   d. The worksheet should have a footer with the word *CONFIDENTIAL* in the center section and the date automatically inserted into the right section.
   e. Only cells **A8:AG28** should be printed.
9. The *Scores* worksheet should be named **Gradebook**.
10. Save and close the workbook.

chapter 5

Adding Charts and Analyzing Data

In this chapter, you will learn the following skills:

- Create and format charts
- Create and format tables
- Sort and filter data
- Conduct what-if analysis using Goal Seek and data tables
- Create PivotTables and PivotCharts

skills

introduction

This chapter introduces data analysis. You will learn to use charts to visualize data; to use tables and PivotTables to quickly sort, filter, and summarize data; and to conduct what-if analyses using Goal Seek and data tables.

Skill 5.1 Exploring Charts

A **chart** is a graphic that represents numeric data visually. In a chart, the values selected in the worksheet, the **data points**, are transformed into graphic **data markers**. Data markers can be columns, bars, pie pieces, lines, or other visual elements. Related data points, usually in the same row or column, are grouped into a **data series**. Some chart types allow you to plot multiple data series.

Figure EX 5.1 shows a column chart with a single data series—*Services-Individual*. You can tell at a glance that the FEB column is the shortest and, therefore, that February has the fewest sales for individual services.

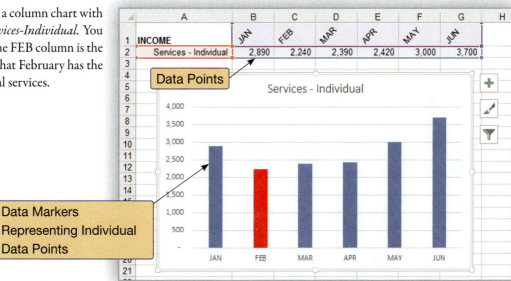

FIGURE EX 5.1

Figure 5.2 is a pie chart using the same data as Figure 5.1. Each individual data point is represented by a piece of the pie. In this chart, it is not as obvious that FEB is the smallest data point.

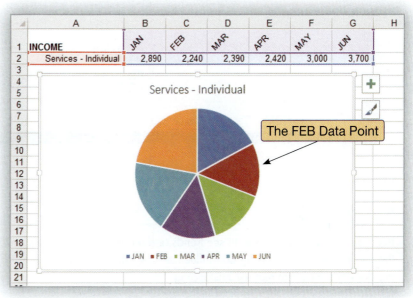

FIGURE EX 5.2

All charts, except pie charts and doughnut charts, plot data along two axes. The **y axis** goes from bottom to top. It is the vertical axis. The **x axis** goes from left to right. It is the horizontal axis. Typically, but not always, values are plotted against the y axis and categories are listed along the x axis.

When working with charts, there are a few other common chart elements you should be familiar with:

❱ The **plot area** is the area where the data series are plotted.

❱ The **chart area** is the area that encompasses the entire chart including the plot area and optional layout elements, such as title and legend.

❱ The **chart title** is a text box above or overlaying the chart. To change the title text, click the box to select it and edit the text directly in the text box. You can also type new text in the formula bar and then press (⏎ Enter).

❱ The **legend** tells you which data point or data series is represented by each color in the chart.

When a chart is selected, two contextual tabs are available: the *Chart Tools Design* tab and the *Chart Tools Format* tab. On the *Chart Tools Format* tab, in the *Current Selection* group, the *Chart Elements* box displays the name of the chart element that is currently selected. This can be helpful if you need to ensure that you have selected the chart area, the plot area, or another chart element. To select a specific chart element, expand the **Chart Elements** list and select the chart element you want to select.

FIGURE EX 5.3

tips & tricks

Because charts make it easier to see trends and relationships, they are an important tool for analyzing data. However, the chart type and formatting can influence how others perceive the data. Be careful that the chart does not present the data in a way that may be misleading.

tell me **more**

If the chart is located on the same worksheet as its data, Excel will highlight that data when you select certain chart elements. For example, select the chart area or the plot area, and Excel highlights the cells containing the data point values in blue, the data series labels in red, and the category labels in purple. If you select a single data series, only that data will be highlighted.

let me **try**

Open the student data file **EX5-01-IncomeAndExpenses** try this skill on your own:

1. Begin with the *Column Chart* sheet. Click any of the data markers to select the entire data series. Use the *Chart Elements* box to verify that you have selected the data series. Observe how the worksheet data are represented by the column data markers.
2. Go to the *Pie Chart* sheet. Select the chart legend. Use the legend to match the pie pieces to the data point values.
3. Go to the *Line Chart* sheet. Select the line representing the Merchandise data series. Observe that when the Merchandise series is selected, cells B4:G4 (the data points) are highlighted in blue.
4. Select the x axis, and then select the y axis. Use the *Chart Elements* list if necessary.
5. Save the file as directed by your instructor and close it.

from the perspective of . . .

COLLEGE STUDENT

I use Excel to track my monthly budget. Before I started using charts, the spreadsheets were just numbers. I knew how much money was going out each month, but I didn't really understand how much of my money I was spending on unnecessary expenses. Once I starting using pie charts, it was obvious that I was spending more on lattes than on transportation! I bought a coffee maker, and now I have a little extra cash each month to put away for a rainy day.

Skill 5.2 Using the Recommended Charts Feature

One trick to working with charts is to select the correct chart type. Excel 2013 makes this easier by recommending specific chart types based on the data you have selected in the worksheet. The recommended charts are available from both the Quick Analysis tool and the *Chart Options* dialog.

To add a recommended chart to a worksheet using the Quick Analysis tool:

1. Select the data you want to visualize as a chart.

2. The Quick Analysis Tool button appears near the lower right corner of the selected range. Click the **Quick Analysis Tool** button, and then click the **Charts** tab.

3. Hover the mouse cursor over each chart type to see a live preview of the chart. Click the button for the chart type you want. Recommended charts may include multiple versions of the same chart type. Check the live preview carefully to ensure that the data display exactly as you want.

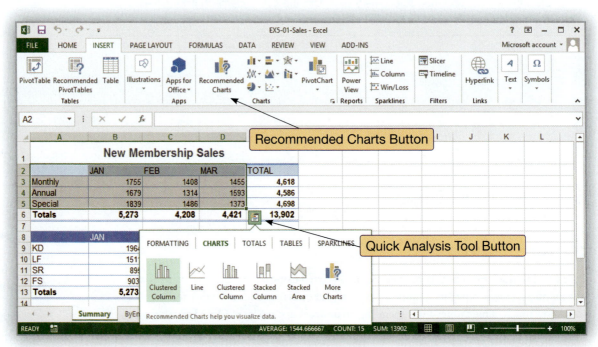

FIGURE EX 5.4

If none of the recommended charts presented in the Quick Analysis tool are precisely what you want, use the *Insert Chart* dialog instead:

1. Select the data for the chart.

2. Click the **Quick Analysis Tool** button.

3. Click the **Charts** tab, and then click the **More Charts** button to open the *Insert Chart* dialog. You can also open the *Insert Chart* dialog from the *Insert* tab, *Charts* group, by clicking the **Recommended Charts** button.

4. The first tab in the *Insert Chart* dialog, *Recommended Charts,* displays the same chart options as the *Charts* tab in the Quick Analysis tool, plus a few more. When you select a chart type, a preview of the chart appears in the right pane of the dialog.

5. Click **OK** to insert the selected chart into the worksheet.

This pane shows a preview of the selected chart type.

FIGURE EX 5.5

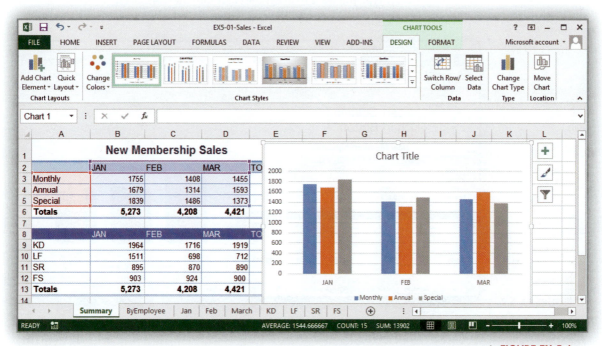

FIGURE EX 5.6
A clustered column chart inserted into the worksheet

tips & tricks

The Quick Analysis tool is only available if the data selected for the chart are in contiguous cells—a group of cells that are all next to one another without any cells left out of the group.

let me try

Open the student data file **EX5-02-Sales** and try this skill on your own:
1. If necessary, verify that the *Summary* sheet is active, and cells **A2:D5** are selected.
2. Insert a **Clustered Column** chart based on the first recommended chart type.
3. Save the file as directed by your instructor and close it.

Skill 5.3 Inserting a Column Chart or a Bar Chart

Column charts work best with data that are organized into rows and columns like a table. Data point values are transformed into columns, with the values plotted along the vertical (y) axis. Each row in the table is grouped as a data series. Excel uses the column labels as the categories along the horizontal (x) axis.

In the clustered column chart shown in Figure EX 5.7, each column represents a single data point. The data points are grouped (clustered) together by category. Each data series is represented by a single color as shown in the legend below the chart.

To insert a column chart:

1. Select the data you want to include in the column chart.

2. On the *Insert* tab, in the *Charts* group, click the **Insert Column Chart** button.

3. Click the chart type you want to insert the chart into the worksheet.

FIGURE EX 5.7

Bar charts are like column charts turned on their side. The categories are displayed on the vertical axis, and the data point values are plotted along the horizontal axis.

The clustered bar chart in Figure EX 5.8 displays the same data as Figure EX 5.7. Each bar represents a single data point. However, in this bar chart, the sales values are plotted along the horizontal axis, grouped into data series by membership type, and the months are displayed along the vertical axis.

To insert a bar chart:

1. Select the data you want to include in the bar chart.

2. On the *Insert* tab, in the *Charts* group, click the **Insert Bar Chart** button.

3. Click the chart type you want to insert the chart into the worksheet.

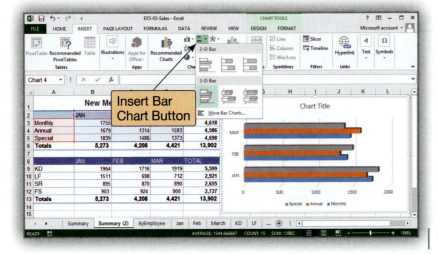

FIGURE EX 5.8

If you don't like the way Excel grouped the data series, you can switch them, making the categories the data series and the data series the categories. On the *Chart Tools Design* tab, in the *Data* group, click the **Switch Row/Column** button. Figure EX 5.9 charts the same data as Figure 5.8 with the rows and columns switched, so the data points are organized into data series by column instead of by row.

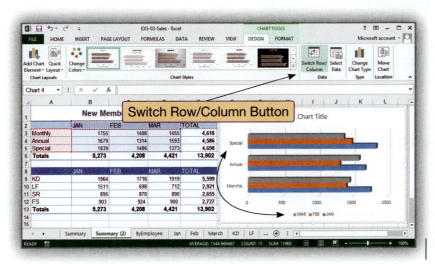

FIGURE EX 5.9

another **method**

You can also insert a column chart or a bar chart from the *Insert Chart* dialog, *All Charts* tab.

let me **try**

Open the student data file **EX5-03-Sales** and try this skill on your own:

1. If necessary, verify that the *Summary* sheet is active, and cells **A2:D5** are selected.
2. Insert a **3-D Clustered Column** chart (the first chart type in the *3-D Column* section of the *Insert Column Chart* menu).
3. Switch to the second sheet, *Summary (2)*, and if necessary, select cells **A2:D5**.
4. Insert a **3-D Clustered Bar** chart (the first chart type in the *3-D Bar* section of the *Insert Bar Chart* menu).
5. Switch the rows and columns in the chart, so the data points are grouped into data series by column.
6. Save the file as directed by your instructor and close it.

Skill 5.4 Inserting a Pie Chart

Pie charts represent data as parts of a whole. They do not have *x* and *y* axes like column charts. Instead, each value is a visual "slice" of the pie. Pie charts work best when you want to evaluate values as they relate to a total value—for example, departmental budgets in relation to the entire budget, or each employee's bonus in relation to the entire bonus pool.

In Figure EX 5.10, the total sales for each sales person is represented by a slice of the pie.

To add a pie chart:

1. Select the data you want to include in the pie chart.

2. On the *Insert* tab, in the *Charts* group, click the **Insert Pie Chart** button.

3. Click the chart type you want to insert the chart into the worksheet.

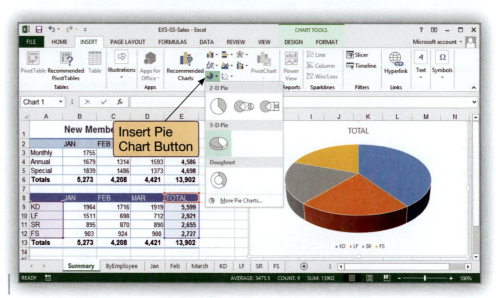

FIGURE EX 5.10

tips & tricks

In an "exploded" pie chart, each slice is slightly separated from the whole. You can "explode" a single slice by clicking it and dragging it away from the rest of the slices. Exploding a single slice of data gives it emphasis.

tell me more

Doughnut charts are similar to pie charts, but they can display more than one series. Each series is represented by a ring around the doughnut. Each data point in the series is represented by a piece of the ring proportional to the total. Doughnut charts can be confusing and are not commonly used.

another method

You can also insert a pie chart from the *Insert Chart* dialog, *All Charts* tab.

let me try

Open the student data file **EX5-04-Sales** and try this skill on your own:
1. If necessary, verify that the *Summary* sheet is active, and cells **A9:A12** and cells **E8:E12** are selected.
2. Insert a **3-D Pie** chart.
3. Save the file as directed by your instructor and close it.

Skill 5.5 Inserting a Line Chart

Line charts feature a line connecting each data point—showing the movement of values over time. Line charts work best when data trends over time are important.

The line chart in Figure EX 5.11 shows sales over a three-month period. Each data series represents a type of membership sales. This type of line chart, called a **line with markers**, includes dots along the line for each data point.

To add a line chart:

1. Select the data you want to include in the line chart. Be sure to include both values and the related cells that represent time segments (dates, calendar quarters, etc.).

2. On the **Insert** tab, in the *Charts* group, click the **Insert Line Chart** button.

3. Click the chart type you want to insert the chart into the worksheet.

FIGURE EX 5.11

tips & tricks

While line charts are a good choice if the data set has many data points, use a line chart with markers only if there are relatively few data points.

another method

You can also insert a line chart from the *Insert Chart* dialog, *All Charts* tab.

let me try

Open the student data file **EX5-05-Sales** and try this skill on your own:

1. If necessary, verify that the *Summary* sheet is active, and cells **A2:D5** are selected.

2. Insert a **Line with Markers** chart (the first chart type in second row of the *2-D Column* section of the *Insert Line Chart* menu).

3. Save the file as directed by your instructor and close it.

Skill 5.6 Moving a Chart

When you first create a chart, Excel places the chart in the middle of the worksheet. Often, you will need to move the chart so it doesn't cover the worksheet data.

You can move a chart to a new position on the sheet by selecting it and then dragging it anywhere on the worksheet. To move a chart by dragging:

1. Click in the chart area of the chart you want to move. (Be careful not to click in the plot area, or you will move just the plot area instead of the entire chart.) Your mouse cursor will change to the move cursor.

2. With your left mouse button depressed, drag the chart to the new location on the worksheet, and then release the mouse button to "drop" the chart at the new location.

If your chart is large or complex, you may want the chart to appear on its own worksheet. To move a chart to a new sheet:

1. If necessary, select the chart. If you just created the chart, it will still be selected.

2. On the *Chart Tools Design* tab, in the *Location* group, click the **Move Chart** button.

3. The *Move Chart* dialog opens.

4. In the *Move Chart* dialog, click the **New sheet** radio button to move the chart to its own worksheet. If you want to specify a name for the new sheet, type it in the *New sheet* box. To move the chart to an existing worksheet, click the **Object in** radio button, and then select the name of the sheet you want to move the chart to.

5. Click **OK.**

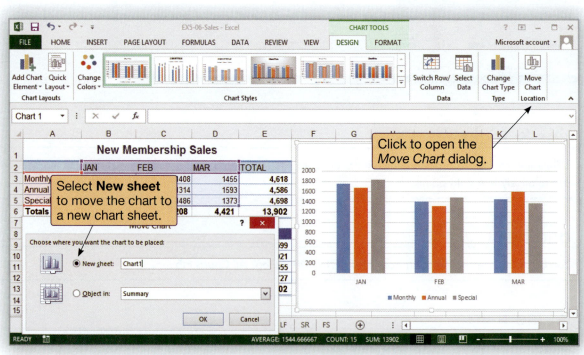

FIGURE EX 5.12

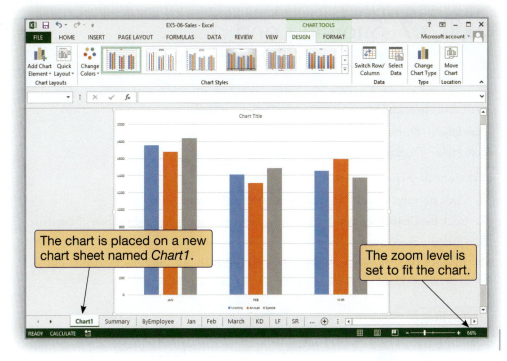

The chart is placed on a new chart sheet named *Chart1*.

The zoom level is set to fit the chart.

FIGURE EX 5.13

When you use the *Move Chart* dialog to move a chart to its own sheet, Excel creates a special type of worksheet called a **chart sheet**. The chart sheet does not include the columns, rows, and cells you are used to seeing in Excel; it contains only the chart object. The new chart sheet automatically changes the zoom level so the entire chart is visible.

tell me **more**

When the chart area is selected, you can resize the chart by clicking one of the resize handles located at the four corners and the middle of each side of the chart area. You cannot resize a chart in a chart sheet.

another **method**

Right-click an empty area of the chart and select **Move Chart...** to open the *Move Chart* dialog.
You can also use the cut, copy, and paste commands to move a chart from one sheet to another.

let me **try**

Open the student data file **EX5-06-Sales** and try this skill on your own:
1. If necessary, select the chart on the *Summary* sheet.
2. Move the chart to the empty area of the worksheet to the right of the data.
3. Move the chart to a new worksheet.
4. Save the file as directed by your instructor and close it.

Skill 5.7 Showing and Hiding Chart Elements

Showing and hiding chart elements such as the chart title, axes, and gridlines can make a chart easier to read. Other common chart elements include:

Data labels—Display data values for each data marker.

Data table—Displays a table of the data point values below the chart.

To hide or show chart elements:

1. Click any empty area of the chart area to select the chart.
2. Click the **Chart Elements** button that appears near the upper right corner of the chart.
3. Click the check boxes to show or hide chart elements.
4. To select a specific placement option for the chart element, click the arrow that appears at the right side of the element name, and then click an option.

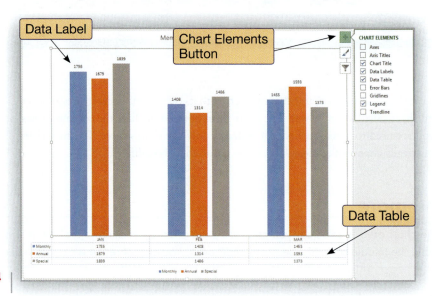

FIGURE EX 5.14

tell me **more**

You can apply a combination of chart elements at once by selecting one of the Quick Layout options from the *Chart Tools Design* tab, *Chart Layouts* group.

another **method**

You can hide or show chart elements and control their appearance and position from the *Chart Tools Design* tab, *Chart Layouts* group. Click the **Add Chart Elements** button, point to the chart element you want, and click an option.

let me **try**

Open the student data file **EX5-07-Sales** and try this skill on your own:

1. If necessary, select the chart on the *Chart1* sheet.
2. Hide the axes.
3. Hide the gridlines
4. Display the data labels at the outside end of each data marker (the top of the columns).
5. Display the data table, including the legend keys.
6. Save the file as directed by your instructor and close it.

Skill 5.8 Applying Quick Styles and Colors to Charts

You can change the style of a chart using the predefined **Quick Styles**. Quick Styles apply combinations of fonts, line styles, fills, and shape effects. You can also change the color scheme from a preset list of colors that coordinate with the workbook theme.

To change the chart style:

1. Select the chart.

2. On the *Chart Tools Design* tab, in the *Chart Styles* group, click the style you want to use, or click the **More** button to see all of the Quick Styles available.

3. To change the color scheme, on the *Chart Tools Design* tab, in the *Chart Styles* group, click the **Change Colors** button and select the color scheme you want.

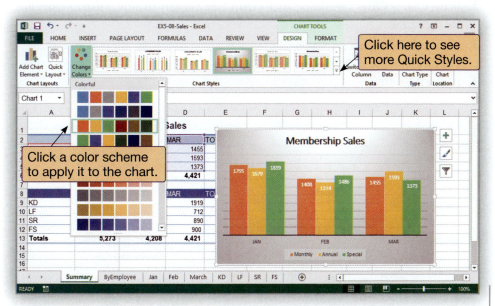

FIGURE EX 5.15

another **method**

Quick Styles and color schemes are also available from the *Chart Styles* button ✎ that appears near the upper right corner of the chart when it is selected.

let me **try**

Open the student data file **EX5-08-Sales** and try this skill on your own:

1. If necessary, select the chart on the *Summary* sheet.
2. Apply the **Style 4** Quick Style.
3. Apply the **Color 3** color scheme from the *Colorful* section.
4. Save the file as directed by your instructor and close it.

Skill 5.9 Changing the Chart Type

Remember that the chart type you select affects the story your chart tells. If you find that your initial chart selection wasn't quite right, you can change the chart type from the *Change Chart Type* dialog without having to delete and recreate the chart.

The clustered column chart in Figure EX 5.16 shows a separate column for sales of each membership type per month, but it doesn't depict the total sales for all memberships. By changing the chart type to a stacked column, each column now represents the total sales for the month, and individual sales for each membership type are represented by a piece of that column. Using this chart type makes it easier to compare total sales as well as sales for each individual type of membership.

To change the chart type:

1. On the *Chart Tools Design* tab, in the *Type* group, click the **Change Chart Type** button.
2. In the *Change Chart Type* dialog, click a chart type category to display that category in the right pane.
3. Click one of the chart types along the top of the right pane to see the options available, and then click the chart type you want.
4. Click **OK**.

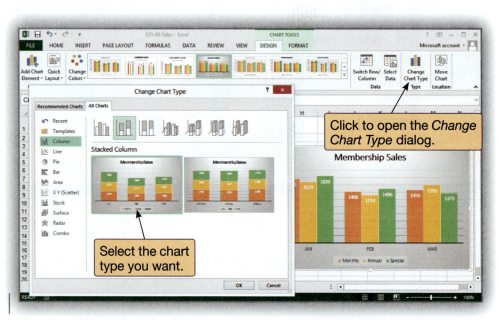

FIGURE EX 5.16

another method

To change the chart type, you can also right-click in the chart area and select **Change Chart Type...**

let me try

Open the student data file **EX5-9-Sales** and try this skill on your own:
1. If necessary, select the chart on the *Summary* sheet.
2. Change the chart type to the first stacked column option.
3. Save the file as directed by your instructor and close it.

Skill 5.10 Filtering Chart Data

Excel 2013 includes a new feature that allows you to hide and show data in a chart without having to filter the source data. The chart in Figure EX 5.17 shows the series options filtered to show just the Monthly and Annual series with a preview of what the chart would look like if the Annual series were the only series option selected.

To filter chart data:

1. Select the chart.
2. Click the **Chart Filters** button that appears near the upper right corner of the chart.
3. Click the check boxes to add or remove data series or categories from the chart.
4. Click the **Apply** button to apply the changes.

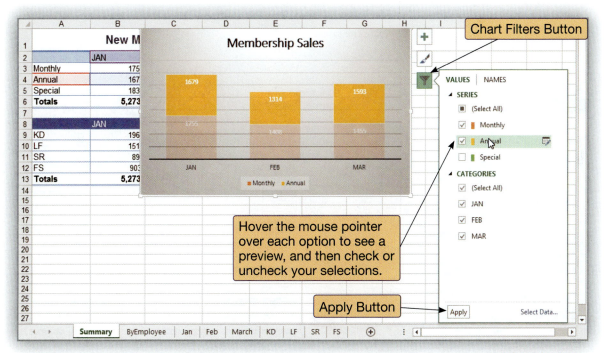

FIGURE EX 5.17

tips & tricks

Notice that when you hover the mouse pointer over the chart filter options, the live preview does not take into account the options that are checked or unchecked. The preview shows what the chart would look like if the highlighted option were the only one checked by dimming all the other series or categories.

let me try

Open the student data file **EX5-10-Sales** and try this skill on your own:

1. If necessary, select the chart on the *Summary* sheet.
2. Filter the chart so only the **Monthly** and **Annual** series are visible.
3. Save the file as directed by your instructor and close it.

Skill 5.11 Converting Data into Tables

In Excel, you can define a series of adjacent cells as a **table**. When you define data as a table, Excel provides a robust tool set for formatting and analyzing the data. In the table, the header row automatically includes filtering and sorting. When you add data to the right of the table, Excel includes the new column in the table automatically.

To define data as a table:

1. Click any cell in the data range. You do not need to select the entire range.

2. On the *Home* tab, in the *Styles* group, click the **Format as Table** button to display the *Table Styles* gallery.

3. Click the style you want to use for your table.

4. Excel will automatically populate the *Format As Table* dialog with the entire data range.

5. Be sure to check the **My table has headers** check box if appropriate.

6. Click **OK** to create the table.

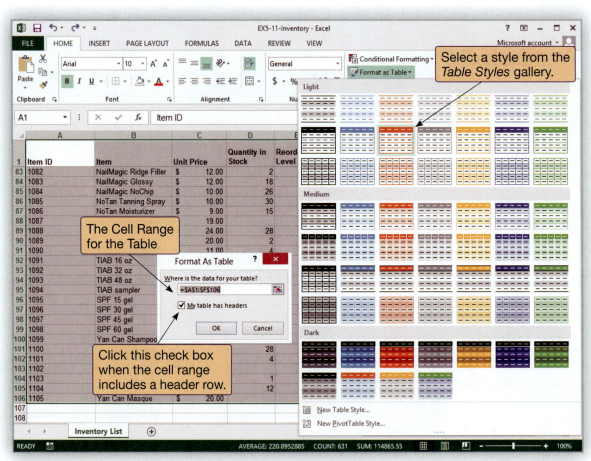

FIGURE EX 5.18

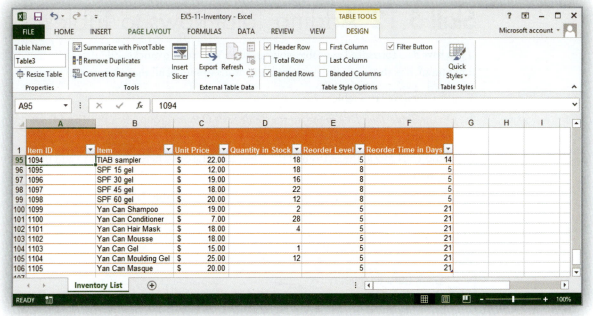

FIGURE EX 5.19
The cell range
converted to a table.

tips & tricks

You cannot create a table in a shared workbook. If your workbook contains a table, you will need to convert the table back to a normal cell range before sharing the workbook.

tell me more

One of the most useful features of tables is the ability to reference table column names in formulas. When you enter a formula in a table, you can reference column names by enclosing the column header text in brackets. For example, to add a new column to the table in Figure EX 5.19 to calculate the value of each inventory item, you would enter the formula **[Unit Price]*[Quantity in Stock]** in the first row of the new column. Excel will copy the formula to the remaining cells in the table column automatically.

another method

To insert a table without specifying the table formatting:
1. Select any cell in the data range for the table.
2. On the *Insert* tab, in the *Tables* group, click the **Table** button.
3. Excel will populate the *Insert Table* dialog automatically with the appropriate data range.
4. Be sure to check the **My table has headers** check box if appropriate.
5. Click **OK** to create the table. Excel will format the table with the most recent table style used.

let me try

Open the student data file **EX5-11-Inventory** and try this skill on your own:
1. If necessary, click any cell in the range **A1:F106**.
2. Convert the cell range to a table using table style **Table Style Light 10**.
3. Save the file as directed by your instructor and close it.

skill 5.11   Converting Data into Tables

Skill 5.12 Adding Total Rows to Tables

If you have data formatted as a table, you can add a **Total row** to quickly calculate an aggregate function such as the sum, average, minimum, or maximum of all the values in the column.

To add a Total row to a table:

1. On the *Table Tools Design* tab, in the *Table Style Options* group, click the **Total Row** check box.

2. In the Total row at the bottom of the table, click the cell where you want to add the function.

3. Click the arrow, and select a function. Excel inserts the formula for you.

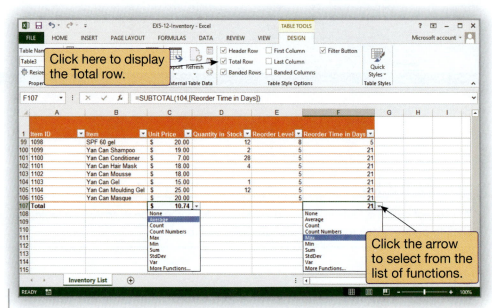

FIGURE EX 5.20

tips & tricks

The **Count** option can be useful when filtering records in a table. Count tells you how many records are included in the filtered table. The Count option from the Total row uses the COUNTA function.

tell me more

When you enable the Total row, the first cell in the Total row displays the word "Total" automatically and the last cell in the Total row calculates the sum of the values in that column (if the column contains numbers).

another method

To add the Total row to the table, right-click any cell in the table, point to **Table,** and click **Total Row.**

let me try

Open the student data file **EX5-12-Inventory** and try this skill on your own:
1. Add a Total row to the table.
2. In the Total row, display the average value for the *Unit Price* column.
3. In the Total row, display the minimum value for the *Reorder Time in Days* column.
4. Save the file as directed by your instructor and close it.

Skill 5.13 Applying Quick Styles to Tables

When you are working with a table, use the *Table Tools Design* tab to apply formatting. This contextual tab is available when you select any cell in the table. From the *Table Styles* gallery, you can select a Quick Style to apply a combination of font colors, fill colors, and banding options. **Banding** applies a fill color to alternating rows or columns, making the table easier to read.

To apply a table Quick Style:

1. Click anywhere in the table.

2. On the *Table Tools Design* tab, in the *Table Styles* group, click the **Quick Styles** button to display the full *Table Styles* gallery. Depending on the width of your Excel window, you may see part of the *Quick Styles* gallery displayed in the Ribbon. In this case, click the **More** button ⤓ to expand the entire gallery.

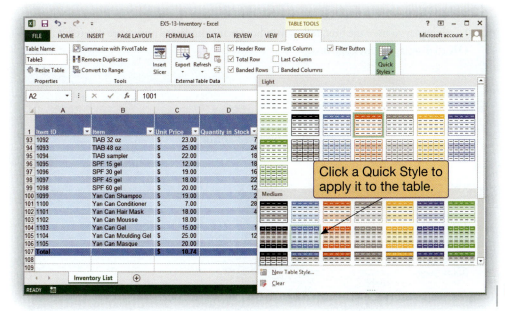

FIGURE EX 5.21

tips & tricks

If your table includes a header row and/or a Total row like the one in Figure EX 5.21, select a style that includes formatting for the first and last rows to help them stand out from the rest of the table.

tell me more

Use the check boxes in the *Table Style Options* group to customize the table formatting by adding or removing banding for rows or columns.

let me try

Open the student data file **EX5-13-Inventory** and try this skill on your own:
1. If necessary, click any cell in the table.
2. Apply the **Table Style Medium 9** Quick Style.
3. Save the file as directed by your instructor and close it.

Skill 5.14 Removing Duplicate Rows from Tables

If you have a large table, it may be difficult to identify rows with duplicate data. Excel includes a tool to find and remove duplicate rows. A "duplicate" can be an exact match, where every cell in the row contains the same data, or you can specify matching data for certain columns only.

To remove duplicate rows from a table:

1. Select any cell in the table.
2. On *Table Tools Design* tab, in the *Tools* group, click the **Remove Duplicates** button.
3. By default, all the columns are selected in the *Remove Duplicates* dialog and Excel will remove duplicates only where the data in the rows are 100 percent identical. To identify duplicate rows where only some of the columns have duplicate data, click the check boxes to uncheck column names. Now Excel will identify rows as duplicates only when the checked columns have the same data.
4. Click **OK** to remove duplicate rows from the table.
5. Excel displays a message box, telling you how many duplicate rows were deleted. Click **OK** to dismiss the message box.

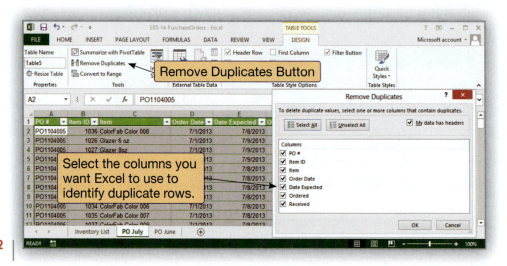

FIGURE EX 5.22

another method

If the data are not formatted as an Excel table, you can access the *Remove Duplicates* command from the *Data* tab, *Data Tools* group.

let me try

Open the student data file **EX5-14-PurchaseOrders** and try this skill on your own:
1. If necessary, click any cell in the table on the *PO July* sheet.
2. Remove duplicate rows where data in all the columns are identical.
3. Save the file as directed by your instructor and close it.

excel 2013   chapter 5 Adding Charts and Analyzing Data

Skill 5.15 Converting Tables to Ranges

Although Excel tables are extremely useful, there are times when you do not want your data formatted as a table. Certain data analysis tools, including creating subtotals and grouping outlines, are not available if data are formatted as a table.

To convert a table to a normal range:

1. On the *Table Tools Design* tab, in the *Tools* group, click the **Convert to Range** button.
2. Excel displays a message box asking if you want to convert the table to a normal range. Click **Yes.**
3. Notice that any table formatting such as banding is still applied to the range.

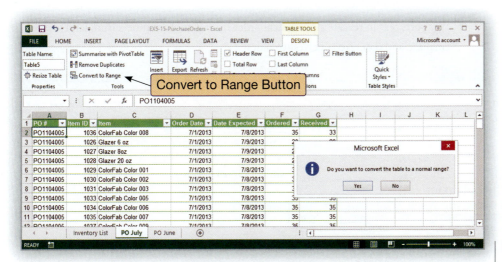

FIGURE EX 5.23

tips & tricks

If you want to use one of the table styles but do not want the data formatted as a table, begin by formatting the range as a table, applying the table style you want, and then convert the table back to a normal range.

another method

You can also right-click anywhere in the table, point to **Table,** and select **Convert to Range.**

let me try

Open the student data file **EX5-15-PurchaseOrders** and try this skill on your own:
1. If necessary, click any cell in the table on the *PO July* sheet.
2. Convert the table to a normal range.
3. Save the file as directed by your instructor and close it.

Skill 5.16 Sorting Data

Sorting rearranges the rows in your worksheet by the data in a column or columns. You can sort alphabetically by text, by date, or by values. Sorting works the same whether or not the data have been formatted as a table.

To sort data:

1. Click any cell in the column you want to sort by.

2. On the *Data* tab, in the *Sort & Filter* group, click the button for the sort order you want:

 》 ![AZ↓] sorts text in alphabetical order from A to Z, numbers from smallest to largest, and dates from oldest to newest.

 》 ![ZA↓] sorts text in reverse alphabetical order from Z to A, numbers from largest to smallest, and dates from newest to oldest.

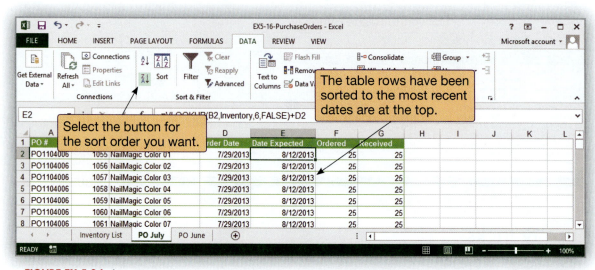

FIGURE EX 5.24

When a table column has been sorted, the column header will display an arrow indicating which way the column has been sorted: **Item ID** ↴↑ An arrow pointing up indicates an A-Z sort order; an arrow pointing down indicates a Z-A sort order.

another **method**

Sort options are also available from the *Home* tab, *Editing* group. Click the **Sort & Filter** button and then select the option you want.

You can also right-click any cell in the column you want to sort by. Point to **Sort,** and select the option you want.

let me **try**

Open the student data file **EX5-16-PurchaseOrders** and try this skill on your own:

1. Verify that the *PO July* sheet is active.
2. Sort the **Date Expected** column so the newest dates are listed first.
3. Go to the *PO June* sheet, and sort the **Item ID** column so the smallest numbers are listed first.
4. Save the file as directed by your instructor and close it.

excel 2013   chapter 5 Adding Charts and Analyzing Data

Skill 5.17 Filtering Data

If your worksheet has many rows of data, you may want to **filter** the data to show only rows that meet criteria you specify. If your data are formatted as a table, filtering is enabled automatically. If your data are not formatted as a table, you must first enable filtering:

1. On the *Home* tab, in the *Editing* group, click the **Sort & Filter** button.

2. Click the **Filter** button to enable filtering. An arrow will appear in each cell of the heading row just as if the data were formatted as a table.

Once filtering is enabled, it works the same whether or not the data have been formatted as a table.

To filter data:

1. Click the arrow at the top of the column that contains the data you want to filter for.

2. At first, all the filter options are checked. Click the **(Select All)** check box to remove all the check marks.

3. Click the check box or check boxes in front of the values you want to filter by.

4. Click **OK.** Excel displays only the rows that include the values you specified.

If the column values are dates, Excel will group the dates in the filter list if possible. You can click a check box to filter for an entire grouping (such as a specific year or month), or you can expand the group by clicking the + and then clicking the check box for specific dates. There may be multiple nested groups of dates, so be sure to continue expanding the date groupings until you find the exact date(s) you want to filter for.

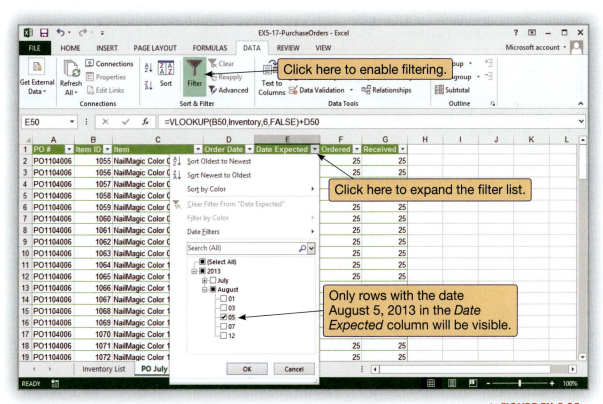

FIGURE EX 5.25

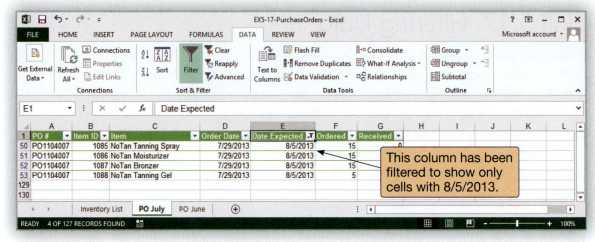

FIGURE EX 5.26

When a filter has been applied to a column, the column header will display a funnel icon: Date Expected To clear the filter, click the funnel icon and select **Clear Filter from 'Name of Column'.**

another method

When filtering is enabled, you can clear the filter and disable filtering from the *Data* tab, *Sort & Filter* group, by clicking the **Filter** button again.

You can also enable or clear filtering from the *Home* tab, *Editing* group, by clicking the **Sort & Filter** button and then making the appropriate choice from the menu.

let me try

Open the student data file **EX5-17-Inventory** and try this skill on your own:
1. Verify that the *PO July* sheet is selected.
2. Filter the **Date Expected** column so only rows with the date **8/5/2013** are shown.
3. Save the file as directed by your instructor and close it.

Skill 5.18 Filtering Table Data with Slicers

A **slicer** is a visual representation of filtering options. You can display multiple slicers and filter the table by multiple values from each. Slicers are only available when the data have been formatted as a table.

To add a slicer:

1. Click anywhere in the table to activate the *Table Tools Design* tab.

2. On the *Table Tools Design* tab, in the *Tools* group, click the **Insert Slicer** button.

3. In the *Insert Slicers* dialog, click the check boxes for the column(s) you want to filter by.

4. Click **OK.**

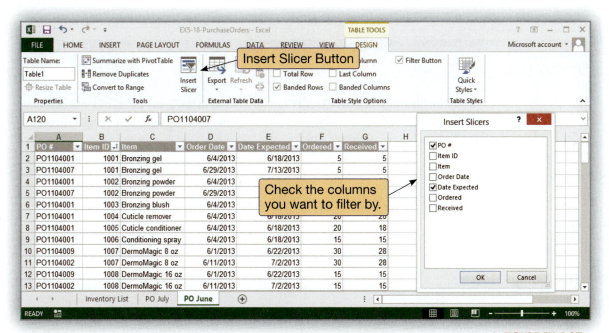

FIGURE EX 5.27

❯ To filter data using a slicer, click the buttons in each slicer to apply filtering to the table.

❯ To display more than one filtering option in a slicer, hold Ctrl as you click your selections.

❯ Notice that as you make selections in one slicer, options in the other slicer may become unavailable—indicating that there are no data available for that option under the current filtering conditions.

The table in Figure EX 5.28 has been filtered to show only rows with **PO1104007** in the *PO #* column and **7/4/2013** in the *Date Expected* column. Notice that all other options in the PO # slicer are disabled—which means that only rows with PO # PO1104007 have an expected date of 7/4/2013. However, there are two other options available in the Date Expected slicer—7/6/2013 and 7/13/2013—indicating that PO1104007 has multiple values in the *Date Expected* column.

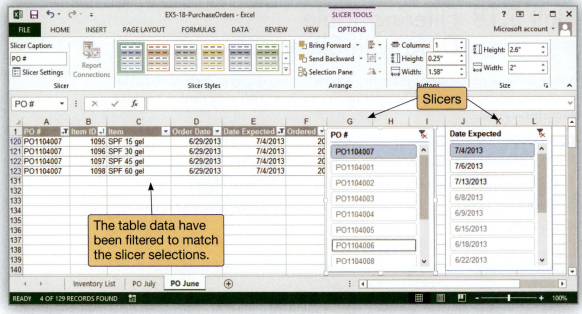

FIGURE EX 5.28

To remove filtering, click the **Clear Filter** ⌧ button in the upper right corner of the slicer. To remove a slicer from the table, click the slicer then press (Delete). Removing a slicer does not clear the filtering from the table.

tips & tricks

Slicers were introduced in Excel 2010 as an easy way to apply filtering to PivotTables. For Excel 2013, Microsoft added this feature to tables.

tell me more

▶ To move a slicer, move your mouse pointer over the slicer. When the cursor changes to the move cursor, click and drag the slicer to a new position on the worksheet.

▶ When a slicer is selected, the *Slicer Tools Options* tab becomes available. From this tab, you can apply a style to the slicer and control slicer settings.

let me try

Open the student data file **EX5-18-PurchaseOrders** and try this skill on your own:
1. If necessary, select the *PO June* sheet and click any cell in the table.
2. Add slicers for **PO #** and **Date Expected.**
3. Using the slicers, filter the table to show only rows for **PO # PO1104007** with an expected date of **7/4/2013.**
4. Save the file as directed by your instructor and close it.

Skill 5.19 Inserting Sparklines

Sparklines represent a series of data values as an individual graphic within a single cell. As you update the underlying data series, the Sparklines update immediately.

To add Sparklines to your worksheet using the Quick Analysis tool:

1. Select the data you want to visualize as Sparklines. If you want the Sparklines to appear in empty cells, ensure that there are empty cells to the right of your selection.

2. The Quick Analysis Tool button appears near the lower right corner of the selected range. Click the **Quick Analysis Tool** button, and then click the **Sparklines** tab.

3. Click the button for the Sparkline type you want.

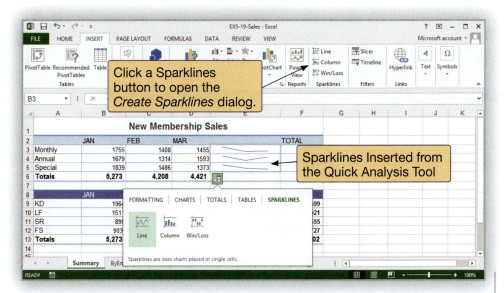

FIGURE EX 5.29

If you do not want Excel to place the Sparklines automatically, or if you are adding Sparklines in a situation where the Quick Analysis tool is not available, use the *Create Sparklines* dialog to specify their location:

1. Select the data range with the data points for the Sparklines.

2. On the *Insert* tab, in the *Sparklines* group, click the button for the type of Sparkline you want to insert: **Line, Column,** or **Win/Loss.**

3. The *Create Sparklines* dialog opens with the selected range added to the *Data Range* box.

4. In the *Location Range* box, enter the cell range where you want the Sparklines to appear. You can type the cell range or click and drag in the worksheet to select the cells.

5. Click **OK** to insert the Sparklines.

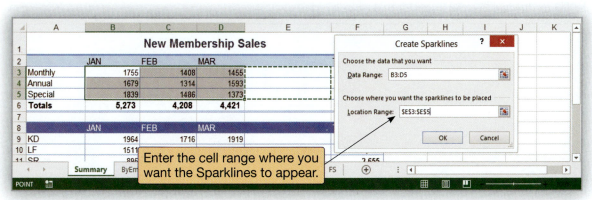

FIGURE EX 5.30

To remove Sparklines, you must select the cells containing the Sparklines, and then on the *Sparkline Tools Design* tab, in the *Group* group, click the **Clear** button.

FIGURE EX 5.31

tips & tricks

Sparklines are not actually chart objects—they are charts in the background of the cells. You can add text and other data to the cells that contain Sparklines. You can also extend the Sparklines over multiple cells using the *Merge & Center* commands.

tell me more

When cells containing Sparklines are selected, the *Sparkline Tools Design* contextual tab becomes active. From this tab you can customize the look of the Sparklines including emphasizing high or low points, changing the type of Sparkline used, and changing colors.

let me try

Open the student data file **EX5-19-Sales** and try this skill on your own:
1. If necessary, select cells **B3:D5** on the *Summary* sheet.
2. Insert Line Sparklines in cells **E3:E6** to visually represent the data in the selected cells.
3. Save the file as directed by your instructor and close it.

Skill 5.20 Analyzing Data with Goal Seek

Excel's **Goal Seek** function lets you enter a desired value (outcome) for a formula and specify an input cell that can be modified in order to reach that goal. Goal Seek changes the value of the input cell incrementally until the target outcome is reached.

To find a value using Goal Seek:

1. Select the outcome cell. (This cell must contain a formula.)
2. On the *Data* tab, in the *Data Tools* group, click the **What-If Analysis** button, and then click **Goal Seek...**
3. Verify that the outcome cell is referenced in the *Set cell* box.
4. Enter the outcome value you want in the *To value* box.
5. Enter the input cell (the cell that contains the value to be changed) in the *By changing cell* box. (This cell must be referenced in the formula in the outcome cell either directly or indirectly and must contain a value, not a formula.)
6. Click **OK.**
7. The *Goal Seek Status* box appears, letting you know if Goal Seek was able to find a solution. Click **OK** to accept the solution, or click **Cancel** to return the input cell to its original value.

In the Goal Seek analysis in Figure EX 5.32, the outcome cell is cell **E15,** the total investor payout for the quarter; the desired outcome value is $25,000; and the input cell is cell **B17,** the investor percentage.

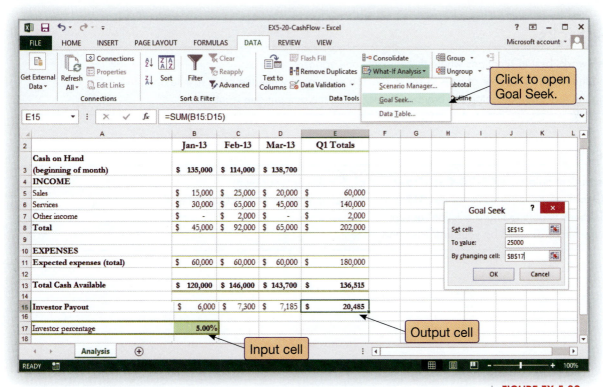

FIGURE EX 5.32

Notice that the formula in cell E15 does not reference cell B17 directly. However, it does reference cells B15:D15, and the formulas in those cells refer to cell B17.

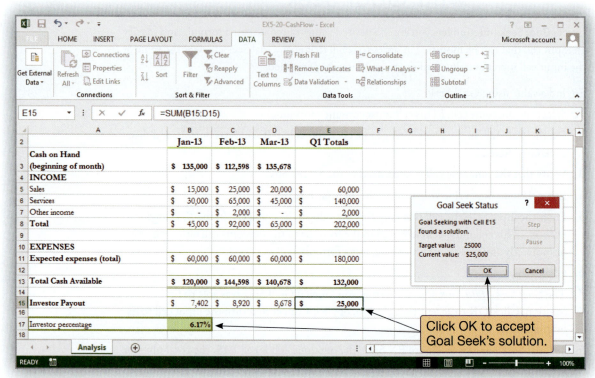

FIGURE EX 5.33

tips & tricks

Goal Seek works best in situations where there is only one variable, such as:
> Finding the required number of units to sell to reach a sales goal when the price is inflexible.
> Finding the required percentage to pay an investor when the amount due is inflexible.

let me try

Open the student data file **EX5-20-CashFlow** and try this skill on your own:
1. Use Goal Seek to find a value for cell **B17** that will result in a value of **$25,000** in cell **E15**.
2. If Goal Seek is able to find a solution, accept it.
3. Save the file as directed by your instructor and close it.

Skill 5.21 Analyzing Data with Data Tables

Data tables provide a quick what-if analysis of the effects of changing one or two variables within a formula. The data table is organized with a series of values for the variable(s) in a column or a row or both.

To create a one-variable data table with a column input format:

1. In a column, type the series of values you want to substitute for the variable in your formula.

2. In the cell above and to the right of the first value, type the formula that references the cell you want to replace with the new values.

3. Select the cell range for the data table, beginning with the empty cell above the first value you entered.

4. On the *Data* tab, in the *Data Tools* group, click the **What-If Analysis** button, and click **Data Table...**

5. In the *Data Table* dialog, the input cell is the cell that contains the original value for which you want to substitute the data table values. In this data table, the output values will be listed in a column, so enter the cell reference in the *Column input cell* box.

6. Click **OK**.

In the one-variable data table in Figure EX 5.34, the formula in cell E4 references the loan term in cell **B5**—the *nper* argument for the PMT function. This is the **column input cell** for the data table. The substitute values for cell B5 are listed in cells **D5:D9.**

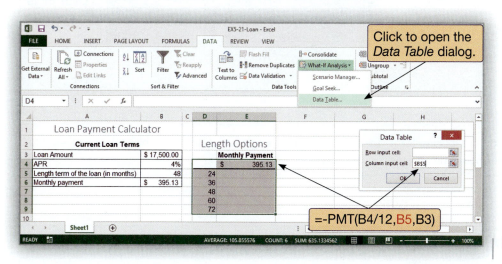

FIGURE EX 5.34

Excel completes the values in the table, using the substitute values in the formula:

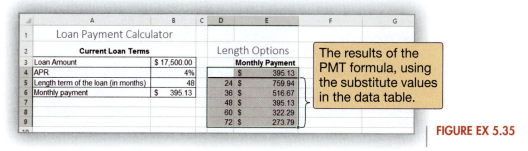

FIGURE EX 5.35

A **two-variable data table** works the same way as a one-variable data table, using inputs for both a column and a row variable. In a two-variable data table, the formula is located in the cell above the column input values and to the left of the row input values.

In the two-variable data table in Figure EX 5.36, the formula in cell E8 references the loan amount in cell **B3**—the *pv* argument for the PMT function. This is the **row input cell** for the data table. The substitute values for cell B3 are listed in cells **F8:I8.** The formula also references the second variable used in the data table, the interest rate in cell **B4**—the *rate* argument for the PMT function. This is the column input cell for the data table. The substitute values for cell B4 are listed in cells **E9:E14.**

In a two-variable data table, you may want to hide the data table formula by changing the cell font color to match the worksheet background. The data table is easier to follow if the cell in the upper left corner of the data table appears blank as shown in Figure EX 5.36. Of course, you can still see the formula in the formula bar.

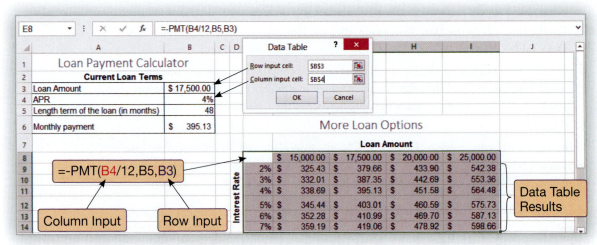

FIGURE EX 5.36

tips & tricks

Use Goal Seek if the result you are looking for is a specific value in a single cell. Use data tables when you want to see multiple possible outcomes based on multiple input options.

let me try

Open the student data file **EX5-21-Loan** and try this skill on your own:
1. If necessary, select the *One Variable* sheet.
2. Insert a one-variable data table in cells **D4:E9** to calculate the monthly loan payment for loan lengths using the following values: **24, 36, 48, 60, 72**
   The formula has been entered for you in cell E4. It references the original loan length in cell **B5.** You will need to enter the substitute values in the data table.
3. Go to the *Two Variables* sheet.
4. Insert a two-variable data table in cells **E8:I14.** The formula in cell E8 has been formatted using the white font color so it appears hidden. Use cell **B3** as the row input cell and cell **B4** as the column input cell for the data table.
5. Save the file as directed by your instructor and close it.

Skill 5.22 Creating PivotTables Using Recommended PivotTables

A **PivotTable** is a special report view that summarizes data and calculates the intersecting totals. PivotTables do not contain any data themselves—they summarize data from a cell range or a table in another part of your workbook.

The easiest way to begin a new PivotTable is to use one of the recommended PivotTables:

1. Select any cell within the table or cell range you want to use for your PivotTable.

2. On the *Insert* tab, in the *Tables* group, click the **Recommended PivotTables** button.

3. Preview each of the options in the *Recommended PivotTables* dialog. Click the one that is closest to how you want your final PivotTable to look.

4. Click **OK** to create the PivotTable in a new worksheet.

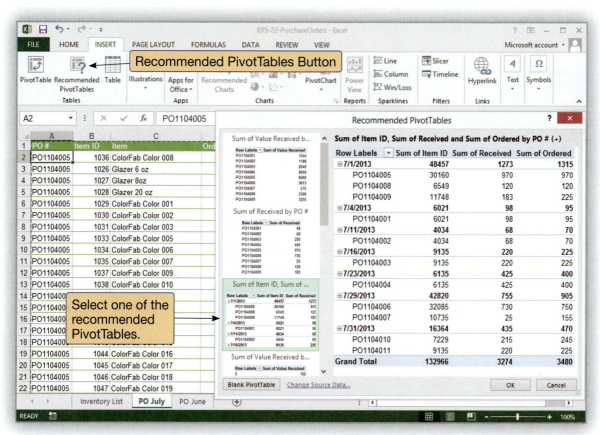

FIGURE EX 5.37

Once the PivotTable is inserted, you can add or remove fields. The *PivotTable Fields* pane shows you the list of available fields—the columns from the PivotTable's data source. In the *PivotTable Fields* pane, check the boxes to add or remove fields from the PivotTable.

❭ Fields that contain text data are added to the Rows section automatically. If there are multiple rows, Excel will attempt to group them in a logical way.

❭ Fields that contain numeric data are added to the Values section automatically. For each row in the PivotTable, Excel summarizes the values in each of the fields listed in the Values section.

You can click and drag the field names to move them between the Filters, Columns, Rows, or Values boxes.

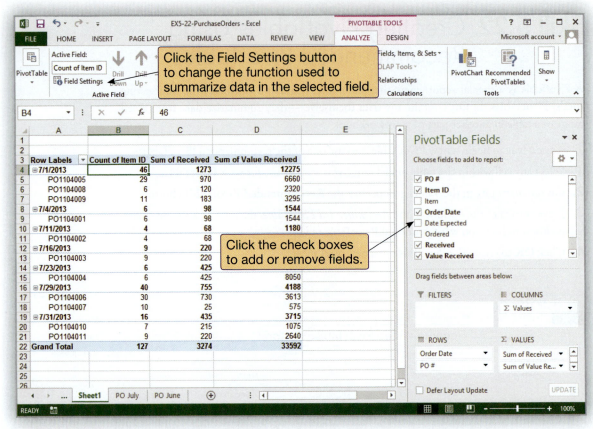

FIGURE EX 5.38

By default, PivotTables calculate totals using the SUM function. To change the calculation type for a field:

1. Click anywhere in the field you want to change.
2. On the *PivotTable Tools Analyze* tab, in the *Active Field* group, click the **Field Settings** button.
3. In the *Value Field Settings* dialog, *Summarize Values By* tab, select the function for the type of calculation you want.
4. Click **OK**.

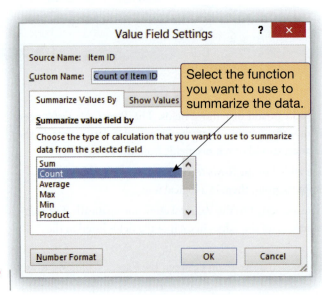

FIGURE EX 5.39

tips & tricks

You can click and drag fields in the *Rows* and *Values* boxes in the *PivotTable Fields* pane to reorder them in the PivotTable.

another method

) If you have the data range for the PivotTable selected, the recommended PivotTables are also available from the *Tables* tab in the Quick Analysis tool.

) You can also open the *Value Field Settings* dialog by clicking the arrow next to the field name in the Values box, and then selecting **Value Field Settings...**

let me try

Open the student data file **EX5-22-PurchaseOrders** and try this skill on your own:

1. Verify that the *PO July* sheet is active and one of the cells in the data range is selected.
2. Insert a recommended PivotTable, using the **Sum of Item ID, Sum of Received and Sum of Ordered by PO #** option.
3. Add the **Value Received** field to the PivotTable.
4. Remove the **Ordered** field from the PivotTable.
5. Modify the **Item ID** field to use the **COUNT** function instead of the SUM function.
6. Save the file as directed by your instructor and close it.

Skill 5.23 Creating a PivotChart from a PivotTable

A **PivotChart** is a graphic representation of a PivotTable. In a column chart, the category fields are represented along the x (horizontal) axis while the data values are represented along the y (vertical) axis.

To create a PivotChart:

1. Select any cell in the PivotTable.

2. On the *PivotTable Tools Analyze* tab, in the *Tools* group, click the **PivotChart** button.

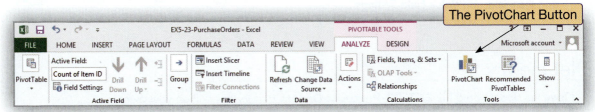

FIGURE EX 5.40

3. Select a chart type from the *Insert Chart* dialog.

4. Click **OK**.

If you need more room to display the PivotChart, you may want to hide the *PivotTable Fields* pane. On the *PivotChart Tools Analyze* tab, in the *Show/Hide* group, click the **Field List** button.

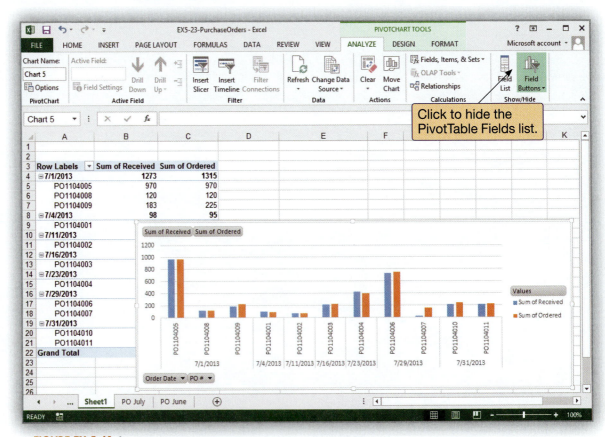

FIGURE EX 5.41

PivotCharts include all the formatting options that regular charts do. You can apply Quick Styles and hide or show chart elements from the *PivotChart Tools Design* tab. You can also resize the PivotChart or move it to its own sheet.

FIGURE EX 5.42
The PivotChart
Tools Design Tab

tell me **more**

To sort or filter the category data in the PivotChart, click the button in the lower-left corner of the PivotChart with the name of the field you want to sort or filter. If your PivotTable used multiple row labels, you will see a button for each.

let me **try**

Open the student data file **EX5-23-PurchaseOrders** and try this skill on your own:
1. If necessary, click anywhere in the PivotChart in the *Sheet1* worksheet.
2. Insert a PivotChart using the first clustered column chart type.
3. Save the file as directed by your instructor and close it.

key terms

Chart	Data table (chart)
Data points	Quick Styles
Data markers	Clustered column chart
Data series	Stacked column chart
Y axis	Table
X axis	Total row
Plot area	Banding
Chart area	Sort
Chart title	Filter
Legend	Slicer
Column charts	Sparklines
Bar charts	Goal Seek
Pie charts	Data table (what-if analysis)
Doughnut charts	Column input cell
Line charts	Two-variable data table
Line with markers	Row input cell
Chart sheet	PivotTable
Data labels	PivotChart

concepts review

1. Data markers are graphic representations of the values of data points in a chart.
   a. True
   b. False

2. _____ charts represent data as parts of a whole.
   a. Column
   b. Line
   c. Pie
   d. Bar

3. _____ apply combinations of fonts, line styles, fills, and shape effects to charts.
   a. Quick Styles
   b. Quick Layouts
   c. Chart Effects
   d. Chart Templates

4. _____ represent each data series as an individual graphic within a single cell.
   a. Sparklines
   b. Charts
   c. Tables
   d. PivotCharts

5. A Total row can be used to quickly calculate the _____ of all the values in a column.
   a. sum
   b. average
   c. both a and b
   d. neither a nor b

6. When you format data as a table, the header row automatically includes filtering and sorting.
   a. True
   b. False

7. The _____ command lets you enter a designated value for a formula and specify an input cell that can be modified in order to reach that goal.
   a. Scenario
   b. Data Table
   c. Consolidate
   d. Goal Seek

8. _____ rearranges the rows in your worksheet by the data in a column or columns.
   a. Sorting
   b. Filtering
   c. Formatting
   d. Grouping

9. The _____ command provides a quick what-if analysis of the effects of changing a single variable within a formula.

   a. Scenario

   b. Data Table

   c. Consolidate

   d. Goal Seek

10. A _____ is a special report view that summarizes data and calculates the intersecting totals.

    a. PivotTable

    b. Table

    c. Chart

    d. Scenario

Data files for projects can be found on
www.mhhe.com/office2013skills

projects

skill review 5.1

In this project, you will analyze data for an event planning company.

Skills needed to complete this project:

- Converting Data into Tables (Skill 5.11)
- Adding Total Rows to Tables (Skill 5.12)
- Sorting Data (Skill 5.16)
- Filtering Data (Skill 5.17)
- Analyzing Data with Data Tables (Skill 5.21)
- Using the Recommended Charts Feature (Skill 5.2)
- Changing the Chart Type (Skill 5.9)
- Applying Quick Styles and Colors to Charts (Skill 5.8)
- Showing and Hiding Chart Elements (Skill 5.7)
- Moving a Chart (Skill 5.6)
- Analyzing Data with Goal Seek (Skill 5.20)
- Inserting a Pie Chart (Skill 5.4)
- Exploring Charts (Skill 5.1)
- Creating PivotTables Using Recommended PivotTables (Skill 5.22)
- Creating a PivotChart from a PivotTable (Skill 5.23)

1. Open the start file **EX2013-SkillReview-5-1** and resave the file as:
   `[your initials] EX-SkillReview-5-1`

2. If the workbook opens in Protected View, click the **Enable Editing** button in the Message Bar at the top of the workbook.

3. Format the data on the *Table* worksheet into a table using one of the table Quick Styles.

    a. Select all the data including the headings, being careful not to select any blank rows or columns.

    b. On the *Home* tab, in the *Styles* group, click the **Format as Table** button to display the *Table Styles* gallery.

    c. Click the **Table Style Light 2** Quick Style.

    d. Verify that the correct cells will be used. Check the **My table has headers** check box. Click **OK.**

4. Add a Total row to the table to count the number of invitations sent.

    a. On the *Table Tools Design* tab, in the *Table Style Options* group, click the **Total Row** check box.

    b. In the Total row at the bottom of the table, note the total count of guests attending.

    c. In the Total row at the bottom of the table, click in the **Street** column, click the arrow, and select the **Count** function to count the invitations sent.

5. Sort the table by last name in alphabetical order:

    a. Click anywhere in the **Last Name** column.

    b. On the *Data* tab, in the *Sort & Filter* group, click the **A-Z** button.

6. Filter the data in the table to show only guests from the city of Rocklin.

    a. Click the arrow in the **City** column header.

    b. Click the (**Select All**) check box to remove all of the check marks.

    c. Click the check box in front of **Rocklin** to filter for only guests from Rocklin.

    d. Click **OK.** Excel displays only the rows for invitations sent to Rocklin.

7. Switch to work with the *Data Table* worksheet and use a data table to estimate costs for different numbers of attendees. Cell C19 contains a formula that sums the costs in cells **C3:C16.** The formulas in those cells all refer to the number of guests in cell **C1.**

    a. Select cells **B19:C26** to use as the data table.

    b. On the *Data* tab, in the *Data Tools* group, click the **What-If Analysis** button, and click **Data Table.**

    c. In the *Column input cell* box, type **C1.** Click **OK.**

    d. Review the data table results computing the party costs for the various numbers of guests.

8. Use the recommended charts feature to create a column chart to compare the cost of various size parties.

    a. Select cells **B18:C26.**

    b. Click the **Quick Analysis Tool** button at the lower right corner of the selected range.

    c. Click the **Charts** tab.

    d. Click the **Clustered Column** option.

9. Change the chart to a line chart.

    a. If necessary, click to select the chart.

    b. On the *Chart Tools Design* tab, in the *Type* group, click the **Change Chart Type** button.

    c. In the *Change Chart Type* dialog, click **Line,** and click the first line chart type.

    d. Click **OK.**

10. Format the chart using a Quick Style. On the *Chart Tools Design* tab, in the *Chart Styles* group, click **Style 2.**

11. Display the chart gridlines and hide the data labels.

   a. Click the **Chart Elements** button that appears near the upper right corner of the chart.

   b. Click the **Gridlines** check box to add a checkmark.

   c. Click the **Data Labels** check box to remove the checkmark.

12. Move the chart to its own sheet in the workbook.

   a. On the *Chart Tools Design* tab, in the *Location* group, click the **Move Chart** button.

   b. In the *Move Chart* dialog, click the **New sheet** radio button.

   c. Click **OK.**

13. Use Goal Seek to determine the most you can afford for dinner per person, on a total $6,000 budget for 100 guests.

   a. Switch back to the *Data Table* sheet.

   b. Select the outcome cell **H19** and review the formula.

   c. On the *Data* tab, in the *Data Tools* group, click the **What-If Analysis** button and click **Goal Seek...**

   d. Verify that the outcome cell **H19** is referenced in the *Set cell* box.

   e. Enter the outcome value of **6000** in the *To value* box.

   f. Enter the input cell **F4** in the *By changing cell* box.

   g. Click **OK** to run Goal Seek.

   h. Click **OK** again to accept the Goal Seek solution.

14. Insert a 3-D pie chart to show the breakdown of the per guest costs.

   a. Select cells **G3:H11.**

   b. On the *Insert* tab, in the *Charts* group, click the **Pie** button, and click the **3-D Pie** option.

   c. Move the chart to the right so it does not cover the worksheet data.

   d. Change the chart title to: **Per Guest Cost Breakdown**

15. Create a PivotTable listing the number attending from each city.

   a. Return to the *Table* worksheet.

   b. Click anywhere in the table.

   c. On the *Insert* tab, in the *Tables* group, click the **Recommended PivotTables** button.

   d. Select the option **Sum of NumAttending by City.**

   e. Click **OK.**

16. Create a PivotChart from the PivotTable.

   a. Select any cell in the PivotTable.

   b. On the *PivotTable Tools Analyze* tab, in the *Tools* group, click the **PivotChart** button.

   c. Verify that the Clustered Column chart type is selected in the *Insert Chart* dialog.

   d. Click **OK.**

   e. Click the title and change it to read: **Number of Guests Attending from Each City**

f. Hide the legend by clicking the **Chart Elements** button that appears near the upper right corner of the PivotChart and clicking the **Legend** check box to remove the checkmark.

g. Move the PivotChart to the right so it does not cover the PivotTable.

17. Save and close the workbook.

skill review 5.2

In this project you will analyze real estate data.

Skills needed to complete this project:

- Converting Data into Tables (Skill 5.11)
- Adding Total Rows to Tables (Skill 5.12)
- Sorting Data (Skill 5.16)
- Filtering Data (Skill 5.17)
- Inserting a Line Chart (Skill 5.5)
- Moving a Chart (Skill 5.6)
- Showing and Hiding Chart Elements (Skill 5.7)
- Exploring Charts (Skill 5.1)
- Applying Quick Styles and Colors to Charts (Skill 5.8)
- Creating PivotTables Using Recommended PivotTables (Skill 5.22)
- Inserting Sparklines (Skill 5.19)
- Creating a PivotChart from a PivotTable (Skill 5.23)
- Analyzing Data with Data Tables (Skill 5.21)
- Analyzing Data with Goal Seek (Skill 5.20)

1. Open the start file **EX2013-SkillReview-5-2** and resave the file as: **[your initials]EX-SkillReview-5-2**

2. If the workbook opens in Protected View, click the **Enable Editing** button in the Message Bar at the top of the workbook.

3. Format the data on the *Sales Data* worksheet as a table using the **Table Style Medium 5** table style:

   a. Select any cell in the data.

   b. On the *Home* tab, in the *Styles* group, click the **Format as Table** button to display the *Table Styles* gallery.

   c. Click the **Table Style Medium 5** style.

   d. Verify that the **My table has headers** check box is checked and that the correct data range is selected.

   e. Click **OK.**

4. Add a Total row to the table to display the number of buyers; the average number of bedrooms and bathrooms for each sale; and the average purchase price, interest rate, and mortgage length.

   a. On the *Table Tools Design* tab, in the *Table Style Options* group, click the **Total Row** check box.

   b. In the Total row at the bottom of the table, click in the **Buyers** column, click the arrow, and select the **Count** function.

c. In the Total row at the bottom of the table, click in the **Bedrooms** column, click the arrow, and select the **Average** function.

d. In the Total row at the bottom of the table, click in the **Bathrooms** column, click the arrow, and select the **Average** function.

e. In the Total row at the bottom of the table, click in the **Purchase Price** column, click the arrow, and select the **Average** function.

f. In the Total row at the bottom of the table, click in the **Rate** column, click the arrow, and select the **Average** function.

g. In the Total row at the bottom of the table, click in the **Mortgage Years** column, click the arrow, and select the **Average** function.

5. Sort the data so the newest purchases appear at the top.

    a. Click anywhere in the **Date of Purchase** column.

    b. On the *Data* tab, in the *Sort & Filter* group, click the **Z-A** button.

6. Filter the data to show only houses sold by **Williman's** with three or more bedrooms.

    a. Click the arrow at the top of the **Agent** column.

    b. Click the **(Select All)** check box to remove all of the checkmarks.

    c. Click the check box in front of **Williman's.**

    d. Click **OK.**

    e. Click the arrow at the top of the **Bedrooms** column.

    f. Click the **(Select All)** check box to remove all of the checkmarks.

    g. Click the check boxes in front of **3, 4,** and **5.**

    h. Click **OK.**

7. Create a line chart showing the purchase prices for houses by date.

    a. Select the **Date of Purchase** data cells. Be careful not to include the column heading. Press and hold `Ctrl` and click and drag to select the **Purchase Price** data cells, again being careful not to include the column heading.

    b. On the *Insert* tab, in the *Charts* group, click the **Insert Line Chart** button.

    c. Select the first line chart type shown.

    d. Click **OK.**

8. Move the chart to its own sheet named *Purchase Prices.*

    a. If necessary, select the chart. On the *Chart Tools Design* tab, in the *Locations* group, click the **Move Chart** button.

    b. In the box type: **Purchase Prices**

    c. In the *Move Chart* dialog, click the **New sheet** radio button.

    d. Click **OK.**

9. Update the chart title and display the data labels as callouts.

    a. Change the chart title to: **Purchase Prices for 3-5 Bedroom Houses**

    b. Click the **Chart Elements** button near the upper right corner of the chart.

    c. Click the **Data Labels** check box to add a checkmark.

    d. Point to **Data Labels,** click the arrow that appears at the right side, and click **Data Callout.**

10. Apply the **Style 15** Quick Style to the chart.

    a. Click the **Chart Styles** button that appears near the upper right corner of the chart.

    b. Scroll to the bottom of the list, and click **Style 15.**

11. Create a PivotTable to summarize the average purchase price of different house types for each agent.

    a. Return to the *Sales Data* worksheet and click anywhere in the table.

    b. Click the **Insert** tab. In the *Tables* group, click the **Recommended PivotTables** button.

    c. Verify that the first recommended PivotTable is **Sum of Purchase Price by Agent.**

    d. Click **OK.**

    e. Select any cell in the **Sum of Purchase Price** column.

    f. On the *PivotTable Tools Analyze* tab, in the *Active Field* group, click the **Field Settings** button.

    g. In the *Summarize value field by* box, select **Average.**

    h. Click **OK.**

    i. Add the **House Type** field to the PivotTable by clicking the check box in the *Fields List* pane. Excel automatically places the *House Type* field in the Rows box and displays the house type data as a subgroup of rows below each agent.

    j. To summarize the house type data for each agent, use the *House Type* field as columns in the PivotTable. Click and drag the **House Type** field from the Rows box to the Columns box in the *PivotTable Fields* pane.

12. Add column Sparklines to the right of the PivotTable.

    a. Select cells **B5:E9** to use as the data for the Sparklines. You do not want to include the grand total column or row.

    b. On the *Insert* tab, in the *Sparklines* group, click the **Column** button.

    c. In the *Create Sparklines* dialog, verify that the cell range **B5:E9** is listed in the *Data Range* box.

    d. Add the range **G5:G9** to the *Location Range* box either by typing the cells range or by clicking and dragging to select it in the worksheet.

    e. Click **OK.**

13. Create a PivotChart from the PivotTable.

    a. Select any cell in the PivotTable.

    b. On the *PivotTable Tools Analyze* tab, in the *Tools* group, click the **PivotChart** button.

    c. Select the first column chart type from the *Insert Chart* dialog. Click **OK.**

    d. Click the **Chart Elements** box near the upper right corner of the PivotChart and click the **Chart Title** check box.

    e. Click the title and change it to: `Average Price by Type of House and Agent`

    f. If necessary, move the PivotChart to another part of the worksheet so it does not cover the PivotTable data.

14. Use the data in the *Loan Worksheet* sheet to run a what-if scenario for a client to show loan payments for a variety of interest rates and loan lengths. This what-if scenario requires a two-variable data table.

    a. Go to the **Loan Worksheet** sheet and familiarize yourself with the formula in cell **B5.** Place close attention to the cell references.

    b. Select cells **B5:E38** to use the payment formula in B5 and the various years and rates as the data table.

    c. On the *Data* tab, in the *Data Tools* group, click the **What-If Analysis** button, and click **Data Table.**

d. In the *Row input cell* box, enter the cell reference for the length of the loan—the *rate* argument from the formula in cell B5: **C2**

e. In the *Column input cell* box, enter the cell reference for the loan interest rate—the *nper* argument from the formula in cell B5: **A2**

f. Click **OK.**

15. Use Goal Seek to determine the most you can afford to borrow, on a $600 per month budget:

    a. On the *Loan Worksheet* sheet, select the outcome formula cell, **H4.**

    b. On the *Data* tab, in the *Data Tools* group, click the **What-If Analysis** button and click **Goal Seek...**

    c. Verify that the outcome cell **H4** is referenced in the *Set cell* box.

    d. Enter the outcome value of **600** in the *To value* box.

    e. Enter the input cell **H9** in the *By changing cell* box.

    f. Click **OK.**

    g. Click **OK** again to accept the Goal Seek solution.

    h. Notice the loan payment changed to $600 and the amount to borrow was computed to be $111,769.

16. Save and close the workbook.

challenge yourself 5.3

In this project, you will analyze shoe sales data and use what-if analysis to determine your commission potential and your sales goal.

Skills needed to complete this project:

- Converting Data into Tables (Skill 5.11)
- Adding Total Rows to Tables (Skill 5.12)
- Removing Duplicate Rows from Tables (Skill 5.14)
- Filtering Data (Skill 5.17)
- Sorting Data (Skill 5.16)
- Inserting a Line Chart (Skill 5.5)
- Filtering Chart Data (Skill 5.10)
- Moving a Chart (Skill 5.6)
- Filtering Table Data with Slicers (Skill 5.18)
- Creating PivotTables Using Recommended PivotTables (Skill 5.22)
- Creating a PivotChart from a PivotTable (Skill 5.23)
- Showing and Hiding Chart Elements (Skill 5.7)
- Inserting Sparklines (Skill 5.19)
- Analyzing Data with Data Tables (Skill 5.21)
- Analyzing Data with Goal Seek (Skill 5.20)

1. Open the start file **EX2013-ChallengeYourself-5-3** and resave the file as: **[your initials]EX-ChallengeYourself-5-3**

2. If the workbook opens in Protected View, enable editing so you can make changes to the workbook.

3. Convert the shoe sales data in the *Sales* worksheet into a table.

   a. Use the **Table Style Light 9** table style.

   b. Add a Total row to the table and display the average for the *# of Pairs* and the *Price Per Pair* columns.

   c. Delete any rows in the table that have duplicate data in all the columns. There are three.

4. Filter to show just the sales for the **California** region.

5. Sort the table by order date with the newest orders first.

6. Insert a line chart to show the total sale amount for each order by order date.

   a. There was an ordering glitch on April 26 that caused a spike in sales. Apply a filter to the chart to hide orders from that date.

   b. If necessary, move the chart so it does not cover the table data.

7. Add a slicer to the table so you can filter by shoe name. Use the slicer to display data for the **Avone** shoe only. Notice the effect on the chart.

8. Create a PivotTable from the data in the *Sales* worksheet. Use the **Sum of Price Per Pair by Region** recommended PivotTable.

   a. Modify the PivotTable so the Price Per Pair data are averaged, not totaled.

   b. Add the Shoe field to the PivotTable. It should appear in the Rows section below the Region field.

   c. Format all the values in the PivotTable using the Accounting Number Format.

9. Create a column PivotChart based on the PivotTable data. Use the first recommended column chart type.

   a. Hide the chart title and legend.

   b. If necessary, move the PivotChart on the worksheet so it does not cover the PivotChart data.

10. Go to the *By Region* worksheet and add Column Sparklines to the right of the data as appropriate.

11. You have been told that you will receive a commission between 5 and 10 percent. On the *Commission* sheet, make a one-variable data table using cells **A4:B14** to determine how much that commission may be. The column input cell is **A4.**

12. You owe $12,000 in student loans and would like to pay it all off with your commissions. Use *Goal Seek* to determine the amount you must sell (cell **G5**) in order for cell **G3** (your commission) to equal $12,000 so you can fully pay off your student loans. Accept the Goal Seek solution.

13. Save and close the workbook.

challenge yourself 5.4

In this project, the local library has received a significant collection of DVDs as a donation and has asked you to provide an analysis of the titles. They need to decide whether they should keep the collection or sell it to raise money for a new computer.

Skills needed to complete this project:

- Converting Data into Tables (Skill 5.11)
- Adding Total Rows to Tables (Skill 5.12)
- Removing Duplicate Rows from Tables (Skill 5.14)
- Applying Quick Styles to Tables (Skill 5.13)

- Sorting Data (Skill 5.16)
- Filtering Data (Skill 5.17)
- Filtering Table Data with Slicers (Skill 5.18)
- Creating PivotTables Using Recommended PivotTables (Skill 5.22)
- Creating a PivotChart from a PivotTable (Skill 5.23)
- Showing and Hiding Chart Elements (Skill 5.7)
- Analyzing Data with Data Tables (Skill 5.21)
- Analyzing Data with Goal Seek (Skill 5.20)

1. Open the start file **EX2013-ChallengeYourself-5-4** and resave the file as:
   `[your initials]EX-ChallengeYourself-5-4`

2. If the workbook opens in Protected View, enable editing so you can make changes to the workbook.

3. Convert the data on the *Videos* sheet into a table using the style **Table Style Light 1**.

   a. Add a Total row to the table and count the number of movie titles and the average purchase price.

   b. Delete all the duplicate rows. Be careful, there may be duplicate rows with the same movie title, but different data in the other columns. When you are finished, there should be 296 unique titles in the collection.

   c. Change the table style to use the **Table Style Medium 1 Quick Style.**

4. Sort the data in the table alphabetically by category.

5. Filter the table to show only Disney and family movies that are rated G or PG.

6. Create a PivotTable from the table data using the **Sum of Price by Rating** recommend PivotTable.

7. Create a pie PivotChart from the PivotTable.

   a. Display the data labels using the **Best Fit** option.

   b. Hide the chart title.

8. On the *Data Table* worksheet, create a one-variable data table to determine the amount of money that would be raised if 100 DVDs were sold at the various prices listed. Review the formula in cell **C7** to identify the appropriate cell to use as the input cell for the data table.

9. What if the selling price for each DVD is set at $1.50? How many DVDs would the library need to sell to raise $535? Use Goal Seek to find a value for cell **F9** that will result in a value of 535 for cell **F7.**

10. Save and close the workbook.

on your own 5.5

In this project, you will be analyzing data about automobile emissions and fuel economy. These green car data were downloaded from the Web site https://explore.data.gov/d/9un4-5bz7 and are explained at this Web site: http://www.epa.gov/greenvehicles/Aboutratings.do. The scores range from 0 to 10, where 10 is best. The vehicles with the best scores on both air pollution and greenhouse gas receive the SmartWay designation.

Skills needed to complete this project:

- Converting Data into Tables (Skill 5.11)
- Filtering Data (Skill 5.17)

- Filtering Table Data with Slicers (Skill 5.18)
- Sorting Data (Skill 5.16)
- Inserting a Column Chart or a Bar Chart (Skill 5.3)
- Showing and Hiding Chart Elements (Skill 5.7)
- Applying Quick Styles and Colors to Charts (Skill 5.8)
- Changing the Chart Type (Skill 5.9)
- Creating PivotTables Using Recommended PivotTables (Skill 5.22)
- Creating a PivotChart from a PivotTable (Skill 5.23)
- Analyzing Data with Data Tables (Skill 5.21)
- Analyzing Data with Goal Seek (Skill 5.20)

1. Open the start file **EX2013-OnYourOwn-5-5** and resave the file as: `[your initials]EX-OnYourOwn-5-5`

2. If the workbook opens in Protected View, click the **Enable Editing** button in the Message Bar at the top of the workbook so you can modify the workbook.

3. The *Data* worksheet contains more than 2,000 rows. That's a lot of data! Use filtering and sorting techniques to display the rows for cars with **8** cylinder engines (*Cyl* column) with an automatic seven-speed transmission (**Auto-7** in the *Trans* column). Narrow the data further to show just four-wheel drives (**4WD** in the *Drive* column). Let's narrow the list down a little bit further and display only cars in the large car class (use the *Veh Class* column). You should end up with six records visible.

4. Sort the data so the cars with the best combination MPG (*Cmb MPG* column) appear at the top.

5. Create a chart comparing the **City MPG, Hwy MPG,** and **Cmb MPG** for the cars shown.

   a. Add and remove chart elements as necessary to make the chart clear and easy to read.

   b. Apply one of the chart Quick Styles.

   c. Try changing the chart to another chart type. Is there another chart type available that's appropriate for the data?

6. Create a PivotTable from the car data to summarize the average City MPG, Hwy, MPG, and Cmb MPG by car class. You may want to start with the **Count of Model by Veh Class** recommended PivotTable and then make changes. Format numbers in the PivotTable as appropriate.

7. Create a PivotChart from the PivotTable data.

8. On the *Commuting Costs* worksheet, create a two-variable data table to calculate the daily cost of gas for a variety of gas prices and a variety of miles driven per day. If you have a daily commute to school or work, use variations on your actual commuting miles in the data table.

   a. The formula to calculate the cost of your daily commute is:
   Commuting miles/your car's MPG*price of gas per gallon

   b. In the data table formula, you can use the MPG in cell B3 or change the value to your car's estimated MPG.

   c. Find a way to hide the data table formula.

   d. Add formatting as appropriate.

9. You're in the market for a new car, and you'd like to reduce your monthly gas costs to around $50. What's the minimum gas mileage you should look for in your new car? Can you use Goal Seek with the data on this worksheet to find an answer?

10. Save and close the workbook.

The staff members of a private college preparatory school have been trying to analyze student data and create what-if scenarios regarding investment decisions. Unfortunately, they've made a mess of this workbook. Can you help them fix it?

Skills needed to complete this project:

- Moving a Chart (Skill 5.6)
- Converting Data into Tables (Skill 5.11)
- Filtering Table Data with Slicers (Skill 5.18)
- Removing Duplicate Rows from Tables (Skill 5.14)
- Adding Total Rows to Tables (Skill 5.12)
- Creating PivotTables Using Recommended PivotTables (Skill 5.22)
- Inserting a Pie Chart (Skill 5.4)
- Changing the Chart Type (Skill 5.9)
- Analyzing Data with Data Tables (Skill 5.21)

1. Open the start file **EX2013-FixIt-5-6** and resave the file as:
   `[your initials]EX-FixIt-5-6`

2. If the workbook opens in Protected View, click the **Enable Editing** button in the Message Bar at the top of the workbook so you can modify the workbook.

3. The data in the *Student Test Data* worksheet has a couple of problems to fix:
   a. The data should be organized alphabetically by subject.
   b. Format the data so the school faculty can use slicers to filter data by month, by subject, or by student or by any combination of the three. Go ahead and display the slicers, but you don't need to apply any filtering.
   c. Find and delete the duplicate records. There should be 90 unique records.
   d. The data should include a Total row to calculate the average score.

4. The faculty members also want a PivotTable to summarize the average scores for each subject for each student by month, but since there wasn't a recommended PivotTable that met their needs exactly, they didn't know how to add one. Go ahead and create the PivotTable for them.

5. The PivotChart on the *Faculty Pivot* sheet should show the size of each department as a proportional part of a whole. A line chart was the wrong choice. Change the chart type to a better choice.

6. The school finance committee has determined that a $14,000 facilities upgrade will be needed in 10 years. An alumnus has donated $10,000. If invested, will it grow to be enough? That depends on the rate of return. On the *Data Table* worksheet, an attempt has been made to use Excel's data table feature to determine the value of the investment after five years at different rates of return. The formula in cell D6 is correct, but something went wrong with the data table. Delete the zeros in cells **D7:D30** and try again. Even if you're not familiar with the PV formula used in cell D6, you should be able to figure this out.

7. Save and close the workbook.

chapter **6**

Exploring Advanced Functions

In this chapter, you will learn the following skills:

> Round numbers using functions

> Use advanced math functions to calculate totals

> Analyze data using statistical functions to calculate averages, count values, and find middle values

> Create formulas with the logical functions AND, OR, and NOT and create nested IF functions

> Work with financial functions to calculate future value, present value, number of payments, and depreciation

> Analyze data using the lookup functions MATCH and INDEX and database functions

> Manage formula errors using the IFERROR function

> Analyze complex formulas

skills

introduction

This chapter expands on Chapter 3's introduction to formulas and functions. You will learn to use advanced mathematical, statistical, financial, logical, lookup, and database functions to find the answers to complex data questions. You will also learn to use the Evaluate Formula feature to troubleshoot formula errors.

Skill 6.1 Rounding with Functions

Rounding refers to adjusting a number up or down to make it more appropriate in the context in which it is being used. Numbers can be rounded up or down to the nearest whole number or the nearest factor of 10, 100, 1000 or any limit. The rounding functions in Excel are used specifically to control the number of digits to the right of the decimal point.

In Figure EX 6.1, the average price per unit is 4.970178926. Nine digits to the right of the decimal is very precise, but it is not a valid number for a price quote. If you apply a number format such as Currency or the Accounting Number Format, the number will appear with only two digits after the decimal, but the number stored in the workbook will remain 4.970178926. By adding one of the rounding functions to the formula, you can ensure that the number is stored exactly as you want.

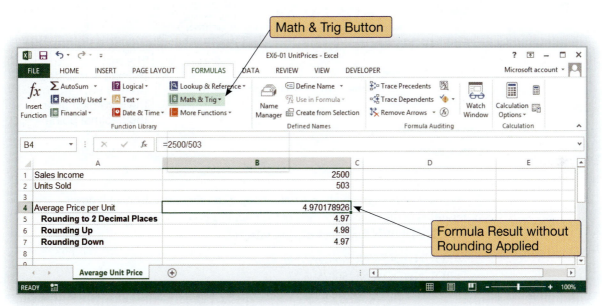

FIGURE EX 6.1

There are three main rounding functions:

ROUND—Rounds the number up or down to the number of decimal places specified in the *Num_digits* argument. The rules of rounding state that if the number immediately to the right of the rounding point is 0, 1, 2, 3, or 4, the trailing digits are cut off. If the number immediately to the right of the rounding point is 5, 6, 7, 8, or 9, the number is rounded up. A formula using the ROUND function looks like this:

=ROUND(*Number,Num_digits*)
=ROUND(2500/503,2)

The result of this formula is 4.97. The number 4.970178926 is rounded down to 4.97 because the *num_digits* argument is 2 and the third digit after the decimal is 0.

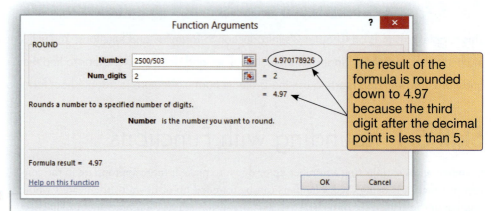

ROUNDUP—Ignores the rules of rounding and automatically rounds up to the next number, regardless of the value to the right of the rounding point. A formula using the ROUNDUP function looks like this:

=ROUNDUP(*Number,Num_digits*)
=ROUNDUP(2500/503,2)

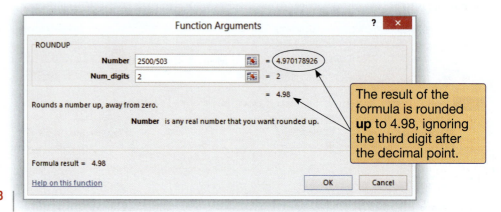

FIGURE EX 6.3

ROUNDDOWN—Ignores the rules of rounding and automatically rounds down, regardless of the value to the right of the rounding point. A formula using the ROUNDDOWN function looks like this:

=ROUNDDOWN(*Number,Num_digits*)
=ROUNDDOWN(2500/503,2)

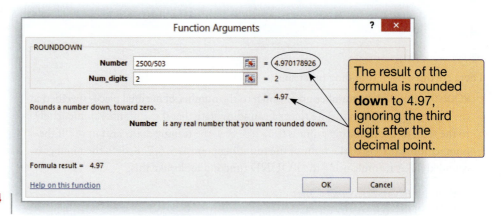

FIGURE EX 6.4

To create a formula using one of the rounding functions:

1. Select the cell where you want to enter the formula.
2. On the *Formulas* tab, in the *Function Library* group, click the **Math & Trig** button.
3. Select the rounding function you want to open the *Function Arguments* dialog.
4. In the *Number* argument box, enter the number, cell reference, or formula you want rounded.
5. In the *Num_digits* argument box, enter the number of digits you want to the right of the decimal.
6. Click **OK.**

tips & tricks

Rounding functions are often used in conjunction with another function such as PMT (used to calculate loan payments). A formula to calculate monthly payments for a 36 month $17,500 loan at 4% annual interest, rounded to two decimal places, looks like this:

=ROUND(PMT(4%/12,36,17500),2)

tell me more

Another rounding function, INT, rounds the number down to the nearest integer (whole number). INT takes only one argument, *Number*. There is no need for the *Num_digits* argument because INT does not allow any digits after the decimal.

If you want to round up to the nearest whole number instead, use the ROUNDUP function with 0 as the *Num_digits* argument.

let me try

Open the student data file **EX6-01-UnitPrices** and try this skill on your own:

1. Enter a formula in cell **B5** to calculate **B1/B2** rounded to **2** decimal places. Use cell references in the formula.
2. Enter a formula in cell **B6** to calculate **B1/B2** rounded up to **2** decimal places. Use cell references in the formula.
3. Enter a formula in cell **B7** to calculate **B1/B2** rounded down to **2** decimal places. Use cell references in the formula.
4. Save the file as directed by your instructor and close it.

Skill 6.2 Calculating Totals with SUMPRODUCT

In mathematics, a **product** is the result of multiplying two or more numbers. The **SUMPRODUCT** function allows you to multiply the corresponding cells in two or more ranges and then sum (add together) the products. This function is very useful when totaling columns of data such as hours worked and hourly rates or unit prices and number of units ordered. To use SUMPRODUCT, arrays do not need to be next to each other, but they must have the same number of rows or columns. If the arrays are different sizes, the formula will return an error.

The formula in Figure EX 6.5 first multiplies each value in the named range *Unit_Price* by its corresponding value in the named range *Units_Ordered* and then sums the products:

=SUMPRODUCT(*Array1*,[*Array2*],[*Array3*]...)
=SUMPRODUCT(Unit_Price,Units_Ordered)

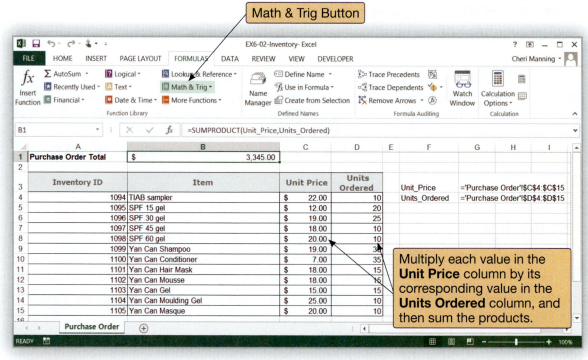

FIGURE EX 6.5

To create a formula using SUMPRODUCT:

1. Select the cell where you want to enter the formula.

2. On the *Formulas* tab, in the *Function Library* group, click the **Math & Trig** button, and select **SUMPRODUCT** to open the *Function Arguments* dialog.

3. In the *Array1* argument box, enter the first cell range or named range.

4. In the *Array2* argument box, enter cell range or named range you want to multiply the values in *Array1* by.

5. Continuing entering *Array* arguments as necessary.

6. Click **OK**.

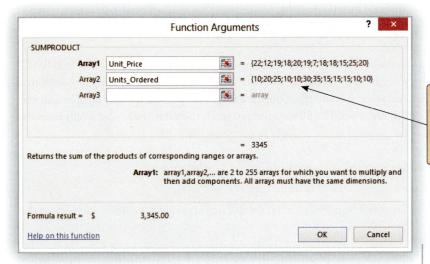

SUMPRODUCT multiplies together the corresponding values in each array (22*10, 12*20, 19*25, etc.) and then adds them together.

FIGURE EX 6.6

tips & tricks

While the example used in this skill uses data arranged in columns, SUMPRODUCT works just as well with data in rows.

let me try

Open the student data file **EX6-02-Inventory** and try this skill on your own:

Enter a formula in cell **B1** using the **SUMPRODUCT** function to calculate the total cost of the purchase order by multiplying the unit prices by the number of units ordered. Use the range names **Unit_Price** and **Units_Ordered.** Save the file as directed by your instructor and close it.

from the perspective of . . .

BRAND MANAGER

Every week I receive sales data from all our retail stores. To calculate totals quickly, I apply range names to the columns of units sold and prices and then use SUMPRODUCT to calculate the grand total. Now all I have to do each week is replace the data in my spreadsheet with the updated sales figures and I'm finished. What a time saver!

Skill 6.3 Using SUMIF and SUMIFS

At this point, you should be able to use SUM to total a range of cells and use SUMPRODUCT to total the product of two cell ranges, but what if you want to sum together only cells that meet specific criteria? You could filter the data and then use SUM, but it is more efficient to use the SUMIF function. The **SUMIF** function totals the values only where cells meet the specified criteria.

SUMIF takes two required arguments and one optional argument:

Range—The range of cells to evaluate against the criteria.

Criteria—The conditions (the criteria) the cell must meet in order to be included in the total.

Sum_range—(Optional) the range of cells containing the values to be summed. *Sum_range* must be the same size as *Range*. This argument is only necessary when the values to be summed are not the same as the values to be evaluated against the criteria.

The formula in Figure EX 6.7 uses SUMIF to calculate the total number of items ordered for the Item ID specified in cell *B1*. SUMIF evaluates the values in the *JuneItems* range (the *Item ID* column). If the value matches the criteria specified in cell *B1*, then the corresponding value in the *JuneOrdered* range (the *Ordered* column) is included in the total.

=SUMIF(*Range*,*Criteria*,[*Sum_range*])
=SUMIF(JuneItems,B1,JuneOrdered)

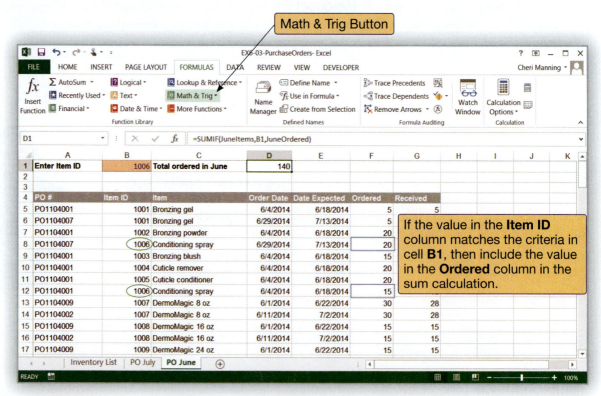

FIGURE EX 6.7

To create a formula using SUMIF:

1. Select the cell where you want to enter the formula.

2. On the *Formulas* tab, in the *Function Library* group, click the **Math & Trig** button, and select **SUMIF** to open the *Function Arguments* dialog.

3. In the *Range* argument box, enter the cell range or named range to evaluate against the criteria.

4. In the *Criteria* argument box, enter the criteria. The criteria can be a text string, numerical value, expression, or cell reference. Text strings and expressions must be enclosed in quotation marks.

5. In the *Sum_range* argument box, enter the cell range or named range containing the values you want to add together. If you omit this argument, SUMIF will total the values in the *Range* argument instead.

6. Click **OK.**

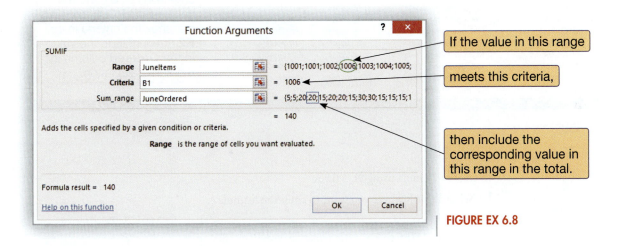

FIGURE EX 6.8

To sum data that meet multiple criteria, use SUMIFS. **SUMIFS** takes arguments for up to 127 pairs of criteria ranges and criteria. The result of SUMIFS is the total of all the cells that meet all criteria.

SUMIFS takes three required arguments and multiple optional arguments:

Sum_range—The range of cells to sum where criteria are met.

Criteria_range1—The range of cells containing the values to be evaluated against the first criteria.

Criteria1—The first criteria.

Criteria_range2—(Optional) the range of cells containing the values to be evaluated against the second criteria.

Criteria2—(Optional) the second criteria.

(continuing up to *Criteria_range127* and *Criteria127*)

The formula in Figure EX 6.9 uses SUMIFS to calculate the sum of the values in the *Ordered* column (the range *JuneOrdered*) where the Item ID (the range *JuneItems*) meets the criteria specified in cell *B1* and the PO # (the range *JunePOs*) meets the criteria specified in cell *B2*.

=SUMIFS(*Sum_range,Criteria_range1,Criteria1,[Criteria_range2],[Criteria2]...*)
=SUMIFS(JuneOrdered,JuneItems,B1,JunePOs,B2)

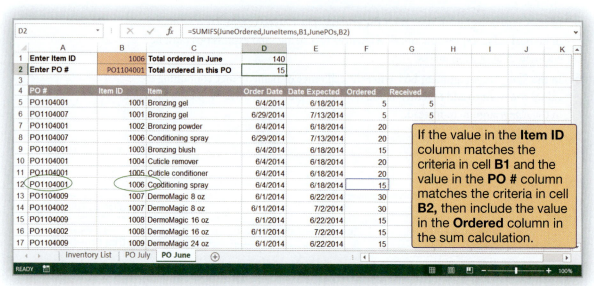

FIGURE EX 6.9

To create a formula using SUMIFS:

1. Select the cell where you want to enter the formula.

2. On the *Formulas* tab, in the *Function Library* group, click the **Math & Trig** button, and select **SUMIFS** to open the *Function Arguments* dialog.

3. In the *Sum_range* argument box, enter the cell range or range name containing the values to be summed if all the criteria are met.

4. In the *Criteria1_range* box, enter the cell range or range name containing the values to be evaluated against the first criteria.

5. In the *Criteria1* argument box, enter text string, number, expression, or cell reference for the first criteria. Text strings and expressions must be enclosed in quotation marks.

6. In the *Criteria2_range* box, enter the cell range or range name containing the values to be evaluated against the second criteria.

7. In the *Criteria2* argument box, enter text string, number, expression, or cell reference for the second criteria. Text strings and expressions must be enclosed in quotation marks.

8. Continue entering criteria range and criteria pairs until you are finished.

9. Click **OK.**

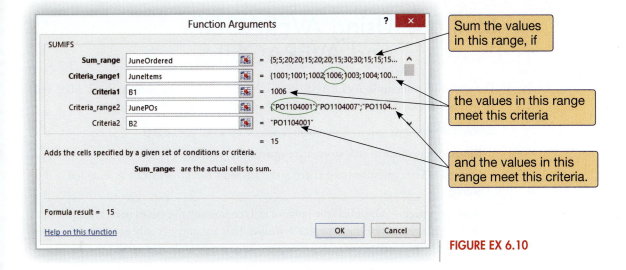

Sum the values in this range, if

the values in this range meet this criteria

and the values in this range meet this criteria.

FIGURE EX 6.10

tips & tricks

It is important to note that while SUMIF and SUMIFS look similar, the arguments are in a different order. SUMIF begins with the cell range to be evaluated against the criteria, while SUMIFS begins with the cell range to be summed. If you find it difficult to remember the difference, stick with SUMIFS. You can use SUMIFS to evaluate against a single criteria range. If the range you are summing is the same as the range you are evaluating, SUMIFS will allow you to use the same cell range in both arguments.

tell me **more**

When entering a numerical expression such as "<10" as the *Criteria* argument, you must enclose the expression in quotation marks. Text criteria must also be enclosed in quotation marks, but cell references or single numerical values do not.

let me **try**

Open the student data file **EX6-03-PurchaseOrders** and try this skill on your own:

1. Enter a formula in cell **D1** using **SUMIF** to calculate the total number of items ordered for the item number specified in cell **B1.** Use the range name **JuneItems** for the *Range* argument and **JuneOrdered** for the *Sum_range* argument.

2. Now enter a formula in cell **D2** using **SUMIFS** to calculate the number of items ordered (use the named range **JuneOrdered**) where the value in the **JuneItems** named range is equal to the value in cell **B1** and the value in the **JunePOs** named range is equal to **B2.**

3. Save the file as directed by your instructor and close it.

Skill 6.4 Using AVERAGEIF and AVERAGEIFS

The statistical functions AVERAGEIF and AVERAGEIFS are similar to SUMIF and SUMIFS. They calculate the average value where cells meet specified criteria.

AVERAGEIF takes two required arguments and one optional argument:

Range—The range of cells to evaluate against the criteria.

Criteria—The conditions (the criteria) the cell must meet in order to be included in the average.

Average_range—(Optional) the range of cells containing the values to be averaged. *Average_range* must be the same size as *Range*. This argument is only necessary when the values to be averaged are not the same as the values to be evaluated against the criteria.

The formula in Figure EX 6.11 uses AVERAGEIF to calculate the average delivery time for items currently on order. AVERAGEIF evaluates the values in the *ReorderStatus* range (the *On Order?* column). If the value matches the criteria specified (*yes*), then the corresponding value in the *DeliveryTime* range (the *Delivery Time in Days* column) is included in the range of values to be averaged. Note that the text criteria *yes* must be enclosed in quotation marks.

=AVERAGEIF(*Range,Criteria,[Average_range]*)
=AVERAGEIF(ReorderStatus,"yes",DeliveryTime)

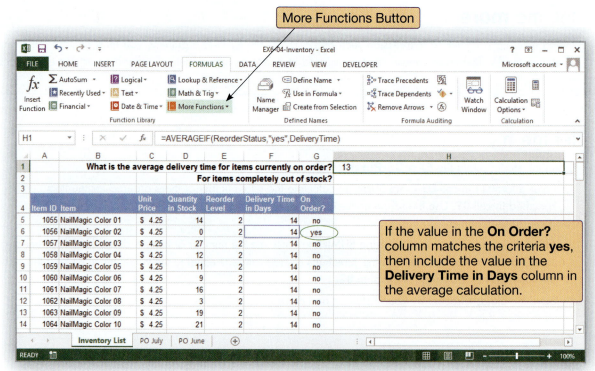

FIGURE EX 6.11

excel 2013   chapter 6 Exploring Advanced Functions

To create a formula using AVERAGEIF:

1. Select the cell where you want to enter the formula.

2. On the *Formulas* tab, in the *Function Library* group, click the **More Functions** button, point to **Statistical,** and select **AVERAGEIF** to open the *Function Arguments* dialog.

3. In the *Range* argument box, enter the cell range or named range to evaluate against the criteria.

4. In the *Criteria* argument box, enter the criteria. The criteria can be a text string, numerical value, expression, or cell reference. Remember, text strings and expressions must be enclosed in quotation marks.

5. In the *Average_range* argument box, enter the cell range or named range containing the values you want to average. If you omit this argument, AVERAGEIF will average the values in the *Range* argument instead.

6. Click **OK.**

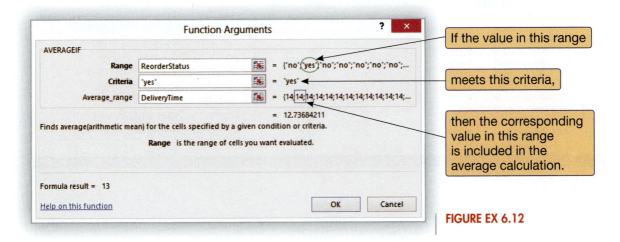

FIGURE EX 6.12

To average data that meet multiple criteria, use AVERAGEIFS. **AVERAGEIFS** takes arguments for up to 127 pairs of criteria ranges and criteria. The result of AVERAGEIFS is the average of all the cells that meet all criteria.

AVERAGEIFS takes three required arguments and multiple optional arguments:

Average_range—The range of cells to average where criteria are met.

Criteria_range1—The range of cells containing the values to be evaluated against the first criteria.

Criteria1—The first criteria.

Criteria_range2—(Optional) the range of cells containing the values to be evaluated against the second criteria.

Criteria2—(Optional) the second criteria.

(continuing up to *Criteria_range127* and *Criteria127*)

The formula in Figure EX 6.13 uses AVERAGEIFS to calculate the average delivery time for items currently on order that are out of stock. The values in the *DeliveryTime* range (the *Delivery Time in Days* column) are included in the range of values to be averaged only where the corresponding value in the *ReorderStatus* range (the *On Order?* column) match the criteria specified (*yes*) and the corresponding value in the *InStock* range (the *Quantity in Stock* column) match the criteria specified (*0*).

=AVERAGEIFS(*Sum_range,Criteria_range1,Criteria1,[Criteria_range2],[Criteria2]...*)
=AVERAGEIFS(DeliveryTime,ReorderStatus,"yes",InStock,0)

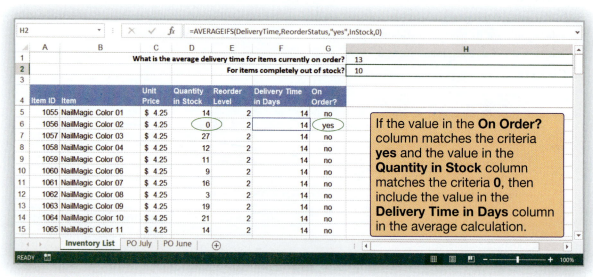

FIGURE EX 6.13

To create a formula using AVERAGEIFS:

1. Select the cell where you want to enter the formula.

2. On the *Formulas* tab, in the *Function Library* group, click the **More Functions** button, point to **Statistical,** and select **AVERAGEIFS** to open the *Function Arguments* dialog.

3. In the *Average_range* argument box, enter the cell range or range name containing the values to be averaged if all the criteria are met.

4. In the *Criteria1_range* box, enter the cell range or range name containing the values to be evaluated against the first criteria.

5. In the *Criteria1* argument box, enter text string, number, expression, or cell reference for the first criteria. Remember, text strings and expressions must be enclosed in quotation marks.

6. In the *Criteria2_range* box, enter the cell range or range name containing the values to be evaluated against the second criteria.

7. In the *Criteria2* argument box, enter text string, number, expression, or cell reference for the second criteria. Remember, text strings and expressions must be enclosed in quotation marks.

8. Continue entering criteria range and criteria pairs until you are finished.

9. Click **OK.**

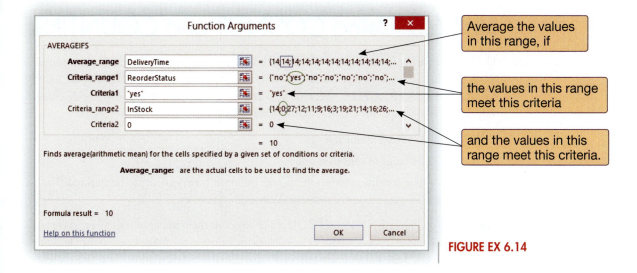

Average the values in this range, if

the values in this range meet this criteria

and the values in this range meet this criteria.

tips & tricks

It is important to note that while AVERAGEIF and AVERAGEIFS look similar, the arguments are in a different order. AVERAGEIF begins with the cell range to be evaluated against the criteria, while AVERAGEIFS begins with the cell range to be averaged. If you find it difficult to remember the difference, stick with AVERAGEIFS. You can use AVERAGEIFS to evaluate against a single criteria range. If the range you are summing is the same as the range you are evaluating, AVERAGEIFS will allow you to use the same cell range in both arguments.

let me try

Open the student data file **EX6-04-Inventory** and try this skill on your own:

1. Enter a formula in cell **H1** using **AVERAGEIF** to calculate the average delivery time for items currently on order (where the value in the *On Order?* column is *yes*). Use the range name **ReorderStatus** for the *Range* argument and **DeliveryTime** for the *Average_range* argument.

2. Now enter a formula in cell **H2** using **AVERAGEIFS** to calculate the average delivery time (use the named range **DeliveryTime**) where the value in the **ReorderStatus** named range is equal to **yes** and the value in the **InStock** named range is equal to **0.**

3. Save the file as directed by your instructor and close it.

Skill 6.5 Using COUNTIF and COUNTIFS

The basic counting functions COUNT, COUNTA, and COUNTBLANK allow you to count the numbers, values, and blank cells in a cell range. Similar to SUMIF/SUMIFS and AVERAGEIF/AVERAGEIFS, there are also counting functions that allow you to count only data that meet specific criteria: **COUNTIF** and **COUNTIFS**.

COUNTIF takes two arguments:

Range—The range of cells to count.

Criteria—The conditions (the criteria) the cell must meet in order to be counted. The criteria can be a text string or numerical value or expression.

The formula in Figure EX 6.15 uses COUNTIF to count the number of cells where there are less than five items in stock. COUNTIF evaluates the values in the *InStock* range (the *Quantity in Stock* column). If the value matches the criteria specified (<5), then the cell is included in the count. Note that the expression criteria <5 must be enclosed in quotation marks:

=COUNTIF(*Range,Criteria*)
=COUNTIF(InStock,"<5")

FIGURE EX 6.15

To create a formula using COUNTIF:

1. Select the cell where you want to enter the formula.

2. On the *Formulas* tab, in the *Function Library* group, click the **More Functions** button, point to **Statistical,** and select **COUNTIF** to open the *Function Arguments* dialog.

3. In the *Range* argument box, enter the cell range or named range to evaluate against the criteria.

4. In the *Criteria* argument box, enter the criteria. The criteria can be a text string, numerical value, expression, or cell reference. Remember, text strings and expressions must be enclosed in quotation marks.

5. Click **OK.**

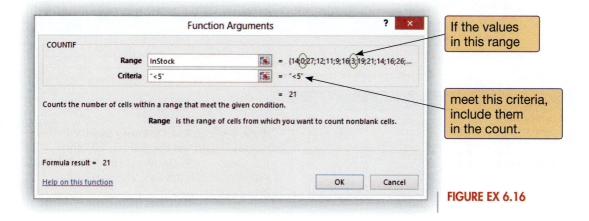

If the values in this range

meet this criteria, include them in the count.

FIGURE EX 6.16

To count data that meet multiple criteria, use COUNTIFS. COUNTIFS takes arguments for up to 127 pairs of criteria ranges and criteria. The result of COUNTIFS is the number of rows or columns that meet all criteria.

COUNTIFS takes two required arguments and multiple optional arguments:

Criteria_range1—The range of cells containing the values to be evaluated against the first criteria.

Criteria1—The first criteria.

Criteria_range2—(Optional) the range of cells containing the values to be evaluated against the second criteria.

Criteria2—(Optional) the second criteria.

(continuing up to *Criteria_range127* and *Criteria127*)

The formula in Figure EX 6.17 uses COUNTIFS to count the number of rows with less than five items in stock and a delivery time of greater than a seven days. COUNTIFS evaluates the values in the *InStock* range (the *Quantity in Stock* column) against the criteria <5 and the values in the *DeliveryTime* range (the *Delivery Time in Days* column) against the criteria >7. Where both criteria are met, the row is included in the count. Note that the criteria expressions <5 and >7 must be enclosed in quotation marks.

=COUNTIFS(*Criteria_range1,Criteria1,*[*Criteria_range2*],[*Criteria2*]...)
=COUNTIFS(InStock,"<5",DeliveryTime,">7")

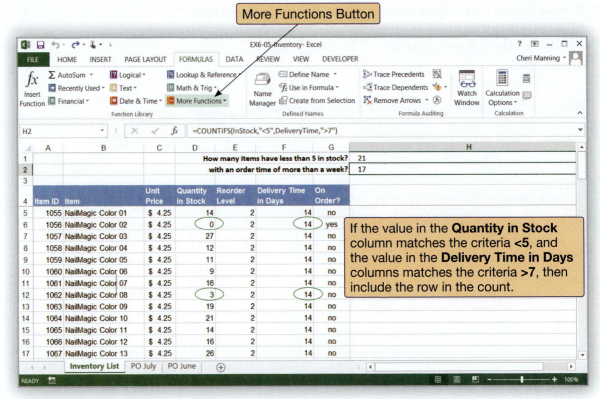

FIGURE EX 6.17

To create a formula using COUNTIFS:

1. Select the cell where you want to enter the formula.

2. On the *Formulas* tab, in the *Function Library* group, click the **More Functions** button, point to **Statistical,** and select **COUNTIFS** to open the *Function Arguments* dialog.

3. In the *Criteria1_range* box, enter the cell range or range name containing the values to be evaluated against the first criteria.

4. In the *Criteria1* argument box, enter text string, number, expression, or cell reference for the first criteria.

5. In the *Criteria2_range* box, enter the cell range or range name containing the values to be evaluated against the second criteria.

6. In the *Criteria2* argument box, enter text string, number, expression, or cell reference for the second criteria.

7. Continue entering criteria range and criteria pairs until you are finished.

8. Click **OK.**

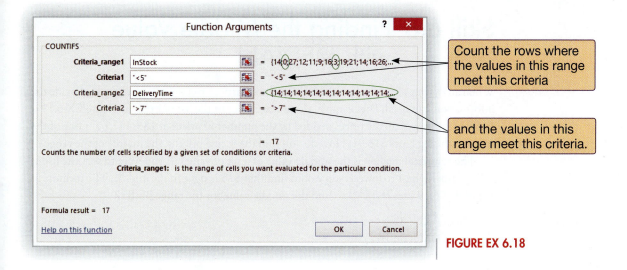

Count the rows where the values in this range meet this criteria

and the values in this range meet this criteria.

FIGURE EX 6.18

tips & tricks

The COUNTIFS function is only compatible with Excel 2007 and later.

tell me more

When working with text criteria, you can use the wildcard characters * and ? to find inexact text matches. The * wildcard replaces any string of characters. The ? wildcard replaces a single character.

❯ Enter the criteria argument "spa*" to return data that begin with the letters *spa*.

❯ Enter the criteria argument "*a" to return data that end with the letter *a*.

❯ Enter the criteria argument "*spa*" to return data that include the letters *spa* anywhere in the string.

❯ Enter the criteria argument "sp?" to return data that end with any single character after *sp* (e.g., *spa* or *spy*).

❯ Enter the criteria argument "sp??" to return data that end with any two characters after *sp* (e.g., *spar* or *spin*).

let me try

Open the student data file **EX6-05-Inventory** and try this skill on your own:

1. Enter a formula in cell **H1** using **COUNTIF** to count the number of cells where the number of items in inventory is **less than 5.** Use the range name **InStock** for the *Range* argument.

2. Now enter a formula in cell **H2** using **COUNTIFS** to calculate the number of rows where the value in the **InStock** named range **less than 5** and the value in the **DeliveryTime** named range is **greater than 7.**

3. Save the file as directed by your instructor and close it.

Skill 6.6 Finding the Middle Value with MEDIAN

When analyzing a list of values, calculating the statistical average may not always provide the information you need. For example, the average price of the list of items in Figure EX 6.19 is $16.91 (the sum of all the prices divided by the number of prices or 186/11), but none of the items in the list costs $16.91. How do you find the actual price in the middle of the range?

The statistical **median** is the middle value of a set of values. If you were to sort the list of prices from highest to lowest, you would find that $15 is right in the middle. The formula in Figure EX 6.19 uses **MEDIAN** to find the middle value for the range B2:B12.

=MEDIAN(*Number1*,[*Number2*]...)
=MEDIAN(B2:B12)

FIGURE EX 6.19

MEDIAN is a fairly simple function to use. Most of the time, you may find it easiest to type the formula directly in the cell or the formula bar. Type: **=MEDIAN(** and then enter the cell range or named range for the *Number1* argument. Type **)** and press ⏎Enter. If you prefer using the *Function Arguments* dialog, on the *Formulas* tab, in the *Function Library* group, click the **More Functions** button, point to **Statistical,** and then click **MEDIAN** to open the *Function Arguments* dialog. MEDIAN takes up to 255 *Number* arguments.

tips & tricks

❭ MEDIAN ignores empty cells and cells that contain text.

❭ If there is an even number of values in the range, MEDIAN will return the average (mean) of the two middle values.

let me try

Open the student data file **EX6-06-Inventory** and try this skill on your own:

Enter a formula in cell **B15** to find the middle value (the median) for prices listed in cells **B2:B12**. Save the file as directed by your instructor and close it.

excel 2013   chapter 6 Exploring Advanced Functions

Skill 6.7 Finding the Most Common Value(s) with MODE.SNGL and MODE.MULT

By now you should know how to find the average (mean) value or the middle (median) value in a list of values, but what if you want to find the most common value? The statistical **mode** is the value that appears most often in a group of values.

In Figure EX 6.20, three values appear twice in the price list B2:B12: $10.00, $15.00, and $25.00. The **MODE.SNGL** function returns a single mode value (the first mode value it finds). If there are no duplicate values, MODE.SNGL will return the error *#N/A*.

=MODE.SNGL(*Number1*,[*Number2*]...)
=MODE.SNGL(B2:B12)

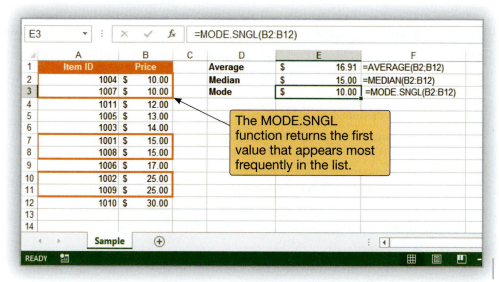

FIGURE EX 6.20

MODE.SNGL is a fairly simple function to use. Most of the time, you may find it easiest to type the formula directly in the cell or the formula bar. If you prefer using the *Function Arguments* dialog, on the *Formulas* tab, in the *Function Library* group, click the **More Functions** button, point to **Statistical,** and then click **MODE.SNGL** to open the *Function Arguments* dialog. You may enter up to 255 cell ranges or range names as arguments.

If your dataset includes more than one mode, you can use the **MODE.MULT** function in an array formula to return multiple values. An **array** formula is capable of conducting multiple calculations, in this case, producing multiple results.

The MODE.MULT function used in Figure EX 6.21 populates cells E4:E6 (the results array) with the three mode values: 10, 15, and 25.

=MODE.MULT(*Number1*,[*Number2*]...)
=MODE.MULT(B2:B12)

Notice that the formula using MODE.MULT is the same as the formula for MODE.SNGL except the formula in Figure EX 6.21 is surrounded by braces. The braces tell Excel that this is an array formula and that the selected cells should be populated with multiple values.

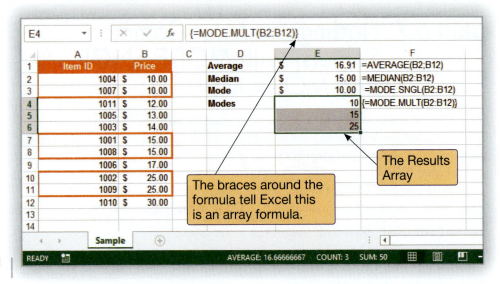

FIGURE EX 6.21

To use MODE.MULT, instead of selecting a single cell, select the range of cells in which you want the results to display. This defines the results array. You do not need to know the exact number of cells to select; if the results array has more cells than there are modes, the extra cells display #N/A.

Use one of these methods to enter the formula:

A. Enter the formula by typing it directly in the formula bar. After typing the formula, press **Ctrl** + **↑ Shift** + **← Enter**. Using this keystroke combination instructs Excel to enter an array formula. Notice that Excel places braces around the formula. You cannot type the braces. You must use **Ctrl** + **↑ Shift** + **← Enter** after typing the formula.

B. Enter the formula using the *Function Arguments* dialog.

1. On the *Formulas* tab, in the *Function Library* group, click the **More Functions** button, point to **Statistical,** and then click **MODE.MULT.**

2. Enter the cell range or range name to evaluate in the argument box.

3. Click **OK.**

4. Place the cursor in the formula bar and press **Ctrl** + **↑ Shift** + **← Enter** before clicking another cell or pressing any other keyboard key.

tips & tricks

Both MODE.SNGL and MODE.MULT are compatible only with Excel 2010 and later.

tell me more

MODE.SNGL and MODE.MULT ignore empty cells and cells that contain text.

let me try

Open the student data file **EX6-07-Inventory** and try this skill on your own:

1. Enter a formula in cell **E3** to display the first mode value in the range **B2:B12.**

2. Enter an array formula in cells **E4:E6** to display the three mode values from the range **B2:B12.** Remember to select the results array before entering the formula.

3. Save the file as directed by your instructor and close it.

Skill 6.8 Exploring More Logical Functions: AND, OR, and NOT

While you could use the logical function IF, introduced earlier, to return text strings "true" and "false," it is easier to use one of the other logical functions designed specifically to return a TRUE or FALSE response: AND, OR, and NOT. As you will see from the examples in this skill, there are multiple correct approaches to asking questions about your data. How you pose the question determines which function you should use to answer it—AND, OR, or NOT?

) If you are looking for a true value to multiple conditions, use AND.

) If you are looking for a true value to any one of multiple conditions, use OR.

) If you are looking for a true value to a question posed in the negative, use NOT.

The logical function **AND** returns TRUE if all the arguments are true, and FALSE if at least one of the arguments is false.

In Figure EX 6.22, the formula used to evaluate whether or not more items should be ordered will only return TRUE if the value in the *Quantity in Stock* column is less than or equal to the value in the *Reorder Level* column. In this case, the AND function requires only one argument: the expression to be evaluated.

=AND(*Logical1*,[*Logical2*]...)
=AND(D4<=E4)

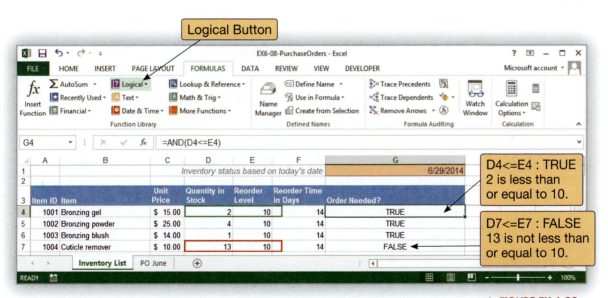

FIGURE EX 6.22

Once you understand how the AND function evaluates an expression and returns TRUE or FALSE, you can create more complex formulas using multiple arguments.

In Figure EX 6.23, the formula used to evaluate whether or not the purchase order line item is closed requires two arguments. The first argument checks whether the value in the *Ordered* column equals the value in the *Received* column. The second argument checks whether the value in the *Date Expected* column is less than (earlier than) the value in the cell named *CompareDate* (cell H1). The AND function returns TRUE only if *both* arguments are true.

=AND(F4=G4,E4<CompareDate)

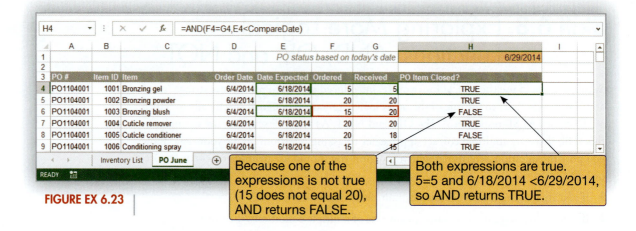

FIGURE EX 6.23

Callout: Because one of the expressions is not true (15 does not equal 20), AND returns FALSE.

Callout: Both expressions are true. 5=5 and 6/18/2014 <6/29/2014, so AND returns TRUE.

To create a formula using the AND function:

1. Select the cell where you want to enter the formula.

2. On the *Formulas* tab, in the *Function Library* group, click the **Logical** button. Select **AND** to open the *Function Arguments* dialog.

3. Enter the first comparison expression in the *Logical1* box. Expressions do not need to be enclosed in quotation marks, but text strings do. Enter additional arguments as necessary. The AND function can take up to 255 arguments. Remember, **all** the arguments must be true in order for the AND function to return TRUE.

4. Click **OK**.

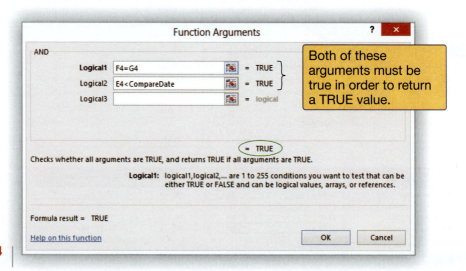

Callout: Both of these arguments must be true in order to return a TRUE value.

FIGURE EX 6.24

The logical function **OR** returns TRUE if at least one of the arguments is true and FALSE if all the arguments are false.

In Figure EX 6.25, we turn the purchase order question on its head. Now we want to know if the PO item is still open instead of closed. The PO item is considered open if the value in the *Ordered* column does not equal the value in the *Received* column **or** the value in the *Date Expected* column is greater than (later than) or equal to the value in the cell named *CompareDate* (cell H1). The OR function returns TRUE if **either** argument is true.

=OR(*Logical1*,[*Logical2*]...)
=OR(G6<>F6,E6>=CompareDate)

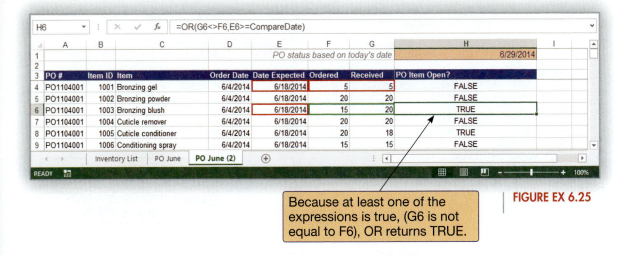

Because at least one of the expressions is true, (G6 is not equal to F6), OR returns TRUE.

FIGURE EX 6.25

To create a formula using the OR function:

1. Select the cell where you want to enter the formula.

2. On the *Formulas* tab, in the *Function Library* group, click the **Logical** button. Select **OR** to open the *Function Arguments* dialog.

3. Enter the first comparison expression in the *Logical1* box. Expressions do not need to be enclosed in quotation marks, but text strings do. Enter additional arguments as necessary. The OR function can take up to 255 arguments. Remember, if *any* of the arguments is true, the OR function returns TRUE.

4. Click **OK**.

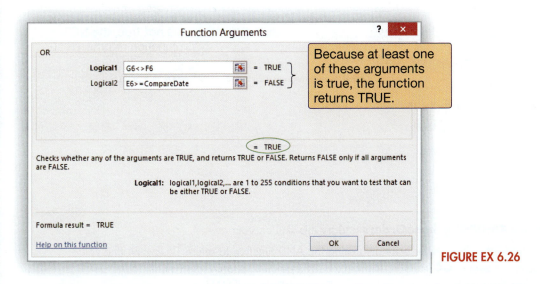

Because at least one of these arguments is true, the function returns TRUE.

FIGURE EX 6.26

The logical function **NOT** returns TRUE if the argument is false, and FALSE if the argument is true. NOT evaluates only one logical test.

Let's return to the inventory question in Figure EX 6.27 and use the NOT function to evaluate whether or not it's time to order. The question is whether the value in the *Quantity in Stock* column is greater than the value in the *Reorder Level* column. If value of the expression is false, this formula returns the value TRUE. In other words, if *Quantity in Stock* is **not** greater than *Reorder Level,* it is time to reorder.

=NOT(*Logical*)
=NOT(D4>E4)

---

skill 6.8   Exploring More Logical Functions: AND, OR, and NOT

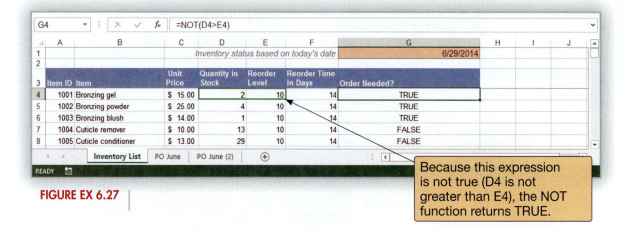

FIGURE EX 6.27

Because this expression is not true (D4 is not greater than E4), the NOT function returns TRUE.

To create a formula using the NOT function:

1. Select the cell where you want to enter the formula.

2. On the *Formulas* tab, in the *Function Library* group, click the **Logical** button. Select **NOT** to open the *Function Arguments* dialog.

3. Enter the expression to evaluate in the *Logical* box. Expressions do not need to be enclosed in quotation marks, but text strings do. Remember, if the expression is false, the NOT function returns TRUE.

4. Click **OK**.

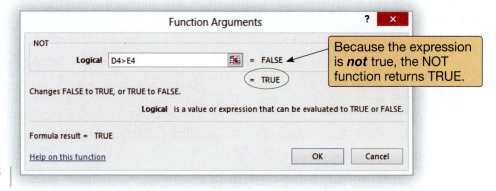

Because the expression is *not* true, the NOT function returns TRUE.

FIGURE EX 6.28

let me try

Open the student data file **EX6-08-PurchaseOrders** and try this skill on your own:

1. In cell **H4** on the *PO June* worksheet, enter a formula using the **AND** function to return TRUE if **F4** (the value in the *Ordered* column) is **equal to G4** (the value in the *Received* column) **and E4** (the value in the *Date Expected* column) is **less than** the value in the cell named **CompareDate** (cell **H1**).

2. Go to the *PO June(2)* worksheet. In cell **H4,** enter a formula using the **OR** function to return TRUE if **F4** (the value in the *Ordered* column) is **not equal to G4** (the value in the *Received* column) **or E4** (the value in the *Date Expected* column) is **greater than or equal to** the value in the cell named **CompareDate** (cell H1).

3. Go to the *Inventory List* worksheet. In cell **G4,** enter a formula using the **NOT** function to return TRUE if **D4** (the value in the *Quantity in Stock* column) is **not greater than E4** (the value in the *Reorder Level* column).

4. Save the file as directed by your instructor and close it.

Skill 6.9 Creating Nested IF Formulas

IF functions become truly powerful when you use them to evaluate a series of logical tests with multiple possible results. These formulas are referred to as **nested IF formulas** because each function is "nested" within the next outer function—like a series of Russian nesting dolls.

Before entering a complex nested IF formula, try working through the logic on paper first. This process will help you identify the optimal logic flow.

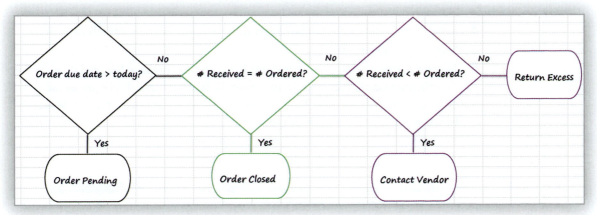

FIGURE EX 6.29

Figure EX 6.30 translates the logic flow diagram into a nested IF statement with three conditions to evaluate:

1. The first logical test is the outermost IF statement. If the value in the *Date Expected* column is greater than the value of the cell named *CompareDate,* then display "order pending."

2. If not, then evaluate if the value in the *Ordered* column is equal to the value in the *Received* column. If true, display "order closed."

3. If not, then evaluate if too few items were received. This is the last function in the logic flow—the innermost IF statement. If the value in the *Received* column is less than the value in the *Ordered* column, display "contact vendor." If not (in other words, if too many were received), display "return excess."

=IF(E4>CompareDate,"order pending",IF(F4=G4,"order closed",IF(F4<G4,"contact vendor","return excess")))

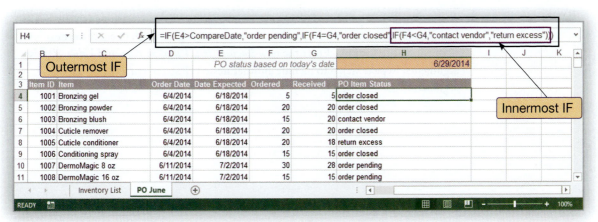

FIGURE EX 6.30

When each of the *Value_if_false* arguments is a nested IF function, the easiest way to build the formula is to use the *Function Arguments* dialog. Once you are comfortable with nested IF formulas, you may find it faster to type the formula directly in the cell or the formula bar.

1. Select the cell where you want to enter the formula.

2. On the *Formulas* tab, in the *Function Library* group, click the **Logical** button and select **IF.**

3. In the *Logical_test* box, enter the condition you want to test for in the outermost IF function.

4. In the *Value_if_true* argument box, enter the text string, value, or formula to use if the *Logical_test* argument is true.

5. To enter a nested IF function, click in the *Value_if_false* argument box, and then click the arrow in the *Name* box to the left of the formula bar to display the list of most recently used functions. If the function you want is not listed (IF), click **More Functions** at the bottom of the list to open the *Insert Function* dialog from which you can open the *Function Arguments* dialog for any function.

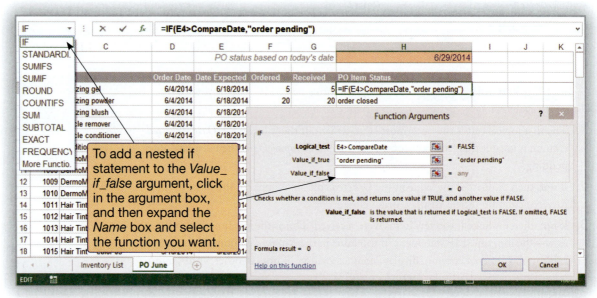

FIGURE EX 6.31

6. A new *Function Arguments* dialog opens. The previous dialog is still open in the computer's memory, but now you have an empty dialog in which to enter the next level of the nested IF formula. Enter the new *Logical_test, Value_if_true,* and *Value_if_false* arguments. Repeat Step 5 to include another nested IF statement as *Value_if_false* argument.

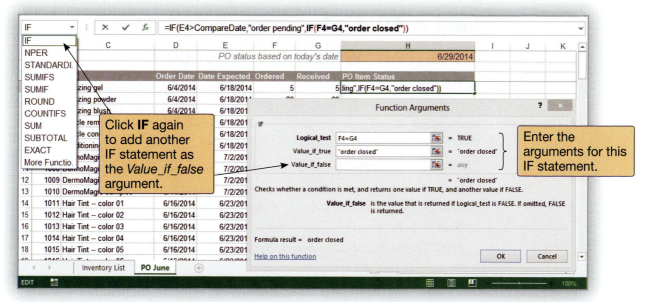

FIGURE EX 6.32

7. You can repeat Steps 5–6 as many times as you need to build the nested formula.

8. When you have entered the arguments for the innermost IF statement, click **OK** to enter the formula into your workbook.

If you want to use this same technique to enter a nested IF statement in the *Value_if_true* argument, you will need to enter the *Value_if_false* argument before the *Value_if_true* argument in the dialog. Once you switch to another *Function Arguments* dialog, you cannot go back to the previous one. Clicking **OK** completes the formula.

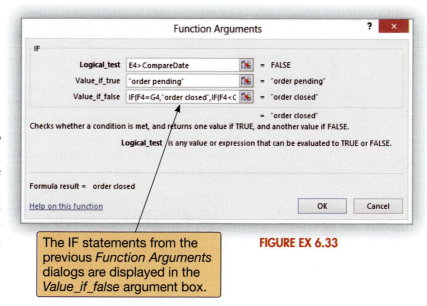

FIGURE EX 6.33

The IF statements from the previous *Function Arguments* dialogs are displayed in the *Value_if_false* argument box.

tips & tricks

Excel displays different color parentheses around the arguments for each nested function. When you are troubleshooting a complex formula, start with the innermost function and work your way out. The color parentheses will help you find the beginning and end of each set of arguments.

let me try

Open the student data file **EX6-09-PurchaseOrders** and try this skill on your own:

Enter a nested IF function in cell **H4** on the *PO June* worksheet to display the text string **order pending** if the *Date Expected* value in cell **E4** is **greater than** the value in the cell named **CompareDate.** Enter a nested IF formula in the *Value_if_false* argument to display the text string **order closed** if the value in **F4** is **equal to** the value in **G4.** Enter another nested IF formula in the *Value_if_false* argument to display the text string **contact vendor** if the *Received* value in cell **F4** is **less than** the *Ordered* value in cell **G4.** Display the text string **return excess** if it is not. Remember to use quotation marks around text strings. Save the file as directed by your instructor and close it.

Skill 6.10 Calculating Future Value with the FV Function

The first financial function you probably learned was how to calculate a loan payment with PMT. Another useful financial function is FV (**future value**). Use the **FV** function to calculate the future value of an investment. For example, if you deposit the same amount of money every period at a steady interest rate, use FV to calculate the future value of your savings.

The FV function has three required arguments and two optional arguments:

Rate—The interest rate. If the interest rate is an annual interest rate, it must be divided by the number of payment periods per year.

Nper—The total number of payments.

Pmt—The amount of each payment. As the payment is money going *out,* it is usually expressed as a negative number.

Pv—(Optional) the present value or how much the investment is worth today. If there is no money in the investment vehicle prior to the first payment, you can omit this argument. When the *Pv* argument is empty, Excel assumes a value of 0.

Type—(Optional) enter 1 for this argument if the payment is made at the beginning of each period. When the *Type* argument is empty, Excel assumes a value of 0 and calculates the result based on payments at the end of each period. Typically, savings accounts and other interest-bearing bank accounts pay interest at the end of each period.

Figure EX 6.34 shows a formula using the FV function to calculate the future value of an investment where cell B3 is the annual interest rate (the *Rate* argument), cell B4 is the number of payments made once a year (the *Nper* argument), and cell B2 is the amount contributed every year (the *Pmt* argument). There is no money in the account at the beginning, so the *Pv* argument is omitted, and the interest is paid at the end of every year, so the *Type* argument is also omitted. Notice that the *Pmt* argument is negative.

=FV(*Rate,Nper,Pmt,*[*Pv*],[*Type*])
=FV(B3,B4,-B2)

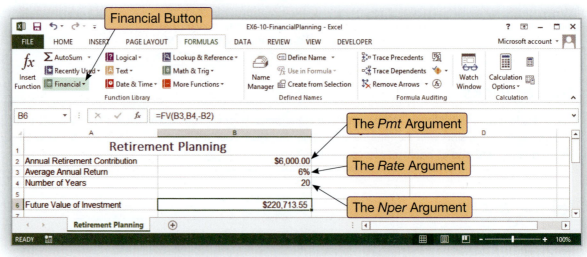

FIGURE EX 6.34

Let's look at another example in Figure EX 6.35 where the annual interest rate is also 6%, but the contributions are made monthly and the interest is paid at the end of every month. In this example, you must divide the ***annual*** interest rate by 12 because contributions are made monthly (twelve times a year).

=FV(B9/12,B10,-B8)

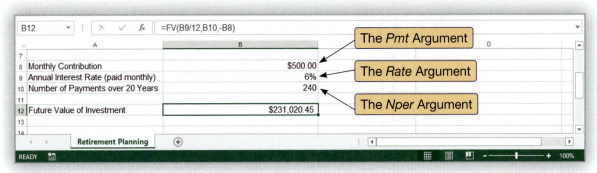

Monthly Contribution $500.00 — The *Pmt* Argument

Annual Interest Rate (paid monthly)   6% — The *Rate* Argument

Number of Payments over 20 Years   240 — The *Nper* Argument

Future Value of Investment $231,020.45

FIGURE EX 6.35

FIGURE EX 6.35

To create a formula using FV:

1. Select the cell where you want to enter the formula.

2. On the *Formulas* tab, in the *Function Library* group, click the **Financial** button. Click **FV** to open the *Function Arguments* dialog.

3. Enter the arguments. In Figure EX 6.36, the interest rate is annual and the payments are monthly, so the interest rate must be divided by 12. Notice that the *Pmt* argument includes a hyphen before the cell reference to make it negative. The *Pv* and *Type* arguments are optional and not necessary in this example.

4. Click **OK**.

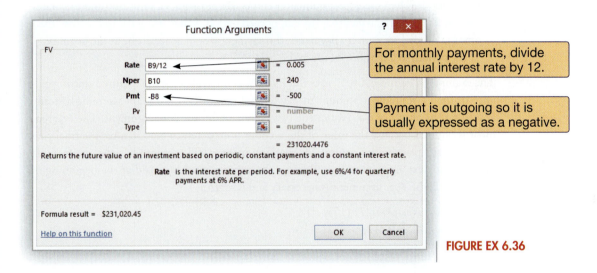

FIGURE EX 6.36

tips & tricks

When working with the financial functions, keep in mind that the *Pmt* argument (the payment) is negative if you are paying out the money, and positive if the money is coming in. This may seem counterintuitive, but you are really making a monthly payment *to* the investment (even if that "investment" is your own savings account).

let me try

Open the student data file **EX6-10-FinancialPlanning** and try this skill on your own:

Enter a formula in cell **B12** using FV to calculate the future value of this investment. Cell **B9** is the annual interest rate. Cell **B10** is the number of monthly payments. Cell **B8** is the amount of payment each month. Remember to express the *Pmt* argument as a negative and divide the annual interest rate by the number of payments per year. Save the file as directed by your instructor and close it.

skill 6.10   Calculating Future Value with the FV Function

Skill 6.11 Using PV to Calculate Present Value when Payments Are Constant

In financial terms, **present value** is the value today of a series of future payments. For example, at today's interest rates, what is the lump sum you would need to fund a retirement account to pay an annuity (a series of constant payments) to yourself? Present value can be calculated using the **PV** function when the payments are constant.

The PV function has three required arguments and two optional arguments:

Rate—The interest rate. If the interest rate is an annual interest rate, it must be divided by the number of payment periods per year.

Nper—The total number of payments.

Pmt—The amount of each payment. Since the payment is money going *out* of the investment, it is usually expressed as a negative number.

Fv—(Optional) the amount of money left after the last payment is made (the future value of the investment). If the final balance in the account is expected to be zero, you can omit this argument. When the *Fv* argument is empty, Excel assumes a value of 0.

Type—(Optional) enter 1 for this argument if the payment is made at the beginning of each period. When the *Type* argument is empty, Excel assumes a value of 0 and calculates the result based on payments at the end of each period. When using PV to calculate the amount needed for annuity payments, the payment would generally be at the beginning of the period, so *Type* must be set to 1.

The example in Figure EX 6.37 uses the PV function to calculate the required starting balance to fund a retirement account to pay $4,000 monthly for 20 years assuming a steady annual rate of return of 6%. Notice the two commas after the *Pmt* argument. The *Fv* argument is omitted because the value of the account is expected to be zero after the final payment, but the placeholder comma for that argument is still required because the formula includes the next argument, *Type*. Because the annuity would be paid at the beginning of every month, the *Type* argument is necessary and is set to 1.

$$=PV(Rate,Nper,Pmt,[Fv],[Type])$$
$$=PV(B15/12,B16*12,-B14,,1)$$

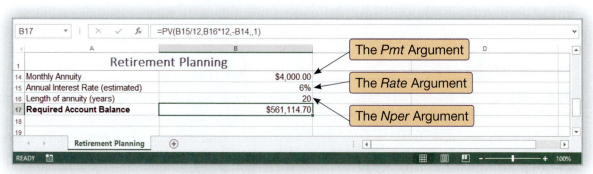

FIGURE EX 6.37

To create a formula using PV:

1. Select the cell where you want to enter the formula.

2. On the *Formulas* tab, in the *Function Library* group, click the **Financial** button. Click **PV** to open the *Function Arguments* dialog.

3. Enter the arguments. In our example, the payments will be monthly, so the annual interest rate (*Rate*) must be divided by 12 and the number of payout years (*Nper*) must be multiplied by 12 as shown in Figure EX 6.38. The *Pmt* argument includes a hyphen before the cell reference to make it negative. The *Pv* argument is omitted, but the *Type* argument is set to 1 because payments will be made at the beginning of every period.

4. Click **OK**.

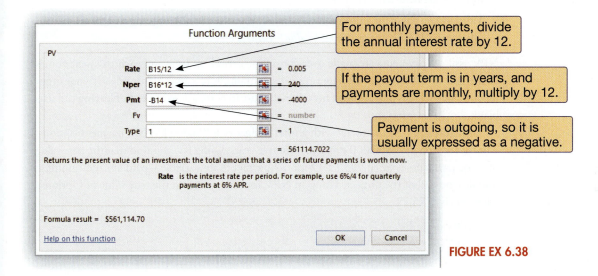

FIGURE EX 6.38

tell me **more**

The concept of the **Time Value of Money (TVM)** is essential to finance. It is the principle that a dollar in hand today is worth more than a promise of a dollar tomorrow because you have the opportunity to invest that dollar today and thus make even more money by tomorrow. The present value (the value today) of a series of future payments is actually less than the sum of those payments. This works **for** you when saving money for future payments to yourself. It can sometimes work **against** you when investing capital today in exchange for a series of future payments. Calculating present value is essential to making good financial decisions.

let me **try**

Open the student data file **EX6-11-FinancialPlanning** and try this skill on your own:

Enter a formula using PV in cell **B17** to calculate the present value needed to pay a monthly annuity over the next twenty years. Cell **B15** is the expected annual interest rate. Cell **B16** is the number of years over which the monthly payments will be made. Cell **B14** is the amount of each monthly payment. Payments will be made at the beginning of every period. Pay attention to the time periods for the interest rate, payout period, and payment schedule. Remember to express the *Pmt* argument as a negative. Save the file as directed by your instructor and close it.

---

skill 6.11   Using PV to Calculate Present Value when Payments Are Constant

Skill 6.12 Using NPV to Calculate Present Value when Payments Are Variable

The **NPV** function is similar to PV, but it allows for variable payment amounts when calculating the present value of future payments. NPV can be especially useful for comparing two investment or payment options.

The NPV function has two required arguments:

Rate—The **discount rate**—the interest rate which would be reasonably expected if the money were invested elsewhere.

Value—The payment amount both incoming (positive) and outgoing (negative). NPV takes up to 254 *Value* arguments (*Value1, Value2,* etc.).

NPV assumes payments are made over consistent periods of time and each payment comes at the end of the period. NPV ignores cells containing text and blank cells. If your argument range includes periods with no values, be sure to enter a zero instead of leaving the cells blank.

In Figure EX 6.39, a project with a total budget of $300,000 has two payment options. The first option pays $60,000 every year for five years. Using PV, you find that the true value of those payments is $270,903.14. Option 2 payments are variable—paid at the beginning, middle, and end of the project. Using an NPV formula, you find the true value of Option 2 payments is $275,721.23.

=NPV(*Rate,Value1,[Value2]...*)
=NPV(F1,C2:C6)

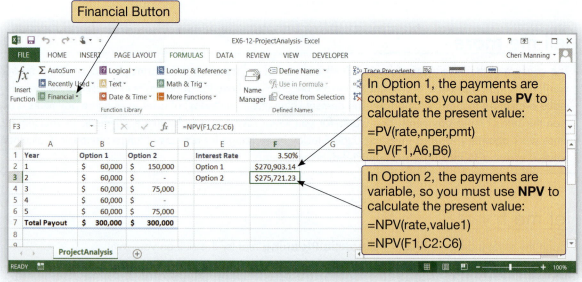

FIGURE EX 6.39

If you are the party paying out the money, Option 1 is the better choice. If you are receiving the payments, however, Option 2 would be better.

To use the NPV function:

1. Select the cell where you want to enter the formula.

2. On the *Formulas* tab, in the *Function Library* group, click the **Financial** button. Click **NPV** to open the *Function Arguments* dialog.

3. In the *Rate* box, enter the interest rate. The NPV *Function Arguments* dialog calls this the discount rate. When working with NPV, the discount rate is the same as the interest rate—just different terminology.

4. The remaining arguments are the payments (negative values) and income (positive values). NPV accepts up to 254 *Value* arguments. You can use cell ranges, named ranges, or individual cell references. If you use a cell range or named range, verify that they do not include blank cells—they will be ignored and the NPV calculation will be wrong.

5. Click **OK.**

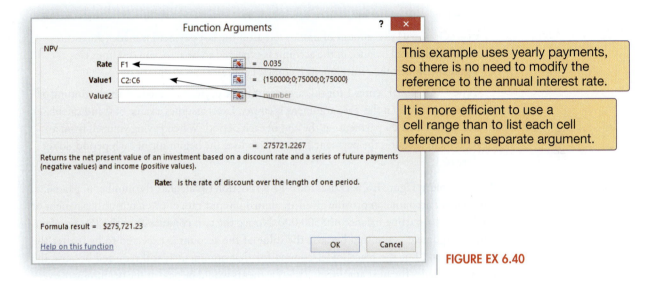

FIGURE EX 6.40

tips & tricks

The financial concept of net present value (also referred to as NPV) does not correspond to Excel's NPV function exactly. Net present value is the value today of future payments minus the cost of the investment—in other words, how much is the investment worth? The Excel function NPV actually calculates present value—the same as the PV function—except it allows for variable value inputs.

tell me more

As with all financial functions that use a *Rate* argument, *Rate* must be expressed in terms of the same time period as the payments. In other words, if you are using an annual interest rate and payments are made monthly, you will need to divide the interest rate by 12 for the *Rate* argument.

let me try

Open the student data file **EX6-12-ProjectAnalysis** and try this skill on your own:

In cell **F3**, enter a formula using the NPV function to calculate the present value of the series of yearly payments in the cell range **C2:C6**. The annual interest rate is in cell **F1**. Use a cell range as a single *Value* argument. Save the file as directed by your instructor and close it.

skill 6.12   Using NPV to Calculate Present Value when Payments Are Variable

Skill 6.13 Calculating the Number of Payments with NPER

Most of the financial functions we've worked with use *Nper* as an argument—the number of payments in the calculation. But what if you know all the variables except the number of payments? You can use the **NPER** function to calculate the number of payments available from a retirement account or due on a loan given a constant interest rate and payment amount.

The NPER function has three required arguments and two optional arguments:

Rate—The interest rate. If the interest rate is an annual interest rate, it must be divided by the number of payment periods per year.

Pmt—The amount of each payment. As the payment is money going *out,* it is usually expressed as a negative number.

Pv—The value of the investment or loan today.

Fv—(Optional) the amount of money left after the last payment is made (the future value). If the final balance in the account is expected to be zero, you can omit this argument. When the *Fv* argument is empty, Excel assumes a value of 0.

Type—(Optional) enter 1 for this argument if the payment is made at the beginning of each period. When the *Type* argument is empty, Excel assumes a value of 0 and calculates the result based on payments at the end of each period. When paying yourself from a retirement account, the payment is usually made at the beginning of each period, so set *Type* to 1.

The example in Figure EX 6.41 uses the NPER function to calculate the number of payments a retirement account can provide given an annual interest rate of 6%, a monthly payment of $3,000, and a starting balance of $500,000. Notice the two commas after the *Pv* argument. The *Fv* argument is omitted because the value of the account is expected to be 0 after the final payment, but the placeholder comma for that argument is still required because the formula includes the next argument, *Type.* Payments would be paid at the beginning of every month, so the *Type* argument is necessary and is set to 1.

=NPER(*Rate,Pmt,Pv,[Fv],[Type]*)
=NPER(B4/12,-B3,B2,,1)

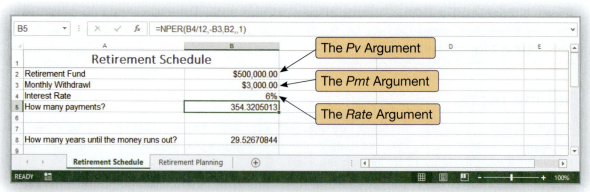

FIGURE EX 6.41

To create a formula using NPER:

1. Select the cell where you want to enter the formula.

2. On the *Formulas* tab, in the *Function Library* group, click the **Financial** button. Click **NPER** to open the *Function Arguments* dialog.

3. Enter the arguments. In our example, the payments will be monthly, so the annual interest rate (*Rate*) must be divided by 12. The *Pmt* argument includes a hyphen before the cell reference to make it negative. The *Fv* argument is omitted, but the *Type* argument is set to 1 because payments will be made at the beginning of every period.

4. Click **OK.**

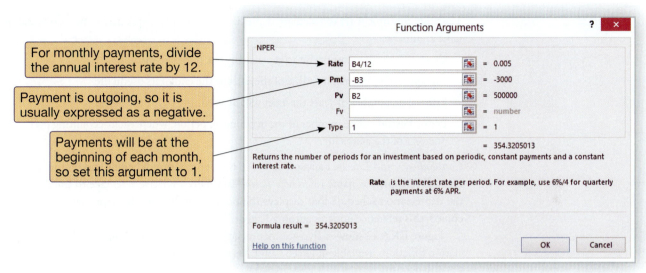

FIGURE EX 6.42

tips & tricks

You might find NPER useful in your personal life. You can use NPER to calculate how long it would take to pay off a student loan or credit card balance with steady monthly payments as long as you know the interest rate, starting balance, and monthly payment you plan to make.

let me try

Open the student data file **EX6-13-Retirement** and try this skill on your own:

In cell **B5** on the *Retirement Schedule* worksheet, enter a formula using NPER to calculate how long your retirement savings will last. The annual interest rate is in cell **B4.** The monthly payment is in cell **B3.** The current value of the account is in cell **B2.** Payments will be made at the beginning of every period. Remember to adjust the interest rate to reflect the same time period as the payments and to express the *Pmt* argument as a negative. Save the file as directed by your instructor and close it.

Skill 6.14 Creating a Depreciation Schedule

When a business purchases a significant asset such as equipment or computer software, generally accepted accounting principles (GAAP) state that the expense must be spread over the asset's useful lifetime. This is referred to as **depreciation**. Depreciation over the life of an asset is figured in a **depreciation schedule**. Depreciation is important because the value of the asset must be stated accurately on financial statements like the business's balance sheet. At the end of each accounting period, the asset's **book value** is recalculated using the initial cost minus the accumulated depreciation.

There are multiple ways to calculate depreciation, but most depreciation functions use the same arguments:

Cost—The initial cost of the asset—usually the purchase price.

Salvage—The fair market value of the asset at the end of its useful life.

Life—The number of years the asset will be used.

Per or **Period**—The number of the accounting period, where each accounting period is one year of the asset's life.

Cost, Salvage, and *Life* are constant values in the depreciation schedule and require an absolute cell reference or name reference. *Period* is usually a relative reference to the column in the depreciation schedule that displays the period number. As the depreciation formula is copied, this reference updates automatically.

Figure EX 6.43 shows a five-year depreciation schedule comparing four different depreciation functions available in Excel. Cell E2 is named *Cost,* cell E3 is named *Salvage,* and cell C3 is named *Life.*

> All the depreciation formulas use cell name references for the *Cost, Salvage,* and *Life* arguments. For simplicity, we've named the cells the same as the argument.

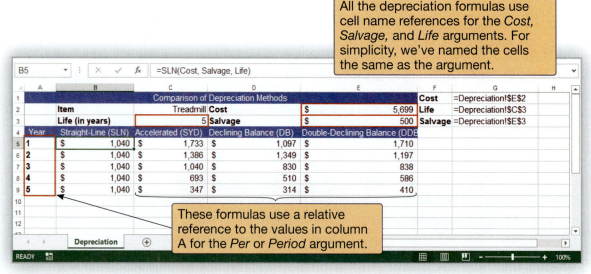

> These formulas use a relative reference to the values in column A for the *Per* or *Period* argument.

FIGURE EX 6.43

STRAIGHT LINE

Straight-line depreciation is the simplest depreciation to figure: the cost of the asset minus the salvage value divided by the life of the asset (in years). Because straight-line depreciation is the same for every period in the depreciation schedule, there is no need for a period argument. To calculate straight-line depreciation, use the **SLN** function.

=SLN(*Cost,Salvage,Life*)
=SLN(Cost,Salvage,Life)

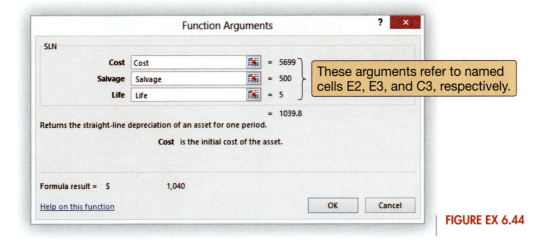

FIGURE EX 6.44

ACCELERATED

Accelerated depreciation assumes that the asset is worth more at the beginning of its lifespan and uses a higher rate of depreciation for early years in the depreciation schedule. In accounting, this is called **sum-of-the-years' digits (SOYD) depreciation**. Use the **SYD** function to calculate SOYD depreciation.

=SYD(*Cost,Salvage,Life,Per*)
=SYD(Cost,Salvage,Life,A5)

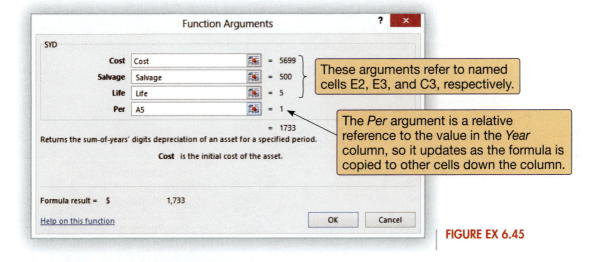

FIGURE EX 6.45

DECLINING BALANCE (DB)

Declining balance depreciation takes into account the declining book value of the asset. Use the **DB** function to calculate declining balance depreciation.

DB includes one optional argument—*Month*. This is used when the asset was in use for only part of the first accounting period. Its value is the number of months the asset was in service. When using this argument in a depreciation schedule, be careful to use it in the cell for period 1 only. Do not copy it to the remaining cells in the column. The formula for period 1 for an asset in use for six months in the first year looks like this:

=DB(*Cost,Salvage,Life,Period,[Month]*)
=DB(Cost,Salvage,Life,A5,6)

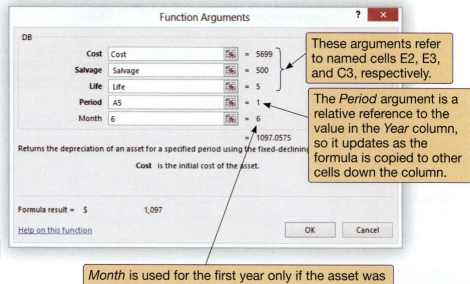

FIGURE EX 6.46

These arguments refer to named cells E2, E3, and C3, respectively.

The *Period* argument is a relative reference to the value in the *Year* column, so it updates as the formula is copied to other cells down the column.

Month is used for the first year only if the asset was not in use for the full year. The DB formula for the remaining years should not include this argument.

DOUBLE-DECLINING BALANCE (DDB)

Double-declining balance depreciation is similar to declining balance depreciation, but it uses a multiplier (usually 2) to accelerate the depreciation. Use the **DDB** function to calculate double-declining balance depreciation.

DDB includes one optional argument—*Factor.* Factor is the multiplier. When this argument is omitted, Excel assumes the factor is 2. A formula using a factor of 1.5 looks like this:

=DDB(*Cost,Salvage,Life,Period,*[*Factor*])
=DDB(Cost,Salvage,Life,A5,1.5)

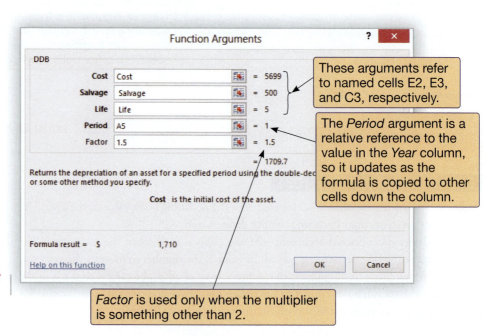

FIGURE EX 6.47

These arguments refer to named cells E2, E3, and C3, respectively.

The *Period* argument is a relative reference to the value in the *Year* column, so it updates as the formula is copied to other cells down the column.

Factor is used only when the multiplier is something other than 2.

To create a depreciation schedule using one of the depreciation functions:

1. First, set up the values for the arguments. Create cells containing the cost, salvage, and life values. Ideally, name the cells the same as the arguments—**Cost, Salvage,** and **Life.** This will make it easier to copy the formulas to the remaining cells in the schedule.

2. List the periods (year numbers) in a column. The depreciation formula will be entered in the column to the right of the period column.

3. Click the cell immediately to the right of the period 1 cell. On the *Formulas* tab, in the *Function Library* group, click the **Financial** button, and then click the depreciation function you want to use.

4. Enter absolute cell references or names for the *Cost, Salvage,* and *Life* arguments. If you selected SLN as the depreciation function, skip to Step 9.

5. Enter a relative cell reference for the *Per* or *Period* argument. Use the first cell in the list of period numbers.

6. If you selected the DB function, and period 1 is a partial period, enter the number of months the item was in use during period 1 in the *Month* argument.

7. If you are using DDB, and the multiplier is something other than 2, enter the multiplier in the *Factor* argument.

8. Click **OK.**

9. Copy the formula to the remaining cells in the depreciation schedule.

   - If you are using DB, copy the formula to the cell for period 2, remove the *Month* argument, and then copy the formula to the remaining cells in the schedule.

   - If you are using SLN, the depreciation schedule will have the same value for every period.

tips & tricks

When calculating the value of assets, the book value of the asset may not be the same as its taxable value. For tax purposes (in the United States), the IRS uses the modified accelerated cost recovery system (MACRS) depreciation schedule. The IRS groups assets in classes and specifies the length of time over which each class can be depreciated.

tell me more

If you format the data as a table, Excel will automatically copy the formula to the remaining cells in the column. If you are using the DB function and you have a value in the *Month* argument for year 1, it is best to not format the data as a table since you will need to modify the formula for the remaining years in the schedule.

let me try

Open the student data file **EX6-14-Depreciation** and try this skill on your own:

1. In cell **B5,** enter a formula using the function for the **Straight-line** depreciation method. Use the cell names **Cost, Salvage,** and **Life** as the function arguments. Copy the formula to cells **B6:B9.**

2. In cell **C5,** enter a formula using the function for the **Accelerated** depreciation method. Use the cell names **Cost, Salvage,** and **Life** as the function arguments. Use a relative reference to cell **A5** for the *Per* argument. Copy the formula to cells **C6:C9.**

3. In cell **D5,** enter a formula using the function for the **Declining balance** depreciation method. Use the cell names **Cost, Salvage,** and **Life** as the function arguments. Use a relative reference to cell **A5** for the *Period* argument. The asset will be in use for only six months in the first period. Modify the function as necessary and copy it to cells **D6:D9.**

4. In cell **E5,** enter a formula using the function for the **Double-declining balance** depreciation method. Use the cell names **Cost, Salvage,** and **Life** as the function arguments. Use a relative reference to cell **A5** for the *Per* argument. Use 1.5 as the multiplier. Copy the formula to cells **E6:E9.**

5. Save the file as directed by your instructor and close it.

Skill 6.15 Finding Data with MATCH and INDEX

Chapter 2 introduced lookup and reference functions with VLOOKUP. Recall that with VLOOKUP, the value you "look up" must match a value in the first column of the data array. But what if the value you want to look up is in a column other than the first? Instead of using VLOOKUP, you can use a combination of two functions: MATCH and INDEX.

MATCH returns the position of a specific value in a single row or column array. **INDEX** returns the value at the intersection of a specified row and column in an array. First use MATCH to find the row or column position of the value you want, and then use the results of MATCH as the row number or column number argument in INDEX.

The MATCH function has two required arguments and one optional argument:

Lookup_value—The text, number, or logical value you want to match.

Lookup_array—The range of cells grouped in a single row or column that contains the value you want to look up. If your data are organized as a table, be careful not to include the header row or label column in the *Lookup_array* range.

Match_type—(Optional) if you want to return only an exact match, you must enter 0 as the argument value. If the lookup array is sorted from smallest to largest, enter 1 (or omit the argument) to find the first position where the value is less than or equal to the lookup value. If the array is sorted from largest to smallest, enter −1 to find the first position where the value is greater than or equal to the lookup value.

The formula shown in Figure EX 6.48 uses MATCH to find the row position in the *InventoryItems* named range for the item entered in cell B1. *Match_type* is set to 0 to ensure an exact match only.

=MATCH(*Lookup_value,Lookup_array,[Match_type]*)
=MATCH(B1,InventoryItems,0)

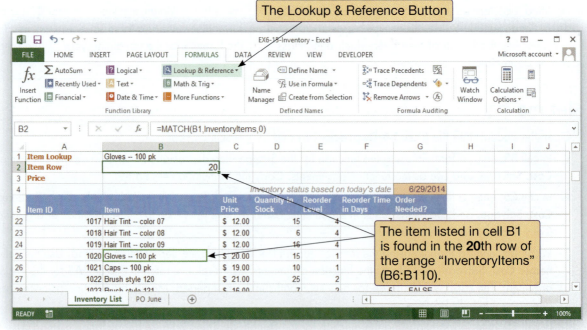

FIGURE EX 6.48

To create a formula using MATCH:

1. Select the cell where you want to enter the formula.

2. On the *Formulas* tab, in the *Function Library* group, click the **Lookup & Reference** button, and select **MATCH** to open the *Function Arguments* dialog.

3. Enter the *Lookup_value* argument. The example in Figure EX 6.48 allows the workbook user to enter an item name in cell B1. The *Lookup_value* argument then references that cell as shown in Figure EX 6.49.

4. Enter the *Lookup_array* argument. In Figure EX 6.49, this argument uses a named range that refers to a vertical range of cells.

5. If necessary, enter the *Match_type* argument. In this example, we want to ensure an exact match, so 0 is entered as the *Match_type* argument.

6. Click **OK.**

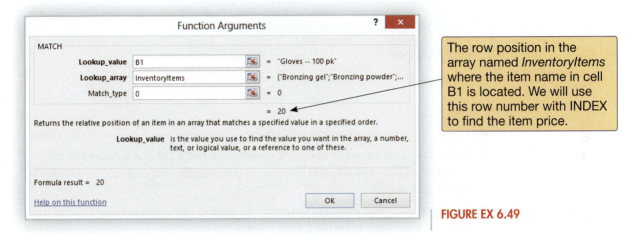

The row position in the array named *InventoryItems* where the item name in cell B1 is located. We will use this row number with INDEX to find the item price.

FIGURE EX 6.49

Now that you have identified the row position, you can use INDEX to find the value at the intersection of the row and column.

The INDEX function in this example has three required arguments:

Array—The range of cells containing the entire data array. If your data include a header row, do not include it in the cell range or named range used for the *Array* argument.

Row_num—The row position in the array for the value you want to look up.

Column_num—The column position in the array for the value you want to look up.

=INDEX(*Array,Row_num,Column_num*)
=INDEX(Inventory,B2,3)

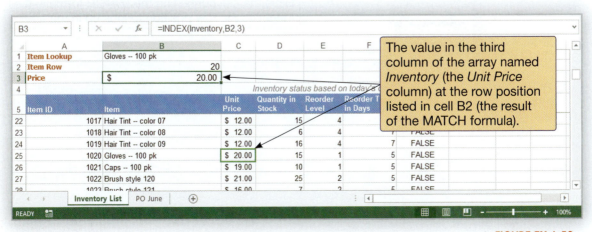

The value in the third column of the array named *Inventory* (the *Unit Price* column) at the row position listed in cell B2 (the result of the MATCH formula).

FIGURE EX 6.50

To create a formula using INDEX:

1. Select the cell where you want to enter the formula.

2. On the *Formulas* tab, in the *Function Library* group, click the **Lookup & Reference** button, and select **INDEX**.

3. There are two possible arguments lists for the INDEX function. Select the **array,row_num,column_num** option. Click **OK.**

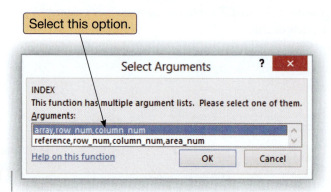

FIGURE EX 6.51

4. In the *Array* argument box, enter the range of cells or the name for the entire data array.

5. In the *Row_num* argument box, enter the reference to the cell that contains the row position you want to look up in the array. In this example, that is the cell containing the MATCH formula.

6. In the *Column_num* argument box, enter the number of the column that contains the data you want displayed in the formula results.

7. Click **OK.**

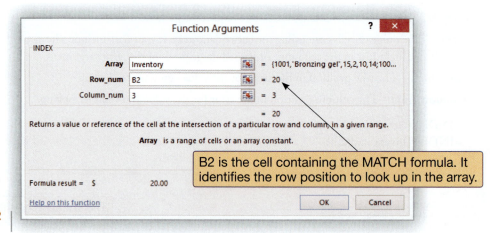

FIGURE EX 6.52

Once you understand how MATCH and INDEX function, you can combine them in a single formula using nested functions.

The formula in Figure EX 6.53 uses a MATCH formula as the INDEX function *Row_num* argument.

=INDEX(*Array*,MATCH(*Lookup_value,Lookup_array,Match_type*),*Column_num*)
=INDEX(Inventory,MATCH(B1,InventoryItems,0),3)

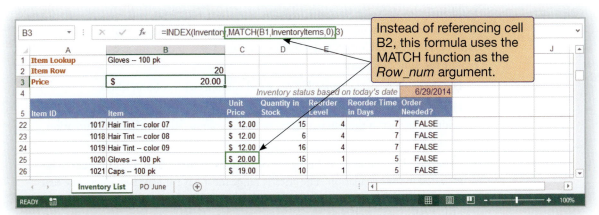

FIGURE EX 6.53

tips & tricks

If you are trying to match or look up a text string, and you're not sure of the exact text, you can use the * and ? wildcard characters. For more information about using wildcards and text strings, refer to the Tell Me More box in the skill *Using COUNTIF and COUNTIFS*.

tell me more

The example here uses a data array with a vertical layout—few columns and many rows. You can apply the same technique to a horizontal layout. Use MATCH to find the column position instead of the row position, and then in the INDEX formula, reference the MATCH formula in the *Column_num* argument instead of the *Row_num* argument.

let me try

Open the student data file **EX6-15-Inventory** and try this skill on your own:

1. In cell **B2** on the *Inventory List* worksheet, enter a formula using MATCH to look up the row position of the item listed in cell **B1** in the array named **InventoryItems**. Require an exact match.

2. In cell **B3,** enter a formula using INDEX to look up the price of the item at the row position in cell **B2.** Use the named range **Inventory** as the *Array* argument. The price is found in the third column of the array.

3. Save the file as directed by your instructor and close it.

Skill 6.16 Using Database Functions

Database functions allow you to perform statistical analysis on data that meet specific criteria by building queries similar to those used when working with a database. You could perform the same analysis by first filtering the data to meet the criteria and then using the regular statistical functions, but using the database versions of the functions is more efficient.

Excel includes database versions of many statistical functions you have already learned. They have the same names, with a "D" added to indicate "database": DSUM, DAVERAGE, DMIN, DMAX, DCOUNT, DCOUNTA, and a few more. All the database functions require the same arguments:

Database—The data arranged in rows and columns with column labels.

Field—The column to use in the calculation. The column can be identified by the column number in the database array or by the column label enclosed in quotation marks.

Criteria—The cell range defining the conditions the data must meet in order to be included in the calculation. The criteria range must have at least two rows. The first row includes labels that match the column labels in the database range. You need only include the columns for which you will enter criteria. The second row is where you enter the criteria. Criteria can be numeric values, expressions, or text.

The formula in Figure EX 6.54 uses the DAVERAGE function to calculate the average quantity in stock for items with a price of $20 or greater in the cell range named *InventoryDB*. (The *InventoryDB* range includes the column labels in row 6.) The *Criteria* argument includes the entire criteria range A3:F4. It would also work with a smaller cell range C3:C4 since that is the only column with criteria entered.

=DAVERAGE(*Database,Field,Criteria*)
=DAVERAGE(InventoryDB,"Qty in Stock",A3:F4)

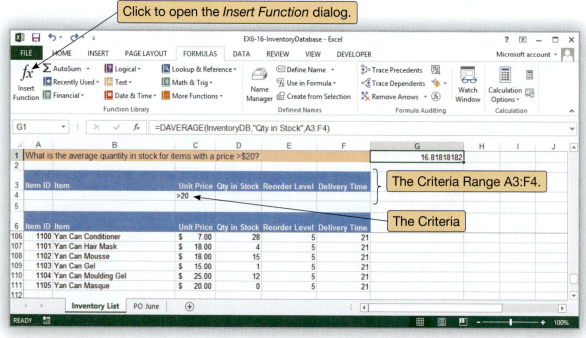

FIGURE EX 6.54

To create a formula using one of the database functions:

1. First, set up the criteria range. If you place the criteria range above the database range, include a blank row between the two ranges.

2. Enter the criteria in the blank row below the appropriate column heading.

3. After setting up the criteria range, select the cell where you want to enter the formula. On the *Formulas* tab, in the *Function Library* group, click the **Insert Function** button to open the *Insert Function* dialog. (Database functions are not accessible from any of the Ribbon buttons.)

4. If necessary, expand the **Or select a category** list and select **Database.**

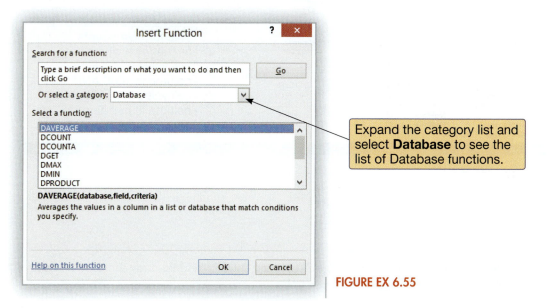

FIGURE EX 6.55

5. Select the function you want, and then click **OK** to open the *Function Arguments* dialog.

6. In the **Database** box, enter the range of cells or the name for the data array. Include the heading row.

7. In the **Field** box, enter the column number or the column label of the column containing the data to use in the calculation. If you use the column label, enclose the text in quotation marks.

8. In the **Criteria** box, enter the range of cells or the name for the criteria range.

9. Click **OK.**

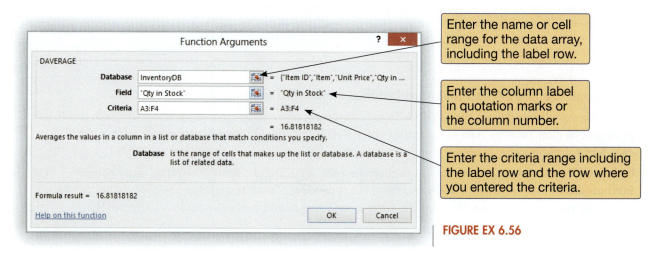

FIGURE EX 6.56

You can include multiple criteria in the criteria range. If you are familiar with creating a query in Access, this process is similar to entering multiple criteria for a query. To include only data that meet all the criteria, enter multiple criteria on the same row. To include data that meet any one of multiple criteria, add more rows to the criteria range, and enter each condition in a separate row.

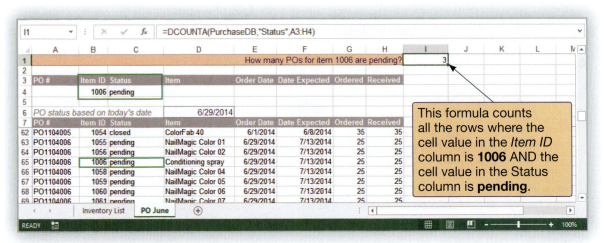

FIGURE EX 6.57

tips & tricks

❯ When using Lookup & Reference functions like VLOOKUP, MATCH, and INDEX, the data array should not include the label row. However, Database functions expect the array to be organized like a database, so the array must include the label row.

❯ If the database range includes a large amount of data, consider setting up a separate worksheet with criteria ranges. Workbooks can include multiple criteria ranges, and they need not be located in the same worksheet as the database range.

tell me **more**

Working with text criteria for database functions can be a little tricky. When you enter text in the criteria range, Excel finds any text string that **begins** with those letters. If you enter *Jones*, Excel will treat *Jones, Jonesy, Jones Park*, etc. as acceptable matches. If you want an **exact** match for the text string *Jones*, you need to create a text expression that begins with = and then encloses the text expression within quotation marks: ="=Jones"

let me **try**

Open the student data file **EX6-16-InventoryDatabase** and try this skill on your own:

1. In the *Inventory List* worksheet, use DAVERAGE to calculate the average quantity in stock for items with a price **greater than 20** in the data array named *InventoryDB*. The criteria range has been set up for you in cells **A3:F4**. Enter the appropriate criteria in the criteria range and then enter the formula in cell G1.

2. In the *June PO* worksheet, use DCOUNTA to count the cells in the **Status** column in the data array named **PurchasesDB** where the item ID is **1006** and the status is **pending.** The criteria range has been set up for you in cells **A3:H4**. Enter the appropriate criteria in the criteria range, and then enter the formula in cell **I1**.

3. Save the file as directed by your instructor and close it.

excel 2013 chapter 6 Exploring Advanced Functions

Skill 6.17 Managing Errors with the IFERROR Function

Most of Excel's functions return an error when a value cannot be found or when the formula cannot be calculated. Rather than displaying an error message to users, it may be more useful to display a text message or a specific value that you define. The **IFERROR** function performs this task.

The VLOOKUP formula in Figure EX 6.58 cannot find a match for the lookup value in cell B1, and so it displays the error #N/A. (If you need a refresher on the VLOOKUP function, refer to the skill *Finding Data Using the VLOOKUP Function*.)

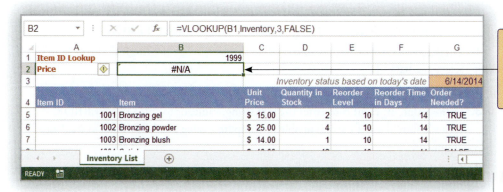

The item ID referenced in cell B1 does not exist, so the LOOKUP function returns the error #N/A.

FIGURE EX 6.58

By adding the IFERROR function around the existing VLOOKUP function, we can make the error message more user-friendly as shown in Figure EX 6.59. The IFERROR function takes two arguments:

Value—The formula to calculate.

Value_if_error—The value, text string, or formula to use if the formula in the *Value* argument results in an error. If you use a text string, enclose it in quotation marks.

=IFERROR(*Value,Value_if_error*)
=IFERROR(VLOOKUP(B1,Inventory,3,FALSE),"item not found")

Notice that IFERROR is used in a nested formula. The first argument contains the formula you want to calculate. The second argument is the text string, value, or formula to display if there is an error.

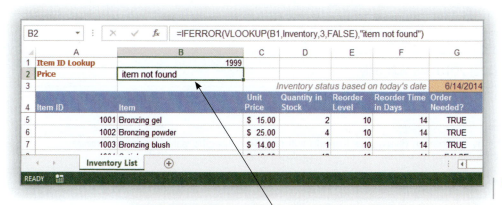

FIGURE EX 6.59

This Item ID still does not exist, but now the formula returns the message *item not found* because the VLOOKUP function is nested inside the IFERROR function.

Often, you will think to add IFERROR only after you notice that the initial formula results in errors. In these cases, it is easier to edit the formula directly in the formula bar or the cell, adding IFERROR and the *Value_if_error* argument without going through the *Function Arguments* dialog.

1. Click in the formula bar or double-click the cell to enter Edit mode.
2. Move the cursor to the beginning of the formula after the = and type **IFERROR(**
3. The existing formula is the *Value* argument. Move the cursor to the end of the formula, type a comma and then type the text string, value, or formula to use as the *Value_if_error* argument. If the *Value_if_error* argument is a text string, remember to enclose it in quotation marks.
4. Type the closing parenthesis **)** and press (← Enter).

To use the *Function Arguments* dialog to create a formula using IFERROR:

1. On the *Formulas* tab, in the *Function Library* group, click the **Logical** button, and select **IFERROR.**
2. In the **Value** box, enter the formula you want to calculate.
3. In the **Value_if_error** box, enter the text string, value, or formula the IFERROR formula should use if Excel is unable to compute a value for the formula in the *Value* argument.
4. Click **OK.**

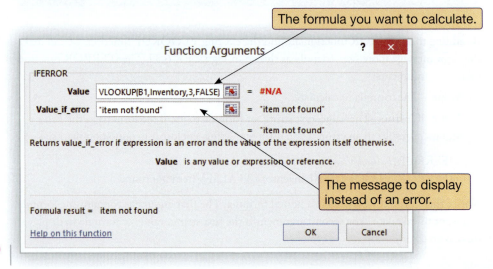

FIGURE EX 6.60

tips & tricks

IFERROR is compatible with Excel 2010 and later only.

tell me more

The *Value_if_error* argument may contain an alternative formula rather than a specific value or cell reference.

let me try

Open the student data file **EX6-17-Inventory** and try this skill on your own:

Modify the VLOOKUP formula in cell **B2** using IFERROR so if the VLOOKUP formula results in an error, the message **item not found** will display instead of the #N/A error. Save the file as directed by your instructor and close it.

Skill 6.18 Analyzing Complex Formulas Using Evaluate Formula

When working with a workbook that contains complex formulas, it can be very helpful to evaluate the formulas step by step before attempting to make any changes. The *Evaluate Formula* feature allows you to view and analyze the current value of each part of a formula. When a cell refers to another cell that contains a formula, you can view the precedent formula directly within the *Evaluate Formula* dialog. (To review the concepts of precedent and dependent formulas, review the skill *Finding Errors Using Trace Precedents and Trace Dependents.*)

To use the Evaluate Formula feature:

1. To evaluate a specific formula, click the cell that contains the formula you want to review.

2. On the *Formulas* tab, in the *Formula Auditing* group, click the **Evaluate Formula** button to open the *Evaluate Formula* dialog for the selected cell.

3. Click the **Step In** button to see the referenced cell highlighted in the worksheet so you can review the precedent formula.

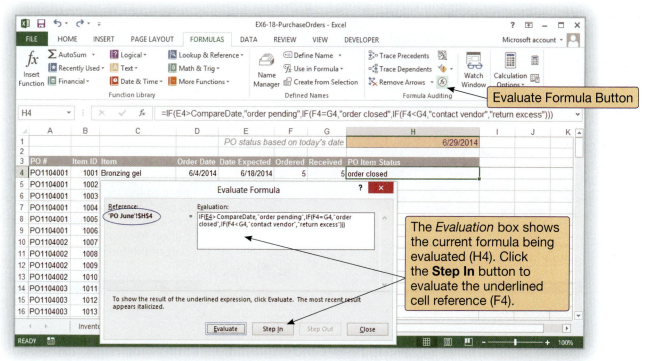

FIGURE EX 6.61

4. If the referenced cell contains a reference to another cell, you can click **Step In** again. The previous formula is still shown in the dialog to help you follow the trail that leads back to the formula in the cell you originally selected.

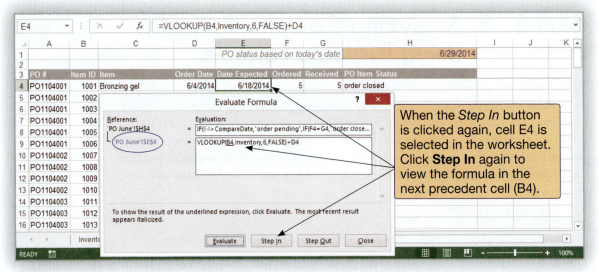

FIGURE EX 6.62

5. Continue clicking **Step In** to review the layers of precedent cells. When you have reached the end, the *Step In* button will be disabled. Click the **Step Out** button to remove the highlighting and go back one level.

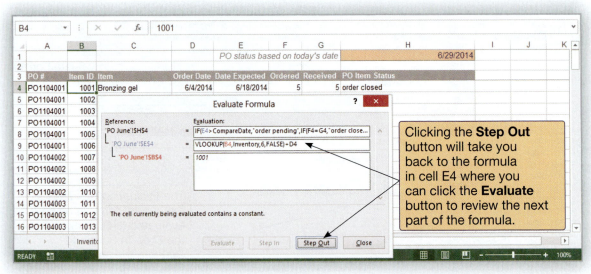

FIGURE EX 6.63

6. At any point, you can click the **Evaluate** button to see the current value for the underlined part of the current formula. Continue clicking **Evaluate** until you have reviewed each part of the formula and the final result is displayed in the *Evaluation* box. If you reach a part of the formula that Excel cannot compute, the *Evaluation* box will display an error message instead of a value.

7. Continue clicking **Step Out** and **Evaluate** until you have examined all parts of the formula, at which point you can click the **Start Over** button to begin the evaluation process from the beginning.

8. Click the **Close** button to dismiss the *Evaluate Formula* dialog.

tips & tricks

Once you click the **Evaluate** button, you cannot go back to review the previous part of the formula. If you find that you wanted to "step in" instead of evaluate that part of the formula, you'll need to click the **Close** button and re-open the *Evaluate Formula* dialog to start over.

tell me **more**

When the worksheet contains an error, the *Evaluate Formula* dialog can be launched directly from the *Error Checking* dialog.

1. On the *Formulas* tab, in the *Formula Auditing* group, click the **Error Checking** button.
2. Click the **Show Calculation Steps** button to open the *Evaluate Formula* dialog for the first cell that contains an error.
3. When you are finished evaluating the formula, click the **Close** button in the *Evaluate Formula* dialog to return to the *Error Checking* dialog.
4. Click the **Resume** button to continue checking the worksheet for errors.

let me **try**

Open the student data file **EX6-18-Inventory** and try this skill on your own:

1. If necessary, select cell **H4** on the *PO June* worksheet.
2. Open the *Evaluate Formula* dialog.
3. "Step in" to review the formula in the first cell reference. Continue "stepping in" until you reach the end of the trail of formulas.
4. Go back one level and evaluate all parts of the formula.
5. Repeat Steps 3–4 until you have reviewed all parts of the formula.
6. Save the file as directed by your instructor and close it.

key terms

Rounding	Present value
ROUND	PV
ROUNDUP	Time Value of Money (TVM)
ROUNDDOWN	NPV
Product	Discount rate
SUMPRODUCT	NPER
SUMIF	Depreciation
SUMIFS	Depreciation schedule
AVERAGEIF	Book value
AVERAGEIFS	Straight-line depreciation
COUNTIF	SLN
COUNTIFS	Accelerated depreciation
Median	Sum-of-the-years' digits (SOYD)
MEDIAN	depreciation
Mode	SYD
MODE.SNGL	Declining balance depreciation
MODE.MULT	DB
Array	Double-declining balance
AND	depreciation
OR	DDB
NOT	MATCH
Nested IF formula	INDEX
Future value	Database functions
FV	IFERROR

concepts review

1. Identify the result of this formula: =ROUNDUP(4.9876021,2)

   a. 4

   b. 4.97

   c. 4.98

   d. 4.99

2. Identify the *Sum_range* argument in this formula: =SUMIFS(JuneOrdered,JuneItems, B1,JunePOs,B2)

   a. JuneOrdered

   b. JunePOs

   c. B1

   d. B2

3. To find the middle value in a list of values, use the _____ function.

   a. AVERAGE

   b. MEDIAN

   c. MODE

   d. DAVERAGE

4. To create an array formula, press _____ after entering the formula in the formula bar.

    a. (Ctrl) + (↑ Shift)

    b. (↑ Shift) + (Alt)

    c. (Ctrl) + (↑ Shift) + (←Enter)

    d. (Ctrl) + (Alt) + (Delete)

5. Identify the result of this formula: =IF(3<4,AND(1<2,5>6),OR(1>2,2<1))

    a. TRUE

    b. FALSE

6. Identify the correct formula to calculate how much money you will have in an investment account where $200 is invested every month for two years at 3.5% annual interest.

    a. =FV(3.5%/12,24,–200)

    b. =PV(3.5%/12,24,–200)

    c. =FV(3.5%,2,–200)

    d. =FV(3.5%/12,2,–200)

7. To calculate the present value of a future investment with variable inflows and outflows of capital, use the _____ function.

    a. PV

    b. FV

    c. NPV

    d. NPER

8. Identify the *Salvage* argument in this function: =SLN(B2,B3,B4)

    a. B2

    b. B3

    c. B4

    d. It's a trick question. The SLN function does not have a *Salvage* argument.

9. When naming a range of cells to be used as the *Array* argument with the INDEX function, should you include the label row?

    a. Yes

    b. No

10. The IFERROR function displays TRUE if the formula results in an error and FALSE if it does not.

    a. True

    b. False

In this project, you will finalize a gradebook by entering formulas to compute final grades and class statistics. You will also create a worksheet to lookup specific assignment grades for one student at a time and answer specific questions about overall class performance.

Skills needed to complete this project:

- Using COUNTIF and COUNTIFS (Skill 6.5)
- Rounding with Functions (Skill 6.1)
- Creating Nested IF Formulas (Skill 6.9)
- Analyzing Complex Formulas Using Evaluate Formula (Skill 6.18)
- Finding the Middle Value with MEDIAN (Skill 6.6)
- Finding the Most Common Value(s) with MODE.SNGL and MODE.MULT (Skill 6.7)
- Managing Errors with the IFERROR Function (Skill 6.17)
- Finding Data with MATCH and INDEX (Skill 6.15)
- Using Database Functions (Skill 6.16)

1. Open the start file **EX2013-SkillReview-6-1** and resave the file as:
   `[your initials]EX-SkillReview-6-1`

2. If the workbook opens in Protected View, click the **Enable Editing** button in the Message Bar at the top of the workbook so you can modify the workbook.

3. Use COUNTIF to compute the number of absences for each student using the criteria *Absent*.

   a. In cell **L2**, enter the following formula: `=COUNTIF(B2:K2,"Absent")`

   b. Use the fill handle to fill the same formula from **L3:L8**.

4. Compute the raw average for each student. Omit absences from the average calculation.

   a. In cell **N2**, enter the following formula: `=SUM(B2:K2)/(10-L2)`

   b. Use the fill handle to fill this formula from **N3:N8**.

5. Compute the rounded average for each student, rounding the value in the *Raw Average* column to zero decimal place.

   a. In cell **O2**, enter the following formula: `=ROUND(N2,0)`

   b. Use the fill handle to fill this formula from **O3:O8**.

6. Use a nested IF statement to determine the final grade for each student.

   a. In cell **P2**, enter the following formula:
   `=IF(O2>93,"A",IF(O2>85,"B",IF(O2>74,"C",IF(O2>69,"D","F"))))`

   b. Fill this formula from **P3:P8**.

7. Use the *Evaluate Formula* feature to review the results of the nested formulas.

   a. Select cell **P2**.

   b. On the *Formulas* tab, in the *Formula Auditing* group, click the **Evaluate Formula** button.

   c. Click the **Step In** button twice to view the formula in cell *N2*.

d. Click the **Evaluate** button until you see the final value *93.9.* Observe the values in the *Evaluation* box each time you click the *Evaluate* button.

e. Click the **Step Out** button, and then click the **Evaluate** button to view the value for cell *O2.*

f. Click the **Step Out** button again, and then click the **Evaluate** button twice to view the value for cell *P2.*

g. Click the **Close** button to close the *Evaluate Formula* dialog.

h. Repeat the same process for cells **N3:N8,** using the **Step In, Evaluate,** and **Step Out** buttons as necessary until you have a clear understanding of how the nested IF formula arrived at the grade result for each student.

8. Determine the middle score (the median) for each assignment.

a. In cell **B10,** enter the following formula:
   `=MEDIAN(B2:B8)`

b. Use the fill handle to fill the cells **C10:K10** with the formula.

9. Determine the average for each assignment.

a. In cell **B11,** enter the following formula:
   `=AVERAGE(B2:B8)`

b. Use the fill handle to fill the cells **C11:K11.**

10. Determine the two most common scores for each assignment (the modes). Remember that the MODE.MULT function is an array function. You will select multiple cells before entering the formula, and then press Ctrl + ↑ Shift + ← Enter to complete it.

a. Select cells **B12:B13.**

b. In the formula bar, type the following formula:
   `=MODE.MULT(B2:B8)` and then press Ctrl + ↑ Shift + ← Enter.

c. Use the fill handle to fill the cells **C12:K13.**

11. Determine the median and average scores and the mode for both the *Raw Average* and *Rounded Average* columns.

a. In cell **N10,** enter the formula to find the middle score:
   `=MEDIAN(N2:N8)`

b. In cell **N11,** enter the formula to compute the average score:
   `=AVERAGE(N2:N8)`

c. In cell **N12,** enter the formula to compute a single mode value as follows:
   `=MODE.SNGL(N2:N8)`

12. Use the IFERROR function to display the message "no mode" instead of an error if no mode value is found.

a. If necessary, select cell **N12** again.

b. In the formula bar, edit the MODE.SNGL formula, placing the IFERROR function and the *Value_if_error* argument as follows:
   `=IFERROR(MODE.SNGL(N2:N8),"no mode")`

13. Copy cells **N10:N12** to cells **O10:O12.**

14. Switch to the *student lookup* worksheet.

15. Enter a nested formula in cell B3 using MATCH and INDEX to find the specific assignment grade for the student listed in cell B1 and the assignment week listed in cell B2. Notice the student name in cell B1 uses a wildcard.

a. Click cell **B3.**

b. On the *Formulas* tab, in the *Function Library* group, click the **Lookup & Reference** button and select **INDEX.**

c. Click **OK** in the *Select Arguments* dialog to select the first set of arguments.

d. Type the name **WeeklyGrades** in the *Array* argument box. This named range has already been defined in the workbook for you. It references *B2:K8* in the *gradebook* worksheet.

e. Click in the **Column_num** argument box. You want to enter the *Column_num* argument before the *Row_num* argument because you are going to use a nested function for the *Row_num*.

f. Enter **B2** as the *Column_num* argument. The value in cell B2 corresponds to the column position for that week's assignment in the *WeeklyGrades* named range.

g. Now click in the **Row_num** argument box where you are going to enter a MATCH function.

h. Click the arrow in the *Name* box to the left of the formula bar. If **MATCH** is listed, select it.

　1. If not, click **More Functions…** at the bottom of the list to open the *Insert Function* dialog.

　2. If necessary, expand the **Or select a category** list and select **Lookup & Reference.**

　3. Click **MATCH,** and then click **OK.**

i. Enter the arguments in the MATCH *Function Arguments* dialog:

　1. Enter **B1** as the *Lookup_value* argument.

　2. Use the named range **Students** as the *Lookup_array* argument. This named range has already been defined for you. It references A2:A8 in the gradebook worksheet.

　3. Enter **0** as the *Match_type* argument. You want to ensure an exact match.

　4. Click **OK.**

j. The final formula in cell B3 should look like this and should result in a value of 89:
```
=INDEX(WeeklyGrades,MATCH(B1,Students,0),B2)
```

16. Use database functions to answer the questions posed on the *semester analysis* worksheet. Begin by setting up the empty criteria ranges for each of the questions. We'll use the same criteria range for both questions.

a. Go to the **gradebook** worksheet.

b. Copy cells **L1:P1.** These are the column labels for the criteria ranges.

c. Go to the **semester analysis** worksheet.

d. Paste the copied cells to **D1:H1** and **D4:H4.** Notice the empty column (*E*) – that was part of the *gradebook* worksheet structure and must be included in the criteria ranges. You may hide the column if you want.

e. Now enter the criteria for the first question "How many students had a final rounded average of >75%?" Type **>75%** in cell **G2** below the *Rounded Average* column label.

f. Click cell **B1.**

g. On the *Formulas* tab, in the *Function Library* group, click the **Insert Function** button. Expand the **Or select a category** list and select **Database.** Click **DCOUNT** and click **OK.**

h. In the *Function Arguments* dialog, enter **gradebook** as the *Database* argument. This named range has already been defined in the workbook for you. It references *B2:K8* in the *gradebook* worksheet.

i. Enter **"Rounded Average"** as the *Field* argument. Remember to enclose the column label in quotation marks.

j. Enter **D1:H2** as the *Criteria* argument. Using the larger criteria range now will make it easier if you want to change the question and the criteria in the future.

k. Click **OK.** The final formula should look like this:

`=DCOUNT(gradebook,"Rounded Average",D1:H2)`

l. Click cell **B4** and repeat Steps g–k to create a formula using **DAVERAGE** to calculate the average number of missed assignments for students who received a **B** grade. Use **gradebook** as the *Database* argument; use the column label **"number of assignments missed"** as the *Field* argument; and use **D4:H5** as the *Criteria* argument. Remember to enter the criteria **B** in cell **H5**. The final formula should look like this:

`=DAVERAGE(gradebook,"number of assignments missed",D4:H5)`

17. Save and close the workbook.

skill review 6.2

In this project, you will create a worksheet to analyze inventory and financial data for a sporting goods store.

Skills needed to complete this project:

- Calculating Totals with SUMPRODUCT (Skill 6.2)
- Finding the Middle Value with MEDIAN (Skill 6.6)
- Finding the Most Common Value(s) with MODE.SNGL and MODE.MULT (Skill 6.7)
- Using SUMIF and SUMIFS (Skill 6.3)
- Using AVERAGEIF and AVERAGEIFS (Skill 6.4)
- Using COUNTIF and COUNTIFS (Skill 6.5)
- Using Database Functions (Skill 6.16)
- Finding Data with MATCH and INDEX (Skill 6.15)
- Managing Errors with the IFERROR Function (Skill 6.17)
- Analyzing Complex Formulas Using Evaluate Formula (Skill 6.18)
- Calculating Future Value with the FV Function (Skill 6.10)
- Calculating the Number of Payments with NPER (Skill 6.13)
- Rounding with Functions (Skill 6.1)
- Using NPV to Calculate Present Value when Payments Are Variable (Skill 6.12)
- Creating a Depreciation Schedule (Skill 6.14)

1. Open the start file **EX2013-SkillReview-6-2** and resave the file as:
`[your initials]EX-SkillReview-6-2`

2. If the workbook opens in Protected View, click the **Enable Editing** button in the Message Bar at the top of the workbook so you can modify the workbook.

3. Start with the *Analysis* worksheet. Use the SUMPRODUCT function to calculate the total value of the inventory. Use the values in the *Selling Price* column and the corresponding values in the *Stock* column as the *Array* arguments.

a. Click cell **B2.**

b. Type `=SUMPRODUCT(`

c. Click the **Inventory** sheet tab, and then click and drag to select cells **G4:G26.**

d. Type **,** and then click and drag to select cells **H4:H26.**

e. Type **)** and press ⏎ Enter .

f. The formula should look like this:

=SUMPRODUCT(Inventory!G4:G26,Inventory!H4:H26)

4. Enter a formula to calculate the average selling price.

    a. Click cell **D2.**

    b. Type **=AVERAGE(**

    c. Click the **Inventory** sheet tab, and then click and drag to select cells **G4:G26.**

    d. Press ⏎ Enter . The formula should look like this:

=AVERAGE(Inventory!G4:G26)

5. Enter a formula to find the middle selling price.

    a. Click cell **E2.**

    b. Type **=MEDIAN(**

    c. Click the **Inventory** sheet tab, and then click and drag to select cells **G4:G26.**

    d. Press ⏎ Enter . The formula should look like this:

=MEDIAN(Inventory!G4:G26)

6. Enter a formula to find the most common selling price.

    a. Click cell **F2.**

    b. Type **=MODE.SNGL(**

    c. Click the **Inventory** sheet tab, and then click and drag to select cells **G4:G26.**

    d. Press ⏎ Enter . The formula should look like this:

=MODE.SNGL(Inventory!G4:G26)

7. What if there are multiple selling prices that are the most common? Enter an array formula in cells G2:G5 to find up to four most common selling prices.

    a. Select cells **G2:G5.**

    b. Type **=MODE.MULT(**

    c. Click the **Inventory** sheet tab, and then click and drag to select cells **G4:G26.**

    d. Press Ctrl + ↑ Shift + ⏎ Enter . The formula should look like this:

{=MODE.MULT(Inventory!G4:G26)}

8. Use the SUMIFS function to calculate the total number of red shoes in inventory. Use the values in the *Cost* column as the *Sum_range* argument. Use the values in the *Item Description* column as the *Criteria_range1* argument and use the criteria **shoes* to find all items that end in the word *shoes*. Use the values in the *Color* column as the *Criteria_range2* argument and use the criteria *red*.

    a. Click cell **B3.**

    b. On the *Formulas* tab, in the *Function Library* group, click the **Math & Trig** button and select **SUMIFS.**

    c. In the *Function Arguments* dialog, verify that the cursor is in the *Sum_range* argument box. Click the **Inventory** sheet tab, and click and drag to select cells **H4:H26.**

    d. In the *Function Arguments* dialog, press Tab ⇆ to move to the *Criteria_range1* argument box.

    e. Click the **Inventory** sheet tab, and click and drag to select cells **A4:A26.**

    f. In the *Function Arguments* dialog, press Tab ⇆ to move to the *Criteria1* argument box.

    g. Type **"*shoes"** to find any text string that ends with the word *shoes*.

h. Press (Tab ⇆). Verify that the cursor is in the *Criteria_range2* argument box.

i. Click the **Inventory** sheet tab, and click and drag to select cells **C4:C26.**

j. In the *Function Arguments* dialog, press (Tab ⇆) to move to the *Criteria2* argument box.

k. Type: **"red"**

l. Click **OK.**

m. The formula should look like this:
```
=SUMIFS(Inventory!H4:H26,Inventory!A4:A26,"*shoes",Inventory!C4:C26,"red")
```

9. Use the AVERAGEIFS function to find the average selling price of red shoes in inventory. Use the values in the *Selling Price* column as the *Average_range* argument. Use the values in the *Item Description* column as the *Criteria_range1* argument and use the criteria **shoes* to find all items that end in the word *shoes.* Use the values in the *Color* column as the *Criteria_range2* argument and use the criteria *red.*

a. Click cell **B4.**

b. On the *Formulas* tab, in the *Function Library* group, click the **More Functions** button, point to **Statistical,** and select **AVERAGEIFS.**

c. In the *Function Arguments* dialog, verify that the cursor is in the *Average_range* argument box. Click the **Inventory** sheet tab, and click and drag to select cells **G4:G26.**

d. In the *Function Arguments* dialog, press (Tab ⇆) to move to the *Criteria_range1* argument box.

e. Click the **Inventory** sheet tab, and click and drag to select cells **A4:A26.**

f. In the *Function Arguments* dialog, press (Tab ⇆) to move to the *Criteria1* argument box.

g. Type **"*shoes"** to find any text string that ends with the word *shoes.*

h. Press (Tab ⇆). Verify that the cursor is in the *Criteria_range2* argument box.

i. Click the **Inventory** sheet tab, and click and drag to select cells **C4:C26.**

j. In the *Function Arguments* dialog, press (Tab ⇆) to move to the *Criteria2* argument box.

k. Type: **"red"**

l. Click **OK.**

m. The formula should look like this:
```
=AVERAGEIFS(Inventory!G4:G26,Inventory!A4:A26,"*shoes",Inventory!C4:C26,"red")
```

10. Use the COUNTIFS function to find the number of red shoe inventory items. Use the values in the *Item Description* column as the *Criteria_range1* argument and use the criteria **shoes* to find all items that end in the word shoes. Use the values in the *Color* column as the *Criteria_range2* argument and use the criteria *red.*

a. Click cell **B5.**

b. On the *Formulas* tab, in the *Function Library* group, click the **More Functions** button, point to **Statistical,** and select **COUNTIFS.**

c. In the *Function Arguments* dialog, verify that the cursor is in the *Criteria_range1* argument box.

d. Click the **Inventory** sheet tab, and click and drag to select cells **A4:A26.**

e. In the *Function Arguments* dialog, press (Tab ⇆) to move to the *Criteria1* argument box.

f. Type **"*shoes"** to find any text string that ends with the word *shoes.*

g. Press <kbd>Tab</kbd>. Verify that the cursor is in the *Criteria_range2* argument box.

h. Click the **Inventory** sheet tab, and click and drag to select cells **C4:C26.**

i. In the *Function Arguments* dialog, press <kbd>Tab</kbd> to move to the *Criteria2* argument box.

j. Type: **"red"**

k. Click **OK.**

l. The formula should look like this:

`=COUNTIFS(Inventory!A4:A26,"*shoes",Inventory!C4:C26,"red")`

11. Now use database functions to analyze inventory data. This method gives you more flexibility in your analysis. Once you set up the formulas, you can change the criteria in the worksheet without changing the formulas. The *InventoryDB* named range has been created for you to use as the *Database* argument. It references *A3:H26* on the *Inventory* worksheet. Notice this named range **includes** the label row.

12. Use the DAVERAGE database function to calculate the average selling price for all items with the word basketball in the item description. Use the wildcard character * before and after the word *basketball* to find all item descriptions with *basketball* anywhere in the text. Use the column label *Selling Price* as the *Field* argument. Remember to enclose the column label in quotation marks.

a. Set up the criteria range.

    1. In cell **D8**, type: **Item Description**

    2. In cell **D9**, type: ***Basketball***

b. Click cell **B9** where you will enter the formula.

c. On the *Formulas* tab, in the *Function Library* group, click the **Insert Function** button.

d. If necessary, expand the **Or select a category** list, and select **Database.**

e. Double-click **DAVERAGE** to open the *Function Arguments* dialog.

f. In the *Database* argument box, type the range name: **InventoryDB**

g. In the *Field* argument box, type the column label: **"Selling Price"**

h. Click in the *Criteria* argument box and then click and drag to select cells **D8:D9.**

i. Click **OK.**

j. The formula should look like this:

    `=DAVERAGE(InventoryDB,"Selling Price",D8:D9)`

13. Use the DCOUNT database function to calculate the number of items in stock where the item description includes the word *Football* and the selling price is less than $30. Use the wildcard character * before and after the word *Football* to find all item descriptions with *Football* anywhere in the text. Use the column label *Stock* as the *Field* argument. Remember to enclose the column label in quotation marks.

a. Set up the criteria range.

    1. In cell **D11**, type: **Item Description**

    2. In cell **D12**, type: ***Football***

    3. In cell **E11**, type: **Selling Price**

    4. In cell **E12**, type: **<30**

b. Click cell **B12** where you will enter the formula.

c. On the *Formulas* tab, in the *Function Library* group, click the **Insert Function** button.

d. If necessary, expand the **Or select a category** list, and select **Database.**

e. Double-click **DCOUNT** to open the *Function Arguments* dialog.

f. In the *Database* argument box, type the range name:
InventoryDB

g. In the *Field* argument box, type the column label:
"Stock"

h. Click in the *Criteria* argument box and then click and drag to select cells **D11:E12.**

i. Click **OK.**

j. The formula should look like this:
=DCOUNT(InventoryDB,"Stock",D11:E12)

14. Now use MATCH and INDEX to look up the item description, quantity in stock, and selling price of an item based on the inventory number. The *Inventory* named range has been created for you to use in these formulas. It references *A4:H26* on the *Inventory* worksheet. Notice this named range does **not** include the label row.

15. First, use MATCH to find the row position for the item listed in cell **B15.** Remember, the *Lookup_array* argument must be a single column. Require an exact match. Use absolute references so you can copy the formula.

   a. Click cell **B16.**

   b. On the *Formulas* tab, in the *Function Library* group, click the **Lookup & Reference** button, and select **MATCH.**

   c. Use an absolute reference to cell **B15** for the *Lookup_value* argument. Type: **$B$15** and then press Tab ⇥.

   d. Verify that the cursor is in the *Lookup_array* argument box. Click the **Inventory** sheet tab and click and drag to select cells **B4:B26.** Edit the cell references to be absolute.

   e. In the *Match_type* argument box, type: **0**

   f. Click **OK.**

   g. The formula should look like this:
   =MATCH($B$15,Inventory!$B$4:$B$26,0)

16. Now add an INDEX function around the MATCH function to find the item description (column **1**) for the row position identified by the MATCH function. Use the named range **Inventory** as the *Array* argument.

   a. If necessary, select cell **B16** again, and then click in the formula bar so you can edit the formula.

   b. After the =, type: **INDEX(Inventory,**

   c. Move the cursor to the end of the formula and type: **,1)**

   d. Press ⏎ Enter.

   e. The formula should now look like this:
   =INDEX(Inventory,MATCH($B$15,Inventory!$B$4:$B$26,0),1)

17. Add an IFERROR function around the INDEX function to hide any error messages by displaying an empty text string (**""**).

   a. If necessary, select cell **B16** again, and then click in the formula bar so you can edit the formula.

   b. After the =, type: **IFERROR(**

   c. Move the cursor to the end of the formula and type: **,"")**

   d. Press ⏎ Enter.

   e. The formula should now look like this:
   =IFERROR(INDEX(Inventory,MATCH($B$15,Inventory!$B$4:$B$26,0),1),"")

18. Copy the formula from cell **B16** to cells **B17:B18.**

19. Modify the formula in cell **B17** to use **8** as the *Column_num* argument for the INDEX function. The formula should look like this:

`=IFERROR(INDEX(Inventory,MATCH($B$15,Inventory!$B$4:$B$26,0),8),"")`

20. Modify the formula in cell **B18** to use **6** as the *Column_num* argument for the INDEX function. The formula should look like this:

`=IFERROR(INDEX(Inventory,MATCH($B$15,Inventory!$B$4:$B$26,0),6),"")`

21. If necessary, apply the **Accounting Number Format** to cell **B18**.

22. If you are having trouble with these formulas, use the **Evaluate Formula** feature to review the results of the nested formulas.

    a. Select the cell containing the formula you want to evaluate.

    b. On the *Formulas* tab, in the *Formula Auditing* group, click the **Evaluate Formula** button.

    c. Use the *Step In, Evaluate,* and *Step Out* buttons as necessary until you have a clear understanding of how the nested INDEX and MATCH formulas work together.

23. Save the file.

24. Hank's Sporting Goods is considering taking out a $25,000 loan to pay for inventory. The details of that loan are shown on the *Financials* worksheet in cells C3:D7. You will help Hank calculate how much money he would make if he invested those same monthly payments in a money market account instead. Calculate the theoretical future value of the same amount deposited monthly in a money market account.

    a. Switch to the **Financials** worksheet.

    b. Click cell **D10**.

    c. On the *Formulas* tab, in the *Function Library* group, click the **Financial** button, and select **FV**.

    d. Enter the *Rate* argument, referring to the interest rate in cell **B5**. The rate is expressed as an annual interest rate, and payments will be monthly, so divide the interest rate by 12: **B5/12**

    e. Enter the *Nper* argument, referring to cell **D6**. There will be monthly payments, so multiple the number of years by 12: **D6*12**

    f. Enter the *Pmt* argument referring to the cell showing the monthly payment amount for the loan: **D5**
    Notice that the loan payment is already expressed as a negative number so there is no need to alter the *Pmt* argument.

    g. There is no value in the investment prior to the first investment period, so you can skip the *Pv* argument.

    h. Deposits would be scheduled for the beginning of each payment period. Enter the appropriate *Type* argument: **1**

    i. Click **OK**. The formula in cell D10 should look like this:
    `=FV(B5/12,D6*12,D5,,1)`

25. Save the file.

26. Hank would like to consider another loan option with the same loan amount and the same interest rate. How many months would it take to pay off the loan if he paid a flat $750 every month?

    a. Click cell **D14**. On the *Formulas* tab, in the *Function Library* group, click the **Financial** button, and select **NPER**.

    b. Enter the *Rate* argument, referring to the loan interest rate in cell **B4**. The rate is expressed as an annual interest rate, and payments will be monthly, so divide the interest rate by 12: **B4/12**

c. Enter the *Pmt* argument referring to the cell showing the new monthly payment amount for the loan: **D13**

Notice that the loan payment is already expressed as a negative number so there is no need to alter the *Pmt* argument.

d. Enter the *Pv* argument referring to the original loan amount in cell **D4.**

e. The loan will be completely paid off, so you can skip the *Fv* argument.

f. Payments would be applied at the end of each payment period, so you can skip the *Type* argument.

g. Click **OK.** The formula in cell D14 should look like this:
```
=NPER(B4/12,D13,D4)
```

27. Hank is easily confused by too many digits after the decimal point, so add a ROUND function to round the number of months to zero decimal places.

a. If necessary, click cell **D14** again.

b. In the formula bar, add the ROUND function using the existing FV function as the *Number* argument and **0** as the *Num_digits* argument. The formula should now look like this:
```
=ROUND(NPER(B4/12,D13,D4),0)
```

28. Hank has another financial question for you. He needs to decide between three equipment purchase options. **Option 1** is the least expensive and will require minimal repairs. It will generate the lowest increase in revenue. **Option 2** is $10,000 more than Option 1 and will generate a higher increase in revenue, but it will require significant repair in year 5 and will begin declining in productivity in year 7. **Option 3** is the most expensive. It will also generate the highest increase in revenue. However, it will require more frequent and expensive repairs than the other two options.

29. Enter the formula to calculate net present value for Option 1 using the revenue schedule in cells **B9:B18.** Use a discount rate of **1.5%.**

a. Click the **Equipment Decision** worksheet.

b. Click cell **B5.**

c. Type: **=NPV(**

d. Type: **1.5%,**

e. Click and drag to select cells **B9:B18.**

f. Type **)** and then press ⏎ Enter to complete the formula:
```
=NPV(1.5%,B9:B18)
```

30. Copy the formula in cell **B5** to cells **C5** and **D5** to calculate the NPV for Option 2 and Option 3.

31. Format cells **B5:D5** with the **Accounting Number Format.**

32. Calculate the true cost of the investment by adding the initial investment (the purchase cost) to the calculated NPV amount:

a. In cell **B6** enter the formula as follows: **=B4+B5**

b. Copy the formula in cell **B6** to cells **C6** and **D6.**

33. Place a thick box border around cells **D3:D6** to highlight the best investment option.

34. Now calculate two alternative depreciation schedules for the selected equipment option. First, set up the values that will be used for the common arguments *Cost, Life,* and *Salvage.*

a. In cell **G3,** enter a reference to cell **D4.** For the depreciation schedule, the cost value should be a positive number, so precede the cell reference with a — character: **=-D4**

b. In cell **G4,** enter the useful life of the equipment: **10**

c. In cell **G5,** enter the salvage value of the equipment. Calculate this as 20% of the cost: **=G3*0.2**

35. In cell **J4,** enter the formula to calculate depreciation for year 1 using the declining balance method.

    a. On the *Formulas* tab, in the *Function Library* group, click the **Financial** button, and then select **DB.**

    b. Enter the *Cost* argument as an absolute cell reference so the reference will not update when you copy the formula: **$G$3**

    c. Enter the *Salvage* argument as an absolute cell reference so the reference will not update when you copy the formula: **$G$5**

    d. Enter the *Life* argument as an absolute cell reference so the reference will not update when you copy the formula: **$G$4**

    e. Enter the *Period* argument as a relative cell reference, so the reference will update when you copy the formula: **I4**

    f. Click **OK.** The formula in cell J4 should look like this: **=DB($G$3,$G$5,$G$4,I4)**

36. Copy the formula to **J5:J13.**

37. In cell **K4,** enter the formula to calculate depreciation for year 1 using the straight-line method.

    a. On the *Formulas* tab, in the *Function Library* group, click the **Financial** button, and then select **SLN.**

    b. Enter the *Cost* argument as an absolute cell reference so the reference will not update when you copy the formula: **$G$3**

    c. Enter the *Salvage* argument as an absolute cell reference so the reference will not update when you copy the formula: **$G$5**

    d. Enter the *Life* argument as an absolute cell reference so the reference will not update when you copy the formula: **$G$4**

    e. Click OK. The formula in cell K4 should look like this: **=SLN($G$3,$G$5,$G$4)**

38. Copy the formula to **K5:K13.** Notice that the straight-line method returns the same depreciation value for each period in the schedule.

39. Apply the **Accounting Number Format** to cells **J4:K13.**

40. Save and close the workbook.

challenge yourself 6.3

In this project, you are an accountant for National Pharmaceutical Sales. You want to make a spreadsheet that contains each sales associate's statistics. Because the company has over 100 sales associates, only a partial spreadsheet will be provided. Please follow the steps below to complete the partial spreadsheet.

Skills needed to complete this project:

- Creating Nested IF Formulas (Skill 6.9)
- Finding the Middle Value with MEDIAN (Skill 6.6)
- Using SUMIF and SUMIFS (Skill 6.3)
- Using AVERAGEIF and AVERAGEIFS (Skill 6.4)
- Using Database Functions (Skill 6.16)
- Analyzing Complex Formulas Using Evaluate Formula (Skill 6.18)
- Managing Errors with the IFERROR Function (Skill 6.17)

1. Open the start file **EX2013-ChallengeYourself-6-3** and resave the file as:
   `[your initials]EX-ChallengeYourself-6-3`

2. If the workbook opens in Protected View, click the **Enable Editing** button in the Message Bar at the top of the workbook so you can modify the workbook.

3. On the *Sales Data* worksheet, calculate the commission rate and commission paid for each sales associate.

4. Beginning in cell **F4,** enter a formula to calculate the commission rate based on the following table. (Hint: Use a nested IF statement.)

IF ANNUAL SALES ARE:	THEN THE COMMISSION RATE IS:
>= 200,000	6%
>= 140,000	4%
>= 80,000	2%
< 80,000	0

5. Fill the formula down through cell **F64.** If necessary, format the range as a percentage, and center the values in the cells.

6. Beginning in cell **G4,** calculate the commission earned by multiplying the annual sales by the commission rate (**E4*F4**).

7. Fill the formula down through cell **G64.** If necessary, format the range using the default **Comma Style** number format.

8. In the *Summary* sheet, calculate average and median sales and commissions. Use the named ranges shown in cells **A23:B26.**

   a. In cell **B5,** enter a formula to calculate the average annual sales for all sales associates. Use the named range **AnnualSales.**

   b. In cell **C5,** enter a formula to calculate the median annual sales for all sales associates. Use the named range **AnnualSales.**

   c. In cell **B6,** enter a formula to calculate the average commission. Use the named range **CommissionEarned.**

   d. In cell **C6,** enter a formula to calculate the median commission. Use the named range **CommissionEarned.**

   e. If necessary, format cells **B5:C6** with the default **Accounting Number Format.**

9. Calculate the total and average sales by region.

   a. In cell **B10,** use a **SUMIF** formula to calculate the sum of **AnnualSales** where the value in the **Regions** named range is equal to the region listed in cell **B9.**

   b. Copy the formula to cells **C10:I10.**

   c. In cell **B11,** use an **AVERAGEIF** formula to calculate the average of **AnnualSales** where the value in the **Regions** named range is equal to the region listed in cell **B9.**

   d. Copy the formula to cells **C11:I11.**

   e. If necessary, format cells **B10:I11** with the default **Accounting Number Format.**

10. The second part of the *Summary* sheet contains a sales associate lookup form, but the appropriate formulas have not been entered yet.

    a. In cell **B18,** enter a formula to calculate the average commission earned for the sales associate last name entered in cell A16. (Hint: Use a database function. Use the named range **Earnings** as the *Database* argument and the column label **Commission Earned** as the *Field* argument. The criteria range should be **A15:B16.**)

b. In cell **B19,** enter a formula to calculate the total commission earned for that same sales associate. (Hint: Use a different database function. The function arguments are the same as those you used in Step 10a.)

c. If necessary, apply the **Accounting Number Format** to cells **B18:B19.**

d. In cell **B20,** enter a formula to calculate the number of clients the sales associate had with annual sales reaching the target set in cell **B16.** (Hint: This time, use the column label **Client** as the *Field* argument. The criteria range should be **A15:B16.**)

e. If necessary, apply the **General** number format to cell **B20.**

f. Test your formulas by entering **Schmidt** as the sales associate's last name (cell **A16**) and **>125000** as the sales target (cell **B16**).

g. Add an **IFERROR** function to the formulas in cells **B18:B20** to display the error text **Associate not found.**

h. If you receive errors, use **Evaluate Formula** to troubleshoot your formulas.

11. Save and close the workbook.

challenge yourself **6.4**

In this project, you will complete a series of budget worksheets, including a home loan analysis and amortization schedule, rental comparison, and savings and retirement planning. The fair market rent information in the *Final_FY2013_Virginia_summary* worksheet was downloaded from the U.S. Department of Housing and Urban Development Web site at http://www.huduser.org.

Skills needed to complete this project:

- Using PV to Calculate Present Value when Payments Are Constant (Skill 6.11)
- Calculating the Number of Payments with NPER (Skill 6.13)
- Rounding with Functions (Skill 6.1)
- Creating Nested IF Formulas (Skill 6.9)
- Finding Data with MATCH and INDEX (Skill 6.15)
- Calculating Future Value with the FV Function (Skill 6.10)
- Using PV to Calculate Present Value when Payments Are Constant (Skill 6.11)
- Using NPV to Calculate Present Value when Payments Are Variable (Skill 6.12)

1. Open the start file **EX2013-ChallengeYourself-6-4** and resave the file as: **[your initials]EX-ChallengeYourself-6-4**

2. If the workbook opens in Protected View, click the **Enable Editing** button in the Message Bar at the top of the workbook so you can modify the workbook.

3. First, you will work on the home loan and amortization worksheets. The loan terms are listed on the *Loan Terms* sheet. You will use that information to create an amortization schedule to track your equity growth. Spend some time familiarizing yourself with the *Loan Terms* worksheet and then go to the **Amortization Schedule** sheet and complete the loan information at the top of the sheet.

a. In cell **B1,** reference the loan amount in cell **B5** on the *Loan Terms* sheet.

b. If necessary, format cell **B1** using the default **Accounting Number Format.**

c. In cell **B2,** reference the monthly payment in cell **E3** on the *Loan Terms* sheet.

d. In cell **E1,** reference the interest rate in cell **B7** on the *Loan Terms* sheet.

e. In cell **E2**, reference the loan term in cell **B6** on the *Loan Terms* sheet.

f. In cell **E3**, reference the total interest in cell **E4** of the *Loan Terms* sheet.

4. Set up the year values in the amortization schedule.

   a. In cell **A7**, type: **1** In cell **A8**, type: **2**

   b. Highlight cells **A7:A8**, and use the fill handle to fill the series down through cell **A36**.

5. In cell **B7**, enter a reference to cell **B1** as the starting balance at the beginning of the loan.

6. In cell **C7**, create an IF statement to find the ending balance for the loan period.

   a. The logical test should evaluate if the period number is less than or equal to the number of years in the loan. Use an absolute cell reference for the years in the loan: **A7<=$E$2**

   b. The *Value_if_true* argument should be the *present value* of the loan. Use absolute cell references for the **PV** function arguments where appropriate. The *Nper* argument should be calculated dynamically by multiplying 12 times the number of years remaining in the loan. The result should be a positive number: **PV($E$1/12,12*($E$2-A7),-$B$2)**

   c. The *Value_if_false* argument should be **0**.

7. In cell **D7**, create a formula that subtracts the ending balance amount from the beginning balance amount.

8. In cell **E7**, use an IF statement to find the interest paid during the loan period.

   a. The *Logical_test* argument should evaluate whether the period number is greater than 0: **A7>0**

   b. The *Value_if_true* argument should be 12 (the number of payments in a year) multiplied by the payment amount minus the principal paid during the period. Use an absolute cell reference where appropriate: **12*$B$2-D7**

   c. The *Value_if_false* argument should be **0**.

9. Ensure that all cells in **B7:E7** are formatted using the default **Accounting Number Format**.

10. Complete the amortization schedule.

   a. In cell **B8**, use a relative cell reference to reference the ending balance in cell **C7**.

   b. Click the fill handle in cell **B8**, and fill the information down through cell **B36**.

   c. Select the range **C7:E7**. Use the fill handle in cell **E7** to fill the range down through cell **E36**.

11. Calculate how quickly you could pay off the loan if you increased the monthly payment. Switch to the **Loan Terms** worksheet.

   a. In cell **D11**, use **NPER** to calculate the number of months to pay off the loan using the new monthly loan payment amount in cell **D10**. Remember to use a negative value for the *Pmt* argument and be careful to reference the loan amount, not the home price. You can omit both the *Fv* and *Type* arguments—home loans are usually set up so the payment is applied at the end of each period.

   b. In cell **D12**, calculate the approximate number of years to pay off the loan by dividing the value in cell **D11** by **12** and then rounding to zero decimal places.

12. Look up the equivalent fair market rents in the same area. This data can be found in the *Final_FY2013_Virginia_summary* worksheet.

   a. In cell **D16**, enter a nested formula using MATCH and INDEX to find the fair market rent for a one bedroom rental unit in the county listed in cell **D15**. We've already defined two named ranges for you to use. **FMR_2013** is the named range to use for the INDEX function *Array* argument. This range includes all the data in cells **A3:O137** in the *Final_FY2013_Virginia_summary* worksheet. The one bedroom rent data is in column **3.** The second named range, **Counties,** can be used as the MATCH *Lookup_array* argument. This range is the column of county names, cells **G3:G137,** in the *Final_FY2013_Virginia_summary* worksheet. Require an exact match for the MATCH function.

   b. In cell **D17,** enter a nested formula using **MATCH** and **INDEX** to find the fair market rent for a two bedroom rental unit in the county listed in cell **D15.** You can use the same formula as in D16, but substitute column **4** for the INDEX *Column_num* argument.

13. Now that you've calculated mortgage and rental options, let's look at savings. Go to the **Savings** worksheet.

   a. You want to save at least $15,000 to buy a new car. In cell **B6,** enter a formula to calculate how much you will have saved by putting away $500 per month for 24 months at a 2% annual interest rate. Use the appropriate cell references. Remember to use a negative value for the *Pmt* argument. There is no money in the account yet and payments are applied at the end of every month, so omit both the *Pv* and *Type* arguments. (Hint: Use the **FV** function.)

   b. You also want to save for retirement. In cell **B12,** enter a formula to calculate how much you will have saved by putting away that same $500 per month for 25 years at 2%. Use the appropriate cell references. Remember to use a negative value for the *Pmt* argument and to adjust the *Rate* and *Nper* arguments to reflect monthly payments. There is no money in the account yet and payments are applied at the end of every month, so omit both the *Pv* and *Type* arguments. (Hint: Use the **FV** function.)

   c. Once you've saved 25 years for retirement, how much can you draw from the retirement account over the next 30 years? In cell **B14,** enter a formula a formula to calculate how much you can pay yourself from the retirement account every month. Assume that at the end of the 30 years, the account balance will be zero and that payments to you will be made at the beginning of every month. Use the appropriate cell references. (Hint: Use the **PMT** function to calculate the payments to yourself. Enter a negative sign before the formula so the result appears as a positive number.)

14. You have two options for additional guaranteed monthly payments in retirement (annuities). Go to the **Annuities** worksheet to calculate the value of each of these options.

   a. The first annuity costs $20,000 and pays you $170 per month for 120 months (10 years). In cell **B5,** enter a formula to calculate the present value of this investment. Remember to express the *Pmt* argument as a negative number and set the *Type* argument to **1** as the payment will be made at the beginning of each month. (Hint: Use the **PV** function.)

   b. The second annuity also costs $20,000 but it pays a variable annual payment. In cell **B13,** enter a formula to calculate the present value of this investment using the annual interest rate in cell **B8** and the payment schedule in cells **B14:B23.** (Hint: Use the **NPV** function.)

15. Save and close the workbook.

In this project, you will complete a personal budget workbook.

- Rounding with Functions (Skill 6.1)
- Finding the Middle Value with MEDIAN (Skill 6.6)
- Finding the Most Common Value(s) with MODE.SNGL and MODE.MULT (Skill 6.7)
- Managing Errors with the IFERROR Function (Skill 6.17)
- Creating Nested IF Formulas (Skill 6.9)
- Calculating the Number of Payments with NPER (Skill 6.13)
- Calculating Future Value with the FV Function (Skill 6.10)

1. Open the start file **EX2013-OnYourOwn-6-5** and resave the file as:
   `[your initials]EX-OnYourOwn-6-5`

2. If the workbook opens in Protected View, click the **Enable Editing** button in the Message Bar at the top of the workbook so you can modify the workbook.

3. Begin with the *Budget* worksheet. We have set up a budget with rows for common personal budget income and expense categories and sample data. You may choose to use the sample data or modify the budget to use your own income and expense categories and data.

   a. In cell **O8,** enter a formula using AVERAGE to calculate the average monthly expense for this category. Be careful not to include the total column (column N). Add the ROUND function to the formula to round the formula result to zero decimal places. Copy the formula to the other cells in the column.

   b. In cell **P8,** enter a formula using MEDIAN to calculate the median monthly expense for this category. Be careful not to include the total column (column N). Copy the formula to the other cells in the column.

   c. In cell **Q8,** enter a formula using MODE.SNGL to find the most common value for each category. Be careful not to include the total column (column N). Copy the formula to the other cells in the column.

   d. Add the IFERROR function to the formula in cell **Q8** to display nothing if there is no mode. (Hint: Use "" as the *Value_if_error* argument.) Copy the formula to the other cells in the column.

4. In cell **B22,** we've set a target goal for monthly expenses. If you are using your own data, change this value to your own monthly expenses goal. In cell **B23,** use a nested IF formula to grade yourself on how well you did in meeting your goal for the month. If your total expenses were less than the goal, display **great.** If total expenses were greater than the goal, but still less than total income, display **ok.** If total expenses were not less than total income, display **not great.** Copy the formula to the other cells in the row through **M23.** (Hint: Use an absolute reference to the target goal in cell B22 so it stays the same when you copy the formula.)

5. Next we'll look at how quickly you might be able to pay off credit card and other loan debt. Go to the **Credit Card and Loan Debt** worksheet. The worksheet is set up with sample data for two credit cards and a loan. You may choose to use the sample data or modify the data to use actual credit card and loan balances and interest rates.

   a. In cell **G3,** enter a formula using **NPER** to calculate the number of months it would take to pay off the credit card balance in cell **B3** using the new monthly payment in cell **F3.** Remember to express the *Pmt* argument as a negative. The loan balance should be zero at the end and payments are applied at the end of every month, so omit both the *Fv* and *Type* arguments.

b. Add a function around the formula in cell **G3** to round the calculation result to two decimal places.

c. Copy the formula in cell **G3** to **G4:G5** to calculate how many months it will take to pay off the other debts based on the new payments.

6. Now that you've calculated how to pay down your debt quicker, let's look at retirement. Go to the **Retirement** worksheet. This part of the project is similar to steps 13.b-c in the *Challenge Yourself 6.4* project. The worksheet is set up with sample data for a simple retirement account with a consistent monthly contribution and a consistent annual interest rate. You may choose to use the sample data or modify the data for your own situation.

a. In cell **B5,** enter a formula to calculate how much money will be in the account when you are ready to retire. Use the appropriate cell references. Remember to use a negative value for the *Pmt* argument and to adjust the *Rate* and *Nper* arguments to reflect monthly payments. There is no money in the account yet and payments are applied at the end of every month, so omit both the *Pv* and *Type* arguments. (Hint: Use the **FV** function.)

b. Once you've saved for retirement, how much can you draw from the retirement account over the next 30 years? In cell **B8,** enter a formula to calculate how much you can pay yourself from the retirement account every month. Assume that at the end of the 30 years, the account balance will be zero and that payments to you will be made at the beginning of every month. Use the appropriate cell references. (Hint: Use the **PMT** function to calculate the payments to yourself. Use the ending balance in the retirement account as the *Pv* argument. Enter a negative sign before the formula so the result appears as a positive number.)

7. Save and close the workbook.

fix it 6.6

In this project, you will work with spreadsheets designed for planning a charity event. In order to determine if the party will meet its fundraising goal, the guest list analysis and expense calculations must be corrected.

Skills needed to complete this project:

- Analyzing Complex Formulas Using Evaluate Formula (Skill 6.18)
- Using SUMIF and SUMIFS (Skill 6.3)
- Using COUNTIF and COUNTIFS (Skill 6.5)
- Using AVERAGEIF and AVERAGEIFS (Skill 6.4)
- Rounding with Functions (Skill 6.1)
- Using Database Functions (Skill 6.16)
- Calculating Totals with SUMPRODUCT (Skill 6.2)
- Finding Data with MATCH and INDEX (Skill 6.15)
- Calculating the Number of Payments with NPER (Skill 6.13)
- Creating Nested IF Formulas (Skill 6.9)

1. Open the start file **EX2013-FixIt-6-6** and resave the file as:
   `[your initials]EX-FixIt-6-6`

2. If the workbook opens in Protected View, click the **Enable Editing** button in the Message Bar at the top of the workbook so you can modify the workbook.

3. Throughout this project, use the Evaluate Formula feature to analyze any formulas you have difficulty troubleshooting.

4. Fix the following errors in the **Guest List** worksheet. Use cell references and named ranges where appropriate. All the named ranges you might need have been defined for you. Refer to the *Named Ranges Reference* sheet for a description of each defined name.

   a. In cell **E3**, the formula to calculate the number of tables should result in a whole number only. Be sure to round the number up so you aren't left with a guess without a seat.

   b. The formula in cell **E4** should calculate the total number of guests from the city listed in cell **D4**.

   c. The formula in cell **E5** should calculate the number of single guests attending from the city listed in cell **D5**.

   d. The formula in cell **E6** should calculate the average number of guests attending from the city listed in cell **D6**. The formula should also round up to a whole number.

   e. In cell **E7**, use a database function to calculate the number of guests from the **city of Auburn** with a **last name beginning with the letter J.** You will need to correct issues in both the formula and in the criteria data. (Hints: DSUM is not the appropriate database function to use in this example. The *Database* arguments should use a named range, but not *GuestList.* Be sure to set the *Criteria_range* argument to include all the column headings so you can change the question and criteria later without having to change the formula. And remember, you are looking for last names that *begin* with the letter J. There's no problem with using "Last Name" as the *Field* criteria.)

5. Fix the following errors in the **Shopping List** worksheet. Use cell references and named ranges where appropriate. All the named ranges you might need have been defined for you. Refer to the *Named Ranges Reference* sheet for a description of each defined name.

   a. The formula in cell **B2** should calculate the total cost of all the shopping items by multiplying the number of items ordered in the *Quantity* column by the cost of each item in the *TotalCostperUnit* column and then summing the values. Be sure to round the final value to 2 decimal places. If necessary, apply the Accounting Number format.

   b. The formula in cell **B4** should allow you to look up the vendor for the item listed in cell **B3**. Using a nested INDEX and MATCH formula is the right idea, but the formula is not quite right. Add an IFERROR function to display **item not found** if the formula results in an error. Also, use absolute references so you can copy the formula to cells **B5** and **B6**.

   c. In cell **B5**, copy and paste the corrected nested INDEX and MATCH formula and then update the *Column_num* argument to find the quantity ordered.

   d. In cell **B6**, copy and paste the corrected nested INDEX and MATCH formula and then update the *Column_num* argument to find the item's total cost per unit. Edit the formula to calculate the total cost by multiplying the result of the INDEX formula by the quantity ordered (cell **B5**). (Hint: Maintain the IFERROR function as the outermost function in the nested formula.) If necessary, apply the Accounting Number Format.

   e. There are three items in the shopping list that are based on the number of guests, but the quantity ordered should be rounded up to the nearest whole number. Add the appropriate rounding function to the formulas in cells **D10**, **D11**, and **D23**.

f. The formula in cell **E4** should calculate how many months it will take to pay off the loan using the total cost in cell **B2** and the loan terms in cells **E2** and **E3**. The formula is using the wrong function and the arguments are in the wrong order. Once you correct this formula, the final cost of the party (cell E5) will be correct as well.

6. Once the guest list analysis and party expenses have been corrected, you can determine whether or not the party will meet the fundraising goal. Go to the **Fundraising Goal** worksheet. The IF formula in cell B10 evaluates whether or not the fundraising goal was met. However, if the goal was not met, the party organizers also want to know if they met at least 75% of the goal.

a. The formula in cell **B10** should display **Goal met!** if the party income (donations, cell **B6, minus** expenses, cell **B8**) is **greater than or equal to** the fundraising goal (cell **B2**). If not, and the income is within 75% of the goal (**greater than or equal to B2*.75**), then the formula should display this message: **within 25% of goal** If the income is not greater than or equal to 75% of the fundraising goal, then the formula should display this message: **less than 75% of goal**.

7. Save and close the workbook.

chapter 7

Exploring Advanced Charts and Graphics

In this chapter, you will learn the following skills:

- ❱ Add a data series to a chart
- ❱ Create a combination chart
- ❱ Apply formatting to charts
- ❱ Create and use a chart template
- ❱ Use trendlines to analyze and forecast values
- ❱ Use Sparklines to visualize data
- ❱ Insert and apply formatting to pictures
- ❱ Insert and apply formatting to shapes
- ❱ Capture and insert a screenshot

skills

introduction

This chapter expands on Chapter 5's introduction to charts. You will learn to modify charts including adding a data series, applying custom formatting, and working with chart templates. You will add and modify trendlines to forecast data. You will also learn to insert and work with graphic elements, including Sparklines, pictures, shapes, and screenshots.

Skill 7.1 Adding a Data Series to a Chart

If your worksheet already includes a chart, you can manipulate the data represented without deleting and recreating the chart. The chart in Figure EX 7.1 includes monthly sales data for two membership types—monthly memberships and annual memberships. You can add another data series, in this case for total monthly memberships, through the *Select Data Source* dialog.

To add another data series to a chart:

1. If necessary, select the chart.
2. On the *Chart Tools Design* tab, in the *Data* group, click the **Select Data** button.

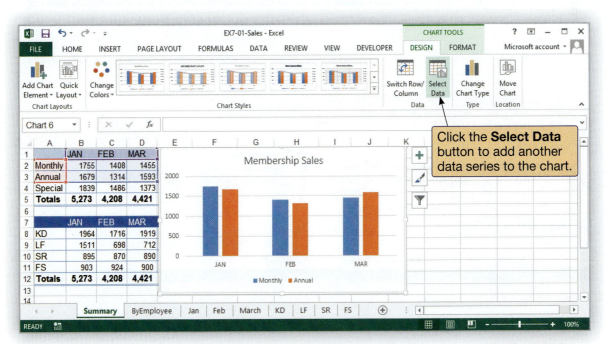

Click the **Select Data** button to add another data series to the chart.

3. The *Select Data Source* dialog opens showing the current data series.

4. Click the **Add** button.

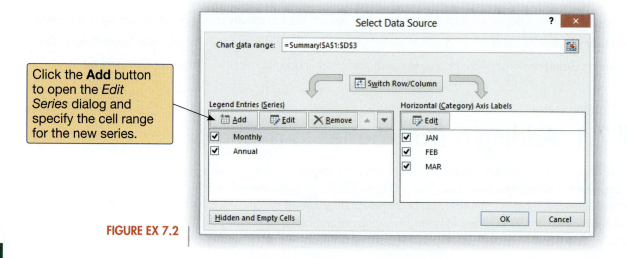

> Click the **Add** button to open the *Edit Series* dialog and specify the cell range for the new series.

FIGURE EX 7.2

5. The *Edit Series* dialog opens. Enter the appropriate cell reference for the new series name in the *Series name* box. You can type or click a cell reference or enter text.

6. Click in the **Series values** box and delete the default entry. Click and drag the new cell range to enter it in the *Series values* box or type the new cell range. Click **OK.**

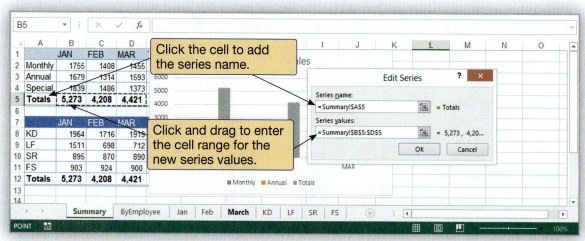

> Click the cell to add the series name.

> Click and drag to enter the cell range for the new series values.

FIGURE EX 7.3

7. The *Select Data Source* dialog opens again with the new data series added. Click **OK** to add the data series to your chart.

The new data series representing total sales per month has been added to the chart.

FIGURE EX 7.4

tips & tricks

You can type the cell references into the *Edit Series* dialog instead of clicking the cells in the worksheet, but this method can be tricky. You must include the sheet reference in both the series name and the series values. If you are adding multiple series, you must separate non-contiguous ranges with commas. It is much easier to click the cells to add the references to the dialog.

tell me more

If the source data for your chart are in contiguous cells, you can extend or reduce the source data range for the chart without opening the *Select Data Source* dialog. When the chart is selected, the source data are highlighted. Click one of the resize handles and drag to change the selected cell range.

another method

There are two other methods to open the *Select Data Source* dialog:

▶ Click the **Chart Filters** button that appears near the top right corner of the selected chart. Click **Select Data...** next to the *Apply* button at the bottom of the *Chart Filters* gallery.

▶ Right-click anywhere in the chart and click **Select Data....**

let me try

Open the student data file **EX7-01-Sales** and try this skill on your own:

1. If necessary, select the chart.

2. Add another data series to the chart. Use cell **A5** as the series name and cells **B5:D5** as the series values.

3. Save the file as directed by your instructor and close it.

Skill 7.2 Creating a Combination Chart

A **combination chart**, or **combo chart**, allows you to specify different chart types for individual data series. The most common combination is a column chart combined with a line chart.

To create a combination chart:

1. Select the data you want to include in the chart.
2. On the *Insert* tab, in the *Charts* group, click the **Combo Chart** button.
3. Click the chart type you want.

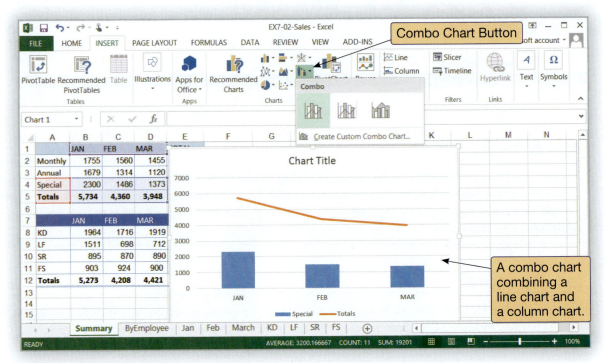

FIGURE EX 7.5

You can also plot one or more of the data series along a secondary axis. This is useful when you want to illustrate related data that have different scales. In Figure EX 7.6, it is easier to see the relationship between "special" sales and total sales once total sales have been plotted along a secondary axis.

To add a secondary axis to a combo chart:

1. If necessary, click the chart to select it.
2. On the *Chart Tools Design* tab, in the *Type* group, click the **Change Chart Type** button.
3. Click the **Primary Axis** or **Secondary Axis** check box next to the series name.

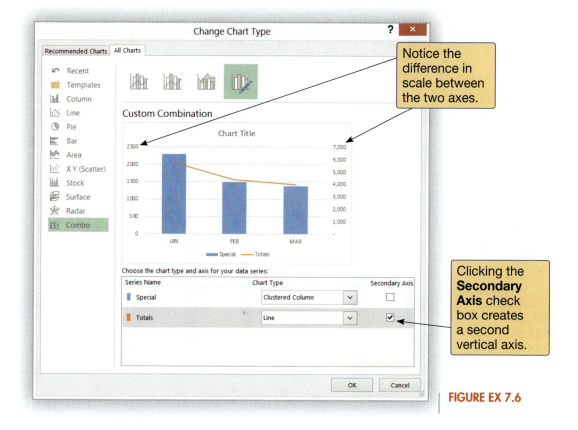

FIGURE EX 7.6

tips & tricks

Combination charts are new for Excel 2013.

tell me **more**

From the *Change Chart Type* dialog, you can also change the chart type for one of the data series. Expand the **Chart Type** drop-down list next to the series name and select the new chart type.

another **method**

You can change the axis for a specific series from the *Format Data Series* task pane.

1. Click any data point in the series to select it.
2. On the *Chart Tools Format* tab, in the *Current Selection* group, click the **Format Selection** button.
3. The *Format Data Series* task pane opens to the *Series Options* panel.
4. Click the **Primary Axis** or **Secondary Axis** radio button to change the axis along which the data series is plotted.

let me **try**

Open the student data file **EX7-02-Sales** and try this skill on your own:

1. If necessary, select the following cell ranges for your chart: **A1:D1** and **A4:D5.**
2. Insert a **clustered column-line combination** chart based on the selected data. The line chart should represent the *Totals* data series. Both data series should be on the primary axis. This is the first chart type in the *Combo Chart* gallery.
3. Modify the chart so the *Totals* data series is plotted along the secondary axis.
4. Save the file as directed by your instructor and close it.

Skill 7.3 Formatting a Data Point or a Data Series

When you apply a chart style or color from the *Chart Tools Design* tab, *Chart Styles* group, it is applied to the entire chart. If you want to override the formatting for an individual data point or data series, select the data point or data series, and then use the options from the *Chart Tools Format* tab, *Shape Styles* group instead.

The *Services— Individual* data series has a Shape Quick Style applied.

The *FEB* data point has an outline color and weight applied.

FIGURE EX 7.7

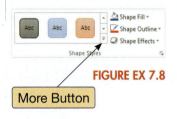

FIGURE EX 7.8

More Button

FIGURE EX 7.9

Before applying formatting changes, always verify that you have the correct data series selected by checking the *Chart Elements* box on the *Chart Tools Format* tab, *Current Selection* group.

Shape Quick Styles allow you to apply a combination of formatting such as borders, rounded corners, and effects with a single command. To apply a Shape Quick Style to a data point or data series:

1. Select the data point or data series you want to change.

2. On the *Chart Tools Format* tab, in the *Shape Styles* group, click the **More** button to expand the *Shape Quick Styles* gallery.

3. Click the style you want.

To apply a fill color to a data point or data series:

1. Select the data point or data series you want to change.

2. On the *Chart Tools Format* tab, in the *Shape Styles* group, click the **Shape Fill** button and click the color you want.

From the *Shape Fill* menu, you can also apply a picture, gradient, or texture to a data series or data point.

To apply an outline to a data point or data series:

1. Select the data point or data series you want to change.
2. On the *Chart Tools Format* tab, in the *Shape Styles* group, click the **Shape Outline** button and click the color you want.
3. To change the outline line width, click the **Shape Outline** button, point to **Weight**, and select the width you want.

To undo changes and return the selected element to the default chart style:

1. Select the data point or data series to want to revert to the original chart style.
2. On the *Chart Tools Format* tab, in the *Current Selection* group, click the **Reset to Match Style** button.

FIGURE EX 7.10

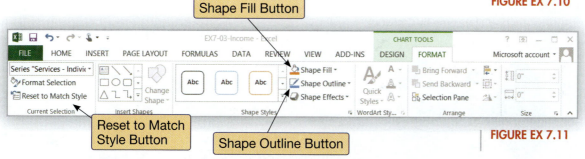

Shape Fill Button

Reset to Match Style Button

Shape Outline Button

FIGURE EX 7.11

tips & tricks

To change the color of a data series in a line chart, change the outline, not the fill.

The *Chart Styles* button that appears near the upper right corner of the selected chart applies to the entire chart, even if you have a single data series or point selected.

another method

You can change the fill and outline options from the *Format Data Point* or *Format Data Series* task pane:

1. Select the data point or data series, right-click, and select **Format Data Point...** or **Format Data Series....**
2. Click the **Fill & Line** button.
3. To change the fill color or style, click **Fill** to expand that section. Click the **Fill Color** button to open the color palette and then click the color you want. Leave the fill type as *Automatic* unless you want to change to a gradient, picture, or pattern.
4. To change the outline, click **Border** to expand that section. Click the **Outline Color** button to open the color palette and then click the color you want. Click in the **Width** box and adjust the outline weight by typing a value or using the increase/decrease arrows. Leave the line type as *Automatic* unless you want to change to a gradient.

let me try

Open the student data file **EX7-03-Income** and try this skill on your own:

1. Select the **Services–Individual** data series and apply the **Subtle Effect–Blue, Accent 1** shape style.
2. Select just the **FEB** data point in the *Services–Individual* data series and change the outline color to **Red.**
3. Change the outline width to **3 pt.**
4. Select the **Services–Packages** data series and change the fill color to **Blue, Accent 5, Darker 25%.**
5. Switch to the **Line Chart** worksheet and reset the **Services–Packages** data series line to match the chart style.
6. Save the file as directed by your instructor and close it.

Skill 7.4 Emphasizing a Data Point in a Pie Chart

Remember that pie charts work best when you want to evaluate data as part of a whole. Each "slice" represents a data point. To emphasize a single data point, you can rotate the pie chart to place the slice where you want it and separate ("explode") that slice from the rest of the pie.

In Figure EX 7.12, the chart has been rotated to place the *Merchandise* data point at the right side of the chart and then that slice has been exploded away from the rest of the pie to give it emphasis.

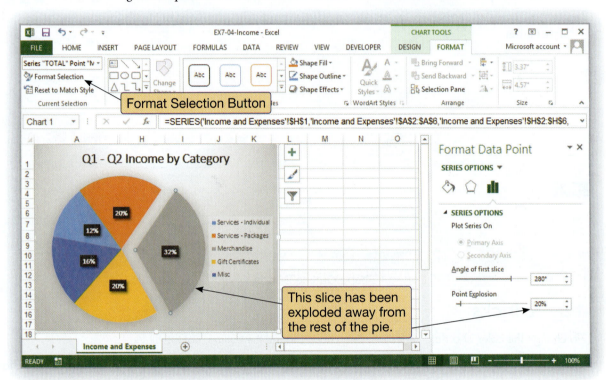

FIGURE EX 7.12

To rotate the pie chart:

1. Click the pie once to select the data series, and then click the data point (slice) you want to emphasize.

2. On the *Chart Tools Format* tab, in the *Current Selection* group, click the **Format Selection** button.

3. The *Format Data Point* task pane opens to the *Series Options* panel. In the *Angle of first slice* box, type the degree of rotation for the chart (from 0 to 360) and press (Enter). You can also use the *Angle of first slice* slider to change the rotation, but it can be difficult to select a precise angle.

To explode a single data point:

1. If it is not already open, open the *Format Data Point* task pane.

2. In the *Series Options* panel, type a percentage in the *Point Explosion* box and press (Enter). The higher the percentage of explosion, the further away the slice will appear. You can use the *Point Explosion* slider to change the degree of explosion, but it can be difficult to select a precise degree of explosion.

excel 2013   chapter 7 Exploring Advanced Charts and Graphics

tips & tricks

You can rotate a pie chart without selecting a specific data point first. Double-click anywhere in the pie to open the *Format Data Series* task pane and then use the *Angle of first slice* option to rotate the chart.

tell me **more**

To apply formatting to an individual data point in a pie chart, use the options in the *Chart Tools Format* tab, *Shape Styles* group or in the *Fill & Line* panel of the *Format Data Series* task pane. Refer to the skill *Formatting a Data Point or a Data Series* for more information.

another **method**

❭ If the pie is already selected, double-clicking a single slice will open the *Format Data Point* task pane.

❭ To format a single data point, right-click the pie slice representing the data point and select **Format Data Point...** to open the *Format Data Point* task pane.

❭ To explode a data point away from the rest of the pie chart, click the slice once to select it, and then drag the mouse so the slice moves away from the rest of the pie.

let me **try**

Open the student data file **EX7-04-Income** and try this skill on your own:

1. Select just the **Merchandise** data point in the *Q1–Q2 Income by Category* pie chart.

2. Rotate the pie chart exactly **280°** so the *Merchandise* data point appears at the right side of the chart near the legend.

3. Explode the *Merchandise* data point by exactly **20%** to move it slightly away from the rest of the pie chart.

4. Save the file as directed by your instructor and close it.

Skill 7.5 Formatting Other Chart Elements

Text-specific formatting options are available for chart elements that include text (the title, legend, data labels, and data table). **WordArt** styles are a preset combination of fill, outline, and text effects which can be applied to any text element.

To apply a WordArt style to a text chart element:

1. Click the chart element to select it. (Always double-check the *Chart Elements* box on the *Chart Tools Format* tab, *Current Selection* group to ensure that the correct chart element is selected.)

2. On the *Chart Tools Format* tab, in the *WordArt Styles* group, click the **WordArt Quick Styles** button to expand the gallery. Click the style you want.

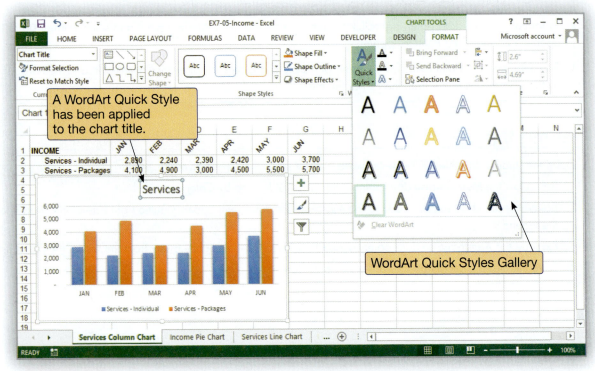

FIGURE EX 7.13

You can apply individual formatting options to text elements using the other buttons in the *WordArt Styles* group:

❭ To change the font color, click the **Text Fill** button and select a color.

❭ To apply a border around each text letter or number, click the **Text Outline** button and select a color. To change the outline line width, point to **Width** and select an option. To change the line style, point to **Dashes** and select an option.

❭ To apply a text effect, click the **Text Effects** button, point to the type of effect you want (**Shadow, Reflection,** or **Glow**), and select an option.

If you want to change the font, font size, or other font formatting characteristics, use the options available on the *Home* tab, in the *Font* group.

To add visual interest to the chart, try applying a gradient to the chart background. A gradient transitions the background from a dark shade to light shade of a single color.

1. If necessary, click an empty area of the chart to select the chart area.

2. On the *Chart Tools Format* tab, in the *Shape Styles* group, click the **Shape Fill** button, point to **Gradient,** and select the gradient you want. Be careful to choose a gradient that doesn't overwhelm the chart data.

In Figure EX 7.14, one of the light gradient variations has been applied to the chart area, so the *Gradient* gallery includes only the light variations, not both the light and dark variations as it would if a gradient had not yet been applied.

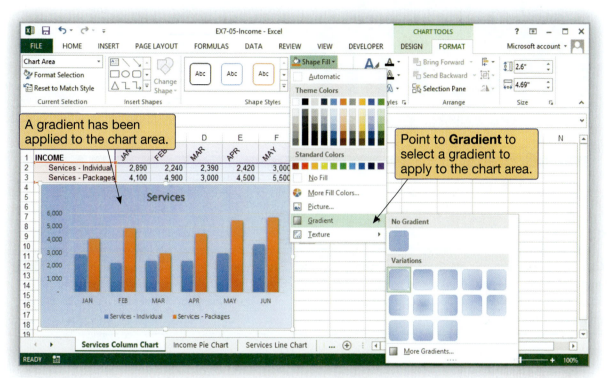

FIGURE EX 7.14

Chart gridlines help the user estimate the values represented by the data markers. They can be an important element in the chart, but they should not be the primary visual focus. Selecting the gridlines can be tricky; it may be easier to use the *Chart Elements* list. In the *Chart Elements* list, the vertical axis gridlines are the lines that run horizontally parallel to the x axis, and the horizontal axis gridlines run up-and-down parallel to the y axis. Pie charts do not have gridlines.

To change the style of the gridlines:

1. On the *Chart Tools Format* tab, in the *Current Selection* group, expand the *Chart Elements* box and select the gridlines.

2. On the *Chart Tools Format* tab, in the *Shape Styles* group, click the **Shape Outline** button and click the color you want.

3. You can also change the style of the lines. Click the **Shape Outline** button again, point to the type of style you want to change (**Width, Dashes,** or **Arrows**) and select an option.

FIGURE EX 7.15

tips & tricks

On the *Chart Tools Format* tab, in the *Current Selection* group, the *Chart Elements* box displays the name of the chart element that is currently selected. This can be helpful if you need to ensure that you have selected the chart area, the plot area, or another chart element. To select a specific chart element, expand the **Chart Elements** list and select the chart element you want to select.

tell me **more**

From the *Chart Tools Format* tab, *Shape Style* group, *Fill* button, you can apply a texture or a picture to the chart background. Use these options sparingly, as they can distract from the chart data.

another **method**

You can use the *Format* task pane for any chart element to apply formatting. Select the chart element, and then on the *Chart Tools Format* tab, in the *Current Selection* group, click the **Format Selection** button to open the appropriate *Format* task pane. Each chart element has its own formatting options, but they are all similar.

let me **try**

Open the student data file **EX7-05-Income** and try this skill on your own:

1. On the *Services Column Chart* worksheet, select the **chart title** and apply the **Pattern Fill–White, Text 2, Dark Upward Diagonal, Shadow** WordArt Quick Style.
2. Select the **chart area** and apply the **Linear Diagonal–Top Left to Bottom Right** gradient fill.
3. Select the **vertical (value) major axis gridlines** and change the color to **Gray-50%, Accent 3.**
4. Change the gridlines to use the **Long Dash Dot Dot** dash style.
5. Save the file as directed by your instructor and close it.

Skill 7.6 Creating a Chart Template

Chart templates can be used to quickly apply a set of chart formatting saved from an existing chart. If you find yourself making the same chart formatting changes over and over again, consider saving the chart as a chart template.

To create a chart template:

1. Right-click an empty part of the chart area and select **Save as Template...** to open the *Save Chart Template* dialog.
2. Excel automatically sets the location to the correct folder and the file type to *.crtx*. The *Save as type* box displays **Chart Template Files (*.crtx).**
3. Type a meaningful name for the template in the *File name* box.
4. Click **Save.**

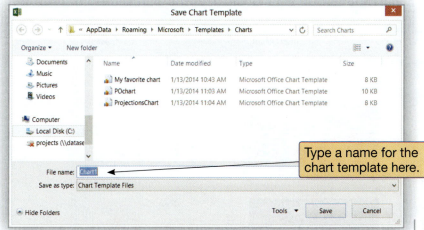

Type a name for the chart template here.

FIGURE EX 7.16

tips & tricks

In Excel 2010, you could create a chart template from a button on the *Chart Tools Design* tab, but this button has been removed in Excel 2013.

tell me more

By default, Excel saves the chart template file to your local drive in the *Users* folder: **C:\Users\[*your user name here*]\AppData\Roaming\Microsoft\Templates\Charts**

let me try

Open the student data file **EX7-06-Income** and try this skill on your own:

1. If necessary, select the chart.
2. Create a new chart template and name the template: **IncomeChart**
3. Save the file as directed by your instructor and close it.

Skill 7.7 Applying a Chart Template

Once you have saved a chart template, it is easy to create a new chart with the options and formatting saved in the template. Creating a new chart from a chart template applies the chart type, shows selected chart elements, and applies formatting to the chart. It does not impact the data selected for the chart.

To use the chart template:

1. Select the data you want to visualize in the chart.
2. On the *Insert* tab, in the *Charts* group, click the **Recommended Charts** button to open the *Insert Chart* dialog.
3. Click the **All Charts** tab.
4. Click **Templates** to view the chart templates you have saved.
5. Click the chart template you want and click **OK.**

Select a chart template to create a new chart using the template's options and formatting.

FIGURE EX 7.17

tell me **more**

You can also apply a custom chart template to an existing chart.

1. On the *Chart Tools Design* tab, in the *Type* group, click the **Change Chart Type** button to open the *Change Chart Type* dialog.
2. Click **Templates.**
3. Select the template you want to apply and click **OK.**

let me **try**

Open the student data file **EX7-07-Income** and try this skill on your own:

1. If necessary, select cells **A1:G3.**
2. Create a chart from the selected cells using the **IncomeChart** chart template.
3. Save the file as directed by your instructor and close it.

Skill 7.8 Adding and Removing Trendlines

A **trendline** is a line that overlays the chart and shows the expected data points based on mathematical analysis of the data. A simple linear trendline calculates the difference between the first two data points and can be used to predict future data points based on that difference.

FIGURE EX 7.18

To add a trendline:

1. Click the chart once to select it.
2. Click the **Chart Elements** button that appears near the upper right corner of the chart.
3. Click the **Trendline** check box to add a checkmark.
4. If the chart has more than one data series, Excel will display a dialog and prompt you to select the series to which the trendline should be added. Select the data series for the trendline and then click **OK.**
5. Excel adds the trendline to the chart using the default trendline type and formatting.

To remove a trendline:

1. Click the chart once to select it.
2. Click the **Chart Elements** button that appears near the upper right corner of the chart.
3. Click the **Trendline** check box to remove the checkmark.
4. If the chart has more than one trendline, Excel will display a dialog and prompt you to select the series from which the trendline should be removed.

tips & tricks

You can add multiple trendlines to a chart, but you must add them one at a time.

another method

To remove the trendline, right-click the trendline and select **Delete.**

let me try

Open the student data file **EX7-08-Sales** and try this skill on your own:

1. Select the chart.
2. Remove the existing trendline.
3. Add a new trendline for the *Egyptian Cotton Towel Set* data series. Use the default trendline type and formatting.
4. Save the file as directed by your instructor and close it.

Skill 7.9 Choosing the Trendline Type

Not every data point may fit into the trendline perfectly. You'll see that while a few data points may be directly on the line, others will be scattered above and below it. For example, if your data points have an exponential relationship, they may not fit well on a linear trendline.

The trendline types you will use most often are:

Linear—Best suited to data that increases (or decreases) at a steady rate.

Exponential—Used for data that increases (or decreases) at an increasing rate.

Logarithmic—Best fits data that increases or decreases rapidly and then levels off.

Moving average—Use for data that swings up and down. Set the number of periods to average.

One tool to help you find the best trendline type for your data is the R-squared value. The **R-squared value** is a statistical measurement of the how well the data fit the trendline. It is a number between 0 and 1; the closer the trendline's R-squared value is to 1, the better the fit. In Figure EX 7.19, the linear trendline has an R-squared value of *0.7644*. You can see that the points on the trendline do not match the actual data point values very well.

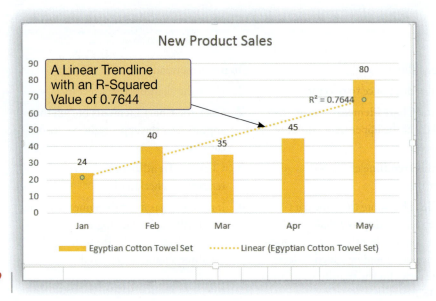

FIGURE EX 7.19

Once you have added a trendline, you can display its R-squared value and change the trendline type through the *Format Trendline* task pane:

1. Click the trendline once to select it.

2. On the *Chart Tools Format* tab, in the *Current Selection* group, click the **Format Selection** button to open the *Format Trendline* task pane.

3. To display the R-squared value, click the **Show R-squared value on chart** check box. (Scroll to the bottom of the task pane if necessary.)

4. To change the type of trendline, click one of the radio buttons at the top of the task pane. Notice that the R-squared value changes when you change the trendline type.

5. To undo any changes you have made, use the *Undo* command.

In Figure EX 7.21, the trendline has been changed to exponential and new the R-squared value is *0.8311,* indicating a better (although still not great) fit.

Change the trendline type by clicking one of these radio buttons.

Check this box to display the R-squared value on the trendline.

Format Trendline

TRENDLINE OPTIONS ▾

▲ TRENDLINE OPTIONS

- ◉ Exponential
- ○ Linear
- ○ Logarithmic
- ○ Polynomial   Order 2
- ○ Power
- ○ Moving Average   Period 2

Trendline Name

- ◉ Automatic   Expon. (Organic Shaving Kit)
- ○ Custom

Forecast

Forward   2   periods
Backward   0.0   periods

☐ Set Intercept   1.0

☐ Display Equation on chart
☑ Display R-squared value on chart

FIGURE EX 7.20

New Product Sales

The trendline has been changed to exponential.

$R^2 = 0.8311$

- Jan: 24
- Feb: 40
- Mar: 35
- Apr: 45
- May: 80

▬ Egyptian Cotton Towel Set   ·····Expon. (Egyptian Cotton Towel Set)

FIGURE EX 7.21

tell me **more**

You can apply formatting to the trendline just as you would to any other chart element. For more information, refer to the skill *Formatting Other Chart Elements.*

another **method**

To open the *Format Trendline* task pane, double-click the trendline or right-click the trendline and select **Format Trendline...**

let me **try**

Open the student data file **EX7-09-NewProductSales** and try this skill on your own:

1. Display the **R-squared** value for the trendline.

2. Change the trendline to **exponential**.

3. Save the file as directed by your instructor and close it.

Skill 7.10 Forecasting Values on a Trendline

Trendlines can show the line along which future data points would be expected based on different statistical growth patterns. This forecasting of future values is also known as **regression analysis**.

Once you have added a trendline, you can extend the trendline to estimate values forward or backward through the *Format Trendline* task pane.

1. Click the trendline once to select it.

2. On the *Chart Tools Format* tab, in the *Current Selection* group, click the **Format Selection** button to open the *Format Trendline* task pane.

3. To extend the trendline and forecast future values, enter a value in the **Forward** box for the number of periods you want to forecast forward. (You may need to scroll to the bottom of the task pane.) Press Enter or Tab to accept the value. You can extend the trendline backward to estimate values for previous periods by entering a value in the *Backward* box.

4. To undo any changes you have made, use the *Undo* command.

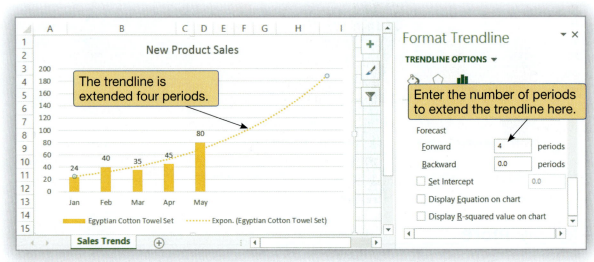

FIGURE EX 7.22

tips & tricks

Mark Twain is often quoted as saying "Facts are stubborn things, but statistics are pliable." As you can see in Figure EX 7.22, forecasting future values with a trendline can be misleading. Accurate forecasting requires having a large enough data set to plot the trendline with a high level of confidence. In this case, five months' sales are probably not enough to accurately predict exponential sales growth for the next four months.

another method

To open the *Format Trendline* task pane, double-click the trendline or right-click the trendline and select **Format Trendline....**

let me try

Open the student data file **EX7-10-NewProductSales** and try this skill on your own:

1. Select the trendline.

2. Extend the trendline to forecast forward four periods.

3. Save the file as directed by your instructor and close it.

Skill 7.11 Changing the Sparkline Type

Chapter 5 introduced the concept of Sparklines. Recall that Sparklines represent a series of data values as an individual graphic within a single cell. As you update the underlying data series, the Sparklines update immediately. Sparklines can be helpful in visualizing data patterns. After inserting Sparklines, you may find that you need to change the Sparkline type to present a clearer picture of your data.

To change the Sparkline type:

1. Click one of the cells containing Sparklines to activate the *Sparkline Tools Design* tab. If necessary, click the tab.

2. In the *Type* group, click the **Line, Column,** or **Win/Loss** button to change the Sparklines to a new format.

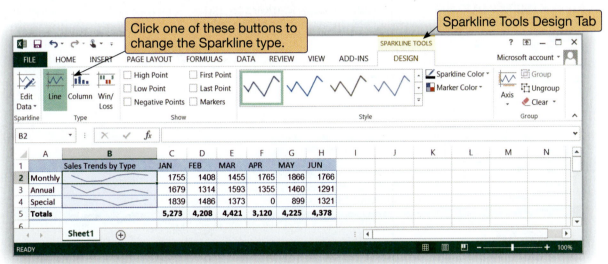

FIGURE EX 7.23

tips & tricks

If you want to know more about the concept of sparklines, check out Edward Tufte's Web site at **http://www.edwardtufte.com.** Edward Tufte is a pioneer in the field of data visualization and information graphics. He discusses sparklines in depth in his book *Beautiful Evidence*.

tell me more

To change the data range or the location range for the Sparklines:

1. Click the **Edit Data** button at the far left side of the *Sparkline Tools Design* tab and select **Edit Group Location & Data.** This opens the *Edit Sparklines* dialog.

2. Edit the cell range in the *Data Range* and *Location Range* boxes as necessary.

3. Click **OK.**

let me try

Open the student data file **EX7-11-Sales** and try this skill on your own:

1. If necessary, click cell **B2** to select the first group of Sparklines.

2. Change the Sparklines from columns to lines.

3. Save the file as directed by your instructor and close it.

Skill 7.12 Adding Markers to Sparklines

Markers are visual representations of data points on a Sparkline. Adding markers can help identify the data points or emphasize high or low points.

To add markers to Sparklines, first click anywhere in the Sparklines, and then check the options you want in the *Sparkline Tools Design* tab, *Show* group:

❭ To add data point markers for every data point, click the **Markers** check box.

❭ To remove data point markers, click the **Markers** check box again to remove the checkmark.

❭ To add a marker for just the highest value, click the **High Point** check box.

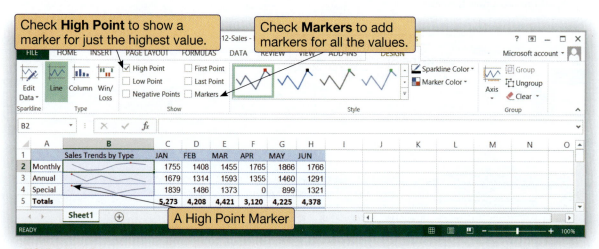

FIGURE EX 7.24

tell me **more**

For information about formatting Sparklines, refer to the skill *Applying Quick Styles and Other Formatting to Sparklines.*

let me **try**

Open the student data file **EX7-12-Sales** and try this skill on your own:

1. If necessary, click cell **B2** to select the first group of Sparklines in this worksheet.

2. Show markers for all the data points in this Sparkline group.

3. Remove the markers from this Sparkline group.

4. Show markers for just the highest values in this Sparkline group.

5. Save the file as directed by your instructor and close it.

Skill 7.13 Applying Quick Styles and Other Formatting to Sparklines

Apply a **Sparkline Quick Style** to change the Sparkline color and marker color(s) at once. You can also specify color for just the Sparklines or individual markers.

To change the Quick Style applied to the Sparklines:

1. Click one of the cells containing Sparklines to activate the *Sparkline Tools Design* tab. If necessary, click the tab.

2. In the *Style* group, if the Quick Style you want is not visible on the Ribbon, click the **More** button to expand the gallery.

3. Click a style to apply it to the Sparklines.

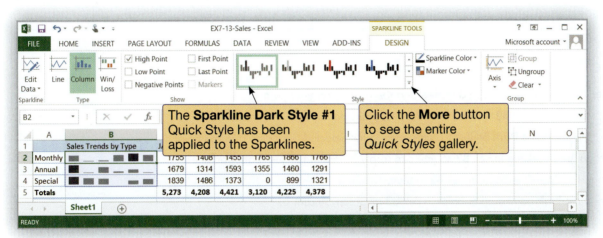

FIGURE EX 7.25

When you create Sparklines, the cells containing the Sparklines are grouped together so any formatting changes you make affect them all. You can remove a single Sparkline from the group to make formatting changes to only that Sparkline.

To change the Sparkline color or the marker color for a single Sparkline:

1. Click the individual Sparkline you want to format separately from the group.

2. On the *Sparkline Tools Design* tab, in the *Group* group, click the **Ungroup** button. Now when you make formatting changes, only the single Sparkline is affected.

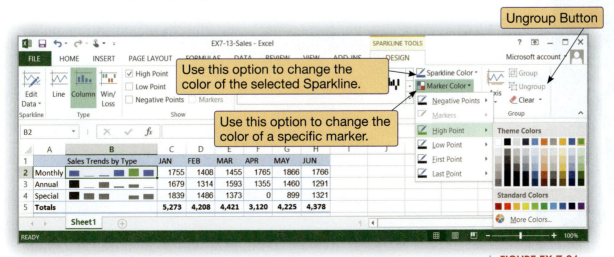

FIGURE EX 7.26

3. To change the Sparkline color, on the *Sparkline Tools Design* tab, in the *Style* group, click the **Sparkline Color** button arrow and select the color you want from the color palette.

4. To change the marker color, on the *Sparkline Tools Design* tab, in the *Style* group, click the **Marker Color** button. Point to the marker you want to change (such as **High Point**) and then select the color you want from the color palette.

tips & tricks

﹥ If you do not select a single Sparkline and remove it from the group before making changes from the *Sparkline Color* button or the *Marker Color* button, the changes will be applied to all the Sparklines in the group.

﹥ If you click the *Sparkline Color* button instead of the button arrow, the most recently used color will be applied automatically to the selected Sparkline(s).

﹥ The *Ungroup* button appears inactive when the selected Sparkline has already been ungrouped.

let me try

Open the student data file **EX7-13-Sales** and try this skill on your own:

1. If necessary, click cell **B2** to select the first group of Sparklines in this worksheet.
2. Apply the **Sparkline Dark Style #1** Quick Style to the selected Sparkline group.
3. Ungroup the Sparkline in cell **B2** so you can apply formatting to just that Sparkline.
4. Change the Sparkline color in cell **B2** to **Blue, Accent 5**.
5. Change the high point marker color in cell **B2** to **Green, Accent 6**.
6. Save the file as directed by your instructor and close it.

from the perspective of . . .

SPORTING GOODS STORE PURCHASING MANAGER

We chart data from our checkout process using trendlines and Sparklines so we can see which merchandise is in high demand. Our inventory keeps current because we watch the trends over time. We can now better predict which items to order for each upcoming season.

Skill 7.14 Inserting a Picture

You can insert a picture you created in another program into your worksheet. There are a number of graphic formats Excel will accept, including those commonly used in Web pages such as JPEG, PNG, and GIF. When you insert a picture into an Excel worksheet, the images are embedded objects, meaning they become part of the workbook. Changing the source file will not change or affect the image in the workbook.

You can insert pictures stored on your local hard drive or connected media storage such as a network drive or a USB key. You can also insert online pictures from the *Office.com Clip Art* gallery and other built-in online sources.

To insert a picture from a local file:

1. On the *Insert* tab, if necessary, click the **Illustrations** button to expand the *Illustrations* group. Click the **Picture** button.

2. The *Insert Picture* dialog opens.

3. If necessary, navigate to the file location. Select the file and click **Insert.**

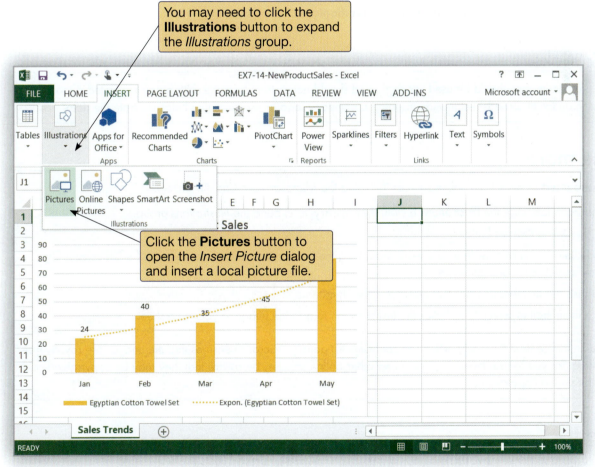

You may need to click the **Illustrations** button to expand the *Illustrations* group.

Click the **Pictures** button to open the *Insert Picture* dialog and insert a local picture file.

FIGURE EX 7.27

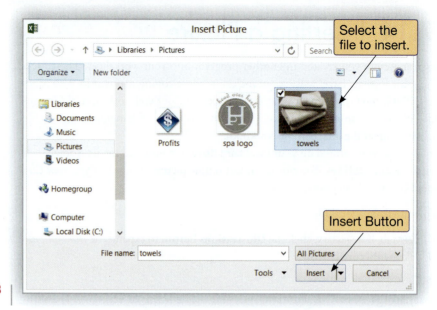

FIGURE EX 7.28

To delete a picture, select the picture and press the (Delete) key.

tips & tricks

In Excel, graphic images should be used sparingly and should not distract from the data being presented. Good uses of images in an Excel spreadsheet include inserting a company logo or a picture that helps illustrate the data.

tell me more

You can also insert pictures from online sources including the *Microsoft.com Clip Art* gallery.

1. On the *Insert* tab, click the **Illustrations** button, if necessary, to expand the *Illustrations* group.
2. Click the **Online Pictures** button.
3. To find clip art from Microsoft, type a word describing the image you want to search for in the **Office.com Clip Art** box and click the **Search** button.
4. Word displays thumbnail results that match the search criteria.
5. Click a thumbnail to select it, and click the **Insert** button to add the image to your worksheet.

If you use an image from the online *Microsoft.com Clip Art* gallery, Microsoft ensures that the images are royalty-free and are legal for you to use. However, if you find other online images, be aware that they may be copyrighted and not legal for you to copy and use.

let me try

Open the student data file **EX7-14-NewProductSales** and try this skill on your own:

1. If necessary, click cell **J1** to set the initial position for the image.
2. Insert the **towels** picture into this worksheet. (The *towels* picture is available with the data files for this book. If you do not have that picture available, use a picture of your choice.)
3. Save the file as directed by your instructor and close it.

Skill 7.15 Resizing and Moving Pictures

You can resize an image by either manually entering the values for the size of the picture or by dragging a resize handle on the image to make it larger or smaller. Entering specific width or height values provides more precise control over the size of the picture.

To resize an image by manually entering values:

1. If necessary, click the picture once to select it.

2. On the *Picture Tools Format* tab, in the *Size* group, type a value in the **Width** or **Height** box.

3. Press (Enter) to accept the change.

To move a picture, point to the image and, when the cursor changes to the move cursor, click and drag the image to the new location.

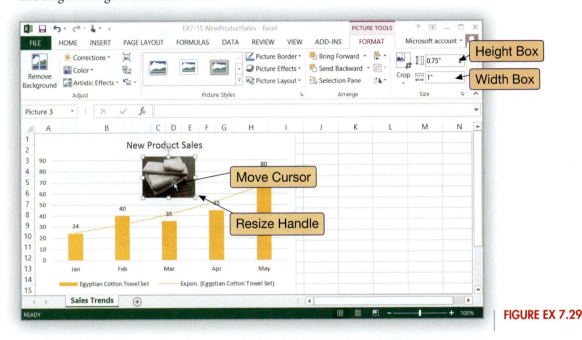

FIGURE EX 7.29

tips & tricks

When you use the *Width* or *Height* box on the *Picture Tools Format* tab to resize a picture, the value in the other box will change automatically to maintain the **aspect ratio**. This means that as the width or height is increased or decreased, the height or width of the image is increased or decreased proportionately. If the aspect ratio did not remain the same, the image would appear stretched or pinched as you resized it.

tell me **more**

To resize a picture by dragging, click a resize handle, and drag toward the center of the image to make it smaller or away from the center of the image to make it larger. To maintain the aspect ratio of the picture, be sure to use one of the resize handles at the four corners of the picture. If you use a resize handle along one of the sides or the top or bottom, you will be resizing the width or height of the picture only.

let me **try**

Open the student data file **EX7-15-NewProductSales** and try this skill on your own:

1. Use the Ribbon to resize the picture to exactly **.75** inches tall. Allow Excel to adjust the width to maintain the aspect ratio.

2. Move the image so it is positioned centered below the chart title.

3. Save the file as directed by your instructor and close it.

Skill 7.16 Applying Quick Styles and Other Formatting to Pictures

FIGURE EX 7.30
Picture Quick Styles

When you insert a picture in a worksheet, the *Picture Tools Format* tab displays. This Ribbon tab contains tools to change the look of the picture including applying Picture Quick Styles, borders, and effects.

Picture Quick Styles allow you to apply a combination of formatting such as borders, rounded corners, and effects with a single command. To apply a Picture Quick Style:

1. If necessary, click the picture once to select it.
2. On the *Picture Tools Format* tab, in the *Picture Styles* group, click the **More** button to expand the gallery.
3. In the *Picture Quick Styles* gallery, click a style to apply it to the picture.

To apply a color border to the picture or change the color of the existing border:

1. On the *Picture Tools Format* tab, in the *Picture Styles* group, click the **Picture Border** button.
2. Select the color you want from the color palette.

Excel includes a variety of effects you can apply to pictures, including a group of preset effects that combine shadows, reflections, glows, and bevels. To apply a preset effect to the picture:

1. On the *Picture Tools Format* tab, in the *Picture Styles* group, click the **Picture Effects** button.
2. Point to **Preset,** and select the effect you want.

FIGURE EX 7.31
Picture Border Menu

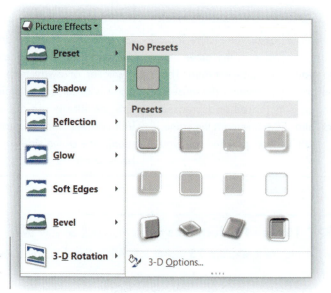

FIGURE EX 7.32
Picture Effects, Preset Effects Gallery

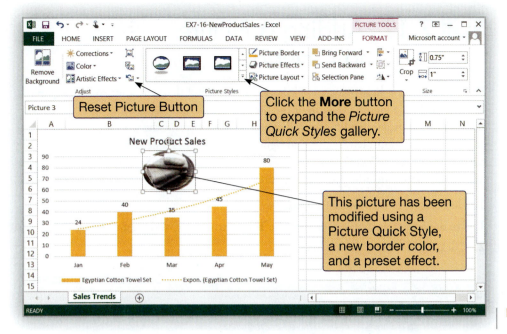

FIGURE EX 7.33

At any time, you can remove formatting and return the image to its original state. On the *Picture Tools Format* tab, in the *Adjust* group, click the **Reset Picture** button.

tell me more

Use the tools in the *Adjust* group to color-correct the image, add colorization, and apply a variety of artistic effects.

another method

❭ The *Picture Quick Styles* gallery is available from the Mini toolbar when you right-click the picture.

❭ More picture formatting options are available from the *Format Picture* task pane. To open the *Format Picture* task pane, click the dialog launcher button in any of the groups on *Picture Tools Format* tab, or right-click the picture and select **Format Picture...**

let me try

Open the student data file **EX7-16-NewProductSales** and try this skill on your own:

1. Apply the **Beveled Oval, Black** Quick Style to the picture.
2. Change the picture border color to **Gold, Accent 4.**
3. Apply the **Preset 7** picture effect to the picture.
4. Reset the picture to its original formatting.
5. Save the file as directed by your instructor and close it.

Skill 7.17 Adding a Picture to a Header

When you create a header for a worksheet, you may find that you want to add a graphic element, such as a logo, to the top of the printed worksheet. Page Layout view shows you exactly how the header and footer will appear when you print the worksheet. The header area has three sections: left, center, and right. When you click a header area, the contextual tab *Header & Footer Tools Design* appears. This tab contains commands for working with the header and footer, including adding a picture.

To add a picture to the worksheet header:

1. On the *Insert* tab, if necessary, click the **Text** button to expand the *Text* group.
2. Click the **Header & Footer** button.

FIGURE EX 7.34

3. Excel switches to Page Layout view with the center section of the header active. If necessary, click the header section where you want the picture to appear.
4. On the *Header & Footer Tools Design* tab, in the *Header & Footer Elements* group, click the **Picture** button.
5. Click the **Browse** button next to *From a file* to insert a file from your local hard drive or an attached drive or storage media.

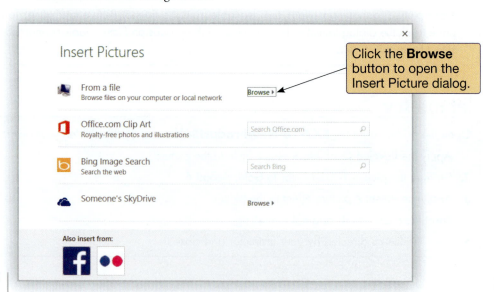

FIGURE EX 7.35

6. Navigate to the file location. Select the file and click **Insert.**

From Page Layout view, when you click the header section where the picture is, you will see the text "&[picture]" instead of the actual image. When you click outside that header section, the image will appear.

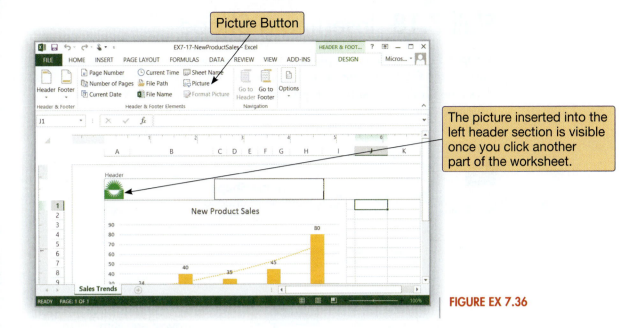

Picture Button

The picture inserted into the left header section is visible once you click another part of the worksheet.

FIGURE EX 7.36

tips & tricks

In Normal view, the picture will not be visible at all because the header is hidden.

tell me **more**

To format a picture in the worksheet header, select the picture and then on the *Header & Footer Tools Design* tab, in the *Header & Footer Elements* group, click the **Format Picture** button. The *Format Picture* dialog opens. From the dialog, you can resize, rotate, crop, and modify the picture. Note that the formatting options available for a picture in the worksheet header are very limited compared to the options available for a picture in the worksheet.

another **method**

To add a picture to a header section from the *Page Setup* dialog:

1. On the *Page Layout* tab, in the *Page Setup* group, click the **Page Setup** dialog launcher.
2. In the *Page Setup* dialog, click the **Header/Footer** tab.
3. Click the **Custom Header** button.
4. Click in the section where you want to position the picture.
5. Click the **Insert Picture** button to open the *Insert Picture* dialog.
6. Navigate to the file location. Select the file, and click **Insert.**
7. Click **OK** to close the *Header* dialog, and then click **OK** again to close the *Page Setup* dialog.

let me **try**

Open the student data file **EX7-17-NewProductSales** and try this skill on your own:

1. Switch to Page Layout view so you can insert a picture into the **left** section of the worksheet header.
2. Add the picture **green logo** to the left section of the worksheet header. (The *green logo* picture is available with the data files for this book. If you do not have that picture available, use a picture of your choice.)
3. Save the file as directed by your instructor and close it.

Skill 7.18 Inserting a Shape

A **shape** is a drawing object that you can add to your spreadsheet to call attention to a cell or group of cells. Excel comes with a number of shapes for you to choose from, including lines, block arrows, callouts, and basic shapes such as rectangles and circles. When you insert a shape into a worksheet, it is not inserted into a specific cell. You can move it to another place in the worksheet without affecting the underlying data or worksheet structure.

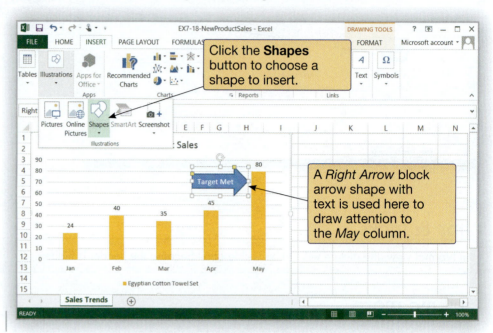

FIGURE EX 7.37

To add a shape:

1. On the *Insert* tab, if necessary, click the **Illustrations** button to expand the *Illustrations* group. Click the **Shapes** button and select an option from the *Shapes* gallery.

FIGURE EX 7.38
Shapes Gallery

2. The cursor changes to a crosshair.

3. Click on the spreadsheet to add the shape. To control the size of the shape more precisely, you can click and drag to draw the shape.

All shapes, except lines, allow you to add text. To add text to a shape:

1. If necessary, click the shape once to select it.

2. Type the text. Click anywhere outside the shape to accept the text.

If you need to edit the shape text, right-click the shape and select **Edit Text.** When you are finished editing the text, you can click outside the shape or right-click the shape again and select **Exit Edit Text.**

tips & tricks

If you have multiple shapes in your worksheet, use the tools in the *Arrange* group to control which image appears on top and group shapes together so they can be manipulated as a single object.

tell me more

Resizing and moving shapes is similar to working with pictures. For more information, refer to the skill *Resizing and Moving Pictures*.

❯ You can resize a shape by either manually entering the values for the size of the shape in the *Width* or *Height* box at the far left side of the *Drawing Tools Format* tab, *Size* group, or by dragging a resize handle on the shape to make it larger or smaller.

❯ To move a shape, point to the shape and, when the cursor changes to the move cursor, click and drag the shape to the new location.

another method

❯ If you have a chart selected, you can also insert a shape from the *Chart Tools Format* tab, *Insert Shapes* groups.

❯ If you have a shape selected, you can add more shapes from the *Drawing Tools Format* tab, *Insert Shapes* group.

let me try

Open the student data file **EX7-18-NewProductSales** and try this skill on your own:

1. Insert a **Right Arrow** block arrow shape to the left of the *May* column in the chart.

2. Add the text **Target Met** to the shape.

3. Save the file as directed by your instructor and close it.

Skill 7.19 Applying Quick Styles and Other Formatting to Shapes

Shape Quick Styles allow you to apply a combination of formatting such as borders, rounded corners, and effects with a single command. When you insert a shape, Excel applies the default Quick Style for the workbook's theme to the shape. To adjust the formatting of the shape you can choose a new Quick Style from the *Shapes Styles* gallery.

To apply a Quick Style to a shape:

1. Select the shape you want to change.

2. On the *Drawing Tools Format* tab, in the *Shape Styles* group, click a Quick Style in the collapsed gallery on the Ribbon.

3. If the Quick Style you want to use does not appear on the Ribbon, click the **More** button to display the gallery and click a Quick Style in the gallery to apply it to the shape.

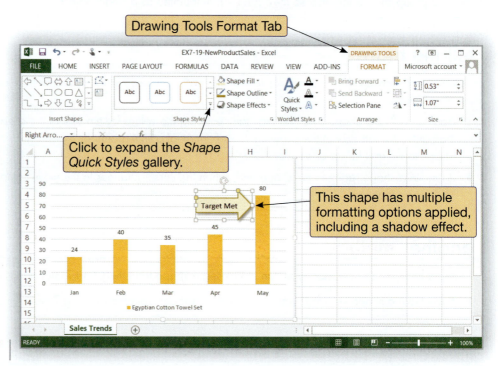

FIGURE EX 7.39

You can further adjust the look of a shape by changing the following:

❭ **Shape fill**—The color that fills the object. You can choose a solid color from the color palette or fill the color with a gradient or texture.

❭ **Shape outline**—The line that surrounds the shape. You can further adjust the outline of shapes by changing the color of the outline, width of the outline, and style of the outline.

❭ **Shape effects**—Graphic effects you can apply to shapes including drop shadows, reflections, glows, and bevels.

To further adjust the formatting of a shape:

1. Select the shape you want to change.

2. Click the **Drawing Tools Format** tab.

3. To change the fill of a shape, in the *Shape Styles* group, click the **Shape Fill** button and select an option from the color palette. To make the shape appear transparent, click the **Shape Fill** button and select **No Fill.**

excel 2013   chapter 7 Exploring Advanced Charts and Graphics

4. To change the outline of a shape, in the *Shape Styles* group, click the **Shape Outline** button.

- Select an option from the color palette to change the color of the outline.
- Point to **Weight** and select a thickness option for the outline.
- Point to **Dashes** and select a dash style for the outline.

5. To apply a shape effect, in the *Shape Styles* group, click the **Shape Effects** button, point to a shape effect, and select an option.

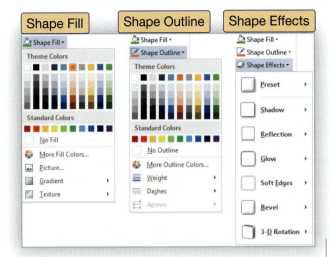

FIGURE EX 7.40

tips & tricks

If the shape includes text, be sure to right-click an empty area of the shape to see the shape formatting options. If you right-click the text area, the right-click menu will show text options instead.

tell me more

More shape formatting options are available from the *Format Shape* task pane. To open the *Format Shape* task pane, click the dialog launcher button in any of the groups on the *Drawing Tools Format* tab, or right-click the shape and select **Format Object....**

another method

❯ To change the Quick Style of a shape, you can right-click the shape and click the **Styles** button on the Mini toolbar.

❯ To change the fill of a shape, you can right-click the shape and click the **Fill** button on the Mini toolbar.

❯ To change the outline of a shape, you can right-click the shape and click the **Outline** button on the Mini toolbar.

let me try

Open the student data file **EX7-19-NewProductSales** and try this skill on your own:

1. Apply the **Colored Outline–Gold, Accent 4** Quick Style to the shape.
2. Change the shape fill color to **Gold, Accent 4, Lighter 80%**.
3. Change the shape outline color to **Gold, Accent 4, Darker 25%**.
4. Apply the **Offset Diagonal Bottom Right** shadow effect to the shape.
5. Save the file as directed by your instructor and close it.

Skill 7.20 Capturing a Screenshot in Excel

A **screenshot** captures the image from the computer screen (such as an open application window or a Web page) and creates an image which can then be inserted and formatted like any other picture. With previous versions of Excel, you had to use another application to create the screenshot and then insert the picture into Excel. In Excel 2010 and later, you can use the *Insert Screenshot* command to capture and insert screenshots into spreadsheets directly from the Excel interface.

To add a screenshot to a worksheet:

1. On the *Insert* tab, if necessary, click the **Illustrations** button to expand the *Illustrations* group. Click the **Screenshot** button.

2. The *Available Windows* section of the *Screenshot* gallery displays a thumbnail of each of the currently open windows.

3. Click a thumbnail to add the entire screenshot of that window to the worksheet.

4. Resize and move the screenshot image as necessary. For more information, refer to the skill *Resizing and Moving Pictures*.

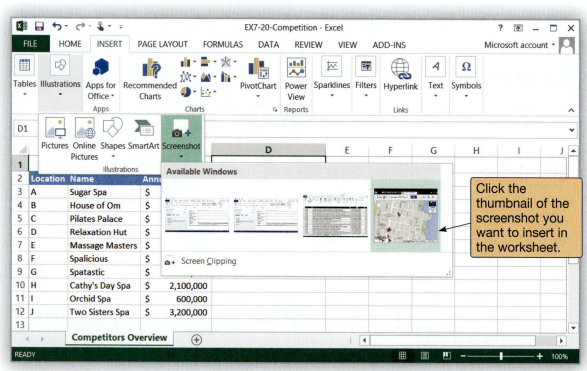

FIGURE EX 7.41

excel 2013   chapter 7 Exploring Advanced Charts and Graphics

If you are using the Internet Explorer browser, you may see a message asking if you'd like to insert a hyperlink.

❭ Click **Yes** to include a link from the screenshot picture to the Web page. If a hyperlink is included with the screenshot picture, when a user clicks the image, the linked Web page will open.

❭ Click **No** to insert a static picture of the screenshot.

❭ If you click the **Remember my choice** check box, you will not see this message again.

FIGURE EX 7.42

Click **Yes** to add a hyperlink to the Web page.

tips & tricks

The *Screenshot* gallery does not display open windows that are minimized.

tell me more

To insert a screenshot of only part of a window or a screenshot of the entire desktop, select **Screen Clipping** from the bottom of the *Screenshot* gallery. The Screen Clipping tool minimizes Excel. Click and drag to select part of the desktop or open window that you want to insert. When you release the mouse button, the Excel interface becomes active again.

let me try

Open the student data file **EX7-20-Competition** and try this skill on your own:

1. Open Internet Explorer or another browser and go to **https://maps.google.com.**
2. Search for the keywords: **day spa Old Town Alexandria VA**
3. If you want, you can collapse the side panel listing the spa businesses so only the map is showing. Zoom in or out until the map shows the points you want. Once the browser window is exactly as you want it for the screenshot, go back to Excel. (Do not minimize the browser window.)
4. From Excel, capture a screenshot of the browser window and insert the picture into the worksheet.
5. If you see the message about including a hyperlink, click **Yes** but do not have Excel remember your choice.
6. Move and resize the picture as necessary so the image appears next to the competition data.
7. Save the file as directed by your instructor and close it.

key terms

Combination chart
Combo chart
Shape Quick Style
WordArt
Chart template
Trendline
Linear trendline
Exponential trendline
Logarithmic trendline
Moving average trendline

R-squared value
Regression analysis
Marker
Sparkline Quick Style
Aspect ratio
Picture Quick Style
Shape
Shape Quick Style
Screenshot

concepts review

1. Which of these is the most common combination for a combo chart?

   a. Pie and line

   b. Column and line

   c. Column and pie

   d. Scatter and line

2. Use the *Chart Styles* button that appears at the upper right corner of a selected chart to change the style for a selected data series or single data point.

   a. True

   b. False

3. Which of these methods allows you to separate a data point in a pie chart?

   a. Enter a value in the *Angle of first slice* box in the *Format Data Point* task pane.

   b. Enter a value in the *Point Explosion* box in the *Format Data Point* task pane.

   c. Enter a value in the *Width* box on the *Chart Tools Format* tab, *Size* group.

   d. Move the data point to a secondary axis.

4. You can apply a chart template that you've saved from which of these methods?

   a. Click the **File** tab and click **Open** to navigate to the chart templates location.

   b. Click the **File** tab. Click **New** and then type the chart template name in the search box.

   c. On the *Insert* tab, in the *Charts* group, click the **Chart Templates** button.

   d. On the *Insert* tab, in the *Charts* group, click the **Recommended Charts** button, and then click the **All Charts** tab.

5. Use a trendline to:

   a. Analyze the relationship between data points in a chart.

   b. Forecast future values on a chart.

   c. Estimate previous values on a chart.

   d. All of the above

6. Which of these would you use for regression analysis?

   a. Line Sparklines

   b. Column Sparklines

   c. Trendline

   d. Line Sparklines with Markers

7. To change the Sparkline type, you must first clear the existing Sparklines.
   a. True
   b. False

8. When you insert a picture into a worksheet, it is inserted into a specific cell.
   a. True
   b. False

9. When you add a picture to a worksheet header, it is not visible in Normal view.
   a. True
   b. False

10. You can insert a screenshot of any open window, even if it's minimized.
    a. True
    b. False

projects

Data files for projects can be found on
www.mhhe.com/office2013skills

skill review 7.1

In this project, you will analyze U.S. population growth over the last 40 years. You will include a screenshot from the 2010 U.S Census Web page.

Skills needed to complete this project:

- Applying Quick Styles and Other Formatting to Sparklines (Skill 7.13)
- Changing the Sparkline Type (Skill 7.11)
- Adding Markers to Sparklines (Skill 7.12)
- Adding a Data Series to a Chart (Skill 7.1)
- Creating a Combination Chart (Skill 7.2)
- Formatting Other Chart Elements (Skill 7.5)
- Formatting a Data Point or a Data Series (Skill 7.3)
- Creating a Chart Template (Skill 7.6)
- Inserting a Shape (Skill 7.18)
- Applying Quick Styles and Other Formatting to Shapes (Skill 7.19)
- Applying a Chart Template (Skill 7.7)
- Adding and Removing Trendlines (Skill 7.8)
- Forecasting Values on a Trendline (Skill 7.10)
- Choosing the Trendline Type (Skill 7.9)
- Capturing a Screenshot in Excel (Skill 7.20)
- Resizing and Moving Pictures (Skill 7.15)
- Applying Quick Styles and Other Formatting to Pictures (Skill 7.16)

1. Open the start file **EX2013-SkillReview-7-1** and resave the file as:

    `[your initials]EX-SkillReview-7-1`

2. If the workbook opens in Protected View, click the **Enable Editing** button in the Message Bar at the top of the worksheet so you can modify the workbook.

3. Add Sparklines to the data and apply a Quick Style.

    a. On the *Population Data* worksheet, select cells **B4:F13.**

    b. On the *Insert* tab, in the *Sparklines* group, click the **Column** button.

    c. In the *Create Sparklines* dialog, verify that B4:F13 is the *Data Range* and specify **G4:G13** as the *Location Range.* Click **OK.**

    d. On the *Sparkline Tools Design* tab, in the *Style* group, apply the **Sparkline Style Accent 1, (no dark or light)** style. Click the **More** button to expand the gallery, then click the first style in the third row.

4. Change the Sparklines to lines with markers for all data points and highlight the high point marker in a different color.

    a. On the *Sparkline Tools Design* tab, in the *Type* group, click the **Line** button.

    b. On the *Sparkline Tools Design* tab, in the *Show* group, click the **Markers** check box.

c. On the *Sparkline Tools Design* tab, in the *Style* group, click the **Marker Color** button, point to **High Point,** and select **Red, Accent 2** (the fifth color from the right in the top row of theme colors).

5. Create a column chart to represent the population data for New York and then add a second series to represent the overall population of the United States.

   a. Select cells **A3:F4.**

   b. On the *Insert* tab, in the *Charts* group, click the **Column Chart** button, and choose **Clustered Column** (the first chart type under *2-D Column*).

   c. Click and drag the chart to reposition it immediately below the data.

   d. On the *Chart Tools Design* tab, in the *Data* group, click the **Select Data** button.

   e. In the *Legend Entries (Series)* box, click the **Add** button.

   f. Click cell **A15** to add the cell reference to the *Series name* box.

   g. Click in the *Series values* box and delete the default entry. Click and drag to select cells **B15:F15.**

   h. Click **OK.**

   i. If you need to reset the column labels (the years) as the x axis labels, in the *Horizontal (Category) Axis Labels* box, click the **Edit** button, and then click and drag to select cells **B3:F3.** Click **OK.**

   j. Click **OK** to accept the changes to the chart.

6. Change the chart type to a combination chart with a secondary axis for the national population data.

   a. On the *Chart Tools Design* tab, in the *Type* group, click the **Change Chart Type** button.

   b. In the list of chart types at the left side of the *All Charts* tab, click **Combo.**

   c. Excel automatically suggests a line chart for the *Total US population* series, but the scale difference between the two series makes the New York data unreadable. Click the **Secondary Axis** check box next to *Total US population* series.

   d. Click **OK.**

7. Add a legend above the chart and format it by applying a style.

   a. Click the **Chart Elements** button that appears near the upper right corner of the chart. Point to **Legend** and click the arrow that appears at the right. Click **Top.**

   b. Click the legend to select it. On the *Chart Tools Format* tab, in the *Shape Styles* group, click the **More** button to expand the gallery. Select the **Subtle Effect–Yellow, Accent 5** style (the second style from the right in the third row from the bottom).

8. Change the fill color of a data point to make it stand out.

   a. Select the data point for *1990* for the series *New York, NY* by clicking the **1990** column once to select the series and then clicking it a second time to select just that data point.

   b. On the *Chart Tools Format* tab, in the *Shape Styles* group, click the **Shape Fill** button and select **Red, Accent 2** (the fifth color from the right in the first row of theme colors).

9. Save this chart as a new chart template.

   a. Right-click an empty area of the chart and select **Save as Template....**

   b. In the *Save Chart Template* dialog, type **Population Combo Chart** in the *File name* box.

   c. Click **Save.**

10. Add a callout to the chart, apply a style to it, and add text.

    a. On the *Chart Tools Format* tab, in the *Insert Shapes* group, click the **More** button to expand the gallery.

    b. Select **Line Callout 1** (the fifth shape from the left in the *Callouts* section).

c. Click anywhere in the chart to insert the shape.

d. Click and drag the shape to reposition it so it is pointing to the highlighted data point.

e. On the *Drawing Tools Format* tab, in the *Shape Styles* group, click the **More** button to expand the gallery. Select the **Subtle Effect–Yellow, Accent 5** style (the second style from the right in the third row from the bottom).

f. Type `What happened here?` and then click anywhere outside the callout.

g. If necessary, make the shape slightly larger so all the text is visible.

11. Create a new chart from the template you saved.

a. Select cells **A3:F5.**

b. On the *Insert* tab, in the *Charts* group, click the dialog launcher to open the *Insert Chart* dialog.

c. In the *Insert Chart* dialog, click the **All Charts** tab.

d. Click **Templates.** If necessary, select the **Population Combo Chart** template.

e. Click **OK.**

f. If necessary, move the chart so it is positioned to the right of the first chart as shown in Figure EX 7.43.

FIGURE EX 7.43

12. Change the outline color of a data series.

a. Select the *Los Angeles, CA* data series by clicking anywhere on the line in the second chart.

b. On the *Chart Tools Format* tab, in the *Shape Styles* group, click the **Shape Outline** button, and select **Gray–50%, Accent 6** (the color at the far right side of the first row of theme colors).

13. Create a clustered column chart for population growth by region. Move the chart to its own chart sheet named *Regional Trends*.

a. Go to the **Census Data by State** worksheet and select cells **A5:L8.**

b. On the *Insert* tab, in the *Charts* group, click the **Insert Column Chart** button and select **Clustered Column** (the first chart under the *2-D Column* section).

c. If necessary, change the x axis labels to match the column headings. On the *Chart Tools Design* tab, in the *Data* group, click the **Select Data** button. In the *Horizontal (Category) Axis Labels* box, click the **Edit** button, and then click and drag to select cells **B3:L3.** Click **OK.** Click **OK** to accept the changes to the chart.

d. On the *Chart Tools Design* tab, in the *Location* group, click the **Move Chart** button.

excel 2013   chapter 7 Exploring Advanced Charts and Graphics

e. Click the **New Sheet** radio button. Type **Regional Trends** in the box and click **OK.**

14. Edit and format the chart title.

a. Click the chart title and type: **Population Trends by Region**

b. On the *Chart Tools Format* tab, in the *WordArt Styles* group, click the **More** button to expand the gallery, and select the **Fill–Green, Accent 1, Shadow** style (the second style from the left in the top row).

c. Click anywhere outside the title.

15. Add trendlines to the chart to forecast exponential growth for the next 40 years.

a. Click the **Chart Elements** button that appears near the upper right corner of the chart. Point to **Trendline**, click the arrow that appears, and click **More Options.**

b. In the *Add Trendline* dialog, click **OK.** (*Northeast* should be selected by default.)

c. In the *Format Trendline* task pane, click the **Exponential** radio button.

d. In the *Forecast* section, type **4** in the *Forward* box.

e. Click the **Fill & Line** button near the top of the task pane.

f. Click in the **Width** box and change the value to **3.**

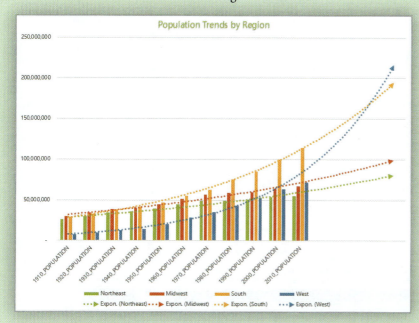

FIGURE EX 7.44

g. Click the **End Arrow** type box and select **Arrow** (the second option in the top row).

h. Right-click any data point in the *Midwest* series and select **Add Trendline....** Apply the same formatting options as you applied to the *Northeast* trendline: **exponential,** forecasting forward for 4 periods, **3 pt** width, and arrow type **End Arrow.**

i. Follow the same steps to add a trendline to each of the other data series using the same formatting options: **exponential,** forecasting forward for 4 periods, **3 pt** width, and arrow type **End Arrow.**

16. Add a screenshot from the U.S. Census Web site.

a. Go to the **Population Migration** worksheet. This is where you will place the screenshot.

b. Open a Web browser window and go to:
   http://www.census.gov/dataviz/visualizations/051

c. Scroll down the page, so you can see the map. You will be taking a screenshot of just the title, *Net Migration between California and Other States: 1955-1960 and 1995-2000,* and the map as shown in Figure EX 7.45, so position the browser window accordingly.

d. Click back to the Excel window. On the *Insert* tab, in the *Illustrations* group, click the **Screenshot** button and select **Screen Clipping.**

e. The computer screen will dim slightly, and the Excel window will minimize, showing you the Web browser window. Click and drag to select the part of the screen image you want to add to the worksheet.

f. When you release the mouse button, Excel becomes active again.

g. If necessary, click and drag the image to position it near the upper left corner of the worksheet.

h. Resize the screenshot image by selecting the resize handle in the lower-right corner of the image and dragging toward the center of the image until the image is approximately the size shown in Figure EX 7.45.

i. On the *Picture Tools Format* tab, in the **Picture Styles** group, click the **Drop Shadow Rectangle** picture style. If this style is not visible on the Ribbon, click the **More** button to expand the gallery and select the fourth style from the left in the top row.

17. Save and close the document.

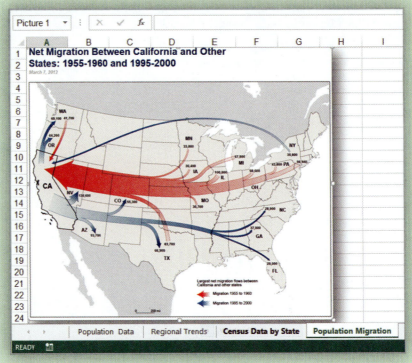

FIGURE EX 7.45

skill review 7.2

In this project, you will work with regional sales data for a shoe company.

Skills needed to complete this project:

- Changing the Sparkline Type (Skill 7.11)
- Adding Markers to Sparklines (Skill 7.12)
- Applying Quick Styles and Other Formatting to Sparklines (Skill 7.13)
- Inserting a Picture (Skill 7.14)
- Resizing and Moving Pictures (Skill 7.15)
- Applying Quick Styles and Other Formatting to Pictures (Skill 7.16)
- Adding a Picture to a Header (Skill 7.17)
- Emphasizing a Data Point in a Pie Chart (Skill 7.4)
- Formatting a Data Point or a Data Series (Skill 7.3)
- Formatting Other Chart Elements (Skill 7.5)

- Inserting a Shape (Skill 7.18)
- Applying Quick Styles and Other Formatting to Shapes (Skill 7.19)

1. Open the start file **EX2013-SkillReview-7-2** and resave the file as:

   `[your initials]EX-SkillReview-7-2`

2. If the workbook opens in Protected View, click the **Enable Editing** button in the Message Bar at the top of the worksheet so you can modify the workbook.

3. On the *By Region* worksheet, change the Sparkline type to columns and apply a Quick Style.

   a. Click any of the cells containing Sparklines (cells **G3:G7**).

   b. On the *Sparkline Tools Design* tab, in the *Type* group, click the **Column** button.

   c. On the *Sparkline Tools Design* tab, in the *Style* group, apply the **Sparkline Style Accent 1, (no dark or light)** style. Click the **More** button to expand the gallery, then click the first style in the third row.

4. Change the color of the high point marker for just the Sparkline in the *Flip* row.

   a. Click cell **G7.** On the *Sparkline Tools Design* tab, in the *Group* group, click the **Ungroup** button.

   b. On the *Sparkline Tools Design* tab, in the *Style* group, click the **Marker Color** button. Point to **High Point,** and click **Teal, Accent 3** (the fourth color from the right in the top row of theme colors).

5. Add the *Flip* picture from your local drive, network, or external media storage device, and then resize and move the picture.

   a. On the *Insert* tab, if necessary, click the **Illustrations** button to expand the *Illustrations* group. Click the **Pictures** button.

   b. Navigate to the local or network drive or storage media where you have downloaded the resource files for this project. Select the **Flip** file and click **Insert.**

   c. On the *Picture Tools Format* tab, *Size* group, type **.75** in the *Width* box. Press (Enter).

   d. Click and drag the picture so it is in approximately cell **B7** and does not overlap with the picture above it.

6. Add a border to the pictures.

   a. Select all five pictures by holding the (Ctrl) key while clicking each picture.

   b. On the *Picture Tools Format* tab, in the *Picture Styles* group, click the **Picture Border** button and click **Purple, Accent 1** (the fifth color in the top row of theme colors).

7. Add the company logo to the left section of the worksheet header.

   a. On the *Insert* tab, if necessary, click the **Text** button to expand the *Text* group. Click the **Header & Footer** button.

   b. Click the left section of the header.

   c. On the *Header & Footer Tools Design* tab, in the *Header & Footer Elements* group, click the **Picture** button.

   d. Click the **Browse** button next to *From a file.* Navigate to the local or network drive or storage media where you have downloaded the resource files for this project. Select the **ShoeLogo** file, and click **Insert.**

   e. Click anywhere outside the worksheet header.

   f. On the status bar, click the **Normal** button to switch back to Normal view.

8. On the *Region 1 Details* worksheet, rotate the chart so the *Flip* slice is at the right side and explode the slice away from the rest of the chart.

   a. Click the **Region 1 Details** worksheet tab.

   b. Click the chart once to select it, and then click the **Flip** slice again to select just that data point.

   c. On the *Chart Tools Format* tab, in the *Current Selection* group, click the **Format Selection** button to open the **Format Data Point** task pane.

d. In the *Angle of first slice* box, type: `90`

e. In the *Point Explosion* box, type: `40%`

9. Apply a Quick Style to just the *Flip* data point.

   a. Verify that the *Flip* data point is still selected.

   b. On the *Chart Tools Format* tab, *Shape Styles* group, click the **More** button to expand the *Shape Quick Styles* gallery, and click **Intense Effect—Gold, Accent 5** (the second style from the right in the last row of styles).

10. Insert, resize, and move and add text to a callout shape.

    a. On the *Chart Tools Format* tab, in the *Insert Shapes* group, click the **More** button to expand the gallery.

    b. Select **Oval Callout** shape (the third shape in the *Callouts* section).

    c. Click anywhere in the chart to insert the shape.

    d. Click and drag the shape to reposition it so it is above the *Flip* slice.

    e. On the *Drawing Tools Format* tab, in the *Shape Styles* group, click the **More** button to expand the gallery. Select the **Colored Outline–Gold, Accent 5** style (the second style from the right in the first row).

    f. Type: `Discontinue this style?`

    g. Make the shape wide enough to view the text by clicking the resize handle in the middle of the right side and dragging to the right until the word *Discontinue* fits on one line without wrapping.

11. Apply a WordArt Quick Style to the chart title and increase the font size.

    a. Click the chart title once to select it.

    b. On the *Chart Tools Format* tab, in the *WordArt Styles* group, click the **WordArt Quick Styles** button and select **Fill—Black, Text 1, Shadow** (the first style). If your screen resolution is wide enough, this style may be visible in the group on the Ribbon.

    c. On the *Home* tab, in the *Font* group, expand the *Font Size* list, and select **20**.

12. Save and close the workbook.

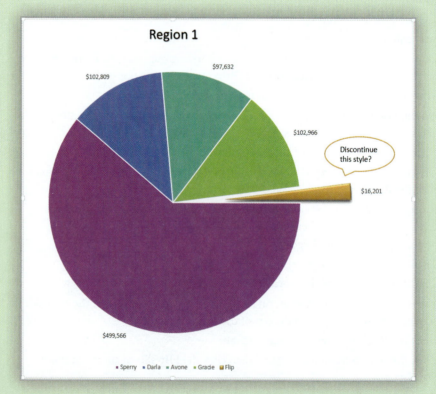

FIGURE EX 7.46

In this project, you will use charts and other graphic elements to analyze climate change data from the United States Environmental Protection Agency Web site (http://iaspub.epa.gov/enviro/datafinder.html?pType=2&pLevel=2&pItem=1023).

Skills needed to complete this project:

- Changing the Sparkline Type (Skill 7.11)
- Adding Markers to Sparklines (Skill 7.12)
- Applying Quick Styles and Other Formatting to Sparklines (Skill 7.13)
- Adding and Removing Trendlines (Skill 7.8)
- Forecasting Values on a Trendline (Skill 7.10)
- Choosing the Trendline Type (Skill 7.9)
- Adding a Data Series to a Chart (Skill 7.1)
- Creating a Combination Chart (Skill 7.2)
- Formatting Other Chart Elements (Skill 7.5)
- Formatting a Data Point or a Data Series (Skill 7.3)
- Inserting a Shape (Skill 7.18)
- Applying Quick Styles and Other Formatting to Shapes (Skill 7.19)
- Inserting a Picture (Skill 7.14)
- Resizing and Moving Pictures (Skill 7.15)
- Applying Quick Styles and Other Formatting to Pictures (Skill 7.16)
- Capturing a Screenshot in Excel (Skill 7.20)

1. Open the start file **EX2013-ChallengeYourself-7-3** and resave the file as:
   `[your initials]EX-ChallengeYourself-7-3`

2. If the workbook opens in Protected View, click the **Enable Editing** button in the Message Bar at the top of the worksheet so you can modify the workbook.

3. Modify the Sparklines on the *World* worksheet.
   a. Change the Sparkline type to **Line.**
   b. Add markers for the low points and the high points.
   c. Apply the **Sparkline Style Accent 2, Lighter 40%** Sparkline Quick Style.
   d. Change the color for the low point markers to **Green** and high point markers to **Red.**

4. Add a trendline to the chart to forecast future values.
   a. Add a linear trendline to the chart on this worksheet.
   b. Forecast the trendline forward **25** periods.
   c. Display the **R-squared value** on the trendline.
   d. Change the trendline type to **exponential.**

5. On the *North America* worksheet, add data for Canada to the chart.
   a. Add a new data series to the chart.
   b. Use cell **A4** as the series name and cells **B4:H4** as the series values.

6. Change the chart type to a combination chart.
   a. In the combination chart, the **Mexico** and **Canada** data series should be clustered column charts.
   b. In the combination chart, the **United States** data series should be a line chart.
   c. Do not add a secondary axis.

7. Add a WordArt Quick Style to the chart title.

    a. Select the chart title.

    b. Apply the **Fill—Black, Text 1, Outline—Background 1, Hard Shadow—Background 1** WordArt Quick Style.

8. Highlight the *1995 Canada* data point.

    a. Change the outline of the **1995 Canada** data point to **Red.**

    b. Change the outline width to **3 pt.**

9. Add a callout to the chart, apply a style to it, and add text.

    a. Add a **Rectangular Callout** to the chart.

    b. Move the callout so it is pointing to the *1995 Canada* data point.

    c. Apply the **Colored Outline—Gray-50%, Accent 3** Shape Quick Style to the callout.

    d. Add the text: `What caused this increase?`

10. Deselect the chart.

11. Add the *CanadaFlag* picture from your local drive, network, or external media storage device, and then resize and move the picture.

    a. Insert the **CanadaFlag** picture.

    b. Resize the picture so it is exactly **.5** inches wide. Maintain the picture aspect ratio.

    c. Move the flag pictures so each image is below the appropriate country name in the chart legend as shown in Figure EX 7.47. *Hint:* If you cannot move the *CanadaFlag* picture below the chart, you probably had the chart selected when you inserted it. Delete the picture, and then verify that you do not have the chart selected and try inserting the picture again.

Combined Methane, Nitrous Oxide, and High GWP Emissions by Country							
	1990	**1995**	**2000**	**2005**	**2010**	**2015**	**2020**
United States	1,066.20	1,072.84	1,076.76	1,054.29	1,114.42	1,188.43	1,278.57
Canada	139.87	190.82	160.15	170.84	184.48	202.08	220.07
Mexico	154.45	156.07	189.99	219.27	254.71	301.17	359.39

FIGURE EX 7.47

12. Add a shadow effect to the pictures.

    a. Select all three pictures by holding the Ctrl key while clicking each picture.

    b. Add the **Offset, Diagonal, Bottom Right** shadow effect. *Hint:* This is an outer shadow picture effect.

13. Add a screenshot from the Environmental Protection Agency's Web site.

    a. Open a Web browser and go to this Web page:
       http://www.epa.gov/climatechange/ghgemissions/global.html

    b. Resize the browser window similar to the screenshot shown in Figure EX 7.48.

    c. Switch back to Excel and navigate to the **EPA Web Site** worksheet.

    d. Insert a screenshot of the browser window.

    e. Move and resize the screenshot picture as necessary so it appears below the URL as shown in Figure EX 7.48.

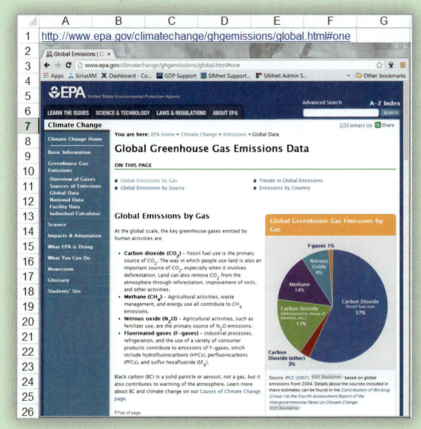

FIGURE EX 7.48

14. Save and close the workbook.

challenge yourself **7.4**

In this project, you will analyze housing trends using charting tools.

Skills needed to complete this project:

- Changing the Sparkline Type (Skill 7.11)
- Adding Markers to Sparklines (Skill 7.12)
- Applying Quick Styles and Other Formatting to Sparklines (Skill 7.13)
- Formatting Other Chart Elements (Skill 7.5)
- Emphasizing a Data Point in a Pie Chart (Skill 7.4)
- Formatting a Data Point or a Data Series (Skill 7.3)
- Inserting a Shape (Skill 7.18)
- Applying Quick Styles and Other Formatting to Shapes (Skill 7.19)

- Adding and Removing Trendlines (Skill 7.8)
- Choosing the Trendline Type (Skill 7.9)
- Inserting a Picture (Skill 7.14)
- Applying Quick Styles and Other Formatting to Pictures (Skill 7.16)
- Resizing and Moving Pictures (Skill 7.15)
- Adding a Picture to a Header (Skill 7.17)

1. Open the start file **EX2013-ChallengeYourself-7-4** and resave the file as:

   `[your initials]EX-ChallengeYourself-7-4`

2. If the workbook opens in Protected View, click the **Enable Editing** button in the Message Bar at the top of the workbook so you can modify the workbook.

3. On the *Summary by Type* worksheet, modify the Sparklines.

   a. Change the Sparklines to columns.

   b. Apply the Quick Style **Sparkline Style Dark #6.**

4. Add a markers to the Sparklines.

   a. Add a marker for the high point.

   b. Change the high point marker color to **Gold, Accent 3.**

5. In the pie chart, change the colors for the individual data labels to match their respective data points and then apply a bevel shape effect to all the data labels. Selecting a single data label is similar to selecting a single data point.

   a. Apply the **Dark Red, Accent 1, Lighter 80%** fill color to the data label for the **Modern** data point.

   b. Apply the **Orange, Accent 2, Lighter 80%** fill color to the data label for the **Condo** data point.

   c. Apply the **Gold, Accent 3, Lighter 80%** fill color to the data label for the **Ranch** data point.

   d. Apply the **Green, Accent 4, Lighter 80%** fill color to the data label for the **Mediterranean** data point.

   e. Select all the data labels and apply the **Circle** bevel shape effect.

6. Emphasize the *Ranch* data point.

   a. Rotate the pie chart **240°** so the **Ranch** data point is at the right side.

   b. Explode the **Ranch** data point away from the pie by **30%.**

   c. Apply the **Circle** bevel shape effect to the **Ranch** data point.

7. In the column chart, change the color of each data point to match the corresponding color in the pie chart. You do not need to change the color of the *Modern* data point.

   a. In the column chart, apply the **Orange, Accent 2** fill color to the **Condo** data point.

   b. In the column chart, apply the **Gold, Accent 3** fill color to the **Ranch** data point.

   c. In the column chart, apply the **Green, Accent 4** fill color to the **Mediterranean** data point.

8. Add a callout to the column chart to emphasize the *Ranch* data point.

   a. Add a **Line Callout 1** shape to the chart.

   b. Add the text: `32% of total`

   c. Resize and position the callout so it is pointing to the *Ranch* column as shown in Figure EX 7.49.

   d. Change the shape style to **Subtle Effect—Gold, Accent 3.**

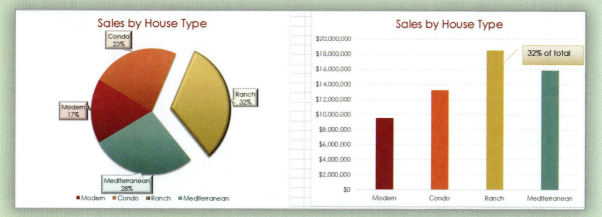

FIGURE EX 7.49

9. Apply the **Fill—Dark Red, Accent 1, Shadow** WordArt style to the column chart title.

10. Apply the **Dash Dot** dashes line option to the column chart gridlines.

11. Add a trendline to the *1 and 2 Bedroom Condo Sales* chart on the *Condo Sales* worksheet.

    a. Switch to the *Condo Sales* worksheet.

    b. Add a trendline.

    c. Change the trendline type to a two period moving average trendline.

12. Modify the *1 and 2 Bedroom Condo Sales* chart background.

    a. Apply the **Black, Text 1** color.

    b. Apply the **From Center** gradient.

13. Add the *SOLD* picture from your local drive, network, or external media storage device, and then apply a style, resize and move the picture.

    a. Insert the **SOLD** picture.

    b. Apply the **Bevel Perspective** picture Quick Style to the picture.

    c. Resize the picture so it is **1.5 inches** wide. Do not change the aspect ratio of the picture.

    d. Reposition the picture so it is located near the bottom right corner of the chart.

14. Add a picture from your local drive, network, or external media storage device to the left section of the worksheet header. Because this worksheet is a chart sheet, you cannot switch to Page Layout view. Excel will open the *Page Setup* dialog instead. If you need help with this method, refer to the *another method* box in the *Adding a Picture to a Header* skill.

    a. Add the **RealtyLogo** picture to the worksheet header.

    b. Preview how the worksheet will look when printed to verify that you inserted the correct picture into the header. It should look similar to Figure EX 7.50.

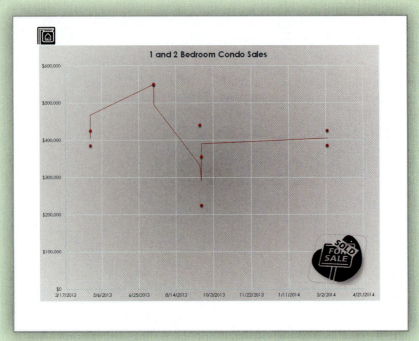

FIGURE EX 7.50

15. Save and close the workbook.

on your own 7.5

In this project, you will analyze football scores using charting and graphics.

Skills needed to complete this project:

- Adding a Data Series to a Chart (Skill 7.1)
- Creating a Combination Chart (Skill 7.2)
- Formatting a Data Point or a Data Series (Skill 7.3)
- Formatting Other Chart Elements (Skill 7.5)
- Inserting a Shape (Skill 7.18)
- Applying Quick Styles and Other Formatting to Shapes (Skill 7.19)
- Adding and Removing Trendlines (Skill 7.8)
- Choosing the Trendline Type (Skill 7.9)
- Inserting a Picture (Skill 7.14)
- Resizing and Moving Pictures (Skill 7.15)
- Applying Quick Styles and Other Formatting to Pictures (Skill 7.16)

1. Open the start file **EX2013-OnYourOwn-7-5** and resave the file as:

   [your initials]EX-OnYourOwn-7-5

2. If the workbook opens in Protected View, click the **Enable Editing** button in the Message Bar at the top of the workbook so you can modify the workbook.

3. The *Chart* worksheet contains a scatter chart of the point differences between the winning and losing Super Bowl scores from 1967 through 2014. Add another series to the chart to represent the total scores for the same periods. Use the data on the *Scores* worksheet. *Hint:* Use cell **G2** on the *Scores* worksheet as the **Series name.** Use the data in the *Year* column as the **Series X values** and the data in the *Total Points* column as the **Series Y values.**

4. Change the chart to a combo chart. Use any combination of chart types that works for you. It is not necessary to use a secondary axis.

5. If necessary, change the color of one or both of the data series to make the chart easier to read.

6. Apply other formatting of your choice to the chart. Include at least one WordArt style.

7. Add shapes to the chart to draw attention to the high point for each data series. Add explanatory text of your choice to each shape. Move, resize, and format the shapes as necessary so the text is easy to read.

8. If possible, apply a linear trendline to one of the data series. If necessary, change the color and the width of the trendline so it is clearly visible.

9. Try changing the trendline to different types until you find one that you feel best represents the data trend.

10. Insert a picture of your choice to illustrate the data (from your local drive or from the Microsoft.com *Clip Art* gallery). Resize and move it as necessary. *Hint:* The author searched for *golden gate* in the Microsoft.com *Clip Art* gallery to find the illustration shown in Figure EX 7-51.

11. Try applying different formatting options to the picture. Try some of the options from the *Picture Tools Format* tab, *Adjust* group. .If you don't like the result, use the *Reset Picture* button to rest the picture back to its original formatting.

12. Save and close the workbook.

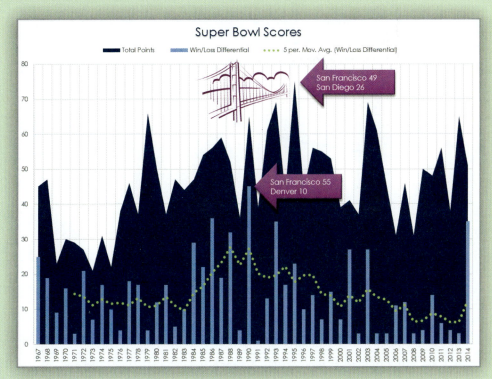

FIGURE EX 7.51

fix it 7.6

In this project, you will fix a salary projections workbook for key departments at a local college.

Skills needed to complete this project:

- Formatting Other Chart Elements (Skill 7.5)
- Choosing the Trendline Type (Skill 7.9)
- Forecasting Values on a Trendline (Skill 7.10)
- Formatting a Data Point or a Data Series (Skill 7.3)
- Changing the Sparkline Type (Skill 7.11)
- Adding Markers to Sparklines (Skill 7.12)
- Resizing and Moving Pictures (Skill 7.15)
- Adding a Data Series to a Chart (Skill 7.1)
- Adding a Picture to a Header (Skill 7.17)

1. Open the start file **EX2013-FixIt-7-6** and resave the file as:

   `[your initials]EX-FixIt-7-6`

2. If the workbook opens in Protected View, click the **Enable Editing** button in the Message Bar at the top of the workbook so you can modify the workbook.

3. Unfortunately, whoever created this workbook made one of the ugliest charts possible. The first thing to do is fix the chart on the *Salary Projections* worksheet. When you are finished, it should look like the chart in Figure EX 7-52.

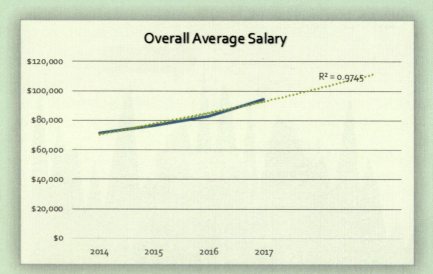

FIGURE EX 7.52

   a. Change the chart background color to **Yellow, Accent 5, Lighter 80%.**

   b. Change the gridlines to **Gray—50%, Accent 6** and reduce the line width to ½ **pt.**

4. The trendline on this chart is wrong. The person who created it chose a logarithmic trendline because it shows the rate of salary increases flattening. However, based on the existing data, that's not the actual trend.

   a. Change the trendline type to the best fit for the existing data. *Hint:* Display the R-squared value and choose the trendline type that has an R-squared value closest to 1.

   b. Forecasting forward 10 periods is very misleading when you only have 4 years of data. Change the trendline to forecast 2 periods.

5. The line representing the *Overall Average Salary* data series should be **Aqua, Accent 4.** The person who created the chart changed the shape fill color and doesn't understand why the line is still red. Please fix this.

6. It's fine to use a WordArt style for the chart title, but the style chosen makes it difficult to read the text. Use the **Fill—Black, Text 1, Shadow** WordArt style instead.

7. The win/loss Sparklines in cells **E12:E18** don't tell us anything about the data.

   a. Change the Sparklines to lines.

   b. Add markers to pinpoint the negative values.

8. The chart on the *Average by Dept* worksheet is better, but it too has a few errors that need correcting.

   a. Someone added the picture of stacked coins to the chart. It is too large and it covers the chart. Move the picture and resize it so it fits below the chart title as shown in Figure EX 7-53.

   b. The English department is listed in the chart legend, but the data from the *Salary Projections* worksheet doesn't appear to be represented on the line chart. Can you fix this? *Hint:* You will need to **edit** the series values for the *English* data series through the *Select Data Source* dialog.

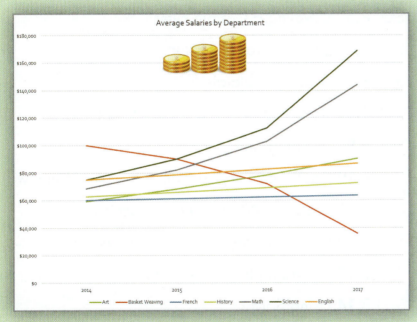

FIGURE EX 7.53

9. Finally, they've forgotten to add the school logo to the headers. Add the picture **CollegeLogo** to the left section of the header for both worksheets. The picture should be located locally wherever you downloaded the data files for this project.

10. Save and close the workbook.

chapter 8

Exploring Advanced Data Analysis

In this chapter, you will learn the following skills:

❭ Use custom conditional formatting to analyze data

❭ Use advanced filtering and sorting techniques

❭ Outline and consolidate data with and without subtotals

❭ Perform what-if analysis using scenarios and Solver

❭ Analyze data using PivotTables and PivotCharts

skills

introduction

The material in this chapter builds on your knowledge of conditional formatting, sorting, and filtering. You will use custom conditional formatting to highlight and then sort and filter data. You will also learn advanced sorting and filtering techniques. You will summarize and outline data and perform what-if analyses using a variety of methods. Finally, you will expand on the basic PivotTable and PivotChart skills that were covered earlier in this book.

Skill 8.1 Creating New Conditional Formatting Rules

Conditional formatting provides a visual analysis of data by applying formatting to cells that meet specific criteria (conditions). Excel offers a wide variety of conditional formatting options from the *Conditional Formatting* menu (available on the *Home* tab, in the *Styles* group). If one of the prebuilt conditional formatting options does not suit your needs, you can specify your own format through the *New Formatting Rule* dialog. In the *New Formatting Rule* dialog, you first select one of the six rule types and then specify the conditions and formatting you want.

To create a new conditional formatting rule:

1. Select the data you want to apply conditional formatting to.
2. On the *Home* tab, in the *Styles* group, click the **Conditional Formatting** button.
3. Click **New Rule...** to open the *New Formatting Rule* dialog.

FIGURE EX 8.1

4. Click the type of rule you want to create from the *Select a Rule Type* box.
5. In the *Edit the Rule Description* box, set the rule parameters and formatting options.
6. When you have made all your selections in the *New Formatting Rule* dialog, click **OK** to apply the new conditional formatting rule.

In the *New Formatting Rule* dialog, the options in the *Edit the Rule Description* box are dependent on the type of rule you selected. Each rule type has its own set of rule description values and formatting options.

The first rule type, *Format all cells based on their values,* applies a variable graphic element (color scale, data bar, or icon set) to the cells based on each cell's value relative to the other cells in the selection.

To create a new conditional formatting rule using an icon set:

1. In the *New Formatting Rule* dialog, *Format all cells based on their values* is selected by default.

2. Expand the **Format Style** list and select **Icon Sets.**

3. If necessary, expand the **Icon Style** list and select the icon set you want.

4. To hide the cell value and display only the icon, click the **Show Icon Only** check box.

5. Enter the values to control when each icon is displayed. You can change the comparison operator, the value, and the type. With icon sets, the default comparison operator is >= and the default type is **percent.** Do not use the % symbol when entering values. In Figure EX 8.2, to show the green icon when values are in the top 75% of values, the comparison operator is >=, the value is **75,** and the type is **percent.** To show the red icon when values are below 25%, the value for the yellow icon (the middle icon) is set to >= **25 percent.**

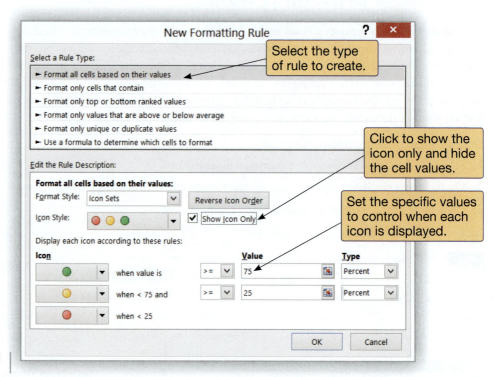

FIGURE EX 8.2

The other rule types all allow you to set cell formatting options instead of applying a graphic element. Although the options for the rules the cell value must meet in order to have the formatting applied change depending on which rule type you selected, setting the cell format is the same.

To create a new conditional formatting rule to format cells that are equal to or above the average value:

1. In the *Select a Rule Type* box, click **Format only values that are above or below average.**

2. Expand the **Format values that are** list and select **equal or above.**

3. Click the **Format...** button to open the *Format Cells* dialog. Notice that this *Format Cells* dialog is slightly different from the one that opens when you format cells in the worksheet.

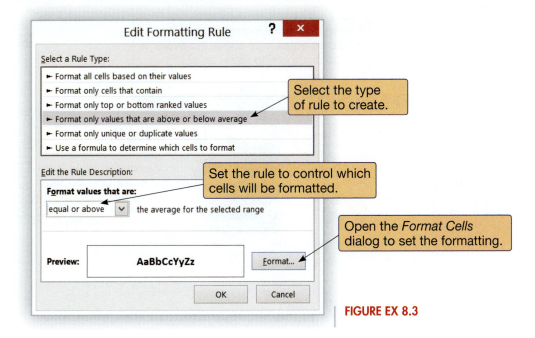

FIGURE EX 8.3

a. To apply a specific number format, click the **Number** tab and select the number format to use.

b. To apply a font change, click the **Font** tab. For conditional formatting, you can change only the font style and the font color. You cannot change the font or font size.

c. To apply a cell border, click the **Border** tab and set the border options.

d. To apply a fill color, click the **Fill** tab and click the color you want.

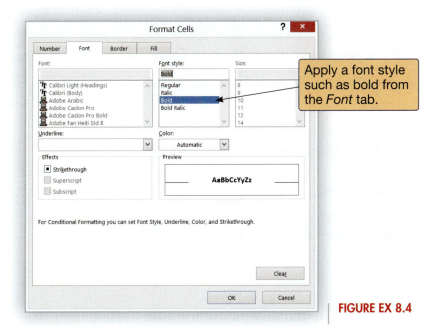

FIGURE EX 8.4

FIGURE EX 8.5

A new conditional formatting rule to bold cells equal to or above the average has been applied to these cells.

A new icon set conditional formatting rule that shows only the icon has been applied to these cells.

tips & tricks

If you are using conditional formatting with icon sets and your worksheet looks too busy, use this trick:

1. Create a copy of the column of data you want to apply the icon set to.
2. Select the copied data, and create a new conditional formatting rule using the icon set.
3. In the *New Formatting Rule* dialog, click the **Show Icon Only** check box.

Now you have two columns—one showing the values and one showing only the icon.

another method

You can open the *New Formatting Rule* dialog from the *More Rules* option at the bottom of each of the formatting submenus off of the *Conditional Formatting* button or from the *New Rule* button in the Conditional Formatting Rules Manager.

let me try

Open the student data file **EX8-01-Sales** and try this skill on your own:

1. Select cells **F3:F33** on the *Jan* worksheet.
2. Apply a new conditional formatting rule with these conditions:
   a. Format all cells in the selected range based on their values.
   b. Change the format style to **Icon Sets** and use the **Three traffic lights (unrimmed)** icon set. This is the default icon set.
   c. Show only the icon, not the cell value.
   d. Show the green light icon when the value is **> = 75.** Leave the type as **percent.**
   e. Show the yellow light icon when the value is **<75 and > = 25.** Leave the type as **percent.**
3. Select cells **E3:E33** on the *Jan* worksheet.
4. Apply a new conditional formatting rule with these conditions:
   a. Format only values that are equal to or above the average for the selected range.
   b. Cells that meet the rule should be **bold.**
5. Save the file as directed by your instructor and close it.

excel 2013   chapter 8 Exploring Advanced Data Analysis

Skill 8.2 Managing Conditional Formatting Rules

When more than one conditional formatting rule is applied to a group of cells, the rules are applied in the order in which they are created. This can sometimes result in conflicts or unexpected results. The **Conditional Formatting Rules Manager** allows you to delete, edit, reorder, and control the way in which conditional formatting rules are applied to your worksheet.

To use the Conditional Formatting Rules Manager:

1. On the *Home* tab, in the *Styles* group, click the **Conditional Formatting** button. Click **Manage Rules...**

FIGURE EX 8.6

2. If necessary, expand the *Show formatting rule for* list and select the part of the workbook you want to manage rules for.

3. From the box next to each formatting rule, you can edit the range of cells to which the rule is applied. If the data in your worksheet have changed since you first created the conditional formatting rule, this is an easy way to update the cell range.

4. When there are multiple formatting rules applied to the same set of cells, click the **Stop If True** check box to prevent later conditional formats from being applied to the cells when the selected condition is true.

Expand the **Show formatting rules for** list and select **This Worksheet** to work with all the rules at once.

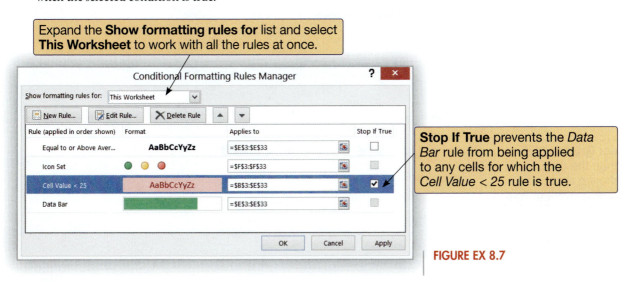

Stop If True prevents the *Data Bar* rule from being applied to any cells for which the *Cell Value < 25* rule is true.

FIGURE EX 8.7

5. To change the order in which rules are applied, click the rule you want to be applied first and then click the **Move Up** button until that rule is at the top of the list.

6. To delete a rule, click the rule you want to delete and then click the **Delete Rule** button.

7. To modify one of the rules, click the rule you want to change and then click the **Edit Rule** button. Make the changes you want and then click **OK.**

8. You can click the **Apply** button to see the effect of the changes on your worksheet before saving them. Click **OK** to save the changes or click **Cancel** to close the Conditional Formatting Rules Manager without making any changes.

When you edit a conditional formatting rule, the options available are dependent on the type of rule you select, just as they are when you create a new conditional formatting rule. Each rule type has its own set of rule description values and formatting options.

To change formatting for a data bar rule:

1. Select the rule in the Conditional Formatting Rules Manger.

2. Click the **Edit Rule...** button.

3. If you do not want the data bars applied to every cell, expand the **Type** list under *Minimum* and *Maximum* and make a different selection.

When you change the type to something other than *Automatic,* you can set specific values to use in the *Value* boxes.

4. To change the fill type for the data bars, expand the **Fill** list and select **Gradient Fill** or **Solid Fill.**

5. To change the color, click the **Color** arrow to display the color palette and select a color.

6. To show only the data bars and hide the cell values, click the **Show Bar Only** check box.

7. Click **OK** in the *Edit Formatting Rule* dialog, and then click **OK** again in the Conditional Formatting Rules Manager to save the changes.

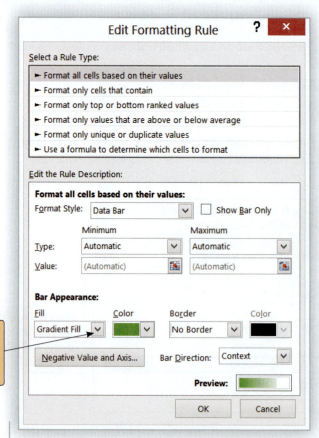

Select **Gradient Fill** to change the data bars to show a range of color from dark to light.

FIGURE EX 8.8

The Data Bar rule is not applied to cell E3 because the Cell Value <25 rule has **Stop If True** applied.

	A	B	C	D	E	F	G
1				New Membership Sales			
2		Monthly	Annual	Special	Daily Total	Daily Total	
3	1-Jan	0	0	20	20	🔴	
4	2-Jan	44	37	113	194	🟢	
5	3-Jan	68	24	29	121	🟡	
6	4-Jan	57	42	49	148	🟡	
7	5-Jan	68	46	57	171	🟡	
8	6-Jan	89	66	79	234	🟢	
9	7-Jan	61	63	101	225	🟢	
10	8-Jan	71	71	57	199	🟢	

Summary | ByEmployee | **Jan** | Feb | March | KD | LF | SR

FIGURE EX 8.9

The data bars are now formatted with a Green, Accent 6 gradient.

tips & tricks

Using the *Clear Rules* command from the *Conditional Formatting* menu on the Ribbon clears **all** the conditional formatting from the selected cells or worksheet. Use the *Delete Rule* command from the Conditional Formatting Rules Manager instead if you want to remove only some of the conditional formatting rules.

tell me more

You can reverse the order of icon sets (for example, reversing the *Three Traffic Lights* icon set applies the red traffic light icon to the highest value instead of the lowest value and applies the green icon to the lowest value instead of the highest value).

1. In the Conditional Formatting Rules Manager, click the Icon Set rule you want to reverse.
2. Click the **Edit Rule...** button.
3. In the *Edit Formatting Rule* dialog, click the **Reverse Icon Order** button. Watch carefully in the *Display each icon according to these rules* section to see the change. The button does not change states when the icon order has been reversed.
4. To reverse the icon order again (to put it back to the original order), click the **Reverse Icon Order** button again.

let me try

Open the student data file **EX8-02-Sales** and try this skill on your own:

1. Select any cell in the *Jan* worksheet.
2. Open the Conditional Formatting Rules Manager.
3. Show the all the formatting rules in this worksheet.
4. Apply the **Stop If True** option to the *Cell Value <25* rule so cells with a value less than 25 will not have the *Data Bar* rule applied to them.
5. Delete the **Equal to or above average** rule.
6. Edit the **Data Bar** rule and change the data bar fill to a gradient. Change the color to **Green, Accent 6** (the last color in the top row of theme colors).
7. Save the conditional formatting changes.
8. Save the file as directed by your instructor and close it.

skill 8.2   Managing Conditional Formatting Rules

Skill 8.3 Filtering and Sorting Using Cell Attributes

You can sort or filter data based on cell color, font color, or icons that were applied with conditional formatting or cell styles. If you need a refresher on sorting and filtering data, refer to the skills *Sorting Data* and *Filtering Data*.

Typically, when you sort data by a single column, you use the *Sort A to Z* or *Sort Z to A* commands available from the *Home* tab, *Editing* group, *Sort & Filter* button or the *Data* tab, *Sort & Filter* group. However, A to Z type sorting does not work with color or icons. Instead, you pick which color or icon appears at the top. Excel moves the rows with the cell attribute you select to the top, and leaves the other rows in their current order.

To sort data by cell attribute:

1. If necessary, on the *Data* tab, in the *Sort & Filter* group, click the **Filter** button to display the AutoFilter arrows at the top of each column. If the data are formatted as a table, these arrows will be available automatically.

2. Click the AutoFilter arrow at the top of the column that includes the cell format you want to sort by.

3. Point to **Sort by Color** and click the option you want to sort by. Excel automatically displays the options available for that particular column: *Sort by Cell Color, Sort by Font Color,* and *Sort by Cell Icon.*

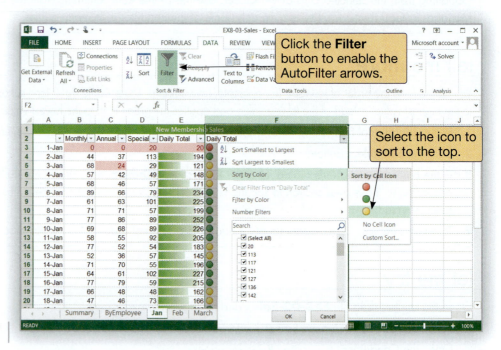

FIGURE EX 8.10

To filter data by cell attribute:

1. If necessary, on the *Data* tab, in the *Sort & Filter* group, click the **Filter** button to display the AutoFilter arrows at the top of each column. If the data are formatted as a table, these arrows will be available automatically.

2. Click the AutoFilter arrow at the top of the column that includes the cell format you want to filter by.

3. Point to **Filter by Color** and click the option you want to filter by. Excel automatically displays the options available for that particular column: *Filter by Cell Color, Filter by Font Color,* and *Filter by Cell Icon.*

FIGURE EX 8.11

tips & tricks

Excel does not recognize data bars and color scales as icons or as cell colors, so you cannot sort and filter cells using those conditional formatting styles.

tell me **more**

You can specify that cells with a specific cell attribute appear at the top of the column and cells with another attribute appear at the bottom of the column. From the *Sort* dialog, use the **Add Level** button to create multiple sort levels and use the *Sort on* list to select **Cell Color, Font Color,** or **Cell Icon.** For more information on using the *Sort* dialog, refer to the skill *Sorting Data on Multiple Criteria.*

another **method**

Right-click a cell that includes the attribute you want to sort or filter by and then point to **Sort** or **Filter** and select the option you want (such as **Put Selected Cell Icon on Top** or **Filter by Selected Cell's Color**).

let me **try**

Open the student data file **EX8-03-Sales** and try this skill on your own:

1. Select cell **F3** in the *Jan* worksheet.
2. Sort the data so cells with the yellow circle icon (the last icon in the list) in column F (the second *Daily Total* column) appear on top.
3. Now filter the data to show only cells with the light red background in column C (the *Annual* column).
4. Save the file as directed by your instructor and close it.

skill 8.3   Filtering and Sorting Using Cell Attributes

Skill 8.4 Sorting Data on Multiple Criteria

Recall that sorting rearranges the rows in your worksheet by the data in a column. If you want to create a multi-level sort so the data are sorted first by one criteria and then sorted again within each group, use the *Sort* dialog. For each sort level, you set the column to sort by, the type of sort, and the order in which you want the data sorted.

To sort data on multiple criteria:

1. Select any cell in the data range.

2. On the *Data* tab, in the *Sort & Filter* group, click the **Sort** button.

3. If your data include a header row, Excel will usually identify that for you and automatically check the *My data has headers* check box.

4. In the *Sort* dialog, expand the **Sort by** list and select the column you want to use for the first sort level.

5. The *Sort On* list defaults to **Value.** If you want to sort by a cell attribute instead, expand the **Sort On** list and select **Cell Color, Font Color,** or **Cell Icon.**

6. The *Order* list detects what type of data are in the column and displays appropriate options such as *A-Z* for text, *Smallest to Largest* for numbers, and *Oldest to Newest* for dates. To change the sort order, expand the list and select another option.

7. Click the **Add Level** button.

8. Expand the **Then by** list and select the column you want for the next sort level.

9. Continue adding levels and building the sort criteria until you are finished.

10. To rearrange the order of sort criteria, click the level you want to move and then use the **Move Up** or **Move Down** arrow.

11. To delete a level from the sort, click the level you want to delete and then click the **Delete Level** button.

12. When you have built all the levels for the sort, click **OK.**

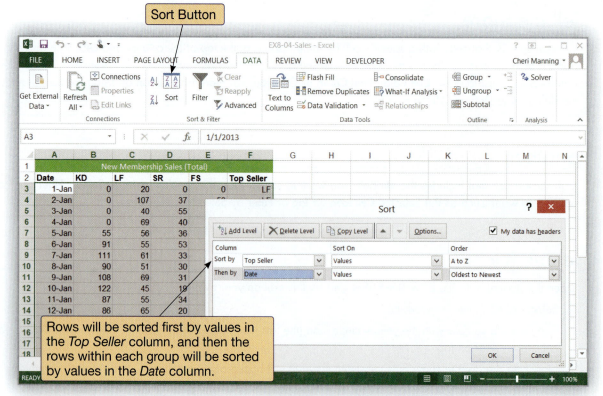

Sort Button

Rows will be sorted first by values in the *Top Seller* column, and then the rows within each group will be sorted by values in the *Date* column.

FIGURE EX 8.12

Rows with *FS* are placed before rows with *KD*.

Where the *Top Seller* value is *FS*, rows are further sorted by date.

FIGURE EX 8.13

tips & tricks

The *Sort* command ignores hidden rows and columns. Be sure to unhide any hidden rows or columns before sorting the data or you may end up with unexpected results.

tell me **more**

By default, Excel ignores text case when sorting. To enforce case sensitivity, click the **Options** button in the *Sort* dialog and check the **Case sensitive** check box. When this option is enabled, identical text will be sorted with initial lowercase before initial uppercase (e.g., "shell" will come before "Shell" in the sort order).

another **method**

To open the *Sort* dialog:

❭ From the *Home* tab, in the *Editing* group, click the **Sort & Filter** button and then click **Custom Sort...**

❭ Right-click any cell in the data set. Point to *Sort* and click **Custom Sort...**

❭ If AutoFilter is enabled, expand the AutoFilter list at the top of any column. Point to one of the sort options and click **Custom Sort...**

let me **try**

Open the student data file **EX8-04-Sales** and try this skill on your own:

1. Select cell **A3** in the *ByEmployee* worksheet.
2. Sort the data first alphabetically by the values in the **Top Seller** column and then by the dates in the **Date** column with the oldest dates first.
3. Save the file as directed by your instructor and close it.

Skill 8.5 Creating a Custom Filter

In addition to filtering by matching exact values or cell attributes, you can filter for values that meet broader criteria. Columns with different data types have different filtering criteria options available.

If the data are formatted as a table, filtering is enabled automatically. If your data are not formatted as a table, you must first enable filtering. On the *Data* tab, in the *Sort & Filter* group, click the **Filter** button.

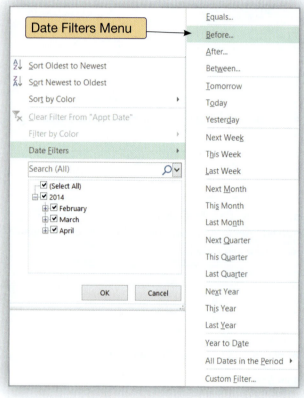

FIGURE EX 8.14

To create a custom date filter:

1. Click the AutoFilter arrow at the top of the column that contains the data you want to filter for and point to **Date Filters.**

2. Click the filter type you want. There is an extensive list of custom date filter options as shown in Figure EX 8.14.

3. The first box in the *Custom AutoFilter* dialog shows the custom filter option you selected. Type the date criteria in the box next to it.

4. You can further refine the filter by expanding the second list and selecting a filter option and then entering the criteria in the box next to it. The filter options available are the same as those in the *Date Filters* menu.

   - The *And* radio button requires that data meet **both** criteria in order to be included in the filter.

   - The *Or* radio button requires that data meet **either** of the criteria.

5. Click **OK** to apply the filter.

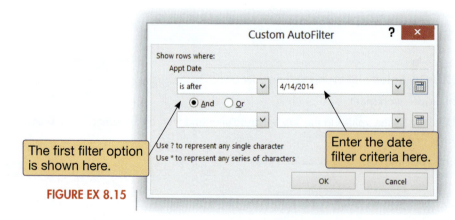

FIGURE EX 8.15

To create a custom text filter or custom number filter, follow the same steps as shown in Figure EX 8.16 and Figure EX 8.17.

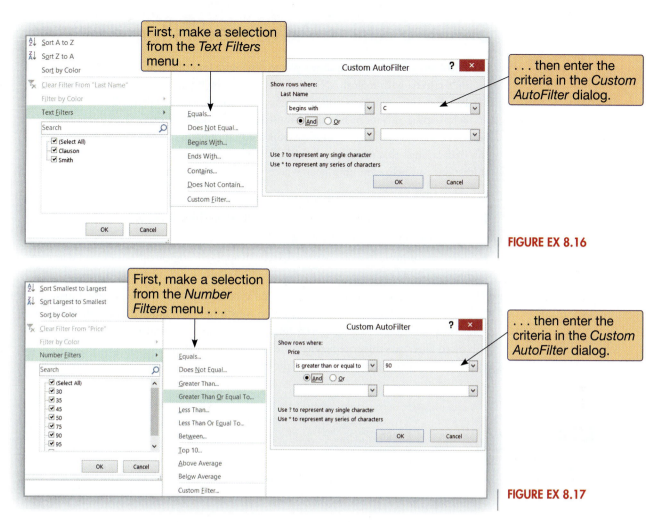

First, make a selection from the *Text Filters* menu . . .

. . . then enter the criteria in the *Custom AutoFilter* dialog.

FIGURE EX 8.16

First, make a selection from the *Number Filters* menu . . .

. . . then enter the criteria in the *Custom AutoFilter* dialog.

FIGURE EX 8.17

When a filter has been applied to a column, the column header will display a funnel icon: . To clear the filter, click the funnel icon and select **Clear Filter from 'Name of Column'.**

another method

On the *Home* tab, in the *Editing* group, click the **Sort & Filter** button and select **Filter** to enable AutoFilter.

To clear the filter:

❭ On the *Data* tab, in the *Sort & Filter* group, click the **Clear** button.

❭ On the *Home* tab, in the *Editing* group, click the **Sort & Filter** button and then select **Clear.**

let me try

Open the student data file **EX8-05-Appointments** and try this skill on your own:

1. On the *Appointments* worksheet, use a custom date filter to show only rows where the appointment date (*Appt Date* column) is **after 4/14/2014.**
2. Clear the filter without removing AutoFilter.
3. Use a custom text filter to show only rows where the customer last name (*Last Name* column) **begins with the letter C.**
4. Clear the filter without removing AutoFilter.
5. Use a custom number filter to show only rows where the service price (*Price* column) is **greater than or equal to 90.**
6. Save the file as directed by your instructor and close it.

Skill 8.6 Using Advanced Filter

Excel's **Advanced Filter** feature allows you to filter data for criteria in multiple columns using multiple criteria with logical AND and OR operators. If you are familiar with using Excel database functions or creating queries in Access, using Advanced Filter will seem familiar.

Before using Advanced Filter, you must set up the **criteria range**. The criteria range can be on the same worksheet or another worksheet in the same workbook. It must include a row of data labels that match the data labels in the data set you are going to filter and include at least one row below the data labels where you will enter the criteria for the filter.

In the criteria range, type the criteria you want to filter for.

❭ If you type criteria in the same row, Excel will use the logical operator AND in the filter—data must meet both criteria.

❭ If you type criteria in separate rows, Excel will apply the logical operator OR—data must meet either criterion.

The criteria range in Figure EX 8.18 is defined as cells A1:H2. The labels in row 1 match the labels for the data set in row 4. The criterion **Smith** has been entered under the label *Last Name* and the criterion >**75** has been entered in the same row under the label *Price*. When Advanced Filter uses this criteria range, the data are filtered to show only rows where the value in the *Last Name* column is **Smith** *and* the value in the *Price* column is **greater than 75.**

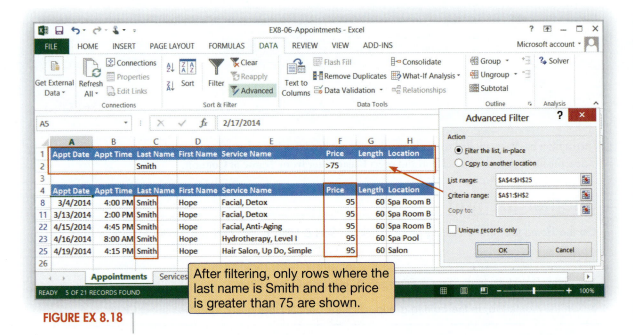

FIGURE EX 8.18

To use Advanced Filter:

1. Click anywhere in the data set you want to filter.

2. On the *Data* tab, in the *Sort & Filter* group, click the **Advanced** button.

3. If necessary, enter the appropriate cell references in the *List range* box. If you begin with a cell in the data set selected, Excel will enter the cell range in the *List range* box for you.

4. Click in the *Criteria range* box and enter the cell references or the name for the criteria range, including the label row. Be careful that your criteria range does not include blank rows.

5. Click **OK.**

To clear the filter from the data, on the *Data* tab, in the *Sort & Filter* group, click the **Clear** button.

tips & tricks

> An easy way to create a criteria range is to insert a few blank rows above the data you want to filter. There should be at least one blank row between the criteria range and the data set. Copy the data label row to the first row of the criteria range and then enter the filter criteria in the row below.

> The first time you define the criteria range, Excel will name the range *Criteria* and then automatically use that criteria range the next time you use Advanced Filter.

> If you name the criteria range *Criteria* before using Advanced Filter, Excel will automatically place the range in the *Criteria* range box for you.

tell me **more**

By default, Advanced Filter will filter the data in-place. You can also elect to copy the filtered data to another location in the workbook:

1. In the *Advanced Filter* dialog, click the **Copy to another location** radio button.

2. In the *Copy to* box, enter the cell reference for the upper left corner of the range where you want Excel to paste a copy of the data labels and the records that meet the criteria. The location where the filtered records are copied is called the **extract range**.

another **method**

You can clear the filter from the *Home* tab. In the *Editing* group, click the **Sort & Filter** button and then click **Clear.**

let me **try**

Open the student data file **EX8-06-Appointments** and try this skill on your own:

1. The criteria range has been set up for you in cells **A1:H2.** Use Advanced Filter to filter the data in place so that only rows where the **Last Name** is **Smith** and the **Price** is **greater than 75** are shown.

2. Save the file as directed by your instructor and close it.

Skill 8.7 Adding Subtotals

Adding **subtotals** is an easy way to outline large amounts of data. In order to use subtotals, the data range must be arranged in columns with the first row containing column headings. The columns must be sorted so the rows you want totaled are grouped together. When you add a subtotal, Excel automatically calculates subtotals based on the grouping you selected. Excel inserts formulas using the SUBTOTAL function in a subtotal row for each group and in a grand total row to summarize all the data in the list.

To create an outline automatically using subtotals:

1. Ensure that your data range is organized in rows, with the first row containing column headings.

2. Sort by the column you want to organize into groups.

3. Once the range is sorted into groups, on the *Data* tab, in the *Outline* group, click the **Subtotal** button.

4. In the *Subtotal* dialog, click the **At each change in** arrow and select the column for which you want to create subtotals—the same column you just sorted by. Excel will create a new subtotal line each time it finds a new value in this column. (That's why you need to sort the data first—so matching values in this column are grouped together before you add the subtotals.)

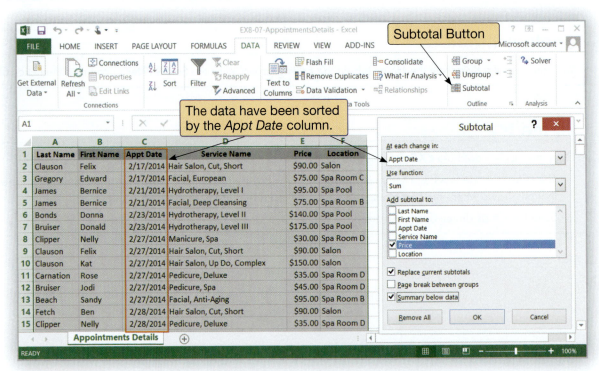

FIGURE EX 8.19

5. Select the function you want to use from the *Use function* drop-down list. Excel can create subtotals with a variety of functions, but SUM and AVERAGE are probably the most common.

6. In the *Add subtotal to* box, check the box(es) for the column(s) containing the data to add subtotals to.

7. Verify that the **Summary below data** check box is selected to place the new subtotal rows below each group. Uncheck this box only if you want the summary row *above* the details instead.

8. Click **OK** to add the subtotals and grouping to your data.

When rows are outlined with subtotals, outline symbols appear to the left of the column headings and row numbers.

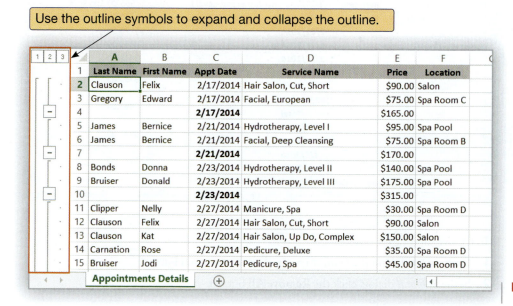

Use the outline symbols to expand and collapse the outline.

	Last Name	First Name	Appt Date	Service Name	Price	Location
1	Last Name	First Name	Appt Date	Service Name	Price	Location
2	Clauson	Felix	2/17/2014	Hair Salon, Cut, Short	$90.00	Salon
3	Gregory	Edward	2/17/2014	Facial, European	$75.00	Spa Room C
4			2/17/2014		$165.00	
5	James	Bernice	2/21/2014	Hydrotherapy, Level I	$95.00	Spa Pool
6	James	Bernice	2/21/2014	Facial, Deep Cleansing	$75.00	Spa Room B
7			2/21/2014		$170.00	
8	Bonds	Donna	2/23/2014	Hydrotherapy, Level II	$140.00	Spa Pool
9	Bruiser	Donald	2/23/2014	Hydrotherapy, Level III	$175.00	Spa Pool
10			2/23/2014		$315.00	
11	Clipper	Nelly	2/27/2014	Manicure, Spa	$30.00	Spa Room D
12	Clauson	Felix	2/27/2014	Hair Salon, Cut, Short	$90.00	Salon
13	Clauson	Kat	2/27/2014	Hair Salon, Up Do, Complex	$150.00	Salon
14	Carnation	Rose	2/27/2014	Pedicure, Deluxe	$35.00	Spa Room D
15	Bruiser	Jodi	2/27/2014	Pedicure, Spa	$45.00	Spa Room D

Appointments Details

FIGURE EX 8.20

To collapse the outline to show just the subtotals, click the **2** outline symbol to the left of the column headings.

Click **2** to collapse the entire outline to show just the subtotals.

	Last Name	First Name	Appt Date	Service Name	Price	Location
1	Last Name	First Name	Appt Date	Service Name	Price	Location
4			2/17/2014		$165.00	
7			2/21/2014		$170.00	
10			2/23/2014		$315.00	
17			2/27/2014		$445.00	
23			2/28/2014 Total		$385.00	
29			3/1/2014 Total		$485.00	
35			3/2/2014 Total		$475.00	
46			3/3/2014 Total		$760.00	
51			3/4/2014 Total		$395.00	

Appointments Details

FIGURE EX 8.21

To show the details for a specific outline group, click the **plus sign** outline symbol next to the row you want to expand.

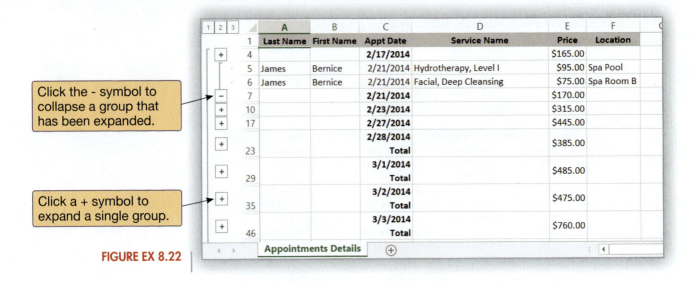

Click the - symbol to collapse a group that has been expanded.

Click a + symbol to expand a single group.

FIGURE EX 8.22

To remove subtotals:

1. On the *Data* tab, in the *Outline* group, click the **Subtotal** button.
2. In the *Subtotal* dialog, click the **Remove All** button.

tips & tricks

To see the SUBTOTAL formulas, click any subtotal cell and look in the formula bar. The SUBTOTAL function requires two arguments. The first argument is a number from 1 to 11 representing the function used to calculate the subtotals. The number 9 is used for the SUM function. The second argument is the range of cells to be subtotaled.

=SUBTOTAL(9,E2:E3)

tell me more

If you add multiple sort levels to your list, you can create subtotals for each level of sorting. Be sure to uncheck the *Replace current subtotals* check box in the *Subtotal* dialog to allow for multiple subtotals.

another method

To expand and collapse outline groups:

1. Click any cell in the summary row or group.
2. On the *Data* tab, in the *Outline* group, click the **Show Detail** button or the **Hide Detail** button.

let me try

Open the student data file **EX8-07-AppointmentsDetails** and try this skill on your own:

1. Select any cell in the data range. The data have been sorted by appointment date in the *Appt Date* column.
2. Create automatic subtotals to **sum** the **price** for each date change in the **Appt Date** column.
3. Collapse the entire outline to show just the subtotals.
4. Display the details for just the **2/21/2014** group.
5. Save the file as directed by your instructor and close it.

Skill 8.8 Using Consolidate to Create Subtotals

One way to subtotal data without formulas and without including the details in an outline format is to use Consolidate. If the data are organized with labels at the top of each column, you can use consolidate to summarize data for each unique value in the first column of the cell range defined as the consolidation reference. The data do not need to be sorted in any particular order.

Use **Consolidate** to create subtotals when you want to further manipulate the data or when you do not want or need the details available.

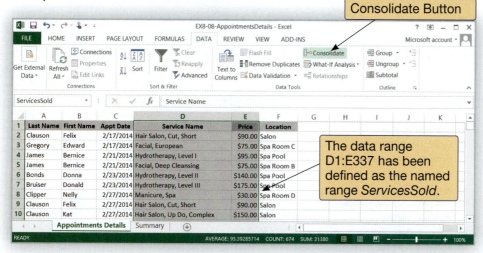

FIGURE EX 8.23

To use Consolidate to create subtotals:

1. Select the cell where you want the upper left corner of the subtotal consolidation to begin. Often this will be cell A1 in an empty worksheet, but it can be an area on the same worksheet as the data you are consolidating. Be sure to leave plenty of room for the summarized data.

2. On the *Data* tab, in the *Data Tools* group, click the **Consolidate** button.

3. In the *Consolidate* dialog, **Sum** is selected in the *Function* list by default. If you want to use another function, expand the list and select the function you want to use.

4. The *All references* box may include references from previous consolidations. If these are not the references you want to use, select each and click the **Delete** button to delete them.

5. Click in the *Reference* box and type the cell range or the range name of the data you want to summarize. If you have only one data range to summarize, you do not need to click the *Add* button. Excel adds the reference to the *All References* box when you click the **OK** button.

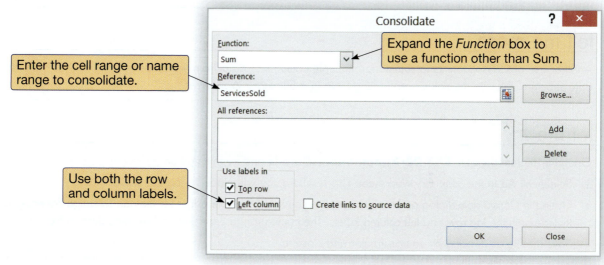

FIGURE EX 8.24

6. Click the **Top row** check box and the **Left column** check box. When the data are organized in rows, you could select just the *Left column* check box as those are the labels used for the consolidation. However, including the *Top row* check box copies the column label above the data that has been subtotaled. This information is often vital to understanding the data.

7. Click **OK**.

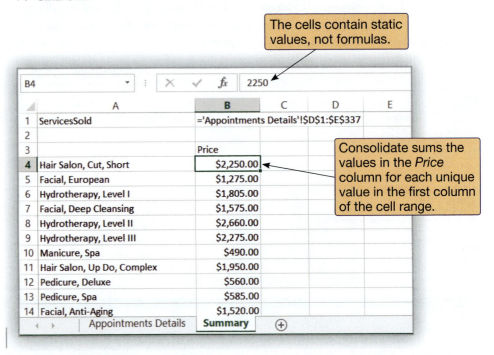

The cells contain static values, not formulas.

Consolidate sums the values in the *Price* column for each unique value in the first column of the cell range.

FIGURE EX 8.25

If your consolidation range includes columns with text or dates between the first column of data in the reference range and the column with values that are summarized, the consolidation will include blank columns. You can safely delete these columns from the consolidation if you do not want them.

tips & tricks

When using Consolidate as a substitute for the *Subtotal* command, you do **not** want to check the **Create links to source data** check box in the *Consolidate* dialog. If you want to summarize a single set of data with subtotals in an outline format, use the *Subtotal* command instead.

tell me more

Another use of Consolidate is to summarize multiple columns of data from worksheets or workbooks with the same data structure. Refer to the skill *Consolidating Data in a Summary Worksheet*.

let me try

Open the student data file **EX8-08-AppointmentsDetails** and try this skill on your own:

1. Select cell **A3** in the *Summary* worksheet. This is where you will place the consolidated data.

2. Open the *Consolidate* dialog and use the **Sum** function to consolidate prices for the named range **ServicesSold.** Include both the **top row** and **left column** labels. The named range *ServicesSold* has been defined for you.

3. Save the file as directed by your instructor and close it.

excel 2013   chapter 8 Exploring Advanced Data Analysis

Skill 8.9 Creating an Outline

If your workbook includes a data range organized with summary rows that include formulas, you can use the **Auto Outline** feature to automatically create groups and subgroups of rows that you can expand and collapse. The summary row for each group must include a formula in a consistent location. Auto Outline automatically groups together the rows above each row that includes the formula.

To create an automatic outline based on summary formulas:

1. Click any cell in the data range.
2. On the *Data* tab, in the *Outline* group, click the **Group** button arrow and click **Auto Outline.**

The Auto Outline feature also works if subtotals are in a column instead of a row. If the data include formulas to calculate subtotals for both rows and columns, Auto Outline will create both row and column groups based on those formulas.

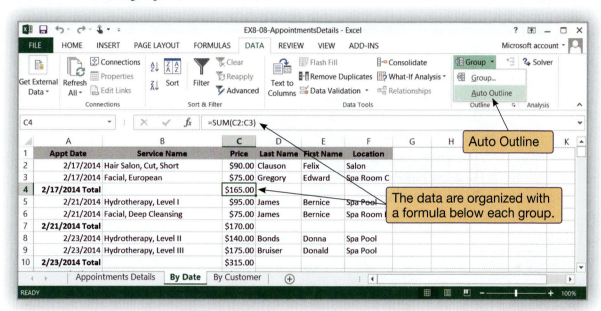

FIGURE EX 8.26

If your data do not include rows with summary formulas, you can outline groups of rows manually. This is useful if you have a large amount of data and you usually work with only part of the data at a time. There must be at least one blank row between each group.

1. Select the rows you want to group. Do not include the blank row.
2. On the *Data* tab, in the *Outline* group, click the **Group** button or click the **Group** button arrow and then select **Group...**
3. In the *Group* dialog, **Rows** is selected by default. If you are grouping by columns instead, click the **Columns** radio button.
4. Click **OK.**
5. Repeat Steps 1–4 for each group of rows you want to define.

When rows are outlined, outline symbols appear to the left of the column headings and row numbers.

) To collapse the outline to show just the subtotals, click the numbered outline symbols to the left of the column headings to collapse or expand all data at that outline level.

) To show the details for a specific outline group, click the + symbol next to the row you want to expand. Click the – symbol to collapse the group.

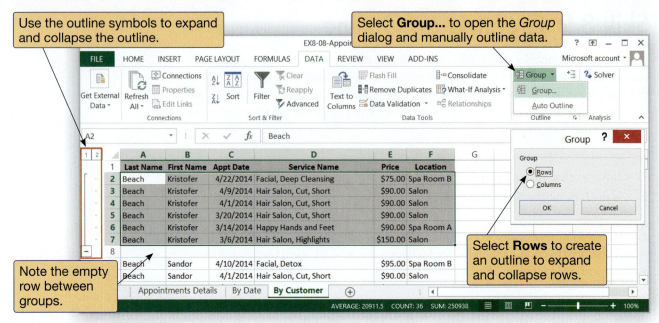

FIGURE EX 8.27

To remove the entire outline:

1. Select any cell in the outline

2. On the *Data* tab, in the *Outline* group, click the **Ungroup** button arrow and select **Clear Outline.**

To ungroup a single group only:

1. Select any cell in the group.

2. On the *Data* tab, in the *Outline* group, click the **Ungroup** button arrow and select **Ungroup.**

tips & tricks

▸ Auto Outline is not available if your data range is formatted as a table. To use Auto Outline, first convert the table to a data range.

▸ Auto Outline can be tricky. If your data include a complicated formula to calculate values, Excel will try to use that formula as the outline point, and Excel may crash (close unexpectedly).

tell me **more**

You can use the *Group* command to create multiple levels of groups within each other.

let me **try**

Open the student data file **EX8-09-AppointmentsDetails** and try this skill on your own:

1. Select cell **A2** on the *By Date* worksheet. Note that the total row for each date uses a SUM function to total the prices.

2. Create an automatic outline from the rows in this data range.

3. Collapse and expand a few groups to get a feel for how Excel outlined the data.

4. On the *By Customer* worksheet, select cells **A2:F7.** Note that the rows are separated into groups by customer name with a blank row between each group.

5. Manually create a group by rows for cells **A2:F7.**

6. Create a few more groups in this worksheet.

7. Collapse and expand a few groups to get a feel for how the manually created groups work.

8. Save the file as directed by your instructor and close it.

Skill 8.10 Analyzing Changes with the Watch Window

With large or complex workbooks, you will often make changes in one part of the workbook that affect cells you cannot see. The **Watch Window** displays the formulas and current values of the cells you add to it, and it stays open and on top of the Excel window until you close it. As you change values throughout your workbook, the *Value* column in the Watch Window updates to show you the effects on the cells you are watching.

To watch cells using the Watch Window:

1. Select the cells you want to watch.
2. On the *Formulas* tab, in the *Formula Auditing* group, click the **Watch Window** button.
3. In the *Watch Window,* click **Add Watch.**
4. The cells you selected are automatically entered in the *Add Watch* dialog. Click **Add.**
5. Click the main Excel window and make changes to cells that are referenced by the cells you are watching. The *Value* column in the Watch Window updates as you work.
6. The Watch Window stays on top of the workbook window until you close it.

FIGURE EX 8.28

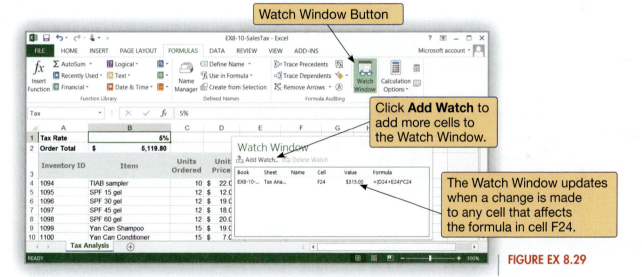

FIGURE EX 8.29

tips & tricks

The Watch Window is really a toolbar. You can drag it to the area beneath the Ribbon, and it will expand to the width of the window and remain anchored there until you move it somewhere else.

tell me more

To remove a watched cell from the Watch Window, click the row in the Watch Window for the cell you want to remove and then click **Delete.**

let me try

Open the student data file **EX8-10-SalesTax** and try this skill on your own:

1. Open the Watch Window and create a new watch for cell **F24.**
2. Change the value in cell **B1** (the sales tax) to **5%** and note the change to cell F24 in the Watch Windows.
3. Save the file as directed by your instructor and close it.

Skill 8.11 Creating What-If Analysis Scenarios

A **scenario** is an alternate version of data values that you create and apply through the **Scenario Manager**. Scenarios allow you to analyze the results of changing values in specific cells (inputs). Each scenario is saved with a name, so you can apply it at any time.

To create a scenario:

1. Open the Scenario Manager. On the *Data* tab, in the *Data Tools* group, click the **What-If Analysis** button and then click **Scenario Manager...**

2. To create a new scenario, click the **Add** button.

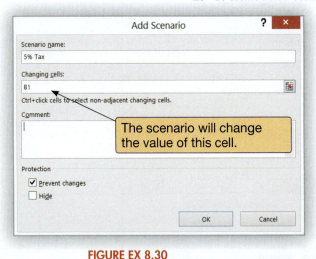

3. The *Add Scenario* dialog opens. Type a name for the scenario in the *Scenario name* box.

4. Enter the cell, range of cells, or range name of the cells you want to change (the inputs) in the *Changing cells* box. The cell(s) you have selected in the worksheet are entered in the box by default.

5. If you want to add a description for this scenario, type it in the *Comment* box.

6. Click **OK** to continue and add the input values for the scenario.

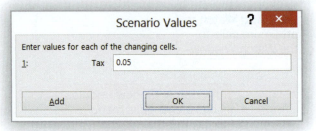

FIGURE EX 8.30

7. In the *Scenario Values* dialog, enter the new value for each input cell.

8. Click the **Add** button to open the *Add Scenario* dialog again and add another cell reference to the scenario, or click **OK** to return to the Scenario Manager.

FIGURE EX 8.31

9. Your new scenario is now included in the *Scenarios* list. To apply the scenario, click the name to select it and then click the **Show** button.

10. To close the Scenario Manager, click the **Close** button.

To delete a scenario:

1. Open the Scenario Manager.

2. Click the scenario name you want to delete.

3. Click the **Delete** button.

Be careful when deleting scenarios! Excel does not ask you to confirm the deletion. Once you click the *Delete* button, the scenario is deleted permanently.

FIGURE EX 8.32

tips & tricks

❯ If you want to keep a copy of your original data, create a scenario without changing any values. Name the scenario "original" or something similar.

❯ If you include cells with formulas in your scenario, the formulas will be changed to the values specified in the scenario and you will lose the formula.

tell me **more**

To edit a scenario:

1. Open the Scenario Manager.
2. Click the scenario you want to edit. Click the **Edit** button.
3. The *Edit Scenario* dialog opens showing the original scenario name and input cells. Make any changes you want and then click the **OK** button to make changes to the input values.
4. Make any changes you want in the *Scenario Values* dialog and then click **OK** to return to the Scenario Manager.

let me **try**

Open the student data file **EX8-11-SalesTax** and try this skill on your own:

1. Select cell **B1**. This is the cell you will be changing in the new scenario.
2. Create a new scenario named **5% Tax** to change the value of cell **B1** to **0.05**. Note that in the *Scenario Values* dialog, the cell name *Tax* is displayed instead of the cell address *B1*.
3. Show the new **5% Tax** scenario. Close the Scenario Manager.
4. Save the file as directed by your instructor and close it.

from the perspective of . . .

A BOOKING AGENT FOR PROFESSIONAL ATHLETES

I can advise clients and "show them the money" with the Scenario Manager. Understanding the impact of collection fees, commissions, and so on is understandable when looking at scenario summary reports.

Skill 8.12 Creating Scenario Summary Reports

Changing cell values through scenarios affects not only the cells defined in the scenario but also any cells that reference the changing cells. If you create multiple scenarios for the same data, use the Scenario Manager to generate a **scenario summary report** summarizing and comparing the effects of the scenarios. At a glance, you will be able to see the cells each scenario affects and decide which scenario provides the results that best fit your needs.

The order total, cell B2, is affected by the scenarios that change the tax rate (the cell named *Tax*, cell B1).

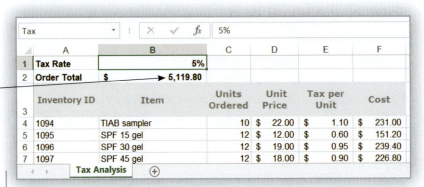

FIGURE EX 8.33

To create a scenario summary report:

1. Open the Scenario Manager. On the *Data* tab, in the *Data Tools* group, click the **What-If Analysis** button and click **Scenario Manager.**

2. Click the **Summary** button.

3. In the *Scenario Summary* dialog, select whether you want the summary report to appear as a new worksheet (**Scenario Summary** radio button) or a new PivotTable (**Scenario PivotTable** report radio button).

4. In the *Result cells* box, Excel will automatically suggest the cell or cells that contain formulas affected by the changing input values for the scenarios.

5. Click **OK** to see the scenario summary report. Notice that Excel automatically creates a new worksheet named *Scenario Summary.*

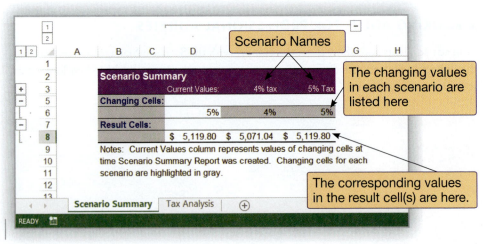

FIGURE EX 8.34

let me try

Open the student data file **EX8-12-SalesTax** and try this skill on your own:

1. Open the Scenario Manager and review the scenarios in this workbook.

2. Create a scenario summary report. Accept the recommended results cells.

3. Save the file as directed by your instructor and close it.

Skill 8.13 Activating the Solver Add-In

Solver is a data analysis tool which you will learn to use in the skill *Using Solver*. However, Solver is not available in Excel by default. You must add it through the *Excel Options* dialog.

To install the Solver add-in:

1. Click the **File** tab.
2. Click **Options** to open the *Excel Options* dialog.
3. Click **Add-Ins.**
4. The *Add-ins* list is divided into *Active Application Add-ins* and *Inactive Application Add-ins.* If Solver is listed in the inactive section, you will need to install it.
5. Near the bottom of the window, the *Manage* box should display *Excel Add-Ins.* If it does not, expand the list and select **Excel Add-Ins.**
6. Click **Go...** to open the *Add-Ins* dialog.
7. Click the **Solver Add-in** check box and click **OK.**

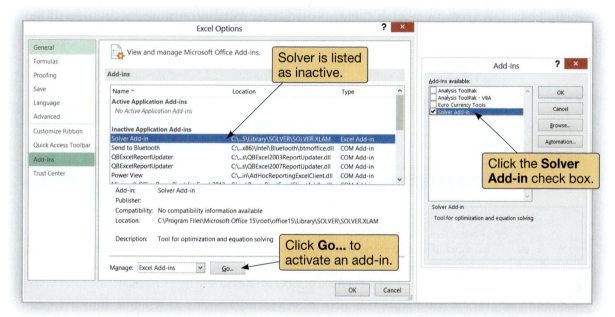

FIGURE EX 8.35

The *Solver* button is now available on the far right side of the *Data* tab in the *Analysis* group.

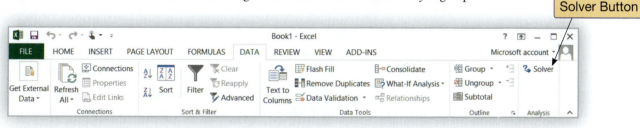

FIGURE EX 8.36

let me try

Try this skill on your own:

1. Open Excel and check to see if the Solver add-in is installed.
2. If the *Solver* button is not available on the *Data* tab, install it.

Skill 8.14 Using Solver

Solver is a data analysis tool that evaluates multiple variables affecting a formula and produces optimal values for those variables within defined constraints to result in a value you specify.

In Figure EX 8.37, we want to find the maximum profit possible from a single shipment. The formula to calculate profit in cell *B1* is the total price of the order minus the total cost of goods. This seems simple enough.

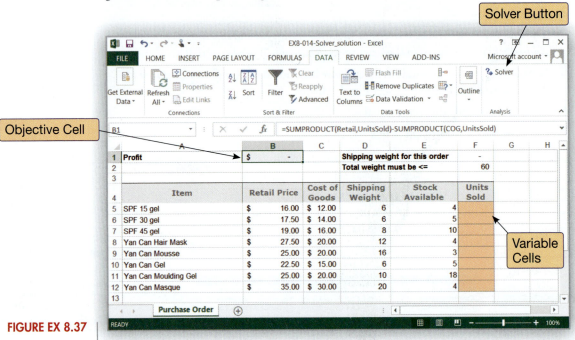

FIGURE EX 8.37

However, there are limitations. The number of units sold must be less than or equal to the number of units in stock, and, in this example, the total shipping weight must be less than or equal to 60 ounces. In addition, the units sold must be integers (whole numbers).

How can we find the optimal number of units to ship for each product in order to maximize profits? Use Solver.

To use Solver:

1. On the *Data* tab, in the *Analysis* group, click the **Solver** button.

2. In the *Solver Parameters* dialog, enter the objective cell reference or cell name in the *Set Objective* box. This is the cell containing the formula you want Solver to solve for. In Figure EX 8.37, cell **B1** is the objective cell.

3. Click the radio button to find the **Max** (maximum) or **Min** (minimum) result value for the formula, or click the **Value Of** radio button and enter a specific value to solve for.

4. In the *By Changing Variable Cells* box, enter the cells you want Solver to manipulate to reach the objective target. These cells must be precedents to the formula in the objective cell. In Figure EX 8.37, the cells in the named range **UnitsSold** (F5:F12) are the variable cells.

5. The **constraints** are limitations you place on the acceptable values for the variable cells. Solver will not produce a result that violates the rules you set here. To add constraints, click the **Add** button next to the *Subject to the Constraints* box.

   In Figure EX 8.38, the value in the *UnitsSold* named range must be *less than or equal to* the parallel value in the *Stock* named range.

FIGURE EX 8.38

- In the *Cell Reference* box, enter the cell containing the variable you want to place limits on. You can use a cell reference or a named range. The reference must be a precedent to the formula in the objective cell.

- Expand the drop-down list in the middle box and select an operator. If you want to restrict values to whole numbers, select **Int** from the list.

- In the *Constraint* box, enter the limit value. This can be a numerical value or a cell reference.

- Click **OK** to add the constraint, or click **Add** to add the constraint and immediately add another constraint.

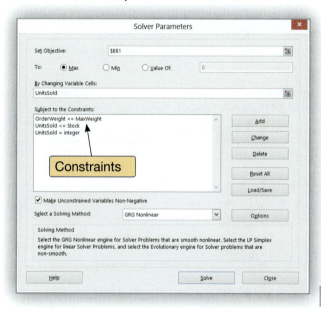

FIGURE EX 8.39

6. When you have added all the constraints, click the **Solve** button. Solver works through all the possible values for the variables and tries to find a solution within the constraints you defined.

7. If Solver is successful, the values are applied to the worksheet. If necessary, move the *Solver Results* dialog so you can see the results.

- If you want to keep the solution results, click **OK.**

- If you do not want to apply the Solver solution right away but may want to come back to it later, you can save it as a scenario. Click the **Save Scenario** button. Enter a name for the scenario and click **OK.** You can show the scenario at any time using the Scenario Manager.

- If you want the cells restored to their original values, click the **Restore Original Values** radio button and then click **OK.**

- If you want to modify the Solver parameters before accepting a change, click the **Return to Solver Parameters Dialog** check box and then click **OK.**

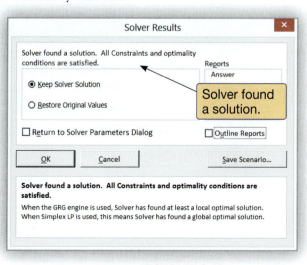

FIGURE EX 8.40

Figure EX 8.41 shows the results of the Solver parameters entered in Figure EX 8.39. The maximum value for the objective cell is $57.00.

	A	B	C	D	E	F
1	Profit	$ 57.00		Shipping weight for this order		60
2				Total weight must be <=		60
3						
4	Item	Retail Price	Cost of Goods	Shipping Weight	Stock Available	Units Sold
5	SPF 15 gel	$ 16.00	$ 12.00	6	4	4
6	SPF 30 gel	$ 17.50	$ 14.00	6	5	1
7	SPF 45 gel	$ 19.00	$ 16.00	8	10	0
8	Yan Can Hair Mask	$ 27.50	$ 20.00	12	4	0
9	Yan Can Mousse	$ 25.00	$ 20.00	16	3	0
10	Yan Can Gel	$ 22.50	$ 15.00	6	5	5
11	Yan Can Moulding Gel	$ 25.00	$ 20.00	10	18	0
12	Yan Can Masque	$ 35.00	$ 30.00	20	4	0

FIGURE EX 8.41

The values Solver found that will maximize the profit calculated in cell B1.

tips & tricks

» Solver may not be able to find a solution that meets the constraints. When this happens, try modifying the variable constraints or the objective target value.

» Some variables, number of units sold or number of people, must be a whole number. If one of the variables must be a whole number, select **int** as the constraint operator in the *Add Constraint* dialog. Solver automatically places *integer* as the constraint value and will only find a solution that returns a whole number for that variable.

tell me **more**

For more information about Solver, visit the official solver Web site at www.solver.com.

let me **try**

Open the student data file **EX8-14-Solver** and try this skill on your own:

1. Use Solver to find the combination of units sold for each product that will result in the maximum profit.
2. Set the objective to find the maximum value for cell **B1.**
3. Use the range name **UnitsSold** as the variable cells.
4. Add the following constraints:
   a. The values in the **UnitsSold** named range must be **less than or equal to** the values in the **Stock** named range.
   b. The value in the **OrderWeight** named range must be **less than or equal to** the maximum weight for the order as defined in the **MaxWeight** named range.
   c. The values in the **UnitsSold** named range must be whole numbers only.
5. Run Solver and accept the solution.
6. Save the file as directed by your instructor and close it.

Skill 8.15 Refreshing Data in a PivotTable

The skill *Creating PivotTables Using Recommended PivotTables* introduces the concept of PivotTables and how to create them, add fields, and change the function used to summarize the data. Recall that PivotTables do not contain any data themselves—they summarize data from another part of your workbook. After you create a PivotTable, if the underlying data change, you must update or refresh the PivotTable to see the changes.

To refresh the data in a PivotTable:

1. Select any part of the PivotTable.
2. On the *PivotTable Tools Analyze* tab, in the *Data* group, click the **Refresh** button.

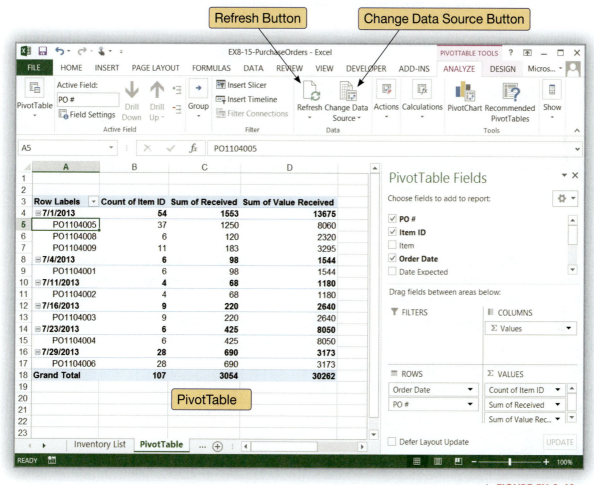

FIGURE EX 8.42

If the source for the PivotTable has been updated with additional rows of data, refreshing the PivotTable is not enough. You will need to update the range of cells used as the PivotTable source:

1. Select any part of the PivotTable.
2. On the *PivotTable Tools Analyze* tab, in the *Data* group, click the **Change Data Source** button.

3. In the *Change PivotTable Data Source* dialog, enter the cell range, named range, or table name in the box. You can also click and drag the appropriate cells in the worksheet to update the cell range.

4. Click **OK.**

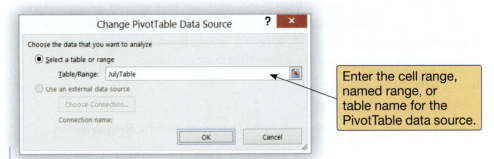

Enter the cell range, named range, or table name for the PivotTable data source.

FIGURE EX 8.43

tips & tricks

) If you find yourself updating the PivotTable source data often because you've added more rows of data, format the source data as a table. When new rows are added to the table, they are included in the PivotTable source automatically. You will not need to update the data source. However, you will still need to refresh the PivotTable to see the updates.

) If your workbook includes a PivotChart, when you refresh data in the source PivotTable, the PivotChart is updated as well.

tell me **more**

You can modify the PivotTable options to refresh the data every time the workbook is opened. This setting is not recommended for PivotTables that use external data that may have changed unexpectedly. By leaving this option unchecked, you have more control over when the PivotTable is updated.

To change the PivotTable option to refresh automatically, select any cell in the PivotTable.

1. On the *PivotTable Tools Analyze* tab, in the *PivotTable* group, click the **Options** button.
2. In the *PivotTable Options* dialog, click the **Data** tab.
3. Click the **Refresh data when opening the file** check box.
4. Click **OK.**

let me **try**

Open the student data file **EX8-15-PurchaseOrders** and try this skill on your own:

1. In the *PO July* worksheet, delete rows **4:11.**
2. Update the PivotTable in the *PivotTable* worksheet.
3. Data was added to the *PO July* worksheet after the PivotTable was created. Update the data source for the PivotTable to use the table named **JulyTable.** Now if more rows are added later, you will not need to update the data source again. You will, however, need to *refresh* the PivotTable.
4. Save the file as directed by your instructor and close it.

Skill 8.16 Adding a Calculated Field to a PivotTable

Recall that PivotTables summarize data and calculate subtotals using functions like SUM and AVERAGE. PivotTables do not contain any data themselves—they summarize data from another part of your workbook. However, you can add new fields to the PivotTable to perform calculations based on that data.

To add a calculated field to a PivotTable

1. On the *PivotTable Tools Analyze* tab, if necessary, click the **Calculations** button to expand the *Calculations* group. Click **Fields, Items, & Sets.** Select **Calculated Field...**

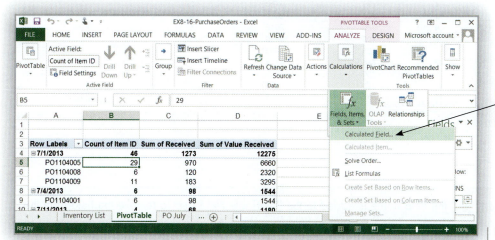

Click **Calculated Field...** to open the *Calculated Field* dialog.

FIGURE EX 8.44

2. In the *Insert Calculated Field* dialog, type a header title for the field in the *Name* box.

3. In the *Formula* box, delete the **0** and type the formula you want to calculate. Do not delete the equals sign.

4. To include fields from the PivotTable, double-click the field name in the *Fields* list (or click the field name once and then click the **Insert Field** button). If the field name includes spaces, Excel will automatically place single quotation marks around the field name. If you type the field name yourself, be sure to include them. This is necessary only for field names that include spaces.

5. Click **OK** to add the calculated field to the PivotTable.

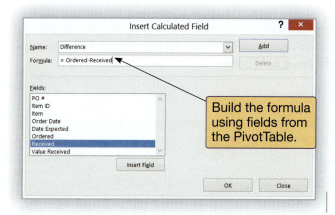

Build the formula using fields from the PivotTable.

FIGURE EX 8.45

The calculated field is added to the PivotTable at the far right side. It is included in the *Pivot-Table Fields* pane as well.

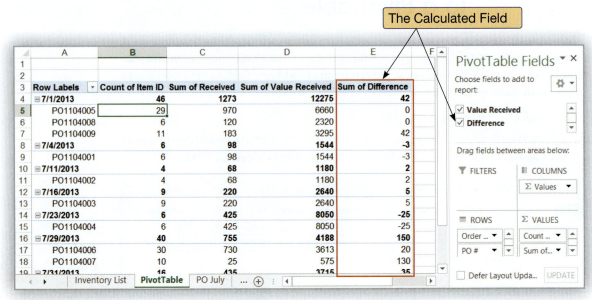

The Calculated Field

FIGURE EX 8.46

tips & tricks

When you create a calculated field, the field name is added to the PivotTable Field List. To remove the field from the PivotTable, click the check box to uncheck it. This removes the field from the PivotTable display without deleting it, so you can display it later without having to re-create it.

tell me more

To delete a calculated field:

1. On the *PivotTable Tools Options* tab, click the **Calculations** button and then click **Fields, Items, & Sets.** Select **Calculated Field.**
2. In the *Insert Calculated Field* dialog, expand the **Name** list and select the name of the calculated field you want to delete.
3. Click the **Delete** button.

another method

To build the formula in the *Insert Calculated Field* dialog, *Formula* box, double-click a field name in the *Fields* list to add it to formula or click the field name once and then click the **Insert Field** button.

let me try

Open the student data file **EX8-16-PurchaseOrders** and try this skill on your own:

1. Select any cell in the PivotTable in the *PivotTable* worksheet.
2. Add a calculated field named **Difference** to summarize the difference between values in the *Ordered* field and the *Received* field: **=Ordered-Received**

    Note that it is not necessary for the *Ordered* and *Received* fields to be visible in the PivotTable.
3. Save the file as directed by your instructor and close it.

Skill 8.17 Grouping Fields in a PivotTable

PivotTables often contain large amounts of data, making it difficult to find the information you want. **Grouping** adds another level of organization to your PivotTable. You can expand or collapse groups to show or hide details as required.

To add grouping:

1. Click a cell in the PivotTable with the type of data you want to group by (a date or number).

2. On the *PivotTable Tools Options* tab, if necessary, click the **Group** button to display the *Group* group. Click the **Group Field** button.

3. In the *Grouping* dialog, Excel automatically detects and enters the start and end values based on the values in the PivotTable.

4. Select how you want the data grouped:

   - For dates, you can select multiple grouping levels, such as months, quarters, and years.

   - For numeric values, enter the increment to group by in the *By* box.

5. Click **OK.**

The PivotTable in Figure EX 8.47 has grouping applied by months and quarters. The details for *Feb* and *Mar* are collapsed.

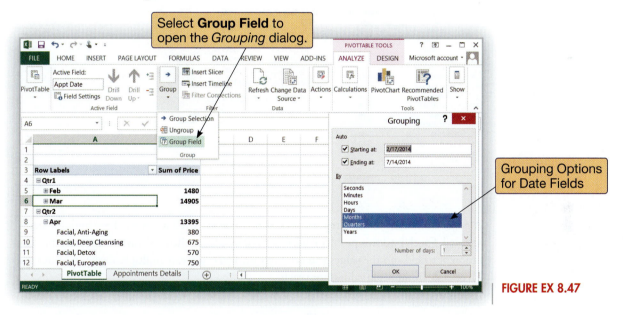

FIGURE EX 8.47

To remove grouping, click one of the grouping level cells and then on the *PivotTable Tools Options* tab, in the *Group* group, click the **Ungroup** button.

another **method**

The *Group* and *Ungroup* commands are also available by right-clicking the cell you want to group or ungroup by.

let me **try**

Open the student data file **EX8-17-AppointmentsDetails** and try this skill on your own:

1. Select any cell in the PivotTable in the *PivotTable* worksheet.

2. Group the data by both month and quarter.

3. Save the file as directed by your instructor and close it.

Skill 8.18 Filtering PivotTable Data

When you create a PivotTable, the column(s) of row labels include an AutoFilter arrow. You can use the options in the AutoFilter menu to filter the PivotTable data just as you would similar data in a table or data range.

You can add additional filters to the PivotTable by clicking a field name in the *PivotTable Fields* pane and dragging it to the *Filters* box in the bottom part of the pane or by moving a field name from one of the other boxes to the *Filters* box. When a field is added to the *Filters* box, a **report filter** is added to row 1 above the PivotTable. Click the filter arrow to select from the list of values.

❭ The report filter is initially set to (All) to show all the values.

❭ To filter for a single value, click the item you want to filter for and then click **OK.**

❭ To filter for multiple values, click the **Select Multiple Items** check box and then click the check box in front of each item you want to include in the filter. Click **OK.**

❭ To remove a filter, click **(All)** again and then click **OK.**

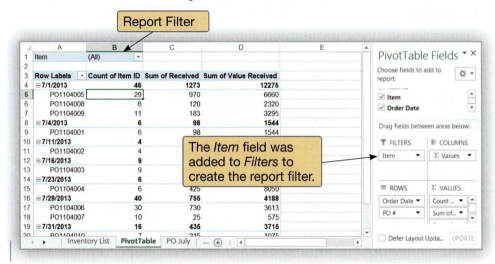

FIGURE EX 8.48

A major limitation to using report filters is that you can't tell when you have multiple items selected. Excel fixed this problem in Excel 2010 by adding slicers. A **slicer** is a visual representation of a field and the values you can filter by. You can create multiple slicers and filter the PivotTable by multiple values from each.

To add a slicer:

1. On the *PivotTable Tools Analyze* tab, in the *Filter* group, click the **Insert Slicer** button.

2. In the *Insert Slicers* dialog, click the check boxes for the fields you want to create slicers for and then click **OK.**

3. A separate slicer opens for each field listing the available values. Notice that a filter icon appears next to the field name in the *PivotTable Fields* task pane to indicate that filtering is available.

4. Click the buttons in each slicer to apply filtering to the PivotTable. To apply more than one option from a slicer, press the Ctrl as you click. Some slicer buttons may become unavailable as you make selections—indicating that there are no data available for that option under the current filtering conditions.

To move a slicer, move your mouse over the slicer. When the cursor changes to the move cursor, click and drag the slicer to the new location.

To clear the selections from a slicer, click the **Clear Filter** button in the upper right corner of the slicer window.

To remove a slicer from your PivotTable, click the slicer, and then press the (Delete) key. Deleting the slicer also removes any filtering options applied from that slicer.

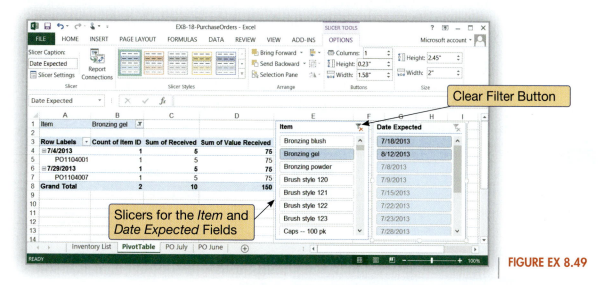

FIGURE EX 8.49

tips & tricks

Slicers are more useful than a report filter because they visually show you which filters are applied to the PivotTable.

tell me more

When a slicer is selected, the *Slicer Tools Options* tab becomes available. From this tab, you can apply a style to the slicer and control slicer settings.

another method

▶ Right-click a field name in the *PivotTable Fields* task pane and select **Add to Report Filter** to create a new report filter for that field.

▶ When a PivotTable is active, the *Slicer* button is available from the *Insert* tab, Filter group.

▶ You can also delete a slicer by right-clicking the slicer and selecting the **Remove** option.

let me try

Open the student data file **EX8-18-PurchaseOrders** and try this skill on your own:

1. Select any cell in the PivotTable in the *PivotTable* worksheet.
2. Add a report filter for the **Item** field.
3. Use the report filter to filter the PivotTable to show only data where the *Item* value is **Bronzing gel.**
4. Add slicers for the **Item** and **Date Expected** fields. Note that the *Item* slicer reflects the filter that was applied through the report filter.
5. Use the slicer to filter the data further to show only data where the *Date Expected* value is **8/12/2013.**
6. Save the file as directed by your instructor and close it.

Skill 8.19 Changing the Look of a PivotTable

You can customize PivotTables in almost any way imaginable. As with other tables, you can apply a Quick Style to a PivotTable to give it a professional, polished appearance.

To apply a Quick Style to a PivotTable:

1. Click anywhere in the PivotTable.

2. On the *PivotTable Tools Design* tab, in the *PivotTable Styles* group, click a style to apply it. To expand the *PivotTable Quick Styles* gallery, click the **More** button.

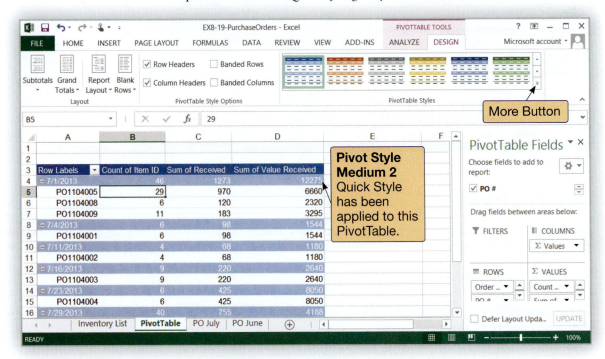

FIGURE EX 8.50

You can also change the layout of a PivotTable. By default, PivotTables use the compact layout, combining all the row fields in a single column. If you have large groups, you may want to use a tabular layout instead to separate the fields into their own columns.

To change the PivotTable layout:

1. On the *PivotTable Tools Design* tab, in the **Layout** group, click the **Report Layout** button and select **Show in Tabular Form.**

2. Now fields are separated into their own columns, but there will be blank cells to the left of each subgroup item.

3. To repeat the item labels in every row, click the **Report Layout** button again and select **Repeat All Item Labels.**

4. To show subtotals for each group, click the **Subtotals** button and select **Show all Subtotals at Bottom of Group** or **Show all Subtotals at Top of Group.**

let me try

Open the student data file **EX8-19-PurchaseOrders** and try this skill on your own:

1. Select any cell in the PivotTable in the *PivotTable* worksheet.

2. Apply the **Pivot Style Medium 2** Quick Style to the PivotTable.

3. Save the file as directed by your instructor and close it.

Skill 8.20 Filtering Data in a PivotChart

PivotCharts do not have a *Chart Filters* button like regular charts do. However, you can use slicers to filter data in a PivotChart. Adding a slicer to a PivotChart is the same as adding one to a PivotTable.

To add a slicer to a PivotChart:

1. On the *PivotChart Tools Analyze* tab, in the *Data* group, click the **Insert Slicer** button.

2. In the *Insert Slicers* dialog, click the check boxes for the fields you want to create slicers for and then click **OK.**

3. Click the buttons in each slicer for the data values you want to display. To select multiple values from a single slicer, press the ⌃Ctrl as you click.

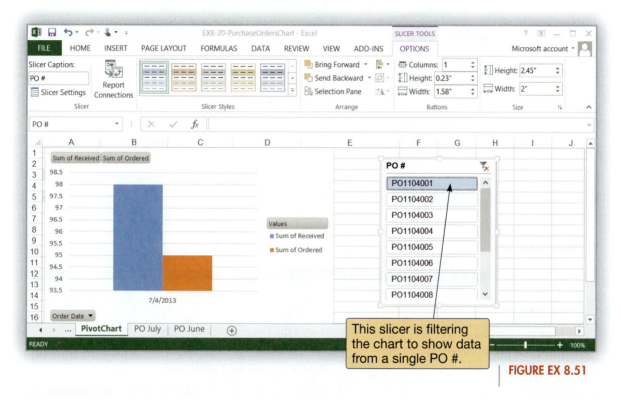

This slicer is filtering the chart to show data from a single PO #.

FIGURE EX 8.51

tips & tricks

As you use the slicer to filter data in the PivotChart, the same changes are applied to the associated PivotTable.

let me try

Open the student data file **EX8-20-PurchaseOrdersChart** and try this skill on your own:

1. Select the PivotChart in the *PivotChart* worksheet.
2. Add a slicer to this PivotChart for the **PO #** field and show only data where the *PO #* value is **PO1104001** (the first button in the slicer).
3. Save the file as directed by your instructor and close it.

Skill 8.21 Changing the Look of a PivotChart

When you create a PivotChart, you have many of the same formatting and design options as you have with regular charts. All the skills for formatting charts can be applied to PivotCharts.

From the *PivotChart Tools Design* tab, you can change the chart type and apply chart layouts and chart styles.

To apply a Quick Style to a PivotChart, on the *PivotChart Tools Design* tab, in the *Chart Styles* group, click the style you want to use or click the **More** button to see all of the Quick Styles available.

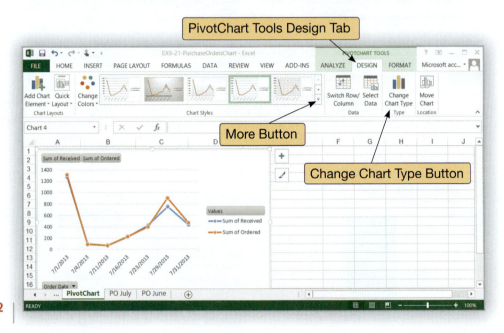

FIGURE EX 8.52

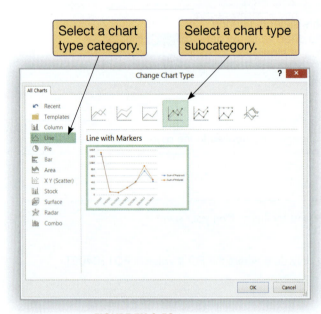

FIGURE EX 8.53

To change the PivotChart chart type:

1. On the *PivotChart Tools Design* tab, in the *Type* group, click the **Change Chart Type** button.

2. In the *Change Chart Type* dialog, click a chart type category to display that category in the right pane.

3. Select a subcategory from the top of the dialog.

4. Click the chart type you want. Notice the dialog shows a preview of how the chart will look.

5. Click **OK.**

From the *PivotChart Tools Format* tab you can modify the format of specific aspects of the chart including applying fills, outlines, and effects to data series and individual data points. You can also insert and format shapes and apply WordArt Styles to text elements.

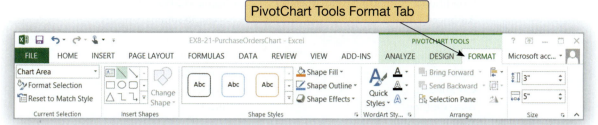

PivotChart Tools Format Tab

FIGURE EX 8.54

tips & tricks

The PivotChart can only display data visible in the associated PivotTable. To show item details in the PivotChart, expand the field in the PivotTable.

tell me **more**

For more details on formatting charts, review the skills *Formatting a Data Point or a Data Series* and *Formatting Other Chart Elements*.

another **method**

Quick Styles are also available from the *Chart Styles* button 📝 that appears near the upper right corner of the Pivot-Chart when it is selected.

let me **try**

Open the student data file **EX8-21-PurchaseOrders** and try this skill on your own:

1. Select the PivotChart in the *PivotChart* worksheet.
2. Change the PivotChart type to the first line chart option.
3. Apply the **Style 4** Quick Style to the PivotChart.
4. Save the file as directed by your instructor and close it.

key terms

Conditional formatting
Conditional Formatting Rules Manager
Advanced Filter
Criteria range
Extract range
Subtotal
Consolidate
Auto Outline
Watch Window

Scenario
Scenario Manager
Scenario summary report
Solver
Constraints
Grouping
Report filter
Slicer

concepts review

1. To open the *Sort* dialog:

   a. On the *Data* tab, in the *Sort & Filter* group, click the **Sort** button.

   b. On the *Home* tab, in the *Editing* group, click the **Sort & Filter** button and click **Custom Sort...**

   c. Right-click any cell in the data set, point to **Sort,** and click **Custom Sort...**

   d. All of the above

2. Which of these options is not available from the *Text Filters* menu?

   a. *Equals*

   b. *Does Not Equal*

   c. *Greater Than*

   d. *Contains*

3. When setting up the criteria range for Advanced Filter, type criteria in separate rows if data must meet any one of the criteria to be included in the filter.

   a. True

   b. False

4. Before adding subtotals with the *Subtotal* command, you must _____ the data.

   a. Filter

   b. Outline

   c. Sort

   d. Group

5. The *Subtotal* command uses which function to create subtotals?

   a. SUM

   b. SUMIFS

   c. SUBTOTAL

   d. OUTLINE

6. If you want to summarize data without using an outline format or including formulas, use which command?

   a. *Auto Outline*

   b. *Outline*

   c. *Subtotal*

   d. *Consolidate*

7. When you show a scenario, any changing cells that included formulas originally will be converted to values.

   a. True

   b. False

8. To install Solver, open the *Excel Options* dialog, and go to which section?

   a. Customize Ribbon

   b. General

   c. Add-Ins

   d. Trust Center

9. When setting up the Solver parameters, which of these cells must include a formula?

   a. Objective

   b. Variable cells

   c. Constraint

   d. All of the above

10. When a PivotTable's source data updates, the PivotTable and PivotChart update automatically.

    a. True

    b. False

projects

Data files for projects can be found on
www.mhhe.com/office2013skills

skill review **8.1**

In this project, you will analyze sales data using consolidation, subtotals, outlines, conditional formatting, advanced filters, PivotTables, and PivotCharts.

Skills needed to complete this project:

- Using Consolidate to Create Subtotals (Skill 8.8)
- Sorting Data on Multiple Criteria (Skill 8.4)
- Adding Subtotals (Skill 8.7)
- Creating an Outline (Skill 8.9)
- Creating New Conditional Formatting Rules (Skill 8.1)
- Filtering and Sorting Using Cell Attributes (Skill 8.3)
- Managing Conditional Formatting Rules (Skill 8.2)
- Using Advanced Filter (Skill 8.6)
- Refreshing Data in a PivotTable (Skill 8.15)
- Adding a Calculated Field to a PivotTable (Skill 8.16)
- Changing the Look of a PivotTable (Skill 8.19)
- Filtering PivotTable Data (Skill 8.18)
- Filtering Data in a PivotChart (Skill 8.20)
- Changing the Look of a PivotChart (Skill 8.21)

1. Open the start file **EX2013-SkillReview-8-1** and resave the file as:
   `[your initials]EX-SkillReview-8-1`

2. If the workbook opens in Protected View, click the **Enable Editing** button in the Message Bar at the top of the workbook so you can modify the workbook.

3. Use Consolidate to create a summary of the sales data by region. The summary will be located on the *Analysis* worksheet.

   a. Go to the **Analysis** worksheet and select cell **A2.**

   b. On the *Data* tab, in the *Data Tools* group, click the **Consolidate** button.

   c. Verify that **Sum** is selected in the *Function* box.

   d. If there are any references in the *All references* box, click each and then click the **Delete** button to remove them.

   e. Click in the **Reference** box and then click the **Sales Data** worksheet tab. Click and drag to select cells **C3:E67.**

   f. Click both the **Top row** and **Left column** check boxes.

   g. Click **OK.**

   h. On the *Analysis* worksheet, delete cells **B2:B10,** allowing the other cells to shift left.

4. Sort the sales data alphabetically by region and then by last name.

   a. Go to the **Sales Data** worksheet and click any cell in the data set.

   b. On the *Data* tab, in the *Sort & Filter* group, click the **Sort** button.

   c. In the *Sort* dialog, expand the **Sort by** list and select **Region.**

d. Click the **Add Level** button.

e. Expand the **Then by** list and select **Last Name.**

f. Click **OK.**

5. Add subtotals to the data to calculate the total commission earned for each sales associate.

a. On the *Data* tab, in the *Outline* group, click the **Subtotal** button.

b. Expand the **At each change in** list and select **Last Name.**

c. Verify that **Sum** is selected in the *Use function* box.

d. Verify that there is a check mark next to **Commission Earned** in the *Add subtotal to* box.

e. Click **OK.**

6. Copy the subtotal data to the *Analysis* worksheet.

a. On the *Sales Data* worksheet, click the outline level **2** button to collapse the list so only the total commission earned for each sales associate is visible. This will make it easier to copy the data.

b. Select cells **A3:G77** and copy them to the Clipboard. Do not include the *Grand Total* row (row 78).

c. Go to the **Analysis** worksheet and paste the copied data beginning in cell **A13.**

7. Notice that when you paste the subtotaled data, Excel removes the subtotal grouping, but keeps the subtotal rows and formulas. You can use the *Outline* command to re-create groups based on the subtotal formulas.

a. Click any cell in the data range.

b. On the *Data* tab, in the *Outline* group, click the **Group** button arrow and select **Auto Outline.**

c. Click the outline level **1** button to collapse the list so only the total commission earned for each sales associate is visible.

8. Remove the subtotals from the *Sales Data* worksheet.

a. Go to the **Sales Data** worksheet and click any cell in the data set.

b. On the *Data* tab, in the *Outline* group, click the **Subtotal** button.

c. In the *Subtotal* dialog, click the **Remove All** button.

9. On the *Sales Data* worksheet, create a new conditional formatting rule to apply an icon set to the values in the *Commission Earned* column.

a. Select cells **G4:G67.**

b. On the *Home* tab, in the *Styles* group, click the **Conditional Formatting** button. Click **New Rule...**

c. In the *Select a Rule Type* box, verify that **Format all cells based on their values** is selected.

d. In the *Edit the Rule Description* box, expand the **Format Style** list and select **Icon Sets.**

e. Expand the **Icon Style** list and select **3 Stars.**

f. In the *Display each icon according to these rules* section, expand the first **Type** list and select **Number.**

g. In the first *Value* box type **10000** to display a gold star when the cell value is greater than or equal to 10,000.

h. Expand the second **Type** list and select **Number.**

i. In the second *Value* box, type **5000** to display a half gold star when the cell value is less than 10,000 and greater than or equal to 5,000.

j. Click **OK.**

10. Sort the sales data so commissions with the gold star appear first.

    a. Click cell **G4**.

    b. On the *Data* tab, in the *Sort & Filter* group, click the **Filter** button to display the AutoFilter arrows for the data columns.

    c. Click the AutoFilter arrow at the top of the **Commission Earned** column. Point to **Sort by Color** and select the solid gold star.

11. Go to the **Sales Data Filter** worksheet.

12. Delete the conditional formatting rule that applies a font format to cells where the value is above average.

    a. On the *Home* tab, in the *Styles* group, click the **Conditional Formatting** button. Click **Manage Rules...** to open the Conditional Formatting Rules Manager.

    b. If necessary, expand the **Show formatting rules for** list and select **This Worksheet.**

    c. Select the **Above Average** rule and click the **Delete Rule** button.

    d. Click **OK**.

13. Use the Advanced Filter feature to find sales greater than $115,000 for George Anderson or Xin Zhu.

    a. Insert four new rows above row 3, so the column label row is now row 7 and there are five blank rows between the title and the column labels.

    b. Copy the range **A7:G7** (the column labels) and paste in **A3:G3**.

    c. Enter the filter criteria in **A4:G5** as follows:

        i. In **A4**, type: `George`

        ii. In **B4**, type: `Anderson`

        iii. In **E4**, type: `>115000`

        iv. In **A5**, type: `Xin`

        v. In **B5**, type: `Zhu`

        vi. In **E5**, type: `>115000`

    d. Click any cell in the data set.

    e. On the *Data* tab, in the *Sort & Filter* group, click the **Advanced** button.

    f. Verify that the **Filter the list, in place** radio button is selected.

    g. The *List range* box should display $A$7:$G$71. If it does not, click in the **List range** box and then click and drag to select cells **A7:G71.**

    h. Click in the **Criteria range** box. Click and drag to select the range **A3:G5** as the criteria range.

    i. Click **OK.**

14. The data in the *Sales Data* worksheet has changed since the PivotTable was created. Refresh the PivotTable to reflect the changes.

    a. Go to the **PivotTable** worksheet and click anywhere in the PivotTable.

    b. On the *PivotTable Tools Analyze* tab, in the *Data* group, click the **Refresh** button.

    c. In the *PivotTable Fields* pane, click **Last Name** to add the *Last Name* field to the *Rows* box.

    d. In the *Rows* box, click **Last Name** and move it above **Client.**

15. Add a calculated field to determine the average commission rate for each row in the PivotTable.

    a. On the *PivotTable Tools Analyze* tab, in the *Calculations* group, click the **Fields, Items, & Sets** button.

    b. Click **Calculated Field...**

c. In the *Name* box, type: `Average Commission Calculated`

d. In the *Fields* box, click **Commission Earned** and then click the **Insert Field** button.

e. Type: `/`

f. In the *Fields* box, double-click **Annual Sales.**

g. The final formula in the *Formula* box should look like this:

`='Commission Earned'/'Annual Sales'`

h. Click **OK** to add the calculated field to the PivotTable.

i. Click any cell in the new calculated column.

j. On the *PivotTable Tools Analyze* tab, in the *Active Field* group, click the **Field Settings** button to open the *Value Field Settings* dialog.

k. In the *Custom Name* box, type: `Average Commission`

l. Click the **Number Format** button at the bottom left corner of the dialog. In the *Category* list, click **Percentage.** If necessary, type **2** in the *Decimal places* box.

m. Click **OK.**

n. Click **OK** again to close the *Value Field Settings* dialog.

16. Apply a Quick Style to the PivotTable.

a. Click anywhere in the PivotTable.

b. On the *PivotTable Tools Design* tab, in the *PivotTable Styles* group, click the **More** button to expand the gallery.

c. Click **Pivot Style Medium 4.**

17. Use slicers to filter the PivotTable by region to show only the NE2 region.

a. On the *PivotTable Tools Analyze* tab, in the *Filter* group, click the **Insert Slicer** button.

b. In the *Insert Slicers* dialog, click the **Region** check box. Click **OK.**

c. In the *Region* slicer, click the **NE2** button.

18. Filter the PivotChart data to show only the NE1 and NE2 regions.

a. Go to the **PivotChart** worksheet and select the chart.

b. On the *PivotChart Tools Analyze* tab, in the *Filter* group, click the **Insert Slicer** button.

c. In the *Insert Slicers* dialog, click the **Region** check box. Click **OK.**

d. In the *Region* slicer, click the **NE1** button. Press the `Ctrl` key and click the **NE2** button.

19. Apply a Quick Style to the PivotChart.

a. Select the PivotChart.

b. On the *PivotChart Tools Design* tab, in the *Chart Styles* group, click the **More** button to expand the gallery.

c. Click **Style 8.**

20. Save and close the workbook.

skill review 8.2

In this project, you will use what-if analysis to analyze real estate options and inventory problems for a sporting goods store. This project uses named ranges extensively. For your reference, the named range list was pasted in the *Names* worksheet.

Skills needed to complete this project:

- Creating What-If Analysis Scenarios (Skill 8.11)
- Creating Scenario Summary Reports (Skill 8.12)
- Creating New Conditional Formatting Rules (Skill 8.1)
- Managing Conditional Formatting Rules (Skill 8.2)
- Activating the Solver Add-Inn (Skill 8.13)
- Using Solver (Skill 8.14)
- Refreshing Data in a PivotTable (Skill 8.15)
- Adding a Calculated Field to a PivotTable (Skill 8.16)
- Filtering Data in a PivotChart (Skill 8.20)
- Changing the Look of a PivotChart (Skill 8.21)

1. Open the start file **EX2013-SkillReview-8-2** and resave the file as:
   [your initials]EX-SkillReview-8-2

2. If the workbook opens in Protected View, click the **Enable Editing** button in the Message Bar at the top of the workbook so you can modify the workbook.

3. The store owner is considering buying a new building. The current loan terms are listed in cells B2:B7 on the *Building Loan* worksheet. Create a scenario to save the original loan terms and then create two more scenarios for alternate down payments.

   a. On the *Data* tab, in the *Data Tools* group, click the **What-If Analysis** button and select **Scenario Manager...**

   b. Click the **Add...** button to create a new scenario.

   c. In the *Scenario* name box, type: **Original Loan Terms**

   d. Click in the **By Changing Cells** box and then click cell **B3** in the *Building Loan* worksheet.

   e. Click **OK**.

   f. For this scenario, leave the *DownPayment* value at 200000. Click **Add** to add another scenario.

   g. In the *Scenario* name box, type: **Large Down Payment**

   h. Verify that **B3** is listed in the *By Changing Cells* box. Click **OK**.

   i. Enter **500000** in the *DownPayment* box. Click **Add** to add another scenario.

   j. In the *Scenario* name box, type: **Small Down Payment**

   k. Verify that **B3** is listed in the *By Changing Cells* box. Click **OK**.

   l. Enter **100000** in the *DownPayment* box. Click **OK** to return to the Scenario Manager.

4. Show the *Large Down Payment* scenario.

   a. In the *Scenarios* box, select **Large Down Payment.**

   b. Click the **Show** button.

5. Create a Scenario Summary Report.

   a. Click the **Summary...** button.

   b. In the *Scenario Summary* dialog, verify that the **Scenario summary** radio button is selected and that **B8** is listed in the *Result cells* box.

   c. Click **OK**.

6. Review the results and then return to the *Building Loan* worksheet.

7. The data in B11:M21 show the monthly payments for combinations of interest rates and loan lengths. Add custom conditional formatting to highlight the highest monthly payments.

   a. Select cells **C12:M21.**

   b. On the *Home* tab, in the *Styles* group, click the **Conditional Formatting** button and select **New Rule...**

   c. In the *Select a Rule Type* box, click **Format only top or bottom ranked values.**

   d. In the *Edit the Rule Description* box, change **10** to **3** to highlight the three largest values.

   e. Click the **Format...** button to define the format.

   f. On the *Font* tab, expand the **Color** palette and select the standard **Red** color.

   g. On the *Border* tab, expand the **Color** palette and select the standard **Red** color. Click the **Outline** button.

   h. Click **OK.**

   i. Review the format in the *Preview* box and then click **OK** to apply the new conditional format to the selected cells.

8. Create another custom conditional formatting rule to highlight the lowest monthly payments.

   a. On the *Home* tab, in the *Styles* group, click the **Conditional Formatting** button and select **New Rule...**

   b. In the *Select a Rule Type* box, click **Format only top or bottom ranked values.**

   c. In the *Edit the Rule Description* box, expand the drop-down list and select **Bottom.** Change **10** to **3** to highlight the three smallest values.

   d. Click the **Format...** button to define the format.

   e. On the *Font* tab, expand the **Color** palette and select the standard **Green** color.

   f. On the *Border* tab, expand the **Color** palette and select the standard **Green** color. Click the **Outline** button.

   g. Click **OK.**

   h. Review the format in the *Preview* box and then click **OK** to apply the new conditional format to the selected cells.

9. Create another custom conditional formatting rule to apply an icon to all the values.

   a. On the *Home* tab, in the *Styles* group, click the **Conditional Formatting** button. Click **New Rule...**

   b. In the *Select a Rule Type* box, verify that **Format all cells based on their values** is selected.

   c. In the *Edit the Rule Description* box, expand the **Format Style** list and select **Icon Sets.**

   d. Expand the **Icon Style** list and select **3 Symbols (Uncircled).**

   e. Click the **Reverse Icon Order** button.

   f. Click **OK.**

10. On the *Home* tab, in the *Cells* group, click the **Format** button and select **AutoFit Column Width.**

11. Manage the conditional formatting rules so the icon rule is applied last and will not be applied to cells that meet one of the other conditions.

    a. On the *Home* tab, in the *Styles* group, click the **Conditional Formatting** button. Click **Manage Rules...**

    b. In the Conditional Formatting Rules Manager, expand the **Show formatting rules for** list and select **This Worksheet.**

c. Click the **Icon Set** rule and click the **Move Down** button twice so the rule is last in the list.

d. Click the **Stop If True** check box next to the *Bottom 3* rule.

e. Click the **Stop If True** check box next to the *Top 3* rule.

f. Click **OK.**

12. To reduce inventory before moving to the new building, the store wants to run a 20% off sale for a limited number of items in stock. Use Solver to find the optimal number of items to put on sale for the maximum profit possible.

13. If necessary, install the Solver add-in. If Solver is already installed, skip to Step 14.

a. Click the **File** tab.

b. Click **Options** to open the *Excel Options* dialog.

c. Click **Add-Ins.**

d. Near the bottom of the window, the *Manage* box should display *Excel Add-Ins.* If it does not, expand the list and select **Excel Add-Ins** and then click **Go...**

e. In the *Add-Ins* dialog, click the **Solver Add-in** check box.

f. Click **OK.**

14. Before setting up the Solver parameters, go to the **Inventory** worksheet and review the formulas in cells **C1** and **F2:F5.** Solver will find the maximum profit possible (C1) by changing the number of items in the named range *SaleStock* (J10:J34) within the constraints imposed on the formulas in cells F2:F5.

a. Click cell **C1.** This is the *Objective* cell containing the formula to calculate profit:

`=SUMPRODUCT(SalePrice,SaleStock)-SUMPRODUCT(Cost,SaleStock)`

b. On the *Data* tab, in the *Analysis* group, click **Solver.**

c. Verify that **$C$1** is entered in the *Set Objective* box.

d. In the *By Changing Variable Cells* box, enter the range `J10:J34` or use the named range `SaleStock`.

e. Click **Add** to add the first constraint: The total number of balls on sale (F2) must be less than or equal to the value in cell G2 (25). In the *Add Constraint* dialog, enter **F2** in the *Cell Reference* box. Verify <= as the comparison operator. Enter **G2** in the *Constraint* box. Click **Add** to add another constraint.

f. The total number of shoes on sale (F3) must be less than or equal to the value in cell G3 (50). Enter **F3** in the *Cell Reference* box. Verify <= as the comparison operator. Enter **G3** in the *Constraint* box. Click **Add** to add another constraint.

g. The total number of items on sale (F4) must be less than or equal to the value in cell G4 (75). Enter **F4** in the *Cell Reference* box. Verify <= as the comparison operator. Enter **G4** in the *Constraint* box. Click **Add** to add another constraint.

h. Items from the manufacturer Nuke cannot be on sale this week. The value in cell F5 must be equal to the value in cell G5 (0). Enter **F5** in the *Cell Reference* box. Expand the comparison operator list and select =. Enter **G5** in the *Constraint* box. Click **Add** to add another constraint.

i. The value of each cell in the *SaleStock* range (J10:J34) must be less than or equal to the value in the *Stock* range (I10:I34). Enter **SaleStock** in the *Cell Reference* box. Verify <= as the comparison operator. Enter **Stock** in the *Constraint* box. Click **Add** to add another constraint.

j. The *SaleStock* values must be whole numbers. Enter `SaleStock` in the *Cell Reference* box. Expand the comparison operator list and select **int**. Click **OK** to return to the *Solver Parameters* dialog.

k. The default solving method, GRG Nonlinear, will not find an appropriate solution. Expand the list and select **Simplex LP** instead.

l. Carefully review all the settings in the *Solver Parameters* dialog and then click the **Solve** button.

m. Keep the Solver solution. In the *Solver Results* dialog, verify that the **Keep Solver Solution** radio button is selected. Click **OK**.

15. Now that the values in the *Inventory* worksheet have been updated by Solver, you need to refresh the PivotTable and PivotChart.

a. Go to the **Inventory PivotChart** worksheet and click anywhere in the PivotTable.

b. On the *PivotTable Tools Analyze* tab, in the *Data* group, click the **Refresh** button.

16. Add a calculated field to summarize the remaining items in stock after the sale in the PivotTable.

a. On the *PivotTable Tools Analyze* tab, in the *Calculations* group, click the **Fields, Items, & Sets** button.

b. Click **Calculated Field...**

c. In the *Name* box, type: `Remaining Stock`

d. In the *Fields* box, click **Stock** and then click the **Insert Field** button.

e. Type: -

f. In the *Fields* box, double-click **Items on Sale.**

g. The final formula in the *Formula* box should look like this:

`=Stock-'Items on Sale'`

h. Click **OK** to add the calculated field to the PivotTable.

17. Apply a Quick Style to the PivotTable.

a. Click anywhere in the PivotTable.

b. On the *PivotTable Tools Design* tab, in the *PivotTable Styles* group, click the **More** button to expand the gallery.

c. Click **Pivot Style Light 2.**

18. Filter the PivotChart data to show data for a single manufacturer.

a. Click the PivotChart to select it.

b. On the *PivotChart Tools Analyze* tab, in the *Filter* group, click the **Insert Slicer** button.

c. In the *Insert Slicers* dialog, click the **Manufacturer** check box. Click **OK**.

d. In the *Manufacturer* slicer, click the **Cole** button.

19. Change the PivotChart to a stacked column chart.

a. Select the PivotChart.

b. On the *PivotChart Tools Design* tab, in the *Type* group, click the **Change Chart Type** button.

c. Click **Stacked Column** (the second column type at the top of the *Change Chart Type* dialog).

d. Click **OK**.

20. In the *Manufacturer* slicer, press Ctrl and click the **Assuage** and **Zinks** buttons to add these manufacturers to the PivotChart.

21. Save and close the workbook.

challenge yourself 8.3

In this project, you will analyze grades for a spreadsheets class and use conditional formatting to highlight grades where you suspect students are cheating. You will work with a PivotTable and PivotChart to analyze grades by section and create scenarios to compare the effects of changing the grading scale.

Skills needed to complete this project:

- Using Consolidate to Create Subtotals (Skill 8.8)
- Sorting Data on Multiple Criteria (Skill 8.4)
- Using Advanced Filter (Skill 8.6)
- Creating an Outline (Skill 8.9)
- Creating What-If Analysis Scenarios (Skill 8.11)
- Creating Scenario Summary Reports (Skill 8.12)
- Creating New Conditional Formatting Rules (Skill 8.1)
- Filtering and Sorting Using Cell Attributes (Skill 8.3)
- Refreshing Data in a PivotTable (Skill 8.15)
- Adding a Calculated Field to a PivotTable (Skill 8.16)
- Changing the Look of a PivotTable (Skill 8.19)
- Changing the Look of a PivotChart (Skill 8.21)
- Filtering Data in a PivotChart (Skill 8.20)

1. Open the start file **EX2013-ChallengeYourself-8-3** and resave the file as:
   `[your initials]EX-ChallengeYourself-8-3`

2. If the workbook opens in Protected View, click the **Enable Editing** button in the Message Bar at the top of the workbook so you can modify the workbook.

3. Use Consolidate to create a summary of the grades by section.

   a. Place the summary in cell **A2** the *Summary by Section* worksheet.

   b. Use the **Average** function.

   c. Consolidate data from the cell range **C3:O26** in the **Gradebook** worksheet.

   d. Use labels from both the top row and the left column.

   e. Do not create links to the source data.

   f. If necessary, Autofit the columns.

   g. On the *Summary by Section* worksheet, center and merge the title across cells **A1:M1**.

4. Sort the data in the *Gradebook* worksheet alphabetically by section and then by last name.

5. Use Advanced Filter to find students who had less than 80 on the midterm *or* had less than 80 on the final.

   a. Copy cells **A3:P3** and paste them starting in cell **A29** for use as the header row in the criteria range.

   b. Enter the criteria in the criteria range to find rows where the value in the **Midterm** column is **<80** *or* the value in the **Final** column is **<80**.

   c. Use Advanced Filter and copy the filtered data to the range beginning with cell **A34.**

6. Manually create an outline group by columns for **D3:M26** and collapse the group so the individual chapter assignments are hidden.

7. Create and show scenarios for different grading scales.

    a. Create a scenario named `Original Scale`. Include cells **S5, R6, S6, R7, S7, R8, S8,** and **R9.** For this scenario, do not change any of the cell values. Note that these cells currently include formulas which will be converted to values when you show a scenario.

    b. Create a second scenario named `Generous Scale`. Change the values for the following cells:

	R	S	T
4	High	Low	Grade
5	100	90	A
6	89	80	B
7	79	70	C
8	69	60	D
9	59		F

    c. Create a third scenario named `Difficult Scale`. Change the values for the following cells:

	R	S	T
4	High	Low	Grade
5	100	95	A
6	94	89	B
7	88	83	C
8	82	77	D
9	76		F

    d. Show the **Generous Scale** scenario.

    e. Show the **Difficult Scale** scenario.

8. Create a scenario summary report showing the changes to cells **P4:P26** (students' final grades).

9. Apply custom conditional formatting and filtering to the data in the *Suspect Grades* worksheet to find suspicious grades.

    a. Apply custom conditional formatting to the data so duplicate values for each assignment use **Red, Accent 2** and **bold** font formatting. You will need to create 10 separate conditional formatting rules—one for each chapter assignment.

    b. Filter each of the columns to show only cells with the red font color. Notice that as you work through the columns, some columns no longer include *Filter by Color* as an option, because all of the cells without red text have been hidden by the filters in previous columns.

    c. When you are finished, there should be five rows visible with two groups of students who suspiciously scored the same on every assignment.

10. The source data for the PivotTable have changed. Go to the **PivotTable** worksheet and update the PivotTable.

11. Add a calculated field named **Difference** to the PivotTable to calculate the difference between the final average and the midterm average for each section. The formula in the *Insert Calculated Field* dialog should look like this: `=Final-Midterm`

12. Apply the **Pivot Style Dark 5** Quick Style to the PivotTable.

13. Change the PivotChart to a combo chart with the **Sum of Difference** series as a line chart on the secondary axis and the other two series as clustered column charts on the on primary axis.

14. Apply the **Style 6** PivotChart Quick Style to the PivotChart.

15. Add a slicer to the PivotChart to filter the data by the **Grade** field. If necessary, move the slicer so it doesn't cover the PivotChart. Display data where the grade is **D** or **F** only.

16. Save and close the workbook.

challenge yourself 8.4

In this project, you will use scenarios and a scenario summary to analyze car purchasing options. A large amount of data about car gas consumption was downloaded from **https://explore.data.gov/d/9un4-5bz7** and are explained at this Web site: **http://www.epa.gov/greenvehicles/Aboutratings.do.** You will use custom filtering to find the data you are interested in and copy it from this very large data set to another worksheet. You will then use Advanced Filter, conditional formatting, sorting, and subtotals to further analyze this subset of data. You will manipulate a PivotTable created from the main vehicle data set. Finally, you will use Solver to solve a business problem to help you pay for your new car.

Skills needed to complete this project:

- Creating What-If Analysis Scenarios (Skill 8.11)
- Creating Scenario Summary Reports (Skill 8.12)
- Creating a Custom Filter (Skill 8.5)
- Using Advanced Filter (Skill 8.6)
- Creating New Conditional Formatting Rules (Skill 8.1)
- Sorting Data on Multiple Criteria (Skill 8.4)
- Adding Subtotals (Skill 8.7)
- Changing the Look of a PivotTable (Skill 8.19)
- Filtering PivotTable Data (Skill 8.18)
- Activating the Solver Add-Inn (Skill 8.13)
- Using Solver (Skill 8.14)

1. Open the start file **EX2013-ChallengeYourself-8-4** and resave the file as:
   `[your initials]EX-ChallengeYourself-8-4`

2. If the workbook opens in Protected View, click the Enable Editing button in the Message Bar at the top of the workbook so you can modify the workbook.

3. You want to purchase a new car. Your current car is worth $2,500 as a trade-in. The base sticker price on the car you want is $21,595. The first financing offer from the dealer is 1.9% APR for 24 months with no cash back. The original financing offer terms are listed in cells A3:B9 on the *Car Loan* worksheet. Cell B10 contains a formula with a PMT function to calculate the monthly payment. Use what-if analysis tools to compare financing options. Create scenarios to compare financing options for the car loan.

    a. Create names for the following cells to make the scenarios easier to follow:

        Name cell **B3**: `Price`

        Name cell **B4**: `TradeIn`

        Name cell **B5**: `CashBack`

        Name cell **B6**: `Loan`

Name cell **B8**: `Months`

Name cell **B9**: `APR`

Name cell **B10**: `Payment`

Name cell **B12**: `TotalCost`

   b. Create a scenario named `Original Financing` to save the original values in cells **B3, B5, B8,** and **B9.**

   c. Create a second scenario named `Intermediate Car`. Change the values as follows:

Cell **B3**: `33999`

Cell **B5**: `1500`

Cell **B8**: `36`

Cell **B9**: `2.4%`

   d. Show the **Intermediate Car** scenario to verify your data entry.

   e. Create a third scenario named `Luxury Car`. Change the values as follows:

Cell **B3**: `56500`

Cell **B5**: `2500`

Cell **B8**: `60`

Cell **B9**: `3.9%`

   f. Show the **Luxury Car** scenario to verify your data entry.

4. Create a scenario summary report to compare the results for cells **B10** (the monthly payment) and **B12** (the total cost of the car including interest).

5. The data in the *MPG Data* worksheet were downloaded from the Web site **https://explore.data.gov/d/9un4-5bz7** and are explained at this Web site: **http://www.epa.gov/greenvehicles/Aboutratings.do.** The greenhouse gas scores range from 0 to 10, where 10 is best. The vehicles with the best scores on both air pollution and greenhouse gas receive the *SmartWay* designation. Use custom filtering to find cars in this data set that meet your criteria and then copy the smaller data set to another worksheet where you can work with it further.

   a. Go to the **MPG Data** worksheet and display the AutoFilter arrows for the data set.

   b. Create a custom number filter to show only rows where the greenhouse gas score is greater than or equal to **8.**

   c. Create another custom number filter to show only rows where the highway MPG is greater than or equal to **35.**

   d. Create a custom text filter to show only rows where the *Trans* column contains the word **auto.**

   e. At this point, the list of more than 2,000 cars should be filtered down to just 27 records.

   f. Copy the filtered data to cell **A1** in the **My Car Data** worksheet. Be sure to include the heading row and paste keeping the source columns widths.

6. On the *My Car Data* worksheet, use Advanced Filter to copy a subset of data to another location on this worksheet.

   a. Copy cells **A1:O1** and paste them below the data set in row **31.**

   b. In cell **A30**, type: `Criteria`

   c. Set up the criteria in the row(s) below row 31. Find cars where the value in the **Fuel** column is **gasoline** *and* the value in the **Hwy MPG** column is **greater than 35.**

   d. In cell **A34**, type: `Filtered Data`

e. Use Advanced Filter to find the rows that meet the criteria and copy the filtered data to another location beginning in cell **A35.**

f. Thirteen rows should have been copied from the main data set to cells **A36:O48.**

7. Format the filtered data set (cells A35:O48) as a table. Use **Table Style Light 9.** Be careful ***not*** to include row 34 in the table data range.

8. Insert a new table column to the left of the **Greenhouse Gas Score** column.

   a. Copy the values from cells **M36:M48** to **N36:N48.**

   b. Type this column label in cell **N35: Cmb MPG Icon**

9. Apply a new custom conditional formatting rule to cells **N36:N48** to show the **4 Ratings** icon set. Show the icon only.

10. Sort the table first alphabetically by the values in the **Model** column and then by icon in the **Cmb MPG Icon** column so the **Signal Meter With Four Filled Bars** icon appears at the top and the **Signal Meter With One Filled Bar** icon appears at the bottom.

11. Go back to the main data set at the top of the *My Car Data* worksheet and add subtotals for each change in **Model** to calculate the **average** for the following: **Air Pollution Score, City MPG, Hwy MPG,** and **Cmb MPG.**

12. Collapse the data to show just the total rows.

13. Go to the **MPG PivotTable** worksheet. This sheet includes a PivotTable created from the data on the *MPG Data* worksheet.

   a. Apply the **Pivot Style Light 14** Quick Style to the PivotTable.

   b. Display a slicer for the **SmartWay** field and show only data where the *SmartWay* value is **Yes.**

14. To pay for the new car, you've decided to start a bakery business out of your home kitchen. You have limited capital and capacity, so you need to make wise decisions about which products to bake each day. Go to the **Bakery Business** worksheet. Cell B1 uses a SUMPRODUCT formula to calculate profit. Carefully review the assumptions and formulas in this worksheet before entering the following Solver parameters:

   a. Find the maximum possible profit (cell **B1**) by changing the values in cells **C7:C10.**

   b. The working hours required (**B3**) must be less than or equal to the number of working hours in the day (**D3**).

   c. The total cost of ingredients (**B4**) must be less than or equal to the available capital (**D4**).

   d. For each item in the range **C7:C10,** the number of items baked cannot exceed the maximum capacity available per day as defined in cells **F7:F10.** This restriction requires four separate constraints in the *Solver Parameters* dialog.

   e. The items in the variable cell range **C7:C10** must be whole numbers.

   f. There should be a total of seven constraints.

   g. Run Solver and accept the Solver solution.

15. Save and close the workbook.

In this project, you will update data for selling back textbooks with your own data and then make copies of the worksheet to analyze with a variety of methods.

Skills needed to complete this project:

- Creating What-If Analysis Scenarios (Skill 8.11)
- Creating Scenario Summary Reports (Skill 8.12)
- Refreshing Data in a PivotTable (Skill 8.15)
- Adding a Calculated Field to a PivotTable (Skill 8.16)
- Changing the Look of a PivotChart (Skill 8.21)
- Filtering Data in a PivotChart (Skill 8.20)
- Creating New Conditional Formatting Rules (Skill 8.1)
- Managing Conditional Formatting Rules (Skill 8.2)
- Filtering and Sorting Using Cell Attributes (Skill 8.3)
- Sorting Data on Multiple Criteria (Skill 8.4)
- Adding Subtotals (Skill 8.7)

1. Open the start file **EX2013-OnYourOwn-8-5** and resave the file as:
   `[your initials]EX-OnYourOwn-8-5`

2. If the workbook opens in Protected View, click the **Enable Editing** button in the Message Bar at the top of the workbook so you can modify the workbook.

3. Update the data in the *Book Inventory* worksheet to reflect your own textbook inventory. Update the sell back rate in cell B2 to reflect the average rate that you receive when selling back textbooks.

4. Create a few scenarios using different sell back rates and generate a scenario summary report.

5. Once you've updated the data, you'll need to refresh the PivotTable and PivotChart in the Pivot worksheet.

6. The PivotTable data source includes the total row from the *Book Inventory* data, but it should not. Update the data source.

7. Add a calculated field to the PivotTable to calculate the difference between the book costs and the resell values.

8. Change the PivotChart type to something other than a combo chart. Choose a chart type that is appropriate for the data.

9. Add slicers to filter the PivotChart.

10. Create a copy of the *Book Inventory* worksheet.
    a. Create custom conditional formatting rules to highlight the books with the highest or lowest resale values.
    b. Create a custom formatting rule using an icon set or data bars to compare resale values.
    c. Use the Conditional Formatting Rules Manager as necessary to re-order the rules.
    d. Sort the data based on cell attributes applied by the conditional formatting rules.

11. Create another copy of the *Book Inventory* worksheet.
    a. Delete the *Total* row.
    b. Sort the data by subject matter and year published.
    c. Add subtotals to calculate the total cost and resell value at each change in subject matter.

12. Save and close the workbook.

fix it 8.6

In this project, you will fix errors in financial data for a restaurant chain to find which locations are the lowest performers and correct the Solver parameters to set target sales goals for next year using reasonable constraints. You will create the missing scenario summary report.

Skills needed to complete this project:

- Managing Conditional Formatting Rules (Skill 8.2)
- Filtering and Sorting Using Cell Attributes (Skill 8.3)
- Sorting Data on Multiple Criteria (Skill 8.4)
- Using Advanced Filter (Skill 8.6)
- Creating a Custom Filter (Skill 8.5)
- Refreshing Data in a PivotTable (Skill 8.15)
- Filtering Data in a PivotChart (Skill 8.20)
- Changing the Look of a PivotChart (Skill 8.21)
- Creating What-If Analysis Scenarios (Skill 8.11)
- Activating the Solver Add-In (Skill 8.13)
- Using Solver (Skill 8.14)
- Creating Scenario Summary Reports (Skill 8.12)

1. Open the start file **EX2013-FixIt-8-6** and resave the file as:
   `[your initials] EX-FixIt-8-6`

2. If the workbook opens in Protected View, click the **Enable Editing** button in the Message Bar at the top of the workbook so you can modify the workbook.

3. There are multiple conditional formatting rules applied to cells in the *Financial Data* worksheet. Make changes to the conditional formatting rules on this worksheet only.

   a. There should be three conditional formatting rules: a Top 2 rule, a Bottom 2 rule, and an Icon Set rule. Delete all the extra rules.

   b. Correct the cell range for the remaining rules. All the rules should be applied to cells **D5:G20.**

   c. Fix the remaining conditional formatting rules so if the value of the cell is in the top 2 values or the bottom 2 values, the icon rule is not applied.

4. Now that the conditional formatting rules have been fixed, sort the data alphabetically by the value in the *Location* column and then by icon in the *Quarter 1* column so rows with the up arrow are at the top and rows with the bottom arrow are at the bottom.

   a. If necessary, be sure to click a cell in the data set to de-select the D5:G20 cell range or the sort will be applied to only the selected cells and your data will be mixed up.

   b. You will need to use the *Sort* dialog as this requires a multi-level sort.

   c. If the sort is performed correctly, the data will be sorted by location, and then within each location, by the icon in the *Quarter 1* column.

5. An advanced filter should be performed to find any locations with a profit/loss for *any* quarter less than or equal to 10,000. The results should be copied to cell **I4.**

   a. The criteria range beginning in cell **A23** is set up incorrectly. The criteria for this filter should include values <10,000 in *Quarter 1 or* <10,000 in *Quarter 2 or* <10,000 in *Quarter 3 or* <10,000 in *Quarter 4.*

   b. The previous attempt at using Advanced Filter used the wrong *Criteria range.*

c. The previous attempt at using Advanced Filter resulted in an incorrect *Copy to* range. Be sure to start the new *Copy to* range in cell **I4.**

d. AutoFit column **K.**

6. Apply a custom number filter to the main data set to show only stores with a profit greater than $55,000 in *Quarter 4.* You will need to select the data range **A4:G20** before enabling *Filter.*

7. The data underlying the PivotTable have been updated since it was created. Update the PivotTable and PivotChart.

8. A slicer should be visible so the user can filter the data in the PivotChart by *Performance Status.* Use the slicer to show only data where the *Performance Status* is **Below Average.**

9. Change the PivotChart style to use **Style 8.**

10. Conditional formatting rules have been applied to the data on the *Financial Targets* worksheet to highlight the two lowest values for each quarter. However, the values for *Quarter 4* are not highlighted. Edit one of the rules in the Conditional Formatting Rules Manager to fix the problem.

11. The *Financial Targets* worksheet has two scenarios for possible sales targets for next year. Show the **20% Increase for All Locations** scenario.

12. The *Financial Targets* worksheet has been set up with Solver parameters to find reasonable target sales goals for the two worst locations for each quarter. Some locations had shown very uneven profit/loss results from quarter-to-quarter. The Solver parameters include constraints to limit the new sales target for each cell to less than or equal to the average quarterly sales for that location.

    Fix the Solver parameters to find the **maximum** possible value for the overall average quarter income (cell **G24**) by changing the values in cells **C10, C15, D15, D19, E15, E19, F10,** and **F19** within the following constraints. It may be easier to delete all of the existing constraints and start over.

    a. For each quarter, the value of the two variable cells for that quarter must be equal to each another. This requires a total of four constraints.

    b. None of the changing cells can have a value greater than half the average for that location (the location average is calculated in column G). This requires a total of eight constraints—one for each variable cell where the value is less than or equal to the value in the average cell for that location.

    c. Fix the Solver parameters and then run Solver.

    d. Keep the Solver solution and create a new scenario named `Solver Results`.

13. Create a scenario summary report to show the changing results for cell **G24** only.

14. Save and close the workbook.

chapter 9

Importing Data, Reviewing, and Finalizing the Workbook

In this chapter, you will learn the following skills:

❱ Import data from external files

❱ Use Flash Fill and Text to Columns to manipulate data

❱ Use data validation tools

❱ Summarize data using Consolidate

❱ Add and review comments

❱ Create hyperlinks

❱ Share and protect workbooks and worksheets

❱ Highlight and accept or reject changes

❱ Save a workbook in alternative formats

❱ Finalize a workbook

skills

introduction

This chapter begins with importing data from external sources. You will then use Excel's Flash Fill and Text to Columns features to manipulate that data. You will learn how adding data validation can help prevent errors and make the workbook more user-friendly and how to use Consolidate to summarize data. As part of the review process, you will work with comments and hyperlinks and apply sharing and protection options to the workbook. You will check the workbook for compatibility with older versions of Excel and export Excel data to other formats. Before finalizing the workbook, you will secure the workbook with a password and remove private and hidden data.

Skill 9.1 Importing Data from Access

Microsoft Access is a relational database program. Data are stored in multiple tables that connect to one another via related fields. Through queries based on table relationships, the database can create a specific view of data combining fields from multiple tables. Organizations often use a database to input and store data and then import that data into Excel to perform statistical and what-if analyses.

To import data from an Access database:

1. On the *Data* tab, if necessary, click the **Get External Data** button to expand the *Get External Data* group. Click the **From Access** button.

2. In the *Select Data Source* dialog, navigate to the folder where the Access database is stored, select the file, and click the **Open** button.

Click to open the *Select Data Source* dialog to import data from an Access database.

Access Databases

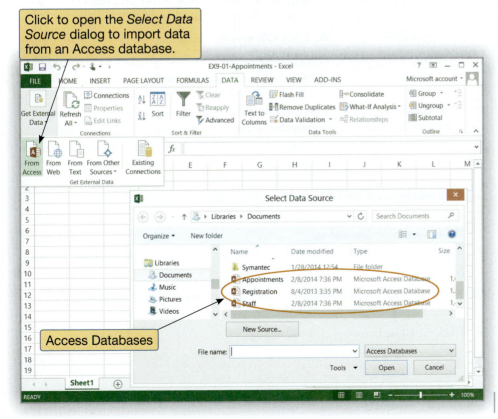

FIGURE EX 9.1

3. In the *Select Table* dialog, select the table or query view you want to import data from, and then click **OK.**

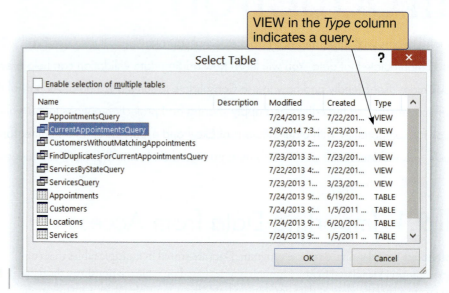

VIEW in the *Type* column indicates a query.

FIGURE EX 9.2

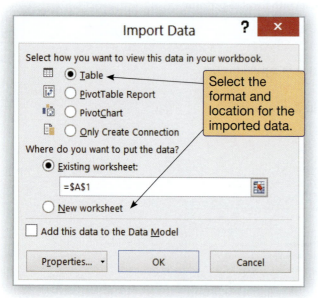

Select the format and location for the imported data.

FIGURE EX 9.3

4. In the *Import Data* dialog, select how you would like the data formatted in Excel. Click the **Table, PivotTable Report, PivotChart,** or **Only Create Connection** radio button. The last option creates the connection but does not import the data.

5. By default, the data will be imported into the selected cell in the current worksheet. You can change the cell reference or click the **New** worksheet radio button to select a different location.

6. Click **OK** to complete the import.

Once the import is complete, the data in the worksheet remain connected to the database.

You can refresh the data from the database connection from the *Data* tab, *Connections* group. Click the **Refresh All** button, and either select **Refresh** to update data only in the selected table, PivotTable, or PivotChart or select **Refresh All** to update all connected data in the workbook.

To disconnect the worksheet data from the database:

1. On the *Data* tab, in the *Connections* group, click the **Connections** button to open the *Workbook Connections* dialog.

2. If necessary, click the name of the connection you want to delete and click the **Remove** button.

3. A warning box appears telling you that the data will no longer be updated from the source. Click **OK.**

4. Click the **Close** button to close the dialog.

Once the worksheet is disconnected from the database, data updates are no longer available.

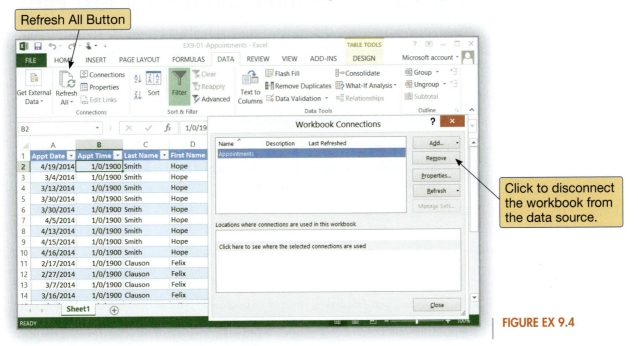

FIGURE EX 9.4

tips & tricks

You do not need to have Access installed on your computer to import data from a database.

tell me more

❯ To manage the data connections in your workbook, on the *Data* tab, in the *Connections* group, click the **Connections** button. From the *Workbook Connections* dialog, you can see where connections are used in the workbook and manage connection properties including setting automatic data update options.

❯ When you open a workbook that has connections to an external data source, the file may open in Protected View. Click the **Enable Content** button in the warning bar to work with the file. For more information about Protected View, refer to the skill *Working in Protected View*.

another method

If you imported the data as a table, tools to manage the connection are included in the *Table Tools Design* tab, *External Table Data* group.

let me try

Open the student data file **EX9-01-Appointments** (or open Excel and create a new, blank workbook) and try this skill on your own:

1. Import data from the *Appointments* Access database, *CurrentAppointments* query.

2. Import the data as a table in cell **A1** of the current worksheet.

3. Update the linked worksheet data.

4. Disconnect the worksheet data from the database.

5. Save the file as directed by your instructor and close it.

Skill 9.2 Importing Data from a Text File

If you work with data from external sources such as vendors or customers, that data may be available only in plain text format. Text files are common for passing data between organizations because they can be read by many different application programs. A text file that includes multiple data fields may separate the fields with a specific character (a **delimiter**). Common delimiters are commas, tabs, and spaces. When you import data from a text file using a delimiter, each data field is imported into a separate column.

To import data from a text file:

1. On the *Data* tab, if necessary, click the **Get External Data** button to expand the *Get External Data* group. Click the **From Text** button.

FIGURE EX 9.5

2. In the *Import Text File* dialog, navigate to find the file you want to import, select it, and click the **Import** button.

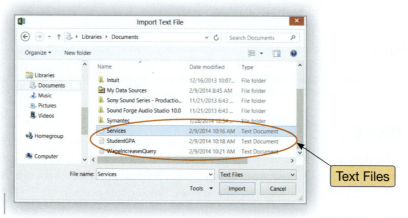

FIGURE EX 9.6

3. The *Text Import Wizard* opens. In Step 1, click the radio button that describes how the data fields are separated— **Delimited** or **Fixed width.** The wizard may detect that the text is delimited and select that option for you. If appropriate, click the **My data has headers** check box.

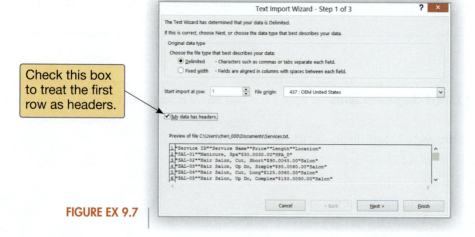

Check this box to treat the first row as headers.

FIGURE EX 9.7

4. Step 2 asks you to select the delimiter character that separates the data fields. Click the appropriate check box. The *Data preview* pane shows how the imported data will be separated into columns.

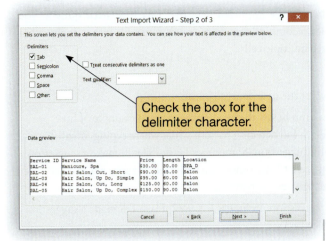

FIGURE EX 9.8

5. In Step 3, if necessary, set the data format for each column. By default, all columns are set to the *General* format. You can always reformat the columns after they have been imported.

6. Click **Finish.**

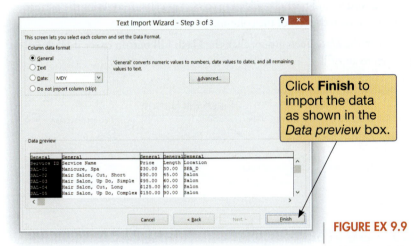

FIGURE EX 9.9

7. In the *Import Data* dialog, select how you would like the data formatted in Excel. Click the **Table, PivotTable Report, PivotChart,** or **Only Create Connection** radio button. The last option creates the connection but does not import the data.

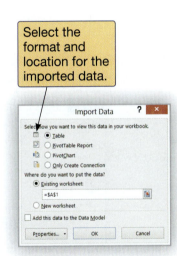

FIGURE EX 9.10

8. By default, the data will be imported into the selected cell in the current worksheet. You can change the cell reference or click the **New** worksheet radio button to select a different location.

9. Click **OK** to complete the import.

let me try

Open the student data file **EX9-02-Appointments** and try this skill on your own:

1. If you are continuing to work with the file **EX9-01-Appointments** from the previous skill, add a new worksheet to the workbook.

2. Import the **Services** tab-delimited text file into the *Sheet2* worksheet. The data include a header row.

3. Save the file as directed by your instructor and close it.

FIGURE EX 9.11

Skill 9.3 Inserting Data Using Flash Fill

Flash Fill detects patterns in your data and autofills the remaining cells for you. This new Excel 2013 feature is useful when you've imported data that isn't formatted quite as you would like. Flash Fill can be used to combine data from contiguous cells into a single cell or to split data from a single cell into multiple cells.

To begin using Flash Fill:

1. Insert a column where you want the new data to appear.

2. In the first cell of the new column below the header row, type an example of how you'd like the data filled. If Flash Fill detects a pattern while you're typing, it will automatically make an autofill suggestion. Sometimes Flash Fill will make a suggestion after you type data in just one cell. Other times, you will need to type two or three examples before Flash Fill recognizes the pattern.

3. Press ⎵Enter to accept the suggestion. In Figure EX 9.12, Flash Fill made a suggestion as soon as **Kat** was typed in cell F3.

There will be cases when Flash Fill does not recognize the pattern automatically. However, you can invoke the *Flash Fill* command manually.

1. Select the first cell below the cell containing the example you want Flash Fill to copy. In Figure EX 9.12, you would begin by selecting cell C3 as cell C2 contains the pattern you want to use to autofill the rest of the column.

2. On the *Data* tab, in the *Data Tools* group, click the **Flash Fill** button to see if Flash Fill can find a pattern to autofill.

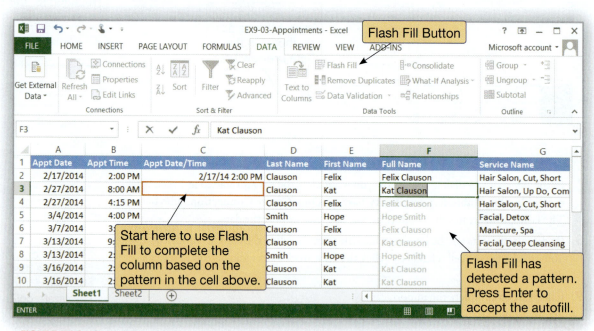

FIGURE EX 9.12

Flash Fill can also be used to add text. In Figure EX 9.13, Flash Fill recognizes that the word *minutes* should be added after the number based on the example in cell E2. Yes, you could accomplish the same result using the CONCATENATE function. However, using Flash Fill fills the cells with static content instead of formulas, making it easier to move and manipulate the data.

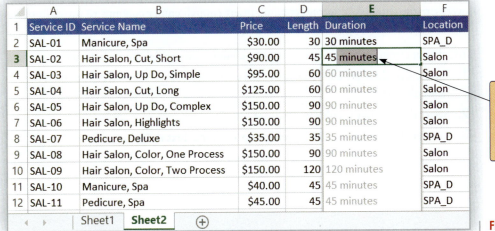

Flash Fill adds the word *minutes* based on the pattern in cell E2 and autofills the rest of the column.

FIGURE EX 9.13

tips & tricks

Flash Fill doesn't always fill the data consistently as you intended. Be sure to check the data after you've accepted Flash Fill's suggestions.

tell me **more**

Flash Fill works on one column at a time. If you want to split data into multiple columns, first use Flash Fill to fill data in the first column using the first part of the pattern, and then use Flash Fill to fill data in the second column using the second part of the pattern.

another **method**

On the *Home* tab, in the *Editing* group, click the **Fill** button and select **Flash Fill.**

let me **try**

Open the student data file **EX9-03-Appointments** and try this skill on your own:

1. On *Sheet1*, in cell **F2,** type `Felix Clauson` and press **Enter.**

2. In cell **F3,** begin typing `Kat Clauson` and when Flash Fill makes an autofill suggestion, accept it. If Flash Fill does not make a suggestion, use the command on the Ribbon.

3. In cell **C3** continue typing the appointment date and time pattern for column C. Flash Fill probably won't recognize the pattern automatically, but you can use the command on the Ribbon to autofill the rest of the column.

4. Go to **Sheet2,** and type `30 minutes` in cell **E2.** Press **Enter.**

5. In cell **E3,** begin typing `45 minutes` and when Flash Fill makes an autofill suggestion, accept it. If Flash Fill does not make a suggestion, use the command on the Ribbon.

6. Save the file as directed by your instructor and close it.

skill 9.3   Inserting Data Using Flash Fill

Skill 9.4 Converting Data to Columns

Excel's Text to Columns feature allows you to split data into separate columns if there is a consistent character at which Excel can split the data (the **delimiter**) or the data can be split at a specific number of characters. If the column to the right of the column you are splitting contains data, Excel will replace the contents of the destination cells. If you do not want to overwrite the data in the second column, insert enough empty columns to the right of the column you are splitting *before* converting the data.

To split data from one column into separate columns using a delimiter character:

1. Ensure that there are enough empty cells to the right of the selected cells to hold the new columns.
2. Select the data in the column you want to split.
3. On the *Data* tab, in the *Data Tools* group, click the **Text to Columns** button.

from the perspective of . . .

INVENTORY MANAGER

One of our main customers sends us purchase orders in Excel with a single column listing the part number followed by a comma and then the part name. Of course, our inventory system expects the part number and the item name to be in separate fields. I use Text to Columns to separate the data into two separate columns.

The customer's system also omits our three-letter company codes from the part numbers. In the past, I used a nested IF formula with CONCATENATE to correct the part numbers. Now with Excel 2013, I use Flash Fill to update the part numbers by typing just a few examples. I'm hiring an assistant soon who doesn't know Excel very well. It will be much easier to show him how to use Flash Fill than to teach him how to use my old formula.

excel 2013   chapter 9 Importing Data, Reviewing, and Finalizing the Workbook

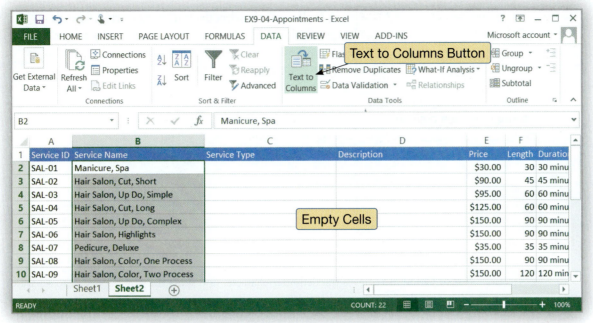

FIGURE EX 9.14

4. The *Convert Text to Columns Wizard* opens.

5. If the data are separated by a common delimiter such as a tab, space, or comma, click the **Next** button to go to Step 2.

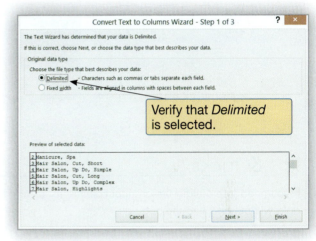

FIGURE EX 9.15

6. Click the check box for one of the common delimiter characters (tab, semicolon, comma, or space) or click the *Other* check box and enter the delimiter character in the box. The *Data preview* box shows how the data will be separated based on the delimiter you selected. Click **Next.**

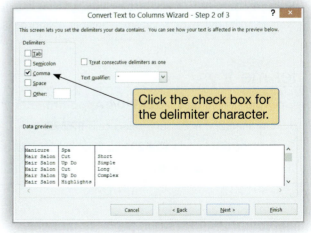

FIGURE EX 9.16

skill 9.4   Converting Data to Columns

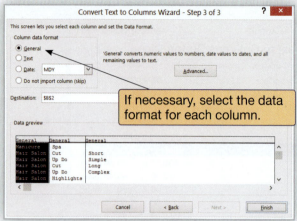

FIGURE EX 9.17

7. If necessary, select the correct data format for each column. The *General* format is selected by default. You can always change the format later.

8. Click **Finish.**

Text to Columns removes the delimiter character and splits the original data into separate columns as shown in Figure EX 9.18.

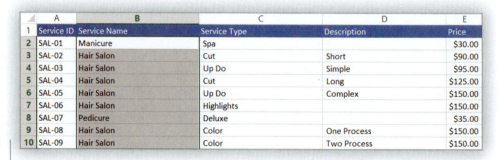

FIGURE EX 9.18

tips & tricks

If you need to maintain the original column, try using Flash Fill instead of Text to Columns to create new columns of data without affecting the original.

tell me more

You can also split cells into columns at specific character intervals. This option works only if the data in the cells you want to split have exactly the same number of characters in each interval in each row.

let me try

Open the student data file **EX9-04-Appointments** and try this skill on your own:

1. On *Sheet2*, if necessary, select cells **B2:B23.**
2. Split the text in cells **B2:B23** into three columns. Use the comma as the delimiter.
3. Save the file as directed by your instructor and close it.

Skill 9.5 Adding Data Validation

One way to prevent errors in your workbooks is to add **data validation rules.** By requiring data validation, you can prevent users from entering invalid data or data that may cause errors in formulas. Data validation rules can limit cell entries to a specific data type (such as whole number or date) or a list of acceptable values.

To add data validation rules:

1. Select the cells to which you want to apply data validation rules.

2. On the *Data* tab, in the *Data Tools* group, click the **Data Validation** button.

3. To restrict data entries to a specific numeric value or values within a range:

   a. From the *Allow* list, select **Whole number** or **Decimal.**

   b. From the *Data* list, select a comparison operator.

   c. Enter the specific value or the minimum and maximum values.

   d. To require a value in every cell, click the **Ignore blank** check box to uncheck it.

4. When you have completed the data validation settings, click **OK.**

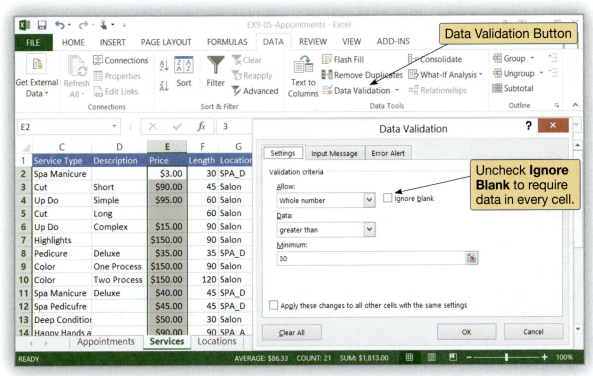

FIGURE EX 9.19

If you added data validation rules after entering data, you may have invalid data in your worksheet. Click the **Data Validation** button arrow, and select **Circle Invalid Data** to identify the invalid data entries in your worksheet. You do not need to select the cells with the data validation rules first.

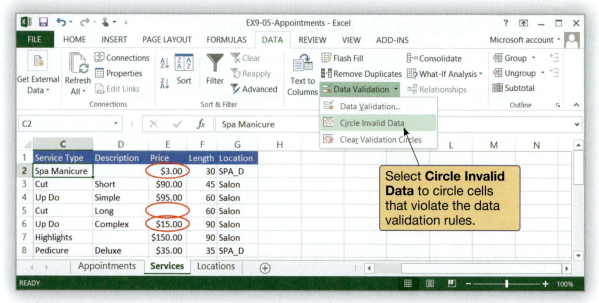

FIGURE EX 9.20

To hide the circles, click the **Data Validation** button arrow and select Cl**ear Validation Circles.**

Clearing the validation circles does not remove the validation rules. To remove data validation rules, click the **Clear All** button in the *Data Validation* dialog.

tips & tricks

❱ To identify cells with data validation rules applied to them, on the *Home* tab, in the *Editing* group, click the **Find & Select** button, and select **Data Validation** from the list.

❱ When you save or close the workbook, Excel hides the validation circles. They will not be visible next time you open the workbook, but the data validation rules will still be in effect.

tell me more

When you enter invalid data in a cell with a validation rule applied, Excel displays a warning message. You can customize the warning message through the *Validation Rules* dialog. For more information, refer to the skill *Creating a Drop-Down List for Data Entry.*

let me try

Open the student data file **EX9-05-Appointments** and try this skill on your own:

1. On the *Services* worksheet, select cells **E2:E23,** if necessary.
2. Every service must have a price listed. Add data validation to the list of prices. Require whole numbers greater than **30.** Do not ignore blank cells.
3. Display the circles to find invalid data.
4. Hide the validation circles.
5. Save the file as directed by your instructor and close it.

Skill 9.6 Creating a Drop-Down List for Data Entry

You can use data validation rules to limit cell entries to a list of acceptable values and create a drop-down menu for users to choose from.

To create a drop-down list for data entry:

1. Select the cell where you want the list to appear.

2. On the *Data* tab, in the *Data Tools* group, click the **Data Validation** button.

3. In the *Data Validation* dialog, from the *Settings* tab, click the **Allow** arrow, and select **List**.

4. In the *Source* box, type the list of acceptable values, separating each value with a comma. You can also reference a named range as the list source. Type **=** followed by the name.

5. To include a drop-down list of values, ensure that the **In-cell dropdown** check box is checked. When the *Allow* option is set to **List,** this box is checked by default.

6. Click **OK**.

When you click in a cell that has a list data validation rule applied, an arrow appears at the right side of the cell. Click the arrow to expand the list and make a selection.

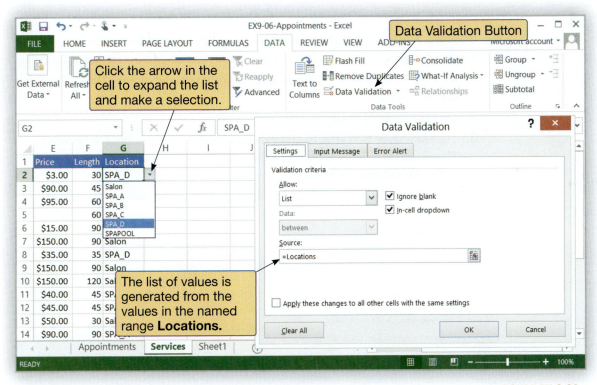

FIGURE EX 9.21

From the *Data Validation* dialog, *Input Message* tab, you can add a prompt that will appear every time the user clicks a cell requiring data validation. Customizing these messages makes your workbook more user-friendly.

1. If the *Data Validation* dialog is not open, select the cells and click the **Data Validation** button to open it.

2. Click the **Input Message** tab.

3. The **Show input message when cell is selected** check box is checked by default. This ensures that the user will always see the input prompt.

4. Enter text for the message title and/or message. Be as brief as possible. A title is not required.

5. Click **OK** to apply the changes.

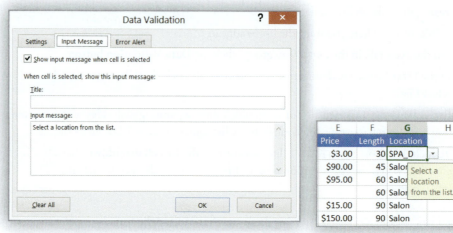

FIGURE EX 9.22

FIGURE EX 9.23

When the user enters data that violates the data validation rule, an error message appears. You can customize the error message from the *Error Alert* tab in the *Data Validation* dialog.

1. If the *Data Validation* dialog is not open, select the cells and click the **Data Validation** button to open it.

2. Click the **Error Alert** tab.

3. The **Show error alert after invalid data is entered** check box is checked by default. This ensures that the error message will display whenever the user attempts to enter data that breaks the data validation rule.

4. Enter text for the message title and/or message. Be as brief as possible. A title is not required.

5. Click **OK** to apply the changes.

FIGURE EX 9.24

FIGURE EX 9.25

tips & tricks

Using a named range as the list source allows you to add and remove values from the in-cell drop-down list without having to modify the validation rule.

tell me **more**

To change data validation rules, including adding or changing input messages and error alerts:

1. Select at least one of the cells that has the data validation rule applied.

2. On the *Data* tab, in the *Data Tools* group, click the **Data Validation** button.

3. In the *Data Validation* dialog, on the *Settings* tab, click the **Apply these changes to all other cells with the same settings** check box. This step isn't necessary if you've already selected all the cells already.

4. Make the changes you want and then click **OK.**

let me **try**

Open the student data file **EX9-06-Appointments** and try this skill on your own:

1. On the *Services* worksheet, select cells **G2:G23**, if necessary.

2. Use data validation to display an in-cell drop-down list of values from the named range: **locations** Allow blanks.

3. Add this input message: `Select a location from the list.`

4. Add the same message as the alert that appears if the user attempts to enter invalid data: `Select a location from the list.`

5. Save the file as directed by your instructor and close it.

Skill 9.7 Consolidating Data in a Summary Worksheet

If your workbook contains multiple worksheets with the same data structure, you can create a master worksheet to summarize the data. You may already be familiar with how to do this using formulas that reference cells in other worksheets, also known as 3-D cell references (see the skill *Creating Formulas Using References to Other Worksheets*). You can also use the Consolidate command. Through the *Consolidate* dialog, you can summarize data from multiple worksheets for a range of cells at once.

Unlike 3-D references, Consolidate gives you the option to link to the source data via formulas or insert a static summary—that is, cells that contain only values, not references to other cells. Use Consolidate to create summary worksheets whenever you want to share the summary as static values without the details. Be sure to uncheck the **Create links to source data** check box in the *Consolidate* dialog when you create the consolidation.

To create the summary worksheet where the data will be consolidated, copy one of the source worksheets and clear the data from the cells containing the values. The summary worksheet is shown in Figure EX 9.26, and the source worksheets are shown in Figure EX 9.27. Notice the identical data structures. You can change the name of the summary worksheet and modify any text or formatting as long as the rows where the data are consolidated are in the same order as the rows in the source worksheets, with the same columns.

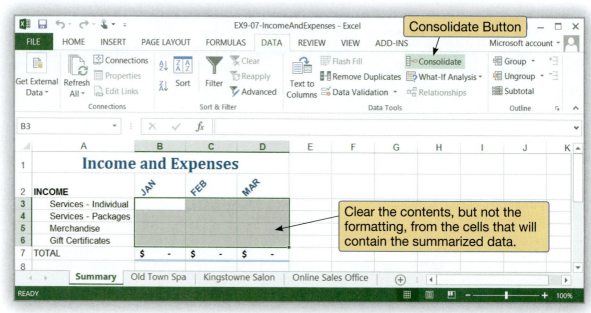

FIGURE EX 9.26

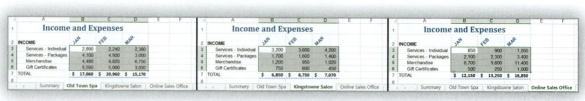

FIGURE EX 9.27

To create a summary totaling data from multiple worksheets:

1. Select the cells that will contain the totals.

2. On the *Data* tab, in the *Data Tools* group, click the **Consolidate** button.

3. In the *Consolidate* dialog, **Sum** is selected in the *Function* list by default. If you want to use another function, expand the list and select the function you want to use.

4. The *All references* box may include references from previous consolidations. If these are not the references you want to use, select each and click the **Delete** button to delete them.

5. Click in the *Reference* box and then click the tab for the first sheet you want to include.

6. Click and drag to select the cell range. When you release the mouse button, Excel returns to the *Consolidate* dialog.

7. Click the **Add** button.

8. Click the next sheet tab you want to add to the consolidation. Notice that you do not need to select the specific cells in the next worksheet. Excel maintains the same cell range in the *Reference* box, changing only the worksheet name.

9. Click **Add.**

10. Continue clicking sheet tabs and clicking the **Add** button until all the worksheets are included.

11. If you want the summary to update automatically when the source data change, in the *Consolidate* dialog, click the **Create links to source data** check box. If you want the consolidation data to be independent of the source, do ***not*** click this check box.

12. Click **OK.**

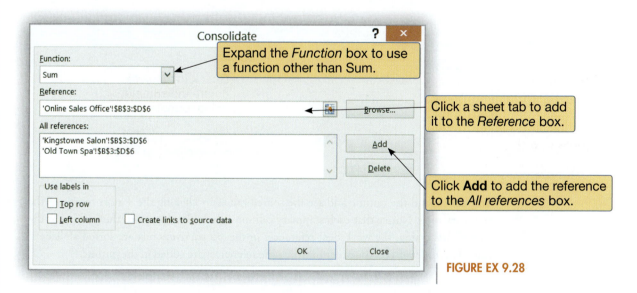

FIGURE EX 9.28

Each cell in the summary sheet displays the total of the values in the corresponding cells in the referenced worksheets. Notice that the cells contain values, not formulas.

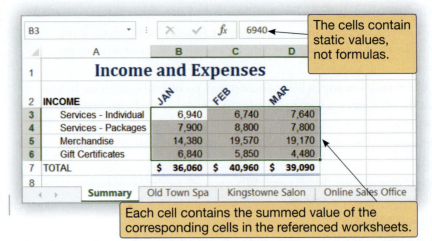

FIGURE EX 9.29

When you check the **Create links to source data** check box in the *Consolidate* dialog, Excel creates links to the source data in outline format. Use this option if you want the values in the summary sheet to update when the data in the source worksheets change.

FIGURE EX 9.30

You can expand the outline and see the source values by clicking the + next to one of the summary rows. Notice that each summary cell sums the cells *above* it in the outline. In the *Consolidate* dialog, the worksheet references in the *All references* box are sorted alphabetically. This order affects the order in which the references are added in the outline.

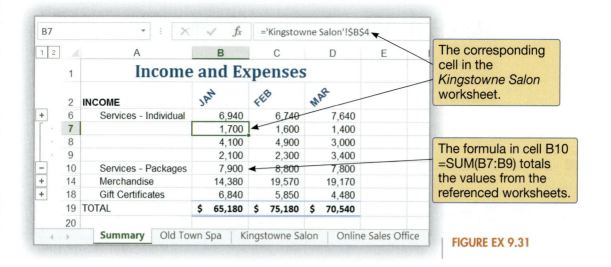

The corresponding cell in the *Kingstowne Salon* worksheet.

The formula in cell B10 =SUM(B7:B9) totals the values from the referenced worksheets.

FIGURE EX 9.31

tips & tricks

In a consolidation with links to the source data, the details for the first row of the consolidation use the formatting from the row above. Often, this row contains formatting for the heading row. You can select the detail cells and change the formatting without affecting the consolidation.

tell me **more**

To use Consolidate to summarize data from worksheets in other workbooks.

1. In the *Consolidate* dialog, click in the *Reference* box, and then switch to the workbook you want to reference. If the workbook is not already open, click the **Browse...** button to open the workbook.

2. Click and drag to select the cells. When you release the mouse button, Excel returns to the original workbook.

3. If you don't want to create links between the workbooks, remember to verify that the **Create links to source data check** box is *not* checked.

let me **try**

Open the student data file **EX9-07-IncomeAndExpenses** and try this skill on your own:

1. If necessary, select cells **B3:D6** on the *Summary* worksheet.

2. In the selected cells, use Consolidate to sum data from the other worksheets. In the *Consolidate* dialog, *Sum* is selected by default. You do not need to change the function for this exercise.

3. If the *References* box includes references, delete them before adding the new references for this exercise.

4. Add cells **B3:D6** from the **Old Town Spa** worksheet to the references.

5. Now add the same cell range (**B3:D6**) from the **Kingstowne Salon** and **Online Sales Office** worksheets and complete the consolidation.

6. Replace the data consolidation in the selected cells. Use the same references, but this time include links to the source data to display subtotals. You do not need to clear the cells first.

7. Save the file as directed by your instructor and close it.

Skill 9.8 Working with Comments

A **comment** is a note you add to a cell in a worksheet. Use comments to add information, descriptions, or instructions to cells. Add and work with comments from the *Review* tab, *Comments* group.

FIGURE EX 9.32

To insert a comment:

1. Select the cell in which you want to insert the comment.

2. On the *Review* tab, in the *Comments* group, click the **New Comment** button.

3. Type your comment text in the balloon that appears.

4. Click outside the balloon when you are finished.

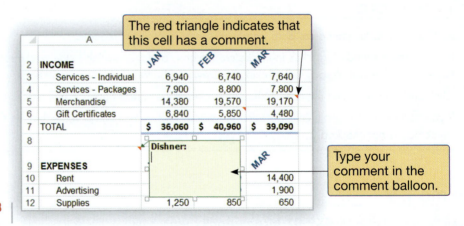

FIGURE EX 9.33

Each cell can have only one comment. When the cell includes a comment, the *New Comment* button changes to *Edit Comment*.

When your worksheet includes comments, there are a few ways to view them:

❯ A red triangle appears in the corner of a cell that has a comment. Point to the cell to make the comment visible. Move your mouse away from the cell to hide the comment.

❯ To display all the comments in a worksheet at once, click the **Show All Comments** button.

❯ To display a specific comment, click the cell, and then click the **Show/Hide Comment** button.

❯ To browse through all the comments in your worksheet, use the **Previous** and **Next** buttons.

To delete a comment, first select the cell that includes the comment you want to delete, and then click the **Delete Comment** button ⌧ Delete .

tips & tricks

When you create a comment, Excel automatically inserts your name (the name used when you installed Excel) so other users know who added the comment. You can edit the name or delete it from the comment, but if you find yourself doing this every time you add a comment, change the user name instead.

To change the Excel user name:

1. Click the **File** tab.
2. Click **Options.**
3. Under *General,* in the *Personalize your copy of Microsoft Office* section, in the *User name* box, type the name you want to appear.
4. Click **OK.**

tell me **more**

❯ To resize a comment balloon: Show the comment. Click a resize handle and drag toward the center of the comment to make it smaller or away from the center of the image to make it larger.

❯ To move a comment balloon: Show the comment. Point to the comment, and when the cursor changes to the move cursor, click and drag the comment balloon to the new location.

another **method**

❯ To insert a comment, right-click the cell in which you want the comment, and select **Insert Comment** or select the cell and press **Shift +F2.**

❯ If a cell has a comment, the right-click menu includes the following commands: *Edit Comment, Delete Comment, Hide Comment* (if the comment is showing), and *Show Comment* (if the comment is hidden).

❯ You can also delete a comment from the *Home* tab, *Editing* group. Click the cell with the comment, then click the **Clear** button and select **Clear Comments.**

let me **try**

Open the student data file **EX9-08-IncomeAndExpenses** and try this skill on your own:

1. If necessary, select cell **A9** on the *Summary* worksheet.
2. Add this comment to the selected cell: `Need links to details here`
3. Display all the comments on this worksheet at once.
4. Delete the comment you just added.
5. Save the file as directed by your instructor and close it.

Skill 9.9 Inserting Hyperlinks

A hyperlink is text or a graphic that can be clicked to open another location in the same file, another file, or a Web page. In Excel, the hyperlink encompasses an entire cell or range of cells rather than text.

To insert a hyperlink:

1. Select the cell or range of cells where you want to create the link.

2. On the *Insert* tab, in the *Links* group, click the **Hyperlink** button to open the *Insert Hyperlink* dialog.

3. If the cell you selected is empty, type the text you want to appear in the cell in the *Text to display* box. If you selected a cell that contains a value or formula already, the *Text to display* box displays <<*Selection in Document*>>.

4. In the *Link to* section on the left side of the dialog, select the type of location you want to link to, and then enter the link details.

   - Click **Existing File or Web Page,** and then select the specific file or Web page to link to.

   - Click **Place in This Document,** and then select the worksheet or named range to link to. If necessary, edit the cell reference in the *Type the cell reference* box. Cell **A1** is selected by default.

   - Click **Create New Document,** and then enter the path and file name for the new document.

   - Click **E-mail Address,** and then enter the email address to link to and a subject. When this link is clicked, Outlook will open a new mail message.

5. Click **OK** to close the *Insert Hyperlink* dialog and insert the hyperlink into your workbook.

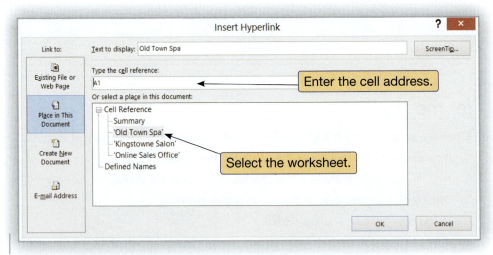

FIGURE EX 9.34

When you add a hyperlink to a cell, the text in the cell appears blue and underlined. Click the link to navigate to the linked location. Once you click the hyperlink, it will appear purple and underlined to indicate that the link has been followed.

There are no Ribbon buttons to remove or edit hyperlinks because once you click the cell to select it, you jump to the linked location.

To edit a hyperlink:

1. Right-click the link and select **Edit Hyperlink.**
2. Make changes in the *Edit Hyperlink* dialog.
3. Click **OK.**

To remove a hyperlink, right-click the cell and select **Remove Hyperlink.**

To edit the contents of a cell with a hyperlink, use the keyboard arrow keys to navigate to and select the cell and then click in the formula bar and edit the cell content from there.

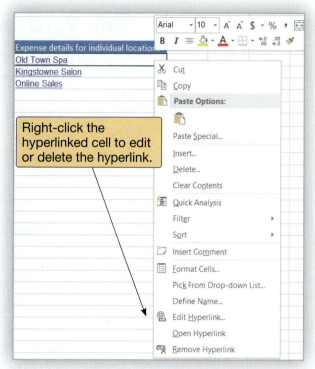

FIGURE EX 9.35

tips & tricks

A ScreenTip is a bubble that appears when the mouse pointer is placed over the link. Add a ScreenTip to include a more meaningful description of the hyperlink. In the *Insert Hyperlink* dialog, click the **ScreenTip** button. In the Set *Hyperlink ScreenTip* dialog, enter the ScreenTip text in the box, and then click **OK.**

another method

To open the *Insert Hyperlink* dialog, you can also:

❯ Right-click the cell and select **Hyperlink...**
❯ Press **Ctrl + K** on the keyboard.

let me try

Open the student data file **EX9-09-IncomeAndExpenses** and try this skill on your own:

1. Add a hyperlink from cell **F11** on the *Summary* worksheet to link to cell **A1** in the **Old Town Spa** worksheet.
2. Remove the hyperlink from cell **F13.**
3. Save the file as directed by your instructor and close it.

Skill 9.10 Sharing a Workbook

When you share a workbook, you allow several people to view and make changes to the workbook at the same time. Shared workbooks are usually saved to a network where multiple users have access, so be careful to save your shared workbook to a secure location where only authorized users have access to it.

To share a workbook:

1. On the *Review* tab, in the *Changes* group, click the **Share Workbook** button.

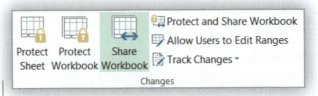

FIGURE EX 9.36

2. In the **Share Workbook** dialog, click the check box to allow sharing. Click **OK.**

FIGURE EX 9.37

3. A message box appears, asking if you want to save the workbook and continue. Click **OK.**

Once the workbook is shared, *[shared]* appears after the file name in the title bar.

At any point, you can see the list of users who have the workbook open by opening the *Share Workbook* dialog again.

To remove sharing, open the *Share Workbook* dialog again and click the check box to remove the check mark and disallow sharing.

tips & tricks

❯ Shared workbooks cannot contain tables. If your workbook contains tables, you will need to convert the tables to normal cell ranges before enabling sharing. For information about removing tables, refer to the skill *Converting Tables to Ranges.*

❯ Once sharing is enabled, you will notice that many of the buttons on the Ribbon are dimmed, meaning you no longer have access to those features. You cannot insert new cells or graphic objects (including charts), nor can you use certain Excel formatting features like conditional formatting.

let me try

Open the student data file **EX9-10-IncomeAndExpenses** and try this skill on your own:

1. Enable sharing so more than one person at a time can work on this workbook.

2. Remove sharing from this workbook.

3. Save the file as directed by your instructor and close it.

Skill 9.11 Protecting Worksheets and Workbooks from Changes

If you intend to share the workbook, you should set worksheet and workbook protection first. You cannot apply protection after the workbook has been shared.

By default, Excel "locks" all the cells in a worksheet, but this does not affect users until you apply worksheet protection. Before adding worksheet protection, you should unlock any cells you want the user to be able to edit.

To unlock cells:

1. Select the cells you want users to be able to edit when worksheet protection is enabled.

2. On the *Home* tab, in the *Cells* group, click the **Format** button.

3. Click **Lock Cell** to remove the highlight and unlock the selected cells.

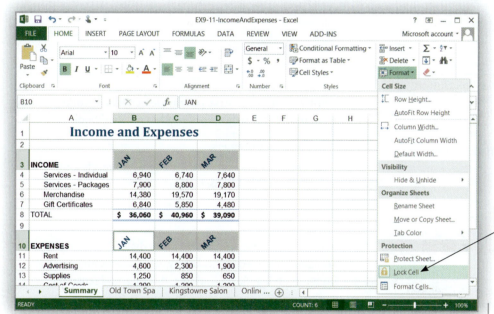

Click **Lock Cell** to remove the highlight and unlock the selected cells.

FIGURE EX 9.38

To enable worksheet protection and set protection options:

1. On the *Review* tab, in the *Changes* group, click the **Protect Sheet** button.

2. In the *Protect Sheet* dialog, notice that the *Select locked cells* option is checked—allowing users to select the cells, not edit them. Allowing users to select locked cells can help them understand the worksheet by viewing formulas in the formula bar. The *Select unlocked cells* option is also checked to allow users to select and edit unlocked cells. They can edit the cells because the cells are *unlocked*. Click the check boxes for any other options you want to give your users. Any unchecked options will be unavailable.

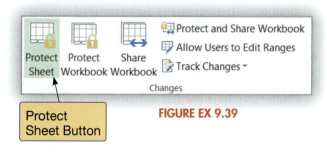

Protect Sheet Button

FIGURE EX 9.39

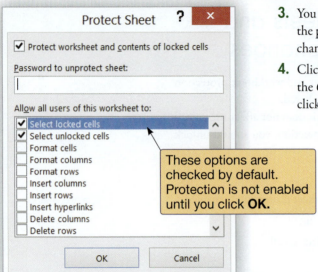

These options are checked by default. Protection is not enabled until you click **OK**.

FIGURE EX 9.40

3. You can add a password to your worksheet to require users to enter the password before they can unprotect the worksheet and make changes. Type the password in the *Password to unprotect sheet* box.

4. Click **OK** to accept your changes. If you have entered a password, the *Confirm Password* dialog will appear. Retype your password and click **OK** to close the dialog and enable worksheet protection.

Protect Workbook Button

FIGURE EX 9.41

Just as you can protect certain elements in a worksheet, you can protect the structure of your overall workbook.

To protect a workbook:

1. On the *Review* tab, in the *Changes* group, click the **Protect Workbook** button.

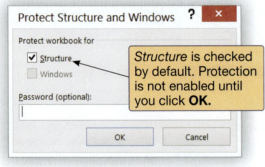

Structure is checked by default. Protection is not enabled until you click **OK**.

FIGURE EX 9.42

2. In the *Protect Structure and Windows* dialog, notice that the *Structure* check box is checked by default. This prevents users from modifying moving, adding, deleting, and renaming worksheets.

3. Type a password in the *Password* box to require a password to unlock the workbook.

4. Click **OK** to accept your changes. If you have entered a password, the *Confirm Password* dialog will appear. Retype your password and click **OK** to close the dialog and lock your workbook.

tips & tricks

❯ If you intend to share the workbook and track changes, you should set worksheet and workbook protection *first.* You cannot apply protection after the workbook has been shared.

❯ When a worksheet is protected, the *Unprotect Worksheet* button is unavailable when the workbook is shared. To unprotect the worksheet, you must first remove sharing.

❯ The *Windows* option in the *Protect Structure and Windows* dialog cannot be used in Excel 2013. It is included only for compatibility with workbooks created in older versions of Excel that have this level of workbook protection enabled.

tell me **more**

Another way to allow users to edit cells in a protected worksheet is to apply a password to the cells. The cells remain locked, but users can unlock them with a password.

To specify ranges of locked cells that users can modify with a password when the worksheet is protected:

1. On the *Review* tab in the *Changes* group, click the **Allow Users to Edit Ranges** button.
2. In the *Allow Users to Edit Ranges* dialog, click the **New** button to add a new range to the list.
3. In the *New Range* dialog, enter a title for the range. The title appears in the *Allow Users to Edit Ranges* dialog.
4. In the *Refers to cells* box, enter = followed by the cell range or the range name.
5. In the *Range password* box, type the password users will have to enter in order to edit the cells.
6. Click **OK.**
7. Excel will ask you to verify the password. Type the password again and click **OK.**
8. Click **OK** to close the *Allow Users to Edit Ranges* dialog and apply the changes to the worksheet.

another **method**

❯ To unlock cells from the *Format Cells* dialog, *Protection* tab, click the **Locked** check box to uncheck it.

❯ To apply protection from the *File* tab, *Info* page, click the **Protect Workbook** button and select **Protect Workbook Structure** or **Protect Current Sheet.**

❯ To apply protection to the current sheet from the *Home* tab, *Cells* group, click the **Format** button and then click **Protect Sheet.**

let me **try**

Open the student data file **EX9-11-IncomeAndExpenses** and try this skill on your own:

1. If necessary, select cells **B3:D3** and **B10:D10** on the *Summary* sheet.
2. Unlock these cells so the user can edit the cells when the worksheet is protected.
3. Enable worksheet protection for this worksheet so users can **select** both locked cells and unlocked cells.
4. The **Old Town Spa** worksheet has been protected. Unprotect it so users can make changes to locked cells.
5. Enable workbook protection so users cannot change worksheet names.
6. Now, remove workbook protection so users can add new worksheets.
7. Save the file as directed by your instructor and close it.

Skill 9.12 Tracking Changes

When you have multiple people working on a shared workbook, tracking the change history can be important. The change history tracks any deletions, insertions, or changes to data (except formatting changes). The change history also displays which user made the change and when.

To track changes to your workbook:

1. On the *Review* tab, in the *Changes* group, click the **Track Changes** button, and select **Highlight Changes...**

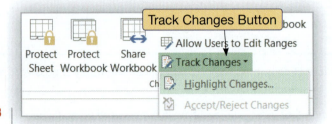

2. In the *Highlight Changes* dialog, click the **Track changes while editing** check box.

3. Specify tracking options, such as highlighting changes since the last time you saved or changes made by a particular user. Click the check box for the type of change you want to highlight, and then select a specific option from the drop-down list.

4. Click the check box to specify where you want to see the changes: **Highlight changes on screen** or **List changes on a new sheet.** (You may be able to select both options.)

5. Click **OK.**

6. Click **OK** again to allow Excel to save the workbook.

Cells that were changed are highlighted with a dark blue triangle in the upper-left corner. Point to a highlighted cell to see a description of the changes made.

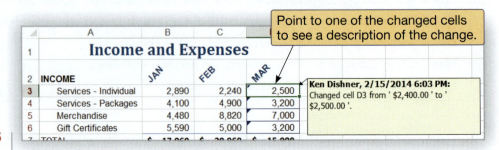

To accept and reject changes in a workbook:

1. On the *Review* tab, in the *Changes* group, click the **Track Changes** button and select **Accept/Reject Changes.**

2. If Excel prompts you to save the workbook, click **OK.**

3. In the *Select Changes to Accept or Reject* dialog, select which changes to review:

   a. **When:** Select changes that have not been reviewed or changes made by a certain date.

   b. **Who:** Select all reviewers or specific reviewers.

   c. **Where:** Enter the cell range or worksheet you want to review. Clearing the *Where* box selects the entire workbook.

Set the options for the type of changes to review.

FIGURE EX 9.46

4. Click **OK** to begin reviewing the changes in the workbook.

5. The *Accept or Reject Changes* dialog displays information about each change: who made the change, when it was made, and what the change was. You must accept or reject a change before being moving to the next change. Notice the changed cell is highlighted in the worksheet to help you identify the change.

   - Click **Accept** to accept the current change.
   - Click **Reject** to reject the current change.
   - To accept all the changes in the workbook, click **Accept All.**
   - To reject all the changes in the workbook, click **Reject All.**

6. When all the changes in the workbook have been reviewed, the *Accept or Reject Changes* dialog closes automatically.

Review and accept or reject each change.

FIGURE EX 9.47

tips & tricks

You can only track changes in a shared workbook. When you turn on the *Track Changes* feature, Excel automatically enables workbook sharing. Recall that shared workbooks cannot include tables. Therefore, you cannot track changes in workbooks that include tables unless you first convert the tables to normal ranges.

tell me more

let me try

Open the student data file **EX9-12-IncomeAndExpenses** and try this skill on your own:

1. Turn on *Track Changes* to highlight all changes made in this workbook since it was last saved.
2. Make the following changes:

   Change the value in cell **D3** to: 2500

   Change the value in cell **D4** to: 3200

   Change the value in cell **D5** to: 7000

   Change the value in cell **D6** to: 3200
3. Review all changes made to this workbook that have not yet been reviewed.
4. Accept the first change.
5. Accept all the remaining changes at once.
6. Save the file as directed by your instructor and close it.

from the perspective of . . .

GRANT WRITER

There are at least a dozen people who have input on our grant budgets. Without tracking the changes, it would be impossible for me to know who made which changes and when they were made. One of our finance managers is notorious for making unnecessary changes. I always review changes made by just that user and then click the *Reject All* button.

Skill 9.13 Checking for Compatibility with Previous Versions of Excel

Some features in Excel 2013 are not available in previous versions of the application. If a workbook uses one of the new features, opening it in a previous version of Excel may cause errors or prevent the workbook from displaying as you intended.

To check your workbook for potential compatibility issues:

1. Click the **File** tab. On *Info* page, click the **Check for Issues** button, and then click **Check Compatibility.**

2. The Compatibility Checker lists the items in your workbook that may be lost or downgraded if you save the workbook in an earlier Microsoft Excel format. The dialog groups the items by loss of functionality and loss of fidelity (formatting) and lists the number of times each issue occurs in the workbook (occurrences).

3. Click the **Find** link next to an issue to go directly to that cell in the workbook. This closes the *Compatibility Checker* dialog.

4. Excel may be able to offer a fix for some compatibility issues. To remove the incompatible functionality from your workbook, click the **Fix** link. Review the compatibility issue carefully before deciding to "fix" it. Removing the functionality may require you to make other changes to the workbook to maintain data integrity.

5. To save a list of the issues found, click the **Copy to New Sheet** button. This closes the *Compatibility Checker* dialog.

6. Click **OK** to close the Compatibility Checker.

Click **Find** to go directly to this issue and close the Compatibility Checker.

FIGURE EX 9.48

Click **Fix** to allow Excel to remove the functionality from the workbook.

tips & tricks

If you often share a workbook with people using an older version of Microsoft Excel, you can set the Compatibility Checker to run every time you save the workbook. Open the *Compatibility Checker* dialog, and then click the **Check compatibility when saving** check box to add a check mark. Click **OK.**

let me try

Open the student data file **EX9-13-Sales** and try this skill on your own:

1. Open the Compatibility Checker to check if this workbook contains elements that are not compatible with earlier versions of Excel.

2. Fix the *Stop if true* conditional formatting compatibility issue, and then close the Compatibility Checker.

3. Save the file as directed by your instructor and close it.

Skill 9.14 Exporting to Text Formats

Text file formats allow Excel data to be read by a variety of applications. The most common text file formats are **Text (Tab delimited)** (**.txt**) and **CSV (Comma delimited)** (**.csv**). When you save in one of the text formats, only the current worksheet will be saved because text formats do not support multiple worksheets in the same file. You will also lose all formatting, and cells with functions will be converted to their current values.

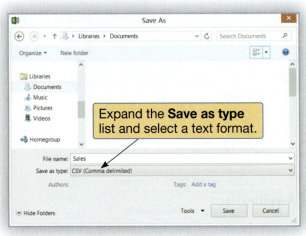

FIGURE EX 9.49

To export a worksheet to a text format:

1. Click the **File** tab.
2. Click **Save As.**
3. In the *Save As* dialog, click the **Save as type** arrow and select the text format you want.
4. Click **Save.**
5. If your workbook includes more than one worksheet, Excel displays a message warning that the text file format does not support multiple worksheets. Click **OK** to dismiss the message.

FIGURE EX 9.50

6. Excel may show yet another warning message that some features might be lost if you save in the selected format. Click **Yes** to continue saving the file.

tips & tricks

If you or someone else is going to import the file into another spreadsheet program or database, comma delimited (.csv) is the most common format to use.

another method

Pressing the **F12** key opens the *Save As* dialog.

let me try

Open the student data file **EX9-14-Sales** and try this skill on your own:

1. Export (save) this worksheet as a CSV comma-delimited text file named: `Sales_CSV`
2. Export (save) this worksheet as a tab-delimited text file named: `Sales_Tab`
3. Close the file.

excel 2013   chapter 9 Importing Data, Reviewing, and Finalizing the Workbook

Skill 9.15 Saving a Workbook in Other Formats

If you have an Excel workbook that you make copies of often to reuse, or if you want to share a workbook with others to use as a sample, try saving it as a template. A **template** is a file with predefined settings that you can use as a starting point for other workbooks.

To save a workbook as a template:

1. Click the **File** tab. Click **Save As.**
2. In the *Save As* dialog, click the **Save as type** arrow and select **Excel Template** or one of the other template formats.
3. Notice that when you change the file format to Excel Template, the *Save As* location changes to **My Documents > Custom Office Templates.** This is the default location for saving new Microsoft Office templates. You can change the location if you want to save the file somewhere else.
4. Click **Save.**

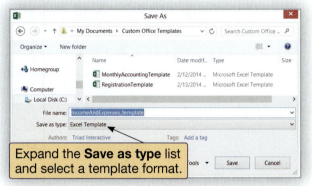

Expand the **Save as type** list and select a template format.

FIGURE EX 9.51

Beginning with Excel 2007, Microsoft changed the default file format for Excel to .xlsx, which is not backward compatible. If you want to share a workbook with people who use an earlier version of Excel, you will need to save the file using the **Excel 97-2003 Workbook** (*.xls) format. Some loss of formatting or functionality may occur.

To save a workbook in a format compatible with older versions of Excel:

1. Click the **File** tab. Click **Save As.**
2. In the **Save As** dialog, click the **Save as type** arrow and select **Excel 97-2003 Workbook.**
3. Click **Save.**

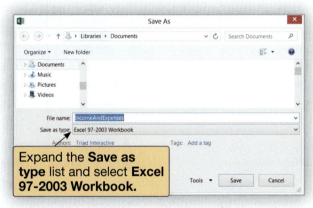

Expand the **Save as type** list and select **Excel 97-2003 Workbook.**

FIGURE EX 9.52

When saving a workbook, be sure to consider who will use the workbook and how they will use it, and select the most appropriate file format.

tell me **more**

When you open a workbook created by a version of Excel older than Excel 2007, you will see *[Compatibility Mode]* in the title bar immediately following the name of the workbook. In **Compatibility mode**, some of the new Excel features and formats are not available (in order to maintain backward compatibility). To convert the workbook to the default Excel 2013 format, click the **File** tab, and click the **Convert** button or click **Save As** and select the **Excel Workbook** format.

let me **try**

Open the student data file **EX9-15-IncomeAndExpenses** and try this skill on your own:

1. Save this workbook as an Excel template named: `IncomeAndExpenses_template`
2. Save the workbook in the format compatible with *Excel 97-2003*. Allow the file to save with compatibility issues. Use the file name: `IncomeAndExpenses_97-2003`
3. Close the file.

Skill 9.16 Adding a Password

The *Info* tab in Backstage displays the current permissions status of the workbook. By default, workbooks are unsecured—anyone can open, copy, and edit any part of the workbook. One way to secure your workbook is to add a password. Users will need to enter the password before they can open the file to view or edit it.

To add a password to your workbook:

1. Click the **File** tab.
2. On the *Info* page, click the **Protect Workbook** button and select **Encrypt with Password.**
3. Type your password in the *Password* box. Notice that the characters you type are hidden and black dots appear instead. Click **OK.**

FIGURE EX 9.53

4. Retype your password in the *Confirm Password* dialog.
5. Click **OK** to add the password to the workbook.

When a workbook has a password, the *Info* page displays a message that a password is required to open the workbook.

FIGURE EX 9.54

tips & tricks

Adding a password will not lock or unlock data in your workbook. You must set worksheet and workbook protection to prevent users from changing data in the workbook once they have it open. Refer to the skill *Protecting Worksheets and Workbooks from Changes* for more information.

let me try

Open the student data file **EX9-16-IncomeAndExpenses** and try this skill on your own:

1. Encrypt the workbook with this password: `abc123`
2. Save the file as directed by your instructor and close it.

Skill 9.17 Finalizing the Workbook

Another way to secure the workbook is to mark it "final." Marking a workbook as final indicates that it will not be edited further. The workbook is converted to read-only status.

Before finalizing the document, you may want to remove certain elements such as personal information in the document properties, comments and hidden rows, columns, and worksheets. The **Document Inspector** allows you to check your file for hidden data and personal information contained in the workbook properties before you finalize the workbook and send it to others.

To inspect your workbook for hidden data or personal information:

1. Click the **File** tab. Click the **Check for Issues** button, and select **Inspect Document.**

2. Excel will prompt you to save changes before running the Document Inspector. Click **Yes.**

3. Review the list of content types that the Documents Inspector will look for. Uncheck any options you do not want to include.

4. Click the **Inspect** button.

5. Click the **Remove All** button next to the items you want to remove from your workbook.

6. To continue inspecting the workbook, click the **Reinspect** button and then repeat Steps 3–5.

7. When you are finished, click the **Close** button to close the Document Inspector.

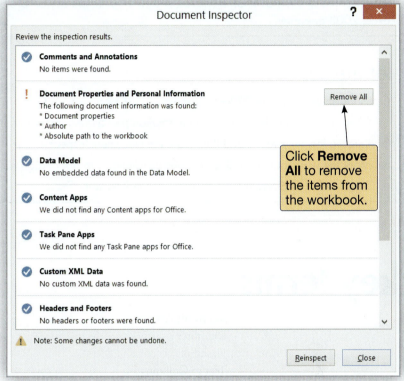

FIGURE EX 9.55

To mark a workbook as final:

1. Click the **File** tab. On the *Info* page, click the **Protect Workbook** button, and select **Mark as Final**.

2. A message box appears letting you know the workbook will be marked as final and saved.

3. Click **OK.**

4. Another message box may appear explaining what features are not available when a workbook has been marked as "final." If you do not want to see this message every time you mark a workbook as final, click the **Don't show this message again** check box. Click **OK** to dismiss the message and finalize the workbook.

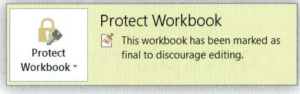

FIGURE EX 9.56

When a workbook has been marked as final, the *Marked as Final* icon appears in the status bar ![icon] and the *Info* page displays a message that the workbook has been marked as final.

MARKED AS FINAL An author has marked this workbook as final to discourage editing. [Edit Anyway]

Click the **Edit Anyway** button to remove a workbook from final status and enable editing.

Marking a workbook as final does not really prevent another user from editing it. When the workbook is opened, the Message Bar displays a warning that the workbook has been marked as final. Any user can click the **Edit Anyway** button to remove the read-only status from the file.

tips & tricks

Files that are marked as final in Microsoft Office 2013 will not be protected with read-only status when opened in Excel 2003 or earlier.

let me try

Open the student data file **EX9-17-IncomeAndExpenses** and try this skill on your own:

1. Check the workbook for personal information and hidden information.
2. Remove the items found and then close the Document Inspector.
3. Mark the workbook as final so it opens as read-only to discourage editing.
4. Save the file as directed by your instructor and close it.

key terms

Microsoft Access	Shared workbook
Delimiter	Compatibility Checker
Flash Fill	Text (Tab delimited) format
Text to Columns	CSV (Comma delimited) format
Data validation rules	Template
Consolidate	Excel 97-2003 Workbook format
Comment	Compatibility mode
Hyperlink	Document Inspector
ScreenTip	Mark as Final

concepts review

1. Which of these commands will update data that was imported from a Microsoft Access database?
   a. Get External Data
   b. Refresh All
   c. Flash Fill
   d. Import Data

2. Which of these characters is *not* a common delimiter for a text file?

   a. Tab

   b. Comma

   c. Semicolon

   d. Hash tag

3. Flash Fill can be used to create multiple columns of data with a single command.

   a. True

   b. False

4. Which of these commands *cannot* be used for similar purposes?

   a. Flash Fill and the CONCATENATE function

   b. Flash Fill and Text to Columns

   c. Text to Columns and the CONCATENATE function

   d. None of the above

5. When you add data validation rules to cells, invalid data are circled automatically.

   a. True

   b. False

6. Using the Consolidate feature always includes links to the source data in an outline format.

   a. True

   b. False

7. Hyperlinks can link to which of these types of locations?

   a. A Web page

   b. An email address

   c. A cell in another worksheet in the workbook

   d. All of the above

8. In order to allow users to edit some cells in a protected worksheet, you must

   a. Unlock the cells and verify that **Selected unlocked cells** is checked in the *Protect Sheet* dialog.

   b. Verify that **Selected locked cells** is checked in the *Protect Sheet* dialog.

   c. Enable the *Track Changes* feature.

   d. Verify that the **Structure** check box is checked in the *Protect Structure and Windows* dialog.

9. Which of these formats supports saving a workbook with multiple worksheets?

   a. Text (Tab delimited)

   b. CSV (Comma delimited)

   c. Excel 97-2003 Workbook

   d. All of the above

10. When a workbook is marked as final, there is no way for a user to edit the workbook.

   a. True

   b. False

projects

Data files for projects can be found on
www.mhhe.com/office2013skills

skill review 9.1

In this project, you will import gradebook data from a Microsoft Access database. You will work with the data to create the final gradebook worksheet. Before finalizing the workbook, you will turn on *Track Changes* and check for compatibility issues with earlier versions of Excel.

Skills needed to complete this project:

- Importing Data from Access (Skill 9.1)
- Adding Data Validation (Skill 9.5)
- Consolidating Data in a Summary Worksheet (Skill 9.7)
- Creating a Drop-Down List for Data Entry (Skill 9.6)
- Working with Comments (Skill 9.8)
- Inserting Hyperlinks (Skill 9.9)
- Converting Data to Columns (Skill 9.4)
- Tracking Changes (Skill 9.12)
- Protecting Worksheets and Workbooks from Changes (Skill 9.11)
- Sharing a Workbook (Skill 9.10)
- Checking for Compatibility with Previous Versions of Excel (Skill 9.13)

1. Open the start file **EX2013-SkillReview-9-1** and resave the file as:
   `[your initials]EX-SkillReview-9-1`
2. If the workbook opens in Protected View, click the **Enable Editing** button in the Message Bar at the top of the workbook so you can modify the workbook.
3. Import student grades from the **WeeklyQuizQry** query (view) in the *Gradebook* Access database.
   a. Go to the **Weekly Quiz** worksheet.
   b. On the *Data* tab, in the *Get External Data* group, click the **From Access** button.
   c. Navigate to the location where the data files for this project were saved. Double-click the **Gradebook** Access database to open it.
   d. In the *Select Table* dialog, click **WeeklyQuizQry.** Click **OK.**
   e. In the *Import Data* dialog, click **OK** to import the data as a table in cell A1 in the existing worksheet.
4. Import student grades from the **HomeworkQry** query (view) in the *Gradebook* Access database.
   a. Go to the **Homework** worksheet.
   b. On the *Data* tab, in the *Get External Data* group, click the **From Access** button.
   c. Navigate to the location where the data files for this project were saved. Double-click the **Gradebook** Access database to open it.
   d. In the *Select Table* dialog, click **HomeworkQry.** Click **OK.**
   e. In the *Import Data* dialog, click **OK** to import the data as a table in cell A1 in the existing worksheet.

5. Import student grades from the **ExtraAssignmentsQry** query (view) in the *Gradebook* Access database.

   a. Go to the **Extra Assignments** worksheet.

   b. On the *Data* tab, in the *Get External Data* group, click the **From Access** button.

   c. Navigate to the location where the data files for this project were saved. Double-click the **Gradebook** Access database to open it.

   d. In the *Select Table* dialog, click **ExtraAssignmentsQry.** Click **OK.**

   e. In the *Import Data* dialog, click **OK** to import the data as a table in cell A1 in the existing worksheet.

6. Remove the Access database connections.

   a. On the *Data* tab, in the *Connections* group, click the **Connections** button.

   b. In the *Workbook Connections* dialog, click each connection listed and then click the **Remove** button.

   c. When prompted by Excel, click **OK** to remove each connection.

   d. When you have removed all connections, click the **Close** button to close the dialog.

7. Add data validation to the imported data to find any grades that are whole numbers and are less than 0 or greater than 100. You will need to do this for each worksheet.

   a. Select cells **C2:L8** on the **Weekly Quiz** worksheet.

   b. On the *Data* tab, in the *Data Tools* group, click the **Data Validation** button.

   c. In the *Data Validation* dialog, expand the **Allow** list and select **Whole Number.**

   d. Verify that the *Data* box displays **Between.**

   e. Type **0** in the *Minimum* box.

   f. Type **100** in the *Maximum* box.

   g. Click **OK.**

   h. On the *Data* tab, in the *Data Tools* group, click the **Data Validation** button arrow and select **Circle Invalid** data. There should be no invalid data in this worksheet.

8. Repeat Steps 7a–h for the **Homework** and **Extra Assignments** worksheets. You should find three invalid entries in the *Homework* worksheet. Fix them as follows.

   a. Edit the values that are negative and remove the – to make the numbers positive.

   b. Edit the value that is greater than 100 and change it to **100.**

   c. When you have edited the grades, there should be no circles on the worksheet.

9. Use Consolidate to create a single grade for each week averaging the grades from the *Weekly Quiz, Homework,* and *Extra Assignments* worksheets.

   a. Go to the **Final Grades** worksheet.

   b. Select cells **B2:K8.**

   c. On the *Data* tab, in the *Data Tools* group, click the **Consolidate** button.

   d. If there are existing references in the *All References* box, remove them by clicking each one and then clicking the **Delete** button.

   e. Expand the *Function* list and select **Average.**

   f. Add the first reference. Click in the **Reference** box.

   g. Click the **Weekly Quiz** worksheet tab and click and drag to select cells **C2:L8.**

   h. Click **Add.**

   i. Click the **Homework** worksheet tab and then click **Add.**

   j. Click the **Extra Assignments** worksheet tab and then click **Add.**

   k. Verify that the **Create links to source data** check box is *not* checked.

   l. Click **OK.**

10. Add a drop-down list to limit extra credit to specific values.

    a. On the **Final Grades** worksheet, select cells **N2:N8.**

    b. On the *Data* tab, in the *Data Tools* group, click the **Data Validation** button.

    c. In the *Data Validation* dialog, expand the **Allow** list and select **List.**

    d. In the *Source* box, type: `10,25,50`

    e. Click **OK.**

    f. Verify that the in-cell drop-down list appears as expected, and add the extra credit value **25** to the first student in the gradebook.

11. Add a comment about the changed grade.

    a. Select cell **Q2.**

    b. On the *Review* tab, in the *Comments* group, click the **New Comment** button.

    c. In the *Comment* balloon, type: `Grade bumped to B with extra credit`

    d. Click outside the balloon.

12. Add a hyperlink to link to the *Grade Scale* worksheet.

    a. Select cell **Q1.**

    b. On the *Insert* tab, in the *Links* group, click the **Hyperlink** button.

    c. Under *Link to,* select **Place in this Document.**

    d. In the *Or select a place in this document* box, click **Grade Scale.**

    e. Verify that the cell reference in the *Type the cell reference* box is **A1.**

    f. Click **OK.**

    g. Test the link by clicking cell **Q1.**

13. Before adding worksheet protection, you should separate the student first and last names into separate columns.

    a. On the **Final Grades** worksheet, insert a new column to the right of the student names.

    b. Change the text in cell A1 to: `First Name`

    c. Press **Tab** and type `Last Name` in cell **B1.**

    d. Select cells **A2:A8.**

    e. On the *Data* tab, in the *Data Tools* group, click the **Text to Columns** button.

    f. In Step 1 of the wizard, verify that **Delimited** is selected. Click **Next.**

    g. In Step 2 of the wizard, if necessary, check the **Space** check box to separate the names at the space between the first name and the last name. Click **Next.**

    h. Review the *Data preview* box to verify that the text will be separated as you expect and then click **Finish.**

14. Unlock the extra credit cells so changes can be made after you apply worksheet protection to the gradebook.

    a. On the *Final Grades* worksheet, select cells **O2:O8.**

    b. On the *Home* tab, in the *Cells* group, click the **Format** button. Click *Lock Cell* to remove the highlight.

15. Apply worksheet protection so users can only select cells that are locked, not edit them.

    a. On the *Review* tab, in the *Changes* group, click the **Protect Sheet** button.

    b. Verify that the **Protect worksheet and content of locked cells** check box is checked.

    c. Verify that **Select locked cells** and **Select unlocked cells** are the only two options checked.

    d. Click **OK.**

16. Recall that shared workbooks cannot include tables. Before turning on *Track Changes* and sharing the workbook, you will need to convert the imported tables to ranges.

    a. Click the **Weekly Quiz** worksheet tab. Select any cell in the table. On the *Table Tools Design* tab, in the *Tools* group, click the **Convert to Range** button. Click **OK.**

    b. Repeat Step 16a for the **Homework** and **Extra Assignments** worksheets.

17. Turn on *Track Changes* to highlight any changes to the workbook that have not yet been reviewed.

    a. On the *Review* tab, in the *Changes* group, click the **Track Changes** button, and select **Highlight Changes…**

    b. In the *Highlight Changes* dialog, click the **Track changes while editing. This also shares your workbook.** check box.

    c. Expand the **When** box, and select **Not yet reviewed.**

    d. Verify that the **Highlight changes on screen** check box is checked.

    e. Click **OK.**

    f. Click **OK** again to save the workbook.

18. Add a 10 point extra credit bonus for Manual Topaz.

    a. On the **Final Grades** worksheet, click cell **O8.**

    b. Click the arrow and select **10** from the list.

    c. Note that you can edit this cell because you unlocked it previously.

19. Accept all changes made to this workbook that have not yet been reviewed.

    a. On the *Review* tab, in the *Changes* group, click the **Track Changes** button and select **Accept/Reject Changes.**

    b. Click **OK** when prompted to save the workbook.

    c. In the *Select Changes to Accept or Reject* dialog, click **OK.**

    d. Review the change and click the **Accept** button.

20. Check for any possible compatibility issues in this workbook.

    a. Click the **File** tab.

    b. Click the **Check for Issues** button and select **Check Compatibility.**

    c. In the Compatibility Checker, review the issues, but do not make any changes.

    d. Click **OK** to close the Compatibility Checker.

21. Close the workbook.

skill review 9.2

In this project, you will create a summary worksheet to consolidate sales data from different regions. You will import addresses from a text file and manipulate the imported data.

Skills needed to complete this project:

- Consolidating Data in a Summary Worksheet (Skill 9.7)
- Adding Data Validation (Skill 9.5)
- Inserting Hyperlinks (Skill 9.9)
- Working with Comments (Skill 9.8)
- Importing Data from a Text File (Skill 9.2)
- Inserting Data Using Flash Fill (Skill 9.3)
- Converting Data to Columns (Skill 9.4)

- Protecting Worksheets and Workbooks from Changes (Skill 9.11)
- Checking for Compatibility with Previous Versions of Excel (Skill 9.13)
- Finalizing the Workbook (Skill 9.17)

1. Open the start file **EX2013-SkillReview-9-2** and resave the file as: `[your initials]EX-SkillReview-9-2`

2. If the workbook opens in Protected View, click the **Enable Editing** button in the Message Bar at the top of the workbook so you can modify the workbook.

3. Use Consolidate to create a summary sheet totaling sales from the *Northeast, Southeast, Southwest,* and *Northwest* worksheet. Include links to the source data.

    a. Go to the **Summary** worksheet.

    b. Select cells **B4:E11.**

    c. On the *Data* tab, in the *Data Tools* group, click the **Consolidate** button.

    d. If there are existing references in the *All References* box, remove them by clicking each one and then clicking the **Delete** button.

    e. Verify that **Sum** is selected in the *Function* list.

    f. Add the first reference. Click in the **Reference** box.

    g. Click the **Northeast** worksheet tab and click and drag to select cells **B3:E10.**

    h. Click **Add.**

    i. Click the **Southeast** worksheet tab and then click **Add.**

    j. Click the **Southwest** worksheet tab and then click **Add.**

    k. Click the **Northwest** worksheet tab and then click **Add.**

    l. If necessary, click the **Create links to source data** check box to add a checkmark.

    m. Click **OK.**

4. Expand the details for the Equipment sales type category and add data validation to find any individual sales less than 75,000.

    a. On the *Summary* worksheet, click the ⊕ next to *Equipment.*

    b. Select cells **B4:E7.**

    c. On the *Data* tab, in the *Data Tools* group, click the **Data Validation** button.

    d. In the *Data Validation* dialog, expand the **Allow** list and select **Whole Number.**

    e. Expand the **Data** list, and select **greater than.**

    f. Type **70,000** in the *Minimum* box.

    g. Click **OK.**

    h. On the *Data* tab, in the *Data Tools* group, click the **Data Validation** button arrow and select **Circle Invalid** data.

5. Add a hyperlink from the circled cell to the cell in the source worksheet.

    a. On the *Summary* worksheet, click cell **D6.** Look in the address bar to see the cell reference for this particular value.

    b. On the *Insert* tab, in the *Links* group, click the **Hyperlink** button.

    c. Under *Link to,* select **Place in this Document.**

    d. In the *Type the cell reference* box, type: **D3**

    e. In the *Or select a place in this document* box, click **Southeast.**

    f. Click **OK.**

    g. Test the link by clicking cell **D6.**

6. Add a comment.

    a. Select cell **D3** in the *Southeast* worksheet.

    b. On the *Review* tab, in the *Comments* group, click the **New Comment** button.

    c. In the *Comment* balloon, type: `Why the drop in sales here?`

    d. Click outside the balloon.

7. Import sales associate addresses from the tab-delimited text file *SalesAssociateAddressList.* You will create a new worksheet when you import the data.

    a. On the *Data* tab, in the *Get External Data* group, click the **From Text** button.

    b. Navigate to the location where the data files for this project were saved. Double-click the **SalesAssociateAddressList** text file to open it.

    c. In Step 1 of the wizard, verify that delimited is selected. Click **Next.**

    d. In Step 2 of the wizard, click the **Tab** check box if it is not already checked. Click **Next.**

    e. Click **Finish.**

    f. In the *Import Data* dialog, click the **New worksheet** radio button under **Where do you want to put the data?**

    g. Click **OK.**

8. Double-click the new worksheet tab and rename it: `AddressList`

9. Remove the text file connection.

    a. On the *Data* tab, in the *Connections* group, click the **Connections** button.

    b. In the *Workbook Connections* dialog, click the connection listed and then click the **Remove** button.

    c. When prompted by Excel, click **OK** to remove the connection.

    d. Click the **Close** button to close the dialog.

10. Use Flash Fill to correct the phone number format.

    a. On the *AddressList* worksheet, type `Fixed Mobile Phone Format` in cell **D1.** Make the column wider if necessary.

    b. Type the new phone number format in cell **D2:** `(916) 555-1324`

    c. Press **Enter** or click in cell **D3.**

    d. On the *Data* tab, in the *Data Tools* group, click the **Flash Fill** button.

    e. Delete column **C.**

11. Use Text to Columns to separate the address into columns for the street address, the city, the state, and the zip code.

    a. On the *AddressList* worksheet, insert three columns to the right of the **Address** column.

    b. Change the text in cell B1 to: `Street Address`

    c. Press **Tab** and type `City` in cell **C1.**

    d. Press **Tab** and type `State` in cell **D1.**

    e. Press **Tab** and type `Zip` in cell **E1.**

    f. Select cells **B2:B9.**

    g. On the *Data* tab, in the *Data Tools* group, click the **Text to Columns** button.

    h. In Step 1 of the wizard, verify that **Delimited** is selected. Click **Next.**

    i. In Step 2 of the wizard, if necessary, check the **Comma** check box. Click **Next.**

    j. Review the *Data preview* box to verify that the text will be separated as you expect and then click **Finish.**

12. Unlock the address and mobile phone cells so changes can be made if you later apply worksheet protection to the workbook.

   a. On the *AddressList* worksheet, select cells **B2:F9.**

   b. On the *Home* tab, in the *Cells* group, click the **Format** button. Click **Lock Cell** to remove the highlight.

13. Apply worksheet protection so users can only select cells that are locked, not edit them.

   a. On the *Review* tab, in the *Changes* group, click the **Protect Sheet** button.

   b. Verify that the **Protect worksheet and content of locked cells** check box is checked.

   c. Verify that **Select locked cells** and **Select unlocked cells** are the only two options checked.

   d. Click **OK.**

14. Check for any possible compatibility issues in this workbook.

   a. Click the **File** tab.

   b. Click the **Check for Issues** button and select **Check Compatibility.**

   c. In the Compatibility Checker, review the issue, but do not make any changes.

   d. Copy the issue to a new worksheet in the workbook by clicking the **Copy to New Sheet** button at the bottom left of the dialog. This will close the Compatibility Checker.

15. Mark the workbook as final.

   a. Click the **File** tab.

   b. Click the **Protect Workbook** button and select **Mark as Final.**

   c. Click **OK** to dismiss any messages Excel displays about marking the document as final.

16. Close the workbook.

challenge yourself **9.3**

In this project, you will create a summary worksheet to consolidate real estate sales data for different types of properties. You will import sales data from a text file and manipulate the imported data.

Skills needed to complete this project:

- Consolidating Data in a Summary Worksheet (Skill 9.7)
- Importing Data from a Text File (Skill 9.2)
- Creating a Drop-Down List for Data Entry (Skill 9.6)
- Adding Data Validation (Skill 9.5)
- Working with Comments (Skill 9.8)
- Inserting Data Using Flash Fill (Skill 9.3)
- Inserting Hyperlinks (Skill 9.9)
- Protecting Worksheets and Workbooks from Changes (Skill 9.11)
- Checking for Compatibility with Previous Versions of Excel (Skill 9.13)
- Finalizing the Workbook (Skill 9.17)

1. Open the start file **EX2013-ChallengeYourself-9-3** and resave the file as:
   `[your initials]EX-ChallengeYourself-9-3`

2. If the workbook opens in Protected View, enable editing so you can make changes to the workbook.

3. Use Consolidate to create a summary of real estate sales for all property types. Place the consolidated data on the *Summary* worksheet in cells **B3:C15.** Use the **Average** function to consolidate the data from cells **B2:C14** in the **Condo, Townhouse,** and **Single Family** worksheets. Include links to the source data.

4. Import individual sales data from the tab-delimited text file **Select Sales Data 2013-2014.** Import the data as a table in cell **A1** of the **Select Sales** worksheet.

5. Remove the data connection when the import is complete.

6. In the *Select Sales* worksheet, add data validation to restrict values in the *House Type* columns (cells **B2:B139**) to the values in the cell range named **PropertyTypes.** Include a drop-down list of values in the cells to assist in data correction.

7. Apply data validation circles to any values that violate the data validation rules you just created.

8. Add a comment to cell **B1** in the *Select Sales* worksheet that reads: `We need to fix this data`

9. Add a hyperlink to cell **B1** to link to the named range (defined name) **PropertyTypes.** Test the link.

10. Use Flash Fill to add a new column of data to display the number of bedrooms/the number of bathrooms.

    a. In cell **F1,** type the heading: **BR/BR**

    b. Complete the column of data using this pattern in cell **F2:** `1 BR/1 BA`

    You will need to enter at least two samples in order for Flash Fill to suggest the correct autofill data. Check your work carefully.

11. Apply worksheet protection so users can only select cells, not edit them. Do not unlock any cells.

12. Check for any possible compatibility issues in this workbook.

13. Mark the workbook as final.

14. Close the workbook.

challenge yourself 9.4

In this project, you will use data validation to identify missing and incorrect data. You will create a summary worksheet to consolidate data about vaccine shipments, and then you will import data from the *Vaccines* Access database and manipulate the data.

Skills needed to complete this project:

- Adding Data Validation (Skill 9.5)
- Working with Comments (Skill 9.8)
- Protecting Worksheets and Workbooks from Changes (Skill 9.11)
- Creating a Drop-Down List for Data Entry (Skill 9.6)
- Inserting Hyperlinks (Skill 9.9)
- Consolidating Data in a Summary Worksheet (Skill 9.7)
- Converting Data to Columns (Skill 9.4)
- Importing Data from Access (Skill 9.1)
- Checking for Compatibility with Previous Versions of Excel (Skill 9.13)
- Finalizing the Workbook (Skill 9.17)

1. Open the start file **EX2013-ChallengeYourself-9-4** and resave the file as: `[your initials]EX-ChallengeYourself-9-4`

2. If the workbook opens in Protected View, enable editing so you can make changes to the workbook.

3. Apply data validation rules to cells **F15:F24** on the **2013 Shipments** worksheet and cells **F15:F26** on the **2014 Shipments** worksheet.

   a. Require whole numbers between 100 and 5,000.

   b. Do not allow blanks.

   c. Circle invalid data in both the **2013 Shipments** and **2014 Shipments** worksheets.

4. Add this comment to cell **F20** on the **2014 Shipments** worksheet: `Need to look up cost`

5. Unlock the blank cells so someone can update the data after the worksheet protection has been applied. *Hint:* There is one cell on the *2013 Shipments* worksheet and one cell on the *2014 Shipments* worksheet. Use the data validation circles to find them.

6. Apply data validation rules to cells **C15:C24** on the **2013 Shipments** worksheet and cells **C15:C26** on the **2014 Shipments** worksheet.

   a. Values for these cells must come from the **Locations** named range.

   b. Include an in-cell drop-down list. Do not allow blanks.

   c. Circle invalid data in both the **2013 Shipments** and **2014 Shipments** worksheets.

7. Add a hyperlink to cell **C16** on the **2013 Shipments** worksheets to link to cell **A26** on the **Locations** worksheet. Test the link.

8. Use Consolidate to create a summary of total units shipped and total cost to date.

   a. Place the consolidated data on the **Summary** worksheet in cells **B2:C10**.

   b. Use the **Sum** function to consolidate the data from cells **B3:C11** in the **2013** and **2014** worksheets.

   c. Include links to the source data.

9. Use Consolidate to create a summary of average total units shipped and total cost to date.

   a. Place the consolidated data on the **Summary** worksheet in cells **B31:C39**.

   b. Use the **Average** function to consolidate the data from cells **B3:C11** in the **2013** and **2014** worksheets.

   c. *Do not* include links to the source data.

10. On the **Locations** worksheet, use Text to Columns to separate the city and country names into separate columns.

    a. The city name should remain in column B, and the country name should be moved to column C.

    b. Add the text `Country` to cell **C1**.

    c. Use Format Painter to copy the formatting from cell **B1** to cell **C1**.

11. Import data from the **Vaccines** table in the **Vaccines** Access database to cell **A1** in the **Vaccines** worksheet. The database should be located in the folder where the data files for this project were saved. When you are finished with the import, delete the data connection.

12. Check for any possible compatibility issues in this workbook.

13. Mark the workbook as final.

14. Close the workbook.

In this project, you will work with a university registration workbook. You will import data from an Access database and manipulate the data in workbook to create a summary worksheet.

Skills needed to complete this project:

- Consolidating Data in a Summary Worksheet (Skill 9.7)
- Adding Data Validation (Skill 9.5)
- Importing Data from Access (Skill 9.1)
- Creating a Drop-Down List for Data Entry (Skill 9.6)
- Working with Comments (Skill 9.8)
- Protecting Worksheets and Workbooks from Changes (Skill 9.11)
- Inserting Hyperlinks (Skill 9.9)
- Exporting to Text Formats (Skill 9.14)
- Checking for Compatibility with Previous Versions of Excel (Skill 9.13)
- Finalizing the Workbook (Skill 9.17)

1. Open the start file **EX2013-OnYourOwn-9-5** and resave the file as:
   `[your initials]EX-OnYourOwn-9-5`

2. If the workbook opens in Protected View, click the **Enable Editing** button in the Message Bar at the top of the workbook so you can modify the workbook.

3. This workbook includes four worksheets of student GPA and average credit hour data. Create a summary worksheet to calculate average GPA and credit hours for all students for each of the advisors.

4. Apply data validation rules to restrict the credit hours in each worksheet to values appropriate for that level of university student.

5. Import the **Class, Course, Department,** and **Professor** tables from the **University Registration** Access database. The database should be located in the folder where the data files for this project were saved. Remember to remove the data connections when you are finished importing the data.

6. Apply data validation rules to restrict future data entry as appropriate. Try creating a named range of all the department codes and applying a data validation rule wherever department codes are references.

7. Create a hyperlink somewhere in the workbook to link to an appropriate Web page on your school's Web site listing departments or faculty.

8. Save one of the worksheets in a variety of text formats. Be sure to save a copy of the workbook in the default Excel Workbook format before saving as a text file or you will lose your work!

9. Open the Excel Workbook version of your file, and try re-importing data from the text files you saved. How does the imported data compare to the original worksheet you exported?

10. Run Compatibility Checker and Document Inspector before saving the workbook as final.

11. Save the workbook as final and close it.

fix it 9.6

In this project, you will make corrections to a party planning workbook. Some of the data in this worksheet was imported from other programs and is not formatted correctly for purposes of this workbook.

Skills needed to complete this project:

- Inserting Data Using Flash Fill (Skill 9.3)
- Converting Data to Columns (Skill 9.4)
- Inserting Hyperlinks (Skill 9.9)
- Consolidating Data in a Summary Worksheet (Skill 9.7)
- Protecting Worksheets and Workbooks from Changes (Skill 9.11)

1. Open the start file **EX2013-FixIt-9-6** and resave the file as:
   `[your initials]EX-FixIt-9-6`

2. If the workbook opens in Protected View, click the **Enable Editing** button in the Message Bar at the top of the workbook so you can modify the workbook.

3. Use Flash Fill to complete the missing data on the *Guest List* worksheet.

   a. In the *Name Tag* column, please complete the list of name. The names should be in all upper case letters similar to the name in cell **C3.**

   b. In order to send the addresses to the printer, the city, state, and zip code need to be in a single column in the format **City, State Zip.** Complete the data in column **H.**

4. On the *Places to Shop* worksheet, use Text to Columns and Flash Fill to fix the following issues:

   a. The address should be separated into separate columns for Street, City, State, and Zip.

   b. The phone number should use the format ###-####. Someone used Flash Fill previously to complete the data, but the phone numbers were not autofilled correctly. You will need to re-do the Flash Fill using a couple of examples and verify that the autofill works as expected.

5. On the *Week Before* worksheet, the hyperlink in cell **A2** links to the wrong cell in the *Places to Shop* worksheet. It should link to cell **A11,** not cell A12.

6. Add links to the source from the data consolidation in cells **C2:C16** in the **Total Budget** worksheet. When you open the *Consolidate* dialog, the references are there for you. All you need to do is generate the links to the source data.

7. Before saving the file, protect *all* the worksheets so no changes can be made and protect the workbook so the structure cannot be modified.

8. Save and close the workbook.

chapter **10**

Working with Macros

In this chapter, you will learn the following skills:

- Understand macro security warnings
- Define a trusted location
- Add the Developer tab to the Ribbon
- Use, record, and modify macros
- Work with VBA in the Visual Basic Editor
- Add macros to the Ribbon and the Quick Access Toolbar

Skill **10.1** Opening a Macro-Enabled Workbook

Skill **10.2** Changing the Trust Center Settings

Skill **10.3** Adding the Developer Tab to the Ribbon

Skill **10.4** Running a Macro

Skill **10.5** Saving a Macro-Enabled Workbook or Template

Skill **10.6** Recording a Macro

Skill **10.7** Modifying a Macro Using VBA

Skill **10.8** Adding a Macro to a Form Button Control

Skill **10.9** Adding a Custom Tab to the Ribbon

Skill **10.10** Customizing the Quick Access Toolbar

skills

introduction

In this chapter you will work with macro-enabled workbooks. First, you will learn to enable and use existing macros, and then you will record and edit a macro on your own. You will add a custom button to the workbook to run a macro. Finally, you will customize the Excel interface by adding a new tab and group to the Ribbon and adding a macro to the Quick Access Toolbar.

Skill 10.1 Opening a Macro-Enabled Workbook

A **macro** is a custom set of programming commands written in the **Visual Basic for Applications (VBA)** language. Macros are often used to simplify repetitive tasks—saving you time and effort. Instead of performing the same set of actions over and over, you can just run the macro. Macros are also useful when other, less-experienced users need to work on the workbook. You can provide them with a set of macros to use instead of expecting them to try to figure out the Excel commands on their own.

Macros are only available in macro-enabled workbooks. A workbook that can include macros has the file extension **.xlsm;** macro-enabled templates use the file extension **.xltm.** Macro-enabled files also use a slightly different file icon as shown in Figure EX 10.1.

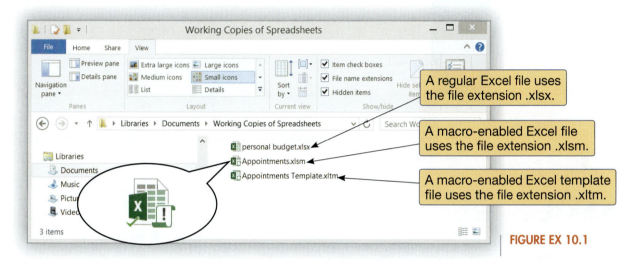

FIGURE EX 10.1

When you open a workbook that contains macros, the Message Bar appears below the Ribbon with a security warning that macros have been disabled. You must click the **Enable Content** button to enable macros in the workbook. Clicking *Enable Content* enables macros for this session only. If you re-open the file again later, you will see the same message and will need to click **Enable Content** again.

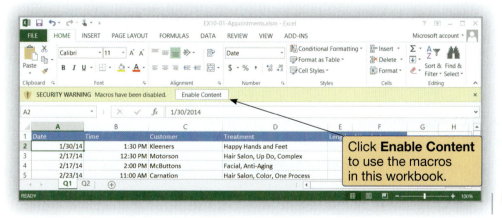

FIGURE EX 10.2

If you do not want this warning to appear every time the workbook is opened, you can make the workbook a **trusted document**. Marking the workbook as trusted allows all active content to run without warning including macros, data connections, and ActiveX controls.

To make a workbook a trusted document:

1. Click the **File** tab.

2. On the Info page, click the **Enable Content** button and select **Enable All Content.**

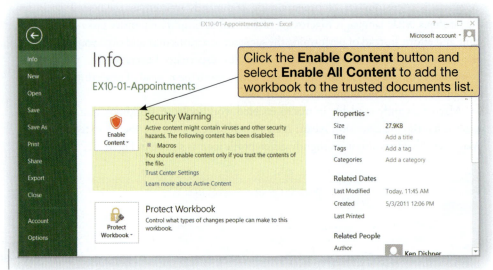

FIGURE EX 10.3

For more information about working with trusted documents, refer to the skill *Changing the Trust Center Settings.*

tips & tricks

> If you begin working without enabling the content, the message disappears, but Excel will not allow you to run macros without first closing the workbook and re-opening it with active content enabled.

> If you are working in a computer lab or other environment where the administrator has restricted permissions, you may not be able to enable macros or add the workbook to the trusted documents list.

tell me more

In Windows 8, to display the file name extensions in the Explorer window, on the *View* tab, click the **File name extensions** check box.

let me try

Open the student data file **EX10-01-Appointments** and try this skill on your own:

1. Enable the active content in this workbook for just this session.

2. Always enable this workbook's active content by making it a trusted document.

3. Save the file as directed by your instructor and close it.

Skill 10.2 Changing the Trust Center Settings

By default, Excel allows you to open all files that contain macros, but disables the macros unless you explicitly enable the content. If you open a file that you know contains macros, but you do not see the *Enable Content* button on the Message Bar, Excel may be set to disable all macros automatically without warning.

To check the macro security settings, open the **Trust Center**:

1. Click the **File** tab.

2. Click the **Options** button to open the *Excel Options* dialog.

3. Click **Trust Center** and then click the **Trust Center Settings...** button to open the Trust Center.

4. Click **Macro Settings** and review the current setting. If necessary, click the **Disable all macros with notification** radio button and click **OK.**

5. Click **OK** to close the *Excel Options* dialog.

Verify the macro security settings in the Trust Center.

FIGURE EX 10.4

If you work extensively with macro-enabled files, you may want to store them in a folder designated as a **trusted location**. Files that are opened from a trusted location do not use Protected View and active content is allowed without requiring you to enable it each time you open the file. Be careful. Any changes you make to the Trust Center apply to the Excel application, not just the open workbook.

To add a location to the *Trusted Locations* list:

1. Open the Trust Center.

2. Click **Trusted Locations.**

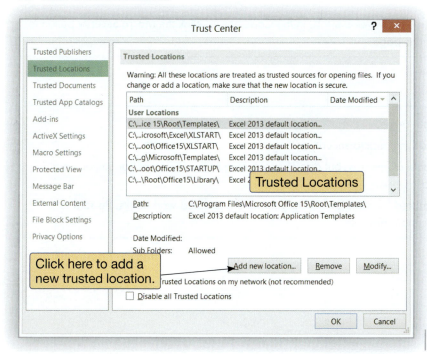

Trusted Locations

Click here to add a new trusted location.

FIGURE EX 10.5

FIGURE EX 10.6

3. Click the **Add new location...** button.
4. Click the **Browse...** button and navigate to the folder you want to use as a trusted location. Select the folder and click **OK.**
5. Verify the folder location in the *Path* box and click **OK.**
6. The folder is added to the list of trusted locations.
7. Click **OK** to close the Trust Center.
8. Click **OK** again to close the *Excel Options* dialog.

tips & tricks

Because a macro runs computer code written in Visual Basic for Applications, it has the potential to contain malicious actions. You should never allow macros to run in files unless you are certain that they come from trustworthy sources.

tell me more

To remove a trusted location:

1. Open the Trust Center.
2. Click **Trusted Locations.**
3. Click the path in the trusted locations list and click **Remove.**

another method

) If there is a security warning active on the Info page, you can click the **Trust Center Settings** link to open the Trust Center.

) If you have the *Developer* tab enabled, on the *Developer* tab, in the *Code* group, click the **Macro Security** button to open the Trust Center to the Macro Settings page.

let me try

Open any Excel file and try this skill on your own:

1. Open the Trust Center and review the current macro security settings.
2. If necessary, change the setting to disable all macros, but display a warning in the Message Bar so you can choose to enable them on a case-by-case basis.
3. If you have permission, create a new trusted location for storing your macro-enabled workbooks. Be sure to use this location only for files you are certain are safe.

Skill 10.3 Adding the Developer Tab to the Ribbon

Before working with macros, you should add the *Developer* tab to the Ribbon. The **Developer tab** provides easy access to macro tools in the *Code* group. Throughout the macro skills, we use the *Developer* tab as the primary method for working with macros. Most actions are also available from the *View* tab, *Macros* group.

To add the *Developer* tab to the Ribbon:

1. Click the **File** tab.
2. Click **Options** to open the *Excel Options* dialog.
3. Click **Customize Ribbon.**
4. On the right side of the *Customize the Ribbon* window, the *Customize the Ribbon* list shows all the tabs and groups available. Click the **Developer** check box to add the *Developer* tab to the Ribbon.
5. Click **OK.**

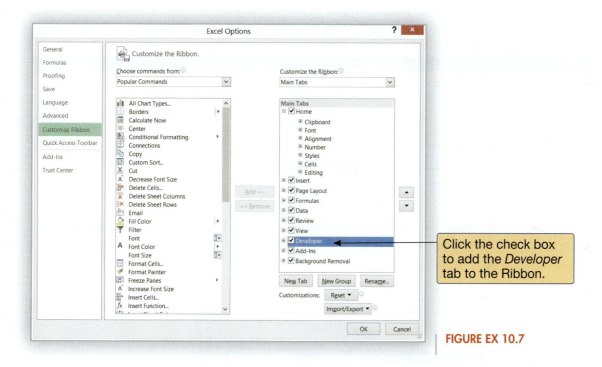

FIGURE EX 10.7

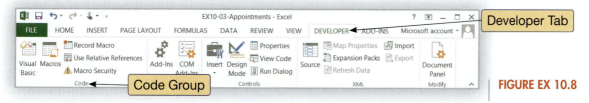

FIGURE EX 10.8

another **method**

Right-click any area of the Ribbon and select **Customize the Ribbon...** to open the *Excel Options* dialog to the Customize Ribbon page.

let me **try**

Open any Excel file and try this skill on your own:

Add the *Developer* tab to the Ribbon.

Skill 10.4 Running a Macro

Figure EX 10.9 shows data imported from an Access database. The macro named *FormatImport* includes all the steps that must be completed to format the data properly.

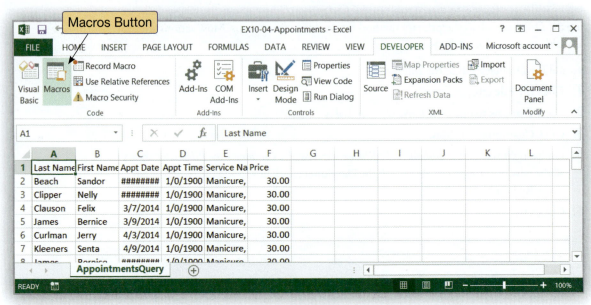

FIGURE EX 10.9

To run a macro:

1. If necessary, click the **Enable Content** button in the Message Bar to enable macros in the current workbook.

2. On the *Developer* tab, in the *Code* group, click the **Macros** button.

3. In the *Macro* dialog, click the name of the macro you want to run. Notice that a description of the purpose of the macro appears near the bottom of the dialog.

4. Click the **Run** button.

FIGURE EX 10.10

Figure EX 10.11 shows the results after running the macro. The *FormatImport* macro formatted the imported data as a table, applied a time format to column D, applied a number format to column F, and sorted the data.

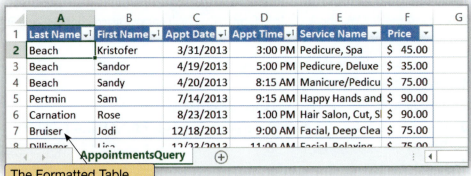

The Formatted Table after Running the Macro

FIGURE EX 10.11

tips & tricks

› You can run a macro stored in any open workbook, not just the workbook you are working on. By default, the *Macro* dialog displays available macros from all open workbooks. When the macro is from another workbook, the workbook name will precede the macro name in the *Macro* dialog.

› To see only the macros contained within a specific workbook, either expand the *Macros in* list and select the workbook file name from the list or select **This workbook** to see only macros in the current workbook.

tell me more

Many macros have a keyboard shortcut associated with them. To find the keyboard shortcut for a macro, open the *Macro* dialog, select the macro you want, and then click the **Options** button.

another method

On the *View* tab, in the *Macros* group, click the **Macros** button arrow and then click **View Macros** to open the *Macros* dialog.

let me try

Open the student data file **EX10-04-Appointments** and try this skill on your own:

1. If necessary, enable the active content in this workbook.
2. Start with cell **A1** selected.
3. Run the **FormatImport** macro.
4. Save the file as directed by your instructor and close it.

Skill 10.5 Saving a Macro-Enabled Workbook or Template

If you add macros or other VBA code to the workbook, you will need to save it using the **Excel Macro-Enabled Workbook** (***.xlsm**) format. Excel will not save macros or other code in workbooks saved in the regular .xlsx format.

To save the file in a format that supports macros:

1. Click the **File** tab and click **Save As.**

2. Navigate to the location where you want to save the file.

3. In the *Save As* dialog, click the **Save as type** arrow and select **Excel Macro-Enabled Workbook.**

4. Click **Save.**

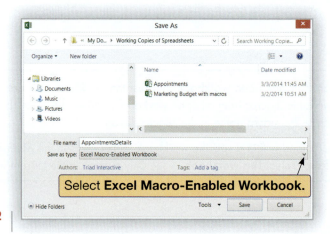

Select **Excel Macro-Enabled Workbook.**

FIGURE EX 10.12

Follow the same steps to save the file as a macro-enabled template. Select the file type **Excel Macro-Enabled Template**. If you have file extensions enabled, you will see the extension ***.xltm.** Notice that when you change the file format to *Excel Macro-Enabled Template,* the *Save As* location changes to **My Documents > Custom Office Templates.** This is the default location for saving new Microsoft Office templates. You can navigate to another folder if you want to save the file in another location.

tips & tricks

If you record a macro in a "regular" workbook, when you save or close the file, Excel will display a message stating that the workbook contains a VB project that cannot be saved in a macro-free workbook. Click the **No** button to open the Save As page so you can save the workbook in another format.

Before adding macros to a workbook, it is a good practice to save it in the macro-enabled format so you don't accidentally close the workbook without choosing the new format and lose your work.

let me try

Open the student data file **EX10-05-AppointmentsDetails** and try this skill on your own:

1. Save the file as a macro-enabled workbook and then close it.

2. Open the student data file **EX10-05-AppointmentsDetailsTemplate.**

3. This file will be used as a template. Save it with the template format that allows macros and then close it.

Skill 10.6 Recording a Macro

There are two ways to create a macro. If you are familiar with the VBA programming language, you can open the Visual Basic Editor and write the programming code to instruct Excel to perform each task in the macro. The easier way to create a macro is to record it. When you record a macro, you complete all the actions you want the macro to perform, and Excel converts your keystrokes and mouse clicks to VBA code.

Macro-recording actions are available from the *Developer* tab, *Code* group.

When you have the *Developer* tab enabled, the status bar includes a button to begin recording a new macro. When a macro recording is running, this button changes to a *Stop* button.

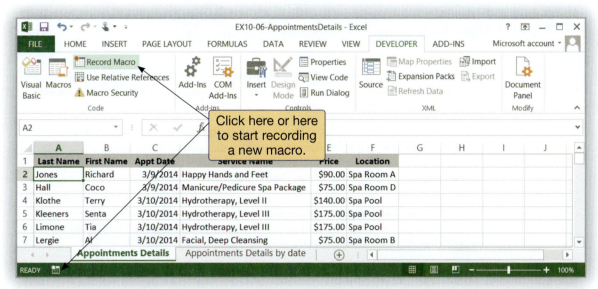

FIGURE EX 10.13

To record a macro:

1. On the *Developer* tab, in the *Code* group, click the **Record Macro** button or click the button on the status bar.

2. In the *Record Macro* dialog, enter a name for the macro in the *Macro name* box.

3. If you want to create a keyboard shortcut for the macro, type the upper- or lowercase letter in the *Shortcut key* box.

   - If you type a lowercase letter, the keyboard shortcut will be Ctrl + the letter you enter.
   - If you type an uppercase letter, the keyboard shortcut will be Ctrl + Shift + the letter you enter.

4. By default, Excel stores the macro in the current workbook. If you want to store the macro in a new workbook instead, expand the **Store macro in** list and select **New Workbook.** Select **Personal Macro Workbook** to store the macro in a hidden workbook that is available whenever you use Excel. (Refer to the *Tips & Tricks* box for more information about using the personal workbook.)

5. In the *Description* box, enter a description of the tasks the macro will perform and/or the circumstances under which the macro should be used.

6. Click **OK** to begin recording the macro.

FIGURE EX 10.14

7. Excel is now recording your typing and mouse clicks to create the macro. Perform all the actions you want the macro to perform. If you make minor mistakes, you can correct them in the VBA code later.

8. When you are finished, on the *Developer* tab, in the *Code* group, click the **Stop Recording** button ▪ Stop Recording or click the button on the status bar READY ▢.

When you record a macro, you can choose whether Excel should capture cell reference as absolute or relative. By default, Excel records macros with absolute references. If you use relative cell references instead, the actions performed by the macro will be relative to the cell you select when you start the macro. On the *Developer* tab, in the *Code* group, click the **Use Relative References** button ▣ Use Relative References to enable or disable this option. The button appears highlighted when the option is enabled.

tips & tricks

If you want macros to be available whenever you use Excel, select **Personal Macro Workbook** as the *Store macro in* option in the *Record Macro* dialog. The personal workbook is a hidden workbook file named *PERSONAL.XLSB*. It is always open in the background when you use Excel, so the macros stored there are always available.

1. To delete or edit a macro stored in your personal workbook, you first need to unhide the workbook. On the *View* tab, in the *Window* group, click the **Unhide** button. In the *Unhide* dialog, click the **PERSONAL.XLSB** file, if necessary, and then click **OK.**

2. Once the file is unhidden, you can open the *Macro* dialog and edit or delete macros as needed.

3. Hide the *PERSONAL.XLSB* workbook when you are finished. Do not close the file. Excel will close it automatically when you exit Excel.

another method

If the *Developer* tab is not available, you can work with macros from the *View* tab, *Macros* group.

❭ To start recording a macro, click the **Macros** button arrow and select **Record Macro.**

❭ To stop recording a macro, click the **Macros** button arrow and select **Stop Recording.**

❭ To enable or disable recording with relative references, click the **Macros** button arrow and select **Use Relative References.**

let me try

Open the student data file **EX10-06-AppointmentsDetails** and try this skill on your own:

1. Record a new macro with the following specifications:

   a. Macro name: **AddSubtotals**

   b. Location: **This Workbook**

   c. Shortcut key: **Ctrl + Shift + S**

   d. Description: **Sort by last name and then add subtotals**

2. Record these actions in the macro:

   a. Sort the data from A-Z by the *Last Name* column.

   b. Add subtotals (*Data* tab, *Data Tools* group, **Subtotal** button). At every change in **Last Name, Sum** the values in the **Price** column.

3. Save the file as directed by your instructor and close it.

from the perspective of . . .

SMALL BUSINESS OWNER

Our accountant is an Excel expert. She develops great spreadsheets for us to analyze cash flow and inventory bottlenecks. When I first started working with these spreadsheets, I was extremely intimidated. They are full of fancy macros and complicated formulas! However, as I started recording my own macros and working with the VBA code, I began to understand what was going on behind the scenes. I'm still not a VBA programmer, but I can open the Visual Basic Editor and make simple changes on my own.

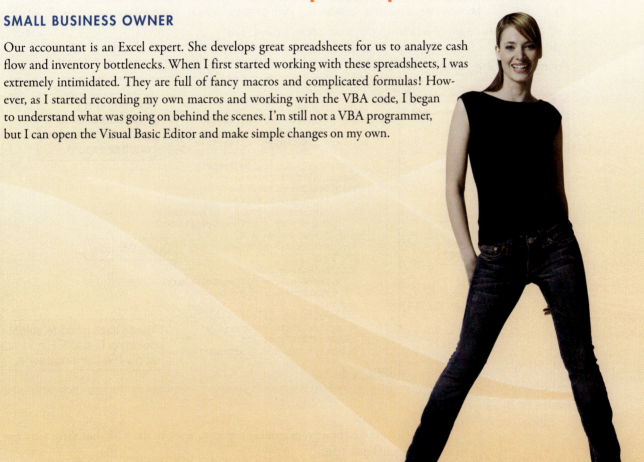

Skill 10.7 Modifying a Macro Using VBA

If you need to make a simple change to a macro, there is no need to rerecord it. Instead, you can edit the underlying VBA code in the **Visual Basic Editor (VBE)**.

Select the macro to edit and then click the **Edit** button to open the Visual Basic Editor.

FIGURE EX 10.15

To edit a macro in the Visual Basic Editor:

1. On the *Developer* tab, in the *Code* group, click the **Macros** button to open the *Macro* dialog.

2. Select the macro you want to edit and then click the **Edit** button.

The Visual Basic Editor opens in a new window with the macro code displayed in the **code window**. If there are multiple macros stored in the same module, the VBE will open at the point where the macro you selected starts.

To navigate to the beginning of the code for another macro, if necessary, double-click the module name in the Project Explorer window, and then expand the **Procedure** list in the upper right corner of the code window and select the name of the macro you want to go to.

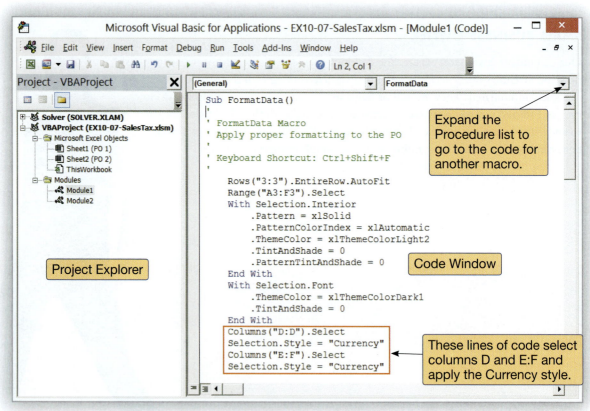

Expand the Procedure list to go to the code for another macro.

Project Explorer

Code Window

These lines of code select columns D and E:F and apply the Currency style.

FIGURE EX 10.16

You do not need to be a programming expert to work in the VBE, but there are a few basics you should know first.

The Visual Basic Editor is a separate program that runs in its own window.

Each Excel file has its own set of VBA code called a **project**. Projects are listed in the VBE **Project Explorer** window.

Projects are made up of **modules** and **objects** that contain groups of code called **procedures**. In Excel, objects refer to the individual worksheets and the overall workbook. Procedures in objects are intended for use in that object only. Procedures in modules are usually available to any open Excel workbook. The code for each macro is stored in its own procedure within a *module* (not an object). A single module may contain the procedures for multiple macros.

Procedures that perform actions but do not return a value are called **subroutines**. The code for a subroutine procedure begins with the word *Sub* followed by the name of procedure (or macro) and a set of empty parentheses:

```
Sub FormatData()
```

Every programming instruction in a procedure begins on a new line. This makes it easy to find the specific instruction you want to edit. Much of the code is written in such a way that you can figure out what it does by working through it logically.

In Figure EX 10.16, the lines of code to select a column and then apply a number style look like this:

```
Columns("D:D").Select
Selection.Style = "Currency"
Columns("E:F").Select
Selection.Style = "Currency"
```

When the macro was recorded, the user selected column D, applied the *Currency* style, and then selected columns E:F and applied the *Currency* style again. You can edit the code to combine the instructions and apply the *Comma* style instead.

```
Columns("D:F").Select
Selection.Style = "Comma"
```

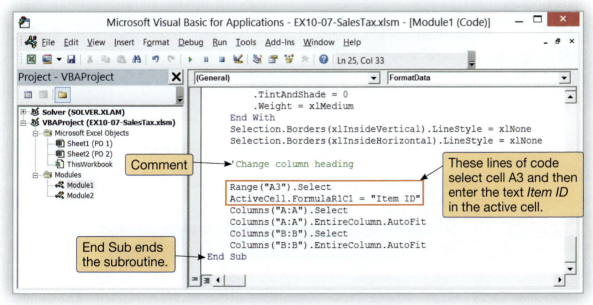

FIGURE EX 10.17

The two lines of code to select a single cell and then enter text look like this:

```
Range("A3").Select
ActiveCell.FormulaR1C1 = "Item ID"
```

To change the text *Item ID* to *Inventory ID,* edit the second line to:

```
ActiveCell.FormulaR1C1 = "Inventory ID"
```

The last line in a subroutine tells Excel that the procedure is finished and to stop executing code:

```
End Sub
```

Comments about the procedure appear in green text, and each line begins with an apostrophe. The apostrophe at the beginning of the line tells VBA to ignore the line—do not execute it as code. When you record a macro, the macro name, keyboard shortcut, and description are automatically added to the beginning of the VBA code as comments:

```
'

' FormatData Macro
' Apply proper formatting to the PO
'

' Keyboard Shortcut: Ctrl+Shift+F
'
```

To add a new comment:

1. Go to the end of the line where you want to insert the comment.

2. Press (Enter) twice to create a new line in the code.

3. Type an apostrophe and then type the comment text.

4. Press (Enter) again to place a blank line after the comment.

The blank lines before and after the comment aren't necessary, but they help break up the code visually.

When you are finished with your changes, click the **Save** button in the VBE toolbar, and then click the red **X** to close the VBE window and return to Excel. These commands are also available from the VBE *File* menu.

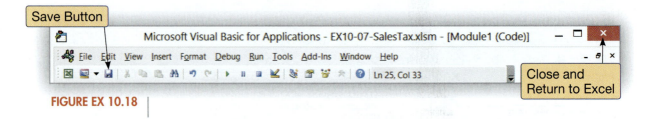

FIGURE EX 10.18

Figure EX 10.19 shows the effect of running the modified macro.

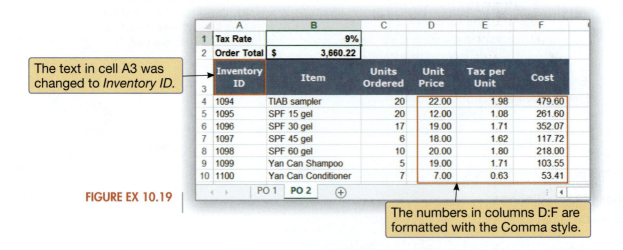

FIGURE EX 10.19

tips & tricks

tell me **more**

The Properties window in the Visual Basic Editor lists the properties for the selected object or module. Show or hide the Properties window from the VBE *View* menu.

another **method**

You can also open the Visual Basic Editor and edit macros from the *View* tab.

1. On the *View* tab, in the *Macros* group, click the top half of the **Macros** button to open the *Macro* dialog.
2. Select the macro you want to edit, and then click the **Edit** button.

let me **try**

Open the student data file **EX10-07-SalesTax** and try this skill on your own:

1. Edit the code for the **FormatData** macro in the Visual Basic Editor.
2. Find the lines of code that select columns D and E:F and apply the *Currency* style.

```
Columns("D:D").Select
Selection.Style = "Currency"
Columns("E:F").Select
Selection.Style = "Currency"
```

3. Modify the code to select columns **D:F** with a single command. (*Hint:* You should end up with two lines of code instead of four.)
4. Modify the code to apply the **Comma** style.
5. Find the lines of code that select cell A3 and enter the text Item ID.

```
Range("A3").Select
ActiveCell.FormulaR1C1 = "Item ID"
```

6. Modify the code to enter the text **Inventory ID** instead of *Item ID*.
7. Insert a new comment **Change column heading** above the block of code you just modified. Include a blank line before and after the new comment.
8. Add other comments throughout the code to identify what each block of code does.
9. Save the changes and close the Visual Basic Editor.
10. Go to the **PO 2** worksheet and run the modified **FormatData** macro.
11. Save the file as directed by your instructor and close it.

Skill 10.8 Adding a Macro to a Form Button Control

If you use a certain macro often, consider adding a **form button control** to the worksheet to call it. Calling the macro from a button is also useful if you are going to use the workbook as a template. You can give the button a friendly name and other workbook users won't need to know which macro to select to run.

To add a form button control to run a macro:

1. On the *Developer* tab, in the *Controls* group, click the **Insert Controls** button and click the **Command Button (Form Control)** button.

2. Click and drag on the worksheet to draw the button.

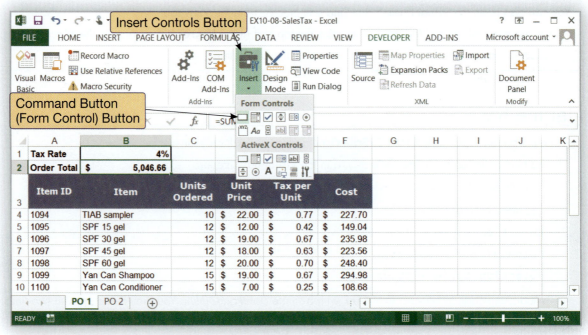

FIGURE EX 10.20

3. When you release the mouse button, the *Assign Macro* dialog opens.

4. Click the name of the macro you want and then click **OK.**

FIGURE EX 10.21

Once you've created the button, clicking it will call the macro. If you want to modify the button instead, right-click it and select an action from the right-click menu.

The button shows the default text **Button [1]** where **[1]** is the number assigned to the button by Excel. To change the button label text, right-click the button and select **Edit Text.** Click outside the button when you are through editing the text.

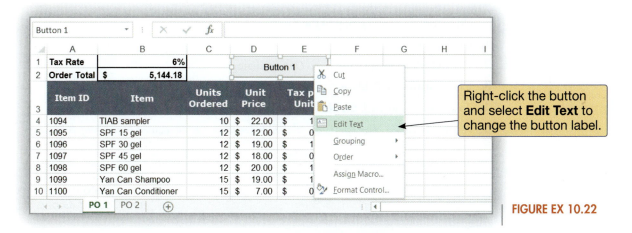

FIGURE EX 10.22

You can modify the look of the button text from the *Format Control* dialog. Right-click the button and select **Format Control...** to open the *Format Control* dialog. From this dialog you can change the look of the button text and change the button properties.

To delete a button control, right-click the button to select it and then press (Delete).

tips & tricks

The *Insert Controls* gallery has two groups of buttons: **form controls** and **ActiveX controls**. Form controls can call macros directly. ActiveX controls require that you write the code for the button action directly in the Visual Basic Editor.

tell me more

In the *Assign Macro* dialog, before you select an existing macro to assign to the button, Excel displays a new button name similar to *Button1_Click* in the *Button name* box. This is the default name for the macro or VBA procedure if you want to create a new macro to assign to the button.

❭ To record a new macro, click the **Record...** button to open the *Record Macro* dialog.

❭ To write a VBA procedure from scratch, click the **New** button to open the Visual Basic Editor.

let me try

Open the student data file **EX10-08-SalesTax** and try this skill on your own:

1. Edit the code for the **FormatData** macro in the Visual Basic Editor.

2. Add a from control button to run the **ApplyDCTax** macro. The button should be placed at approximately cells **D1:E2.**

3. Change the button label text to: **Show DC Tax**

4. Save the file as directed by your instructor and close it.

Skill 10.9 Adding a Custom Tab to the Ribbon

If you have a group of macros you use often, consider adding them to a custom Ribbon tab or group.

To add a custom tab and group to the Ribbon:

1. Click the **File** tab.
2. Click **Options** to open the *Excel Options* dialog.
3. Click **Customize Ribbon.**
4. To add a new tab, click the **New Tab** button located below the *Customize the Ribbon* list.
5. A new tab named *New Tab (Custom)* is added with one group named *New Group (Custom).*

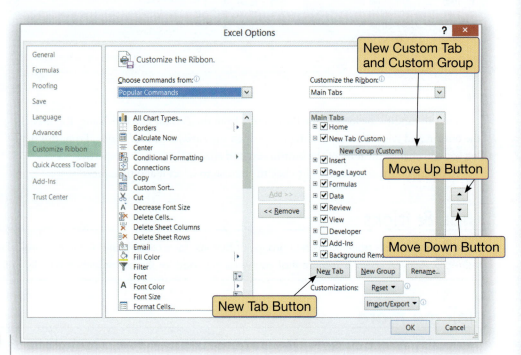

FIGURE EX 10.23

FIGURE EX 10.24

6. To rename the tab, select the tab name in the *Customize the Ribbon* list and then click the **Rename** button.
7. In the *Rename* dialog, type the new tab name in the *Display name* box and then click **OK.**

8. Follow the same steps to rename the new group. When you rename a group, you can also select an icon. This is the image that shows on the group button when the Excel window is too narrow to show the group completely.

9. To add another group to the tab, select the tab name in the *Customize the Ribbon* list and then click the **Add Group** button.

10. To change the order in which tabs appear on the Ribbon, select the tab name and then click the **Move Up** or **Move Down** button.

Now that you have a custom tab and group, you need to add commands to the group.

To add a command to a custom group:

1. In the *Customize the Ribbon* list, select the custom group you want to add commands to.

2. On the left side of the *Customize the Ribbon* window, expand the **Choose commands from** list and select the option you want. Select **Macros** to see the list of macros included in all open workbooks. Select the command you want to add and click the **Add** button.

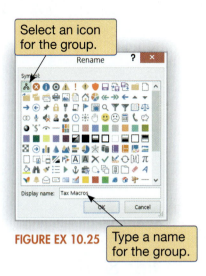

FIGURE EX 10.25

Select an icon for the group.

Type a name for the group.

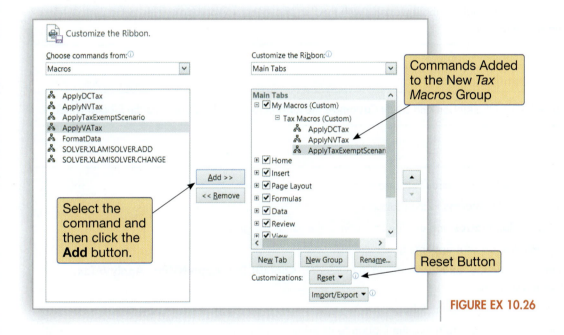

Commands Added to the New *Tax Macros* Group

Select the command and then click the **Add** button.

Reset Button

FIGURE EX 10.26

3. To change the order in which commands appear in a custom group, select the command name and then click the **Move Up** or **Move Down** arrow.

4. Once you have added a command to a custom group, you can rename the command button using the **Rename** button.

When you are finished customizing the Ribbon, click **OK.** The custom tab and groups will be available whenever you use Excel.

Custom Tab

FIGURE EX 10.27

To remove a custom group or tab, select it in the *Customize the Ribbon* list and then click the **Remove** button. Removing a custom group or tab deletes it permanently. Removing a command from a custom group only removes the command from the group. You cannot delete commands.

To undo all customizations and return both the Ribbon and the Quick Access Toolbar to their original states:

1. In the *Excel Options* dialog, *Customize the Ribbon* page, click the **Reset** button and select **Reset all customizations.**

2. Excel displays a message to verify that you want to reset all Ribbon and Quick Access Toolbar customizations. Click **Yes.**

Caution: Resetting the Ribbon will remove the *Developer* tab. If you need it, you will need to re-enable it again.

tips & tricks

If you have macros that you want to add to a custom Ribbon tab and group, consider storing them in the Personal Macro Workbook. For more information about working with the Personal Macro Workbook, refer to the *Tips & Tricks* box in the *Recording a Macro* skill.

another method

You can right-click anywhere on the Ribbon and select **Customize the Ribbon** to open the *Customize the Ribbon* window.

let me try

Open the student data file **EX10-09-SalesTax** and try this skill on your own:

1. Add a custom tab named **My Macros** to the Ribbon.
2. Rename the new group **Tax Macros** and use the first icon in the list as the group icon.
3. Move the new **My Macros** tab so it appears first in the list.
4. Add the following macros to the **Tax Macros** group in this order: **ApplyDCTax, ApplyNVTax, ApplyVATax,** and **ApplyTaxExemptScenario.**
5. Click **OK** and review the changes to the Ribbon.
6. Reset all workbook customizations to return the Ribbon to its original state.

Skill 10.10 Customizing the Quick Access Toolbar

The Quick Access Toolbar is located at the top of the application window above the *File* tab. The Quick Access Toolbar, as its name implies, gives you quick one-click access to common commands. You can add commands to and remove commands from the Quick Access Toolbar.

To add common commands to the Quick Access Toolbar:

1. Click the **Customize Quick Access Toolbar** button located on the right side of the Quick Access Toolbar.
2. Options with check marks next to them are already displayed on the toolbar. Options with no check marks are not currently displayed.
3. Click an option to add it to the Quick Access Toolbar.

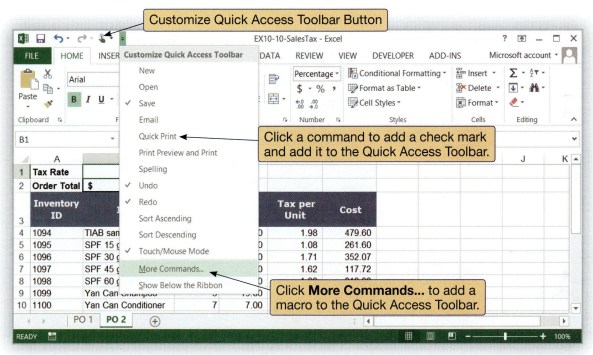

FIGURE EX 10.28

You can also add other commands, including macros, to the Quick Access Toolbar.

1. Click the **Customize Quick Access Toolbar** button and select **More Commands...**
2. The *Excel Options* dialog opens to the *Customize the Quick Access Toolbar* page.
3. Expand the **Choose commands from** list and select **Macros.**
4. Select the macro name and click the **Add** button.
5. You can reorder commands by selecting a command in the list and using the **Move Up** and **Move Down** buttons.
6. When you are finished customizing the Quick Access Toolbar, click **OK.**

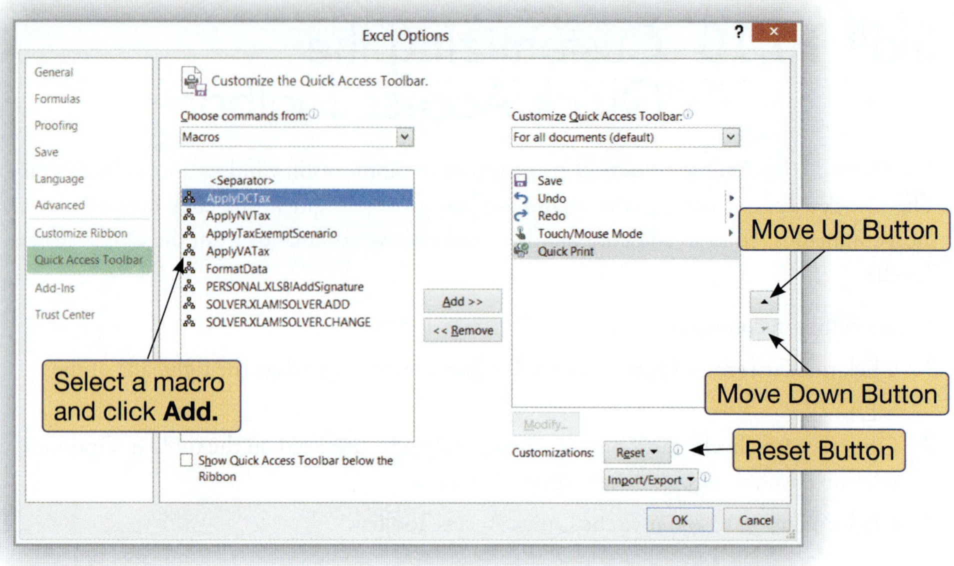
Excel Options
General
Formulas
Proofing
Save
Language
Advanced
Customize Ribbon
Quick Access Toolbar
Add-Ins
Trust Center
Customize the Quick Access Toolbar.
Choose commands from:
Macros
<Separator>
ApplyDCTax
ApplyNVTax
ApplyTaxExemptScenario
ApplyVATax
FormatData
PERSONAL.XLSB!AddSignature
SOLVER.XLAM!SOLVER.ADD
SOLVER.XLAM!SOLVER.CHANGE
Add >>
<< Remove
Customize Quick Access Toolbar:
For all documents (default)
Save
Undo
Redo
Touch/Mouse Mode
Quick Print
Move Up Button
Move Down Button
Select a macro and click Add.
Reset Button
Modify...
Customizations:
Reset
Import/Export
Show Quick Access Toolbar below the Ribbon
OK
Cancel

FIGURE EX 10.29

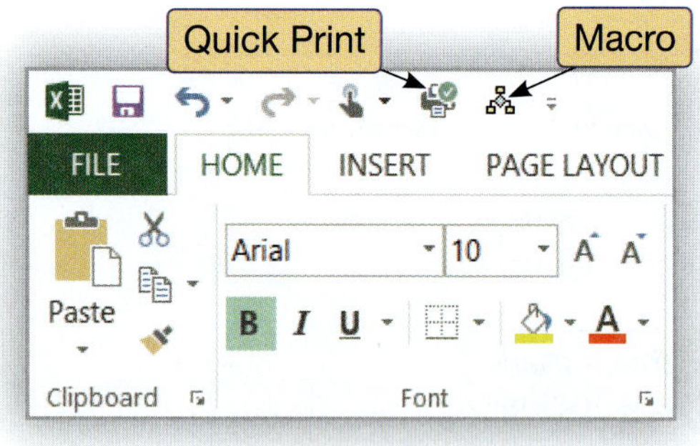
Quick Print
Macro
FILE
HOME
INSERT
PAGE LAYOUT
Paste
Arial
10
B
I
U
Clipboard
Font

FIGURE EX 10.30

Figure EX 10.30 shows the modified Quick Access Toolbar with the *Quick Print* command and the *ApplyDCTax* macro added.

To reset the Quick Access Toolbar to its original state:

1. In the *Excel Options* dialog, *Customize the Quick Access Toolbar* page, click the **Reset** button and select **Reset only Quick Access Toolbar.**
2. Excel displays a message to verify that you want to reset the Quick Access Toolbar customizations. Click **Yes.**

tell me more

When customizing the Quick Access Toolbar through the *Excel Options* dialog, you have the option of making the change to all of Excel or just the open workbook. To make the changes to the open workbook only, expand the **Customize Quick Access Toobar** list on the right side of the dialog and select the workbook title.You do not have this option when customizing the Ribbon.

another method

To open the Customize Quick Access Toolbar page:

- Click the *File* tab and click *Options* to open the *Excel Options* dialog. Click **Quick Access Toolbar.**
- Right-click the Quick Access Toolbar and select **Customize Quick Access Toolbar...**

let me try

Open the student data file **EX10-10-SalesTax** and try this skill on your own:

1. Add the **Quick Print** command to the Quick Access Toolbar.
2. Add the macro **ApplyDCTax** to the Quick Access Toolbar.
3. Click **OK** and review the changes to the Quick Access Toolbar.
4. Reset just the Quick Access Toolbar to its original state.

Macro	Project
Visual Basic for Applications (VBA)	Project Explorer
Trusted document	Module
Trust Center	Object
Trusted location	Procedure
Developer tab	Subroutine
Excel Macro-Enabled Workbook	Comment
Excel Macro-Enabled Template	Form button control
Personal workbook	Form control
Visual Basic Editor (VBE)	ActiveX control
Code window	Quick Access Toolbar

concepts review

1. Macros are written in which programming language?

   a. ASP.net

   b. Visual Basic for Applications

   c. C#

   d. Visual Basic.net

2. A trusted document:

   a. Warns the user before running macros and requires the user to allow active content to run.

   b. Allows macros to run without warning the user that the workbook contains active content.

   c. Disables all macros and other active content.

   d. Must be saved in a trusted location.

3. The *Developer* tab must be enabled before you can run a macro.

   a. True

   b. False

4. A macro-enabled workbook uses which file extension?

   a. .xlsx

   b. .xltx

   c. .xlsm

   d. .xltm

5. The command to begin recording a new macro is located where:

   a. *Developer* tab, *Code* group

   b. *View* tab, *Macros* group

   c. Status bar

   d. All of the above

6. Macros are always saved to the personal macro workbook.

   a. True

   b. False

7. In VBA, the code for each macro is stored in its own _____.

    a. Module

    b. Object

    c. Procedure

    d. Project

8. In VBA, comments must begin with which character?

    a. Comma

    b. Semi-colon

    c. Hash tag

    d. Apostrophe

9. Which control should you use to add a button to run a macro?

    a. Form button control

    b. ActiveX button control

    c. *Macro* button

    d. None of the above

10. You can add a macro to the Quick Access Toolbar.

    a. True

    b. False

projects

skill review 10.1

This project begins with data imported from a text file. You will create, edit, and run a macro to format the imported inventory data for three store locations.

Skills needed to complete this project:

- Saving a Macro-Enabled Workbook or Template (Skill 10.5)
- Adding the Developer Tab to the Ribbon (Skill 10.3)
- Recording a Macro (Skill 10.6)
- Modifying a Macro Using VBA (Skill 10.7)
- Running a Macro (Skill 10.4)
- Adding a Macro to a Form Control Button (Skill 10.8)
- Customizing the Quick Access Toolbar (Skill 10.10)

1. Open the start file **EX2013-SkillReview-10-1.**

2. If the workbook opens in Protected View, click the **Enable Editing** button in the Message Bar at the top of the workbook so you can modify the workbook.

3. Save the file as a macro-enabled workbook with this file name:
   `[your initials]EX-SkillReview-10-1`

   a. Click the **File** tab.

   b. Click **Save As.**

   c. Navigate to the location where you want to save the workbook.

   d. In the *Save As* dialog, expand the **Save as type** list, and select **Excel Macro-Enabled Workbook.**

   e. Click **Save** to save the workbook with macros.

4. Display the *Developer* tab. (If you already have the *Developer* tab enabled, skip to Step 5.)

   a. Click the **File** tab.

   b. Click **Options** to open the *Excel Options* dialog.

   c. Click **Customize Ribbon.**

   d. In the *Customize the Ribbon* list, click the **Developer** check box.

   e. Click **OK.**

5. Start on the *Alexandria* worksheet.

6. Create a macro to format the inventory data and add totals.

   a. On the *Developer* tab, in the *Code* group, click the **Record Macro** button.

   b. In the *Record Macro* dialog, in the *Macro name* box, type: `Inventory`

   c. In the *Record Macro* dialog, click in the *Shortcut key* box, press **Shift,** and type: `I`

   d. Verify that *This Workbook* is selected in the *Store macro in* box.

   e. In the *Description* box, type: `Format inventory`

   f. Click **OK.**

7. Record the Inventory macro.

    a. Select cells **A1:H1**.

    b. On the *Home* tab, in the *Alignment* group, click the **Merge & Center** button.

    c. On the *Home* tab, in the *Styles* group, click the **More** button to expand the *Styles* gallery. Select the style **Accent 1.**

    d. Select cells **A2:H2**.

    e. On the *Home* tab, in the *Alignment* group, click the **Merge & Center** button.

    f. On the *Home* tab, in the *Styles* group, click the **More** button to expand the *Styles* gallery. Select the style **60% - Accent 1.**

    g. Select cells **A3:H3**.

    h. On the *Home* tab, in the *Font* group, click the **Bold** button.

    i. Click cell **A4**.

    j. On the *Home* tab, in the *Styles* group, click the **Format as Table** button and select **Table Style Light 9.**

    k. In the *Format as Table* dialog, verify that the cell range *A1:H29* is selected and the *My table has headers* check box is checked. Click **OK.**

    l. Notice that the table includes the titles in cells A1:H2. You will fix this later by editing the macro in the Visual Basic Editor.

    m. On the *Developer* tab, in the *Code* group, click the **Stop Recording** button to stop recording the macro.

8. Fix the errors in the macro by editing the code in the Visual Basic Editor.

    a. On the *Developer* tab, in the *Code* group, click the *Macros* button.

    b. Click the **Edit** button. The Inventory macro should be selected by default.

    c. In the Visual Basic Editor, scroll down through the code to find the line `Range("A4").Select` and click to place the cursor at the end of the line.

    d. Press (Enter) to insert a blank row in the code where you can type a comment.

    e. Type the comment `Fixed cell range for the table` as shown in Figure EX 10.31. Remember to type an apostrophe before the comment text.

    f. In the next line of code, correct the cell reference for the table range to `Range("$A$3:$H$29")` as shown in Figure EX 10.31.

    g. Save your changes by clicking the **Save** button on the VBE toolbar.

    h. Click the **File** menu and select **Close and Return to Microsoft Excel.**

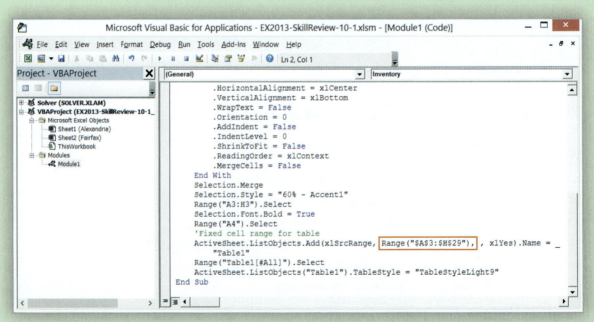

FIGURE EX 10.31

9. Click anywhere in the table. On the *Table Tools Design* tab, in the *Tools* group, click the **Convert to Range** button and then click **Yes** to convert the table back to a regular cell range so you can run the modified macro.

10. Press **Ctrl + Shift + I** to run the modified Inventory macro.

11. When you see a message that merging cells keeps only the upper left cell value and discards the other values, click **OK.**

12. Look at the last two lines of code in Figure EX 10.31. The two lines of code that apply the table style refer to the table named *Table1.* When the macro was recorded and Excel created the new table, it was automatically named *Table1.* If you run the macro again on another set of data, Excel will name the new table *Table2,* but the macro will look for a table named *Table1* when applying the style. To eliminate this problem, rename the current *Table1* to something else before running the macro on a new set of data.

   a. On the *Formulas* tab, in the *Defined Names* group, click the **Name Manager** button.

   b. The *Table1* name is selected by default. Click the **Edit...** button.

   c. Type **Alexandria** in the *Name* box to rename the table.

   d. Click **OK.**

   e. Click **Close** to close the Name Manager.

13. Add a form button to the *Fairfax* worksheet to run the Inventory macro.

   a. Click the **Fairfax** worksheet tab.

   b. On the *Developer* tab, in the *Controls* group, click the **Insert Controls** button and then click the **Button (Form Control)** button.

   c. Click and drag to draw the button to cover cells **J2:K3.**

   d. In the *Assign Macro* dialog, click **Inventory** and then click **OK.**

14. Change the button label text.

   a. Right-click the button and select **Edit Text.**

   b. Delete the text **Button 1** and type: **Format Inventory**

   c. Click outside the button.

15. Click the **Format Inventory** button to run the Inventory macro on the data in this worksheet.

16. Rename the new *Table1* table.

   a. On the *Formulas* tab, in the *Defined Names* group, click the **Name Manager** button.

   b. Click **Table1** to select it. Click the **Edit...** button.

   c. Type **Fairfax** in the *Name* box to rename the table.

   d. Click **OK.**

   e. Click **Close** to close the Name Manager.

17. Rather than creating a new button for every new sheet of inventory data, it might be easier to access the macro from the Quick Access Toolbar.

   a. Click the **Customize Quick Access Toolbar** button at the far right side of the Quick Access Toolbar.

   b. Select **More Commands...**

   c. Expand the **Choose commands from** list and select **Macros.**

   d. Click the **Inventory** macro and click the **Add** button.

   e. Expand the **Customize Quick Access Toobar** list on the right side of the dialog and select the name of your workbook to save the custom version of the Quick Access Toolbar with this workbook only.

   f. Click **OK.**

18. Go to the **Montgomery** worksheet and click the **Inventory** button that now appears on the far right side of the Quick Access Toolbar.

19. Save the workbook.

20. If you are going to submit this project in SIMnet, save a copy of it as a regular Excel workbook (without macros).

21. Close the workbook.

skill review 10.2

In this project, you will create, edit, and run macros to format the imported hourly billing information for a law firm and consolidate the data.

Skills needed to complete this project:

- Saving a Macro-Enabled Workbook or Template (Skill 10.5)
- Adding the Developer Tab to the Ribbon (Skill 10.3)
- Recording a Macro (Skill 10.6)
- Modifying a Macro Using VBA (Skill 10.7)
- Adding a Macro to a Form Control Button (Skill 10.8)
- Adding a Custom Tab to the Ribbon (Skill 10.9)
- Running a Macro (Skill 10.4)

1. Open the start file **EX2013-SkillReview-10-2.**

2. If the workbook opens in Protected View, click the **Enable Editing** button in the Message Bar at the top of the workbook so you can modify the workbook.

3. Save the file as a macro-enabled workbook with this file name:
   [your initials]EX-SkillReview-10-2

   a. Click the **File** tab.

   b. Click **Save As.**

   c. Navigate to the location where you want to save the workbook.

   d. In the *Save As* dialog, expand the **Save as type** list and select **Excel Macro-Enabled Workbook.**

   e. Click **Save** to save the workbook with macros.

4. Display the *Developer* tab. (If you already have the *Developer* tab enabled, skip to Step 5.)

   a. Click the **File** tab.

   b. Click **Options** to open the *Excel Options* dialog.

   c. Click **Customize Ribbon.**

   d. In the *Customize the Ribbon* list, click the **Developer** check box.

   e. Click **OK.**

5. Begin with the *Month 1* worksheet active.

6. Create a macro to add totals to the billing data.

   a. On the *Developer* tab, in the *Code* group, click the **Record Macro** button

   b. In the *Record Macro* dialog, in the *Macro name* box, type: **Totals**

   c. Do not include a shortcut key for this macro.

   d. Verify that *This Workbook* is selected in the *Store macro in* box.

   e. In the *Description* box, type: **Calculate totals**

   f. Click **OK.**

7. Record the Totals macro.

    a. Click cell **I1** and type: `Total`

    b. In cell **I2,** enter the following formula: `=SUM(D2:G2)*H2`

    c. Click the AutoFill handle and drag to copy the formula to cells **I3:I14.**

    d. Select cell **D15** and enter the formula: `=SUM(D2:D14)`

    e. Click the AutoFill handle and drag to copy the formula to cells **E15:G15.**

    f. Select cells **H2:I14.**

    g. On the *Home* tab, in the *Number* group, click the **Accounting Number Format** button.

    h. Select cells **A15:I15.**

    i. On the *Home* tab, in the *Font* group, click the **Borders** button arrow and select **Top and Double Bottom Border.**

    j. Select cells **A1:I1.**

    k. On the *Home* tab, in the *Styles* group, click the **More** button to expand the *Styles* gallery. Select the style **Accent 3.**

    l. On the *Developer* tab, in the *Code* group, click the **Stop Recording** button to stop recording the macro.

8. Edit the macro code to change the number style applied to cells H2:I14 to use the style *Currency [0]* to show zero digits after the decimal.

    a. On the *Developer* tab, in the *Code* group, click the **Macros** button.

    b. Click the **Edit** button. The Totals macro should be selected by default.

    c. In the Code window, locate this line of code:
```
Selection.Style = "Currency"
```
    and change it to this:
```
Selection.Style = "Currency [0]"
```
    Be sure to include the space after the word *Currency.*

    Hint: If you applied the Accounting Number Format using a method other than the Ribbon button, locate and change this line of code instead:
```
Selection.NumberFormat = "_($* #,##0.00_);_($* (#,##0.00);_($* ""_""??_);_(@_)"
```

    d. Save your changes by clicking the **Save** button on the VBE toolbar.

    e. Click the **File** menu and select **Close and Return to Microsoft Excel.**

9. Create another macro to consolidate the data.

    a. Click the **Summary** worksheet.

    b. Click the **Record Macro** button on the status bar.

    c. In the *Record Macro* dialog, in the *Macro name* box, type: `Consolidate`

    d. Do not include a shortcut key for this macro.

    e. Verify that *This Workbook* is selected in the *Store macro in* box.

    f. In the *Description* box, type: `Consolidate totals`

    g. Click **OK.**

10. Record the Consolidate macro.

    a. On the *Summary* worksheet, click cell **D2.**

    b. On the *Data* tab, in the *Data Tools* group, click the **Consolidate** button.

    c. In the *Consolidate* dialog, verify that *Sum* is selected in the *Function* box.

    d. Click the **Month 1** worksheet tab.

    e. Click and drag to select cells **D2:I14.**

    f. Click the **Add** button.

g. Click the **Month 2** worksheet tab.

h. Click the **Add** button.

i. Click the **Month 3** worksheet tab.

j. Click the **Add** button.

k. Verify that the *Create links to source data* check box is ***not*** checked.

l. Click **OK.**

m. Click the **Stop Recording** button on the status bar to stop recording the macro.

11. Add a form button to the *Summary* worksheet to run the Consolidate macro.

a. On the *Developer* tab, in the *Controls* group, click the **Insert Controls** button and then click the **Button (Form Control)** button.

b. Click and drag to draw the button to cover cells **K2:M3.**

c. In the *Assign Macro* dialog, click **Consolidate** and then click **OK.**

12. Change the button label text.

a. Right-click the button and select **Edit Text.**

b. Delete the text **Button 1** and type: **Update Summary Data**

c. Click outside the button.

13. Create a new Ribbon tab and group to display the macros.

a. Click the **File** tab and click **Options** to open the *Excel Options* dialog.

b. Click **Customize Ribbon.**

c. Click the **New Tab** button.

d. In the list on the right side of the dialog, click **New Tab (Custom)** and then click the **Rename...** button.

e. Type **My Macros** in the *Display name* box and click **OK.**

f. If necessary, click the **My Macros (Custom)** tab to select it.

g. Click the **Move Up** button as many times as necessary so the *My Macros (Custom)* tab appears at the top of the list.

h. Click **New Group (Custom)** and then click the **Rename...** button.

i. Click the icon that looks like a pair of scales (the last icon in the third row).

j. Type **Billing Summary** in the *Display Name* box and click **OK.**

k. If necessary, click **Billing Summary (Custom)** to select the group.

l. Expand the **Choose commands from** list and select **Macros.**

m. Click **Consolidate** and then click the **Add** button.

n. Click **Totals** and then click the **Add** button.

o. Click **OK.**

p. On the Ribbon, click the **My Macros** tab and verify that the two macros are included in the *Billing Summary* group.

14. Run the Totals macro on the *Month 2* and *Month 3* worksheets.

a. Click the **Month 2** worksheet tab.

b. On the *My Macros* tab, in the *Billing Summary* group, click the **Totals** button.

c. Click the **Month 3** worksheet tab.

d. On the *My Macros* tab, in the *Billing Summary* group, click the **Totals** button.

15. Click the **Summary** worksheet tab and click the **Update Summary Data** button. Notice how the summary data updates to include the totals from the *Month 2* and *Month 3* worksheets.

16. Remove the custom tab from the Ribbon.

   a. Click the **File** tab and click **Options** to open the *Excel Options* dialog.

   b. Click **Customize Ribbon.**

   c. Click **My Macros (Custom)** in the list on the right side of the dialog.

   d. Click the **Remove** button.

   e. Click **OK** to close the *Excel Options* dialog.

17. Save the workbook.

18. If you are going to submit this project in SIMnet, save a copy of it as a regular Excel workbook (without macros).

19. Close the workbook.

challenge yourself 10.3

In this project, you will record a macro to calculate grade totals and modify it in VBA. You will then run the macro on a second set of grades.

Skills needed to complete this project:

- Saving a Macro-Enabled Workbook or Template (Skill 10.5)
- Adding the Developer Tab to the Ribbon (Skill 10.3)
- Recording a Macro (Skill 10.6)
- Modifying a Macro Using VBA (Skill 10.7)
- Customizing the Quick Access Toolbar (Skill 10.10)
- Adding a Custom Tab to the Ribbon (Skill 10.9)
- Adding a Macro to a Form Control Button (Skill 10.8)
- Running a Macro (Skill 10.4)

1. Open the start file **EX2013-ChallengeYourself-10-3.**

2. If the workbook opens in Protected View, enable editing so you can make changes to the workbook.

3. Save the file as a macro-enabled workbook with this file name :
   `[your initials]EX-ChallengeYourself-10-3`

4. Display the *Developer* tab. (If you already have the *Developer* tab enabled, skip to Step 5.)

5. Begin with the *ClassAnalysis* worksheet active.

6. Create a macro to calculate yearly totals and yearly averages for each student.

   a. Name the new macro: **Grades**

   b. Include the keyboard shortcut: **Ctrl + Shift + G**

   c. Include the description: **Calculate student totals and averages**

7. Record the Grades macro following these steps:

   a. In **G1**, create a column heading: `Year Total`

   b. In **H1**, create a column heading: `Year Average`

   c. Click cell **A2.**

d. Format the data as a table using the **Table Style Medium 6** table style. Be sure to include the table header row.

e. In the *Year Total* column, use the SUM function to calculate the yearly total for each student.

f. In the *Year Average* column, use the AVERAGE function to calculate the yearly average for each student.

g. Autofit columns **G** and **H.**

8. Edit the Grades macro to use the **Table Style Medium 5** table style instead of **Table Style Medium 6.** *Hint:* Edit this line in the VBA code:

```
ActiveSheet ListObjects("Table1") TableStyle = "TableStyleMedium6"
```

9. Add the **Grades** macro to the Quick Access Toolbar for just this workbook.

10. Create a macro to display the table *Total* row and display the class average for each assignment. *Hint:* to display the table *Total* row, check the **Total Row** check box on the *Table Tools Design* tab, *Table Style Options* group.

a. Name the new macro: **ShowTotalRow**

b. Do not include a keyboard shortcut.

c. Include the description: **Show Total row with averages**

d. Display the table *Total* row.

e. Change the text in the first cell of the *Total* row to: **Class Averages**

f. Select **Average** in the *Total* row for columns **C:H.**

11. Create a macro to hide the table *Total* row. *Hint:* This macro has only one action: Uncheck the **Total Row** check box on the *Table Tools Design* tab, *Table Style Options* group.

a. Name the new macro: **HideTotalRow**

b. Do not include a keyboard shortcut.

c. Include the description: **Hide the Total row**

12. If you have permission, create a new custom Ribbon tab for the macros.

a. Name the new custom tab: **My Macros**

b. Name the new custom group: **Challenge Macros**

c. Add the three macros you created during this project.

13. Add a form button to the *ClassAnalysis* worksheet to run the Grades macro.

a. Place the button to cover cells **J1:L2.**

b. Edit the button label text to: **Calculate Grades**

14. Add a form button to the *ClassAnalysis* worksheet to run the ShowTotalRow macro.

a. Place the button to cover cells **J4:L5.**

b. Edit the button label text to: **Show Assignment Averages**

15. Add a form button to the *ClassAnalysis* worksheet to run the HideTotalRow macro.

a. Place the button to cover cells **J7:L8.**

b. Edit the button label text to: **Hide Assignment Averages**

16. Test the **Show Assignment Averages** and **Hide Assignment Averages** buttons.

17. Clear all content and formatting from rows **1:10. Caution:** If you delete the rows, you will delete the buttons as well. Instead, use the *Clear All* command from the *Home* tab, *Editing* group.

18. Go to the **Class101B** worksheet and copy the data in cells **A1:F10.**

19. Go to the **ClassAnalysis** worksheet and paste the copied data beginning in cell **A1.**

20. Run the **Grades** macro using any method.

21. Use the **Show Assignment Averages** button to run the ShowTotalRow macro.

22. Save the workbook.

23. If you are going to submit this project in SIMnet, save a copy of it as a regular Excel workbook (without macros).

24. If you added a custom tab to the Ribbon, you may want to remove it before closing the workbook.

25. Close the workbook.

challenge yourself 10.4

In this project you will work with a macro-enabled workbook that includes three macros. You will edit one of the macros and run it to format data that have been imported into the workbook. You will create form button controls to run the other macros. Finally, you will record you own macro and add it to the Quick Access Toolbar.

Skills needed to complete this project:

- Opening a Macro-Enabled Workbook (Skill 10.1)
- Saving a Macro-Enabled Workbook or Template (Skill 10.5)
- Adding the Developer Tab to the Ribbon (Skill 10.3)
- Adding a Custom Tab to the Ribbon (Skill 10.9)
- Modifying a Macro Using VBA (Skill 10.7)
- Running a Macro (Skill 10.4)
- Adding a Macro to a Form Control Button (Skill 10.8)
- Recording a Macro (Skill 10.6)
- Customizing the Quick Access Toolbar (Skill 10.10)

1. Open the start file **EX2013-ChallengeYourself-10-4.**

2. Enable the active content so you can work with the macro in this workbook.

3. Save the file as a macro-enabled workbook with this file name :
   [your initials] EX-ChallengeYourself-10-4

4. Display the *Developer* tab. (If you already have the *Developer* tab enabled, skip to Step 5.)

5. If you have permission, create a new custom Ribbon tab for the three macros included in this workbook.

   a. Name the new custom tab: **Pet Store Macros**

   b. Name the new custom group: **Custom Macros**

   c. Add the three macros included with this project.

6. The workbook includes a macro to automatically apply formatting after data have been imported. Edit the **Format** macro to change the fill color to the theme color **Accent 4.** *Hint:* Edit this line in the VBA code: .
   ThemeColor = xlThemeColorAccent6

7. Run the **Format** macro on the data in the *import* sheet. *Hint:* The keyboard shortcut is listed in the comments at the beginning of the macro subroutine procedure code.

8. Add a form button to the *import* worksheet to run the **AddSubtotals** macro.

   a. Place the button to cover cells **I1:J1.**

   b. Edit the button label text to: `Add Subtotals`

9. Add a form button to the *import* worksheet to run the **RemoveSubtotals** macro.

   a. Place the button to cover cells **I3:J4.**

   b. Edit the button label text to: `Remove Subtotals`

10. Test the buttons.

11. Record a new macro to autofit the columns.

    a. Name the new macro: `AutoFit`

    b. Do not include a keyboard shortcut.

    c. Include the description: `AutoFit the columns`

12. Record the AutoFit macro to autofit each of the columns **A:G.**

13. Add the **AutoFit** macro to the Quick Access Toolbar for just this workbook.

14. Go to the **January** worksheet and run the **AutoFit** macro.

15. If you are going to submit this project in SIMnet, save a copy of it as a regular Excel workbook (without macros).

16. If you added a custom tab to the Ribbon, you may want to remove it before closing the workbook.

17. Close the workbook.

on your own 10.5

In this project, you will record macros to format data in a sample personal budget. You will then create your own budget and modify and run the macro to format that data.

Skills needed to complete this project:

- Saving a Macro-Enabled Workbook or Template (Skill 10.5)
- Adding the Developer Tab to the Ribbon (Skill 10.3)
- Recording a Macro (Skill 10.6)
- Adding a Custom Tab to the Ribbon (Skill 10.9)
- Customizing the Quick Access Toolbar (Skill 10.10)
- Modifying a Macro Using VBA (Skill 10.7)
- Adding a Macro to a Form Control Button (Skill 10.8)
- Running a Macro (Skill 10.4)

1. Open the start file **EX2013-OnYourOwn-10-5.**

2. If the workbook opens in Protected View, click the **Enable Editing** button in the Message Bar at the top of the workbook so you can modify the workbook.

3. Save the file as a macro-enabled workbook with this file name :
   `[your initials]EX-OnYourOwn-10-5`

4. Display the *Developer* tab. (If you already have the *Developer* tab enabled, skip to Step 5.)

5. Record macros to format the budget in the **Sample Budget** worksheet.

  a. Record a macro to apply formatting to the table and calculate annual totals and averages for each budget category. Apply appropriate number formatting where necessary.

  b. Record a macro to calculate total expenses for each month. Apply appropriate number and cell formatting as necessary.

  c. Record a macro to create a chart to display the annual total for each expense category as part of the entire annual budget. Try using a pie chart. Apply a chart style of your choice. If you include a chart title, change the title text.

6. If you have permission, create a new custom Ribbon tab to store the macros you created.

7. Add at least one of the macros to the Quick Access Toolbar for this workbook.

8. Go to the **My Budget** worksheet and update the data to reflect your personal budget. Add new rows as necessary for your budget categories that were not included in the sample.

9. Before working with the VBA code and running the macros on your own data, you might want to copy the worksheet as a backup in case the macros do not work as you intend. This way you'll have a clean copy of the data to try again with.

10. Edit the VBA code as necessary for each of the macros you created so you can run them on the data in the *My Data* worksheet.

  a. If you added rows to the data, you will need to update the cell ranges where the category totals and averages are calculated. In the example shown in Figure EX 10.32, one row was added to the data. Every reference to row 7 was updated to row 8.

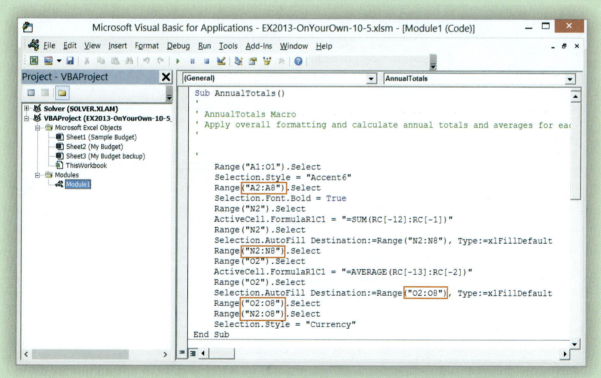

FIGURE EX 10.32

b. If you added rows to the data, you will need to update the cell range where the monthly totals are calculated. In the example shown in Figure EX 10.33, one row was added to the data. Every reference to row 8 was updated to row 9. We also changed the offset for the SUM function's relative reference range from `"=SUM(R[-6]C:R[-1]C)"` to `"=SUM(R[-7]C:R[-1]C)"` to increase the cell range for the SUM function argument by one.

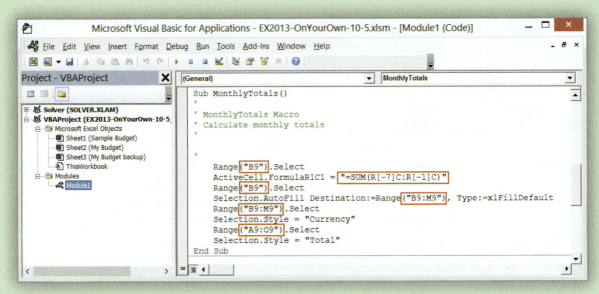

FIGURE EX 10.33

c. If you added rows to the data, you will need to update the cell range for the pie chart. In the example shown in Figure EX 10.34, one row was added to the data. Every reference to row 7 was updated to row 8.

d. Update the sheet name in the code that selects the data source for the chart and update the cell references if necessary as shown in Figure EX 10.34.

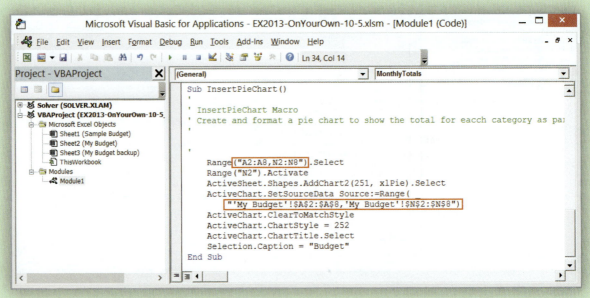

FIGURE EX 10.34

11. Add at least one form button to the *My Budget* worksheet to run one of the macros you created.

12. Run the updated macros on the data in the *My Budget* worksheet.

13. Save the workbook

14. If you are going to submit this project in SIMnet, save a copy of it as a regular Excel workbook (without macros).

15. Save a copy of the workbook as a macro-enabled template so you can use it again for your personal budget.

16. If you added a custom tab to the Ribbon, you may want to remove it before closing the workbook.

17. Close the workbook.

fix it 10.6

This project file includes a macro with an error and a missing calculation. Your task is to correct the macro and run it on the data in the file. Skills needed to complete this project:

- Opening a Macro-Enabled Workbook (Skill 10.1)
- Saving a Macro-Enabled Workbook or Template (Skill 10.5)
- Adding the Developer Tab to the Ribbon (Skill 10.3)
- Modifying a Macro Using VBA (Skill 10.7)
- Running a Macro (Skill 10.4)
- Adding a Macro to a Form Control Button (Skill 10.8)

1. Open the start file **EX2013-FixIt-10-6** and resave the file as a macro-enabled workbook with the file name:
   `[your initials] EX-FixIt-10-6`

2. Enable the active content so you can work with the macro in this workbook.

3. Display the *Developer* tab. (If you already have the *Developer* tab enabled, skip to Step 4.)

4. The workbook contains a macro named **Scholarships** to calculate the number of scholarships in the table named **ScholarshipData.** The keyboard shortcut is **Ctrl + Shift + S.** If you run the macro, you'll find there is an error. Fix the error, and then run the corrected macro.

   a. When you try to run the macro, a message box should appear telling you that there is an application-defined or object-defined error. This means there is a problem with the macro code. Click the **Debug** button to open the Visual Basic Editor with the line containing the error highlighted.

   b. Fix the error. *Hint:* The table name is incorrect in the highlighted line of code. Save your changes, and then close the VBE window. A message will appear telling you that closing the VBE window will stop the debugger. Click **OK.**

   c. Run the modified macro to test your work.

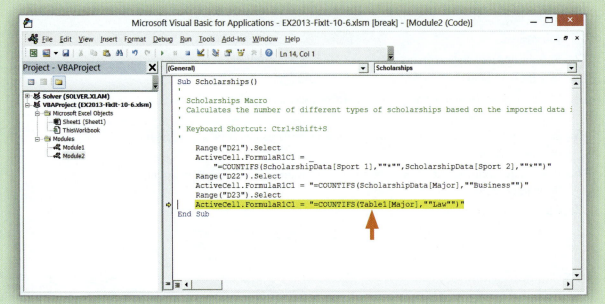

FIGURE EX 10.35

5. The macro does not include a calculation to find the number of communications majors (cell **D24**). Edit the VBA code for the Scholarships macro subroutine procedure to include this calculation.

   a. Copy the two lines of code that calculate the number of law majors and then change the code to select cell **D24** and count the number of cells with the word **Communications.**

   b. Run the **Scholarships** macro again. This time it should calculate values for cells **D21:D24.** If you encounter an error, run the debugger again and find and fix your error.

6. The form button to run the Scholarships macro should display the label text **Count Scholarships.** Edit the button text.

7. Save the workbook

8. If you are going to submit this project in SIMnet, save a copy of it as a regular Excel workbook (without macros).

9. Close the workbook.

Office 2013 Shortcuts

Office 2013 Keyboard Shortcuts

ACTION	KEYBOARD SHORTCUT
Display Open page in Backstage view	Ctrl + O
Create a new blank file (bypassing Backstage view)	Ctrl + N
Copy	Ctrl + C
Cut	Ctrl + X
Paste	Ctrl + V
Undo	Ctrl + Z
Redo	Ctrl + Y
Save	Ctrl + S
Select All	Ctrl + A
Help	F1
Bold	Ctrl + B
Italic	Ctrl + I
Underline	Ctrl + U
Close Start page or Backstage view	Esc
Close a file	Ctrl + W
Toggle between hiding and showing the Ribbon	Ctrl + F1
Switch windows	Alt + Tab

Excel 2013 Keyboard Shortcuts

ACTION	KEYBOARD SHORTCUT
Open a new blank workbook	Ctrl + N
Display Open page in Backstage view	Ctrl + O
Open the *Open* dialog	Ctrl + F12
Move to cell A1	Ctrl + Home
Save	Ctrl + S
Cut	Ctrl + X
Copy	Ctrl + C
Paste	Ctrl + V
Undo	Ctrl + Z
Redo	Ctrl + Y
Bold	Ctrl + B
Italic	Ctrl + I
Underline	Ctrl + U
Open the Quick Analysis tool	Ctrl + Q
Open the *Find and Replace* dialog with the *Find* tab displayed	Ctrl + F
Open the *Find and Replace* dialog with the *Replace* tab displayed	Ctrl + H
Edit mode (insertion point appears within the cell)	F2
Add a line break within a cell	Alt + ←Enter
Hide row	Ctrl + 9
Hide column	Ctrl + 0
Unhide row	Ctrl + ↑Shift + 9
Insert dialog (cell, row, or column)	Ctrl + ↑Shift + =
Insert worksheet	↑Shift + F11
Insert chart	Alt + F1
Fill selected cell(s) with the value from the cell above it	Ctrl + D
Fill selected cell(s) with the value from the cell to the left of it	Ctrl + R
Open *Insert Function* dialog	↑Shift + F3

Appendix A

ACTION	KEYBOARD SHORTCUT
Toggle between displaying formulas in cells and showing the formula results	Ctrl + `
Apply percent style	Ctrl + ↑ Shift + 5
Insert the SUM function	Alt + =
Toggle between cell reference states in a formula (absolute, mixed with relative column and absolute row, mixed with absolute column and relative row, relative)	F4
Open *Paste Name* dialog	F3
Open the *Spelling* dialog	F7
Open the Print page in Backstage view	Ctrl + P
Add a new worksheet to the left of the current worksheet	↑ Shift + F11
Instruct Excel to enter an array formula	Ctrl + ↑ Shift + ←Enter

glossary of key terms

Office 2013 Overview

a

Account page: Page in Backstage view that lists information for the user currently logged in to Office. This account information comes from the Microsoft account you used when installing Office.

b

Backstage: Tab that contains the commands for managing and protecting files, including Save, Open, Close, New, and Print.

c

Contextual tabs: Contain commands specific to the type of object selected and are visible only when the commands might be useful.

e

Enhanced ScreenTip: A ScreenTip that displays the name of the command, the keyboard shortcut (if there is one), and a short description of what the button does and when it is used.

f

File Properties: Information about a file such as the location of the file, the size of file, when the file was created and when it was last modified, the title, and the author. File properties can be found on the Info page in Backstage view.

File tab: Tab located at the far left side of the Ribbon. Opens the Microsoft Office Backstage view.

g

Groups: Subsections of a tab on the Ribbon; organizes commands with similar functions together.

h

Home tab: Contains the most commonly used commands for each Office application.

k

Keyboard shortcuts: Keys or combinations of keys that, when pressed, execute a command.

l

Live Preview: Displays formatting changes in a file before actually committing to the change.

m

Metadata: All the information about a file that is listed under the Properties section of the Info page in Backstage view.

Microsoft Access: A database program. Database applications allow you to organize and manipulate large amounts of data.

Microsoft Excel: A spreadsheet program. Originally, spreadsheet applications were viewed as electronic versions of an accountant's ledger. Today's spreadsheet applications can do much more than just calculate numbers—they include powerful charting and data analysis features.

Microsoft PowerPoint: A presentation program. Such applications enable you to create robust, multimedia presentations.

Microsoft Word: A word processing program. Word processing software allows you to create text-based documents. Word processing software also offers more powerful formatting and design tools, allowing you to create complex documents, including reports, résumés, brochures, and newsletters.

Mini toolbar: Provides access to common tools for working with text. When text is selected and then the mouse is rested over the text, the Mini toolbar fades in.

n

New command: Creates a new file in an Office application without exiting and reopening the program.

o

Office Help: System for searching topics specifically tailored for working with an application.

OneDrive: Microsoft's free cloud storage where you can save documents, workbooks, presentations, videos, pictures, and other files and access those files from any computer or share the files with others.

p

Protected View: Provides a read-only format that protects your computer from becoming infected by a virus or other malware.

q

Quick Access Toolbar: Toolbar located at the top of the application window above the *File* tab. The Quick Access Toolbar gives quick one-click access to common commands.

r

Ribbon: Located across the top of the application window and organizes common features and commands into tabs.

s

ScreenTip: A small information box that displays the name of the command when the mouse is rested over a button on the Ribbon.

Shortcut menus: Menus of commands that display when an area of the application window is right-clicked.

Start page: Displays when you first launch an application. The Start page gives you quick access to recently opened files and templates for creating new files in each of the applications.

t

Tab: Subsection of the Ribbon; organizes commands further into related groups.

Tags: Keywords used for grouping common files together or for searching.

Excel 2013

3-D reference: A formula that references the same cell(s) on multiple sheets.

a

Absolute reference: A cell reference whose location remains constant when the formula is copied. The $ character before a letter or number in the cell address means that part of the cell's address is absolute (nonchanging).

Accelerated depreciation: Depreciation method that uses a higher rate of depreciation for the early years of an asset's life. In accounting this is called *sum-of-the-years' digits (SOYD) depreciation*. Use the *SYN function* to calculate SOYD depreciation.

Accounting Number Format: Aligns the $ at the left side of the cell, displays two places after the decimal, and aligns all numbers at the decimal point. Zero amounts are displayed as dashes (–).

ActiveX control: A graphical user interface element that you can add to the Excel worksheet, such as a shape or image. When the user interacts with the control (clicks the button or checks the check box), the control runs VBA code called an event procedure.

Advanced Filter: Feature that filters data for conditions defined in the criteria range. Capable of filtering data in multiple columns using multiple criteria with logical AND and OR operators.

Alignment: Refers to how text and numbers are positioned within the cell both horizontally and vertically.

AND: Logical function that returns TRUE if all the arguments are true and FALSE if at least one of the arguments is false. A formula using the AND function looks like this:
=AND(*Logical1*,[*Logical2*], . . .)

Argument: The part of the formula (input) that the function uses to calculate a value.

Array: A formula that is capable of conducting multiple calculations, in this case, producing multiple results.

Aspect ratio: When resizing an image, as the width or height is increased or decreased, the height or width of the image is increased or decreased proportionately.

Auto Outline: Feature used to automatically create groups and subgroups of rows based on a data range organized into rows with subtotals or summary rows that have a formula in a consistent location.

AutoFill: Feature used to fill a group of cells with the same data or to extend a data series.

AutoSum: Allows you to insert common functions (SUM, AVERAGE, COUNT, MIN, and MAX) with a single mouse click.

AVERAGE: A statistical function that is used to calculate the average value of a group of values. A formula using the AVERAGE function looks like this: =AVERAGE(*Number1*,[*Number2*], . . .)

AVERAGEIF: A statistical function that is used to calculate the average value where cells meet specified criteria. A formula using the AVERAGEIF function looks like this:
=AVERAGEIF(*Range*,*Criteria*,[*Average_range*])

AVERAGEIFS: A statistical function that is used to calculate the average value where cells meet multiple criteria. A formula using the AVERAGEIFS function looks like this:
=AVERAGEIFS(*Sum_range*,*Criteria_range1*,*Criteria1*, [*Criteria_range2*],[*Criteria2*], . . .)

b

Banding: Applies a fill color to alternating rows or columns, making a table easier to read.

Bar charts: Chart type that works best with data that are organized into rows and columns like a table. The categories are displayed on the vertical (y) axis, and the data points are plotted along the horizontal (x) axis.

Book value: Initial cost of an asset minus its accumulated depreciation.

c

Cascade window arrangement: Places the windows in a staggered, overlapping, diagonal arrangement.

Cell address: The column and row position that defines a cell. For example, the cell at the intersection of column B and row 4 has a cell address of B4.

Cell range: A contiguous group of cells. A cell range is identified by the address of the cell in the upper left corner of the range, followed by a colon, and then the address of the cell in the lower right corner of the range. The cell range B3:D5 includes cells B3, B4, B5, C3, C4, C5, D3, D4, and D5.

Cell reference: A cell's address when it is used in a formula.

Cell style: A combination of effects that can be applied at one time. Styles can include formatting such as borders, fill color, font size, and number formatting.

Cell: The intersection of a row and column in a spreadsheet.

Chart area: Encompasses the entire chart including the plot area and optional layout elements, such as title and legend.

Chart sheet: A special type of worksheet that contains only the chart object.

Chart template: Custom chart type with predefined settings that can be used as a pattern to create a new chart.

Chart title: A text box above or overlaying the chart.

Chart: A graphic that represents numeric data visually.

Clustered column chart: Chart type where each column represents a single data point. The data points are grouped (clustered) together by category. Each data series is represented by a single color.

Code window: Area of the Visual Basic Editor that displays the lines of VBA code.

Color scales: A conditional formatting style in Excel that colors cells according to one of the color scales (e.g., red to green [bad/low to good/high] or blue to red [cold/low to hot/high]).

Column charts: Chart type that works best with data that are organized into rows and columns like a table. Data point values are transformed into columns, with the values plotted along the vertical (y) axis. Each row in the table is grouped as a data series. Excel uses the column labels as the categories along the horizontal (x) axis.

Column input cell (data table): The cell that contains the original value for which you want to substitute the data table values when the substitute values are listed in a column.

Column selector: The box with the column letter at the top of the worksheet grid. Clicking this box will select the entire column.

Column: A vertical group of cells. Columns are identified by letters. For example, the fourth column is labeled with the letter D.

Combination chart: A chart that allows you to specify different chart types for individual data series. The most common combination is a column chart combined with a line chart.

Combo chart: See *Combination chart*.

Comma Style format: Number format similar to the Accounting Number Format, but without the currency symbol.

Comment: Note you add to a cell in a worksheet. Use comments to add information, descriptions, or instructions to cells.

Comment (VBA): A note beginning with an apostrophe and appearing as green lines of text in a VBA procedure. The apostrophe beginning each line tells VBA to ignore the line—do not execute it as code. Comments in VBA code are used to describe the purpose of the procedure and provide additional information to users.

Compatibility Checker: Feature that lists the items in the workbook that may be lost or downgraded if the file is saved in an earlier Microsoft Excel format.

Compatibility mode: Mode in which files saved in older file formats are opened in Excel. Some of the new Excel features and formats are not available (in order to maintain backward compatibility).

CONCATENATE: Function used to combine the text values of cells. For example, if you have two columns for first name and last name, but you need a third column displaying the full name, you can use CONCATENATE to combine the values of the first two columns. A formula using the CONCATENATE function looks like this: =CONCATENATE(*Text1*,[*Text2*],...)

Concatenate: Means to link items together.

Conditional Formatting Rules Manager: Allows you to delete, edit, reorder, and control the way in which conditional formatting rules are applied to your worksheet.

Conditional formatting: Provides a visual analysis of data by applying formatting to cells that meet specific criteria (conditions).

Consolidate: Data tool that can be used to summarize data from multiple worksheets, with or without links back to the source data. It can also be used to summarize data by row or column labels.

Constraints: Limitations you place on the acceptable values for the variable cells when using Solver.

Copy: Command that places a duplicate of the selected cell(s) or object on the Clipboard without changing the file.

COUNT: Counts the number of cells that contain numbers within a specified range of cells. A formula using the COUNT function looks like this: =COUNT(*Value1*,[*Value2*],...)

COUNTA: Counts the number of cells that are not blank within a specified range of cells. Use COUNTA if your cell range includes both numbers and text data. A formula using the COUNTA function looks like this: =COUNTA(*Value1*,[*Value2*],...)

COUNTBLANK: Counts the number of blank cells within a specified range of cells. A formula using the COUNTBLANK function looks like this: =COUNTBLANK(*Range*)

COUNTIF: Statistical function that counts the number of times a specific value occurs within a range of cells. A formula using the COUNTIF function looks like this: =COUNTIF(*Range*,*Criteria*)

COUNTIFS: Statistical function that counts data that meet multiple criteria. COUNTIFS takes arguments for multiple ranges—each with its own criteria. The result of COUNTIFS is the number of rows and columns that meet all criteria. A formula using the COUNTIFS function looks like this:
=COUNTIFS(*Criteria_range1*,*Criteria1*,[*Criteria_range2*],[*Criteria2*],...)

Criteria range: Area defined for use with a database function or the Advanced Filter feature. The criteria range includes at least one column label and one cell with a criteria value.

CSV (Comma delimited) format: Text format where each column of data is followed by a comma. When you save a workbook in this format, only the current worksheet will be saved because text formats do not support multiple worksheets in the same file.

Currency format: Number format that places the $ immediately to the left of the number, so columns of numbers do not align at the $ and at the decimal as they do with Accounting Number Format.

Cut: Command that removes the selected cell(s) or object from the file and places it on the Office Clipboard for later use.

d

Data bars: A conditional formatting style in Excel that displays a color bar (gradient or solid) representing the cell value in comparison to other values (cells with higher values have longer data bars).

Data labels: Display data values for each data marker in a chart.

Data markers: Columns, bars, pie pieces, or other visual elements in a chart that represent data point values.

Data points: Values from a cell range plotted on a chart.

Data series (AutoFill): A sequence of cells with a recognizable pattern (used with the AutoFill feature).

Data series (chart): A group of related data points plotted on a chart.

Data table (chart): Displays a table of the data point values below the chart.

Data table (what-if analysis): Provides a quick what-if analysis of the effects of changing one or two variables within a formula. The data table is organized with a series of values for the variable(s) in a column or a row or both.

Data validation rules: Prevent users from entering invalid data or data that may cause errors in formulas by limiting cell entries to a specific data type (such as whole number or date) or a list of acceptable values.

Database functions: Allow you to perform statistical analysis on data that meet specific conditions defined in the criteria range. Data must be organized into records (rows) with the first row containing a label for each field (column).

DB: Financial function used to calculate declining balance depreciation. DB includes one optional argument—month. This is used when the asset was in use for only part of the first accounting period. Its value is the number of months the asset was in service. A formula using the DB function looks like this:
$=DB(Cost,Salvage,Life,Per,[Month])$

DDB: Financial function used to calculate double-declining balance depreciation. DDB includes one optional argument—factor. Factor is the multiplier. When this argument is omitted, Excel assumes the factor is 2. A formula using the DDB function looks like this: $=DDB(Cost,Salvage,Life,Per,[Factor])$

Declining balance depreciation: Depreciation method that takes into account the declining book value of the asset. Use the DB function to calculate declining balance depreciation.

Defined name: The names you created and names that Excel creates automatically when you define a print area or print titles.

Delimiter: Character at which data will be split into separate columns when converting text to columns or importing a text file.

Dependent: The cell containing a formula that references the value or formula in the selected cell.

Depreciation schedule: Schedule for calculating the depreciation of an asset over the number of years in its life.

Depreciation: The reduction in the value of an asset over its useful life.

Developer tab: Tab on the Excel Ribbon that contains macro tools in the *Code* group.

Discount Rate: The interest rate that the money could earn elsewhere if it were not used for the investment in NPV calculations.

Document Inspector: Feature in Excel that allows you to check your file for hidden data and personal information contained in the workbook properties before you finalize the workbook and send it to others.

Double-declining balance depreciation: Depreciation method that takes into account the declining book value of the asset including a multiplier (usually 2) to accelerate the depreciation. Use the DDB function to calculate double-declining balance depreciation.

Doughnut charts: Chart type similar to a pie chart with the capability to display more than one series. Each series is represented by a ring around the doughnut. Each data point in the series is represented by a piece of the ring proportional to the total.

e

Edit mode: The data entry method used in Excel to change only part of the cell data by double-clicking the cell, and then moving the cursor within the cell to insert or delete data.

Excel 97–2003 Workbook format: Excel format that allows you to share your workbook with people who have earlier versions of Excel. The file extension for Excel 97–2003 Workbook formats is *.xls.*

Excel Macro-Enabled Template: File format that allows you to save a file as an Excel template that contains macros. The file extension of a macro-enabled workbook is **.xltm.**

Excel Macro-Enabled Workbook: File format that allows you to save a workbook that contains macros. The file extension of a macro-enabled workbook is **.xlsm.**

Exponential trendline: Trendline that is used for data that increases (or decreases) at an increasing rate.

Extract range: When copying filtered data to another location in the worksheet, it is the location where the filtered records are copied.

f

Fill color: Solid color that shades a cell.

Fill Handle tool: Appears at the lower-right corner of a selected cell or group of cells and can be used to implement the AutoFill feature.

Filter: Limits the spreadsheet rows displayed to only those that meet specific criteria.

Find: Command that locates specific text, data, or formatting in a spreadsheet.

Flash Fill: Excel feature that detects patterns in your data and auto-fills the remaining cells for you.

Font: Refers to a set of characters of a certain design. The font is the shape of the character or number as it appears on-screen.

Footer: Text that appears at the bottom of every page.

Form button control: Object you can add to a worksheet that, when clicked, will run a macro.

Format Painter: Tool that copies and pastes formatting styles.

Formula AutoComplete: Displays a list of potential matches (functions and other valid reference names) after an = has been typed in a cell in Excel.

Formula bar: Data entry area directly below the Ribbon and above the worksheet grid.

Formula: An equation used to calculate a value.

Freeze: Excel command that keeps column headings and row labels visible as you scroll through your data.

Function: Preprogrammed shortcuts for calculating complex equations (like the average of a group of numbers).

Future value: Investment worth at a future date given consistent payments and a steady interest rate.

FV: Financial function used to calculate the future value of an investment based on consistent payments at a steady interest rate. A formula using the FV function looks like this:
=FV(*Rate,Nper,Pmt*, [*Pv*],[*Type*])

g

General horizontal alignment: Default alignment of cells. When cells are formatted using the General horizontal alignment, Excel detects the type of content in the cell. Cells that contain text are aligned to the left, and cells that contain numbers are aligned to the right.

General number format: Number format that right-aligns numbers in the cells but does not maintain a consistent number of decimal places (43.00 will appear as 43, while 42.25 appears as 42.25) and does not display commas (so 1,123,456 appears as 1123456).

Goal Seek: Feature that lets you enter a desired value (outcome) for a formula and specify an input cell that can be modified in order to reach that goal.

Gridlines (chart): Optional horizontal or vertical lines on a chart to help the user estimate values represented by the data markers.

Gridlines (worksheet): The lines that appear on the worksheet defining the rows and columns.

Group: Multiple worksheets with the same structure that you can make changes to at the same time.

Grouping: Combining data in a PivotTable by date or numeric increments. You can expand or collapse groups to show or hide details as required.

h

Header: Area that appears at the top of every page.

Headings: The numbers at the left of rows and the letters at the top of columns.

Highlight Cells Rules: A conditional formatting style in Excel that allows you to define formatting for cells that meet specific numerical or text criteria (e.g., greater than a specific value or containing a specific text string).

HLOOKUP: Function that finds a value or cell reference in a cell range and returns another value from the same column. A formula using HLOOKUP looks like this:
=HLOOKUP(*Lookup_value,Table_array,Row_index_num*, [*Range_lookup*])

Horizontal scroll bar: The scrollbar located at the bottom of the window. Click the arrows at the ends of the scroll bars to move left and right to see more cells in an individual worksheet.

Horizontal window arrangement: Places the windows in a row next to each other.

Hyperlink: Text or a graphic that can be clicked to open another location in the same file, another file, or a Web page. In Excel, the hyperlink encompasses an entire cell or range of cells rather than text.

i

Icon sets: Conditional formatting style in Excel that displays a graphic in each cell representing the cell value in relation to other values.

IF: Logical function that returns one value if a condition is true and another value if the condition is false. A formula using the IF function looks like this: =IF(*Logical_test,Value_if_true,Value_if_false*)

IFERROR: Logical function used to display an alternate text string, value, or computation if the formula in the value argument results in an error. A formula using the IFERROR function looks like this: =IFERROR(*Value,Value_if_error*)

INDEX: Lookup function that returns the value at the intersection of a specified row and column in an array. A formula using the INDEX function looks like this:
=INDEX(*Array,Row_num,Column_num*)

l

Landscape orientation: Page orientation where the width of the page is greater than the height.

Legend: A key for a chart defining which data series is represented by each color.

Line charts: Chart type that features a line connecting each data point—showing the movement of values over time.

Line with markers: Line chart type that includes dots along the line for each data point.

Linear trendline: Trendline that is best suited to data that increases (or decreases) at a steady rate.

Logarithmic trendline: Trendline that best fits data that increases or decreases rapidly and then levels off.

Long Date format: Excel date format that displays the day of the week, and then the name of the month, the two-digit date, and the four-digit year (Monday, September 05, 2011).

LOWER: Function that converts the text string to all lowercase letters. A formula using the LOWER function looks like this: =LOWER(*Text*)

m

Macro: Custom set of programming commands written in the Visual Basic for Applications (VBA) language. Macros can simplify repetitive tasks.

Margins: The blank spaces at the top, bottom, left, and right of a page.

Mark as Final: Feature in Excel that marks a file indicating that is should not be edited further.

Marker: Visual representation of data points on a Sparkline or line chart.

MATCH: Lookup function that returns the position of a specific value in a single row or column array. A formula using the MATCH function looks like this: =MATCH(*Lookup_value,Lookup_array,* [*Match_type*])

MAX: Statistical function that will give the highest value in a range of values. A formula using the MAX function looks like this: =MAX(*Number1,*[*Number2*], . . .)

Mean: The sum of a group of values divided by the number of values in the group.

MEDIAN: Statistical function that returns the middle value of a set of values. A formula using the MEDIAN function looks like this: =MEDIAN(*Number1,*[*Number2*], . . .)

Median: The middle value of a set of values.

Message Bar: Displays a warning at the top of the window, below the Ribbon, when a file is opened in Protected View.

Microsoft Access: The relational database program that is part of Microsoft Office.

MIN: Statistical function that will give the lowest value in a range of values. A formula using the MIN function looks like this: =MIN(*Number1,*[*Number2*], . . .)

Mixed reference: A combination cell reference with a row position that stays constant with a changing column position (or vice versa).

MODE.MULT: Statistical function used in an array formula to return multiple mode values. An array formula using the MODE. MULT function looks like this: {=MODE.MULT(*Number1,*[*Number2*], . . .)}

MODE.SNGL: Statistical function that returns a single mode value (the first mode value it finds). A formula using the MODE.SNGL function looks like this: =MODE.SNGL(*Number1,* [*Number2*], . . .)

Mode: The value that appears most often in a group of values.

Module: Group of procedures in VBA that are usually available to any open Excel workbook. The code for each macro is stored in its own procedure within a module. A single module may contain the procedures for multiple macros.

Moving average trendline: Trendline that is used for data that swings up and down. Set the number of periods to average.

n

Name Box: Appears at the left side of the formula bar and displays the address of the selected cell or the name of a named range.

Name Manager: Lists all the named ranges used in your workbook, the current value for each, the cells to which the name refers

(including the sheet name), the scope of the name (whether it is limited to a specific worksheet or applies to the entire workbook), and comments (if there are any).

Name: A word or group of words assigned to cells or ranges of cells to give your cell references names that are more user-friendly. Also called a named range or a range name.

Named range: A word or group of words assigned to cells or ranges of cells to give your cell references names that are more user-friendly. Also called a name or a range name.

Nested IF formula: A formula with a series of IF functions used to evaluate a series of logical tests with multiple possible results. A nested IF formula looks like this: =IF(*Logical_test,*[*Value_if_true*], IF(*Logical_test,*[*Value_if_true*],[*Value_if_false*]))

Normal view: The typical working view in Excel. In Normal view, Excel shows the aspects of the worksheet that are visible only on-screen. Elements that are visible only when printed (like headers and footers) are hidden.

NOT: Logical function that returns TRUE if the argument is false and FALSE if the argument is true. NOT evaluates only one logical test. A formula using the NOT function looks like this: =NOT(*Logical*)

NOW: Function that inserts the current date and time. A formula using the NOW function looks like this: =NOW()

NPER: Financial function that calculates the number of payments available from a retirement account or due on a loan given a constant interest rate and payment amount. A formula using the NPER function looks like this: =NPER(*Rate,Pmt,Pv,*[*Fv*],[*Type*])

NPV: Financial function used to calculate the value today of a series of future payments when the payments are variable. The Excel function NPV actually calculates present value—the same as the PV function—except it allows for variable value inputs. A formula using NPV looks like this: =NPV(*Rate,Value1,*[*Value2*], . . .)

Number format: An Excel cell format that stores data as numbers and shows two decimal places by default (so 43 displays as 43.00) but does not include commas.

o

Object: Group of procedures in VBA specific to individual worksheets and the overall workbook. Procedures in objects are intended for use in that object only.

OR: Logical function that returns TRUE if at least one of the arguments is true and FALSE if all the arguments are false. A formula using the OR function looks like this: =OR(*Logical1,*[*Logical2*], . . .)

Order of operations (precedence): A mathematical rule stating that mathematical operations in a formula are calculated in this order: (1) exponents and roots, (2) multiplication and division, and (3) addition and subtraction.

Orientation: Refers to the direction the worksheet prints.

p

Page Break Preview view: Allows you to manipulate where page breaks occur when the worksheet is printed.

Page Layout view: Shows all the worksheet elements as they will print. Page Layout view includes headers and footers.

Paste: Command that is used to insert text or an object from the Clipboard into a file.

Percent Style format: Displays numbers as % with zero places to the right of the decimal point.

Personal workbook: Hidden workbook file named PERSONAL. XLSB that is always open in the background while you use Excel.

Picture Quick Style: Allows you to apply a combination of formatting such as borders, rounded corners, and effects with a single command.

Pie charts: Chart type that represents data as parts of a whole. Pie charts do not have x and y axes like column charts. Instead, each value is a visual "slice" of the pie.

PivotChart: A graphic representation of a PivotTable.

PivotTable: A special report view that summarizes data and calculates the intersecting totals. In Excel, PivotTables do not contain any data themselves—they summarize data from a range or a table in another part of your workbook.

Plot area: The area of the chart where the data series are plotted.

PMT: Function that can be used to calculate loan payments. The PMT function is based upon constant payments and a constant interest rate. A formula using the PMT function looks like this: $=PMT(Rate,Nper,Pv,[Fv],[Type])$

Portrait orientation: Page orientation where the height of the page is greater than the width.

Precedent: The cell containing the formula or value the selected cell refers to.

Present value: The value today of a series of future payments.

Print area: A range of cells that you designate as the default print selection.

Procedure: Group of code contained within a module or object in a macro project.

Product: In mathematics, the result of multiplying two or more numbers.

Project Explorer: Area of the Visual Basic Editor that lists open VBA projects.

Project: Set of VBA code specific to a workbook. VBA projects are made up of objects and modules.

PROPER: Function that converts the text string to proper case (the first letter in each word is capitalized). A formula using the PROPER function looks like this: $=PROPER(Text)$

Protected View: Provides a read-only format that protects your computer from becoming infected by a virus or other malware.

PV: Financial function used to calculate the value today of a series of future payments when the payments are constant. A formula using the PV looks like this: $=PV(Rate,Nper,Pmt,[Fv],[Type])$

q

Quick Access Toolbar: Toolbar located at the top of the application window above the File tab. The Quick Access Toolbar gives quick one-click access to common commands.

Quick Analysis tool: Feature that helps you easily apply formatting, create charts, and insert formulas based on the selected data.

Quick Styles: A group of formatting, including text formatting, borders, fills, and effects, that can easily apply to cells, tables, charts, or other objects.

r

Ready mode: The data entry method used in Excel to change the contents of the entire cell by clicking the cell once and then typing the data.

Redo: Reverses the *Undo* command and restores the file to its previous state.

Regression analysis: Predicting future values based on the current relationship between two variables. In Excel, this can be illustrated by forecasting values on a trendline.

Relative reference: A cell reference that adjusts to the new location in the worksheet when the formula is copied.

Replace: Used with the *Find* command to replace specified data or formatting in a file with new data or formatting.

Report filter: Filter applied to a PivotTable by adding a field to the *Filters* section of the *PivotTable Fields* pane.

ROUND: Mathematical function that rounds the number up or down to the number of decimal places specified in the *Num_digits* argument. A formula using the ROUND looks like this: $=ROUND(Number,Num\_digits)$

ROUNDDOWN: Mathematical function that ignores the rules of rounding and automatically rounds down, regardless of the value to the right of the rounding point. A formula using the ROUNDDOWN looks like this: $=ROUNDDOWN(Number,Num\_digits)$

Rounding: Adjusting a number up or down to make it more appropriate in the context in which it is being used.

ROUNDUP: Mathematical function that ignores the rules of rounding and automatically rounds up to the next number, regardless of the value to the right of the rounding point. A formula using the ROUNDUP looks like this: $=ROUNDUP(Number,Num\_digits)$

Row input cell (data table): The cell that contains the original value for which you want to substitute the data table values when the substitute values are listed in a row.

Row selector: The box with the row number at the left side of the worksheet grid. Clicking this box will select the entire row.

Row: A horizontal group of cells. Rows are identified by numbers. For example, the third row is labeled with the number 3.

R-squared value: A statistical measurement of the how well the data fit the trendline. It is a number between 0 and 1; the closer the trendline's R-squared value is to 1, the better the fit.

Range name: A word or group of words assigned to cells or ranges of cells to give your cell references names that are more user-friendly. Also called a name or a named range.

s

Scale: Specifies that the worksheet will print at a percentage of the original size or at a maximum number of pages wide and/or tall.

Scenario Manager: Allows you create and apply scenarios.

Scenario summary report: Report that summarizes and compares the effects of scenarios.

Scenario: An alternate version of data values that you create and apply through the Scenario Manager. Scenarios allow you to analyze the results of changing values in specific cells (inputs).

Screenshot: An image of what is currently displayed on the computer screen (such as an open application window or a Web page).

ScreenTip: A bubble with text that appears when the mouse pointer hovers over a hyperlink. Typically, a ScreenTip provides a description of the hyperlink.

Shape Quick Style: Allows you to apply a combination of formatting such as borders, rounded corners, and effects with a single command.

Shape: Drawing object that can be added to a worksheet to call attention to a cell or group of cells. Shapes include lines, block arrows, callouts, rectangles, and circles.

Shared workbook: Workbook that allows several people to view and make changes at the same time. Shared workbooks are usually saved to a network to which multiple users have access.

Short Date format: Excel number format that displays the one- or two-digit number representing the month, followed by the one- or two-digit number representing the day, followed by the four-digit year (9/5/2011).

Slicer: A visual representation of filtering options. You can display multiple slicers and filter by multiple values from each. Slicers are only available when the data have been formatted as a table or PivotTable.

SLN: Financial function used to calculate straight-line depreciation. A formula using the SLN function looks like this: $=SLN(Cost,Salvage,Life)$

Smart Tag: Icon that appears next to a formula with a potential error and displays a menu for resolving the issue.

Solver: Data analysis tool that evaluates multiple variables affecting a formula and produces optimal values for those variables within defined constraints to result in a value you specify.

Sort: Arranges the rows in a table, worksheet, or datasheet in either ascending (A–Z) or descending (Z–A) alphabetical or numeric order.

Sparkline Quick Style: Allows you to change the Sparkline color and marker color(s) at once.

Sparklines: Represent a series of data values as an individual graphic within a single cell.

Stacked column chart: Chart type that shows each data point as part of a whole where the column represents the sum of the values in the series. Use a stacked column chart instead of a pie chart when you want the chart to show multiple series.

Status bar: Appears at the bottom of the worksheet grid and can display information about the selected data, including the number of cells selected that contain data (count) and the average and sum (total) of the selected values (when appropriate).

Straight-line depreciation: The cost of the asset minus the salvage value divided by the life of the asset (in years). To calculate straight-line depreciation, use the SLN function.

String: Text in a function.

Subroutine: VBA procedure that performs actions but does not return a value.

Subtotal: Data tool used to summarize data in place by adding subtotals to groupings of data. Before applying the *Subtotal* command, you must sort the data so rows for which you want a subtotal calculated are grouped together.

SUMIF: Mathematical function used to total the values only where cells meet the specified criteria. A formula using the SUMIF function looks like this: $=SUMIF(Range,Criteria,[Sum\_range])$

SUMIFS: Mathematical function used to sum data that meet multiple criteria. A formula using the SUMIFS function looks like this: $=SUMIFS(Sum\_range,Criteria\_range1,Criteria1,[Criteria\_range2],[Criteria2]...)$

Sum-of-the-years' digits (SOYD) depreciation: See *Accelerated depreciation.*

SUMPRODUCT: Mathematical function used to multiply the corresponding cells in two or more ranges and then sum (add together) the products. A formula using the SUMIPRODUCT function looks like this: $=SUMPRODUCT(Array1,[Array2],...)$

SYD: Financial formula that calculates sum-of-the-years' digits (SOYD) depreciation. A formula using the SYD function looks like this: $=SYD(Cost,Salvage,Life,Per)$

Table: A range of cells may be explicitly defined as a table in Excel with additional functionality such as a Total row.

Template: A file with predefined settings that can be used as a pattern to create a new file.

Text (Tab delimited) format: Text file format where each column of data is followed by a Tab character. When you save a workbook in this format, only the current worksheet will be saved because text formats do not support multiple worksheets in the same file.

Text String: Text in a function.

Text to Columns: Excel feature that allows you to split data into separate columns if there is a consistent character at which Excel can split the data (the delimiter) or the data can be split at a specific number of characters.

Theme Colors: Aspect of the theme that limits the colors available from the color palette for fonts, borders, and shading.

Theme Effects: Aspect of the theme that controls how graphic elements appear.

Theme Fonts: Aspect of the theme that controls which fonts are used for built-in cell styles. Changing the theme fonts does not limit the fonts available from the Font group on the Ribbon.

Theme: A group of formatting options applied to an entire Office file. Themes include font, color, and effect styles that are applied to specific elements in a file.

Tiled window arrangement: Places the windows in a grid pattern.

Time Value of Money (TVM): The financial principle that a dollar in hand today is worth more than a promise of a dollar tomorrow because you have the opportunity to invest that dollar today and thus make even more money by tomorrow.

TODAY: Function that inserts the current date. A formula using the TODAY function looks like this: =TODAY()

Top/Bottom Rules: Excel conditional formatting style that automatically finds and highlights the highest or lowest values or values that are above or below the average in the specified range of cells.

Total row: A row that calculates an aggregate function, such as the sum or average, of all the values in the column. Total rows can be added to defined tables in Excel.

Trendline: Graphic element that helps visualize the relationship between data points in a chart by showing the line along which data points would be expected based on different statistical growth patterns.

Trust Center: Area in Excel where you can modify macro security settings.

Trusted document: Workbook that has been designated as safe, allowing all active content to run without warning including macros, data connections, and ActiveX controls.

Trusted location: Folder designated as safe for opening files containing macros. Files that are opened from a trusted location do not use Protected View and active content is allowed without requiring you to enable it each time you open the file.

Two-variable data table: Provides a quick what-if analysis of the effects of changing two variables within a formula. The data table is organized with a series of values for the variables in both a column and a row.

U

Undo: Reverses the last action performed.

UPPER: Function that converts the text string to all uppercase letters. A formula using the UPPER function looks like this: =UPPER(*Text*)

V

Vertical scroll bar: The scrollbar located along the right side of the window. Click the arrows at the ends of the scroll bars to move up and down to see more cells in an individual worksheet.

Vertical window arrangement: Places the windows in a stack one on top of the other.

Visual Basic Editor (VBE): Application used for writing and editing VBA code.

Visual Basic for Applications (VBA): Programming language used with Office applications for macros and other procedures.

VLOOKUP: Function that finds a value or cell reference in a cell range and returns another value from the same row. A formula using the VLOOKUP function looks like this:
=VLOOKUP(*Lookup_value*,*Table_array*,*Col_index*,
[*Range_lookup*])

W

Watch Window: Window that displays the formulas and current values of cells that you add to it. The Watch Window stays open and on top of the Excel window until you close it. As you change values in your workbook, the *Value* column in the Watch Window updates to show you the effects on other parts of your workbook.

WordArt: Predefined graphic styles applied to text. These styles include a combination of color, fills, outlines, and effects.

Workbook: An Excel file made up of a collection of worksheets.

Worksheet: An electronic ledger where you enter data in Excel (also called a sheet). The worksheet appears as a grid made up of rows and columns where you can enter and then manipulate data using functions, formulas, and formatting.

X

X axis: The horizontal axis in a chart. It goes from left to right.

Y

Y axis: The vertical axis in a chart. It goes from bottom to top.

Z

Zoom slider: Slider bar that controls how large or small the file appears in the application window.

office index

Opening files, OF-6–OF-7
Options dialog, OF-13

p

Paragraph formatting, OF-12
Parents, OF-14
Paste command, OF-10
Photo, user, OF-15–OF-16
Picture formatting, OF-12
Presentation programs, OF-4
Printer icon (Help toolbar),
    OF-21
Protected View, OF-18, EXG-2
Pushpin icon (Help toolbar),
    OF-21

q

Quick Access Toolbar, OF-11,
    EXG-2
Quick Print button, OF-11
Quick Styles, OF-12

r

Relational databases, OF-4
Reports, database, OF-4
Ribbon, OF-9, EXG-2

s

Save command, OF-10
Saving files, OF-23–OF-26
    and closing files, OF-8
    to local drive, OF-23–OF-24
    with new names, OF-26
    to OneDrive, OF-25
ScreenTips, OF-12, EXG-2
Searching in Office Help, OF-21
Security settings, OF-18
Shape styles, OF-12
Sharing OneDrive documents,
    OF-25
Shortcut menus, OF-10, EXG-2
SmartArt, OF-12
Spreadsheet applications, OF-3
Start page, OF-14, EXG-2

t

Tables, OF-4, OF-12
Tabs, OF-9, EXG-2; *see also specific tabs*
Tags, OF-22, EXG-2
Templates, OF-20
Themes, OF-17
Trust Center, OF-18

u

Undo command, OF-10
User interface, OF-9–OF-13
User photo, changing, OF-15–OF-16

v

View, Protected, OF-18

w

Windows 7, OF-5
Windows 8, OF-4
Word processing software, OF-3

excel index

Symbols

a

chart type, EX-210, EX-325
data validation rules, EX-449
fonts, font size, and font color,
    EX-66–EX-67
formatting for data bar rules,
    EX-380
order of conditional formatting
    rules, EX-380
order of tabs on Ribbon, EX-503
orientation, EX-175
PivotChart appearance,
    EX-414–EX-415
PivotTable appearance, EX-412
Sparkline type, EX-339
status bar display, EX-26
tab color, EX-155
trendline type, EX-337
Trust Center settings,
    EX-487–EX-488
user name, EX-455
view, EX-169
workbook arrangement,
    EX-32–EX-33
zoom level, EX-27–EX-28
Character intervals, splitting text at,
    EX-444
Chart area, EX-198, EXG-3
Chart elements, EX-197–EX-198,
    EX-208, EX-330–EX-332
Chart Elements box, EX-332
Chart sheets, EX-207, EXG-3
Chart Styles button, EX-209, EX-327,
    EX-415
Chart templates, EX-333, EX-334,
    EXG-3
Chart title, EX-198, EXG-3
Chart Tools Design tab, EX-198,
    EX-208
Chart Tools Format tab, EX-198,
    EX-351
Charts, EX-191–EX-211,
    EX-321–EX-338
    applying Quick Styles and colors to,
        EX-209
    bar, EX-202–EX-203, EXG-2
    changing type of, EX-210, EX-325,
        EX-414
    clustered column, EX-210, EXG-3
    column, EX-202–EX-203, EX-232,
        EXG-3
    combination, EX-324–EX-325,
        EXG-3
    components of, EX-197–EX-199

data points, EX-326–EX-329
data series, EX-321–EX-323,
    EX-326–EX-327
defined, EX-197, EXG-3
doughnut, EX-204, EXG-4
filtering data in, EX-211
inserting, EX-202–EX-205
line, EX-205, EX-327, EXG-5
line with markers, EX-205,
    EXG-5
moving, EX-206–EX-207
pie, EX-204, EX-328–EX-329,
    EXG-7
PivotCharts, EX-232–EX-233,
    EX-406, EX-413–EX-415,
    EXG-7
recommended charts feature,
    EX-200–EX-201
stacked column, EX-210, EXG-8
trendlines, EX-335–EX-338
Checking
    Compatibility Checker, EX-465,
        EXG-3
    error, EX-128–EX-129, EX-297
    spelling, EX-34
Clear All command, EX-82
Clear commands, EX-82–EX-83
Clear Comments command, EX-82
Clear Contents command, EX-82
Clear Formats command, EX-82
Clear Hyperlinks command, EX-82
Clear Rules command, EX-381
Clearing
    cell content, EX-82–EX-83
    filters, EX-220, EX-387–EX-389
    print area, EX-89
    validation circles, EX-446
Clustered column charts, EX-210,
    EXG-3
Code window, EX-496, EXG-3
Col_index_num argument, EX-126
Collapse Dialog button, EX-104,
    EX-117
Collapsing outline groups, EX-391,
    EX-392, EX-395–EX-396
College students, EX-31, EX-199
Color(s)
    changing conditional rules on,
        EX-380
    for charts, EX-209
    of data series, EX-327
    fill, EX-70–EX-71, EX-326,
        EX-327, EX-377, EXG-4

filtering data by, EX-382–EX-383
font, EX-66–EX-67, EX-70,
    EX-382–EX-383
sorting data by, EX-382
of Sparklines, EX-341–EX-342
of tabs, EX-155
Theme, EX-66, EX-161, EXG-8
Color scales, EX-76, EX-77, EX-383,
    EXG-3
Column charts, EX-202–EX-203,
    EX-232, EXG-3
Column input cell, EX-227, EXG-3
Column selector, EX-5, EXG-3
Column width, EX-57, EX-132,
    EX-162–EX-163
Column_num argument,
    EX-287–EX-289
Columns
    autofit for, EX-163
    converting data to, EX-442–EX-444
    defined, EX-3, EXG-3
    deleting, EX-165
    freezing/unfreezing, EX-166
    hiding/unhiding, EX-167
    inserting, EX-164, EX-165
    names of, in formulas, EX-213
    repeating, EX-178
    selecting, EX-5
    splitting data into, EX-441–EX-444
    Text to Columns, EX-63,
        EX-442–EX-444, EXG-8
Combination charts, EX-324–EX-325,
    EXG-3
Combining text, EX-113
Combo charts; see Combination charts
Comma [0] cell style, EX-13
Comma cell style, EX-13
Comma delimited (CSV) format,
    EX-466, EXG-3
Comma Style button, EX-12
Comma Style format, EX-12, EX-13,
    EXG-3
Comments (VBA), EX-498, EXG-3
Comments (worksheet), EX-82,
    EX-454–EX-455, EXG-3
Compare Side by Side feature, EX-33
Comparing workbooks, EX-33
Comparison operator (icon set),
    EX-376
Comparison values, EX-74
Compatibility Checker, EX-465,
    EXG-3
Compatibility mode, EX-467, EXG-3

Hyperlinks
    clearing, EX-82
    defined, EXG-5
    inserting, EX-355, EX-456–EX-457

i

Icon sets
    conditional formatting with, EX-77
    creating conditional rules with,
        EX-376, EX-377
    defined, EXG-5
    reversing order of, EX-381
Identifying invalid data, EX-445
IF formulas, nested, EX-271–EX-273
IF logical function, EX-120–EX-121,
    EX-271–EX-273, EXG-5
IFERROR function, EX-293–EX-294,
    EXG-5
Importing data, EX-435–EX-449
    adding data validation,
        EX-445–EX-446
    converting data to columns,
        EX-442–EX-444
    creating drop-down lists for data
        entry, EX-447–EX-449
    inserting data with Flash Fill,
        EX-440–EX-441
    from Microsoft Access,
        EX-435–EX-437
    from text files, EX-438–EX-439
Increase Decimal button, EX-13
INDEX function, EX-286–EX-289,
    EX-292, EXG-5
Inexact text matches, EX-263
Input cell (Goal Seek function), EX-225
Insert button, EX-165
Insert Charts dialog
    inserting bar/column charts with,
        EX-203
    inserting line charts with, EX-205
    inserting pie charts with, EX-204
    recommended charts from,
        EX-200–EX-201
Insert command, EX-165
Insert Copied Cells command, EX-52
Insert Cut Cells command, EX-52
Insert dialog, EX-58
Insert Function dialog,
    EX-103–EX-105
Insert Hyperlink dialog, EX-456,
    EX-457
Insert tab, EX-171

Inserting; *see also* Adding
    cells, EX-58–EX-59
    charts, EX-202–EX-205
    comments, EX-454, EX-455
    data with AutoFill, EX-16–EX-17
    data with Flash Fill,
        EX-440–EX-441
    hyperlinks, EX-355,
        EX-456–EX-457
    page breaks, EX-172–EX-173
    pictures, EX-343–EX-344
    rows/columns, EX-164, EX-165
    shapes, EX-350–EX-351
    Sparklines, EX-223–EX-224
    SUM function, EX-23
    worksheets, EX-153
Installing Solver, EX-401
Instructions worksheets, EX-31
Instructors, EX-121
Int constraint operator, EX-404
INT function, EX-249
Interest rates, EX-122
Internet Explorer, EX-355
Intervals, splitting text into columns at,
    EX-444
Invalid data, EX-445
Inventory managers, EX-442
IRS, depreciation schedule of,
    EX-285
Italic, EX-64–EX-65

k

Keep Source Column Widths (paste
    option), EX-53, EX-55
Keep Source Formatting (paste option),
    EX-53
Keyboard shortcuts, EXA-2–EXA-3
    for bold, italic, and underline for-
        matting, EX-65
    Copy command, EX-52
    Cut command, EX-52
    Fill command, EX-17
    for finding and replacing data,
        EX-85
    for hiding/displaying formulas,
        EX-132
    Increase/Decrease Decimal buttons,
        EX-13
    for line breaks, EX-11
    for macros, EX-491, EX-493
    Paste command, EX-52,
        EX-54

Quick Analysis tool, EX-75
Redo command, EX-56
Undo command, EX-56

l

Label row, in database functions,
    EX-292
Labels
    data, EX-208, EXG-4
    as range names, EX-114
    repeating, EX-178
Landscape orientation, EX-175, EXG-5
Layout
    page; *see* Page Layout tab; Page Layout
        view
    PivotTable, EX-412
Legend, EX-198, EXG-5
Life argument, EX-282–EX-285
Line breaks, EX-11
Line charts, EX-205, EX-327, EXG-5
Line with markers (chart), EX-205,
    EXG-5
Linear trendlines, EX-336, EXG-5
Link (paste option), EX-54
Linked Picture (paste option), EX-54
Links
    to external data sources, EX-452,
        EX-453
    hyperlinks, EX-82, EX-355,
        EX-456–EX-457, EXG-5
Lists
    of compatibility issues, EX-465
    drop-down, EX-447–EX-449
    of named ranges, EX-117
Live Preview, EX-72, EX-77
Loan payments, EX-122–EX-123
Local files, inserting pictures from,
    EX-343–EX-344
Location range, Sparkline, EX-339
Locations, trusted, EX-487–EX-488,
    EXG-9
Logarithmic trendlines, EX-336,
    EXG-5
Logical functions
    AND, EX-267, EXG-5
    IF, EX-120–EX-121,
        EX-271–EX-273, EXG-5
    NOT, EX-267, EX-269–EX-270,
        EXG-6
    OR, EX-267–EX-269, EXG-6
Logical operators, filtering data with,
    EX-388–EX-389

photo credits